The Internet of Things:

Breakthroughs in Research and Practice

Information Resources Management Association
USA

www.igi-global.com

Published in the United States of America by
    IGI Global
    Information Science Reference (an imprint of IGI Global)
    701 E. Chocolate Avenue
    Hershey PA, USA 17033
    Tel: 717-533-8845
    Fax: 717-533-8661
    E-mail: cust@igi-global.com
    Web site: http://www.igi-global.com

Library of Congress Cataloging-in-Publication Data

Names: Information Resources Management Association, editor.
Title: The internet of things : breakthroughs in research and practice /
  Information Resources Management Association, editor.
Description: Hershey PA : Information Science Reference, [2017] | Includes
  bibliographical references.
Identifiers: LCCN 2016045995| ISBN 9781522518327 (hardcover) | ISBN
  9781522518334 (ebook)
Subjects: LCSH: Internet of things. | Internet of things--Security measures.
Classification: LCC TK5105.8857 .I64 2017 | DDC 004.67/8--dc23 LC record available at https://lccn.loc.gov/2016045995

British Cataloguing in Publication Data
A Cataloguing in Publication record for this book is available from the British Library.

All work contributed to this book is new, previously-unpublished material. The views expressed in this book are those of the authors, but not necessarily of the publisher.

For electronic access to this publication, please contact: eresources@igi-global.com.

List of Contributors

Table of Contents

Section 2
Health and Welfare

Section 3
Security, Privacy, and Forensics

Section 4
Strategic Innovation and Data Management

Preface

The constantly changing landscape surrounding the Internet of Things makes it challenging for experts and practitioners to stay informed of the field's most up-to-date research. That is why IGI Global is pleased to offer this single-volume comprehensive reference collection that will empower students, researchers, and academicians with a strong understanding of these critical issues by providing both broad and detailed perspectives on cutting-edge theories and developments. This compilation is designed to act as a single reference source on conceptual, methodological, and technical aspects, as well as to provide insight into emerging trends and future opportunities within the discipline.

The Internet of Things: Breakthroughs in Research and Practice is organized into four sections that provide comprehensive coverage of important topics. The sections are:

1. Community Engagement and Governance
2. Health and Welfare
3. Security, Privacy, and Forensics
4. Strategic Innovation and Data Management

The following paragraphs provide a summary of what to expect from this invaluable reference source:

Section 1, "Community Engagement and Governance," opens this extensive reference source by highlighting the shifting landscape of community involvement and practices in modern society. Through perspectives on education, social interaction, and consumer behavior, this section demonstrates how the Internet of Things is transforming the potential of emerging technologies. The presented research facilitates a better understanding of the prevalence of interconnectivity in the digital era.

Section 2, "Health and Welfare," includes chapters on the various aspects of citizen welfare and quality of life considerations. Including discussions on healthcare, assistive technology, and environmental concerns, this section presents research on the integration of computing devices into societal infrastructures. This inclusive information assists in advancing current practices in health and welfare contexts.

Section 3, "Security, Privacy, and Forensics," presents coverage on the current state of security concerns in society's age of interconnected technology. Through innovative discussions on system communication, smart forensics, and crowdsensing, this section highlights the growing issue of information protection and individual privacy. These inclusive perspectives contribute to the available knowledge on assuring security with modern technology.

Section 4, "Strategic Innovation and Data Management," discusses research perspectives on data and network analysis trends, as well as applications for the Internet of Things. Through discussions on big data, 5G networks, and business models, this section contains pivotal information on novel data and computing solutions. The presented research facilitates a comprehensive understanding of emerging innovations and data analysis trends.

Although the primary organization of the contents in this work is based on its four sections, offering a progression of coverage of the important concepts, methodologies, technologies, applications, social issues, and emerging trends, the reader can also identify specific contents by utilizing the extensive indexing system listed at the end.

As a comprehensive collection of research on the latest findings related to *The Internet of Things: Breakthroughs in Research and Practice*, this publication provides researchers, administrators, and all audiences with a complete understanding of the development of applications and concepts surrounding these critical issues.

Section 1
Community Engagement and Governance

Chapter 1
Exploring the Educational Potential of Internet of Things (IoT) in Seamless Learning

Veysel Demirer
Süleyman Demirel University, Turkey

Betül Aydın
Süleyman Demirel University, Turkey

Şeyma Betül Çelik
Ministry of National Education, Turkey

ABSTRACT

One of the new concepts that appear in the learning revolution with emerging technological advances is seamless learning. This type of learning involves the continuity of learning experiences by means of technology regardless of environment and time, and without any interruption. A necessary and useful technology in realizing seamless learning is "Internet of Things". IoT technology is an infrastructure on which things can communicate with one another or with human beings by connecting to the Internet, and which has the capability of simultaneously storing and exchanging the collected data on cloud computing systems. With its potential in a wide area of applications in the future, this technology is expected to be used in education as well. Furthermore, it has a huge potential to contribute to seamless learning experiences. Development and expansion of this technology will make future educational institutions feel the necessity to accept and adapt this technology. In this regard, this study aimed to introduce IoT technology and to explore educational potential of seamless learning.

INTRODUCTION

Dramatic changes in information and communication technologies has transformed our lives and the way we learn. Therefore, learning goes beyond the walls of the classroom. "The world is becoming a mobigital virtual space where people can learn and teach digitally anywhere and anytime" (Şad &

DOI: 10.4018/978-1-5225-1832-7.ch001

Göktaş, 2014, p. 606). Besides, individuals have gained the habit of rapid knowledge acquisition and sharing. One of the new concepts that appear in the learning revolution based on technological advances is seamless learning. This concept, independent of the technology as an essential component, was initially defined by American College Personnel Association (1994) as connecting in and out of classroom student experiences within the campus to ensure their seamless learning. Moreover, Kuh (1996) emphasized that this process was of high significance regarding students' out of campus experiences. Later on, Chan et al. (2006) stated that interconnected mobile devices had the potential of initiating a new era in technology-enhanced learning by ensuring the continuity of learning. Today, mobile technologies, which are owned by almost every individual, do not only support learning but they also provide constant communication for learners through social networks and other ways of communication, establishing a perpetual link between virtual and the real world, and access to information by joining the networks (Looi et al., 2010). Regardless of time and space, these technologies simplify individuals' activities of communication, collaboration, sharing and learning with peers, friends and family members (Looi et al., 2010). Thus, learners can learn everything they are curious about uninterruptedly on the basis of individual or social interaction in formal or informal learning environments (Chan et al., 2006). In this regard, seamless learning can be defined as the continuity of learning in real or virtual world based on individual or group cooperation in in-school or out-of-school, formal and informal learning environments by means of personal technological devices (Looi et al., 2010; Wong & Looi, 2011; Wong, 2012). In seamless learning, learners are able to learn everything they need in different environments and situations using their personal mobile devices easily and quickly. While this learning can be individual, it can also take place among peers, in small or larger groups, even with teachers at school, in the outside world, in museums, in virtual environments, in social networks and in short, virtually everywhere (Milrad et al., 2013). Interconnected mobile devices in the seamless learning process have a significant role in providing support services to learners and their access to learning content via digital networks, in enriching the learning process, learning resources, learning opportunities and experiences, and the continuation of learning activities in a seamless way. With mobile devices, learning experiences show continuity in different environments. One of the necessary and useful technologies in realizing seamless learning is the "Internet of Things (IoT)" technology. IoT enables learners to learn any content at any given time in an uninterrupted manner by making every object in learning environment digital, intelligent and connected to a network. Therefore, IoT provides a technological background for seamless learning environments (Xue, Wang & Chen, 2011). IoT is anticipated to change our world and our habits. Also, the learning habits of individuals are also subject to change. Individuals experience seamless learning processes and share the gained experiences with the rise of devices connected to the Internet. In this sense, IoT technology is regarded as one of the effective means of technology that can mediate the experience sharing process of seamless learning. For this purpose, IoT technology is introduced and its potential use in the field of education is discussed in this section.

INTERNET OF THINGS

Internet of Things is a concept which was first coined by Kevin Ashton in 1999 in one of his presentations (Ashton, 2009). This concept is also called Internet of Everything (IoE). There are several definitions of IoT. This concept expresses a broad technology that consists of networks through which all objects can communicate with one another by means of different communication protocols and connect to the Internet

(Liu & Lu, 2012; Zuerner, 2014). In 2012, International Telecommunication Union (ITU) defined IoT as "a global infrastructure for the information society that enables advanced services by interconnecting (physical and virtual) things based on existing and evolving interoperable information and communication technologies". IoT makes complete use of things to offer services to all kinds of applications through utilization of identification, data capture, processing and communication capabilities. From a broader viewpoint, IoT can be perceived as a vision with technological and societal implications.

The IERC (European Research Cluster on the Internet of Things, 2014) definition states that IoT is "a dynamic global network infrastructure with self-configuring capabilities based on standard and interoperable communication protocols where physical and virtual "things" have identities, physical attributes, and virtual personalities and use intelligent interfaces, and are seamlessly integrated into the information network". All in all, IoT is an infrastructure which can interconnect animate and inanimate objects, and communicate with them connecting to the Internet, store data by collecting them through sensors in cloud systems, and provide real-time information to people or machines.

The first example of interconnected devices is Trojan Room Coffee Pot or XCoffee product created in 1991 when 15 researchers, including Quentin Stafford-Fraser and Paul Jardetzky, at the University of Cambridge Computer Lab shared a coffee machine located in a rather uninspiring area known as the Trojan Room, away from the location where all the researchers worked. Offices of another group of researchers were two or three flights of stairs away and they must travel some distance in search of coffee, often to find those closer at hand have beaten them to it. There were computers in this room, one of which had a video frame-grabber attached. A camera was fixed to a retort stand, pointed at the coffee machine in the corridor, and they ran the wires under the floor to the frame-grabber in the Trojan Room. Jardetzky and Fraser wrote a "client" program, which ran on that machine, captured images of the pot every few seconds at various resolutions, connected to the server, and displayed an icon-sized image of the pot in the corner of the screen. The image was only updated about three times a minute, but that was fine because the pot filled rather slowly, and it was only greyscale, which was also fine, because so was the coffee. This way, real-time information from an object connected to the network was obtained (Fraser, 1995).

IoT brought a new dimension to the concept of communications, and over time, in addition to human-to-human and human-to-machine communications, machine-to-machine communication has become available through "Internet of Things." IoT connects real and virtual worlds and utilizes M2M interaction in an effective way. Communication of things is also referred to as the speech between things. All things in the near future are assumed to stay connected to the Internet. Transition from information era to "the connected age" has started. This transformation process, which began with the introduction of Internet to our lives, has led to developments such as the concept of "connected things" that take place in our lives in a way where each object has a unique ID, an IP address, is connected to each other via a network, exchanging information and transmitting the data related to the environment with embedded sensor systems. Evans (2011) estimates that IoT was "born" sometime between 2008 and 2009, and looking to the future, it is predicted that there will be 25 billion devices connected to the Internet by 2015 and 50 billion by 2020 (Figure 1).

IoT seems to have the power to change our lives. With this technology, in the near future, it is highly possible to encounter smart systems such as connected cities, houses, ecosystems, etc. or even smarter environments. Many innovative solutions such as operation of house ventilation systems even when you are far away, alerting the nearest health facility in case the patient has a high fever, and routing your car to the most convenient track will make our lives easier.

Figure 1. The yearly distribution of devices connected to the Internet
Source: Cisco IBSG, 2011, as cited in Evans, 2011

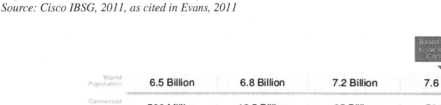
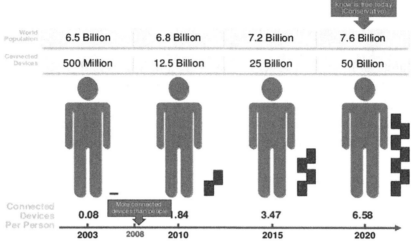

What Is the Difference Between the Internet and Internet of Things?

There are some differences between the Internet and Internet of Things. According to Goldman Sachs (2014), IoT has key attributes that distinguishes it from the "regular" Internet such as "Sensing, Efficient, Networked, Specialized, Everywhere". Key attributes of IoT and how it differs from the "regular" Internet are shown in Table 1.

The Internet is a constantly evolving technology that becomes more significant with the spread of broadband connections. The Internet has started as the "Internet of Computers." With Web 2.0, it has evolved into the Internet of People and is progressing towards the Internet of Things.

Table 1. Key attributes of the IoT and how it differs from the "regular" Internet (Goldman Sachs, 2014)

Sense	What the Internet of Things Does	How It Differs from the Internet
Sensing	Leverages sensors attached to things (e.g. temperature, pressure, acceleration)	More data is generated by things with sensors than by people.
Efficient	Adds intelligence to manual processes (e.g. reduces power usage on hot days)	Extends the internet's productivity gains to things, not just people.
Networked	Connects objects to the network (e.g. thermostats, cars, watches)	Some of the intelligence shifts from the cloud to the network's edge ("fog" computing).
Specialized	Customizes technology and process to specific verticals (e.g. healthcare, retail, oil)	Unlike the broad horizontal reach of PCs and smartphones, the IoT is very fragmented.
Everywhere	Deployed pervasively (e.g. on the human body, in cars, homes, cities, factories)	Ubiquitous presence, resulting in an order of magnitude more devices and even greater security concerns.

Related Technologies

IoT is closely related to the Internet, mobile communication networks and wireless sensor networks. In this section, radio frequency identification technology, sensor technologies, cloud computing, big data and near field communication are discussed. The first one is Radio Frequency Identification (RFID) Technology. Juels (2006) defines RFID technology as an automated identification technology of objects and humans. According to Want (2006), RFID enables identification from a distance. RFID tags have single and unique IDs. They include additional data such as manufacturer and product type. They can even measure environmental factors such as temperature. Moreover, RFID systems can discern many different tags located in the same general area without human assistance (Deepti, Ganesh, & Prasad, 2011).

Other related technologies are sensors. Human-beings make sense of the world using their five senses. Similarly, electronic tools have special senses to recognize sources in a physical environment. The most frequently encountered definitions of a sensor is based on the definition given by American National Standards Institute (ANSI, 1975): a device that provides usable output in response to a specific measurement such as temperature, pressure, acceleration (National Research Council, 1995). Wireless sensor networks (WSN) are important elements of IoT technology. The benefits of linking both WSN and other IoT elements go beyond distant access, as heterogeneous information systems could collaborate and provide common services (Alcaraz, Najera, Lopez et al., 2010).

Another related technology is Cloud Computing. Armbrust et al. (2010) define Cloud computing as "both the applications delivered as services over the Internet and the hardware and software in the data centers that provide those services". Cloud computing has virtually unlimited capabilities in terms of storage and processing power, and is a much more advanced technology (Botta, Donato, Persico et al., 2014). Moreover, Cloud computing can offer an effective solution for IoT security, data service management and data storage.

One of the most important related technologies is "Big Data". The term Big Data applies to information that cannot be processed or analyzed using traditional processes or tools (Zikopoulos, Eaton, deRoos et al., 2012). According to CISCO's 2014-2019 global estimates, the data created by IoT devices will be 269 times larger than the amount of data being transmitted to data centers from end-user devices currently. And it will be 49 times higher than total data center traffic by 2019. As could be understood from these figures, a huge volume of raw data will be available in the future. It is necessary to process this raw data produced by things and obtain a value as a result of this process, since this raw data is not meaningful on its own.

NFC technology can also be included within the scope of IoT. NFC is one of the short-range wireless technologies. As a result of IoT new services and different communication technologies emerge. SIM cards, low-power Bluetooth, GPS and sensors can be listed as examples of these technologies.

THE USES OF IoT TECHNOLOGY

The IoT application areas are limitless as far as one could imagine (Figure 2). In his study, Tarman (2014) lists IoT technology applications in the fields of environmental monitoring, industries, energy, healthcare, living areas and transportation.

Figure 2. The uses of Internet of Things technology
Source: Growthcap, 2014

With the help of sensors used in IoT technologies, performed air and water pollution analyses can be transferred to different units connected to the same network. Additionally, with IoT technology in industries, an analysis of production speed is determined and obtained production requirement information is transferred through established connections and as a result, production rate could be altered based on current circumstances. One issue that became a common problem for the whole world in recent years is energy. When energy consuming devices are connected to the Internet, remote control is possible and significant energy savings could be achieved. Especially, avoiding unnecessary energy consumption will result in significant profits for the country's economy in the short run.

One of the areas of IoT technology implementation is the health sector. The physical conditions of individuals and other living creatures can be monitored with the help of sensors. For example, while away from a health care facility, the flow of important health data could be provided in terms of health with the help of medical devices inserted in the body or placed on the patient's skin. This technology can be used without any pain to the patient and without disrupting their daily activities (Aktaş, Çeken, & Erdemli, 2014; Çınar, 2015). Along with the patient's family, physicians can also track patients' heartbeat and blood glucose (Hoy, 2015). One of the other uses of IoT technology is the automation of electrical systems in buildings over the Internet. With this system used in smart home appliances, which we have started to see in recent years, individual's lives are made easier, while energy savings and safety are ensured. IoT, which could be used outside the buildings as well as inside, can also be used in the regulation of traffic, cargo, transportation, and communication with vehicles. Besides all these, during preservation of food products, they are watched and tracked by various devices, and thus, preventing possible health problems. Another product of IoT technology is BiKN. With this technology, any lost belonging can be found via a smartphone, and when the smartphone is lost, it can be tracked and found via GPS even when its battery has died out (Johnson, Adams Becker, Estrada, & Freeman, 2015). Moreover, the use and future of IoT technology in the educational field is explained as follows:

An example of the use of IoT technologies for educational purposes is the use of cheap, easy-to-produce chip and sensors in campus areas. For example, the Twine product is a small box described as "the simplest way to connect stuff to the Internet". This product allows users to link almost any physical object to a local area network. Twine integrates sensors with a cloud-based service, allowing for easy setup and data transfer. Even people with no knowledge in coding software can receive text and email updates (Selinger et al., 2013). Selinger et al. (2013) emphasized that, in the near future, user-friendly technologies like Twine may soon be available for higher education, and sensor kits will also be used in K–12 level widely. Considering this aspect, thanks to the Internet of Things technology, many objects will attain a position that could serve educational purposes.

One of the educational institutions using IoT technology is the College of the Holy Cross in Massachusetts, USA. Biology lab freezer sensors at this college send email alerts when their temperatures drift out of the acceptable range. Thus, when the laboratory temperature is within unacceptable range, potential problems can be avoided. Moreover, IoT technology has a role in facilitating the lives of students in classrooms, laboratories, and the burden on facilities management. For example, students in the Massachusetts campus are able to use their smartphones to check whether washers are free in the dormitory laundry room (Peterson, 2014).

As is known, generally schools have limited resources. IoT technology can be useful in utilizing these limited resources efficiently and reducing energy costs. For example, the New Richmond Exempted Village Schools, located in Tipp City, Ohio, save $128,000 annually due to an energy conservation program that involved building automation retrofits and more accurate monitoring of energy consumption (Lutz, 2014). The use of devices which send a warning message to the staff in charge when energy consuming devices are left on during non-working hours can provide quite substantial savings in the medium term.

In many countries, one of the common concerns of parents is the safety of their children at school. It is known that many projects and studies were conducted on school and student safety. At this point, it is possible that the IoT technology could be an effective tool. For this purpose, cameras that communicate with security officers, administrators or parents, motion sensors and customized locking systems can be used. In Japan's Tokyo Rikkyo primary school, a RFID card application was initiated to accurately monitor the comings and goings of students in real time. RFID cards were requested to be mounted on students' personal belongings (e.g. bag, coat). Via these active RFID cards, student's arrival and departure times were recorded and controlled in real time. Through the RFID application, tracking students' school arrival and departure times are published at an identified web site and location of active RFID tags (in the classroom, in the canteen, in library etc.) could be verified through camera recordings in real-time. Additionally, school management and families are warned and informed in the case of a possible accident or natural disasters.

Educational Potential of IoT in Seamless Learning

In the contemporary world, learners want to keep connected to the Internet anywhere at any time without spending an effort (Demir & Kuzu, 2015). The need and commitment to technology and the Internet are significant in educational settings too. Individuals are experiencing seamless learning especially with the help of new technologies regardless of time and space. In this sense, traditional learning methods and tools are outdated and inadequate for some of today's learners (Castronova, 2002; Darling-Hammond, 2006). The platforms through which learners get, share, and use information has changed with the spread of the Internet and learning activities have mostly became Internet-based. The new generation smart

Figure 3. The model of IoT in seamless learning

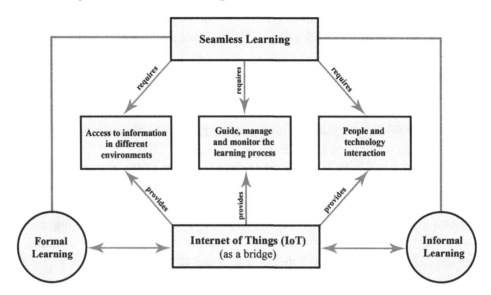

object technology can calculate elements such as cost, age, temperature, color, pressure and humidity and transfer them instantly. Students can annotate them with descriptions, instructions, tutorials, pictures, links to other objects, etc. IoT would allow access to these data easily (Johnson et al., 2013). According to 2015 Horizon Report, this technology is expected to become prevalent in higher education (Johnson et al., 2015). In this section, the relationship between IoT and seamless learning is identified. Also, the educational potential of IoT in seamless learning is discussed with a reference to the existing literature.

In seamless learning, individuals achieve learning experiences across different scenarios and contexts (Chan et al, 2006). IoT enables learners to learn any learning content at any given time in an uninterrupted way by making every object in learning environment digital, intelligent and connected to a network. Therefore, IoT provides technological background for seamless learning environments (Xue, Wang & Chen, 2011). Based on this idea, researchers have suggested the following model (Figure 3):

Figure 3 shows the role of IoT in the realization of seamless learning. Various requirements must be provided for the effective realization of seamless learning. First, seamless learning requires the opportunity to access information in different environments (D'Aniello, Gaeta, Orciuoli et al., 2015). The second requirement is the use of technology to guide, manage and monitor the learning process (Sharples, 2015). One another requirement is the interaction between people and machines in order to ensure information exchange (Milrad et al., 2013). IoT, having technologies such as sensor, RFID, NFC and cloud computing, can meet all the requirements of seamless learning. Technologies, such as mobile devices, can assist this exchange of information by allowing students to achieve learning experiences at home, outdoors, and in enriched locations such as museums or field trips, and then examine these experiences in the classroom environment (Selinger et al., 2013; Wong & Looi, 2011). One of the greatest developments of the 21st century is the fact that learning environments do not include only the quality, but also the place and type of learning. With advancing technologies, students spend more time in such 'informal' settings than in 'formal' settings (Looi et al., 2009). Therefore, a bridge could be built between formal and informal learning through IoT technologies in order to achieve seamless learning. When related literature is reviewed, it could be observed that IoT has a potential to provide seamless learning. This potential will be further discussed in the following section.

Mobile devices are used more frequently for different purposes, particularly for educational ones (Şad, Göktaş, & Ebner, 2016). Today, mobile devices that are enriched with sensors can gather information from the nearby area and they can communicate with one another (Specht & Klemke, 2013). Since these technologies are easy-to-use and wearable, they enable students to share their experiences instantly. Mobile technologies open up new opportunities for connecting and bridging the contexts, and this is linked to seamless support of learning events distributed across time, space, and social contexts (Specht & Klemke, 2013). Thanks to these interconnected mobile devices, learners can get the information in any space and time they need it, and they can share this information with their friends, peers and teachers. Furthermore, IoT technology allows teachers or schools to gather information about their students and they can exchange data with students and teachers in full-time. With the future IoT technology, communication between different information sources will be effective in ensuring seamless learning.

Sensor technology is used for receiving information about individuals' daily activities such as diet, fitness, health, lifestyle, productivity and learning process performances. Especially regarding the learning process, sensors can give detailed information about individuals' learning styles and thus, a regulation or restructuring of the learning process might become possible. Gathering information about learners and their learning progress are at the core of computer based educational environments. Especially, adaptive learning environments use assessment and user tracking for personalization of interaction with the learner (Specht & Klemke, 2013). In this context, IoT technology can be useful to provide data infrastructure for creating adaptive learning environments. Particularly, big data about learners (collected through sensors) can be analyzed and each learner's learning style and needs can be specified. The more information collected about the learners, the more adaptive and individualized systems could be created.

Analyzing the big data and translating it into action has now gained importance (Lutz, 2014). A huge amount of data is being generated as a result of forum discussions, exam results, student information, attendance and request status by the recently popular platform of Massive Open Online Courses (MOOC). According to Çınar (2015), with the help of these statistical data, it is possible to track the time spent on each lesson and topic or determine the attractive aspects of any lesson. Thus, customized learning environments and learning content can be shaped according to the needs of students. Moreover, feedback received from the students enables finding more about strengths and weaknesses of the learning environments. IoT technologies are used to collect these data and makes them more valuable and functional (Lutz, 2014).

Expansion of wearable technologies into our lives will enlarge the use of the IoT technologies. Wearable devices are technologies which surround the human body with their sensors and display units, and these technologies offer the opportunity to understand and experience the reality by addressing multiple senses (Erbaş & Demirer, 2014). These devices -with a mobility feature- provide ubiquitous access to learning resources. With these features, these devices can be named as a seamless learning assistants. In this regard, these devices provide data exchange by connecting to the Internet and they will make every moment of future learners' lives a seamless learning experience.

Libraries are one of the areas of educational use of the IoT technology (Hoy, 2015). One of the areas of library use of the IoT technology is Beacon. Beacon is a smartphone application working with a transmitter and sends location-triggered information and services that matches the interests of individual customers. Libraries use these triggers to announce their events, provide navigation and recommendations (Sarmah, 2015). The use of IoT technology in libraries is not limited to this. A study was conducted in 2015 to evaluate librarians' familiarity with and views about the Internet of Things and related technologies, in order to find out how to integrate these technologies into library functions. It was reported that

IoT technology could be used for inventory control, mobile payments, ticketing and event registration, climate and room configuration, accessibility, way-finding, and increasing resource availability (OCLC, 2015). A similar technology called iBeacon is used in the museums. With this technology, objects, text, video, audio or multimedia content is transferred in the form of a story. When all these are taken into account, these objects, which are connected to the Internet, enable students to be informed by massive resources and social observation data (Hancock, 2014). In this regard, IoT can be used in order to achieve authentic learning experiences in different places such as libraries, museums, and historical areas.

Devices connected to the Internet can make the lives of students with special needs easier in different environments. For instance, a card with personal information can be handed to a student with sight problem. When this learner swipes this card to the computer, text font on the screen can become bigger or screen contrast can be improved by making the background white and the text font black. Calls to teachers can be sent by students who need help. Thus, a suitable environment is provided that matches the student's individual needs. In this case, it will also save time for students and teachers. Transportation of learners with sight and speech problems to school could be facilitated by providing the shuttle location via GPS. Thus, a sense of confidence and independence would be given to disabled individuals with special needs. In their study, Coetzee and Olivrin (2012) suggest that a person with disability can use microphones, automatic speech recognition or press a help button on an interactive display, or through accessing a city service from his smart mobile device. A similar application was conducted in Australia for students with special needs. Sensor gloves are being explored to provide feedback to children learning Australian sign language with a computer. A learner attempts to sign while wearing the glove; the information is transferred to the computer, which gives the learner a feedback on the accuracy of his/her signing. Research shows that learning is enhanced when the feedback is received timely and correctly (Selinger et al., 2013).

CONCLUSION

The IoT technology, which is thought to have a transformative effect on society, is regarded to affect educational settings as well. Literature review revealed that sample applications of these technologies were quite few, but a widespread future use is a high possibility. IoT is considered to be one of the key technologies that will contribute to the construction of seamless learning environments. This technology can be integrated to seamless learning through connected objects. Initially, technology was not considered as an essential component of seamless learning (Wong, Chin, & Tay, 2011). However, with the increasing prevalence of mobile and wireless devices, the technology use in formal and informal learning settings has become inevitable. Kuh (1996) emphasized the significance of creating the connection between in-class and out-of-class learning experiences in ensuring seamless learning. Chan et al. (2006) underlined the use of mobile devices connected to the Internet to ensure this connection. Accordingly, IoT technologies can enrich the learning process by introducing a technological dimension to seamless learning.

The IoT concept can be an effective way of using technology. In this sense, curriculum programs, which help learners to develop, structure and comprehend future technologies, should be developed. It is now known that maker culture should be taught in future schools. One of the prerequisites for this is developing problem-based and project-based learning activities. It is very important to consider all these factors when developing new curriculum for programming objects that can be connected to the internet. Creative workshops for developing software should be integrated to the schools. Based on this idea, the United Kingdom Open University redesigned the computer science undergraduate program. One of the lessons in this program called "My digital life" was designed within the framework of IoT. By doing so, instead of explaining the IoT concept technically, the aim was that students could perceive IoT by understanding their own world, questioning it and realizing their roles. Also, it was stated that the use of learning analytics in massive open online courses would get more efficient results in future studies (Kortuem, Bandara, Smith et al., 2013). The IoT training should be developed via joint efforts of the academia and industry (Ning & Hu, 2012). For example, China has developed a strategic program based on the development of core technologies and applications in the IoT field, focusing on agriculture, logistics, transportation, electricity, public health and other important industries (Wang, 2012). It is also observed that companies such as CISCO, IBM and Intel are cooperating with universities on IoT education. Intel is in agreement with various academies for the training of personnel who will develop these objects in the future.

Consequently, with increasing Internet use, a large amount of data has accumulated. However, storage and management of this data and its use naturally has become quite significant. Besides many benefits of IoT technology, there are also limitations such as privacy and security. Nonetheless, on an educational perspective, IoT technology is expected to contribute to educational institutions in the fields of communication, interaction, ergonomics, and safety. Even though managers and teachers are not as open to technology as students, acceptance and adaptation of the IoT technology will become mandatory as a result of the extensive use of cloud computing and mobile devices. Additionally, this and other similar technologies shall not be seen as an element of consumption, but instead they should be utilized for production. Application development in this field should be a priority to help learners to take advantage of the unique opportunity provided by IoT technologies. The use of IoT technology in educational settings and organizing training in IoT for future generations with an innovative perspective will become quite significant.

When the educational use of IoT technologies will become widespread, learning will become more authentic with out-of-setting participation that would be independent of the classroom. In this context, IoT technology has a strong potential for the realization of seamless learning. IoT, which provides seamless learning anywhere with an Internet connection, can be preferred in the learning experience by enabling a universal status, without being limited to specific areas. One of the targets of IoT is to communicate anytime, anywhere, using any media (Zhou & Chao, 2011). Similarly, in seamless learning, reaching accessing the information or the learning environment anytime, anywhere, and using any educational media is significant. Through IoT, new learning environments, which can be defined as "seamless learning environments with interconnected devices," could be developed. These interconnected devices can be useful tools in ensuring lifelong seamless learning. Therefore, future studies should seek answers for the following questions: "How to use interconnected objects in seamless learning environments", "What type of seamless learning activities can be realized with interconnected devices?" As a result, IoT has a long way to go in achieving seamless learning in formal or informal educational settings and more research is required in the educational context.

REFERENCES

Aktaş, F., Çeken, C., & Erdemli, Y. E. (2014). *Biyomedikal uygulamaları için nesnelerin interneti tabanlı veri toplama ve analiz sistemi*. Tıp Teknolojisi Ulusal Kongresi, Kapadokya.

Alcaraz, C., Najera, P., Lopez, J., & Roman, R. (2010). Wireless sensor networks and the internet of things: Do we need a complete integration? In *1st International Workshop on the Security of the Internet of Things (SecIoT'10)*.

American College Personnel Association. (1994). *The student learning imperative: Implications for student affairs*. Washington, DC: Author.

Armbrust, M., Fox, A., Griffith, R., Joseph, A. D., Katz, R., Konwinski, A., & Zaharia, M. et al. (2010). A view of cloud computing. *Communications of the ACM, 53*(4), 50–58. doi:10.1145/1721654.1721672

Ashton, K. (2009). That 'internet of things' thing. *RFiD Journal, 22*(7), 97–114.

Botta, A., de Donato, W., Persico, V., & Pescapé, A. (2014, August). On the integration of cloud computing and internet of things. In *Future internet of things and cloud (FiCloud),2014 International Conference on* (23-30). IEEE. doi:10.1109/FiCloud.2014.14

Castronova, J. A. (2002). Discovery learning for the 21st century: What is it and how does it compare to traditional learning in effectiveness in the 21st century. *Action Research Exchange, 1*(1), 1–12.

Chan, T. W., Roschelle, J., Hsi, S., Kinshuk, , Sharples, M., Brown, , & Hoppe, U. et al. (2006). One-to-one technology-enhanced learning: An opportunity for global research collaboration. *Research and Practice in Technology Enhanced Learning, 1*(1), 3–29. doi:10.1142/S1793206806000032

Çınar, D. (2015). *Öğrenme nesnelerinin interneti (iolt)*. Retrieved January 03, 2016, from http://www.egitimdeteknoloji.com/ogrenme-nesnelerinin-interneti-iolt/

Cisco Global Cloud Index. (n.d.). *Forecast and methodology, 2014–2019*. Retrieved January 02, 2016, from http://www.cisco.com/c/en/us/solutions/collateral/service-provider/global-cloud-index-gci/Cloud_Index_White_Paper.pdf

Coetzee, L., & Olivrin, G. (2012). *Inclusion through the Internet of Things*. INTECH Open Access Publisher. doi:10.5772/31929

D'Aniello, G., Gaeta, A., Orciuoli, F., Rossi, P. G., & Tomasiello, S. (2015). Handling continuity in seamless learning via opportunistic recognition and evaluation of activity cohesion. In *Intelligent Networking and Collaborative Systems (INCOS), 2015 International Conference on* (pp. 429-434). IEEE. doi:10.1109/INCoS.2015.55

Darling-Hammond, L. (2006). Constructing 21st-century teacher education. *Journal of Teacher Education, 57*(3), 300–314. doi:10.1177/0022487105285962

Deepti, M. V., Ganesh, L., & Prasad, S. D. (2011). Turbo coding based high performance technique to minimise privacy and safety issues in RFID. *International Journal of Engineering Research and Applications, 1*(3), 879–883.

Demir & Kuzu. (2015). Giyilebilir teknolojiler ve eğitimde kullanımı. In B. Akkoyunlu, A. İşman & H. F. Odabaşı (Eds.), Eğitimde teknoloji okumaları 2015 (pp. 251-266). Ankara: Academic Press.

Erbaş, Ç., & Demirer, V. (2014). Eğitimde artırılmış gerçeklik uygulamaları: Google Glass örneği. *Journal of Instructional Technologies & Teacher Education, 3*(2), 8–16.

Evans, D. (2011). The internet of things: How the next evolution of the internet is changing everything. *CISCO White Paper, 1*, 1-11. Retrieved January 02, 2016, from http://www.cisco.com/c/dam/en_us/about/ac79/docs/innov/IoT_IBSG_0411FINAL.pdf

Fraser, Q. S. (1995). *The Trojan Room Coffee Pot*. Retrieved January 03, 2016, from https://www.cl.cam.ac.uk/coffee/qsf/coffee.html

Goldman Sachs. (2014). *The internet of things: Making sense of the next mega-trend*. Retrieved January 02, 2016, from http://www.goldmansachs.com/our-thinking/outlook/internet-of-things/iot-report.pdf

Growthcap. (2014). *Internet of Things: overhyped or investment opportunity?* Retrieved January 04, 2016, from https://growthcap.co/articles/?p=360

Hancock, M. (2014). *Ubiquitous everything and then some*. Retrieved January 03, 2016, from http://er.educause.edu/articles/2014/9/ubiquitous-everything-and-then-some

Hoy, M. B. (2015). The "Internet of Things": What it is and what it means for libraries. *Medical Reference Services Quarterly, 34*(3), 353–358. doi:10.1080/02763869.2015.1052699 PMID:26211795

IERC. (2014). *Internet of things*. Retrieved January 03, 2016, from http://www.internet-of-things-research.eu/about_iot.htm

ITU. (2012). *Overview of the Internet of things*. Retrieved January 10, 2016 from https://www.itu.int/rec/dologin_pub.asp?lang=e&id=T-REC-Y.2060-201206-I!!PDF-E&type=*items*

Johnson, L., Adams Becker, S., Cummins, M., Estrada, V., Freeman, A., & Ludgate, H. (2013). *NMC Horizon Report: 2013 Higher Education Edition*. Austin, TX: The New Media Consortium.

Johnson, L., Adams Becker, S., Estrada, V., & Freeman, A. (2015). *NMC Horizon Report: 2015 Higher Education Edition*. Austin, TX: The New Media Consortium.

Juels, A. (2006). RFID security and privacy: A research survey. *Selected Areas in Communications. IEEE Journal on, 24*(2), 381–394.

Kortuem, G., Bandara, A. K., Smith, N., Richards, M., & Petre, M. (2013). Educating the internet-of-things generation. *Computer, 46*(2), 53–61. doi:10.1109/MC.2012.390

Kuh, G. D. (1996). Guiding principles for creating seamless learning environments for undergraduates. *College Student Development, 37*(2), 135–148.

Liu, T., & Lu, D. (2012). The application and development of IOT. In *Information Technology in Medicine and Education (ITME), 2012 International Symposium on* (Vol. 2, 991-994). IEEE.

Looi, C. K., Seow, P., Zhang, B., So, H. J., Chen, W., & Wong, L. H. (2010). Leveraging mobile technology for sustainable seamless learning: A research agenda. *British Journal of Educational Technology*, *41*(2), 154–169. doi:10.1111/j.1467-8535.2008.00912.x

Lutz, R. (2014). *The implications of the internet of things for education.* Retrieved January 12, 2016, from http://www.systech.com/the-implications-of-the-internet-of-things-for-education

Milrad, M., Wong, L. H., Sharples, M., Hwang, G. J., Looi, C. K., & Ogata, H. (2013). Seamless learning: An international perspective on next-generation technology-enhanced learning. In Z. L. Berge & L. Y. Muilenburg (Eds.), *Handbook of Mobile Learning* (pp. 95–108). New York: Routledge.

National Research Council. (1995). *Expanding the vision of sensor materials.* Washington, DC: National Academy Press.

Ning, H., & Hu, S. (2012). Technology classification, industry, and education for future internet of things. *International Journal of Communication Systems*, *25*(9), 1230–1241. doi:10.1002/dac.2373

OCLC. (2015). *Libraries and the Internet of Things.* Retrieved January 12, 2016, from https://www.oclc.org/publications/nextspace/articles/issue24/librariesandtheinternetofthings.en.html

Peterson, T. (2014). *The internet of things goes to college.* Retrieved January 12, 2016, from http://www.edtechmagazine.com/higher/article/2014/05/internet-things-goes-college

Şad, S. N., & Göktaş, Ö. (2014). Preservice teachers' perceptions about using mobile phones and laptops in education as mobile learning tools. *British Journal of Educational Technology*, *45*(4), 606–618. doi:10.1111/bjet.12064

Şad, S. N., Göktaş, Ö., & Ebner, M. (2016). Prospective teachers—are they already mobile? In Mobile, Ubiquitous, and Pervasive Learning Fundaments, Applications, and Trends (pp. 139-166). Springer.

Sarmah, S. (2015). *The internet of things plan to make libraries and museums awesomer.* Retrieved January 04, 2016, from http://www.fastcompany.com/3040451/elasticity/the-internet-of-things-plan-to-make-libraries-and-museums-awesomer

Selinger, M., Sepulveda, A., & Buchan, J. (2013). *Education and the internet of everything: How ubiquitous connectedness can help transform pedagogy.* White Paper. Cisco.

Sharples, M. (2015). Seamless learning despite context. In L.-H. Wong, M. Milrad, & M. Specht (Eds.), *Seamless learning in the age of mobile connectivity* (pp. 41–55). Springer Singapore.

Specht, M., & Klemke, R. (2013) Enhancing learning with technology.*Proceedings of the Third International Conference on e-Learning*.

Tarman, F. (2014). *Şeylerin (nesnelerin) interneti nedir?* Retrieved January 13, 2016, from http://www.teknomani.com/2014/12/internet-of-things.html

Wang, Y. (2012). *China pushes development of internet of things.* Retrieved January 26, 2016, http://news.xinhuanet.com/english/china/2012-02/14/c_131410233.htm

Want, R. (2006). An introduction to RFID technology. *Pervasive Computing, IEEE*, *5*(1), 25–33. doi:10.1109/MPRV.2006.2

Wong, L. H. (2012). A learner-centric view of mobile seamless learning. *British Journal of Educational Technology, 43*(1), 19–23. doi:10.1111/j.1467-8535.2011.01245.x

Wong, L. H., Chin, C. K., & Tay, B. P. (2011). A wiki technology-supported seamless learning approach for Chinese language learning. *US-China Education Review, 7*(1), 891–902.

Wong, L. H., & Looi, C. K. (2011). What seams do we remove in mobile-assisted seamless learning? A critical review of the literature. *Computers & Education, 57*(4), 2364–2381. doi:10.1016/j.compedu.2011.06.007

Xue, R., Wang, L., & Chen, J. (2011, July). Using the IOT to construct ubiquitous learning environment. In *Mechanic Automation and Control Engineering (MACE), 2011 Second International Conference on* (7878-7880). IEEE.

Zhou, L., & Chao, H. C. (2011). Multimedia traffic security architecture for the internet of things. *IEEE Network, 25*(3), 35–40. doi:10.1109/MNET.2011.5772059

Zikopoulos, P., Eaton, C., deRoos, D., Detusch, T., & Lapis, G. (2012). *Understanding big data: Analytics for enterprise class hadoop and streaming data*. New York: McGraw.

Zuerner, H. (2014). The Internet of things as greenfield model: A categorization attempt for labeling smart devices in internet of things (WF-IoT). *IEEE World Forum.*

KEY TERMS AND DEFINITIONS

Big Data: All the data we have obtained from different sources is transformed into meaningful and actionable format.

Cloud Computing: A common information sharing service between computing devices.

Internet of Things: A network of items -each embedded with sensors- which are connected each other via Internet.

Near Field Communication: A short-range wireless technology. It enables simple and safe communication between devices by locating them in a short distance.

Radio Frequency Identification: An automated identification technology for objects and humans.

Seamless Learning: The seamless integration of the learning experiences across various dimensions.

Sensor: A device that provides usable output in response to a specified measured.

This work was previously published in Digital Tools for Seamless Learning edited by Süleyman Nihat Şad and Martin Ebner, pages 145-159, copyright year 2017 by Information Science Reference (an imprint of IGI Global).

Chapter 2
Establishing Governance for Hybrid Cloud and the Internet of Things

Martin Wolfe
IBM Corporation, USA

ABSTRACT

This chapter is focused on the current and future state of operating a Hybrid Cloud or Internet of Things (IoT) environment. This includes tools, data, and processes which allow an organization to use these assets to serve business goals. Examining governance in this context shows how it works today and how it should change, using some real-world examples to show the impacts and advantages of these changes. It is a high level overview of those important topics with prescriptive detail left for a future and follow-on analysis. Finally, all of the lessons learned, when combined together form a governance fabric, resulting in a set of techniques and actions which tie together into a supporting framework and set of processes. The important questions include: Why does governance matter in the deployment and operation of Hybrid Cloud and IoT? If governance already exists how must it change? What are the important and salient characteristics of governance which need special focus? Thus, this analysis gives a context of how today's governance approach should change when moving to a Hybrid Cloud or IoT model.

INTRODUCTION

The focus of this chapter is a review on the unique perspective of governance when deploying, operating or using a Hybrid Cloud or Internet of Things (IoT) technical infrastructure. This type of governance has many unique considerations, but understanding the similarities with traditional ITIL-style governance ensures the most important foundations are not ignored. It is the combination of new and existing techniques which are key to the success of governance in this rapidly changing style of technology deployment. It is these similarities and differences which are key guiding principles in how to establish a governance process when working with different service providers, in different locations, all with different approaches to security, deployment and operations. The need for technical integration, for the

DOI: 10.4018/978-1-5225-1832-7.ch002

Figure 1. The important stages of hybrid governance

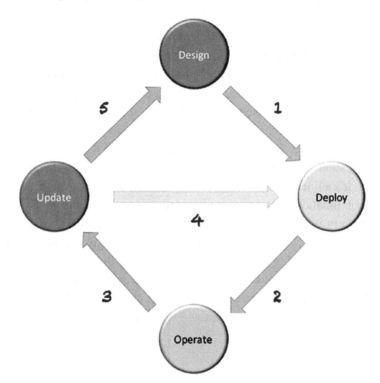

sharing of data and resources, is the typical and seemingly obvious entry being the first thing considered for change or update. The more important and vital need is to establish a set of processes where it is *well understood* how services interact, how they are chosen, how they are secured, how they are deployed, how they are updated and how they are operated.

Throughout this chapter, the various stages of governance as it applies to Hybrid Cloud or the IoT will be covered. It is important to understand how governance may change and is applied when deploying an infrastructure versus when it is being operated or updated. In addition, in this chapter the terms *infrastructure* or *environment* are used interchangeably throughout the text. The broader relationship between the key governance stages is shown in Figure 1.

Many organizations and companies, small and large, are using services from various providers, and they are doing it now, either with the blessing of their Information Technology (IT) staff and just as often without IT knowing that it is happening, a common phenomenon called Shadow IT (Raden, 2005). For those companies which are relatively new, say less than 5 years old and around 100-1000 employees, this is likely how they are currently opperating. Their base assumption is focused on the idea that IT infrastructure is not something they need to own, but just use as needed, much like power and water. Everything treated as a utility. For existing organizations, who have legacy assets with stricter data and compliance protocols, there is a mix of these existing assets (data, servers, policies, and processes) and the need and desire to use new capabilities, often provided by outside vendors and in fact managed by those vendors. They want to use and experiment in an agile fashion, with new business models while keeping the cost of this experimentation as low as possible. While it always depends on the size and type of company, the mindset of the IT team is often different from those focused on business goals. Thus, governance, rules, and policies on how technology is used to meet business goals are going to have a different focus in each of these groups.

The application of governance for these new deployment models, such as Hybrid Cloud and IoT, requires special consideration of the audience or constituency which will create the model and who will be the users impacted by the processes and model when put into practice. Furthermore, the creation of this model needs to take into account whether it is applied differently for different situations or events. In a similar fashion to standard ITIL based governance, when applying to Hybrid Cloud and IoT, the application of incident, problem, and change management processes will need to be applied in a way that matches the event being governed. For example, if there is a network outage this is handled primarily through incident management with problem and change management being invoked to prevent this from occurring in the future. It's a linear progression and application of core governance processes. However for those events such continual data assurance and security perimeter control, just two of many types of examples, the application of incident management should be considered to be in parallel with problem and change management. These two types of events require that the governance processes have a different *temporal applicability*, once being linear and one being in parallel. Thus the event type and audience applying the governance processes need to be considered. Given this, there are some really important guiding principles when it comes to governance and the relationship to Hybrid Cloud and IoT. This is not just about governance but why it is important and what should be done to get started and keep the momentum going into steady state operations.

Guiding Principles

While this might be obvious in some cases, in nearly every Hybrid deployment, governance turns out to be overlooked and is the missing key component. Agreeing on these early on, makes it all much easier, and less expensive in the long run:

- **The Basics are the Same:** The governance processes and model for both Hybrid Cloud and the Internet of Things are the same. How incident, problem, and change management are handled is not fundamentally different.
- **Hybrid Cloud is the Foundation:** It's easier to leverage or deploy IoT resources, tools and components if you start by using Hybrid Cloud. An IoT hosting platform and the "things" it connects can only run in a Hybrid Cloud hosting environment. IoT needs Hybrid Cloud to work properly.
- **Data Lineage is Vitally Important:** Knowing the path your data travels is really important. Knowing the data lineage is the basis for both Hybrid Cloud and IoT Security.
- **Different Deployment Makes Sense:** Hybrid Cloud and IoT can be entirely "off-premises", entirely "on-premises" or a combination of on and off premises. There are many different deployment patterns where governance applies.
- **The Network is Key:** Net-centric operating principles (such as synchronous and asynchronous integration), including complex connectivity across physical and logical locations, form the core of the governance model.
- **Governance May Change:** Depending on the phase in which governance is being used, governance may be applied differently. Phases such as initial design, deployment to the end user, or operation of the environment, plus the management disciplines such as incident, problem, change, and security management disciplines can be applied differently

Which Characteristics Are Impacted?

Understanding the impacts of a Hybrid Cloud or Internet of Things style of technology deployment is important in determining the right governance model to put in place. There are some key impacts to consider both when there is some type of governance in place as well as when there is not any governance in place. In both situations, determining where and how to apply governance processes is important to ensure it can be effective in these new deployment models. More detail is provided throughout this chapter describing how real-world experiences are influenced and how those change how governance is applied.

Design and Deployment

One of the most important aspects of deploying or using a Hybrid Cloud technology infrastructure and, for that matter, using an Internet of Things platform to connect devices is overlooked and typically handled reactively instead of proactively. The ability for these types of technology environments to just work is not enough, they must be something that can be actually deployed and operated once deployment is complete. Understanding the integration between the processes needed to operate a Hybrid Cloud or IoT environment and those processes used to run the rest of IT while aligning with key governance processes used by the business is important in defining a Hybrid governance model. Governing both the design and deployment is important, but if it cannot be effectively operated, then all the work to design the model is merely academic. It is also important to note one of the important factors in governance of this type of complex deployment is tracking and management of the assets or "bill or materials" of those services and platforms being used in runtime environment. This is all part of the governance of a runtime system.

Security

The massive growth, both predicted and realized, in the deployment of devices and sensors creates an integrated web of connected "instances" both physical and logical. Given this growth, in both the number of devices and the number of service providers, all supporting the same solution, the movement of data and the number of possible entry points increases dramatically (Meulen, 2015). With each new connection and each new device, these become a new "door" or entry point for a hacker to try and penetrate. The key aspects of incident management are important in responding to breaches rapidly, where problem and change management need to be in place to prevent or mitigate the likelihood of future security incursions. Ensuring the feedback loop between operating an environment, updating, and then re-deploying that environment to handle security issues is something that needs to be addressed in these three areas of governance.

Operations

Data Quality and Assurance

In an environment with a heterogeneous set of service providers, data sources, integration points and different approaches to security and incident, problem, and change management, the lineage of data as it moves throughout a system of services and components needs to be both well understood and monitored. This is one of the most important foundations for assuring the quality and integrity of the data, in line with some of the precepts of Defense in Depth ("Defense in Depth", 2015). Furthermore, data lineage is key to root cause analysis (RCA). Determining where problems arise in these types of complex systems, where many providers and "things" are being integrated takes on additional complexity. Knowing where and how data moves is important in getting to root cause quickly, ultimately increasing availability and reducing operational expense.

Reusability

In part, this analysis focuses on the important aspects of governance and how it should be used and possibly adjusted to support a Hybrid Cloud or IoT deployment. However, one of the key guiding principles is that existing ITIL style governance does not have to be re-written but can be modified in some cases and used "as-is" in other cases. Some of the client examples, elsewhere in this chapter, discuss these type of examples. Thus, reusing an existing governance model with, what in the larger scheme of impacts are minor adjustments to support a service bureau and elastic consumption model, saves significant time and money for an organization. This is especially true for existing organizations, but it also has real value for new organizations. For new organizations, their ability to take an existing governance model and adapt it to their goals and needs, also has significant savings in time and money. It really makes sense to use an existing governance model, while making adjustments to the model, in specific ways, supporting this ability to consume technology resources in an elastic model, like a utility, and to support multiple technology deployment models. These types of deployments include on-premises, off-premises and multiple combinations of these models as needed for a particular organization or company. One of the key assumptions in this chapter is the ability to reuse an existing governance model, leveraging ITIL techniques as a guide and making modifications to it to support the service bureau and service broker style of delivery between IT to the business in an organization.

BACKGROUND

In deploying and using a Hybrid Cloud model, there are several important concepts and assumptions which are typically applied when talking about the design, deployment and operation of this type of technical infrastructure. As described elsewhere in this chapter, many of these key concepts apply not only to Hybrid Cloud but also to using and deploying devices and data to an Internet of Things platform. This topic of governance is more important than is typically understood. Without some kind of governance in place, and the needed updates and enhancements in order to support Hybrid Cloud and IoT, these types of environments and technical infrastructures will not be able to operate. In the worst cases, determining the root cause of problems and ensuring data integrity across the connective fabric of these systems will be nearly impossible to determine and mitigate. Thus, the inspiration for this chapter and this topic is to help assure that when dealing with the highly complex nature of these integrated physical and logical systems, there is a foundation and set of processes in place to help operate and maintain the availability, resiliency and reliability of these environments. This work is inspired not by analysts reports or presentations but by real-world implementation experience through anecdotal evidence from many types of engagements and deployments.

Moreover, this chapter contains a focus on how an IT organization would operate a Hybrid Cloud style infrastructure or how it would leverage IoT technology to connect devices and objects both physical and logical. While reviewing the content here, it is important to understand there is both explicit and implied bias towards IT. However, governance is equally valuable to both an IT organization and the business entities it supports. Governance is the fabric to tie together the ability of IT and the business to successfully deliver capability in support of the organization's goals and measurements.

Where and How Does Governance Apply?

Think about the two types of organizations and the most important questions to address when applying governance in this Hybrid world:

1. For existing organizations, how do they have a common "management" and "governance" set of steps, which responds at the speed of their business, both for existing assets and these new capabilities, which they want to rapidly integrate into their toolset?
2. For new organizations, what is the path of evolution from their combined model of operating to separation of concerns in their organization and yet leverage a common operating model (instead of just yelling across the office when there's a problem, college dorm room style)?

Furthermore, examining Figure 1, the application of governance will be slightly different in each phase of a governance lifecycle.

Design

During the design phase, this is where the deployment specifications are created, including a definition of the functionality provided, such as cloud services from a Hybrid Cloud or the connection of devices and systems through an IoT deployment. In addition to the functionality, the question of "how well" the system will work is specified through Service Level Agreements (SLA) and Service Level Objectives (SLO) in line with the ITIL model of governance. The design phase is key since this sets the tone for how much governance will be needed to deploy, update, and operate a Hybrid Cloud environment. The transition from designing to deployment is dependent on a sufficient level of design, and specifying these different service levels drives how much monitoring will be required for the Operate phase. Also covered during the design phase are the services, versus service levels, provided. Services such as infrastructure, connectivity or specific business functions are candidates for inclusion in a catalog of services. The design phase defines the initial set of these services which drive the SLA and SLO definitions for the deployed Hybrid Cloud or IoT environment.

Deploy

The deploy phase is where the actual implementation, installation, and configuration start. The result should be a running environment in support of the initial set of services in the catalog with the ability to extend in support of future services. The first instances of incident, problem, and change management will be encountered during this phase, as they apply typically to a runtime environment.

Operate

Once deployment is complete, transition into the Operate phase is next. The focus will be on incident and Problem Management specifically. Incident and Problem management are in flight considerations.

Update

Change management will be the key process during any updates to a deployed Hybrid Cloud or IoT environment. During the Update phase, change management is key especially given the complexity of multiple on-premises and off-premises systems. Any change to a single component will have a potential ripple effect across multiple systems. This is the same issues encountered when migrating from a traditional environment to a Hybrid Cloud environment, the affinity between systems must be understood. It is this affinity and inter-dependence between systems which requires an effective change management process to ensure that these cross-system effects are well understood. Once the update phase is complete, and there has been effective Change Management, re-deployment can occur ensuring all the right steps are in place and initial testing can take place.

Multiple Systems, Processes, and Integrations

What happens when we take the model of multiple components and multiple integrations to it's logical evolution? Having a combination of systems of record, systems of insight and systems of engagement both on premise and off premise is the typical pattern of complexity in this heterogeneous deployment. The key questions are how this be effectively managed and governed, and why is that important?

In fact, if you think about it, everyone is using this Hybrid model. We pay someone to collect our trash, pay the water company for just the amount of water we use and the power company for just the power we use. The utility model. It's a pay per use model in much of our daily lives and it is this Hybrid environment, comprising many components, systems, rules, laws, policies, and processes that we live in every day.

When it comes to consuming IT assets and technology imagine the issues when trying to use a utility style of consumption every day. Changes in how budgets are appropriated (from pre-defined to just-in-time), a different set of roles in IT, expectations from the business side of the house that more flexibility and speed of deployment are not only possible but are now an assumed minimum capability. In this new delivery model, and this is especially important with the increasing complexity of this truly distributed system of "pieces", management, governance, data integrity, and problem determination are more complex than ever. It is increasingly, and even exponentially difficult, to just "talk to the server team" or "talk to the network team" or "talk to the web server team" to figure out why the website is down, or SAP is not available. It's challenging to use this approach since it requires finding and bringing together just the right personnel to know the status of resources or the sources of problems in the runtime environment. For example, what happens when an organization's payroll does not get distributed on time. Since this is probably the most important business function in any organization, the entire IT staff typically organizes a series of root cause analysis and recovery sessions. Thus, governance is key. The ability to rapidly identify an event or incident, feed that into a problem management process, and leverage an effective change management method allows for the ability to learn from previous mistakes and problems and work to prevent them in the future.

In this review of Hybrid Cloud and IoT Governance, some fairly deep analysis is included, conclusions are provided, and some examples are provided in order to understand the context of where a Hybrid Governance Fabric should and would be applied.

How can we track the movement of data and track down the various issues that arise when these types of heterogeneous systems are used to build applications for the business? In this heterogeneous deployment, the data used by various applications is moving back and forth, on and off-premise, and the number of integrations between systems are significantly higher than a single system. This increases the complexity in trying to provide a governance framework, end to end, for these systems. Moreover, each point of integration between components and data sources has its own service level, support structure, and technology stack. The *composite nature* of these applications makes it much harder and more complex to manage changes, updates to releases, incidents and issues as well as ensuring security and compliance.

Regardless of the name applied to this governance approach, the truth about using this utility "cloud" model for delivering functionality, in support of the business is there will always be some "systems" which remain on-premises and some that are off-premises. All of these will likely be based on a variable set of technologies. It can be argued there are some organizations and enterprises which will use only those capabilities which they do not own. In this case everything will be consumed as a utility. However, for every case where there are no on-premises IT systems or on-premises data, there is at least one scenario where some piece of enterprise collateral will remain on their premise, at their site and/or in their possession. The "ground truth" is there will always be data sources and "business and technology assets" on premise which may or may not be core to the business. It is vital to bring these together in the proper order and in the proper context.

All enterprises and organizations, regardless of size, will retain some data or technical component "on their premise" and thus governance is needed to track, check, and maintain this cross-premise deployment of data, business logic, and applications. They will build more and more of these applications which integrate various components and data sources, both on and off-premise.

Bringing all of these aspects together is a model called the Hybrid Governance Fabric. This fabric is a compilation of important components. These include processes, existing and modified support models, data lineage and security, root cause analysis and multi-location deployment. Brought together these components form a tapestry which needs to be correctly and properly woven together.

Comparing Hybrid Governance to Your Life

This idea of the Hybrid Cloud and the Internet of Things (IoT) models being both similar to each other and essentially the same theme as how people live their daily lives, is illustrated in these views. In Figure 1, the deployment models of on and off-premise are mapped to ownership, incorporating also management as it applies to ownership and locality. The important factor is to understand the differences between each sector of the picture, which could easily be open for debate, and how they relate to the way utilities are consumed, such as power, water, food, etc. In Figure 2, you can see how the typical utilities which power society's infrastructure have a relationship to the various technology and IT related services consumed in an enterprise. In both scenarios, the connectivity between various systems, the location of those systems, and the importance of how data and information moves between them is key. Just as it is important that the power company properly meter the usage of power, it's important that the usage of compute, storage, network, data and applications be metered in manner that supports the ability to consume these resources in an elastic model.

Figure 2. The hybrid and IoT operational model

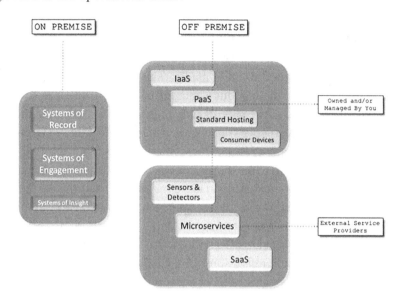

The ability to apply policies and to actually meter and monitor the usage of different systems is the vital element in ensuring that you can actually ensure security, compliance, and reliability of interconnected, heterogeneous, and location independent components. This interconnected and dispersed model is the foundation and key assumption in the deployment of a Hybrid Cloud infrastructure and an Internet of Things system of devices and data.

Hybrid Cloud and IoT can Use the Same Governance

The Internet of Things and Hybrid Cloud have emerged as commonly agreed upon models of deployment, they are typically considered different especially in the use cases they support. Experience in real-world deployments has shown that an IoT deployment is dependent on a Hybrid Cloud model and thus they are actually complimentary deployment models with many key similarities when it comes to governance, management, and operations. Thus, deploying governance in this type of heterogeneous mode, the steps and lifecycle of governance in support of *Connected Things* and in support of a Hybrid Cloud or IoT operating model share many of the same characteristics.

What are the key similarities between the Hybrid Cloud (sometimes called Hybrid IT) and Internet of Things (IoT) models? Let's take a look at the generic definitions of each, using Wikipedia, typically a generic enough source:

Hybrid cloud is a composition of two or more clouds (private, community or public) that remain distinct entities but are bound together, offering the benefits of multiple deployment models. Hybrid cloud can also mean the ability to connect collocation, managed and/or dedicated services with cloud resources. Gartner, Inc. defines a hybrid cloud service as a cloud computing service that is composed of some combination of private, public and community cloud services, from different service providers. A hybrid cloud service crosses isolation and provider boundaries so that it can't be simply put in one category of

Figure 3. Your life follows the integrated and interdependency model

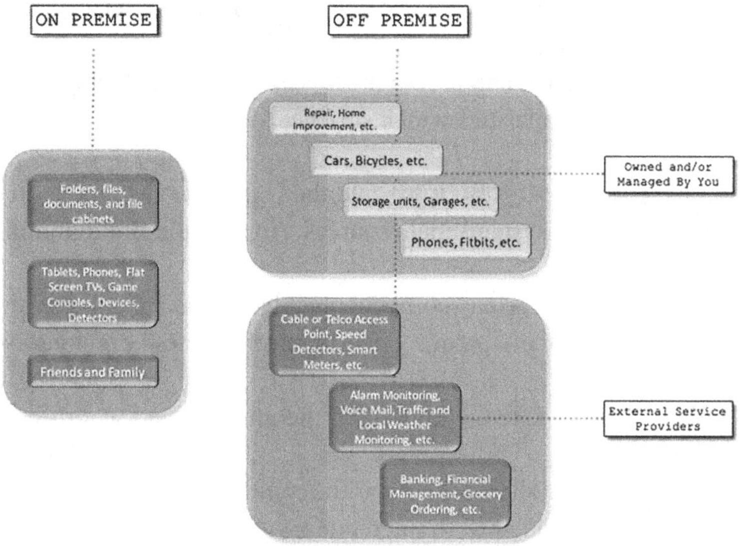

private, public, or community cloud service. It allows one to extend either the capacity or the capability of a cloud service, by aggregation, integration or customization with another cloud service (Cloud Computing, Hybrid Cloud section).

and

The Internet of Things (IoT) is the network of physical objects or "things" embedded with electronics, software, sensors, and network connectivity, which enables these objects to collect and exchange data. [1] The Internet of Things allows objects to be sensed and controlled remotely across existing network infrastructure,[2] creating opportunities for more direct integration between the physical world and computer-based systems, and resulting in improved efficiency, accuracy and economic benefit. Each thing is uniquely identifiable through its embedded computing system but is able to interoperate within the existing Internet infrastructure. (Internet of Things, 1ˢᵗ paragraph)

Evaluating the two commonly agreed upon definitions, there are a number of similarities and one key difference. Does this difference matter when it comes to governance? The important difference between Hybrid Cloud and the Internet of Things is it's dependence on physical devices and the connectivity between those devices. It does not rule out the ability for virtual devices and "things" (such as software defined radios, applications running in containers, virtual network switches, and other "appliances"), but there is a clear expectation that IoT assumes physical devices are connected across a heterogeneous network fabric, which can include both physical and logical devices and assets. This dependence, at least in terms of the definition of IoT, on physical sensors and devices, does not change how incidents, problems, and changes are handled. The process and method for handling this governance is essentially the same, while the tools used might (and will likely) be different. Thus, the biggest difference between a Hybrid Cloud and the Internet of Things is more of a distinction without being a real difference, in the broadest sense governance will be the same. What's key is these being two different definitions, but from a governance perspective they are treated one and the same. The model is the same. The impacts are the same. The governance and management are the same.

When looking at the definitions and comparing those with real world deployment experiences, there are a number of really important similarities which surface.

1. **Heterogeneous Interconnectivity:** Both IoT and the Hybrid model are based on connecting and running different components, systems, data sources, Application Programming Interfaces (API), and networks
2. **Location Independence:** The various components, assets, and functionality of a system can be located in different places, on or off-premise, in different countries or regions. Net-Centricity (Net-centric, 1st Section)
3. **Data Lineage:** While security is really important, the integrity and security of data is the core

Thus, one of the most of important shared aspects is the combination of incorporating a heterogeneous set of assets and functionality, and the need to interconnect these in a single operating environment to ensure data integrity, reliability and resilience.

In a Hybrid and IoT Connected Model, Governance is Important and Vital

It's important to note that this is IT governance versus just generic governance, so it's not as broad in scope as governance needed by formal governments or across an entire enterprise. However, it's scope is cross-enterprise in the sense of where technology assets are used, thus there are specific and numerous integrations between IT governance and corporate governance. While these integration points deserve their own detailed treatment, when establishing a governance model, the commonalities become clear. Thus, there are many similarities, but what's important for the context of the Hybrid Governance Fabric, is a focus on how this affects the operating model when using IT in support of providing business functionality. The IT governance Institute's definition is:

"... leadership, organizational structures and processes to ensure that the organization's IT sustains and extends the organization's strategies and objectives." (IT Governance Institute, p. 6)

HYBRID CLOUD AND IoT REQUIRE ADHERENCE TO GOVERNANCE

The set of Hybrid Cloud use cases is useful in understanding where and how governance may or may not apply. The really interesting observation is how close Hybrid Cloud and the Internet of Things are when it comes to governance and management of these environments.

When evaluating how to define a special governance model for Hybrid Cloud and IoT, understanding where there is overlap is important in determining where to focus. Notice that Hybrid Cloud is appropriate in nearly every use case, and this makes sense as the Internet of Things require a Hybrid Cloud style deployment foundation in order for it to effectively tie together all the various physical and logical devices and end points.

Figure 4. Mapping hybrid cloud and IoT to the key use cases

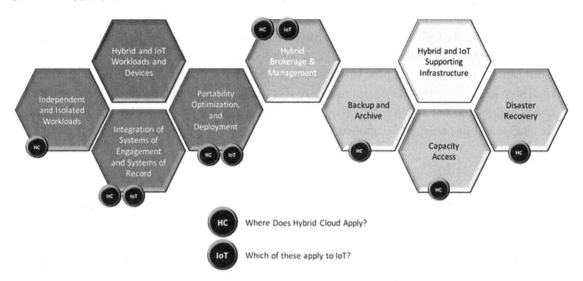

In evaluating how to define the more optimized governance model, specifying how many aspects of governance are affected provides a good foundation for establishing the best processes and role definitions.

Incident, Problem, and Change Management

While there are standardized definitions for incident, problem, and change management, typically spoken of as "ICP", the view used in this chapter will be one based on real-world and anecdotal experience from across a good number of organizations.

Incident Management is focused on the tracking and monitoring events which occur, typically, when some kind of technology based outage or error occurs in the use of a technology infrastructure. Sometimes this also includes reports of unofficial functionality which, while not an error, are unexpected.

Consider this representative list of important considerations for incident, problem, and change management:

1. Does the incident cross the boundaries of more than one environment? This is important in Hybrid Cloud, sincere there are multiple providers in multiple locations however it is even more important when it comes to IoT. Security is key and is at higher risk with IoT so understanding the root cause of an incident in a multi-environment and multi-device world is fundamentally important.
2. Once the problem has been identified, how can it be remediated? There is a key dependency on have good cross-site, cross-environment and cross-device incident management, so the root cause can be identified and documented. Now that the event has been documented, going through the full root cause analysis and remediation process is important so that this can be prevented in the future, if possible. Quite often, dealing with a problem is managed through the "fire drill phone call" or meeting where everyone who might be involved gets together and tries to figure out if this is the real problem, if the cause is known and how it could be fixed or remediated. This will not scale in a world where there are numerous end points, devices, cloud environments and technical platforms

with an exponentially larger number of interconnections between systems and components. Problem Management must be modified in order to more rapidly determine root cause and remediation. This can be achieved through more pro-active monitoring, asset tracking for interconnections, devices, and components, and well defined services which have well specified interfaces.

3. How can an existing problem be prevented from happening again? Change management is the final step in ensuring that future problems are less likely through making sure changes go through a well understood and documented process. Change management does not have to change to make this happen, it just needs to be applied.

Security

The challenge with security, in this Hybrid Cloud and IoT deployment approach, is less about the number of components and more focused on being able to easily add new services, end points, and devices nearly at will. Thus, complexity increases but more importantly the number of end points offering potential access into the overall system increases and at an unpredictable rate. Security is all about knowing what is deployed and what will be deployed. Tracking the impact of this unpredictable change in complexity is key. Asset management is a core capability to ensure is included. Modern IoT platforms, at least the ones where security exposure is being considered, have asset management and tracking built into the system. Further this asset management needs to focus on both the components and their interconnections.

SOLUTIONS AND RECOMMENDATIONS

Creating a Fabric for Hybrid Cloud and IoT Governance (HGF)

In terms of computing, IT, technology and applications, the idea of *fabrics* are a fundamental deployment concept. This interconnected set of processes is something called a "governance fabric". It is a single approach to managing the movement of data between service providers, different services, data sources, and heterogeneous infrastructures. The definition of a fabric is a really important foundation for the governance fabric. The definition has some important characteristics:

Fabric computing or unified computing involves constructing a computing fabric consisting of interconnected nodes ... Usually the phrase refers to a consolidated high-performance computing system consisting of loosely coupled storage, networking and parallel processing functions linked by high bandwidth interconnects ... but the term has also been used.. to describe platforms ... where the common theme is interconnected nodes that appear as a single logical unit ... The fundamental components of fabrics are "nodes" ... and "links". While the term "fabric" has also been used in association with storage area networks and switched fabric networking, the introduction of compute resources provides a complete "unified" computing system. Other terms used to describe such fabrics include "unified fabric", "data center fabric" and "unified data center fabric". (Fabric Computing, 1ˢᵗ paragraph)

Governance needs to be treated as its own fabric since it is the glue and the unifying approach to ensuring a Hybrid Cloud or IoT deployment can be effectively managed and operated. Furthermore, governance is much more challenging to effectively implement given the different types of integration

Table 1. The most important design, deployment, and operational considerations

Characteristic	Criteria
Security and Compliance	Focused on topics such as encryption, key management, regulatory compliance, compensating controls, intrusion detection, and auditing • Does the data need to be encrypted in flight or at rest (or both)? Do the transactions need to be encrypted? • Who will own management of encryption keys? • What types of auditing (e.g. level of detail or specific compliance) need to be supported once the workload is deployed? • What level of monitoring needs to be recorded and stored? • Will special intrusion detection (at the network, storage, and compute layers) be required? • What are the regulatory and/or compliance requirements (including FDA, HIPPA, PCI, FFIEC, etc.)? • Does the data need to stay within country and/or locale and does this include both application data and management system data? • Now that we are moving into the Cloud, are there compensating controls and/or reporting that can be put in place to achieve same result?
Capacity	Capacity requirements (the initial capacity needs) and capacity management (the needs during steady state) are some of the first things to understand including how much compute, storage, and network capacity is required • What initial capacity is needed to get the system initially up and running (understanding that you can scale up later) ? • What is the steady state capacity needed? • If the workload is re-engineered / re-architected when moving into a Cloud environment, how do the capacity requirements change? • What are the different levels of capacity needed for development, test, QA, and production?
Connectivity	The method for connecting from the existing enterprise network to a Cloud provider needs to be defined • What amount of bandwidth will be required for development, test, QA, and production deployments? • Are clients on the current network allowed direct workstation VPN client connectivity to an off-premise Cloud or must they go through a corporate VPN? • Is an IPSEC VPN required between the client and the cloud network? • Will the current environment and the target (cloud) environment be co-located in the same data center? • Will parts of the workload/application be located in different cloud data centers and across different Cloud providers? (e.g. leading to Hybrid Cloud)
Services Management (ITSM)	Defining how incidents, problems, and changes (requests) are handled now that the workload will be running in the Cloud • What is the process/workflow needed to support incident, problem, and change management once a workload is deployed into a Cloud environment? • How do these processes need to change in development, test, QA, and Production contexts? (Experience tells us there will surely be changes needed especially in a "Hybrid Cloud" scenario • Monitoring – How will monitoring be performed and who will have access to the monitoring data?
Managed Services	This topic is focused on providing management and oversight and is tightly linked to services management • Does corporate IT want full management from a vendor or partial "a la carte" management? (e.g. such as software patch management for a specific set of Cloud workloads, etc.) • Will the vendor's managed services (outsourcing) team be managing deployment of workloads to a single Cloud vendor or multiple service providers? • Metering – How will the use of the Cloud be measured? How does the client wanted to be charged? Will there be a need for an internal chargeback within the client's environment? • Will the managed services vendor have visibility to the data or only ping, power, and pipe?
Performance	Determining the level of performance (scalability, reliability, availability, etc.) required once in the Cloud will guide many other decisions • When moved to the Cloud, will the same level of performance be required in development, test, QA, and/or production use cases? • How is performance measured? • Who will execute performance testing and will the same scripts and use cases be used once the workload is moved to the Cloud?

between data sources, services, components, and service providers. Ensuring data integrity and determining the lineage of data are more challenge as is the determination of the root cause of incidents and problems that arise in the deployment and operation of these complex systems.

The Most Important Hybrid and IoT Deployment Considerations

Governance is focused on many different aspects of ensuring the Hybrid Cloud and IoT deployment models will effectively meet the goals set for the functionality needed, either by the business, IT organizations, or customers of an enterprise. One the most important phases is the actual deployment which includes both initial deployment and iterative re-deployment and updating of functionality. To prepare for deployment, there are a number of important focus areas that need to be addressed. Not surprisingly, this list is the same for both Hybrid, IoT, or more legacy deployment models. The details are key.

When evaluating each important consideration, there are some fundamental topics to cover and question to ensure all of the core characteristics are covered. In this table, many of the guiding principles and considerations are covered and some evaluation criteria are provided to ensure the governance model is being structured properly:

Real Client Examples

Figuring out how best to implement governance, and just the right amount of governance, is best understood through some examples. These are from real-world experiences, in different industries. These should hold up in pretty much any geography. I will cover compliance and security concerns where applicable, but mostly this will focus on incident, problem and change management.

EXAMPLE 1: GLOBAL MANUFACTURER

Organization Summary

This enterprise is a global manufacturing company, with revenue between $50B and $100B, selling and manufacturing their products in all major geographies including North America, Europe, Middle East, Africa, and Asia-Pacific. They have and continue to acquire smaller manufacturers primarily to grow their presence in a particular geography. The challenges of evolving their current IT governance model while integrating with the governance that their acquisitions already have in place coupled with local and global compliance and security requirements leaves them in a state where most incidents, problems, and changes are handled through *heroic* work. Given this environment let's focus on a particular pattern of components and processes that IT is having to deploy, with the help of vendors, all in this fluid and changing environment.

Scenario

In this scenario, the client is upgrading core SAP 'basis' components and migrating from DB2 and Oracle to use SAP's HANA environment, deployed globally, each location has its own applications and some are shared across all regions. They leverage a managed services vendor to operate their systems which

Characteristic	Criteria
Roles and Access	Focused on the ability to consume and access of the workload once it's deployed into a Cloud environment • Who will be accessing the workload? business users? IT administrators? Developers? Third party vendors? • How will each user group access the workload? via API? via UI? via Reporting? via status provided by an outsourcing team? • How will access and status of the workload be determined? Who will have access to monitoring data and how will they access it? • How will ID's and the management of user IDs be managed and governed?
Data	The ownership and location of data is vitally important • Data Integrity - What is the location of data and how is that different as it relates to development, test, QA, and production? • Will the data be located separately from the application? (if yes, does that require its own secure connection?) • Is the data in scope of any specific compliance and/or regulatory requirements? • Who will own the data? • Data Lineage - What is lineage of the data? What is the golden master version?
Deployment Model	Where will the workload be deployed? • Is off-premise or on-premises required? • Does the workload map to existing items in the Cloud catalog? • Will this be Bring Your Own License (BYOL)? • Is cross-site, cross-geo and/or multi-provider required? • Will the deployment model be determined by the service levels of the providers or a centralized governance model? • Will it be deployed to a single or multiple environment(s)? • What is the bill of materials and/or list of assets to be deployed, integrated and managed
Workload Architecture and Integration	The architecture of the workload and its external dependencies are important to know up front • Does the workload require integrations/connections to systems or data sources in other cloud or non-cloud environments? • Is the architecture of the workload 'cloud ready', 'cloud native', or requiring dedicated hardware, network, and storage resources? • Will the application and data be separated or co-located?

include traditional assets such as mainframes, dedicated Linux and windows servers, as well virtualized environments using VMWare. Further, there is an Analytics environment used to collate the data from appliances connected via an IoT platform and an IoT platform, both of which are off-premise. Taking a look at the environment, you can see it's a mix of on and off-premise with some assets owned by the client and some by third party vendors.

For this enterprise, they will continue to need both on and off-premise capabilities and thus the ability to have connectivity between heterogeneous components is key. Moreover, the need to not be tied to location and knowing the flow and lineage of their data is vitally important. The key technologies and workstreams include: SAP HANA, Managed Services, Internet of Things, Mainframe, Analytics, and ServiceNow

Current Approach

Incidents are handled, typically, through a combination of manual processes, recent use of ServiceNow to track incidents, and "Crisis conference calls" to determine the scope of the incident. Identification of incidents is a manual process. Since there is little match between the servers and physical IT assets and the running applications, determining root cause of an issue is a complex effort requiring the time of many technical experts from both corporate IT, regional IT groups and any 3rd party vendors.

Tools and technologies are used in the typical fashion. The managed services, outsourcing, managed operations provider uses their own set of tools to both meter usage and track operational issues. Manual integration (e.g. phone calls and e-mails) between the 3rd party managed operations team and corporate IT (using ServiceNow). This includes no centralized CMDB, essentially "spreadsheet based" change management.

When an incident occurs, typically there's a ticket submitted and all the relevant resources (people) are gathered together. Typically, the outsourced operations team, which has a good track record of responding to issues, does not have visibility to all incidents, especially if they are not submitted into the ServiceNow system (which many are not). So the main challenge for this organization in handling incidents is understanding:

1. The root cause of the incident,
2. Having predictive insights into potential issues and
3. Well defined and rapid processes to respond and remediate the cause of the incident.

Hybrid Governance Enhancements

Some of the recent enhancements made to address improvements supporting multi-site, heterogeneous integration, and improved data linage management include:

- Recent inclusion of automation tools used by the outsourcing team has sped up and added more standardization
- The process is still handled, for the most part, manually.
- The organization has initiated the creation of a common services catalog
- The organization wants common visibility across all applications and server to server connectivity to understand the root cause of the incidents
- Recently an assessment was completed of their major data centers to understand how servers (both physical and logical) are interconnected as a source of information for root cause analysis (RCA)
- Response times are marginally faster than before, overall the number of incidents has decreased through more monitoring and more automation.
- The impact on operations is still determined through a largely manual process and restoration leveraging either backups or a DR process is still far too time consuming
- Traceability of the incident is partially available via the ServiceNow system and tools used by the managed operations team
- There's more of a need to secure in flight data as it moves from on-premises to off-premise

Next Steps

The next phases of improvements include:

- Traceability of an incident from initiation/discovery through the problem management and change management processes.
- The combination of SAP HANA + Managed Services + Internet of Things + Mainframe + Analytics + ServiceNow adds cross-site governance complexity to both the movement of data and to ensure that when incidents occur in one system the cascade effects of those incidents are known.

EXAMPLE 2: GLOBAL RETAILER

Organization Summary

A retailer with a recently deployed e-commerce online presence and over 1000 brick and mortar stores in North America supported by a global supply chain and various global product manufacturers. They have over $50B in annual revenue and a fairly large IT budget as it relates to overall enterprise revenue and profit. Their IT department is run in a fairly traditional centralized and project based manner, as overall IT budget is largely determined and allocated through project definition. Thus, the total number of projects is combined to make up the overall budget allocated. Each project leverages a common infrastructure but can request additional physical or logical infrastructure for just their project.

Scenario

Currently, they have deployed a global e-commerce solution but the supporting services in only a small portion of their locations. The solution comprises many different components including order management, e-commerce and payment solutions, as well as delivery and fulfillment. Integration with supply chain and purchasing is not yet implemented directly, but there are asynchronous connections with these systems through queuing, thus they are indirect. The Hybrid Cloud characteristics include connectivity between on and off-premise systems with integration to both systems owned by this organization as well as those of external service and functionality providers.

Current Approach

Governance, including operations, development, and testing processes are driven by this organization but actually executed by several service providers. These external providers cover both application and infrastructure management, and have their own management and governance processes. The integration of governance and management between these providers and the main organization is largely manual requiring constant preparation but using little or no automation when an incident occurs. The overall change management process is project focused and thus does not have the context of shared services, thus lessons learned are not well integrated into future enhancements.

Hybrid Governance Enhancements

No enhancements to the processes have been implemented. However, one of the key service providers has implemented a rigorous preparation scheduled for major events ensuring that if an incident does occur, there's a clear escalation and ownership process in place. This is one of the key foundational steps to ensure the eventual use of policy based automation will be effective in deploying incident, problem, and change management in a cross-site and multi-vendor deployment.

Next Steps

Automation is the theme.

1. Establishing automation when incidents occur and to take lessons learned and incorporate them into the broader change management process is key
2. Allowing for better portability of the components of a Hybrid Deployment through the use of container technology will support the deployment a governance fabric since this will be a more loosely coupled deployment.

In both of these examples there are several important themes which are common and which are typically found in many organizations.

- Visibility across all components is important in understand where problems occur (incident management), how to repair and remediate problems (problem management), and how to lessen the likelihood these issues will happen in the future (change management)
- Understanding the escalation and ownership process when trying to operate this type of complex environment
- Establishing an effective Backup and DR strategy is both important and much more complex given the unpredictable nature of adding new services (Hybrid Cloud) and devices (Internet of Things)

CONCLUSION

The Importance of Net-Centric Operating Principles in a Hybrid Governance Fabric

In defining the most important characteristics of an HGF, using aspects of the ITIL governance framework is valuable, but the core tenants of net-centricity have equally or more important applicability. When looking at the definition of the "net-centric" operating model:

Net-centric, or "network-centric", refers to participating as a part of a continuously-evolving, complex community of people, devices, information and services interconnected by a communications network to optimize resource management and provide superior information on events and conditions needed to empower decision makers. Many experts believe the terms "information-centric" or "knowledge-centric" would capture the concepts more aptly because the objective is to find and exploit information, the network itself is only one of several enabling factors along with sensors, data processing and storage, expert analysis systems and intelligent agents, and information distribution. (Net-centric, 1ˢᵗ paragraph)

Heterogeneous Integration is a Core Guiding Principle

The importance of governance becomes clear, usually in hindsight, when integrating many different components and data sources. Typically, there is a large deployment of some monolithic application or "system" and it is assumed, since there is a typically an available set of API functions, that integration is fairly straight forward. This *technical* integration, while important and sometime fraught with difficulty, is actually not the major challenge. The ability to determine where the root cause of a flaw in that integration, especially when dealing with things like security breaches, data corruption, or performance issues, is where a large amount of OpEx is spent.

This net-centric integration of different devices and components affects incident, problem, and change management. When dealing with an incident, essentially and event that occurs, typically there is a gathering of as many of the people and information available to determine the current state of the incident and the initial steps to take in order to resolve the incident moving it into the problem management phase. The manual approach to dealing with incidents simply does not scale when addressing events in a heterogeneous integration scenario especially when there are different technologies in place, each potentially with their own support models and paths to resolve problems. Automation and policy based resolution are key to dealing with incidents. Policies are really important here. Leveraging a policy and template based approach to handling incidents allows for a set of tools to automatically respond to incidents, gather the core supporting data and to bring together those personnel who may have supporting information in addressing the incident and preparing for a root cause analysis.

It is important to address the results of identifying an incident throughout it's entire lifecycle, bringing the resulting problem to resolution. Moreover, preventing the problem in the future is key. In a Hybrid and IoT environment, dealing with an initial incident and determining the root cause are hard enough, however when there are a multitude of integrations between both physical and logical components, services, and assets, the ability to manage the resolution to a problem and to further prevent future occurrences of that problem are much more complex. Thus, the problem management process, needs the ability to track the changes needed across the many different components and different locations, the order of these changes in order to support a Hybrid style of change management.

Location Independence is Typical

In both the Hybrid Cloud and Internet of Things deployment models, net-centricity is one of the important governing principles, and is the reason why cross-site and multi-location deployment is not only possible but actually the most likely and typical scenario. Given the regularity of using multiple locations in a Hybrid model, applying incident, problem, and change management requires accounting for multiple locations, but interestingly these locations can change rapidly and regularly. This is what is atypical about the Hybrid and IoT models. Not only is cross-site typical, the addition and removal of new services, devices, and assets to the overall working system or operating environment happens both rapidly but also quite unexpectedly. These services can come from any provider that meets the basic service levels needed, and this clearly implies that services came come from different locations and thus different locations are typical.

Dealing with incidents in an environment where locations can change frequently, rapidly, and unexpectedly, means that automation could be limited. This is where the importance of using policy based control is key. Policies can be created to reduce the response time when an incident occurs, even if automation is not readily available. Of course, when automation can be used it definitely accelerates the ability to respond. Responding to incidents in a distributed and multi-site deployment does not require changes to a typical ITIL style incident management process, but it does require a better feedback loop from problem and change management lessons learned. In addition to this feedback loop, a multi-site deployment supporting Hybrid or IoT environments requires the ability to incorporate many different service levels, service definitions, and support models from many different providers in order to more rapidly get to root cause.

Data Lineage is Vital for Reliability, Security, and Resiliency

The one aspect of changing to a new operating model is the ability to trace and track the movement and storage of data. Data is, in reality, the most important possibly the only important asset for any organization. It is the reason that an organization has a mission or it's the result of their mission. It is the core. In the Hybrid and IoT models, ensuring that data, as it moves through the network and is both accessed and affected by the various services and service levels, is a much more complicated task. The typical terminology for following the flow of data is called Data Lineage. Data Lineage (Harreis, 2015) is not specifically the tracking of data but it is ensuring that the integrity and security of the data is maintained at the level required by the owning organization. In the Hybrid and IoT models, dealing with incidents and the incident management process, is unique due to the multi-location, heterogeneous integration, and of course data lineage expectations.

When an incident occurs, typically these are not just generic events but typically something that is not supposed to happen. The loss of access to data, the loss of data, the unplanned distribution of data or the corruption of data quality and accuracy are often the root causes of an incident. The typical incident management process needs to be amended to not only identify that an atypical event has occurred but it needs to prevent further affect on the lineage of data. The process needs to stop any further impact to the data, while beginning to analyze the root cause of the incident and as a preparation for the problem management process.

Governance is Complicated in a Hybrid and Connected Things Operating Environment

Applying governance is more than just looking up definitions in the most recent version of the ITIL standard or installing a tool that "implements governance" or defining patterns of architectures. The purpose of governance, and this comes out in the definition, is to ensure that the assets and tools being used to run the organization are in fact effectively ensuring the organization is achieving its business goals. Both the journey and the destination are important when it comes to deploying governance.

FUTURE DIRECTIONS AND CONSIDERATIONS

How Do You Know If You Need Hybrid Governance?

There are a set of important questions and topics that must be addressed when defining how governance a Hybrid Cloud or IoT deployment should be formulated.

1. Is there existing, *documented*, governance in place?
2. If there is existing governance is it tracked, metered, and *measured*?
3. How much governance is needed? Is it needed just for compute, storage, and/or network?
4. How many providers of services will need to be tied or integrated together in governance model?
5. Do all services, systems, or components need the same level of governance?

6. How should governance be handled before, during and post migration of workloads from on-premises to off-premise.
7. Does data lineage tracking and metering already exist?
8. Is deployment to multiple locations required or already in place?

In addition to these important topics, one of the rapidly emerging use cases, especially for those enterprises with fairly complex IT topologies, is using services from various external providers in conjunction with their existing systems.

A good example of this is with the Internet of Things (IoT) where various sensors, devices, mobile apps (systems of engagement) and legacy information sources (systems of record) are combined. Many of the key characteristics of Services Oriented Architecture (SOA) apply here, but now in a geographically distributed and cross-provider model.

Integrated Services Management

In this Hybrid model, whether it's Hybrid Cloud or the Internet of Things, it is important to take a look at the most common governance processes and examine if these need to be changed, when they need to changed, and if they need to be changed. With the assumption that Hybrid Cloud and IoT really expect and leverage the same style of governance, the Incident, Problem, and Change Management models can be looked at as one set of processes in this same context. Moreover, updates to these processes are needed, but those modifications are specific and do not result in a fundamental re-engineering of these foundational governance processes.

Handling Data Provenance: Data Lineage and Traceability (DLT)

Governance is not just about dealing with problems but also focused on best practices for monitoring and securing various parts of a system. When an organization uses a combination of components and systems, deploying in various sites with many different interconnections and service levels, ensuring data integrity is key and surely more complex.

- The lineage of data, as it passes and has passed through the various components of a Hybrid Cloud or IoT deployment, is important in determining root cause of an issue. It is important to isolate the cause and the various components of a system using a forensic style approach. Understanding the original source of the data and knowing the form of the golden master version is vital to understand how it has changed and if that change matters. Managing the incident and bringing it to resolution through a problem management process are almost entirely dependent on knowing the original source. Incident and Problem Management processes need to be adjusted to ensure that both data integrity and the lineage of the original source of the data are well understood before a proper root cause can be determined.
- Change Management is focused on managing the process for implementing changes but, just as importantly, this process is used to clarify those changes that are needed and especially when changes are not required. The Change Management process should be modified to include steps to ensure that the results of incidents and problems result in well managed instead of haphazard changes to the golden master versions of data. Thus, changes will happen but they must be done in

way that ensures the integrity of the original form of the data so the incident management process has the necessary foundation to compare original versus current forms, as these will show where and how changes occur and their impacts on the overall system. Understanding both data lineage and it's impacts on data integrity are key guiding principles.

Hybrid Root Cause Analysis (HRCA)

One of the most challenging aspects of Hybrid Cloud, where many different components, systems, and data sources are stitched together to form a single business function is to determine how to resolve functional and delivery issues as they arise. Hopefully good design of each "service" lessens the possibility of functional or operational problems.

The key aspect is to create incident, problem, and change management processes that take into account having a heterogeneous set of functionality, service providers and methods of connectivity (APIs, Middleware, and Network infrastructure). There are early aspects of this described in early work done in the SOA Governance and Maturity Model (SGMM), but here are the main points:

- Incident and Problem Management need to take into account not just functional issues but the interconnections between those systems, the various APIs being used, and the movement of data and how it may have changed as it moves between services and service providers. Handling and identifying an incident that likely spans multiple components in multiple locations is the key here.
- Change Management is the place where leveraging DevOps and Continuous Integration techniques are really valuable. It's vitally important that both building services and the integration of those services is merged into the overall process of operations governance.

The most important IT capability is not servers, networks, services or databases, but it's the data that is most important. This is the most interesting and the most cutting edge aspect of establishing common governance. The ability to know the location, status, and security of data is vital as it moves between services and components especially from on-premises to off-premise locations. To assure the integrity of the data is key and thus knowing the linage of the data and have the ability to trace and track its movement across systems is key to being able to adequately govern data which is, above and beyond all other things, the most important asset an enterprise or organization owns.

Establishing common governance in a Hybrid Cloud model has turned out to be the most important aspect to going beyond just deploying tools for Hybrid Cloud and consuming Cloud services. Being able to assure the integrity of data as it moves between the components in a Hybrid deployment and integrating with a process to determine the root cause of problems and manage changes is key to successful deployment.

Blockchain

Blockchain is essentially a secure ledger supporting the combination of specific blocks (events and entries) into chains where the blocks are tied together to show a complete lineage of a transaction. This allows for there to be no single owner of the chain and is fully transparent to all those participating in the chain. This makes it perfect for digital currencies, tracking a physical or logical supply chain, and it can be applied to the manufacturing and distribution industries to ensure all needed components are in place. When it comes to Hybrid Cloud and IoT, the integration and interconnectivity of services is a key requirement. One of the challenges is to ensure the lineage of data, described in other sections, and the other is to allow for the elasticity of connections between services. The ability to connect, disconnect, and re-connect services into the whole system is required to make Hybrid Cloud and IoT function and for these types of system to allow for some type of governance mechanism to work effectively. The Blockchain model can be applied to the interconnectivity of services and devices in a Hybrid Cloud or Internet of Things composite system of components. As these two models evolve, Blockchain techniques make sense in tying together the various components and devices in a way that assures connectivity and the lineage of data as it moves between systems. Given this evolution, the techniques and examples for Hybrid and IoT governance covered in this analysis can be applied to ensure the "chain" of components in these systems stay tied together.

REFERENCES

Cloud Computing and Hybrid Cloud. (n.d.). Retrieved May 09, 2016 from https://en.wikipedia.org/wiki/Cloud_computing#Hybrid_cloud

Corporate Governance of Information Technology. (n.d.). Retrieved May 09, 2016 from https://en.m.wikipedia.org/wiki/Corporate_governance_of_information_technology

Create, W.The Project? (n.d.). Retrieved on May 10, 2016 from https://www.hyperledger.org/

Fabric Computing. (n.d.). Retrieved May 09, 2016 from https://en.wikipedia.org/wiki/Fabric_Computing

Harreis, H., Lange, M., Machado, J., Rowshankish, K., & Schraa, D. (2015). *A marathon, not a sprint: Capturing value from BCBS 239 and beyond*. McKinsey & Company. Retrieved May 09, 2016 from http://www.mckinsey.com/~/media/mckinsey/business%20functions/risk/our%20insights/a%20marathon%20not%20a%20sprint%20capturing%20value%20from%20bcbs%20239%20and%20beyond/a_marathon_%20not_a_sprint_capturing_value_from_bcbs_239_and_beyond.ashx

Internet of Things. (n.d.). Retrieved May 09, 2016 from https://en.wikipedia.org/wiki/Internet_of_Things

IT Governance Institute. (2003). *Board Briefing on IT Governance* (2nd ed.). Rolling Meadows, IL: IT Governance Institute. Retrieved May 09, 2016 from http://www.isaca.org/restricted/Documents/26904_Board_Briefing_final.pdf

Meulen, R. V. (2015, November 10). *Gartner Says 6.4 Billion Connected*. Retrieved May 05, 2016 from http://www.gartner.com/newsroom/id/3165317

National Security Agency. (2015). *Defense in Depth, A practical strategy for achieving Information Assurance in today's highly networked environments*. Ft. Meade, MD: National Security Agency, Information Assurance Solutions Group – STE 6737. Retrieved May 09, 2016 from http://www.iad.gov/iad/library/reports/defense-in-depth.cfm

Net-centric. (n.d.). Retrieved May 09, 2016 from https://en.wikipedia.org/wiki/Net-centric

Raden, N. (2005). Shadow IT: A Lesson for BI. *BI Review Magazine*.

What is ITIL® Best Practice ? (n.d.). Retrieved on May 10, 2016 from https://www.axelos.com/best-practice-solutions/itil/what-is-itil

KEY TERMS AND DEFINITIONS

Blockchain: Blockchain is a peer-to-peer distributed ledger technology for a new generation of trans-actional applications that establishes trust, accountability and transparency while streamlining business processes. Think of it as an operating system for interactions. It has the potential to vastly reduce the cost and complexity of getting things done. The key to Blockchain is assuring data integrity and data lineage (Why Create The Project, 1ˢᵗ paragraph).

Defense in Depth: Originally a military a strategy for ensuring redundancy when systems and pro-cedures fail, this is typically applied to technology deployments. Focused on both security "at the edge" and the redundancy of each component in a system of systems context, this approach ensures that any one component will not reduce the reliability of the whole system.

Governance: Generically governance is a set of processes and models that define roles and how people and technology are used to both influence and control the design, delivery and operation of a system. This view on governance has a technology bias, but is generally applicable to most any context.

Hybrid Cloud: This a cloud deployment model that combines several cloud environments, typically more than one. These remain separate environments but are connected together, combining on-premises collocation, managed services and off-premises cloud-native services. All of this can be presented to the consumer as a single service providing a specific functionality. Furthermore, the intent of a Hybrid Cloud is to allow for simple services to be enhanced through the combination with other services in a single pool of capability (Cloud Computing, Hybrid Cloud section).

Internet of Things (IoT): This is a connected network of physical and logical objects, devices, and structures. It combines both physical and logical objects where logical objects could include specific data sources, all interconnected and sharing information in a chain of connectivity. It relies on a Hybrid Cloud model in order to function effectively (Internet of Things, 1ˢᵗ paragraph).

ITIL: This is an acronym for Information Technology Infrastructure Library and is intended as a guide for describing the processes and procedures used to govern a technology environment, especially infrastructure and data centers. Included in this are the roles and delivery plans focused on topics such as incident, problem, and change management. ITIL advocates that IT services are aligned to the needs of the business and support its core processes. It provides guidance to organizations and individuals on how to use IT as a tool to facilitate business change, transformation and growth (What is ITIL Best Practice?, 2016). A large number of processes are addressed both for pre-delivery, runtime, operations, and post-delivery. This is not specific to an organization but is intended as a foundation for an organiza-tion to define their specific processes, procedures, roles, and delivery plans.

Net-Centric / Net-Centricity: A continuously-evolving, complex community of people, devices, information and services interconnected by a communications network to achieve optimal benefit of resources and better synchronization of events and their consequences (Net-centric, 1ˢᵗ paragraph).

Chapter 3
User–Centric Social Interaction for Digital Cities

Kåre Synnes
Luleå University of Technology, Sweden

Juwel Rana
Luleå University of Technology, Sweden

Matthias Kranz
University of Passau, Germany

Olov Schelén
Luleå University of Technology, Sweden

ABSTRACT

Pervasive computing was envisioned by pioneers like Mark Weiser but has yet to become an everyday technology in our society. The recent advances regarding Internet of Things, social computing, and mobile access technologies converge to make pervasive computing truly ubiquitous. The key challenge is to make simple and robust solutions for normal users, which shifts the focus from complex platforms involving machine learning and artificial intelligence to more hands on construction of services that are tailored or personalized for individual users. This chapter discusses Internet of Things together with Social Computing as a basis for components that users in a "digital city" could utilize to make their daily life better, safer, etc. A novel environment for user-created services, such as social apps, is presented as a possible solution for this. The vision is that anyone could make a simple service based on Internet-enabled devices (Internet of Things) and encapsulated digital resources such as Open Data, which also can have social aspects embedded. This chapter also aims to identify trends, challenges, and recommendations in regard of Social Interaction for Digital Cities. This work will help expose future themes with high innovation and business potential based on a timeframe roughly 15 years ahead of now. The purpose is to create a common outlook on the future of Information and Communication Technologies (ICT) based on the extrapolation of current trends and ongoing research efforts.

1. INTRODUCTION

By the end of 2008 a milestone was reached, there was now more people living in the cities than outside. This has of course affected and will even more affect people's life in the future. A higher density of people creates its challenges, problems and needs.

DOI: 10.4018/978-1-5225-1832-7.ch003

Today's society and economy is totally depending on a working and always accessible Internet 24/7. This fact changes and creates opportunities among people in cities and elsewhere. In the cities there is a high density of almost everything and therefore the need of services is special - citizen centric services.

Early 2010 the topic Smart Cities was not very much known in the research community of Future Internet (FI). So far FI had focused on the next generation Internet, building large-scale test-beds, having in mind that this is a 30 year old design. Visions like 50 billion connected devices by the year 2020 (Ericsson), Internet of things creates new opportunities.

The last ten years another topic called Living Labs, sometimes also described as open user driven innovation, entered the European research scene. Methods, tools and processes have been developed in how to involve users as co-creators and this in parallel to FI research. Today there are tools ready to be used involving end users, many end users, to participate in the development of new services and products as co-creators. Not in the end of the product development cycle but early, for, with and by, the users of the new services/products. These new services can be developed by the end-users in the cities (citizens).

Up to now many services that already from the start didn't attract a huge amount of potential customer was never created. Phenomena like the entry of the iPhones and Android mobile phones completely changed the game plan in the telecom world. Services for a very small group of users was possible to develop to a small cost and by the users of their own. Still though, you have to be a rather skilled 'programmer' to create a mobile 'app' or service so the challenge today is to lower the threshold, the barriers of becoming a 'programmer'.

By providing the users, the citizens with tools in order to make their own mobile services the expectation is booming regarding potential new needs to be solved by citizens developing their own services. Internet of things, 50 billion connected devices, open and accessible public data, both from static servers in the city but also by dynamic sensor data in the street will create a totally new scenario about a more intelligent use of smart technology creating a better quality of life and entrepreneurship in cities.

One definition of a Smart City is 'We believe a city to be smart when investments in human and social capital and traditional (transport) and modern (ICT) communications infrastructure fuel sustainable economic growth and a high quality of life, with a wise management of natural resources, through participatory governance' (Caragliu et al, 2009).

The trend is to allow anybody to become a developer of services, even for a small target group usually not in focus by telecom operators and thereby contribute to a better society in many aspects, step by step. Smart Cities is very close to the thematic research area of Digital Cities and the importance of citizen centric services can not enough be seen as a strong driver of new services, products and companies but to reach full effect, there is also a need to lower the threshold, provide the tools, and utilize peoples creativity and the cities advantage as a multicultural melting pot driving societal changes will reach its full potential.

This book discusses the creation of personal, social, and urban awareness through pervasive computing. Although pervasive computing services are foreseen as potentially revolutionary, there is yet little adaption in industry. This paradox is similar to the predicted potential of artificial intelligence and later machine learning, which are successfully applied within a few applications, but which are not generally adopted. Though, this topic recently received again a lot of attention within the context of embodied AI, that is AI within technical systems. The reason for the lack of real-world adoption of pervasive computing for social interaction is potentially due to the inherit complexity of such systems that needs to span both heterogeneous networks and organizations. There are also inherent usability problems in pervasive systems (Drugge et al, 2004). How can then pervasive computing succeed better? The authors of this chapter believe that there are clear incentives, which will be discussed further later in this chapter. It however builds on three pillars: access to open data, novel interaction techniques and enabling end-users to visually compose mobile/pervasive components.

In the following, we introduce in Section 2 the characteristics for grid architectures for Internet of Things, which enables citizen-centric services based on open data. Section 3 presents a discussion of Social Web of Things. Section 4 presents initial work on a framework of social components enabling citizens to easily create their own mobile social apps. Section 5 summaries the chapter, highlights the trends, identifies future challenges and presents recommendations based on the presented work.

2. GRID ARCHITECTURES FOR THE INTERNET OF THINGS

There are several proposed architectures for storing, indexing and presenting large scale sensor (ESNA, 2009)(Sensei, 2008)(Smart Santander, 2008)(Castellani et al, 2010)(Enokido et al, 2010)(Krantz et al, 2010). However, there is more research needed to fully exploit the Internet of Things (IoT) and Crowd scenario across wireless domain and a distributed cloud of multiple players in providing application services. Experiences from these earlier architectures should be considered.

Earlier results in real-time and client-server scenarios should be reused. There are systems focusing on real-time streaming of sensor data to sinks (Schneidman et al, 2004). More recently there is a trend towards advanced sensor nodes that have capabilities to act as servers providing their data through light-weight RESTFUL approaches (Tsiftes et al, 2011). Methods for advertising and discovering data are needed (Aloisio et al, 2006)(Botts et al, 2009). Protocols for communications in resource-constrained environments are developed in the IETF (McGregor et al, 2012).

The objective would be to provide technology and infrastructure for an open business environment of both free data (Yuriyama et al, 2010) and data provided commercially on equal terms. Security considerations must be explored (Kapadia et al, 2010)(Poolsappasit et al, 2011).

Grid Architectures for Internet of Things and Future Media

The Internet of Things is expected to grow quickly to 50 billion devices and beyond (Ericson IoT, 2012) (Ericsson 2020, 2012). The solutions will include sensor networks and machine-to-machine communication. Applications may range over dynamic services in smart cities, advanced annotated media, supporting industrial and business processes, etc. In such networks, sensors and other input-devices will produce vast amounts of data that need to be collected, disseminated, stored, classified and indexed in a scalable way for various application purposes. Sensor data must in some cases be provided in real-time to large numbers of receivers and in some cases be stored and indexed for retrieval of large numbers of applications.

Research has emerged on the above-described aspects but most proposals are point solutions for specific scenarios, requirements, and problem domains. Consequently, the objective of this focus area is to support more research on scalable solutions for Internet of Things scenarios. This includes supporting crowd services where the crowd can be both producers and consumers of data. Besides meeting technical requirements, a clear objective is to promote open and generic distributed cloud solutions where a diversity of players can interact on reasonable and equal business terms to jointly provide unprecedented end services.

Research direction includes generative grid architectures that can scale over the data collection domain and application domain involving multiple users and organizations cooperating for the common objectives. Some specific research issues are mentioned in the following sections and at the end some related work is listed.

Security (Authentication, Authorization, Encryption)

The solutions must be completely open and promote equal opportunities (e.g. business terms) to different players, however this does not necessarily mean that all data is free and available to anyone. Therefore authentication, authorization and encryption are essential elements that need to be researched in this context.

Performance and Scalability

The vast number of producers and consumers where many entities will assume both roles, require specific research on performance and scalability in this context. The scalability solutions must be applied across all other requirements as here listed.

Decentralization, Open Interfaces, Business Interfaces

A key objective is that there must be an open market place with open interfaces and open business terms. Much data may be free and unrestricted (possibly funded by advertisements), but diversity of players that refine data and services is normally increasing if there is support to charge for and protect access to such data.

Wireless Aspects

Wireless devices may be the norm in Internet of Things and crowd scenarios. The architecture must support efficient resource usage (e.g. battery and power) and some degree of service continuity in scenarios where mobile devices (producers or consumers of data) only have occasional connectivity.

Resource Discovery

The vast amount of data provided must be discoverable by entities that want to use them. It is expected that data offered in the crowd scenario may in some cases be hard to find and in some cases be very redundant. In either case it is a matter of resource efficiency and service availability to be able to determine how and where to retrieve data.

Storage, Classification and Indexation

Large-scale (big data) storage of information in Internet of Things networks is a critical issue. For data that is timeless or of typical historical value this is a natural issue. However, even for typical real-time data it may be desirable to store some history for following up on failures etc. Existing data store technologies may need adaptation for effective storage and indexation of such data. Also, machine generated data from multiple sources is often hard to combine and interpret for humans. Automated methods to interpret data and classify it into real-world status and events are essential.

Applications

The key drivers for Internet of Things grid networks come from specific and creative applications in smart city scenarios, both addressing citizens and organizations/enterprises. Besides bringing clear values, the technologies mentioned previously should be evaluated both quantitatively and qualitatively in such application scenarios.

3. SOCIAL WEB OF THINGS

The on-going connection of appliances, the increasing adoption of smartphones, and emerging instrumentation of items with QR-codes and RFID provide the basis for a comprehensive layer of connectedness to objects, products, things and people. People are becoming part of digital social networks driven by personal interests and aspiration. The feeling of belonging to a community and the perpetual drive of getting connected from real life find it continuation in digital networks.

Both the digital integration of things and people starts to embrace our daily lives and enables for new interaction, new experiences and new behaviors. We can remotely query and control appliances of a smart home, we can participate in the experiences and opinions of our friends about product while shopping, and we can share our activities, our preferences instantly? (Michahelles et al, 2012)(Kranz et al, 2013)

The technological developments with respect to computing power, sensing systems, communication technologies, identification systems, middleware systems and infrastructure have resulted in a large number of uniquely identifiable systems and objects allow the sensing and actuation of real world phenomena on a large scale, not possible before. These embedded systems and the information embedded therein (Schmidt et al, 2004) is mainly designed for machine-to-machine communication (M2M), but also facilitate human-machine communication (M2H), also called human-computer interaction (HCI).

This provides novel chances for future services, especially with respect to the integration into people's everyday life. Technology becomes, as envisioned by Weiser, part of it, indistinguishable and woven into the fabric of everyday life: *'In the 21st century the technology revolution will move into the everyday, the small and the invisible'* (Weiser, 1991). In the following text we discuss the novel challenges and potentials of the proliferation of these developments, just entering our environment and emerging markets.

Private and Public Sensing as Basis for Open Data and Big Data

Networked sensing systems on all scales are on the verge of entering different environments of public and private life: intelligent power grids, vehicular communication systems such as vehicle-to-vehicle (V2V) and vehicle-to-infrastructure communication (V2I) (Schmidt et al, 2008)(Schmidt et al, 2010) (Rusu et al, 2006), smart home sensing, or crowd-sourced data, both acquired explicitly (manually inputted or automatically acquired) and implicitly (e.g. such as the traffic data generated by GSM base station changes from travellers using navigation services, such as TomTom HD traffic) or by explicitly incorporating the smartphone of the user (Diewald et al, 2011). This data is complemented by the release of governmental data, such as geo-referenced data sets (e.g. maps, pollution data, air quality data, health information) or other institutional data. This data is shared, online (e.g. using services such as former Pachube) or offline, in near-real time or even real time. The data originates from both public (e.g. governmental institutions, research agencies) and private sources (companies, private persons). This can be use to create novel socio-technical networks optimizing e.g. personal mobility (Diewald et al, 2012).

Solutions making use of the data will not only be required to make sense of all the sensing (such as employing techniques from machine learning), but also will need to handle this big data (immense amount of potentially heterogeneous data sources and data types that need processing, potentially in short periods of time). This requires novel tools and methods, especially novel middleware solutions (Roalter et al, 2010)(Atzori et al, 2010)(Rusu et al, 2006). While current social networks and social interaction platforms such as Facebook feature 1,000,000,000 users, the amount of sensor systems will be several magnitudes higher, assuming 50 to 100 devices per person will result in 50,000,000,000 to 100,000,000,000 data sources and sinks that produce data, at several Herz per second, and potentially of high dimension (multiple sensors per device) or size (full HD imagery).

The availability of data, provided that privacy and other legal issues are appropriately addressed, forms the basis for novel business models, services and markets by the end of 2020.

Embedded Interaction: Distributed Sensor and Actuator Systems

Technological advances and new usage models can cause computing to undergo a stark transformation. Automatic object identification (such as RFID or Near Field Communication, and visual markers), ubiquitous connectivity, improved processing and storage capabilities, various new display technologies, sensor device availability, and decreasing hardware costs all lay the foundation for a new computing era. We can now build vehicles, devices, goods, and everyday objects to become a part of the Internet of Things. (Kranz et al, 2010).

The resulting artifacts are equipped with sensors and actuators that let users seamlessly manipulate digital information and data in the context of real-world usage. This means data is not only sensed, but also used for control purposes (such as intelligent heating and climate control (HVAC – heating, ventilation, air conditioning)). This development does not only increasingly show in the process industry (which, according to today's standards and the state of research is in urgent need for applied solutions to increase efficiency and environmental balance), but also the private and public sector. The control might occur automatically in many cases (e.g. based on machine-to-machine (M2M) communication) to control and steer systems, but it will often enough involve human users that want to modify their environment according to their social needs and social contexts (Kranz et al, 2010).

This sensing and actuation will more increasingly be done via embedded systems and embedded devices. This trend is already immanent, looking e.g. at CPU sales where embedded CPUs have already by far outnumbered classical CPUs for desktop or enterprise computing. These embedded devices and systems will, in addition to their use in automated systems, become important points of interaction between humans and the environment, both in the private domain and in the public space. Miniaturization does not only allow us already to include technology e.g. in clothing (so-called wearables), but to further decrease the costs for a constant amount of computing power. The technological development of the ten recent years has made it possible to transfer this from prototypical objects (Kranz et al, 2005) used in research into smart products for the mass market. This results in networked embedded systems being deployed in public infrastructure, from waste containers, to parks, public spots, etc., allowing data exchange not only with an a-priori known central infrastructure, but spontaneously with e.g. mobile devices of users, both via network-only connection, but also by more natural means such as public-private interaction. These services will be available citywide and moving and following their human users. Further research will be necessary on how to develop, deploy and maintain these large-scale services for citizens (Möller et al, 2012).

We expect, given the existence of initial field studies and case in 2012 (such as in the city of Oulu, Finland, public data sets from smart cities like Amsterdam, Netherlands, and several others), the availability of first citywide interactive services, enabled by embedded interaction sensor-actuator systems, by 2025 or even thereafter. One major issue to be resolved will be the legal framework that ensures privacy and the algorithms for ensuring trust (between service providers and consumers – both technical and human). An example for a challenge in this dimension is, e.g. ensuring or detecting the trustworthiness of sensor data as basis for calculations.

Crowd City Services

A governance infrastructure is the collection of technologies, people, policies, practices, resources, social norms, and information that interact to support governing activities. Smart governance infrastructures augment society's ability to organize, interact, and govern. Novel instances of smart governance infrastructures already exist and are regularly emerging in distributed organizations and online (social) communities. (Johnston, 2005)

The governments of Europe aim at integrating their citizens more directly in all administrative and governance processes. This trend, fostering community and social interaction, will not be limited to governance, but also be extended to all parts of the daily life. We in the following sketch some ideas for services that could evolve in future smart cities, given the current trends and potential future developments foresighted in this report.

The availability of distributed, networked sensor-actuator system will allow for a novel level of participation and social interaction in future smart cities (Erickson, 2010). This poses the question how future participatory systems need, from a methodological point of view, need to be designed to integrate with the societal goals and digital cities.

Future participatory services will, by combining both machine and human intelligence, allow for a faster and more efficient than the information systems and electronic services today (King et al, 2005). We distinguish between services using information push (to the citizen) and information pull (from the citizen).

Classical participatory services for eliciting information are e.g. MobileWorks[1] (e.g. used for large-scale research studies to overcome the current limitations of user-involvement in research projects (Kranz et al, 2013), or Amazon's Mechanical Turk[2] where not only pure information is solicited, but 'artificial intelligence' is simulated, e.g. to overcome the limitations of current machine learning systems (e.g. when Steve Fosset's plane crashed, satellite imagery was bought, put online, and participants asked to find potential crash sites and respective reports were financially awarded).

Further examples of current solutions for crowd sourcing and participatory sensing are shortly presented here: The service Waze[3] uses user-generated geo-references movement data to build up maps e.g. of street networks and to generate and maintain additional information, such as the traffic information. User-contributed content is elicited in a gamified approach where points are awarded e.g. based on the type of data and its novelty (a road that hundreds of people have taken results in less points than a road only few have taken). WheelMap[4] uses also a user-based approach to generate information on accessibility of transportation networks (such as public sidewalks, places, etc.). The service EyeQuest[5] aims at providing up-to-date, on-demand imagery of physical locations. An example could be to ask the community about a photo of places to be visited soon. Users then take pictures of the desired spots and share them. The project 'Kleinwassersensor'[6] democratizes environmental and pollution sensing (today still a domain for the public authorities), at the example of water quality sensing. Finally, services like FixMyStreet[7] or SeeClickFix[8] try to include the user in identifying potentially problematic issues in the city and to raise awareness of the authorities to them. These services today do not 'match' to still predominant governance style. Additionally, they usually lack integration in today's ICT systems. Future digital cities might very well benefit from these and similar services – if the challenges and hurdles can be overcome: lack of middleware and data exchange, lack of trust models of public and user generated/sensed data, scalability (e.g. of public responses to thousands of reports), etc., and finally a model how this more efficient reporting can result in more efficient solutions (demanding for cheaper fixes to the problems).

Data from future networked sensor-actuator systems will demand for an in-depth research on what value-added services can be composed, by e.g. providing the data and eliciting information from the citizen. This might, in a simple case be, e.g. the display of a picture of a spot in the city and the annotation of pollution.

But different data will put different demands on the users, some information will be harder to generate (and potentially not be possible to elicit from everyone), so novel approaches will be needed to develop these services. Gamification might be one of many possible solutions. This methodological research will be required prior to the availability of the digital city's data, so that to-be-identified day0 use cases can be implemented and further speed up development, acceptance and proliferation of these services.

Additional research questions will include a formalized development methodology, an identification of key parameters of these services (from input to output, users, fields of applications, etc.), and finally the societal, economical and social goals that shall be supported, from increasing social interaction if potentially anonymous mega cities, to increased community perception and awareness, well-being and health, citizen-involving governance, or many other possible goals. We are currently, after more then a decade of research, only in the beginning towards and understanding of future digital cities (Ishida, 2000)(Ishida, 2002).

The challenge includes finding methods, tools and approaches that e.g. increasing social interaction in society, by linking data from the digital city (digital networks), to e.g. Facebook (social networks) to physical human 'ad-hoc' networks (find a group to solve, in a community approach, specific problems, community networks).

As Virtanen and Malinen formulate the problem: "there is a growing interest to use online communities to support social interaction also in geography-based communities" (Virtanen et al, 2008).

How could these extensions of current social networks be achieved with the goal of fostering and increasing social interactions in the real world (and not decreasing it by the introduction of technology and data)?

Personal User-Configured Services

Large-scale deployments and large scale sensing solutions are enabled and supported by the expected technological developments. But the resulting services will need more than ever before be able to adapt to situations, contexts, and user-preferences. One size fits all solutions will no longer be adequate – we see here the same trend away from the 'personal computer' to 'ubiquitous computing' where users have multiple computational devices, probably even one device per task.

Personalization and Individualization: Individualization of the Society

Successful services will have to support end-user composition (see below in this report) and end-user configuration of the services, allowing the user to personalize the data, service and user interface. The need for personalization is driven by the societal trend of individualization of the particular members of our society. The larger mega cities become, the more mass production and consumption are at the centre, the more important it becomes for the people to live their individuality. This trend, so far, is at least visible in the western societies and in the growing generation E.

Many anthropologists state that there are great generational differences that can be forseen today, where the new generation is intrinsically accustomed to computers and mobile technologies. Ida Hult, CEO of Trendethnography, defines these as 'Moklofs' or 'Mobile kids with lots of friends'. This Generation E is used to getting rapid feedback on their opinions and actions, through a big flora of tools[9].

Those ages 8 to 18 spend more than 7,5 hours a day with such devices, compared with less than 6,5 hours 5 years ago, when the study was last conducted. And that does not count the 1,5 hours that youths spend texting, or the 0,5 hour they talk on their cell phones. And because so many of them are multitasking – say, surfing the Internet while listening to music – they pack on average nearly 11 hours of media content into that 7,5 hours. (Kevin Drum, MotherJones.com)

The challenges include to develop novel tools that allow the development of these services, the education of users to compose their own services, and the development of mental models for end-users that foster the understanding of the underlying processes. Understanding will be a crucial part of the acceptance of the services, and in turn also of the acquisition of the underlying data. Shared ownership will be crucial and important to achieve for the stakeholders, the citizens, of future digital cities.

From Personalized and Individualized Production to Personalized and Individualized Consumption: Example for Novel Services

We currently see the personalization of mass production. The hot topics are how to facilitate one-of production scenarios (instead of mass market), that is, efficiently (with respect to resource and machine usage) produce one customized item for one customer after each other. Instead of producing the same product or service after another, one different service or product will follow another different product or service. This, as we currently see it, requires immense changes in the manufacturing industry, process optimization to facilitate cheap one-of production in generalized plants and fabrication; networked manufacturing (from initial production of raw materials, to refinement, to production, to delivery), etc., and includes the complete supply and manufacturing chain until the delivery of the good or service.

We see this individualization or socialization of production also in the rise of novel tools, allowing already the individual to produce his own goods: laser cutters, 3D printers, fab labs, etc. are getting more and more popular. Today, individuals have access to highly sophisticated manufacturing equipment. This trend in physical production is accompanied by first approaches to deliver personalized and contextualized services. Though, today's technology is not able to reliably sense or infer human contexts outside the laboratory yet.

Given current trends of e.g. cloud computing and the commercial availability of compute services for individuals (e.g. Amazon's Elastic Compute Cloud (Amazon EC2)) and extrapolating this, in several years it will be possible and economically feasible to reliably enough determine citizens' contexts and combine this with the data from the smart city. Socializing e.g. consumption (my quarter, my town) using e.g. social network data and open data, could result in a socialization again that in he end might result in more awareness. Other future trends will very certain include personal robotics, both as e.g. household helpers, but also as facilitators of social interaction. An other example could be unmanned aerial vehicles (UAV) that e.g. substitute current bike messengers, for both delivering physical goods (e.g. mail, pizza,...) and virtual goods (e.g. call a movie – where a projector equipped UAV delivers the movie and the presentation service). In these examples again, the computational demands will be lifted to the cloud and combined there with the data from the networked distributed sensor-actuator systems.

4. SOCIAL COMPONENTS FOR APP DEVELOPMENT BY EMPOWERED CITIZENS

This part presents a framework of social components for the Satin app development environment (Satin2, 2012), which provides a systematic way of designing, developing and deploying social components, e.g. for social network applications. We discuss the life cycle of developing social apps (that is information applications designed for a great number of users and personalized towards specific social target groups), where the social app development environment is targeting end-users. We consider here persons that have no dedicated programming skills and more specifically have not programmed using languages such as HTML5, JavaScript or other similar scripting languages. As proof-of-concept, several social components have been deployed to the Satin Editor, which can be used to compose mobile social apps. We report on the specific results of this deployment, and extrapolate trends for social interaction in future digital cities.

Social Media

At present, there is a huge interest from the users in social media such as Facebook[10], LinkedIn[11], Google+[12], YouTube[13], Twitter[14], and others (Faloutsos et al, 2012). Smartphones are becoming more and more apps driven, with people using apps as specialized front end to different data sources and sinks. One of the major areas of apps development is social media, which covers different kind of communication and media distribution needs (Böhmer et al, 2011)(Cui et al, 2011). Moreover, popular social networking services such as Facebook, Twitter, Google+ are offering developer-oriented APIs to produce new apps on basis of these platforms.

End-users, though, are due to their lack of expert-level programming skills, excluded from 'developing' novel applications or personalizing existing services to their needs. This excludes an immense number of people (with other skills than programming) from contributing to social applications and services. Comparing 1,000,000,000 Facebook users to several thousand active developers highlights this imbalance. We argue that, next to user empowerment, including these people in a structured, self-driven development process can leverage an immense potential.

Social web-based mash-ups are a means allowing for end-user to compose mash-up applications without programming dedicated knowledge (Liu et all, 2007)(Wong, 2007). In our proposed component-based social apps development framework, we aim to minimize this gap between traditional application developer and non-technical users with the goal to enable these end-users to develop social apps in a drag-and drop manner. For example, a component could retrieve a user's friends' birthday, process the information and e.g. compute an action, and eventually another component could send a SMS with personalized birthday wishes. By combining these components, a user is able to form, from existing components, a novel and personalized app for this purpose. Social components show important aspects of social apps composition by offering new ways of managing contacts and initiating communication. For example, based on social components, users will be able to generate mash-ups to visualize global contacts (e.g. across several independent social networks), forming groups of people by adapting to contexts and by connecting participants, e.g. to organize a group video chat on a special topic (such as organizing a birthday present for the aforementioned friend).

Software structures are, also in other areas, evolving towards component-based architectures that support dynamic, high-level composition through wrapping and adaptors. We expect that open component libraries will be available for end-users that enable individual components to be reusable for visual end-user composition.

Another important problem in this context (Rana et al, 2009, 2010, 2012) is communication and social data aggregation. There are few theoretical models proposed to access social data generated from heterogeneous data sources in a unified manner. However, the proposed solutions do not cover appropriate cases where social data aggregation is essential and appropriate apps on that. By the proposed component based social apps creation framework, now it's being possible for the end-user to fuse social and communication data from different sources and develop attractive apps out of it. For example, collaborative social apps creation where collaborators from different networks need to be invited was complicated due to partition in social networking mechanism. However, compose-able component of such networks may cross that partition and invite each other to perform collaboration.

Social data is increasingly available in more and more areas of our daily life, which makes this data interesting for app developers. Data from these apps and their usage is also fed back to (groups in) social networks. Creating your own personalized apps based on the available social data by visual editing will, in the future, be offered by several platforms.

Note that the notion of a dynamic group can be used for many of these social components for media distribution (Rana et al, 2009)(Hallberg et al, 2007). These dynamic groups could be created at need or be managed over time, and be used to control access to real-time collaborative applications (Parnes et al, 1999). Making components that are easily included in mobile apps support otherwise complex user management in a good way.

Social media distribution is often time critical (posing real-time demands on the delivery) and usually unpredictable beforehand (except examples e.g. from the sports domain, e.g. on a final baseball game). These circumstances inflict that it is complicated to handle, even for (temporary) homogenous social groups. Even despite the availability of a-priori knowledge on the sharing interest similarity allowing to generate patterns that define when and how users generally share content (Gilbert et al, 2009). Therefore, frequently access to a user's real-time content is very resource demanding in terms of data-capturing, or computational complexity of data processing. The research problem addressed here is: 'How does a framework support social components to capture social data and utilize those components for real-time social apps composition?'

Related Work on Social App Development and End-User Service Composition

The literature lists several graphical tools (Rana et al, 2009, 2012)(Roalter et al, 2011) where user can create different kind of (desktop) applications or (mobile) apps without any programming knowledge. In most cases, users can, by using the 'Drag-and-Drop' metaphor, or by simply connecting (e.g. by clicking via a direct manipulation interface such as a mouse or a tangible user interface) different visual or physical objects to create the desired apps. The source code of the components is shielded from the user, the functionality of the components are embedded within these visual or physical objects.

Liu et al (2007) have proposed a mash-up creation architecture by extending a mash-up creating SOA models. In this architecture, they present a mash-up component model allowing the user to create own services by the composition of individual, smaller components.

Wong presented 'MARMITE', a visual tool that offers different kinds of graphical objects and allows users with no programming knowledge to create one's own mash-ups (Wong, 2007). Required programming scripts and logic are here, again, embedded within these graphical objects.

Web technology giants like Yahoo[15] and Microsoft[16] also provide environments for creating mash-ups by the end users. Using 'Yahoo Pipes' or 'Microsoft Popfly', end-users (with no programming knowledge) can create mash-ups. Both tools provide graphical editors where the user can drag and drop and interconnect the individual component to create the resulting mash-ups. Microsoft Popfly provides a platform where user can create apps ranging from games to small applications and eventually share these again. Ennals et al (2007) presents the 'Intel Mash Maker' that is the web extension of the user's existing web browser. It allows the user to expand the current page that the user browsed to with additional information from other websites (which potentially poses security risks e.g. due to cross-site scripting etc.). A user can create a new mash-up and add it to the current web site with the 'Intel Mash Maker' tool. After learning about the new mash-up, 'Intel Mash Maker' suggests this new mash-up to other users. 'Intel Mash Maker' provides a platform for building and exchanging these new mash-ups. 'Intel Mash Maker' depends on the developer community who will 'teach' it about the structure and semantics of web pages (supported of course by the structuring HTML/XHTML/XML elements embedded in the pages).

Jung and Park proposed an ontology-based mash-up creation system that uses different kinds of web data sources to construct mash-ups by end-users without any programming knowledge (Jung et all, 2011). This system proposed a 'mash-up rule language'. This system gets parameters from the users and uses a rule-based language to construct new mash-ups.

Berners-Lee and et al. proposed a platform called 'Tabulator' which links RDF data with the semantic web browser in order to create new applications based on the RDF data sources (Berners-Lee et al, 2008). 'Tabulator' allows users to search a RDF graph in a tree structure and to browse nodes to find more information about them. An outliner mode is used which enables 'Tabulator' to create tables, Google maps, calendars, timelines, etc. Morbidoni et al (2008) present 'Semantic Web Pipes' which is a tool to create RDF based mash-ups. This tool aggregates and manipulates the content from different RDF data. This Semantic Web Pipe' can perform operations starting from straightforward aggregation to complex collaborative editing and filtering of distributed graphs.

Social Apps Development Lifecycle

This section describes a potential social apps development life cycle. The life cycle consists of four different conceptual steps of the component development process, namely the business model, the component development model, the composition model and evaluation model. Figure 1 depicts the iterative development flow of the proposed life cycle, which is similar to life-cycles for general system development but has an increased focus on the interaction between component developers and users/composers of apps (such as their creation of business models).

Business Model

There are different categories of mobile apps available in the various apps stores. We identified, based upon a qualitative investigation, a list of components from representative example apps in these app stores. Without loss of generalization we assume that comparable apps exist for all major platforms (such as Google's Android or Apple's iOS). When it comes specifically to social apps, their components have a lot of importance in user-centric mobile apps development. These components might include means to manipulate and process the users' social information, contact information, and communication history, and by utilizing this information, provide a means to create more personalized and contextualized mobile applications for improved communication experiences. An appropriate business model could help component developer and apps developer to understand the need for useful apps development and make use for a commercialization (e.g. by respective advertisement, or just by providing more appropriate services to the user).

Component Development Model

Components, within the context of this work, are considered as a building blocks of program logic or program code that performs a specific task in the context of social apps development. For example, a Facebook data aggregator is a component in the Satin Editor (Satin2, 2012) that captures the user's Facebook

Figure 1. Social application development life cycle

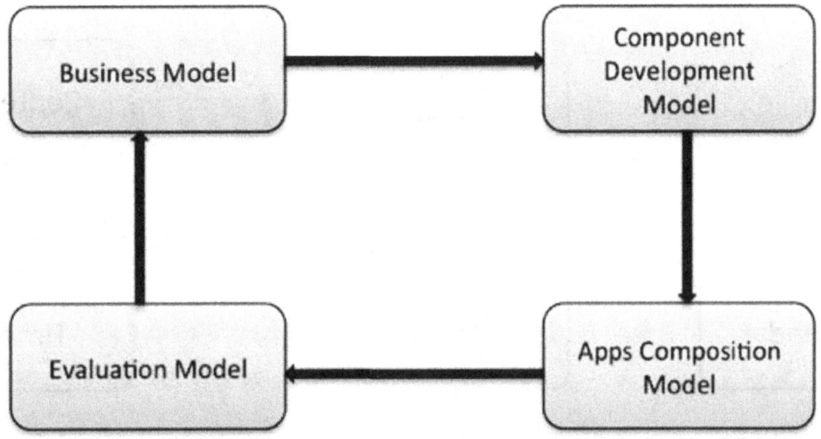

data from this platform through the respective platform's API. In general, a black-box approach has been followed to develop the components within the Satin context. After the development, the components provide inputs/output interfaces to the users via a graphical object that can be configured using a direct manipulation interface. To perform the composition of a mobile app, the components need to be connected via their input/output labels of the components in a graphical editor. All of the processing is hidden to the end-user. The details of the component development framework are discussed to the next section.

Apps Composition Model

The apps composition model describes how various components can be used for creating different kind of social applications. The individual social components could be used for different purposes in order to create various social apps that fulfill the user's specific requirements. A component can be composed through input/output interfaces. During the building session, the composition provides a web link to access the apps. In our apps composition model, there are several components that can be used for capturing social data, while there are other components for representing and filtering social data and finally there exist other components for visualizing data.

Figure 2 shows a high-level composition of an app for providing alerts for coffee breaks, where the blocks represent different single components. The 'Group Former' is a social data collector component that gathers and creates groups from a user's social connections based on a given context. 'Context' represents a supporting component that provides an input option for the apps user. The other three components 'Calendar', 'Alert' and 'Timer' performs specific tasks, as indicated by their name. In another scenario, a user might want an application that could help him to identify a location based on social connections. In this task, the user needs data adapters for instance for Facebook and/or LinkedIn (and/or other social network data adapters) in order to gather his social data from these data sources. A social data aggregator component will then aggregate the necessary information of these stored data. A data analyzing component will finally identify and sort the user's specific locations (e.g. Europe) based on the user's friends connected in different social networks and eventually suggest a location, e.g. to meet.

Figure 2. Apps COMPOSITION

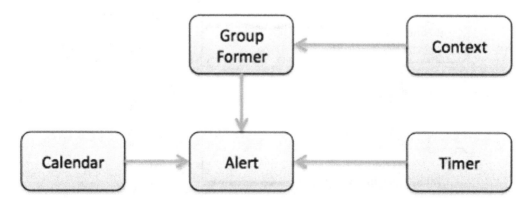

Evaluation Model

The evaluation model allows the users to study or provide feedback based on the app creation. The user's experiences of the app creation using these components will be collected here with the goal to improve the components in terms of compatibility, composition with other components, scalability, and simplicity. Moreover, in the evaluation model we have included some validation parameters. Evaluation for the proposed components will be carried out based on these parameters. Selected validation parameters are listed below:

- **Social Acceptance:** A user could evaluate if the social component based apps are acceptable from a societal point of view.
- **Positive Affect:** A user could evaluate if the social components allow for composition of any useful apps that make users' life more comfortable.
- **Quality of Experience:** A user could evaluate if the social apps are more useful and/or user friendly compared to commercial apps available.
- **Control:** A user could evaluate if he feels in control over the apps composition process.
- **Ownership:** A user could evaluate if the ownership of the newly generated apps remains with the user itself (and not with the platform provider).

Social Component Framework

Figure 3 shows a generalized, high-level framework for social components. It contains different layers of the social components development model that we previously described. In the lower layer, social data sources are connected to fetch the users' social networking data such as (e.g. Facebook, Twitter, LinkedIn, etc.). The middle layer provides a temporary storage of the users' social data, performs initial analysis on the data to offer different extended functionalities in the components placed on the top layer. Social data aggregation and analysis are performed in the middle layer. The social components itself constitute from the top layer.

During the component development, it is well recognized that different components have different levels of complexity (such as varying rights to use the contained data, richness of the data types and models, etc). A challenge is to express the components such that they can adapt to varying data sources, where the adoption naturally needs to be done per individual component. In the case of social components, most of the components are based on internal or external web APIs of social networks and social services (some of these APIs are based on open standards, such as OpenSocial). Therefore, we find it crucial to start with the identification what class of social components we need to develop. Primarily, two groups of components have been identified, which we call core components and supporting components (c.f. Figure 4).

Core components are the main social components such as social filters, social data adapter and so on. Many of these components have been implemented and deployed for illustration and research purposes in the Satin Editor. There are also some components that support these core components, e.g. in triggering or labeling of web apps, which we therefore called supporting components. We find it important to provide a classification of the components to help social apps developers in assessing what is there and by providing a joint naming scheme. The classification is illustrated in Figure 4. The different types of core components that would be suitable for social apps creation are as follows:

Figure 3. Social component framework

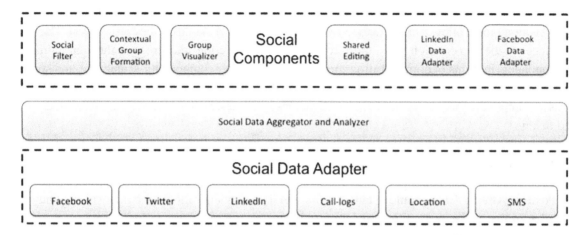

- **Social Data Adapter:** This class of components adapts social data from the social networking sites (which are made available through the users' credentials). The data is stored in a (computational) cloud for context reasoning.
- **Social Data Connector:** This class of components provides an interface to communicate between data sources and other components that utilize data.
- **Social Data Processing:** These components apply unified data representation to enhance data mining within social data components.
- **Social Data Reasoning:** These components implement different program logic or semantic functions on the social data for the user's desired apps.
- **Visualization:** Visualization components display different forms of social data. For example, if a processing and reasoning component forms a social group based on the user's social data, the visualization components can show this group in e.g. a grid view or a graphical tree view.
- **Smart Object:** Smart object components provide interfaces for lightweight devices with messaging and web connectivity functionalities.
- **Messaging:** These components provide different options of sending and receiving messages such as email, posting to social networks, SMS, and so on.
- **Location:** These components use the location APIs and social networks location- based services, such as Checkin.

Implementation

As discussed above, different kinds of core social components along with some supporting components have been developed towards a fully working prototype in an explorative and constructive approach to investigate this important research field. The users' social data is embedded within a social data component and deployed in a platform that allows our target groups (end users without any programming knowledge) to create their own social application.

Additionally, other social components embed 'intelligence' that can exploit the social data to create social applications to provide novel services. In our case, the so-called Satin Editor is used as the test-bed for simulating and evaluating the proposed social component-based application creation environment. As the background and details of the Satin Editor are beyond the scope of this work, we would like to refer the interested reader to the research project's web site with the full documentation (Satin2, 2012). Social components are based on web technologies (i.e., HTML5, JavaScript, AXIS2 web Services, etc.), which enable users to run and test their applications regardless the specific type of devices used. Therefore any modern web browser (both in desktop and mobile versions) should be able to run Satin-based mobile applications.

Data adapting (or collecting) components along with other supporting components aggregate the users' different social network(s) data. The data aggregating components 'understand' the format of the stored social data (e.g. by respective XML or similar resource descriptions) and aggregate it as a single data resource either based on context key or as a whole. Later, this data resource can be analyzed

Figure 4. A classification of components for social apps development

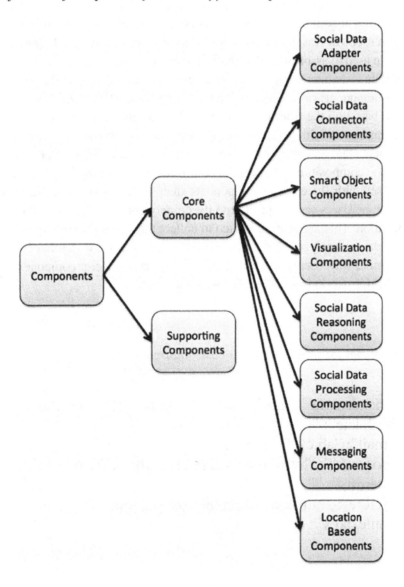

and reused by the data analyzer component in order to create personalized social applications. Data analyzer components are performing different kinds of data processing and analysis, such as the user's social interaction, his social behavior, interests, etc. Data visualization components are used to show e.g. user's aggregated social graph (a graph created from the relationships in various independent social networks, showing persons that e.g. have a temporary interest, e.g. as organizing a birthday present - c.f. the examples discussed above) either as graphical form or text form.

Different kinds of social data adapters (e.g., *LinkedIn Data Adapter*, *Facebook Data Adapter*, *Gmail Log Adapter*, etc.) have been developed and tested in order to collect users' data from these data sources. In the implementation, all collected data from different data sources are stored in as common JSON properties. The same JSON data format is applied to other data-sources to e.g. solve data aggregation problem. Figure 5 shows an example of the data format of profiling friend's basic information through social components.

In this example, the *JSON properties Reader* component has been developed to parse important information from social data and developing interesting apps. Moreover, there are components that aggregate data from different sources and provide a personalized data source. To implement this, a new indexing based upon user's access in multiple social data sources is conducted. The JSON properties of the index file are then used to associate users multiple social identities and social data sources are shown in figure 6. Social data visualizer component could be used to visualize social data.

Another social component was created which we called *Social Data Filter*, which filters users, aggregates social data based on the filtering parameters. For instance this *Social Data Filter* component could be used to create group with the users social connections based on users' interest. There are also other social components that are used to share user social resources with his/her connections.

Figure 7 shows the composition of an application in the Satin Editor. In this example one supporting component is used with three social components such as *Facebook Data Adapter*, *JSON Reader* and *Social Data Viewer*. Users can drag and drop the components in the canvas of the Satin Editor and compose the application. This application is used to collect the user's Facebook friend's data and view the whole collected data to analyze it further or to use this information with other components to create further apps. In a similar way, users can use different social data collector components to amass his/her social connections' information from different social data sources.

Figure 5. JSON properties for profiling friends basic information

```
{
        "Friendsname": "abc" , "userid": 519817106, "username": "ab.c",
        "birthdate": "0",
        "email": "ab.c@facebook.com",
        "profileurl": "https ://www.1212121/ab.c", "movies": "",
        "interests": "",
        "picture": "https://a.akamaihd.net/hp/3 t.jpg",
        "contextkey": "p,q,r,s,t,u"
}
```

Figure 6. JSON properties for associating user's identities in multiple social data sources

{"index":[{"asguser":"1323732759" ,"data":
    {"username":"1323732759" ,"socialIDs":
        {"facebookId":"1323732759" ,
        "linkedinId " : "UQxEWbiYX5" ,
        "googlePlusId " : " 109570210223523334209 " } ,
        "socialDataPaths"
        {"facebook":"../../jsonfiles/facebook/1323732759",
        "linkedin":"../../jsonfiles/linkedin/UQxEWbiYX5",
        "googleplus":"../../jsonfiles/googleplus/109570"}}}
    ]
}

Figure 7. Sample social apps composition in the Satin Editor

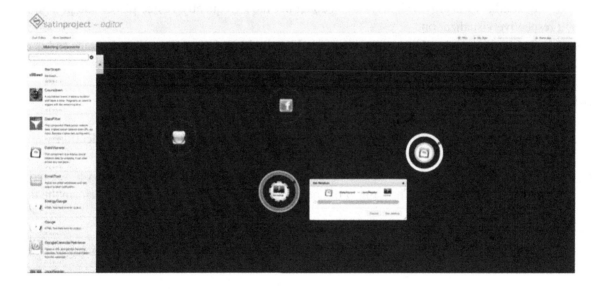

Evaluation

The ultimate aim of this work is that any user after a 15-20 minutes introduction should be able to easily create simple social apps on their own. The objective of this study was however to indicate whether this would be achievable at all, as even visual composition can be challenging for normal users as data paths and sequential dependencies still are hard to understand, and thus provide feedback on social apps development for the next iteration of the Satin Editor. A small user study was therefore initiated, which was based on the evaluation model and which was limited to 10 users with some prior knowledge of mobile apps (they were for instance required to at least have used apps before). The limited set of users and their a-priori knowledge makes the results no more than indicative, but they are still very valuable as feedback for the next generation of the Satin Editor. To conduct the study, we prepared three different scenarios (described below) of apps development. Before the users start with the app composition, the available components for social apps were introduced to the users by providing written descriptions of the components, as well as demonstrating apps composition using the Satin Editor. In this subsection, description of the scenarios is presented.

Scenarios

The following three scenarios of app compositions were used to evaluate the described approach and concepts in the user study:

Scenario 1: Bob is planning an outdoor party in a newly explored and interesting place. He wants to invite all his Facebook friends to join the party from wherever they are. Thus, Bob intends to publish an app to his Facebook timeline in order to invite his friends, as well as a to provide a map to direct them to the party place in a comfortable way.

Scenario 2: Alice wants to know which places are of most interest to her. So, she creates an app that automatically logs her current location if she stays at a place for more that 30 minutes. At the end of the month, she is provided information about her most frequently visited places and potentially a respective visualization.

Scenario 3: Charlie is going for a coffee break, and he would like to send an alert message to his co-workers so that they can have the break at the same time.

Data Collection

The following parameters have been taken into consideration during the test for data collection:

- **App Composition Time:** The time that a user has spent to compose an app on a given scenario.
- **Number of Components:** The number of components that have been selected to perform the final composition.
- **App Formation:** The user is able to build an apps and able to run the apps
- **App Functionality:** Logs whether the app that are composed by the users is functioning correctly with respect to the scenarios described above.

Figure 8 shows the snapshot of the apps generated during the user tests. Figure 8 (a) shows the apps based on scenario 1. Figure 8 (b) shows apps based on scenario 2 and Figure 8 (c) is based on scenario 3. The functionalities are not fully compliant with the described scenarios. For example, apps for the scenario 1 share the invitation through the Facebook 'Like' operation, which could also be done with other options.

Evaluation Results

Figure 9 shows the users' ratings for evaluating social apps as gathered in the user study. The ratings are taken within the scale of 1 to 5, where 1 is the most negative response while 5 is the most positive response. In general, from most of users we received positive responses.

Figure 8. Social apps generated by the Satin users for scenarios 1 to 3

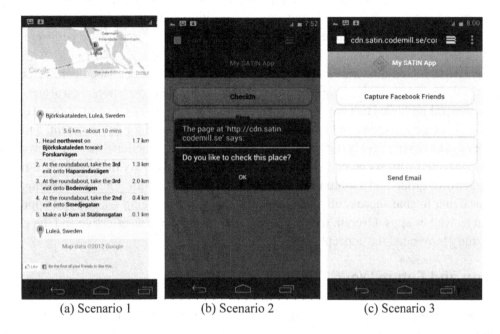

| (a) Scenario 1 | (b) Scenario 2 | (c) Scenario 3 |

Figure 9. Users' rating for evaluating social apps

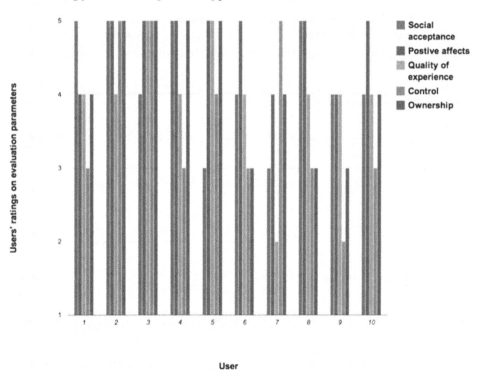

Figure 10 shows time durations for social apps composition. Although there are significant amount of assistance have been given before or during apps composition to the users, however the time duration varies highly from user to user. Average time is calculated to 29.3 minutes required per user to compose apps based on the given scenarios.

Moreover, we collected the users' individual opinions based on the described parameters from the evaluation model such as social acceptance, positive affect, quality of experience, control and ownership. Some of the general problems that we have identified are common amongst most of users during apps development. As of now, they are not comfortable enough with the editor environment, and they need more support to identifying appropriate components to accomplish functionalities. However, those are not directly connected with social components, but valid comments to fix those before re-running the study for larger user group and a more mature version of the Satin Editor. The positive impact that we got that after being to able successfully apps creation, the users are being relaxed and appreciates the environment as well as apps. Overall, the approach has been validated as effective and the participants of the user study have rated the concept positively.

Discussion and Future Work

We have proposed components for social app development environment via a high-level, four-phase social app development life cycle. Each of the phases of life cycle has been briefly discussed. The business model does not provide any technological challenges, however it describes the social components from the business and usability point of view. The business model is important, as it will help to understand the users' needs and wishes and thus be an important driving factor.

The component development model mainly addresses social aspects of the app development. It identifies different core components and supporting components to compose social apps. We also provided a

Figure 10. Time durations for social apps composition

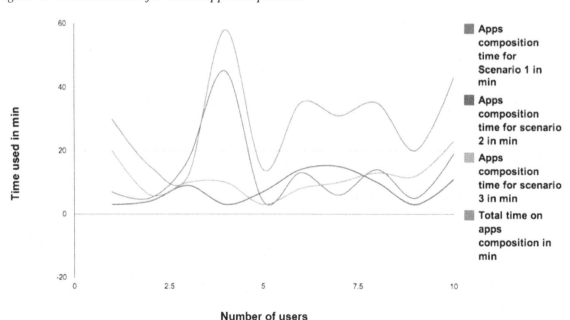

classification of components to provide developers with an overview of what kind of components that could add value to the mobile apps development environment. We argue that there are huge domains of components that need to be developed and classified for diverse apps development, and that is one of the targets for the future work.

From the user study we identified the users' difficulties to understand the composition scheme of the Satin Editor, however having initial support from a instructors, users could soon get proficient in app composition. By our validation model, we achieved useful feedback from the users even though the scale of user study was limited.

The research question addressed in this work ('How can be the user's social and communication data captured from the social and communication data sources be utilized to compose real-time social apps?') considers social data as one of the important area of component development. Facebook and LinkedIn data components got users attractions as they being able to develop social components based on those. We have shown that the social component framework provides a standard way of developing social components to capture data from social media sources. It also shows different kinds of social data collector components developed in Satin platform. The framework could be used as model for other social component developer and could adapt our JSON properties to make their components possible to compose with Satin-based social data components. Thus, new component developers may be benefitted to design and implement their social component in Satin environment. Another aspect of future works is to cover different domains of apps developments such as games, mobile OS based native apps, and so on.

The challenge will be creating an open platform for components-based visual design of apps requires standardization or an industrial de-facto. For user-composed and personalized services to become ubiquitous, the challenge is to create such an open platform based on recognized (de-facto) standards.

Due to use of smart devices, social apps are becoming part of everyday life. Social apps could be very beneficial in social media distribution, group formation, lightweight collaboration and so on. If users being able to adapt social components to build their own apps, then it will open up a new and efficient way of social development. The user of the Satin Editor logically does not require any programming knowledge to develop mobile apps. From the user study and deployed social components in the Satin Editor, it show that proposed social component development framework could be used to develop social component using different kind of social networks and social media data. The social component development life cycle and classification of component may help other developer to develop useful components to generate not only social components but also diverse type of mobile apps in general.

A key technological challenge is to manage to link openly available software components with smart devices and tangible artifacts. This challenge builds on open and standardized APIs.

Our recommendation is to study component-based visual editing of apps that utilize open data, social data and personal preferences, such that personalized apps can be easily constructed by any end-user for use with a smart device.

5. SUMMARY AND DISCUSSION

We have presented three areas of research necessary to achieve personal, social and urban awareness through pervasive computing. The argument made is that pervasive computing services are likely to be driven by user-needs, where three pillars enable these services. These are free access to open data, novel interaction techniques based on the social web of things and the vast potential behind end-users able to easily visually compose mobile/pervasive apps. In other words, that awareness is accomplished by personalizing apps through easy visual composition of components based on open (urban) data connected to social facets that allows for effective filtering, prioritization and recommendation of information and services. What drives the next age of computing is then highly personalized services that harness information from the social web of things.

The vision of pervasive computing is thus likely to be achieved, at least in part, not by inherent complex architectures and services but on simple building blocks that just about anyone can combine into useful services. These services are naturally first deployed in mobile devices, but is likely later also deployed into smart environments when available. Techniques such as tangible computing may then bloom from the few applications available today, to a full range of personalized applications applied to various areas of society such as teaching tools for children, smart homes for elder care, environments for social and tangible communication, etc.

The path towards this development can be plotted by currents trends in this area, which also highlight challenges to overcome and thus recommendations for how to achieve the vision above. A few trends, challenges and recommendations based on the work above is identified in the following sections.

Trends

- Software structures are constantly evolving towards component-based architectures that support dynamic high-level composition through wrapping and adaptors. By 2016, open component libraries will be available that enable single components to be reused for visual end-user composition.
- Social data is increasingly interesting for app developers, so is feeding back information to (groups in) social networks. By 2018, creating your own personalized apps based on social data by visual editing will be offered by several platforms.
- Personalized Physical and Digital Services: Individualization of the members of the society will further increase the demand for personalized services, extending significantly the current services that are designed for the mass.
- The amount of data sensed (and available for control) will grow exponentially. This trend is mainly grounded in the development of the so-called Internet of Things and results in many challenges regarding capturing, filtering, storing, managing and utilizing Big Data.

Challenges

- Creating an open platform for components-based visual design of apps requires standardization or an industrial de-facto. For user-composed and personalized services to become ubiquitous, the challenge is to create such an open platform based on recognized (de-facto) standards.
- A key technological challenge is to manage to link openly available software components with smart devices and tangible artifacts. This challenge builds on open and standardized APIs.
- Provision of a European-wide legal framework for sensing and open data: future smart cities will be providing and collecting a lot data to and on their citizens. Before this data can be used as basis for novel services, clear rules have to be defined on the extent this data may be used and how e.g. the privacy of the digital citizens can be ensured.
- Physical and Digital Rural Depopulation: The size of cities will further grow. Today already more than half of the population lives in cities. In the future, more and more people will live in con-

nected mega cities. The rural areas will need to develop services that, if not stopping this trend, make it at least convenient and possible for the remaining population to stay there. This will most probably concern elderly people that are more reluctant to move, but have special needs and demands, such as connected healthcare.

- The trend for individualization of inhabitants of mega cities requires the society to take counter-measures against a future 'digital loneliness'. The data and digital cities will need to use the digital data to create spaces that foster physical real cooperation, co-living and interaction. This can potentially also support virtual communities, sprung from a common need or understanding, that can offer the benefits of smaller communities in a mega city (digital villages).
- Social interaction and responsibility should, using the available data of the connected artifacts, be employed to increase the participation of the digital citizens in all social and societal issues, e.g. co-governance or to-be-developed services like FixMyDigitalCity 2.0.

Recommendations

- Study component-based visual editing of apps that utilize open data, social data and personal preferences, such that personalized apps can be easily constructed by any end-user for use with a smart device.
- Use Sweden, due its leading position with respect to widespread availability of high-bandwidth internet connectivity (esp. in rural areas), the availability of electronic IDs for digital services, and spearhead projects for digital cities, like in Skellefteå, Sweden, as a test-bed for Europe due to the widespread acceptance and adoption of new technology
- The lack of a common legal framework across the borders of the EU member states will be hindering the development of future digital city services. As can be foreseen now, most probably it will be multi-national companies that will be developing these novel services, due to the challenges from big data and the from the Internet of Things. The associated costs are higher due to the different existing legislative frameworks. A 'legal standardization' will both provide security for the investments and also be valuable for the citizens as users as clear rules will have to ensure their rights, esp. privacy.
- Standardization of middleware and service APIs allowing the interconnection of services, data, etc., while ensuring trust, authenticity and privacy. Application areas benefitting from this range from e-government, citizen service, social interaction to novel business opportunities. This will include the need for modeling and developing a 'transparency' layer for open/big/user centric data in future digital cities and economies.

6. CONCLUSION

End-users in Digital Cities able to compose personalized services within a short span of time through component-based visual composition will drive the development of truly pervasive computing services, first deployed in smart phones and later in smart environments. Components will leverage of open data from both urban and private environments as well as on the advent of novel interaction techniques such as tangible interaction devices. Personal, social and urban awareness through pervasive computing is thus accomplished by a wide variety of novel personalized services, based on users' needs.

REFERENCES

Aloisio, G., Conte, D., Elefante, C., Epicoco, I., Marra, G. P., Mastrantonio, G., & Quarta, G. (2006). Sensorml for grid sensor networks. In *Proceedings of the 2006 International Conference on Grid Computing & Applications, GCA 2006*. Las Vegas, NV: CSREA Press.

Atzori, L., Iera, A., & Morabito, G. (2010). The internet of things: A survey. *Computer Networks*, *54*(15), 2787–2805. doi:10.1016/j.comnet.2010.05.010

Berners-Lee, T., Hollenbach, J., Lu, K., Presbrey, J., Prud'hommeaux, E., & Schraefel, M. M. C. (2008). Tabulator redux: Browsing and writing linked data. In *Proceedings of CEUR Workshop*. CEUR-WS.

Böhmer, M., Hecht, B., Schöning, J., Krüger, A., & Bauer, G. (2011). Falling asleep with angry birds, Facebook and Kindle: A large scale study on mobile application usage. In *Proceedings of the 13th International Conference on Human Computer Interaction with Mobile Devices and Services* (MobileHCI '11). ACM.

Botts, M., & Robin, A. (2009). *Sensor model language (SensorML)*. Retrieved from http://www.ogc-network.net/SensorML

Caragliu, A., Del Bo, C., Kourtit, K., & Nijkamp, P. (2009). *Performance of smart cities in the north sea basin*. Retrieved from http://www.smartcities.info/files/13%20-%20Peter%20Nijkamp%20-%20 Performance%20of%20Smart%20Cities.pdf

Castellani, A. P., Bui, N., Casari, P., Rossi, M., Shelby, Z., & Zorzi, M. (2010). Architecture and protocols for the internet of things: A case study. In *Proceedings of PerCom 2010 Workshops*. Mannheim, Germany: PerCom. doi:10.1109/PERCOMW.2010.5470520

Cui, Y., & Honkala, M. (2011). The consumption of integrated social networking services on mobile devices. In *Proceedings of the 10th International Conference on Mobile and Ubiquitous Multimedia, MUM '11*. ACM.

Diewald, S., Möller, A., Roalter, L., & Kranz, M. (2011). Mobile device integration and interaction in the automotive domain. In *Proceedings of AutoNUI: Automotive Natural User Interfaces Workshop at the 3rd International Conference on Automotive User Interfaces and Interactive Vehicular Applications* (AutomotiveUI 2011). AutomotiveUI.

Diewald, S., Möller, A., Roalter, L., & Kranz, M. (2012). MobiliNet: A social network for optimized mobility. In *Proceedings of the 4th International Conference on Automotive User Interfaces and Interactive Vehicular Applications* (AutomotiveUI 2012). AutomotiveUI.

Drugge, M., Nilsson, M., Liljedahl, U., Synnes, K., & Parnes, P. (2004). Methods for interrupting a wearable computer user. In *Proceedings of ISWC 2004, the Eighth International Symposium on Wearable Computers*. IEEE.

Ennals, R., Brewer, E., Garofalakis, M., Shadle, M., & Gandhi, P. (2007). Intel mash maker: Join the web. *SIGMOD Record*, *36*(4), 27–33. doi:10.1145/1361348.1361355

Enokido, T., Xhafa, F., Barolli, L., Takizawa, M., Uehara, M., & Durresi, A. (Eds.). (2010). *The 13th international conference on network-based information systems* (NBiS 2010). Takayama, Japan: IEEE.

Erickson, T. (2010). *Geocentric crowdsourcing and smarter cities: Enabling urban intelligence in cities and regions.* Paper presented at the 1st International Workshop on Ubiquitous Crowdsourcing. New York, NY.

Ericsson 2020. (2012). *Vision 2020 – 50 billion connected devices.* Retrieved from http://www.slideshare.net/EricssonFrance/vision-2020-50-billion-connected-devices-ericsson

Ericsson IoT. (2012). *The internet of things comes alive through smart objects interoperability.* Retrieved from http://labs.ericsson.com/

ESNA. (2009). *European sensor network architecture (ESNA).* Retrieved from https://www.sics.se/esna/

Faloutsos, C., & Kang, U. (2012). Managing and mining large graphs: Patterns and algorithms. In *Proceedings of SIGMOD Conference.* ACM.

Gilbert, E., & Karahalios, K. (2009). Predicting tie strength with social media. In *Proceedings of the SIGCHI Conference on Human Factors in Computing Systems* (CHI '09). ACM.

Hallberg, J., Norberg, M. B., Kristiansson, J., Synnes, K., & Nugent, C. (2007). Creating dynamic groups using context-awareness. In *Proceedings of the 6th International Conference on Mobile and Ubiquitous Multimedia* (MUM '07). ACM.

Ishida, T. (2000). Understanding digital cities. In *Digital Cities, Technologies, Experiences, and Future Perspectives.* Berlin: Springer-Verlag. doi:10.1007/3-540-46422-0_2

Ishida, T. (2002). Digital city Kyoto. *Communications of the ACM, 45*(7), 76–81. doi:10.1145/514236.514238

Johnston, E. W. (2010). Governance infrastructures in 2020. *Public Administration Review, 70*(1), 122–128. doi:10.1111/j.1540-6210.2010.02254.x

Johnston, E. W., & Hansen, D. L. (2005). Design lessons for smart governance infrastructures. In American Governance 3.0: Rebooting the Public Square? National Academy of Public Administration.

Jung, H., & Park, S. (2011). Mash-up creation using a mash-up rule language. *J. Inf. Sci. Eng., 27*(2), 761–775.

Kapadia, A., Myers, S., Wang, X., & Fox, G. (2010). Secure cloud computing with brokered trusted sensor networks. In *Proceedings of CTS.* IEEE.

King, S. F., & Brown, P. (2007). Fix my street or else: using the internet to voice local public service concerns. In *Proceedings of the 1st International Conference on Theory and Practice of Electronic Governance* (ICEGOV '07). ACM.

Kranz, M., Murmann, L., & Michahelles, F. (2013). Research in the large: Challenges for large- scale mobile application research - A case study about NFC adoption using gamification via an app. store. *International Journal of Mobile Human Computer Interaction.* doi:10.4018/jmhci.2013010103

Kranz, M., Roalter, L., & Michahelles, F. (2010). Things that Twitter: Social networks and the internet of things. In *Proceedings of the What can the Internet of Things do for the Citizen (CIoT) Workshop at The Eighth International Conference on Pervasive Computing* (Pervasive 2010). IEEE.

Kranz, M., & Schmidt, A. (2005). Prototyping smart objects for ubiquitous computing. In *Proceedings of the International Workshop on Smart Object Systems in Conjunction with the Seventh International Conference on Ubiquitous Computing*. ACM.

Kranz, M., Schmidt, A., & Holleis, P. (2010). Embedded interaction: Interacting with the internet of things. *IEEE Internet Computing, 14*(2), 46–53. doi:10.1109/MIC.2009.141

Liu, X., Hui, Y., Sun, W., & Liang, H. (2007). Towards service composition based on mashup. In *Proceedings of IEEE SCW*. IEEE.

McGregor, A., & Bormann, C. (2012a). *Constrained RESTful environments (CoRE) (Tech. rep.). Internet Engineering Task Force*. IETF.

McGregor, A., & Bormann, C. (2012b). *IPv6 over low power wireless personal area networks (Tech. rep.). Internet Engineering Task Force*. IETF.

Michahelles, F., Kranz, M., & Mandl, S. (2012). *Social networks for people and things (SoNePT)*. Retrieved from http://www.theinternetofthings.eu/social-networks-people-and-things-sonept

Möller, A., Michahelles, F., Diewald, S., Roalter, L., & Kranz, M. (2012). Update behavior in app. markets and security implications: A case study in Google play. In *Proceedings of the 3rd International Workshop on Research in the Large*. ACM.

Morbidoni, C., Le Phuoc, D., Polleres, A., Samwald, M., & Tummarello, G. (2008). Previewing semantic web pipes. In *Proceedings of the 5th European Semantic Web Conference on the Semantic Web: Research and Applications* (ESWC'08). Berlin: Springer-Verlag.

Parnes, P., Synnes, K., & Schefström, D. (1999). Real-time control and management of distributed applications using IP-multicast. In *Proceedings of Integrated Network Management, Distributed Management for the Networked Millennium*. IEEE. doi:10.1109/INM.1999.770730

Poolsappasit, N., Kumar, V., Madria, S., & Chellappan, S. (2011). Challenges in secure sensor-cloud computing. In *Proceedings of the 8th VLDB International Conference on Secure Data Management, SDM'11*. Springer-Verlag.

Rana, J., Kristiansson, J., Hallberg, J., & Synnes, K. (2009). Challenges for mobile social networking applications. In *Proceedings of First international ICST Conference on Communications, Infrastructure, Systems and Applications in Europe* (EuropeComm 2009). London, UK: EuropeComm.

Rana, J., Kristiansson, J., Hallberg, J., & Synnes, K. (2009). An architecture for mobile social networking applications. In *Proceedings of the First International Conference on Computational Intelligence, Modelling and Simulation* (CSSim 2009). IEEE.

Rana, J., Kristiansson, J., & Synnes, K. (2010a). Enriching and simplifying communication by social prioritization. In *Proceedings of ASONAM 20110, the International Conference on Advances in Social Network Analysis and Mining*. ASONAM.

Rana, J., Kristiansson, J., & Synnes, K. (2010b). Modeling unified interaction for communication service integration. In *Proceedings of UBICOMM 2010, The Fourth International Conference on Mobile Ubiquitous Computing, Systems, Services and Technologies*. IARIA.

Rana, J., Kristiansson, J., & Synnes, K. (2012a). Supporting ubiquitous interaction in dynamic shared spaces through automatic group formation based on social context. In *Proceedings of SCI 2012, the ASE International Conference on Social Informatics*. IEEE.

Rana, J., Kristiansson, J., & Synnes, K. (2012b). Dynamic media distribution in ad-hoc social networks. In *Proceedings of the 2nd International Conference on Social Computing and its Applications (SCA2012)*. IEEE.

Roalter, L., Kranz, M., & Möller, A. (2010). A middleware for intelligent environments and the internet of things.[LNCS]. *Proceedings of Ubiquitous Intelligence and Computing, 6406*, 267–281. doi:10.1007/978-3-642-16355-5_23

Roalter, L., Möller, A., Diewald, S., & Kranz, M. (2011). Developing intelligent environments: A development tool chain for creation, testing and simulation of smart and intelligent environments. In *Proceedings of the 7th International Conference on Intelligent Environments (IE)*. IE.

Röckl, M., Gacnik, J., Schomerus, J., Strang, T., & Kranz, M. (2008). Sensing the environment for future driver assistance combining autonomous and cooperative appliances. In *Proceedings of the Fourth International Workshop on Vehicle-to-Vehicle Communications* (V2VCOM). V2VCOM.

Rusu, R. B., Maldonado, A., Beetz, M., Kranz, M., Mösenlechner, L., Holleis, P., & Schmidt, A. (2006). Player/stage as middleware for ubiquitous computing. In *Proceedings of the 8th Annual Conference on Ubiquitous Computing* (Ubicomp 2006). ACM.

Satin. (2012). *SATIN editor*. Retrieved from http://satinproject.eu/

Schmidt, A., Kranz, M., & Holleis, P. (2004). Embedded information. In *Proceedings of Workshop Ubiquitous Display Environments at UbiComp 2004*. ACM.

Schmidt, R. K., Leinmüller, T., & Böddeker, B. (2008). V2x kommunikation. In *Proceedings of 17th Aachener Kolloquium*. Academic Press.

Schmidt, R. K., Leinmüller, T., Schoch, E., Kargl, F., & Schäfer, G. (2010). Exploration of adaptive beaconing for efficient intervehicle safety communication. *IEEE Network Magazine, 24*, 14–19. doi:10.1109/MNET.2010.5395778

Sensei. (2008). *SENSEI - Integrating the physical with the digital world of the network of the future*. Retrieved from http://www.ict-sensei.org/

Shneidman, J., Pietzuch, P., Ledlie, J., Roussopoulos, M., Seltzer, M., & Welsh, M. (2004). *Hourglass: An infrastructure for connecting sensor networks and applications (Tech. rep.)*. Harvard.

Smart Santander. (2008). *Smart santander - Future internet research & experimentation*. Retrieved from http: //www.smartsantander.eu/

Tsiftes, N., & Dunkels, A. (2011). A database in every sensor. In *Proceedings of the 9th ACM Conference on Embedded Networked Sensor Systems* (SenSys '11). ACM.

Virtanen, T., & Malinen, S. (2008). Supporting the sense of locality with online communities. In *Proceedings of MindTrek 2008, International Digital Media & Business Festival*. MindTrek.

Weiser, M. (1991). The computer for the 21st century. *Scientific American, 265*(3), 66–75. doi:10.1038/scientificamerican0991-94 PMID:1754874

Wong, J. (2007). Marmite: Towards end-user programming for the web. In *Proceedings of VL/HCC*. IEEE.

Wong, J., & Hong, J. I. (2007). Making mash-ups with marmite: Towards end-user programming for the web. In *Proceedings of CHI*. ACM.

ENDNOTES

[1]   https://www.mobileworks.com
[2]   http://www.mturk.com
[3]   http://www.waze.com
[4]   http://www.wheelmap.org/
[5]   http://www.eyequest.de/
[6]   http://kleinwassersensor.com/
[7]   http://www.fixmystreet.com/
[8]   http://www.seeclickfix.com/
[9]   Dagens Nyheter 2010-06-15 "Generation E går sin egen väg?" http://www.dn.se/insidan/insidan-hem/generation-e-gar-sin-egen-vag
[10]   https://www.facebook.com/
[11]   https://www.linkedin.com/
[12]   https://plus.google.com/
[13]   https://www.youtube.com/
[14]   https://www.twitter.com/
[15]   http://pipes.yahoo.com/pipes/
[16]   http://www.popfly.ms/

Chapter 4
Factors Influencing Consumer Acceptance of Internet of Things Technology

Chung Sim Liew
Universities Malaysia Sabah, Malaysia

Wai Kin Koh
Universities Malaysia Sabah, Malaysia

Ju Min Ang
Universities Malaysia Sabah, Malaysia

Shy Yin Tan
Universities Malaysia Sabah, Malaysia

Yee Teen Goh
Universities Malaysia Sabah, Malaysia

Ru Yi Teh
Universities Malaysia Sabah, Malaysia

ABSTRACT

The aim of this research is to examine factors influencing consumer acceptance of Internet of Things Technology (IoT) guiding by the Technology Acceptance Model (TAM). This quantitative research involves 204 respondents approached via convenience sampling at a public higher learning institution. Data was analyzed using multiple regression and results revealed that the dimension of perceived usefulness is the most influencing factor on the consumers' acceptance of IoT technology and consumers' behavioural intention to use. In the Malaysian context, this research provides additional information in narrowing the research gap with regard to understanding behavioural intention to use the IoT technology. Next, the framework will be used for future exploration to address the issue of people who have never utilized an IoT innovation react.

INTRODUCTION

The Internet has become a need for many people as the technology advanced. It satisfies people with its multiple services in different types of sector. The Internet is used for communication, as a search engine, entertainment, and even purchases of products or services. Internet of Things (IoT) was introduced in 1999 by Ashton, a British technology pioneer who help develop the concept (Gubbi, Buyya, Marusic, & Palaniswami, 2013). The IoT technology purpose is to enlarge the advantages of the consistent internet

DOI: 10.4018/978-1-5225-1832-7.ch004

such as frequent connectivity, the ability of remote control, and sharing of data (Peoples, Parr, Mcclean, & Morrow, 2013). With IoT technologies, people in many fields such as transportation, logistics, and finance can work more efficient and easy because the technology includes of fitting objects by using a microchip and a communications antenna (Welle, 2013). IoT technology help corporations by using radio frequency identification (RFID) to monitor their inventories, use Homeland Security to scan passports, and for fare cards reading at subway terminals. Prior to its functionality, IoT technologies have become a technological revolution that will change our life and the world (Schlick, Ferber & Hupp, 2013).

However, a more practical question for IoT technology practitioners is: what characteristics create consumer awareness that this technology is useful, effortless to use, enjoyable, and can be trusted? Therefore, this research focus on the hypothetical fields of the Technology Acceptance Model (TAM) such as usefulness, ease of use, trust, social influence, and enjoyment from the industrial, social background and individual perceptions, to advance an unified framework. Thus, this framework integrates that the consumer acceptance of IoT technologies will be affected by these variables (Ha & Stoel, 2009). This study creates knowledge that will be beneficial to IoT technology practitioners. This knowledge will help practitioners understand more about the impact of consumers' certainty about IoT technologies such as the way to attract more consumers to try this technology.

The objective of this research is to investigate the consumer recognition towards the Internet of things technology and identify the features influencing IoT acceptance among students. This study is comprises of two major independent variables: perceived ease of use and perceived usefulness. For a student, the factor that affects his acceptance on IoT might be different according to his own preference. However, the feature that has the most effective on the acceptance of IoT is one of the main outcomes of this research.

Prior studies have not effectively addressed the effects of technology features, characteristics of individual and social context on consumer acceptance towards the technologies. According to Schlick *et al.* (2013), researchers mainly focus on the usage and design of the technologies from the industry or company's point of view. This study proposes an extension to the current model of IoT technology acceptance. The second section is about the background hypothetical foundation from prior literature and develops the research model and hypotheses. Thirdly, the proposed model will be tested by the research method, and the next section will shows the analysis and result of the study. Furthermore, the research finding will be discussed in the fifth section. Final section will concludes the limitation and implication of the study and also recommendation for future research.

LITERATURE REVIEW

According to Uckelmann, Harrison and Michahelles (2011), the IoT is defined as things that can be used to connect via internet. Generally, the discussions on IoT focused on the future of communications and computing as it is a technological revolution. IoT has been used in many areas recently, for example, digital logistics, supply chain management, stock control, urban planning, library management, retail tracking, mobile payment, efficient transportation, home automation, warehouse management, healthcare and the private domain (Ding, 2013). It also offers many advantages for many industries and their benefits to consumers, for example substantial efficiencies. (Sundamaeker, Guillemin, Friess & Woelffle, 2010).

In this circumstance, consumers' behaviour might be affected from the internet of things technologies on few aspects of the consumers' daily routine. (Li, & Wang, 2013). For instance, IoT consumers might get advantage from technologies that used in smart fridges which can monitor the consumption of food and beverages and also rearrange goods automatically.

Perceived Usefulness

Perceived usefulness refers to a person believes that using a specific system would develop his or her job enactment (Davis, 1989). This study believes that the control to attract users lies in the technology's usability and usefulness. Consumers are only willing to accept transformation if those transformation provides a distinctive advantage (Rogers, 1995). Additionally, the perceived usefulness of IoT technologies are likely to be high because their service convenience would definitely increase consumer's satisfaction level. This will somehow affecting consumers perceptions towards enhanced performance as well as affects consumers intention. However, perceived usefulness also depends on the services IoT technologies offered such as faster processes, convenience, transferring money abroad, obtaining relevant information and also maintaining their efficiency (Wang, Lei, & Li, 2013).

The IoT technology is beneficial to consumers in so many ways. The TAM indicates that perceived usefulness is a significant factor of behaviour aim to use. (Lee, Park, Chung, & Blakeney, 2012). Similarly, perceived usefulness is an essential aspect in determining adaptation of advances. As a consequence, the greater the perceived usefulness of using the IoT technologies, the more likely the IoT technologies will be adopted by consumers. Hence, this study proposes that:

H1: Perceived usefulness has a positive influence on the behavioural intention to use IoT technologies.

Perceived Ease of Use

Perceived ease of use is like exertion anticipation of Unified Theory of Acceptance and Use of Technology (UTAUT) and the unpredictability of Integrated Device Technology (IDT), (Venkatesh, Morris, Davis, & Davis, 2003). It is worried with clients' apparent applied endeavours when utilizing the IoT innovations/administrations. For IoT clients to receive IoT, they have to feel that IoT is anything but difficult to utilize. Perceived ease of use, in contrast, refers to the degree to which a person believes that using a particular system would be free of effort. Exertion is a limited asset that a man may allot to the different exercises for which he or she answerable (Radner & Rothschild, 1975). Extensive previous studies express that apparent convenience is a huge determinant of behavioural goals to the innovation (Lee *et al.*, 2012). Hence, we recommend:

H2: Perceived ease of use show a positive influence on the behavioural intention to use IoT technologies.

Trust

Trust can be defined as a firm belief in the reliability, truth, or ability of someone or something (Definition of Trust, n.d.). It also can be known as commit someone or something to the safekeeping of. The innovations of IoT need the trust from consumers because advancements typically accompany danger (Cho, 2004).

Users feel more concern and sensitive risk in their adoption result because the exclusive characteristics of IoT technologies are incapability to straightforwardly see and touch an item, and high level of IT inclusion. The sensitive level of a piece of privacy is determined by owner's feeling. Therefore, the piece of privacy will have many sensitive levels. Trust is one of the most effective tools for reducing uncertainty and risks and generating a sense of safety (Lin, 2011) because of the significance of trust is decreasing hazard and encouraging appropriate use of conduct, we incorporate trust in TAM and extra arrangement of positive connection in the middle of trust and the behavioral expectation to utilize IoT advances. Thus, this study suggests:

H3: Trust has a positive influence on the behavioural intention to use IoT technologies

Social Influence

Social influence is the change in feelings, opinions and behaviour that changed a person in another sentience (Rashotte, 2002). It has a great power to affect a person in making decision process on technological innovations. Those impact may originate from ones' companion, family and even the media which may impact clients' expectation to embrace IoT advancements and administrations. When a new technological innovations of product and services is launched, the majority of the consumers' insufficiency of reliable information of the latest product and service aspects. Therefore, social context has assumed an imperative part by giving suggestions for consumer which may help in assessing the products' value (Hsu & Lu, 2004). These related information can easily obtained by accessing social network. It also enable mobile IoT gadgets to turn into a trend for consumers who to involved in the change of technological innovations.

The acknowledgement of technological innovations in social context occupied with the behaviour of other individuals perceive. Ventatesh, Morris, Davis, & Davis (2003) stated that it is closely related with the subjective norm of Theory of reasoned action (TRA). Thus, it is indicated that social influence has crucial impacts on consumer intention to adopt mobile IoT commerce. In conclusion, this study examined that:

H4: Affection of social influence has a positive impact on the behavioural intention to use IoT technologies.

Perceived Enjoyment

Perceived enjoyment is the degree to which the action of utilizing a particular framework is seen to be pleasurable in its own right, beside any authorization outcomes coming about because of framework use (Ventatesh *et al.*, 2003). This study shows that the original TAM has been extended by including the perceived enjoyment on IoT innovation as one of the components. This is because of perceived enjoyment has been found to rouse clients to embrace another innovation as a noteworthy characteristic inspiration (Bruner & Kumar, 2005). Users usually will be naturally motivated to adopt IoT technologies when the use of IoT technologies is convenience as well as fun and pleasure. This is because users care more on the enjoyment of IoT technologies. Taking into account the confirmation from past studies, enjoyment in shopping is seen as a vital variable of why purchasers shop (Lu & Su, 2009).

The investigation on the part of enjoyment in versatile trade recommended the significance of pleasure on use purposes and practices (Kim, Park, & Oh, 2008). It is important to focus on users' usage intentions because it will directly affect the enjoyment on the users' enjoyment. Therefore, we can assume that the usefulness of IoT technologies can affect the perceived enjoyment of users. Based on Kim *et al.* (2008), perceived enjoyment is found to affect the intention to use short message service. Because users are expected to be more enjoyed with long messages service. As a consequence, the greater the perceived enjoyment of using the IoT technologies, the more likely the IoT technologies will be adopted by consumers. Hence, this study proposes that:

H5: Perceived enjoyment has a positive influence on the behavioural intention to use IoT technologies.

Perceived Behavioural Control

Perceived behavioural control refers to the people's perception of their ability to perform a given behavioural Perceived behavioural control is a component that encourages individuals' engagement in looking for the pertinent data when utilizing IoT innovation. On the most fundamental level, the IoT includes fitting items with a microchip and an interchanges reception apparatus (Welle, 2013). Consumers are rational and make systematic use of information that available to them when making decisions. At the point when individuals trust that they have little control over performing the conduct because of the absence of imperative assets and opportunities, then their aims to perform the conduct may be low regardless of the fact that they have great states of mind and or subjective standards concerning execution of the conduct.

Perceived behavioural control regularly serves as a substitute for genuine control, and seeing that apparent control is a reasonable assessment of real control. Bandura (1977) has given exact confirmation that individuals' conduct is emphatically affected by the certainty they have in their capacity to perform the conduct. Perceived behavioural control will affect the behavioural expectation to utilize the IoT advances. The IoT innovation will give awesome efficiencies crosswise over numerous commercial ventures and their advantages to purchasers are significant (Uckelmann *et al.*, 2011). For instance, clients may profit by IoT innovations utilized as a part of brilliant ice chests that independently screen the utilization of nourishment and drinks and re-request products (Sundamaeker *et al.*, 2010). Anxiety of control and positive evaluation of the IoT technology is a must. Support of the positive role on behavioral intention is provided (Casalo, Flavia, & Guinaľıu, 2010; Lu, Zhou, & Wang, 2009; Mathieson, 1991). Hence, this study proposes:

H6: Perceived behavioural control has a positive influence on the behavioural intention to use IoT technologies.

Behavioural Intention to Use

Behavioural intention is the mark which a person has formulated mindful plans to perform or not perform some stated future behaviour. The original Technology Acceptance Model (TAM) recommends that two variables which is perceived ease of use and perceived usefulness are substantial elements of behavioural intention to use a technology or system. However, other factors like the opinions of other persons will also affect a users' acceptance towards adoption of IoT (Venkatesh, Thong, & Xu, 2012). Moreover, users will not able to perform a behaviour without the essential resources and skills (Ajzen, 2011). Thus, this unique TAM variables is not effectively explain vital causes influencing customer acceptance of IoT technology. Therefore, original TAM need to be extending in order to explain more accurately towards behavioural intention to use.

Beliefs about enjoyment, social influence, trust, and perceived behavioural control has been found as the key factors influencing consumer acceptance of new technology (Zhang & Mao, 2008). Thus, this study proposes the expanded TAM which included six independent variables that influencing consumer's acceptance towards IoT technology such as perceived usefulness, perceived ease of use, trust, social influence, perceived enjoyment, and perceived behavioural control. These variables has become the new significant determinant of behavioural intention to use IoT technology. As a consequence, the greater of the belief on variables, the more likely the IoT will be adopted by consumers. Hence, this study suggests that:

H7: All the independent variables has a positive influence on the behavioural intention to use IoT technologies.

METHODOLOGY

Participants and Procedure

The data were collected from students at two faculties: Labuan Faculty of International Finance (LFIF) and Faculty of Computing and Informatics (FCI). 204 sets of questionnaire functioning finalized ques-

Figure 1. Proposed Theoretical Framework

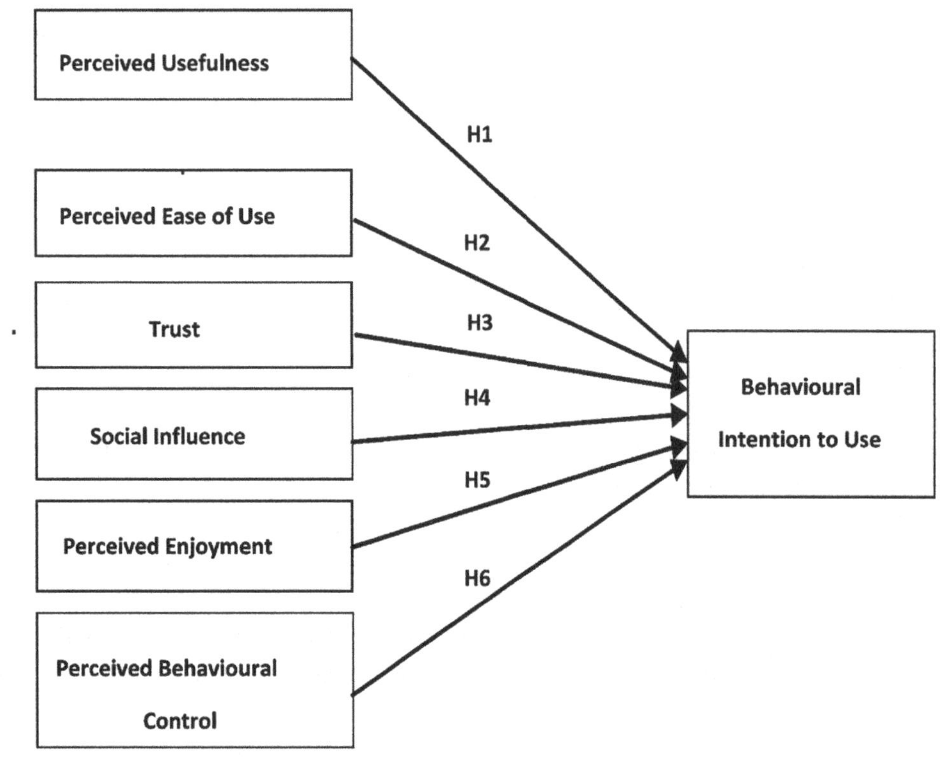

tionnaires were given to confirm that the data collected met the size requirement for valid quantitative data analysis. All respondents are randomly selected at these faculties, utilizing the convenience sampling technique. Data were collected from 21st of September to 30th of September 2015 and respondents were required to circle the response which best describe their level of preference with each of the questionnaire items. Therefore, all of the 204 responses were fully answered and it was useful in our research.

Questionnaire Development and Instrument

A close-ended questionnaire was developed based on the objectives of this study. The questionnaire comprises of 3 sections. Section A inquire about respondents' demographic profile and their prior experience in IoT technology. Section B evaluates the variables that affect consumer's acceptance of IoT technology which are perceived usefulness, perceived ease of use, trust, social influence, perceived enjoyment, perceived behavioural control and behavioural intention to use. Section C consists of perception of consumers' acceptance of IoT. This study utilized a five-point Likert scale ranging from 1- Strongly disagree to 5- Strongly agree.

Data Analysis

A well-known computer software, the IBM Statistical Package for Social Sciences (SPSS) version 21 was used for the data analysis. Using the SPSS, several analyses were performed on the data. Firstly, descriptive analysis consisting of several analyses such as mean, standard deviation, and also correlation analysis were conducted. The demographic profile of the respondent was presented in the form of frequency and percentage. Next, reliability test was carried out to measure the reliability of the data collected. Cronbach's alpha is a reliability coefficient that indicates how well the items in a set are positively correlated to one another (Cronbach, 1946). The closer Cronbach's alpha is to 1, the higher the internal consistency reliability (Sekaran & Bougie, 1992). This study utilised the criteria of Cronbach's alpha as suggested in previous literatures (i.e. George & Mallery, 2003; Kline, 2000), as follows: (i) excellent ($\alpha \geq 0.9$), (ii) good ($0.7 \leq \alpha < 0.9$), (iii) acceptable ($0.6 \leq \alpha < 0.7$), (iv) poor ($0.5 \leq \alpha < 0.6$), and (v) unacceptable ($\alpha < 0.5$). Then, correlation analysis was conducted to find out the correlation coefficients among the variables. Finally, stepwise multiple linear regression analysis multiple regression analysis was administered in order to examine the causal relationships between each set of variables according to the hypothesis developed.

RESULTS

Demographic Profile of Respondents

Table 1 illustrates the respondents' demographic profile. Out of 204 respondents, 119 of them are male (58%) while 85 were female (42%). 74% of respondents were aged more than 19 years old. The minority of respondents (9%) were aged less than 15 years old whereas the remaining of the respondents are between the age of 16 to 18 years old was 16.7%. In terms of race, Malay made up 32% of the sample,

Table 1. Demographic profile of respondents

Variables	Categories	Frequency	%
Gender	Male	119	58.3
	Female	85	41.7
Age (years)	< 15	18	8.8
	16-18	34	16.7
Race	Malay	65	31.9
	Chinese	61	29.9
	India	32	15.7
Education	SPM	52	25.5
	Degree	152	74.5

Chinese made up 30% of the sample. Meanwhile, minority of respondents 16% are India and 22% are Bumiputera. More than three-quarter of the respondents who are undertaking Degree holder (74.5%), 152 out of 204 respondents and 52 of them are SPM holder (25.5%).

Prior Experience in Internet of Things (IoT) Technology

Table 2 describes the respondent's prior experience in Internet of Things (IoT) Technology. Of the 204 respondents, 72 of the respondents spent more than 4 hours a day on the internet (35.3%) whereas only 8 of them spend around 1-2 hours a day on the internet (3.9%). However, the remaining three categories which are less than one hour a day, 2-3 hours a day and 3-4 hours a day shows a moderate frequency of time spend on the internet of around 19 (9.3%), 51 (25%) and 54 (26.5%) respectively. A majority of 71 respondents (34.8%) use social networking websites while browsing the internet whereas only 6 respondents (2.9%) out of 204 play music while browsing the internet. Other activities chosen by respondents while browsing the internet are purchase products or services (19 respondents), pay bills (16 respondents), research academic articles or books (38 respondents), make travel arrangement (12 respondents) and also play games (42 respondents). Besides, respondents preferred using English language while browsing the internet as compared to Malay and Chinese language (198/97.1%, 1/0.5% and 5/2.5% respectively). In terms of browser, majority respondents preferred using Google Chrome (100 students/ 49.0%) as compared to Mozilla Firefox and Internet Explorer. Of the 204 respondents, 100 (49%) of them preferred using smartphone to connect to the internet whereas no respondents used computer tablet and enterprise digital assistant (EDA). The remaining categories which are laptop computer, personal digital assistant (PDA) and desktop computer have 83(40.7%), 1(0.5%) and 20(9.8%) respondents respectively.

Reliability Analysis

Reliability analysis was conducted to determine the validity of each items of measurement. Cronbach's alpha is used to measure how closely related the variables are as a group. Results showed in Table 3 indicate that all variables are positively contributing to the general reliability. The Cronbach's alpha value

Table 2. Prior experience in internet of things technology

Variables	Categories	Frequency	%
Time spend on the Internet in a day	< 1 hours a day	19	9.3
	1-2 hours	8	3.9
	2-3 hours	51	25.0
	3-4 hours	54	26.5
	> 4 hours a day	72	35.3
Activities in browsing Internet	Purchase products or services	19	9.3
	Pay bills	16	7.8
	Research academic articles or books	38	18.6
	Use social networking websites	71	34.8
	Make travel arrangement	12	5.9
	Play music	6	2.9
	Play games	42	20.6
Language use while browsing Internet	English	198	97.1
	Malay	1	0.5
	Chinese	5	2.5
Type of preferred browser used	Google Chrome	100	49.0
	Mozilla Firefox	18	8.8
	Internet Explorer	86	42.2
Type of devices used to connect Internet	Laptop Computer	83	40.7
	Personal digital assistant (PDA)	1	0.5
	Desktop Computer	20	9.8
	Smartphone	100	49.0

Table 3. Reliability analysis

Variables	No. of Items	Cronbach's α
Perceived Usefulness (PU)	3	0.796
Perceived Ease of Use (PEOU)	3	0.832
Trust (TR)	3	0.700
Social Influence (SI)	3	0.737
Perceived Enjoyment (PE)	3	0.713
Perceived Behavioural Control (PBC)	3	0.761
Behavioural intention to use (BI)	5	0.753

for all variables of consumer's acceptance towards internet of things (IoT) technology range from 0.700 to 0.832. Perceived ease of use shows the highest Cronbach's alpha, α value at (0.832) while trust shows the lowest value at (0.700). The remaining variables which are perceived usefulness, social influence, perceived enjoyment, perceived behavioural control and behavioural intention to use has Cronbach's alpha, α value at 0.796, 0.737, 0.713, 0.761 and 0.753 respectively. Cronbach's alpha, α above 0.70 is considered to be highly reliable. In other words, consumers' acceptance towards internet of things (IoT) technology and consumers' response all have high reliability.

Correlation Analysis

The Pearson correlation coefficient was performed to indicate significant two way correlation between specific variables. The scope of correlation coefficient (r) value is between -1 shows a negative correlation to +1 shows a positive correlation. The values which closer to ± 1 indicate a strong relationship than values closer to 0. Table 4 illustrate that all variables have positively correlated with consumers' behavioural intention to use the Internet of Things (IoT) technology. As the result shown, independent variable of perceived usefulness has the strongest correlation coefficient $r = 0.643$ value with consumers' behavioural intention. This indicate that consumers' behavioural intention is dependent on consumer's perceived usefulness. However, the least correlated coefficient lies between perceived behavioural control and behavioural intention to use which is $r = 0.141$.

Besides that, perceived ease of use ($r = 0.380$), trust ($r = 0.500$), social influence (r=0.468) and perceived enjoyment ($r = 0.407$) also show a significant results. All the variables of correlation coefficient values were less than 1, and particularly below 0.85 where statistically significant at the p < 0.05 level ratifying a positive correlation among all the variable. Therefore, it constructed a multicollinearity does not exist in the study (Allen & Bennett, 2010; Field, 2009). The mean for all hypotheses as shown in the Table 4 with a range from 4.2059 to 3.7516. This results conclude that most of the respondents had positive behavioural intention to use the Internet of Things (IoT) technology based on the Likert scale of 1=strongly disagree to 5=strongly agree. The highest mean lies on variable of perceived ease of use. In additional, the skewness of all the variable ranges from -1.473 to -0.805, below ±2.0. Similarity, the

Table 4. Correlation analysis

	1	2	3	4	5	6	7
Perceived Usefulness	1						
Perceived Ease of Use	0.235**	1					
Trust	0.701**	0.280**	1				
Social Influence	0.470**	0.393**	0.370**	1			
Perceived Enjoyment	0.328**	0.282**	0.307**	0.338**	1		
Perceived Behavioural Control	0.040	0.071	0.069	0.132	0.099	1	
Behavioural Intention to Use	0.643**	0.380**	0.500**	0.468**	0.407**	0.141*	1
Mean	4.1863	4.2059	4.0899	3.8709	3.7516	4.0147	4.1333
Standard Deviation	0.66019	0.64334	0.64164	0.74807	0.78462	0.80929	0.62072
Skewness	-0.805	-0.924	-1.473	-1.273	-1.017	-0.836	-1.211
Kurtosis	0.428	1.105	3.134	1.449	0.299	0.074	1.939

Note: **Correlation is significant at the 0.01 level (two-tailed).

*Correlation is significant at the 0.05 level (2-tailed).

value for kurtosis range from 0.074 to 3.134 which well below the edge ± 10. Both of the skewness and kurtosis values are well underneath the given limits, thus, with the implying the study scores approximate a "normal distribution" or "bell-shaped curve".

Multiple Regression Analysis

Multiple regression analysis was conducted to determine the relationship between the factors influencing consumers' acceptance of IoT technology and consumers' behavioural control. Based on Table 5, results computed that all the independent variables have variance inflation factor (VIF) values extending from 1.025 to 2.221 which is below than the cut-off point of 10. On the other hand, the tolerance values of all the items extent from 0.450 to 0.976 which is directly above the limit of 0.10. Thus, it indicates multicollinearity is absent. However, for the p- value which lower than 0.05 (p<0.05) have to discard the null of non-significant and presume that the independent variable is significant predictor to the dependent variable.

The results shown in Table 5 infer hypothesis 1-6 posited the existence of a direct relationship between the factors influencing consumers' acceptance of IoT technology and consumers' behavioural intention to use. The findings indicate three components of factors have positive influence on consumers' behavioural intention to use in IoT showed in Model 1, namely perceived usefulness, perceived ease of use and perceived enjoyment. The estimated coefficient for perceived usefulness ($\beta_1 = 0.487$, t-value=6.540, p < 0.05), perceived ease of use ($\beta_2 = 0.171$, t-value = 3.071, p < 0.05) and perceived enjoyment ($\beta_5 = 0.150$, t-value = 2.720, p < 0.05) which are statistically significant influence the consumers' behavioural intention to use. Thus, the H1, H2 and H5 are accepted in this research. However, another three components of factors which are trust ($\beta_3 = 0.022$, t-value = 0.303, p>0.05), social influence ($\beta_4 = 0.103$, t-value = 1.686, p > 0.05) and perceived behavioural control ($\beta_6 = 0.0.79$, t-value=1.566, p > 0.05) has an insignificant relationships with consumers' behavioural intention to use IoT. This means that the H3, H4 and H6 are not acknowledged. Furthermore, the results proved that the dimension of perceived usefulness is the most influencing factor on the consumers' acceptance of IoT technology and consumers' behavioural intention to use. Figure 1 shows the normal probability plot (P-P) while Figure 2 clarifies the scatter plot of the model where no significant deviations from standards exist, with the scores' majority rectangular distributed at the right.

Table 5. Multiple regression analysis

		Standardized Coefficients	t	Sig.	Collinearity Statistics	
		Beta			Tolerance	VIF
Model 1	Perceived Usefulness	0.487*	6.540	0.000	0.450	2.221
	Perceived Ease of Use	0.171*	3.071	0.002	0.804	1.244
	Trust	0.022	0.303	0.762	0.491	2.037
	Social Influence	0.103	1.686	0.093	0.670	1.493
	Perceived Enjoyment	0.150*	2.720	0.007	0.819	1.221
	Perceived Behavioural Control	0.079	1.566	0.119	0.976	1.025

Dependent Variable: Behavioural Intention to Use; Notes: *p < 0.05

DISCUSSION

This research examined the relationship between integrative model of factors and the acceptance of IoT technologies from consumers. Empirical results of multiple regression analysis showed that out of seven hypotheses investigated, three hypotheses were supported where the acceptance of IoT technologies from customers was affected positively by factors such as perceived usefulness, perceived ease of use, and perceived enjoyment.

The empirical results found that perceived usefulness is the most influential factors that affected the acceptance of IoT technologies from consumers ($\beta_1 = 0.487$, t-value=6.540, p < 0.05) has significant influence on the acceptance of IoT from consumers, inferring H1 is persistent. With this, consumers believe that IoT technologies is very useful for them. This is because most of the consumers agreed that by using IoT technologies will help them for quicker procedures, lead to less lining time, and enhance administration quality saw by clients. This findings is comparable with that of prior studies (Davis, 1989; Hart & Porter, 2004; Lee *et al.*, 2012; Lu & Su, 2009; Song *et al.*, 2008) which found that perceived usefulness has a positive impact on the behavioral intention to use IoT technologies.

Besides that, perceived ease of use have a significant relationship with the acceptance of IoT technologies from consumers ($B_2 = 0.171$, t-value = 3.071, p < 0.05), implying H2 is accepted. Which means perceived ease of use has a positive impact on the behavioral intention to use IoT technologies. The present survey findings showed that perceived ease of use is a critical determinant of behavioral expectations to the innovation (Davis, 1989; Lee *et al.,* 2012). Results infer that consumers agreed that IoT has the usability of online ticketing services, and easily to get information on what consumers need. Moreover, based on the survey, consumers feels convenience in booking, searching, transaction, and payment procedures by using IoT technologies.

With regards to trust affect the behavioral expectation to utilize IoT advancements, results revealed insignificant relationship ($\beta_3 = 0.022$, t-value = 0.303, p > 0.05), implying H3 is not reinforced. Results infer that trust does not affect an individual's intention and decision to accept the IoT technologies. This is not consistent with the previous study (Lin, 2011), which showed that trust is one of the most effective tools for reducing uncertainty and risks and generating a sense of safety. The survey showed that, consumers' disagreement with the chance of having a technical failure in an online transaction is small, online purchasing cannot be trusted and there are too many uncertainties. Besides that, consumers also believe that using IoT technologies will gives them smaller uncertainty and decrease the risk in their adoption decision.

Next, the results of social influence also showed insignificant relationship ($\beta_4 = 0.103$, t-value = 1.686, p < 0.05), implying H4 is not accepted. The present survey findings showed that consumers rely minimally on the recommendations of others like friends and family members in determining their acceptance of IoT technologies. Results infer that social pressure does not affect an individual's intention and decision on attitude and behavior. This is not consistent with the previous study (Hsu & Lu, 2004), which stated social connection assumes an essential part in the choice procedure.

Further examination of the study uncovered that the perceived enjoyment is also significantly affected the acceptance of IoT technologies from consumers with standardized coefficients beta of 0.150, t-value of 2.720 at p<0.05, representing H5 is held by the data. Similarly, this results supports with Kim *et al.* (2008). This study confirmed that consumers' intentions are dependent on the perceived enjoyment. Based on the survey, most of the consumers agreed that perceived enjoyment is the major intrinsic motivations to drive users adopt a new technology, use of IoT technologies can bring fun and pleasure to the users, and perceived enjoyment influences expectation to utilize short message administration.

With regards to perceived behavioral control has a positive effect on the behavioral intention to use IoT technologies, results revealed insignificant relationship ($\beta_6 = 0.079$, t-value =1.566, p > 0.05), implying H6 is not accepted. This results is not align with the previous studies (i.e. Casalo *et al*, 2010; Lu *et al*, 2009; Mathieson, 1991). Therefore, this study showed that consumer's intentions are not dependent on the width of their resources, time, and opportunities to accept IoT technologies. This means they do not control factors such as money, time, and effort, which effect their actual environmental behavior and intention to use IoT technologies in their life.

CONCLUSION AND RECOMMENDATIONS

The results of this study propose a new awareness of the findings of earlier studies that could be importance to researchers and practitioners in understanding the factors that influencing consumer acceptance of internet of things (IoT) technology, particularly in the UMSLIC context. The results indicate three components of factors are accepted that have greatest influence on consumers' behavioural intention to use in IoT which are perceived usefulness, perceived ease of use and perceived enjoyment. Whereas trust, social influence and perceived behavioural control were found insignificant to influence behavioural intention to use Iot technology. Furthermore, the results proved that the dimension of perceived usefulness is the most influencing factor on the consumers' acceptance of IoT technology and consumers' behavioural intention to use.

IoT administration suppliers are suggested to offer clients a helpful, diversion reason and more proficient and viable administrations through the outline of IoT. The consequences of this study can assist IoT with overhauling suppliers to enhance the nature of IoT innovation. The findings also contributes for future specialists which recognize them to comprehend customers' behavioural goal to utilize IoT innovation. Other than that, it is prescribed for future studies should address the issue of people who have never utilized an IoT innovation react.

This research has few limitations. Firstly, this study did not fuse genuine utilization conduct into the proposed model. Nevertheless, significant observational confirmation exists with respect to the causal connection in the middle of aim and use conduct (Lee *et al.,* 2012). Second, it ought to be noticed that a cross-sectional examination configuration does not give as much understanding as does a longitudinal exploration plan. Consequently, future exploration ought to embrace longitudinal information, keeping in mind the end goal to further investigate the time arrangement of the connections among builds. Moreover, future research needs to repeat the study utilizing distinctive IoT item classes to enhance generalizability of the exploration model. Subjective examination is additionally urged for future exploration to increase better comprehension of what buyers' points of view towards IoT innovation.

REFERENCES

Aizen, I. (2011). The theory of planned behaviour: Reactions and reflections. *Psychology & Health*, *26*(9), 1113–1127. doi:10.1080/08870446.2011.613995 PMID:21929476

Allen, P., & Bennett, K. (2010). *Pasw statistics by SPSS: A practical guide (version 18.0)*. Cengage Learning.

Bandura, A. (1977). Self-efficacy: Toward a unifying theory of behavioural change. *Psychological Review, 84*(2), 191–215. doi:10.1037/0033-295X.84.2.191 PMID:847061

Bruner, G. C. II, & Kumar, A. (2005). Explaining consumer acceptance of handheld internet devices. *Journal of Business Research, 58*(5), 553–558. doi:10.1016/j.jbusres.2003.08.002

Casaló, L. V., Flaviá n, C., & Guinal ıu, M. (2010). Determinants of the intention to participate in firm-hosted online travel communities and effects on consumer behavioral intentions. *Tourism Management, 31*(6), 898-911.

Cho, J. (2004). Likelihood to abort an online transaction influences from cognitive evaluations, attitudes, and behavioral variables. *Information & Management, 41*(7), 827–838. doi:10.1016/j.im.2003.08.013

Cronbach, L. J. (1946). Response sets and test validity. *Educational and Psychological Measurement, 6*(4), 475–494.

Davis, F. (1989). Perceived usefulness, perceived ease of use and user acceptance of information technology. *Management Information Systems Quarterly, 13*(3), 319–340. doi:10.2307/249008

Definition of Trust. (n.d.). Retrieved from Merriam Webster: www.merriam-webster.com

Ding, W. (2013). *Study of smart warehouse management system based on the IOT. In Intelligence Computation and Evolutionary Computation* (pp. 203–207). Berlin: Springer. doi:10.1007/978-3-642-31656-2_30

Field, A. P. (2009). *Discovering Statistics using SPSS* (3rd ed.). London, UK: Sage Publication Ltd.

George, D., & Mallery, P. (2003). *SPSS for Windows step by step: A simple guide and reference (11.0 update)* (4th ed.). Boston: Allyn & Bacon.

Gubbi, J., Buyya, R., Marusic, S., & Palaniswami, M. (2013). Internet of things (IoT): A vision, architectural elements, and future directions. *Future Generation Computer Systems, 29*(7), 1645–1660. doi:10.1016/j.future.2013.01.010

Ha, S., & Stoel, L. (2009). Consumer e-shopping acceptance: Antecedents in a technology acceptance model. *Journal of Business Research, 62*(5), 565–571. doi:10.1016/j.jbusres.2008.06.016

Hart, M., & Porter, G. (2004). The impact of cognitive and other factors on the perceived usefulness of OLAP. *Journal of Computer Information Systems, 45*(1), 47–57.

Hsu, C.-L., & Lu, H.-P. (2004). Why do people play on-line games? An extended TAM with social influences and flow experience. *Information & Management, 41*(7), 853–868. doi:10.1016/j.im.2003.08.014

Kim, G. S., Park, S. B., & Oh, J. (2008). Investigating antecedents of behavioral intentions in mobile commerce. *Journal of Internet Commerce, 25*(8), 769–786.

Kline, P. (2000). *The handbook of psychological testing* (2nd ed.). London: Routledge.

Lee, Y.-K., Park, J.-H., Chung, N., & Blakeney, A. (2012). A unified perspective on the factors influencing usage intention toward mobile financial services. *Journal of Business Research, 65*(11), 1590–1599. doi:10.1016/j.jbusres.2011.02.044

Li, X. J., & Wang, D. (2013). Architecture and existing applications for internet of things. *Applied Mechanics and Materials, 347*(1), 3317–3321. doi:10.4028/www.scientific.net/AMM.347-350.3317

Lin, H.-F. (2011). An empirical investigation of mobile banking adoption: The effect of innovation attributes and knowledge-based trust. *International Journal of Information Management, 31*(3), 252–260. doi:10.1016/j.ijinfomgt.2010.07.006

Lu, H.-P., & Su, P. Y.-J. (2009). Factors affecting purchase intention on mobile shopping web sites. *Internet Research, 19*(4), 442–458. doi:10.1108/10662240910981399

Lu, Y., Zhou, T., & Wang, B. (2009). Exploring Chinese users' acceptance of instant messaging using the theory of planned behavior, the technology acceptance model, and the flow theory. *Computers in Human Behavior, 25*(1), 29–39. doi:10.1016/j.chb.2008.06.002

Mathieson, K. (1991). Predicting user intentions: Comparing the technology acceptance model with the theory of planned behavior. *Information Systems Research, 2*(3), 173–179. doi:10.1287/isre.2.3.173

Peoples, C., Parr, G., Mcclean, S. B., & Morrow, P. (2013). Simulation modeling practice and theory. *Performance Evaluation of Green Data Centre Management Supporting Sustainable Growth of the Internet Things, 34*, 221–242.

Radner, R., & Rothschild, M. (1975). On the allocation of effort. *Journal of Economic Theory, 10*(3), 358–376. doi:10.1016/0022-0531(75)90006-X

Rashotte, L. (2002). Social Influence. *Electronic Journal of Sociology*.

Rogers, E. (1995). *Diffusion of innovations*. New York, NY: The Free Press.

Schlick, J., Ferber, S., & Hupp, J. (2013). *IoT applications: Value creation for industry*. Aalborg: River Publisher.

Sekaran, U., & Bougie, R. (1992). *Research methods for business: A skill-building approach* (2nd ed.). New York: Wiley.

Song, J., Koo, C., & Kim, Y. (2008). Investigating antecedents of behavioral intentions in mobile commerce. *Journal of Internet Commerce, 6*(1), 13–34. doi:10.1300/J179v06n01_02

Sundamaeker, H., Guillemin, P., Friess, P., & Woelffle, S. (2010). Vision and challenges for realising the internet of things. *Cluster of European Research Projects on the Internet of Things, European Commission- Information Society and Media DG*.

Uckelmann, D., Harrison, M., & Michahelles, F. (n.d.). An architectural approach towards the future internet of things. *Architecting the Internet of Things*.

Venkatesh, V., Morris, M. G., Davis, G. B., & Davis, F. D. (2003). User acceptance of information technology: Toward a unified view. *Management Information Systems Quarterly, 27*(3), 425–478.

Venkatesh, V., Thong, J., & Xu, X. (2012). Consumer acceptance and use of information technology: Extending the unified theory of acceptance and use of technology. *Management Information Systems Quarterly*, *36*(1), 167–178.

Wang, X. F., Lei, X., & Li, L. (2013). The design of railway information system integration based on IOT. *Advanced Materials Research*, *694*(1), 3336–3339.

Welle, D. (2013). *Internet of things' holds promise, but sparks privacy concerns*. Available at: www. dw.de/internet-of-things-holds-promise-but-sparks-privacy-concerns/a-15911207-1

Zhang, J., & Mao, E. (2008). Understanding the acceptance of mobile SMS advertising among young Chinese consumers. *Psychology and Marketing*, *25*(8), 787–805. doi:10.1002/mar.20239

This work was previously published in the Handbook of Research on Leveraging Consumer Psychology for Effective Customer Engagement edited by Norazah Mohd Suki, pages 186-201, copyright year 2017 by Business Science Reference (an imprint of IGI Global).

Section 2
Health and Welfare

Chapter 5
Social Internet of Things in Healthcare:
From Things to Social Things in Internet of Things

Cristina Elena Turcu
University of Suceava, Romania

Corneliu Octavian Turcu
University of Suceava, Romania

ABSTRACT

This chapter presents a future vision for healthcare, which will involve smart devices, Internet of Things, and social networks, that make this vision a reality. The authors present the necessary background by introducing the Social Internet of Things paradigm. Agent technology seems to be a promising approach in the adoption of the Social Internet of Things in collaborative environments with increased autonomy and agility, like healthcare is. Also, it is examined challenges to the adoption of the Social Internet of Things in healthcare in order to facilitate new applications and services in more effective and efficient ways.

INTRODUCTION

The healthcare industry is constantly bound to adapt to the many occurring changes, from advances in diagnostic and therapeutic procedures to the most advanced information technology, in order to increase the overall quality of patient care, and also to reduce healthcare costs (Riazul Islam, Kwak, Humaun Kabir, Hossain, & Kwak, 2015).

Various worldwide surveys conducted in relation to this field reveal that one of the biggest current technological initiatives in the healthcare industry is the Internet of Things (IoT) (IoT to Revolutionize Healthcare, 2015; State of the Market, 2015). In recent times, there has been a growing interest in building Social Internet of Things (SIoT) (Atzori 2011a, 2012, 2013).

DOI: 10.4018/978-1-5225-1832-7.ch005

This chapter examines challenges to the adoption of the Social Internet of Things in healthcare in order to facilitate new applications and services in more effective and efficient ways. Several papers and studies have focused their attention on this new paradigm. We present the necessary background by introducing the SIoT paradigm. Subsequently, we provide a survey of the applications of SIoT in different domains. Some solutions for SIoT are also presented, each with its own strengths and weaknesses. We consider various enabling technologies that could be exploited in order to extend the current applications in the healthcare area. The movement of healthcare out of the hands of healthcare providers (hospital, laboratory, etc.) and into people's homes will be greatly facilitated with the latest remote sensing devices of all kinds connected to physicians and care givers. The examples are numerous and the potential for cost savings and improved care is overwhelming. We also address social networks that can be used for storing and sharing information of interest for the SIoT interactions. Agent technology seems to be a promising approach in the adoption of the Social Internet of Things in collaborative environments with increased autonomy and agility, like healthcare is. If a physical entity is linked via a unique identifier to an agent, then the identifiable entity could be easily integrated in SIoT as a social thing. For things in SIoT to understand each other, sharing a common understanding of the structure of information among them is required. Ontologies offer a solution to represent information, including the relationships between things in SIoT and to share knowledge as well. Moreover, ontologies allow the dynamic integration of knowledge in different domains into SIoT. Finally, we highlight the lessons to be learnt from the past, open challenges and some possible directions for future research.

This chapter is organized as follows: background of research fields of Internet of Things and Social Internet of Things is investigated in the second section. The next section presents the enabling technologies that could be exploited in order to extend the current applications in the healthcare area. Next, some consideration related to evolution of medicine models and potential implications of SIoT adoption in healthcare are presented. Next section presents some practical benefits enabled by SIoT for people suffering from asthma. Finally, future research direction and conclusions are pointed out.

BACKGROUND

According to various studies, e.g. (Davis, 2004; Fisher, 2003), healthcare systems around the world, face rising costs and uneven quality, thus generating significant variations, both within the United States and internationally. It is a common fact that U.S. adults often do not receive the proper level of care recommended for a certain condition. One study indicates that on average, individuals received only about 55 percent of the recommended medical care for common illnesses (McGlynn et al., 2003), whereas preventive care is often overlooked.

But various studies reveal that a large number of people tracks health indicators or symptoms for themselves or for someone else. For example, according to (Health Fact Sheet, 2015), 60% of U.S. adults track their weight, diet, or exercise routine; 33% of U.S. adults track health indicators or symptoms, like blood pressure, blood sugar, headaches, or sleep patterns; 12% of U.S. adults track a health indicator on behalf of someone they care for. The technology offers the potential to help people to track all these data. For example, according to (Susannah, & Duggan, 2012), 31% of cell phone owners, and 52% of smartphone owners, have used their phone to look up health or medical information. Thus, the advancements in technology, like Internet, Web-based, smartphone, etc. have encouraged the development of technology-based applications aimed at supporting people in both easily tracking health indicators or symptoms, and diagnosing and managing various diseases.

A report by PwC's Health Research Institute (HRI) reveals patients' attraction to social media sites such as Facebook and Twitter in order to find and share medical information (Social media, 2012). According to this survey of 1,060 U.S. adults, about one-third of consumers are using the social space as a place for healthcare discussions. And 42% of consumers have used social media to access health-related consumer reviews.72% of Internet users say they looked online for health information within the past year, according to (Susannah, & Duggan, 2013) and 27% of US internet users had tracked health data online, (Health Fact Sheet, 2015). Consequently, in trying to reduce the costs of providing care and to increase efficiency, many healthcare organizations adopt a social media oriented strategy in order to interact with patients and provide them services and information that could impact their healthcare decisions.

Current development of the traditional medical model toward P6 medicine model can be amplified by the Internet of Things (IoT) paradigm.

The Internet of Things (IoT) infrastructure allows connections between different entities (i.e., human beings, wireless sensors, mobile robots, etc.), using different but interoperable communication protocols and makes a dynamic multimodal/ heterogeneous network. In this infrastructure, these different entities (viewed as "things") have the ability to discover and explore one another, gather, provide, or transmit information to IoT. Thus, according to (ITU Internet Reports, 2005, p. 8), "from anytime, anyplace connectivity for anyone, we will now have connectivity for anything", not only for anyone. According to (Botterman, 2009, p. 5), the Internet of Thing integrates "things having identities and virtual personalities operating in smart spaces, using intelligent interfaces to connect and communicate within social, environmental, and user contexts". And, "from objects that communicate to objects that socialize in the Internet" (Iera, 2011), there is only one step. Thus, a novel paradigm of the Social Internet of Things (SIoT) was introduced: a "social network of intelligent objects" that is "based on the notion of social relationships among objects", according to (Atzori,Iera, & Morabito, 2011b).

The authors of (Zorzi, Gluhak, Lange, & Bassi, 2010; Uckelmann, Harrison, & Michahelles, 2011; Ortiz, Hussein, Park, Han, & Crespi, 2014) present a phased approach of the evolution of Internet of Thing from Intranet of Things or of Extranet of Things to Social Internet of Things. They also discuss how the situation of many "Intranets" of Things should evolve into a much more integrated and heterogeneous system, namely the Internet of Things. According to (Ortiz, Hussein, Park, Han, & Crespi, 2014), "IoT enables the creation and composition of new services and applications, offering to individual users a new ecosystem where different intranets of things can collaborate". Also, "things should be socialized for allowing humans to establish relationships with them in an easy way". In the same paper, the authors present visually the evolution of IoT from Intranet of Things to SIoT (Figure 1), considering that "the cluster between Internet of Things (IoT) and social networks (SNs) enables the connection of people to the ubiquitous computing universe".

The Internet of Things is viewed as an evolutionary process, rather than a completely new one. And the Social Internet of Things, dealing with some IoT related issues, is part of evolution. According to (Atzori, Carboni, & Iera, 2013, p. 13), "the driving motivation is that a social-oriented approach is expected to put forward the discovery, selection and composition of services and information provided by distributed objects and networks that have access to the physical world".

According to (IoT to Revolutionize Healthcare, 2015) the range of "things" that can be part of an IoT or a SIoT solution is practically unlimited. From the small and simple to the large and complex, the

Figure 1. Evolutionary history
Source: Ortiz, Hussein, Park, Han, & Crespi, 2014.

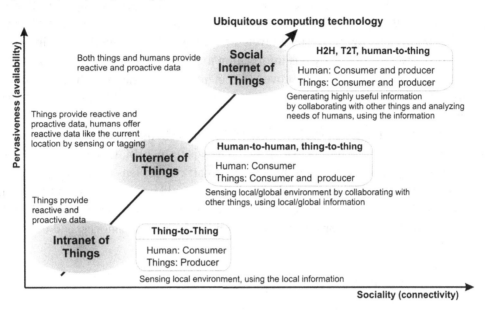

possibilities are enormous. Next we present some medical monitoring devices that can be connected to IoT or SIoT in order to improve the overall quality of patient care.

State of the Art of SIoT Enabling Technologies

Medical Monitoring Devices

Common to everyday living, wearable and wireless implantable medical devices, as well as home monitoring devices, are endowed with transmitting capabilities (Natarajan, Prasath, & Kokila, 2016) that make information about a patient available for hospital staff analysis. For example, these devices may be wireless interconnected with sensors that measure the glucose level, the heart rate, the blood pressure, the weigh, and other medical parameters. These characteristics will turn these devices into a real part of IoT. In this sense, various applications are currently deployed, especially regarding the measurement and monitoring of a patient's vital signs, including glucose level sensing, electrocardiography, and blood pressure monitoring.

Glucose Level Testing/Glucose Monitoring

It is a common fact that carbohydrates are the main sources of glucose, essential for providing energy for both the brain and the body. Nevertheless, a high level of blood glucose over a prolonged period of time might cause diabetes. The World Health Organization estimates that more than 380 million people are suffering from this disorder, and these figures will double by 2030 (What is Diabetes? (n.d.)).

During the last decade, several non-invasive methods for glucose monitoring were used. For example, in 2003 Caduff et al. (Caduff, Hirt, Feldman, Ali, & Heinemann, 2003) described an experiment using a new, non-invasive, non-optical continuous glucose monitoring system, based on impedance spectroscopy. Later on, they used a multisensor system, combining sensors for dielectric and optical characterization of skin (Caduf et al. 2009). In 2006, the concept of Continuous Glucose Monitoring (CGM) was introduced (Hovorka, 2006). Actually, blood sugar levels are recorded using a CGM sensor implanted under the skin of a diabetic patient, and that sends information to a wireless device. In 2011, Istepanian et al. (Istepanian, Hu, Philip, & Sungoor, 2011) proved the potential of Internet of m-health Things "m-IoT" for non-invasive glucose level sensing. Looking towards the future 4G health applications, this concept embedded both m-health and IoT functionalities.

Many companies have developed CGMs using Bluetooth technology to transmit glucose levels to a compatible smart device (i.e. Medtonic, Dexcom, Glucowise). In 2014, Google and the Swiss health care group Novartis announced that they were testing a smart contact lens able to measure the glucose level from tears. Therefore, a new way to deal with diabetes would be to endow such lenses with transmitting capabilities. Also, BodyTel from Germany sells a Bluetooth 4.0 device with a blood glucose meter (GDH-FAD, n.d.) that communicates with Android and iOS smartphones, and transmits data to a medical data cloud.

Electrocardiogram Monitoring

Electrocardiography (ECG or EKG) is a diagnostic tool which records the electrical activity of the heart over a period of time. The electrocardiogram is not used only to measure the rate and rhythm of the heartbeat, but also to diagnose different diseases like arrhythmia, ischemia etc. ECG is very important, especially for the evaluation of patients with possible heart problems.

The Belgian company Imec developed a Smart ECG necklace used to monitor every-day cardiac activity (Wearable health monitoring, n.d.). The device is based on a commercial low-power microcontroller and a low-power radio, and has wireless communication capabilities within 10 m range. Also, the company designed a prototype which stores heart rate and 3D accelerometer data. These data can be transmitted in real time to a receiver located up to 16 km away from the acquiring point.

The Spanish start-up Nuubo, dealing with wearable medical devices for cardiac prevention, diagnostics, and rehabilitation solutions developed a wireless and remote cardiac monitoring platform based on a biomedical e-textile technology - BlendFix Sensor Electrode Technology (NECG Platform, n.d.).

Also, some researches are related to ECG and IoT (Li, 2014; Lu, 2015).

Blood Pressure Monitoring

Researchers and companies showed interest in developing blood pressure devices for IoT integration. In (Xin, Min, & Ji, 2013) the authors proposed an IoT - based blood pressure monitoring system (patent in China), their intelligent terminal being based on the Internet of Things and including the following: a health monitoring device, a data communication device, a locating device, a microprocessor, a storage device, an input-output device, and an electrical power unit.

Many authors implemented various applications for blood pressure monitoring, based on different transmission technologies, usually Bluetooth or Zigbee (Antonovici, 2014; Anurag, 2014). For example, the authors in (Hassanalieragh et al., 2015) use a concentrator to access each individual sensor from an IoT-based architecture.

Different companies released blood pressure monitors that not only check the readings, but also automatically store data in the cloud. For example, QardioArm implements a "tap to pair" system with iPhones and Android, working on Bluetooth 4.0 technology. Data are automatically stored in the Qardio cloud and then shared by actors from the health system or the family.

Aiming to improve the patients' blood pressure, Withings Company and the American Medical Group Foundation finished in 2016 a pilot project (Macala, 2016) that used the Withings Wireless Blood Pressure Monitor. This monitor is connected with the patient's personal iOS or Android device and collected data are transmitted in real time to his personal healthcare team, through a dedicated web portal. Using this device, patients are able to monitor and control their own blood pressure and the medical staff is provided with valuable information regarding the health status of a large group of patients.

Body Temperature Measurement

Body temperature is one of the four main vital signs that must be monitored to ensure safe and effective care (McCallum, & Higgins, 2012). Body temperature sensors are used as a part of various items: wearable bracelet, smart pillow, finger-style device, skin stamp, etc.

Authors in (Mansor, Shukor, Meskam, Rusli, & Zamery, 2013) proposed a remote health monitoring system in which such a sensor sends the body temperature values to a microcontroller through an Xbee wireless communication. Real-time data are stored in a health monitoring database, using a wireless local area network. Another temperature monitoring system was found in (Malhi, Mukhopadhyay, Schnepper, Haefke, & Ewald, 2012). Here, the authors designed and developed a smart noninvasive wearable physiological parameters monitoring device based on Zigbee technology. The deficiency of Zigbee protocol stack is that it might prove too large to handle. Therefore, other authors (Chin, Atmodihardjo, Woo, & Mesbahi, 2015) decided to use the MiWi protocol stack instead. The advantages derived from using this protocol consist in reduced code size, small footprint, and a very low overhead, in comparison to the ZigBee protocol. Authors in (Jian, Zhanli, & Zhuang, 2012) use a OSGi (Open Service Gateway Initiative) to send packages with the body temperature values into an M2M (Machine to Machine) format.

Wireless Body Temperature Monitor from Win-Health is a technologically advanced medical device which allows body temperature recording up to 100 hours. It consists of 2 independent parts: a transmitter, and a receiver; the transmitter monitors the body temperature and transmits the values automatically to the remote receiver.

The US start-up MC 10 released a high-tech tattoo (actually an elastomeric plaster which includes an electronic part) endowed with measuring capabilities (Bachfischer, 2014). It can be used not only to monitor the body temperature in a real-time manner, but also to measure some biometric data (brainwaves, heartbeat, and muscle activity).

All these above presented devices are a few examples from a large range of suitable candidates to "things" that could be connected in IoT/SIoT.

Social Internet of Things

The goal of the Internet of Things is to enable things to be connected anytime, anyplace, with anything and anyone ideally using any path/network and any service (Vermesan, & Friess, 2014).

According to the authors of (Atzori, Iera, & Morabito, 2011b, p. 1193) "the IoT vision can be fully achieved only if objects are able to cooperate in an open way". Thus, in order to exploit the potential of the IoT, the authors believe that trust objects and provided services should be easily discoverable and usable by humans and by other objects. But, the existing solutions for service discovery in IoT do not scale with the number of things that are expected to be connected in IoT. Moreover, although researchers reveal other problems for adopting IoT in reality, various solutions were proposed. In this chapter, we will focus only on the potential offered by social networking to enable IoT.

In (Kleinberg, 2008) the author noticed that the exponential growth of social networking websites usage, along some of the features provided, have attracted the attention of a large number of researchers from various areas. For example, several authors focus on the great potential of using online social networks for enhancing the Internet search (Mislove, Gummadi, & Druschel, 2006; Erola, Castellà-Roca, Viejo, & Mateo-Sanz, 2011), for enabling new forms of information exchange in the Internet (Mislove, Gummadi, & Druschel, 2006), or for optimizing the peer-to-peer networks (Fast, Jensen, & Levine, 2005).

In the last years, social relationships between human beings were extended to social relationships between objects, as solutions to various problems. The authors of (Holmquist al., 2001) were among the first to tackle with the socialization between objects, and they presented a solution for establishing qualitative relations and selective connections between smart wireless devices. In their paper, the authors analyzed temporary relationships between objects and how the owners of those objects should control such a process in the context of ubiquitous computing. In 2001, when the paper was published, both concepts of the IoT and the online social networks were in their beginning stages.

More recent literature focus on several research projects and experimental applications based on a new generation of objects. For example, Bleeckerin (Bleecker, 2006), introduces the neologism "Blogject"- 'objects that blog' in order to distinguish the "things" connected to the Internet from the "things" participating within the Internet of social networks. The researcher presents in his paper the characteristics of Blogjects: they can "track and trace where they are and where they've been"; "have self-contained (embedded) histories of their encounters and experiences; "have some form of agency — they can foment action and participate; they have an assertive voice within the *social web*".

In fact, the Blogject is viewed as a kind of early ancestor to the Spimes, defined by Sterling in (Sterling, 2005) as material instantiations of an immaterial system, digitally manufactured things from virtual plans, trackable in space and time.

Later on, P. Mendes (Mendes, 2011) presents objects able to participate in conversations that were previously reserved to humans only. "Such objects may be intermittently connected most of the time, and may be capable of collecting and processing data without a constant human intervention. The result is a self-organised ecosystem able to make useful data available to people when and where they really need it, augmenting their social and environmental awareness".

With the rapid development of social networking, researchers focused on the benefits social networking could bring to IoT.

D. Guinard et al. (Guinard, Fischer, & Trifa, 2010) proposed the use of the existing online social structures as a solution for enabling the sharing of things in the context of the IoT. Thus, exploiting various features offered by social networks (e.g. Facebook, LinkedIn, Twitter, etc.) and their (open) APIs, the authors build a system for sharing and controlling access to resources supplied by a given Web-enabled device (smart thing).

In order to analyze the behaviors of objects and people as data, L. Ding et al.(Ding, Shi, & Liu, 2010, p. 417) propose a platform to cluster together the Internet, the Internet of Things, and social network. Thus, "since the development of the Internet of Things, objects are involved into the network together with people" they consider that the "social networks can be built based on the Internet of Things" and "are meaningful to investigate the relations and evolution of the objects in the IoT".

In 2010, M. Kranz et al. (Kranz, Roalter, & Michahelles, 2010) present in their paper an investigation regarding both the potential of combining social and technical networks and the implication of so-called "socio-technical networks" in the context of the IoT. Also, the authors describe how to empower physical objects to share pictures, comments, and sensor data via social networks. However, they do not propose any solution for the required architecture and protocols or for how the objects involved can establish social relationships.

Authors of L. Atzori et al. (Atzori, Iera, & Morabito, 2011) define various types of relationships in which things can be engaged: Parental Object Relationship (POR) (built in same period, by the same manufacturer); Co-Location Object Relationship (CLOR) (exist in a common location - cohabitation); Co-Work Object Relationship (CWOR) (work in a common location); Ownership Object Relationship (OOR) (belong to the same owner); Social Object Relationship (SOR) (objects that come into contact due to owners relationships). Based on this last relationship among objects, the paper introduces the concept of Social Internet of Things (SIoT). Moreover, considering a comparison with Social Networks Services (SNS) for human beings, the authors introduce an architectural model of SIoT and imagine some possible application scenarios where objects share best practices. Thus, for example, they propose to establish social relationships between PCs in the same local area network in order to "find solutions to common setting problems, such as those related to the configuration of a tricky network printer". Similarly, social relationships established between devices that visit the same geographical area allow the exchanging of useful information on the physical world. In this scenario, the authors consider the case of handsets that provide data on the radio coverage to new visitors so as improve their connectivity service.

According to L. Atzori et al. (Atzori, Iera, & Morabito, 2011), trustworthiness of the billions of members of the IoT should be a key element in object selection and provided services usage. The problem of the trustworthiness in the Social IoT (how to know which services and objects to trust) is addressed by the authors of (Nitti, Girau, Atzori, Iera, & Morabito, 2012; Nitti, Girau, & Atzori, 2014). In order to build a reliable system on the basis of the behavior of objects, the authors focus on understanding how the information provided by members of the social IoT has to be processed so as to avoid attacks and malfunctions. Therefore, they defined and analyzed two models for trustworthiness management in the social IoT: the subjective and the objective models. The authors plan to use the trustworthiness management, in order to enable the promoting social relations in the social IoT.

The authors of (Nitti, Atzori, & Cvijikj, 2014; Nitti, Atzori, & Cvijikj, 2015) address the problem of network navigability in the Social Internet of Things. In order to find the right object that can provide a desired service, an object can use its own relationships, the friends of its friend, and so on. Considering the selection of the friendships as a key for finding the desired service and, consequently, for a successful deployment of the SIoT, the authors focused on the selection of a narrow set of links, in order to support an efficient management of friendships. Also, they analyze possible strategies for the benefit of overall network navigability.

In (Girau, Nitti, & Atzori, 2013), the authors analyze the major IoT implementations, highlighting their common characteristics that could be re-used for implementing a new platform for the Social Internet of Things. Also, the authors present the major extensions introduced on the existing platforms, in order to offer the features of the SIoT. They describe some possible simple application scenarios that use this platform, "where objects create their own relationships and groups, in order to provide several functionalities to the final users" (p. 5), with minimal human intervention.

Social Internet of Things Platforms

Even though in recent years different models and prototypes of SIoT occurred, practical applications are not very present in literature. Ascribing social attributes to connected devices will open new ways to develop a new generation of applications where human-to-device social relationships will be intensively exploited.

Some examples of SIoT platforms are briefly described below.

Cosmos

Cosmos is an IoT platform, developed in a FP7 project. The declared aim of COSMOS is to "enhance the sustainability of smart city applications by allowing IoT based systems to reach their full potential" ("Cultivate resilient," 2015). The authors proposed this platform in order to endow things with the capacity of acting in an autonomous way, while they become smarter and more reliable. Three representative scenarios were considered in COSMOS: Smart heat and electricity management (London), Smart mobility for public transport (Madrid), IoT Business Eco-System (Taipei). Virtual entities (VE) were used to represent things and groups of things from the real word. VEs act with specific goals and internal mechanisms to achieve them. Multiple interactions between VEs can be established for sharing a common goal, for achieving specific objectives, for advertising properties/attributes actuation service offers etc. (Voutyras, Bourelos, Kyriazis, & Varvarigou, 2014). Further on, the authors considered the social relations and interactions between VEs and introduced two new COSMOS components: Social Monitoring and Social Analysis (Voutyras, Gogouvitis, Marinakis, & Varvarigou, 2014). The first one collects, aggregates, and distributes monitoring data towards collaborating groups, while the second one extracts the VE complex social characteristics, constructs models and patterns for VEs' behaviors, and establishes relations between them. This way, COSMOS became a SIoT platform since, based on social media technologies, it exploits social relations and interactions between the VEs. The result is an interesting social concept: friendship between VEs. Social criteria are used for friends' choice and a valuable advantage of this platform is that each VE is in a relationship of mutual aid with other VEs. Other advantages lie in the possibility of applying this concept to many areas, such as eHealth, environment monitoring, security & emergencies, traffic management, logistics, industrial control, home automation, etc.

ThingsChat

This platform was a subject of a doctoral thesis (Han, 2015). The author considered that connected devices are able to have social relationship with both people and other devices. In this approach, a Web API was used to assure the interaction between online social network (OSN) and devices. Later on, new functionalities were added to the OSN core, and the result, an universal OSN of everything, was named ThingsChat. To include social characteristics into the service framework, a Device Socialization module was added to the architecture presented in (Han, 2015). This module facilitates communication between both devices and SIoT, and devices and human users. A home gateway named ThingsGate is the element that discovers, stores, and transmits device services to ThingsChat. This module is responsible with user grant authorization to ThingsChat and device initialization with social functionalities. In this way the connected device become social entities. ThingsGate plays a vital role in the realization of the socializing device, very important for this platform. In order to fit the device in the SIoT platform, ThingsGate acts like a mediator in the process of device authorizing and customization. It is the module that registers the device in SIoT and adds it to the socialized list, which can be accessed later by user. Message exchanges between users and devices are facilitated by existence of a NLP (Natural Language Processing) interface which converts user messages into machine readable commands, and vice versa. The typical interaction between users and devices identified by the author is that the user asks the device to complete various operations and the device does the job and afterwards replies back to the user. This seems to be similar to the client/server negotiation process in multi-agent technology. Otherwise, we consider that some of the functionalities on/in this platform could be realized by using agents (for example, NLP).

Socialite

For bringing to reality the vision of the SIoT, the authors of (Kim, 2015; Kim, 2016) propose a cloud based distributed collaboration framework, named Socialite. As the authors presented, the Socialite architecture is designed to support the following: the interoperability of different connected devices from various manufacturers performing in different ecosystems; the scalability to handle a large number of data streams from various interactions between devices and/or people; the extensibility, by taking into consideration future devices to be connected and, also, provided services, for achieving the proposed goals based on different types of social relationships. In order to allow participants in Social Internet of Things to collaborate with each other in this framework, the authors define new social relationships between humans and devices, in addition to existing friendships among users in social networks (Kim, 2015; Kim, 2016):

- **Collocation:** Users and/or devices in "the same" location.
- **Friendship:** Relationship between users, as in Social Networks.
- **Kinship:** Devices with a same model and manufacturer.
- **Ownership:** A device registered by its owner.
- **Shared Ownership:** Devices owned by a same user.
- **Thriendship**: Friendship among things/devices of friends.

These newly defined social people-to-device and device-to-device relationships could be used in order to determine how the data generated by users and devices is being exchanged, distributed and received.

The uniform access to different connected devices and people in the system is enabled by the semantic models defined in this framework for users, locations, relationships, services and devices.

Multi-Agent Technology in Healthcare, IoT, and SIoT

In order to solve various problems related to information exchange between different things connected to IoT, agent technology proves to be a viable solution. Before presenting the specific aspects of the problems solved with the help of this type of technology, we briefly introduce the agent technology and several systems developed for healthcare.

There is no universally accepted definition of the term *agent*. However, the definition given by Wooldridge is one of the most comprehensive and frequently used worldwide. According to it, an agent is "a hardware or (more usually) a software-based computer system that enjoys the following properties: autonomy - agents operate without the direct intervention of humans or others, and have some kind of control over their actions and internal state; social ability - agents interact with other agents (and possibly humans) via some kind of agent-communication language; reactivity- agents perceive their environment and respond in a timely fashion to changes that occur in it; pro-activeness - agents do not simply act in response to their environment, they are able to exhibit goal-directed behaviour by taking initiative" (Wooldridge, & Jennings, 1995). The multi-agent system (MAS) paradigm views agents mainly as cooperating entities acting in a group with other agents in order to solve various problems. To enable agents to interoperate ontologies are part of solution. Ontologies represent a formalism which allows the representation of the knowledge related to a certain field, as a model. "Ontologies can be used to represent the structure of a domain by means of defining concepts and properties that relate them" (IGI-GLOBAL Dictionary, 2016).

In fact, researchers agree that agent-based system technology provides a real paradigm for designing and implementing software or integrated systems that offer solutions to various complex and dynamic problems from different domains.

Over time, several multi-agent systems were developed in order to address some of the issues related to various domains, including healthcare.

Remote health monitoring solutions offer great potential help for the disabled, elderly and/or chronically ill patients. This way they have access to good healthcare without regularly visiting their doctors. Over time, various multi-agent systems that offer solutions to remote health monitoring have been developed worldwide.

A multi-agent system for remote healthcare monitoring through computerized clinical guidelines was developed in the SAPHIRE project (Laleci et. al., 2008). This system provides a Clinical Decision Support system for remote monitoring of patients at their homes, and at the hospital to decrease the load of medical practitioners and also of healthcare costs. Also, the system aims to reduce human error in hospital events/complications and finally to provide a feedback system for the medical staff in training.

K4CARE, (K4CARE, 2008), was a research project whose main objective was to create, implement, and validate a knowledge-based healthcare model for the professional assistance of senior patients at home. The main step of the project was to develop a healthcare model to guide the creation of an integrated system of healthcare services for the care of the elderly, the disabled persons, and the patients with chronic diseases, (Bergenti, & Poggi, 2009). The model created during this project defined the actors in the care model (representing the profiles of the subjects involved in the K4CARE model: healthcare professionals, patients and relatives, citizens, and social organisms), their roles and interactions. The concepts behind the model were formalized using ontologies and the chosen language for the ontologies was the OWL (Web Ontology Language).

Also, in the healthcare sectors, various medical systems that cooperate with each other were suggested. Thus, in (Iantovics, 2010), the author proposes a cooperative medical diagnosis multi-agent system called CMDS (Contract Net Based Medical Diagnosis System). This system can flexibly solve a large variety of medical diagnosis problems.

Moreover, the use of agents for gathering the patients' medical electronic records from the information systems of different medical units was addressed in many research papers.

In (Chen, González, Zhang, & Leung, 2010), the authors conducted a study about a secured scheme based on mobile agents, for the systems which manage electronic medical records. The medical staff can instantaneously search for complete information about a patient, by accessing his/her electronic records via the Internet. The mobile agents are used to search for the patients' electronic records in different medical units that provide medical services. Taking into account that a mobile agent communicates with other applications and agents from the network for a faster access to the medical information, the probability of security issues arising is very high. In order to solve the security problems, the authors use a management scheme for access keys based on the interpolation formulas of Lagrange and on hierarchical management structures to increase the security of mobile agents.

In order to gather the information distributed among healthcare centers, authors of (Martin-Campillo, et al., 2009), also take into account the use of mobile agents. The agents developed in the MedIGS system collect all the medical data about a patient by performing a local search at each hospital, part of a predefined group, avoiding the need for a central repository.

Given the different standards used to store the patient's medical records in various health care settings, the use of the ontology is mandatory in order to gather health-related information from many health information systems. The authors of (Chang, Yang, & Luo, 2011), go a step further and "propose an ontology-based agent generation framework for information retrieval in a flexible, transparent, and easy way on cloud environment".

To sum up, we can say that multi-agent technology proves to be a viable solution to various problems encountered in global health care.

Also, the semantic interactions and the interoperability between various things connected to the IoT could be achieved by using a multi-agent system. The adoption of a multi-agent system for an IoT oriented solution is enabled by a natural mapping between a real world entity and an agent. Hence, if a physical entity is linked via its unique identifier (e.g., Radio Frequency IDentification: RFID tag) to an agent, then the identifiable entity could be easily controlled in a complex network of autonomous objects. The distributed software agents will represent the desired IoT things and interact accordingly with the standard defined by the Foundation for Intelligent Physical Agents (FIPA).

Agent technology seems to be a promising approach in the implementation of the Internet of Things in collaborative environments with increased autonomy and agility. Regarding the architecture of an IoT oriented solution, the benefits of an approach based on multi-agent systems (instead of using centralized approaches) are listed below:

- The multi-agent system can work even if one agent (as a component of the system) fails or is compromised;
- It is easy to recover a failed agent or replace it with another one;
- Autonomous agents are less vulnerable to attacks than in a centralized architecture.

But, considering the multiple advantages provided by the agent technology, researchers try to adopt it in implementing the Social Internet of Things. Currently, worldwide there are few applications of the Social Internet of Things using agent technology. Subsequently, we will take a look at some recently published research papers dealing with the adoption of multi-agent technologies in the Social Internet of Things.

Thus, Ciortea et al. (Ciortea, Boissier, Zimmermann, & Florea, 2013) propose to model the autonomous entities in the SIoT as autonomous and proactive agents. The authors' aim is "to enable things as proactive participants in existing social networking services" (p. 1536), extending and transforming social networks by integrating autonomous and proactive things.

The authors of (Hussein, Soochang, & Crespi, 2015) propose a framework for adaptive and personalized smart services provisioning within the Social Internet of Things. Built on the socio-technical net-

Figure 2. Architecture of the NFC-based intelligent agent
Source: Lin, Ho, & Lin, 2014.

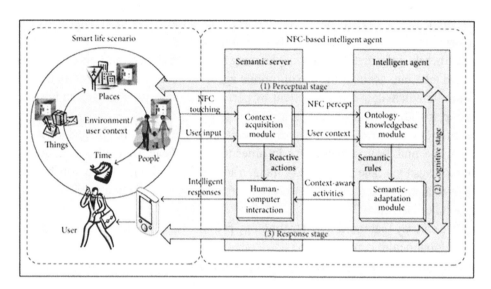

works, it was considered as goal-driven, i.e. cognitive, context-awareness being the core for intelligence generation. The presented results show reduced overhead of contextual data acquisition and processing.

S. Park et al. (Park, Hussein, & Crespi, 2015) presented a "socialization agent to support the evolution toward the SIoT that could be embedded into some of IoT devices by the policy and capacity of themselves" (p. 2). The authors propose an on-site available service discovery architecture which takes into consideration the practical IoT domains' formations and federations, by evolving from smart devices to social devices.

The authors of the (Lin, Ho, & Lin, 2014), define an NFC-based intelligent agent for the Social Internet of Things (presented in Figure 2) and propose a framework for developing this kind of agent, which combines the NFC technique with context-acquisition, ontology-knowledgebase, and semantic-adaptation modules, a credit-based incentive scheme to encourage social cooperation and to recommend relevant services. In order to enable the accommodation to the uncertain real-world environments, "this study also defines intelligent and social functionalities for the proposed NIA to achieve three indispensable abilities: reactive actions, proactive achievements, and social cooperation. In order to support context-aware computing, this study develops several mechanisms to support the abilities of location, time, activity, and social awareness" (p. 15). The resulting social-advertising system shows that this framework can support context awareness in the SIoT environments and a wide range of different functionalities.

The Social Internet of Things represents the extension of Internet of Things, which has great potential for various applications. Although, it lacks intelligence and cannot comply with the increasing application performance requirements from different domains, agent technology seems to be a promising approach in the implementation of the Social Internet of Things.

The next section briefly summarizes a historical evolution of medicine models and potential implications of SIoT adoption in healthcare.

Table 1. The evolution of medicine models

Feature	P0 Medicine	P3 Medicine	P4 Medicine	P5 Medicine	P6 Medicine
Personalized	No	Yes	Yes	Yes	Yes
Predictive	No	Yes	Yes	Yes	Yes
Preventive	No	Yes	Yes	Yes	Yes
Participatory	No	No	Yes	Yes	Yes
Psycho-cognitive	No	No	No	Yes	Yes
Public	No	No	No	No	Yes

MEDICINE MODELS AND SIoT

Over the years various P*n* medicine models (where *n* takes values from 0 to 6) have been considered. Their evolution, taking into consideration their main features, is briefly summarized in Table 1.

The P0 medicine model, strongly centered on the physician, is seen as the dawn of medicine, according to (Bragazzi, 2013). Gradually, we evolved from P0 medicine to P3 medicine, a model defined as personalized, predictive, and preventive. But paradigm changes with an additional feature of the new medicine model: participatory. The editors of Journal of Participatory Medicine, Jessie Gruman and Charles W. Smith, define participatory medicine as "a cooperative model of health care that encourages, supports and expects active involvement by all parties (clinicians, patients, caregivers, administrators, payers and communities) in the prevention, management and treatment of disease and disability and the promotion of health" (Gruman, & Smith, 2009, p. 1). In fact, several terms have been used for this new model, such as: personalized medicine, precision medicine and P4 medicine. We consider that the first two terms do not express the four features of this paradigm, and, therefore we opt for the term P4 medicine. In comparison to traditional medicine, the P4 approach was regarded visionary. However, according to (Gorini, & Pravettoni, 2011, p. 1), this approach "lacks a consideration of the psychological needs and values that make each individual unique". Consequently, the authors suggest adding the 'fifth P' standing for the psycho-cognitive aspects. And *n* was incremented, transforming P4 medicine into 'P5 medicine'. P6 medicine (i.e., personalized, predictive, preventive, participatory, psycho-cognitive, public) entails the addition of the public feature as a conceptual evolution of P5 medicine. In fact, P6 medicine was defined by G. Cumming and others as "P4 + C^n Hippocratic revolution", where, according to Cumming G. et al. (Cumming, Fowlie, & McKendrick, 2013), C^n stands for "community, collaboration, self-caring, co-creation, co-production, and co-development using technologies delivered via the Internet". In accordance with (Bragazzi, 2013), "patients do not limit themselves to browse health-related information on the Web, but they actively exploit all of the Web's potential", including the social networks. In fact, according to (Topol, 2012), "our go-to source for health and medical information is moving away from our doctor—it is increasingly by crowdsourcing and friend sourcing our entrusted social network."

We propose to extend these models. In fact, adopting Social Internet of Thing in healthcare could favor the development of a new form of medicine that ensures the fulfillment of healthcare delivery criteria as presented in (Srini, 2011):

- Content;
- Context;
- Communication;
- Convenience;
- Customization.

These are briefly described as $P6 + C^5$.

In this context, the meaning of the word "community" considered in the definition of P6 medicine $(P4 + C^n)$ must be understood not only in human terms, but as a community of things (living and non-living entities).

The use of this new medicine model, encouraged by the adoption of SIoT in healthcare is in compliance with the right principles of healthcare delivery, presented in (Srini, 2011):

- Right Care (right to access and right to waive);
- Right Time;
- Right Place;
- Right Delivery Model/Channel;
- Right Price;
- Right Personnel;
- Right Partnerships.

These are described as $P6 + C^5 => 7R$.

Next section evaluates the potential and implications of Social Internet of Things approach for people suffering from asthma.

SIoT-Based Benefits for People with Asthma

Further on, we focus on presenting a Social Internet of Things (SIoT) approach to solve some problems encountered by the many people suffering from asthma. In fact, those who suffer from this chronic disease (children and adults alike) are not the only ones affected. Family members and friends may also be dealing with the issues, because they have to adjust their lives according to the special requirements of the patient. The use of information technology holds promise for improving the patients' overall safety and for enhancing the quality of medical services.

In order to meet the needs of asthma patients and to prevent asthma attacks, we propose a smart living, cost-effective and real-time solution based on a Social Internet of Things approach. Acute, severe asthma exacerbations or attacks can be life-threatening and therefore must be prevented by the use of medications and by reducing exposure to the environmental factors known as triggers. But because these triggers differ from case to case, a good asthma management implies identifying those specific to a certain patient in order to limit exposure or to avoid them completely. In this context, the Social Internet of Things can prove really useful for enabling the efficiency of various information related to medical problems. In fact, the SIoT approach can be perceived as a natural extension of the current implementations which must take into consideration important additional IoT based resources and capabilities.

Asthma attacks are the result of some cumulative factors, such as exposure to cold air, pollution, dust, pet dander, exhaustion or even secondhand smoke. More important than recognizing the early warning signs of an asthma attack, is the attempt to prevent it. Some important living or non-living things, located indoors or outdoors, are included in this architecture. Things linked to people are a special category to be considered. Different types of sensors, moving at the same time with the patient, could be used to monitor his health parameters. For example, breath rate sensors developed by PASCO (PASPORT Respiration. (n.d.)) measure the breathing rate based on the air pressure in a mask worn by the patient. Usually, this sensor is used indoors, but if it communicates with another thing, like a mobile phone or a tablet, it would be included in the considered SIoT architecture. The values of breath rate and breath rate average parameter can be sent to the living things of the architecture, e.g. personal general practitioners, specialists, emergency team members, care giver, or family members. Moreover, the patient can wear different types of biosensors or an intelligent T-shirt (Monitoring patients using intelligent t-shirts, 2011), that can measure his temperature or can generate an electrocardiogram. There are many choices available on the market for global positioning system (GPS) receivers that could provide the patient's position (latitude, longitude, and altitude). When the values of the measured parameter exceed the patient's personal presets limits, the data are communicated to other things (especially to the emergency staff, if necessary).

Home things could also bring benefits when the patient's status is monitored. For example, indoor sensors or companion robots can be sources of environment status parameters sent to other things connected in a social relationship to the SIoT. Also, home appliances can tell something about the patient's activities (for example, the moment when the patient uses the vacuum-cleaner implies dust).

The patient could receive alerts from other things connected to the SIoT, such as, air quality monitoring stations, wireless pollution sensors, weather stations or even traffic monitoring systems. Based on these alerts signals, the patient (if pedestrian) can avoid polluted areas in the city, and thus preventing the occurrence of an asthma attack.

If we consider outdoor asthma triggers, the IoT local weather report can enable patients with asthma to monitor the weather conditions and the air quality. Based on their social relationships in SIoT, people with asthma could receive information regarding location-based real-time index levels for pollen, asthma sensitivity, as well as the local weather forecast. Extreme hot, cold, or even humid weather, or rapidly changing climate conditions (e.g., changes in temperature and humidity, barometric pressure or strong winds, etc.) may also be asthma triggers. Also, patients with asthma living in areas where forest fires are common during the summer must pay attention to the poor quality of air. Regular exercise is healthy for patients with asthma, but the air quality must be taken into consideration. Thus, based on the local weather report, patients can schedule their outdoor activities when the air quality is suitable for their health status, thus avoiding exposure to high levels of pollen or pollution. Moreover, this kind of report helps patients to decide whether to use the air conditioner in order to filter the air coming into their home.

Using their social relationships in SIoT, people suffering from asthma have access to exact and real-time information regarding potential symptom triggers in their close environment.

CONCLUSION AND FUTURE WORK

The latest in advanced treatments and information technology came with the promise of improved efficiency in healthcare.

In this chapter we have focused on the social-oriented approach that we believe to be the gap between current medicine models and practice. Starting from the idea that the evolution of the Internet of Things to Social Internet of Things supports this approach, the present chapter aims to examine the adoption of the Social Internet of Things in healthcare. We address a broad range of techniques, methods, models, functionalities, middleware solutions, systems and applications related to SIoT. Next, some consideration related to evolution of P's medicine models and potential implications of SIoT adoption in healthcare are presented.

Additionally, this chapter provides an overview of the impact of the SIoT in healthcare, and tackles with the inherent challenges of making the use of SIoT a reality in the field. The Social Internet of Things has great potential for healthcare organizations and society. The benefits can be enormous, both for people and for healthcare organizations, if the development of SIoT is properly managed.

As healthcare professionals cannot afford to take risks, significant research is needed to make SioT at healthcare a reality. Thus, according to J. A. Stankovic (Stankovici, 2014, p. 6), "new research problems arise due to the large scale of devices, the connection of the physical and cyber worlds, the openness of the systems of systems, and continuing problems of privacy and security". Besides the IoT challenges, SIoT brings its own challenges in order to facilitate new applications and services in more effective and efficient ways. Some of these challenges are the following:

- Ownership;
- Defining/enabling relationship between things;
- The heterogeneous nature of the connected devices (resolving this problem will increase inter-things communications in the SIoT);
- Concurrent access to connected devices; aiming to limit costs, medical units must determine the optimal number of devices that provide the same service. On the other hand, in SIoT, multiple users can simultaneously try to access the same equipment, which can lead to blockages in the system. Establishing a system of priorities in accessing connected devices or temporally limiting the access to them, may be part of the solution to this problem;
- Conflicts between devices;
- Function redundancy;
- The establishing of a level of trustworthiness between connected devices that are "friends" (Chen, Bao, & Guo, 2014; Nitti, 2014; Nitti, 2015);
- Non-standardization.

Despite the many problems faced by the adoption of SIoT in healthcare, this paradigm promises to deliver to human users and connected devices the possibility to discover, select, and use proper services found through scanning their friends network.

REFERENCES

Antonovici, D. A., Chiuchisan, I., Geman, O., & Tomegea, A. (2014). Acquisition and management of biomedical data using Internet of Things concepts. *Fundamentals of Electrical Engineering (ISFEE), 2014 International Symposium*. doi:10.1109/ISFEE.2014.7050625

Anurag, M., Rahmani, A.M., Westerlund, T., Yang, G., Liljeberg, P., & Tenhunen, H. (2014). Pervasive Health Monitoring Based on Internet of Things: Two Case Studies. *Proc. of IEEE International Conference on Wireless Mobile Communication and Healthcare (MobiHealth'14)*. doi:10.4108/icst.mobihealth.2014.257395

Atzori, L., Carboni, D., & Iera, A. (2013). Smart Things in the Social Loop: Paradigms, Technologies, and Potentials. *Ad Hoc Networks*.

Atzori, L., Iera, A., & Morabito, G. (2011a). *Making things socialize in the Internet -- Does it help our lives?* ITU Kaleidoscope.

Atzori, L., Iera, A., & Morabito, G. (2011b). SIoT: Giving a Social Structure to the Internet of Things. *IEEE Communications Letters*, *15*(11), 1193–1195. Retrieved from http://ieeexplore.ieee.org/stamp/stamp.jsp?tp=&arnumber=6042288&isnumber=6083590

Atzori, L., Iera, A., Morabito, G., & Nitti, M. (2012). The Social Internet of Things (SIoT) – When social networks meet the Internet of Things: Concept, architecture and network characterization. *Computer Networks*, *56*(16), 3594–3608. doi:10.1016/j.comnet.2012.07.010

Bachfischer, N. (2014). *The Internet-of-Medical-Things: Five innovative examples, 2014*. Retrieved from http://www.i-q-i.net/

Bergenti, F., & Poggi, A. (2009). Multi-Agent Systems for E-health: Recent Projects and Initiatives. *Proceedings of the 10th International Workshop on Objects and Agents*.

Bleecker, J. (2006). Why Things Matter: A Manifesto for Networked Objects — Cohabiting with Pigeons, Arphids and Aibos. *Internet of Things*. Retrieved from www.nearfuturelaboratory.com/files/WhyThingsMatter.pdf

Botterman, M. (2009). *Internet of Things: an early reality of the Future Internet*. European Commission. Retrieved June, 2015 from ftp://ftp.cordis.europa.eu/pub/fp7/ict/docs/enet/iot-prague-workshop-report-vfinal-20090706_en.pdf

Bragazzi. N. L. (2013). From P0 to P6 Medicine, a model of highly participatory, narrative, interactive and "augmented" medicine: Some considerations on Salvatore Iaconesi's clinical history. *Patient Preference and Adherence, 7*, 353–359.

Caduff, A., Hirt, E., Feldman, Y., Ali, Z., & Heinemann, L. (2003). First human experiments with a novel non-invasive, non-optical continuous glucose monitoring system. *Biosensors & Bioelectronics*, *19*(3), 209–217. doi:10.1016/S0956-5663(03)00196-9 PMID:14611756

Caduff, A., Talary, M. S., Mueller, M., Dewarrat, F., Klisic, J., Donath, M., & Stahel, W. A. et al. (2009). Non-invasive glucose monitoring in patients with Type 1 diabetes: A Multisensor system combining sensors for dielectric and optical characterisation of skin. *Biosensors & Bioelectronics*, *24*(9), 2778–2784. doi:10.1016/j.bios.2009.02.001 PMID:19286364

Chang, Y. S., Yang, C. T., & Luo, Y. C. (2011). An Ontology based Agent Generation for Information Retrieval on Cloud Environment. *Journal of Universal Computer Science*, *17*(8), 1135–1160.

Chen, I.R., Bao, F., & Guo, J. (2014). Trust-based Service Management for Social Internet of Things Systems. *IEEE Transactions on Dependable and Secure Computing*. doi: 10.1109/TDSC.2015.2420552

Chen, M., Gonzalez, S., Zhang, Q., & Leung, V. (2010). Code-centric RFID system based on software agent intelligence. *IEEE Intelligent Systems*, *25*(2), 12–19. doi:10.1109/MIS.2010.44

Chin, C. S., Atmodihardjo, W., Woo, L. W., & Mesbahi, E. (2015). Remote temperature monitoring device using a multiple patients-coordinator set design approach. *ROBOMECH Journal*, *2*(1), 4. doi:10.1186/s40648-015-0027-x

Ciortea, A., Boissier, O., Zimmermann, A., & Florea, A. M. (2013). Reconsidering the social web of things: position paper. *Proceedings of the 2013 ACM conference on Pervasive and ubiquitous computing adjunct publication*, (UbiComp '13 Adjunct). ACM. doi:10.1145/2494091.2497587

Cultivate resilient smart Objects for Sustainable city applications. (2015). Retrieved from http://www.sido-event.com/public/exposants_files/COSMOSNewsletterIssue1.pdf

Cumming, G., Fowlie, A., & McKendrick, D. (2013). H = P4 + C and Health Web Science: "A Hippocratic Revolution in Medicine". *Proceedings of the ACM WebSci '11 3rd International Conference on Web Science*. Retrieved April, 2014 from http://www.websci11.org/fileadmin/websci/Papers/Health_WS_Workshop-A_Hippocratic_Revolution.pdf

Davis, K. (2004). *Mirror, Mirror on the Wall: Looking at the Quality of American Health Care Through the Patient's Lens*. Commonwealth Fund.

Ding, L., Shi, P., & Liu, B. (2010). The clustering of internet, internet of things and social network. *Proc. of the 3rd International Symposium on Knowledge Acquisition and Modeling*. doi:10.1109/KAM.2010.5646274

Erola, A., Castellà-Roca, J., Viejo, A., & Mateo-Sanz, J. M. (2011). Exploiting social networks to provide privacy in personalized web search. *Journal of Systems and Software, 84*(10), 1734-1745. Retrieved from http://www.sciencedirect.com/science/article/pii/S0164121211001117

Fast, A., Jensen, V., & Levine, B. N. (2005). Creating social networks to improve peer-to-peer networking. In *Proc. of ACM KDD'05*. doi:10.1145/1081870.1081938

Fisher, E. (2003). The Implications of Regional Variations in Medicare Spending: Part I. The Context, Quality, and Accessibility of Care. *Annals of Internal Medicine*, *138*(4), 273. doi:10.7326/0003-4819-138-4-200302180-00006 PMID:12585825

GDH-FAD blood glucose meter / Bluetooth. (n.d.). Retrieved from http://www.medicalexpo.com/prod/taidoc-technology/product-70247-729754.html

Girau, R., Nitti, M., & Atzori, L. (2013). Implementation of an Experimental Platform for the Social Internet of Things, *Seventh International Conference on Innovative Mobile and Internet Services in Ubiquitous Computing (IMIS)*, (pp. 500-505). doi:10.1109/IMIS.2013.90

Gorini, A., & Pravettoni, G. (2011). P5 medicine: A plus for a personalized approach to oncology, Nat. Rev. *Clinical Oncology*, *8*(7), 444. doi:10.1038/nrclinonc.2010.227-c1 PMID:21629214

Gruman, J., & Smith, C. W. (2009). Why the Journal of Participatory Medicine? *Journal of Participatory Medicine, 1*. Retrieved from http://www.jopm.org/opinion/editorials/2009/10/21/why-the-journal-of-participatory-medicine/

Guinard, D., Fischer, M., & Trifa, V. (2010). Sharing using social networks in a composable Web of Things. *Proceedings of IEEE PERCOM.* doi:10.1109/PERCOMW.2010.5470524

Han, N. S. (2015). *Semantic service provisioning for 6LoWPAN: powering internet of things applications on Web* (Doctoral dissertation). Available from Institut National des Telecommunications. (tel-01217185)

Hassanalieragh, M., Page, A., Soyata, T., Sharma, G., Aktas, M., Mateos, G.,... Andreescu, S. (2015, June). Health monitoring and management using internet-of-things (IoT) sensing with cloud-based processing: Opportunities and challenges. In *Services Computing (SCC), 2015 IEEE International Conference on* (pp. 285-292). IEEE.

Health Fact Sheet. (2015). *Health Fact Sheet. Pew Internet Project's research related to health and health care.* Retrieved from http://www.pewinternet.org/fact-sheets/health-fact-sheet/

Holmquist, L. E., Mattern, F., Schiele, B., Alahuhta, P., Beigl, M., & Gellersen, H. W. (2001). Smart-its friends: A technique for users to easily establish connections between smart artefacts, *Proceedings of the 3rd international conference on Ubiquitous Computing, UbiComp '01.* Springer-Verlag. doi:10.1007/3-540-45427-6_10

Hovorka, R. (2006). Continuous glucose monitoring and closed-loop systems. *Diabetic Medicine, 23*(1), 1–12. doi:10.1111/j.1464-5491.2005.01672.x PMID:16409558

Hussein, D., Soochang, P., & Crespi, N. (2015). A Cognitive Context-aware Approach for Adaptive Services Provisioning in Social Internet of Things. *IEEE ICCE Conference Proceeding.* doi:10.1109/ICCE.2015.7066376

Iantovics, B. (2010). Cognitive Medical Multiagent Systems, BRAIN. *Broad Research in Artificial Intelligence and Neuroscience, 1*(1).

Iera, A. (2011). The Social Internet of Things: from objects that communicate to objects that socialize in the Internet. *50th FITCE International Congress Palermo.* Retrieved from https://www.youtube.com/watch?v=sQZDlLPgTWY

IGI Global Dictionary. (2016). Retrieved from http://www.igi-global.com/dictionary/ontology/21117

IoT to Revolutionize Healthcare. (2015). IoT to Revolutionize Healthcare Industry: Survey. *M2M Magazine.* Retrieved from http://www.machinetomachinemagazine.com/2015/04/14/iot-to-revolutionize-healthcare-industry-zebra-survey/

Istepanian, R. S., Hu, S., Philip, N. Y., & Sungoor, A. (2011). The potential of Internet of m-health Things "m-IoT" for non-invasive glucose level sensing. *Proceedings of the 33rd Annual International Conference of the IEEE Engineering in Medicine and Biology Society.*

ITU Internet Reports. (2005). *The Internet of Things. Executive Summary.* International Telecommunication Union. Retrieved from http://www.itu.int/osg/spu/publications/internetofthings/InternetofThings_summary.pdf

Jian, Z., Zhanli, W., & Zhuang, M. A. (2012). *Temperature measurement system and method based on home gateway.* Patent CN 102811185.

K4CARE. (2008). *K4CARE project Web site.* Retrieved from http://www.k4care.ne

Kim, J. E. (2016). *Architecting Social Internet of Things* (Doctoral dissertation). University of Pittsburgh, Pittsburgh, PA.

Kim, J. E., Maron, A., & Mosse, D. (2015, June). Socialite: A Flexible Framework for Social Internet of Things. In *Mobile Data Management (MDM), 2015 16th IEEE International Conference on* (Vol. 1, pp. 94-103). IEEE. doi:10.1109/MDM.2015.50

Kleinberg, J. (2008). The convergence of social and technological networks. *Communications of the ACM, 51*(11), 66–72. doi:10.1145/1400214.1400232

Kranz, M., Roalter, L., & Michahelles, F. (2010). *Things that Twitter: social networks and the Internet of things, What can the Internet of Things do for the Citizen (CIoT).* Workshop at Pervasive.

Laleci, G.B., Dogac, A., Olduz, M., Tasyurt, I., Yuksel, M., & Okcan, A. (2008). SAPHIRE: A Multi-Agent System for Remote Healthcare Monitoring through Computerized Clinical Guidelines. *Agent Technology and e-Health. Whitestein Series in Software Agent Technologies and Autonomic Computing,* 25-44.

Li, H., Miao, C., Zhang, L., Tian, W., & Wang, J. (2014). Research on key technologies of ECG monitoring system based on Internet of things. Application Research of Computers, 38(12).

Lin, C.H., Ho, P.H., & Lin, H.C. (2014). Framework for NFC-Based Intelligent Agents: A Context-Awareness Enabler for Social Internet of Things. *International Journal of Distributed Sensor Networks.* doi:10.1155/2014/978951

Lu, L., & Chen, M. (2015). Implementation of ECG Monitoring System Based on Internet of Things. *Chinese Journal of Medical Instrumentation, 39*(6), 418–420. PMID:27066681

Macala, W. (2016). *A pilot project increased blood pressure monitoring effectiveness to 70 percent.* Retrieved from http://www.psfk.com/2016/02/withings-fitness-tracker-home-blood-pressure-monitoring.html

Malhi, K., Mukhopadhyay, S. C., Schnepper, J., Haefke, M., & Ewald, H. (2012). A Zigbee-Based Wearable Physiological Parameters Monitoring System. *IEEE Sensors Journal, Volume, 12*(Issue:3), 423–430. doi:10.1109/JSEN.2010.2091719

Mansor, H., Shukor, M. H. A., Meskam, S. S., Rusli, N. Q. A. M., & Zamery, N. S. (2013, November). Body temperature measurement for remote health monitoring system. In *Smart Instrumentation, Measurement and Applications (ICSIMA), 2013 IEEE International Conference on* (pp. 1-5). IEEE. doi:10.1109/ICSIMA.2013.6717956

Martin-Campillo, A., Martinez-Garcia, C., Cucurull, J., Marti, R., Robles, S., & Borrell, J. (2009). *Mobile Agents in Healthcare.* Distributed Intelligence Approach.

McCallum, L., & Higgins, D. (2012). Measuring body temperature. *Nursing Times, 108*(45), 20–22. PMID:23240273

McGlynn, E. A., Asch, S. M., Adams, J., Keesey, J., Hicks, J., DeCristofaro, A., & Kerr, E. A. (2003). The Quality of Health Care Delivered to Adults in the United States. *The New England Journal of Medicine, 348*(26), 2635–2645. doi:10.1056/NEJMsa022615 PMID:12826639

Mendes, P. (2011). Social-driven internet of connected objects. *Proc. of the Interconnecting Smart Objects with the Internet Workshop.*

Mislove, A., Gummadi, K. P., & Druschel, P. (2006). Exploiting Social Networks for Internet Search. *Proc. of ACM HotNets.*

Monitoring patients using intelligent t-shirts. (2011). Retrieved from http://portal.uc3m.es/portal/page/portal/actualidad_cientifica/noticias/intelligent_tshirts

Natarajan, K., Prasath, B., & Kokila, P. (2016). Smart Health Care System Using Internet of Things. *Journal of Network Communications and Emerging Technologies, 6*(3). Retrieved from www. jncet. org

NECG Platform. (n.d.). Retrieved from http://www.nuubo.com/index.php?q=en/node/165

Nitti, M., & Atzori, L. (2015). What the SIoT needs: a new caching system or new friendship selection mechanism? *Conference: IEEE 2nd World Forum on Internet of Things (WF-IoT).* doi:10.1109/WF-IoT.2015.7389092

Nitti, M., Atzori, L., & Cvijikj, I. P. (2014). Network navigability in the social Internet of Things. *Internet of Things (WF-IoT), 2014 IEEE World Forum on.* doi:10.1109/WF-IoT.2014.6803200

Nitti, M., Atzori, L., & Cvijikj, I. P. (2015). Friendship Selection in the Social Internet of Things: Challenges and Possible Strategies. *IEEE Internet of Things Journal, 2*(3), 240–247. doi:10.1109/JIOT.2014.2384734

Nitti, M., Girau, R., & Atzori, L. (2014). Trustworthiness Management in the Social Internet of Things. IEEE Transactions on Knowledge and Data Engineering.

Nitti, M., Girau, R., Atzori, L., Iera, A., & Morabito, G. (2012). A subjective model for trustworthiness evaluation in the social Internet of Things. *IEEE 23rd International Symposium on Personal Indoor and Mobile Radio Communications* (PIMRC), (pp. 18-23).

Ortiz, A. M., Hussein, D., Park, S., Han, S. N., & Crespi, N. (2014). The Cluster Between Internet of Things and Social Networks: Review and Research Challenges. *IEEE Internet of Things Journal., 1*(3), 206–215. doi:10.1109/JIOT.2014.2318835

Park, S., Hussein, D., & Crespi, N. (2015). On-site service discovery along user roaming over Internet of Things. *Consumer Electronics (ICCE), 2015 IEEE International Conference on*, (pp. 194-195). Retrieved from http://servicearchitecture.wp.tem-tsp.eu/files/2015/01/On-site-Service-Discovery-along-User-Roaming-over-Internet-of-Things.pdf

Pasport Respiration Rate Sensor. (n.d.). Retrieved from https://www.pasco.com/prodCatalog/PS/PS-2133_pasport-respiration-rate-sensor/

Riazul Islam, S. M., Kwak, D., Humaun Kabir, M., Hossain, M., & Kwak, K. S. (2015). The internet of things for health care: A comprehensive survey. *Access, IEEE, 3*, 678–708. doi:10.1109/AC-CESS.2015.2437951

Social Media. (2012). *Social media "likes" healthcare. From marketing to social business.* Health Research Institute. Retrieved from http://www.pwc.com/us/en/health-industries/publications/health-care-social-media.html

Srini, J. (2011). *The Future of mHealth* [PowerPoint slides]. Retrieved from http://www.slideshare.net/HowardRosen129/the-future-of-mhealth-jay-srini-march-201.1

Stankovic, J. A. (2014). Research Directions for the Internet of Things. *IEEE Internet of Things Journal, 1*(1), 3–9. doi:10.1109/JIOT.2014.2312291

Sterling, B. (2005). *Shaping Things*. Cambridge, MA: MIT Press.

Susannah, F., & Duggan, M. (2012). *Mobile health 2012*. Retrieved from http://www.pewinternet.org/2012/11/08/mobile-health-2012/

Susannah, F., & Duggan, M. (2013). *Health Online 2013*. Available at: http://www.pewinternet.org/2013/01/15/health-online-2013/

Topol, E. J. (2012). The Creative Destruction of Medicine: How the Digital Revolution Will Create Better Health Care. Academic Press.

Uckelmann, D., Harrison, M., & Michahelles, F. (2011). An architectural approach towards the future Internet of Things. *Architecting the Internet of Things*, 1–24. doi:10.1007/978-3-642-19157-2_1

Vermesan, O., & Friess, P. (2014). Internet of Things Applications - From Research and Innovation to Market Deployment, Bringing IP to Low-power Smart Objects: The Smart Parking Case in the CALIPSO Project. The River Publishers.

Voutyras, O., Bourelos, P., Kyriazis, D., & Varvarigou, T. (2014). An Architecture supporting Knowledge flow in Social Internet of Things systems. *Wireless and Mobile Computing, Networking and Communications (WiMob), 2014 IEEE 10th International Conference on.*

Voutyras, O., Gogouvitis, S., Marinakis, A., & Varvarigou, T. (2014). Achieving Autonomicity in IoT systems via Situational-Aware, Cognitive and Social Things. *Proceedings of the 18th Panhellenic Conference on Informatics.* doi:10.1145/2645791.2645854

Wearable Health Monitoring. (n.d.). Retrieved from http://www2.imec.be/be_en/research/wearable-health-monitoring.html

What is Diabetes ? (n.d.). Retrieved January 24, 2016, from http://www.diabetesresearch.org/what-is-diabetes

Wooldridge, M., & Jennings, N. (1995). Agent theories, architectures, and languages: a survey. In *Intelligent agents.* Springer Berlin Heidelberg.

Xin, T. J., Min, B., & Ji, J. (2013). *Carry-on blood pressure/pulse rate/blood oxygen monitoring location intelligent terminal based on internet of things*. Patent no. CN 202875315 U.

Zorzi, M., Gluhak, A., Lange, S., & Bassi, A. (2010). From today's INTRAnet of things to a future INTERnet of things: A wireless- and mobility-related view. *IEEE Wireless Commun., 17*(6), 44–51. doi:10.1109/MWC.2010.5675777

This work was previously published in Internet of Things and Advanced Application in Healthcare edited by Catarina I. Reis and Marisa da Silva Maximiano, pages 266-295, copyright year 2017 by Medical Information Science Reference (an imprint of IGI Global).

Chapter 6
An Internet of Things Governance Architecture with Applications in Healthcare

Adrian Copie
West University of Timișoara, Romania &
Institute e-Austria Timișoara, Romania

Victor Ion Munteanu
West University of Timișoara, Romania &
Institute e-Austria Timișoara, Romania

Bogdan Manațe
West University of Timișoara, Romania

Teodor-Florin Fortiș
West University of Timișoara, Romania &
Institute e-Austria Timișoara, Romania

ABSTRACT

The astonishing expansion of Internet of Things has opened a lot of opportunities for related domains to employ strategies that were successfully used for the "things" governance. Furthermore, because of the technology blending in the most common household devices and wearable items, it becomes very easy for the computers to sense the surrounding environment and to collect information about the inhabitants, therefore transforming the intelligent house in a Home Care System (HCS). For medical conditions like dementia and its associated diseases, it is very convenient to monitor the patients in their living space because the patient will benefit from their home comfort. In addition, the costs for in hospital monitoring will decrease. This chapter proposes an Internet of Things Governance Architecture that can be used to sustain and monitor a complex e-health system, with application especially for patients with dementia and its associated diseases.

1. INTRODUCTION AND MOTIVATION

The increased standard of living in many countries around the world has led to a high level of life expectancy, the demographic profile being significantly changed. Together with the benefits resulting from a better quality of life, the level of elderly population has increased, people live longer with all the implications related to specific potential diseases, often multiple and complicated. At the same time, the number and complexity of issues the health system has to face have increased, being confronted with

DOI: 10.4018/978-1-5225-1832-7.ch006

problems related to the way in which those people benefit from the caring system, how to maintain a high quality level of care and how to maximize the independence of the cared people (Patel *et al.*, 2012).

The advances in computer technology have led to great promises in what concerns the health system, making it possible to change our lifestyle by producing wireless sensors, wearable or implantable in the human body, acting to detect biochemical and psychological phenomenon but also targeted to motion sensing. Their applications reside in a wide range of fields (Cooper & James, 2009; World Alzheimer Report, 2013), one of the most important being the health care: medical monitoring, communication in case of emergency, medical data access and much more.

Providing a continuous monitoring of the patients by using implanted or wearable sensors can offer an early detection of risky situations for people suffering of cognitive and physical disabilities. Psychological sensors help in diagnosis and monitoring of various neurological or cardiovascular diseases. It is usual to have sensors related to physical parameters like fall detection, location tracking or posture detection, contributing to enhance the independence level of the elder people, but there are also a wide range of sensors related to biological and environmental parameters able to give information related to the patient's health.

Dementia is one of those conditions associated with aging and having symptoms ranging from memory loss to decreased reasoning and communication skills (Graham & Warner 2009). According to Kinsella & Phillips (2005), "today, over 35 million people worldwide currently live with the condition and this number is expected to double by 2030 and more than triple by 2050 to 115 million."

The patients suffering from such a disease are cared for in specialized health centers or even at home by professional staff, but a large part of this task is considered administrative work, about filling various forms with health parameters, writing different statistics related to the patient's condition, etc. The digital devices like computers, tablets and smartphones could improve this work by reducing the bureaucracy tied with the paperwork, keeping closer touch with hospitals or specialized medical staff.

Considering the number of people that are expected to develop dementia in the next years, one problem that is raising is related to the caring costs in terms of medications and equipment together with the caring personal and, at the same time, the need to provide quality health services. Continuous monitoring of the patients by using implanted or wearable sensors offers early detection of risky situations for the people suffering from cognitive and physical disabilities.

All these technologies help to reduce the medical costs related to dementia, improving the quality of life for the patients by providing a higher safety level and ease the work of the caring personnel, opening the possibility for extending the number of patients whilst maintaining the same medical staff.

2. THE INTERNET OF THINGS

Inspired by the adoption of the computers in more and more areas of activity, Mark Weiser proposed in 1988 the term of ubiquitous computing as "the third wave in computing [...] the age of calm technology, when technology recedes into the background of our lives". Besides the ubiquitous computing paradigm, other concepts have found their place in current language, like pervasive computing, things that think, physical computing or ambient intelligence. Weiser (1991) enunciate that "the most profound technologies are those that disappear. They weave themselves into the fabric of everyday life until they are indistinguishable from it". According to Satyanarayanan (2001) the environment of the pervasive computing is saturated with computing and communication infrastructure that is so integrated with the users that eventually becomes "technology that disappears", sustaining Weiser's statement. However, the fact that today a lot of surrounding technology is part of our life, is indistinguishable, it is due the advances in distributed systems and mobile computing.

2.1 Technologies and Vision

The advances in the technology of materials and the continuous miniaturization of the electronic sensors have led to their integration in the day to day life. The common 'things' become intelligent, they are able to collect information about their environment/neighborhood and to transmit them to dedicated processing units. This 'Things That Think' (TTT) paradigm is a major research direction, focused to put intelligence in the everyday things. Many examples are revealed in (Hawley *et al.*, 1997), companies like Pampers willing to integrate sensors in the diapers, Levi Strauss embracing the intelligent things in their clothes and furniture producer Steelcase foresees the desktops and cabinets with capabilities to see their content inventory and report it to specialized nodes for further processing. Efforts in this arena are made by sport shoes companies in order to monitor the running cadence or by sports equipment manufacturers to keep the heart rate or other physical parameters under control.

The vision of the interconnected objects goes further, offering a Sci-Fi perspective where common things like cars, houses, medical instruments like small video cameras taking images from inside the human body, all equipped with sensors collecting data about their environment and sending it to specialized repositories to be analyzed and processed. The idea reflecting the miniaturization of things is not new, movies like "Fantastic Voyage" reveal the idea of a submarine which was shrunk together with its crew and introduced in a human body to heal a near assassinated diplomat.

A common support for the interconnected objects is the internet, which makes possible the usage of the same communication protocol as the one used by the computers. To keep track and monitor the interconnected objects, they must be uniquely identified. The adoption of the IPv6 scheme, which allows a number of 2^{128} distinct addresses, allows the attachment of a unique identifier to every active device which has to be recognized and monitored.

The number of interconnected objects is foreseen to be in the order of 26 billion in the next years, until 2020, according to Gartner (2013), creating serious problems regarding the data management. Ericsson's vision (Internet of Things - Ericsson report, 2013) is that the number of interconnected devices will reach 50 billion until 2020 and the Network Society in which "connectivity will be the starting point for new ways of innovating, collaborating and socializing" will take care of all the aspects related to people's life and the operations of enterprises and society.

The data resulted during the acquisition processes has to be directed to the specialized repositories. One aspect that must be considered is the 'bandwidth' of the network infrastructure which has to accommodate the increasing data flow. Another open topic is the 'scalability' of the datastores meant to collect and persist the tremendous amount of information. How much information can we collect from those sensors? Are we able to process it in a reasonable amount of time until it becomes obsolete? There are also topics related to the Big Data paradigm but they also touch Data Mining and the Data Analytics fields.

One of the first technology based on electromagnetic field sensors, started to be developed a few decades ago, called Radio Frequency Identification (RFID) has aimed initially to replace the barcodes on products, serving also for other logistic purposes by reading the information carried by a tag. The traceability and transparency of the products during their life cycle is also made possible using the RFID tags. A more concise definition given by Aggarwal et al. (2013) is "RFID is a technology which allows a sensor (reader) to read, from a distance, and without line of sight, a unique product identification code (EPC) associated with a tag". Even if this technology offers a series of advantages as the tags have no need to be powered on when they are read, and they can be aggregated during the read operation, soon it becomes clear that there is a limit to this technology. The amount of information stored in a RFID tag is limited, the area of interaction with the sensors is relatively small and the reading mechanism is prone to errors due to technological issues. Since the fact that RFID tags can be associated with clothes or other things associated with humans, some data privacy problems can arise related to location detection of the individuals. More than this, concerns related to the privacy of RFID tagged goods outside the warehouses and stores are also emphasized.

New approaches were developed in order to overcome these limitations. The technology was enhanced with sensors able to transmit more information about their environment, being called 'active RFID.' The drawback is that the sensors must be powered by batteries which have a limited life and they must be periodically changed which implies supplementary costs and efforts, considering the large number of devices. On the other hand, researches has been done to add new characteristics to the passive tags, in order to collect and transmit information about their local environment (Vogt, 2002), (Chawla *et al.*, 2007), this approach being called 'passive RFID.' One of the most important disadvantage of this technology is that the tags have to be activated with the reader devices from a distance even smaller that the one needed in the classical RFID tags, in order to transfer enough power to the sensors.

The wireless sensors using internet protocol are a step forward in what concerns the information about the environment collected and transmitted, since they can embed more intelligence but at higher costs when we talk about a large scale solution. They have to be permanently powered on since they have to be in an active state all the time due to the requirements of the TCP/IP protocol.

Mobile devices used for communication like smartphones and tablets have a lot of embedded sensors: video cameras, GPS, accelerometers. The information attached to these kinds of devices is miscellaneous, being focused around the owner or the user of the device. Sharing this information often raises privacy concerns but it is also a problem related to the bandwidth of the supporting network and scalability and reliability of the storage systems holding the acquired data.

All this things have become interconnected in the internet network as the common ground for communication. Some of them are aware of each other, some not, some of them can be configured to exchange information but they eventually constitute a smart communication grid, an intelligent network. This intelligent network of "things" is the cornerstone of the Internet of Things paradigm. Even this phenomenon is not new, there isn't yet a standard definition encompassing all the aspects, but the European Commission (2008) proposes that IoT are referred as "Things having identities and virtual personalities operating in smart spaces using intelligent interfaces to connect and communicate within social, environmental, and user contexts".

A more formal definition for this term is given by Kramp *et al.* (2013):

Internet of Things is a combination of a technological push and a human pull for more and ever increasing connectivity with anything happening in the immediate and wider environment - a logical extension of the computing power in a single machine to the environment: the environment as an interface.

According to Gartner's 2013 Hype Cycle for Emerging Technologies Maps Out Evolving Relationship Between Humans and Machines (2013) there are three important trends that will be embraced by enterprises to improve productivity, make a better experience for customers and seek competitive advantage: augmenting humans with technology, machines replacing humans and machines working alongside each other. This close relationship between humans and machines is possible through the advances in knowledge related research. This same research allows humans to better understand machines, for example using Internet of Things, and vice-versa, the machines understand humans through Artificial Intelligence or voice recognition.

Other important research directions are, according to Stankovic (2014) "massive scaling, architecture and dependencies, creating knowledge and big data, robustness, openness, security, privacy and human-in-the-loop". Important research communities like Internet of Things (IoT), Pervasive Computing (PC), Mobile Computing (MC), Wireless Sensor Networks (WSN) or Cyber Physical Systems (CPS) bring their contribution in enabling the networks of smart devices but advances are also expected in related technologies like signal processing, security and privacy, big data, machine learning or real-time computing.

In Figure 1 one can observe that expectations from the Internet of Things are high, together with other inter-related technologies, like Big Data or Wearable User Interfaces, but it is foreseen that its maturation will come over the next 10 years, together with its marked adoption. The Internet of Things paradigm will impact human life as the internet did in the last twenty years, this is the reason why it is called "the next of internet".

2.2 Ambient Assisted Living (AAL)

The ambient assisted living research domain is strongly related to the ambient intelligence (AmI) domain because it makes use of technologies developed for AmI in order to assist, monitor and observe the inhabitants. The ubiquitous computing and pervasive communication are coined by the ambient intelligence in order to offer a better experience and to improve the quality of life. The main goal of AmI is to create an intelligent system which is able to adapt to the inhabitants' needs.

AmI is responsible for managing the following three main domains: comfort (e.g. home automation, things location, social interaction, infotainment), autonomy enhancement (e.g. energy saving, shopping, training, cleaning)and emergency assistance (e.g. assistance, prediction, prevention). The three aforementioned domains are interdependent when integrated in Home Care Systems (HCS) (Kleinberger *et al.,* 2007).

Ambient intelligence is user centered, thus every interaction is personalized for a user profile, and is based on psychological and physiological measurements as well as other measured parameters which describe the environment in which the user is located.

Nowadays the ambient assisted living has become a potential replacement for in hospital treatment, especially when the patient is not in a severe condition. The development of ambient assisted living has been influenced by major technology advances in various fields and by funding from different organizations (e.g. European Union[1]). Also, when considering wearable devices, a crucial criterion for large acceptance is based on the efforts concentrated towards devices miniaturization. (Darwish & Hassanien 2011) For the patients to live a normal life the devices and sensors attached directly to human body or clothes should be non-intrusive and they should have a small mass.

Another important aspect related to the devices that monitor the human body is the operating range, which should cover the area where the patient is performing a large part of the day to day activities. Therefore, the devices need to have a long range so that information collected from the sensors can be transmitted using one of the available wireless communication standards.

Figure 1. Gartner Hype Cycle of Technologies
(Gartner, 2013).

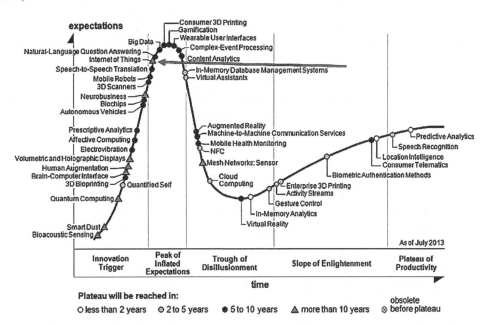

Because the majority of the sensing devices operate on a battery, the period of operation should be maximized and the battery charging should be scheduled when the patients are resting or over the night, when the patients are sleeping.

In some medical cases, like dementia, patients tend to become violent and they try to damage the monitoring equipment. For these special cases the monitoring system should be designed to be resilient and unintrusive in order to diminish the patient's intention to destroy it.

In the field of ambient assisted living (AAL) and ambient intelligence (AmI) a lot of work has been conducted around usage pattern recognition with the purpose of reducing energy consumption and CO_2 emissions (Chen *et al.*, 2013). However, the results can also be used for detecting changes in daily usage patterns, which can act as an early detection phase for dementia because the patients are getting disoriented and tend to skip some of the daily routine tasks.

The tests for dementia should be integrated seamlessly with the smart system that manages the intelligent house so the inhabitants are not restrained from exercising the daily routine. On the other hand the test should interchange and vary the order of the questions because the healthy users will become bored, and the interest for the system usage will diminish.

In the smart house of the future we can envision a wide range of devices designed to aide the inhabitants in performing domestic tasks. One of the futuristic devices presented by the scientific literature is an intelligent bath mirror (Allouch *et al.*, 2009) that can be used to display helpful information while the user is washing his teeth. At the same time the smart mirror can recognize the user and according to the user's profile it can ask a set of questions. This way the memory issues induced by dementia can be tested daily and the results can be compared with the results from the previous tests, and when signs of dementia symptoms are detected a warning can be sent to the specialized medical personnel.

2.3 Complex Event Processing

All the sensors and actuators engaged in patients monitoring are producing a considerable amount of information which describe the patient's health status. Considering that every read from a sensor can be seen as an event generated by a data source, the entire system can be envisioned as a system responsible for complex event processing (CEP) (Gyllstrom *et al.*, 2006).

An approach based on an event-driven architecture for recognizing activities of daily living in AAL is proposed by Storf *et al.* (2009) as a part of the EMERGE project. The authors emphasize the importance of early detection and preventions of the emergency situations at home, therefore limiting the appearance of fatal complications.

Event processing is not a new method for information processing in the IT field. Event driven application are used in active databases (Chakravarthy *et al.*, 1994), business processes orchestration, network management and monitoring. To overcome the issues introduced by the multi-threading programming the events are borrowed by some programming languages and frameworks which are designed from the ground up with event based communication support.

Usually the events that are consumed in a complex event processing architecture are categorized by the scientific literature as primitive and complex events (Xingyi *et al.*, 2008). The primitive events contain atomic information that was collected from a single device that measures and observes a specific environment or the human body (e.g. a single read from the blood pressure sensor). The complex events represent a collection of primitive events, a collection of complex events or a collection that contains both primitive and complex events (e.g. a collection of data gathered from sensors attached to the human body that describes the patient's health condition) (Hinze *et al.*, 2009).

A standard workflow in a CEP architecture is composed from the following phases: the primitive events are stored in a processing queue, in the second phase the events are aggregated and filtered according to certain rules, therefore at this phase complex events may be generated, in the third phase the primitive and complex events are processed for extracting relevant semantic relationships and in the final phase the subscribers are notified depending on the channels they have subscribed. The events delivery to the subscribers is guaranteed by the publisher.

As shown by Zang *et al.* (2007) in the performance evaluation test, event processing proves to be very effective and it is responsible for the increase in responsiveness and agility.

2.4 Distributed Systems

Dealing with a tremendous quantity of information requires a lot of computing resources, that need to be efficiently managed in order to minimize the processing time and to reduce the operational costs. Some of the most utilized platforms for creating distributed systems are presented below.

- **S4 (Simple Scalable Streaming System):** A general purpose, distributed and scalable platform that allows developers to build applications that are able to process continuous streams of data. The S4 architecture is backed by the Actor model this way allowing some of the components to be location agnostic and very flexible, thus it can run on clusters configured on commodity hardware. (Neumeyer *et al.*, 2010)

- **Apache Storm[2]** : An open source realtime computation system incubated by the Apache Foundation. Even though the project is still in the incubation phase it was early adopted by some of the most important players in the Web Industry that need to process a high amount of information.
- **Finagle[3]** : An extensible remote procedure call (RPC) system developed by Twitter, designed to handle concurrency and high performance computations.
- **Akka:** The Akka toolkit is a powerful tool for building concurrent and distributed applications that was built around the "let it crash" syntagm, thus allowing the applications built on top of it to be fault resilient. The actors have a well structured hierarchy where every parent is responsible for managing the failure of the actors situated on the lower levels. The parent actors have different failure strategies implemented that can be employed to handle a child failure (Restart, Resume, Stop, Escalate). In case of a resume, the failed actor continues to function normally. Also a child failure can produce side effects that affect the way other actors running in the system are executing their tasks. A restart command will create a new actor instance which will replace the current running actor. The stop command will stop the running actor in a secure manner by triggering some internal methods to preserve the processed data and to notify the watchers. The escalate command is used when the exception is not handled by the current actor.

2.5 Data Support for Internet of Things

The IoT components generate an enormous volume of data for which special approaches must be considered in terms of storing and allowing particular processing. Data can be classified in different categories, according to Cooper & James (2009): discrete and continuous, automatically generated and input by humans. Regarding data types, one can have RFID, address/unique identifiers, positional and environmental data, descriptive data, historical data, sensor data, physics model and command data.

Data collected from all the building blocks of the IoT architecture is first characterized by an immense quantity. At the same time, there are privacy concerns, since many of the sensors are associated with individuals. This requires caution when handling and processing all this information. One can define public and private access levels for exposing only the necessary data to the consumers. Usually, the information has a limited lifetime in which it is useful, so one can also talk about data expiration, a concept closely related to the IoT.

Taking into account the data format collected inside the IoT architecture, not all types of databases are suitable for storing this data. The information has a punctiform character, usually only a measurement result is collected from a sensor, so the traditional RDBMS systems are not satisfactory candidates for persisting the data. In some situations, RDBMS are used to mime the dedicated storage for IoT, but in most cases, this solution faces scalability problems and cost concerns. Even some of the databases following the NoSQL paradigm are not the best choices to accommodate to IoT, and prove able to adapt to the avalanche of data coming from the sensors network, so a need for something else arises to face the continuous changes concerning the data types and formats, paces and quantities. Because of the tremendous amount of records, data has to be intelligently stored and analyzed using performant and evolutionary algorithms developed in the fields of artificial intelligence or genetics, run in distributed and scalable environments. The particular type of collected data and the huge number of records means that individual records are not relevant but rather the collection of records is. Therefore special attention is paid for data visualization, dedicated graphical and statistical packages are created to sustain the databases themselves. Keeping in mind the source of data, i.e. large sensors networks, web pages, mobile devices and also the sampling rate, this data has a fast growing pace, which requires database to be able to support high writability and also an elastic backend able to spread among many datacenters.

From the wide palette related to the actual databases, there are some choices that fit the demands for data storage inside the Internet of Things paradigm. Some of them are especially tailored to deal with the data collected from the sensors, some of them are for general use but they accommodate well in the context of large data streams and simple data models. A few eligible database are presented as below.

2.5.1 Relational Databases in the Cloud

Even if the traditional RDBMS databases are not appropriate for usage in a distributed environment, the last advances in the technological area and theory of databases shifted focus again from the development of the NoSQL databases to the relational databases, issues like scalability are being addressed in certain circumstances. A new paradigm called NewSQL was born trying to provide relational database services in the cloud. Horizontal scalability is offered for the read operations, when it comes to write operations, the database is manually reconfigured by adding master write nodes in the distributed system. However, the NewSQL databases have their niche for the applications that need an ACID behavior together with a high level of scalability when confronted with many read operations. Some of the existing NewSQL solutions are Xeround[4], NuoDB[5], ClearDB[6] and VoltDB[7].

2.5.2 Key-Value Stores

Based on their internal need to have a highly available, highly writable and highly scalable database, Amazon published in 2007 a paper (DeCandia *et al.,* 2007) describing a new type of database called key-value store which is able to handle "tens of millions customers at peak times using tens of thousands of servers located in many datacenters around the world". The concept implementation was called Dynamo and it has brought many novelties in the database engineering field at that time, one of the most important being the fact that it was built on top of commodity hardware, not on dedicated and expensive servers, but despite this, the level of performance maintained was very high. According to the CAP Theorem (Gilbert & Lynch, 2002) consistency is sacrificed for the availability and partition tolerance, but this is acceptable for certain kinds of applications.

The data has an extremely simple model, based on a map or a dictionary, in which the information is inserted and extracted using unique keys, usually basic strings. There are no specific data types, all the values are treated as Binary Large OBjects (BLOBs), the client of the database has the responsibility for interpreting the data according to the application's needs. In the same trend focused on simplicity, the API is also extremely straightforward, the fundamental Create-Read-Update-Delete (CRUD) operations are exposed through *put*, *get* and *delete* methods. Summing the characteristics of the data model with the fact that the key-value stores are built with scalability in mind, they do not offer support for joins or searching mechanisms and no indexing technology is provided. If a search operation is still needed, it has to be performed in two steps: the first one is to get the value corresponding to a certain key, the second is to interpret the content and search for the specific request. The search method is inefficient and generally not used, the performances of the system suffer visible degradations.

The most representative implementations of key-values stores are Amazon S3[8], which is the commercial implementation of Dynamo, Project Voldemort[9], Tokyo Cabinet[10], MemcacheDB[11], Scalaris[12] and the list could continue.

2.5.3 Time Series Databases

For data that is represented as arrays of numbers indexed in time, the key-value stores have evolved in a special kind of storage system called time-series databases. The novelty element compared with the key-value stores is the fact that the data has a guaranteed temporal ordering. The usual operation against these particular databases are creating, updating, enumerating and destroying the time series. Metadata information facilitating data manipulation and giving a primitive support for data hierarchy, is sustained by most of the existing implementation at this time. The usual queries applied over a time-series databases could be related to (Faloutsos *et al.* 1994): "find past days in which the solar magnetic wind showed patterns similar to today's pattern".

The most representative implementations are Tempo[13] and OpenTSDB[14]. When it comes to cooperation with mission critical applications, IBM's Informix[15] is a strong option due to the integration with Amazon S3 which brings high availability and reliability, but it can also be deployed in private cloud environments too.

2.5.4 Graph Databases

An important segment of the data acquisition devices in the IoT paradigm is made up by the human operators, manipulating smartphones, tablets or computers and even devices acting in humans' behalf. Various relations can be built between data, regardless of content: geographical locations, relationships among people and many more. The correct approach for this is to use graph databases, which do a better job at modeling data and relations between records.

Data is represented based on the concept of mathematical graphs. The elements of a graph database are the nodes, links and properties. The concrete stored objects are in direct relation with the nodes, while the links model the relation between objects. One can add supplementary attributes to the stored objects through properties. The strength of the graph databases is revealed when they are placed in the backend of social networks or other kinds of applications that deal with entities which interact in different forms. Another strength lies in their high scalability, they easily able to accommodate billions of records. They are schemaless, but they support ACID transactions. The most representatives graph databases are Neo4j[16], GraphBase[17], InfoGrid[18].

3. MULTI-AGENT SOLUTIONS FOR CLOUD AND INTERNET OF THINGS GOVERNANCE

Artificial Intelligence (AI) introduced the notion of 'intelligent agent': an autonomous entity which can observe the environment through sensors and can act upon it through actuators, aiming to fulfill certain specific goals. A more concise definition was given by Woolridge (1999): 'an agent is a computer system that is situated in some environment and that is capable of autonomous action in this environment in order to meet its designed objectives'. According to Woolridge (1995) an agent must possess autonomy, which means that it operates without human intervention, social-ability by interacting with other agents using an agent-communication language, reactivity by perceiving their environment and pro-activeness, by being able to take the initiative. In a more extended sense, borrowing certain characteristics from AI, the agents are understood to have all the above features but in the same time deal with some mentalistic notions or even emotions.

Due to their complexity, some problems addressed by the agents cannot be resolved using single entities, but by a collection of them, designed to work together, using various approaches based on different algorithms, functional or procedural paradigms.

In recent years, the multi-agent systems have started to be used in many different fields which are based on independent distributed entities. Because the IoT paradigm covers a large number of intelligent heterogeneous devices which are loosely coupled, the multi-agent approach proves to be the best method to manage such a rich collection of cooperating objects (CO)(Ollero *et al.*, 2008).

Another important aspect related to the multi-agent system is their social ability which is implemented over a communication protocol so that the agents can exchange information about the surrounding environment.

Multi-agent platforms like JADE[19] are able to communicate using ontologies, thus enabling the agents to send a more comprehensive description of the environment by using semantically annotated data. In a dynamic IoT system where the devices are constantly registering and deregistering at runtime the context structure is often altered by these changes so the agents need to adapt to the new context. Even though the communication mechanism is a key point in a multi-agent architecture being implemented over the HTTP which is the backbone of the Internet, when dealing with a plethora of devices ranging from low energy consumption devices to industrial machines different communication protocols can be used. Leppänen *et al.* (2008) propose a mix between the HTTP protocol, which is considered a protocol with a lot of overhead and CoAP a lightweight communication protocol well suited for low power devices. The messages sent using a HTTP protocol to a device using a different communication protocol are translated using a proxy agent.

An IoT system backed by a multi-agent solution (Yu *et al.*, 2013) could also benefit from the agents mobility so that when the processing power of a device is exceeded the agent which needs more computation power can be relocated to another machine by conserving its state and resuming the work after the relocation is completed. The ability to interact with the web services also comes in handy when external data is needed to enhance the knowledge base. For example an agent which monitors the heart beats of a patient can query a web service linked to a medical database in order to calibrate the alarm triggers according to the patient's medical record.

4. INTERNET OF THINGS GOVERNANCE ARCHITECTURE

The term "Internet of Things" encompasses a multitude of solutions tailored to a variety of problems to which different activity domains are confronted. Unfortunately, most of the solutions are very particularly targeted and do not offer a communication interface with other similar systems. The map of the IoT technologies looks, therefore, very fragmented, the isolated islands leading to a metaphor more closely related to many "Intranet of Things" than to a single "Internet of Things". The FP7 project *Internet of Things Architecture* (IoT-A, 2014) aims to find common ground for all the existent platforms, to establish a general Reference Architecture that can be further used to build concrete and interoperable architectures. The identified fields on which IoT have relevance are Transportation/Logistics, Smart Home, Smart City, Smart Factory, Retail, e-Health and Energy and for them, the common elements were identified.

Whatever technological fields they are used in, they will, at some point, be confronted with different problems related to the smart devices and sensors they rely on. Issues like who is responsible with assigning the identifiers, how the object naming is standardized across the IoT, how object addressing is realized, how the collected data security is ensured, which stakeholder is accountable for solving any of the above problems and last but not least, which legal framework should be obeyed by the stakeholders are all solvable by an IoT Governance framework.

The medical field becomes more and more attractive for the new technologies that IoT emphasises. Gathering data from the patients and interpreting it in real time or off-line is the core of the e-Health process, the medical data, regarding individual people or statistically, describing a population of patients, is the foundation of the physicians' decision making process.

Keeping in mind the requirements for an IoT Governance architecture and based on previous existing Cloud governance architectures, a multi-agent solution which can be applied to the e-Health field, in order to allow patients suffering for various diseases, like dementia or Alzheimer to be remotely monitored through an IoT platform, can be built as described in Figure 2.

The collected data managed by the proposed architecture can be interpreted in real time or by request, serving the medical act in making the proper decisions for the monitored patients. Because the things/objects are geographically divided, a multi-agent distributed architecture can serve as a solid basis for this governance architecture. To orchestrate all the services that cooperate inside this framework, many specialized agents are foreseen.

- **Vendor:** Responsible to handle the communication with the cloud providers in order to acquire the cloud resources in terms of computation, storage or network and manage them accordingly to properly run the governance solution.
- **Deployment:** The software that runs on the devices composing the IoT architecture needs to be configured and eventually deployed to support the execution of the IoT governance solution. This agency is responsible for facilitating these tasks and handling the exceptions that could occur during the deployment and commissioning phases.
- **Proxy:** The IoT governance architecture allows the interested third parties (like monitoring or statistical systems) to connect and perform certain operations over the data generated during the IoT governance phases. The proxy agency offers the connectivity point through dedicated APIs which expose only the allowed actions.
- **Audit:** All the activities performed inside the IoT governance solution are closely monitored by this agent and all the anomalies promptly reported to the Audit Management agency for storing.
- **Monitoring:** Obtains information directly from the Things and passes it to the Things Management in order to be eventually stored.
- **Aggregation:** Sometimes the stored data collected from the things has to be aggregated in order to be processed by specialized genetics and evolutionary algorithms, all of this tasks are the responsibility of this agency.
- **User Interface:** Human factor is crucial in this architecture since it is the only one able to draw the main directions of the whole system. System administrators or the other accredited people who need to interact with various processes (for setting various algorithms used by the Aggregation agency, for example) connect to this agency.
- **Software Thing:** This agency acts like a simple Thing and uses the information obtained from the Aggregation agents in order to produce data on its own.

- **Things Management:** The system cannot directly access the storage layer, it has to pass through a proxy level which only allows authenticated agents to store the information in the dedicated databases.
- **Security Management:** Due to the sensitive character of the data stored and processed inside the IoT governance solution, there is an imperative need for a reliable and trustful security system to authenticate and authorize the parties, either humans, agents acting on behalf of humans, or things. This agency is responsible with ensuring the required level of security for all the components of the governance solution.
- **Audit Management:** The data collected from the Auditing agents is analyzed based on a set of given rules and according to the obtained results, certain notifications will be raised or actions taken.
- **Governance Management:** The IoT governance system follows a series of policies and rules describing the data flow and the interaction between the components, which are managed by this agency.

5. INTERNET OF THINGS SERVICES LIFECYCLE

In order to provide a continuous monitoring for patients suffering from dementia and other associated diseases, they have to be equipped with sensors specialized in the acquisition and transmission of differ-

Figure 2. Multi-agent architecture for IoT
(Copie et al. 2013).

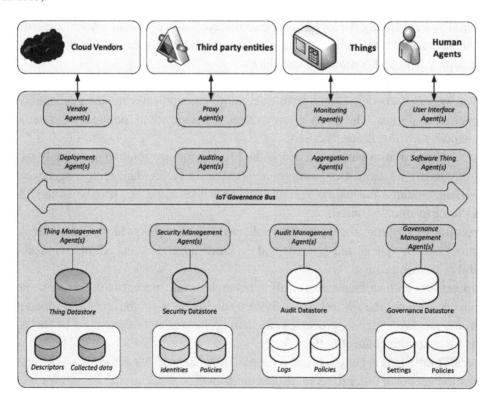

ent physical or chemical parameters, either wearable, implanted or located in the patient's environment. Every patient is different, the diseases require distinct parameters to be observed. One can associate a patient with a collection of different sensors, for example a patient needs to have his temperature and heart rate observed, while another has to be monitored for locomotor functions, falls and diabetes. One can also define a sensor service as a collection of sensors that can be reused for many patients suffering for a specific kind of illness. That sensor service can then be reused as many times as needed.

Then, a specific sensor service is instantiated for a patient and will be in strict correspondence with its owner. It is also possible for more than a sensor service to be instantiated for a patient if many diseases need to be monitored at the same time.

Every sensor service has a distinct life time and it is included in a formal life cycle (see Figure 3). This service needs to be managed from the very beginning when it is registered in the governance system, until it becomes obsolete (patient is removed from the monitoring program, or the sensors are no longer reachable, they fail, or other possible reasons).

According to the schematic architecture represented in Figure 1, some important operation need to be supported:

- **Design Time:** Relates to the phase a sensor service must pass in order to be published in the service repository. The sensor service is described from the syntactic and semantic points of view, establishing the functional parameters and the meaning of the service as a collection of sensors.
- **Provisioning:** Covers the phases in which the services are published and discovered by the interested parties.
- **Deployment:** This is related to the instantiation and commissioning of the sensors services inside the IoT governance framework.
- **Execution:** Treats the services management.
- **Retirement:** Refers to the service retirement due to expiration or other technical reasons.

Since the aim of the sensor services is to collect data from patients and considering the volume of acquired information, a storage layer is needed to store the gathered data together with the information strictly related to the IoT governance process. One can notice from the architecture of the IoT gover-

Figure 3. Services lifecycle schema

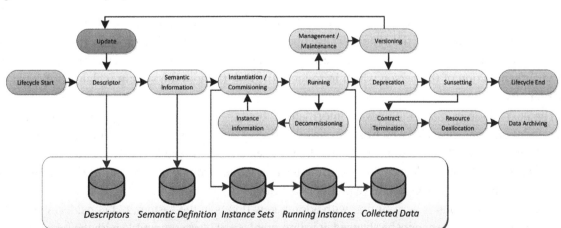

nance and from the sensors services lifecycle schema shown in Figure 3, that there is a close connection between the datastores persisting the crucial information required for the intrinsic act of governance and the phases through which a service crosses during its existence. The architecture of IoT governance emphasises four distinct datastores, as follow: Things Datastore, Security Datastore, Audit Datastore and Governance Datastore.

Things Datastore's purpose is to keep all the necessary information for the sensors services to be published, discovered and instantiated by the consumers but also to store the data collected from the network of 'things'. This is the most complex datastore inside the IoT governance framework, a conglomerate built from different database types that holds heterogeneous information.

The component used to keep the registered sensor services and actions in the discovery phase is the Things Descriptor database. This is the place where sensor services are described from the syntactic point of view and the relations between the monitored disabilities and the required sensors are being documented.

These services are exposed to searches performed by third parties, most of the times human operators. In this respect, the services have to be described as close as possible to the human language. The syntactic description is appropriate for a machine discovery process, but when it comes to a human, the semantic description is the best choice; this high level information is stored in the Semantic Definition database.

The services registered in the IoT governance framework are useful only after they are instantiated and launched in execution. The information about their status at a given moment in time is very important since it can offer valuable information about the condition of the service and could also be used by the monitoring modules. The databases responsible for maintaining the state of the sensors services are Instance Sets and Running Instances.

The sensors' main goal is to collect data from the patients. This information is usually analyzed in real time to facilitate taking of appropriate actions in case of emergency and also stored in the persistence layer for further processing and archiving. All the information retrieved from the sensors is handled by the Collected Data database.

6. USE CASES FOR IOT GOVERNANCE ARCHITECTURE

6.1 Scenario 1

The IoT governance involves the capability to manage things, which is translated in adding, updating or removing things in and from the system. These operations could be complicated since the participating things can be also complex in turn and require several steps, described in Figure 3. The first step is related to the authentication of the person which introduces the new thing in the system which is followed by verifying its authorisation rights.

The next action is to add the relevant information about the new thing, like its identifier descriptor, type, endpoint, characteristics which can be considered a syntactic definition of the thing, used during the discovering process. Because some data could be very sensitive as it relates to privacy, there is the need for a high protection level. Security information must be added, accompanied with different permission rights, since third parties can also have access to the data.

The update operation is very similar with adding new things in the system, but considering that the type of the collected data cannot be changed, it is immutable or at least compatible with the initial format.

Deleting a thing from the system involves archiving all the data related to it and storing it in dedicated data warehouses, followed by a datastore cleaning since the cost of keeping all the data associated to the removed thing in the cloud could be high.

The databases needed to support this scenario must fulfill some particular requirements, in order to provide the necessary functionality, reliability and performance. By correlating this scenario with the architecture of IoT Governance, represented in Figure 2, together with the sequence diagram from Figure 4, one can identify the requirements expected from different databases which form the storage layer, in Table 1.

6.1.1 Identities Database

The Identities database is the core of the IoT Governance authentication mechanism. This should offer high searchability since is the most used operation in this phase. This characteristic fits better with a relational database in the cloud, due to this specific orientation of the IoT Governance architecture.

Figure 4. Sequence diagram for Scenario 1

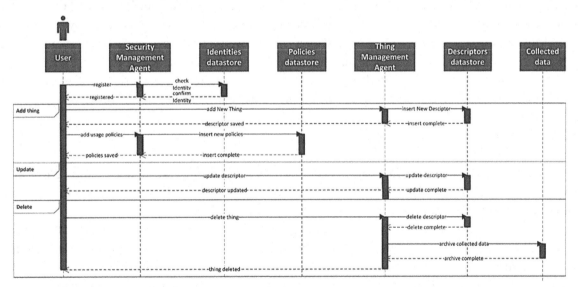

Table 1. Requirements for the databases involved in Scenario 1

Crt. Nr.	Database	Searchability	Transactional Support	Specialized Content
1	Identities	Yes	Yes	No
2	Policies	Yes	Yes	No
3	Descriptors	Yes	Yes	No
4	Collected data	No	No	No

6.1.2 Policies Database

Some types of data collected inside of the IoT Governance are highly sensitive in terms of privacy, implying the need for a protection level composed by different security policies and access rights, which are stored in a dedicated database and attached to a specific users. These policies are consulted very often, when the collected data is accessed for various purposes, so the database must be highly searchable. This also leads to a relational database in the cloud.

6.1.3 Descriptors Database

Every 'thing' managed inside the IoT Governance has its own characteristics in terms of identifier, descriptor, type and endpoint, which are stored on a dedicated database, providing search capabilities, especially for the things discovery phase. The descriptor database is also a relational one in the cloud.

6.1.4 Collected Data Database

In many cases, the amount of data collected from the things is extremely large, but its structure is usually very simple, consisting of different values associated to a timestamp and sometimes containing some metadata. The relational databases are not the best solution in this case, especially due to the fact that a highly writable characteristic is expected, to accommodate the data stream and to not lose any of the value taken from the registered things. Over the last years, many efforts have been made in order to improve the performance and provide databases with high writeability, reliability and fault-tolerance. Depending on the type of collected data, one could choose from key-value datastores, time series databases or graph databases, but there are also some combinations like key-value datastore packaged with a graph database.

6.2 Scenario *2*

This scenario is related to individual patients whose physical parameters are monitored through various sensors or group of sensors. The goal is to analyse all the collected data in real time in order to anticipate possible illness manifestations and prescribe treatments in a timely manner.

To achieve this goal, the governance solution must allow the registration of the things, which could be a single senor or a group of sensors, attached to an individual. Registration also involves collecting semantic information that will be used by humans, during the search operations performed over the collection of things. Together with this data, security and privacy policies could be established. For example one could define the level of data exposure attached to a specific patient, or the persons who can access this data, or the lifetime of the data and much more. Other policies that can be defined refer to the thresholds set in order to monitor the patients and take some actions if they are exceeded. After this setup, the sensors are ready to start collecting data and the patient's monitoring begins.

Based on the values collected from the sensors and compared with the threshold policies, various actions can be performed, for example phone call or message the patient's family or if the physical parameters are critical, a direct call to the ambulance (Figure 5).

Figure 5. Sequence diagram for Scenario 2

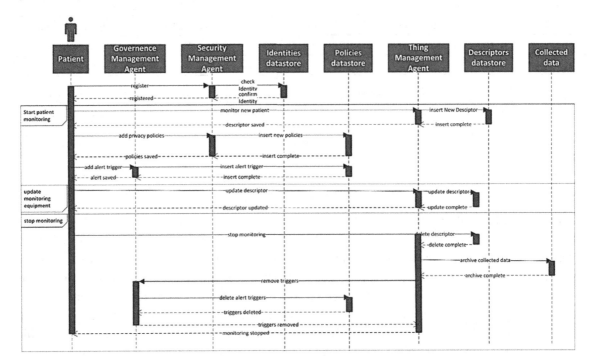

6.2.1 Identities Database

This is the place where patients are registered. Its requirements consist of high searchability since it should be at the medical centers disposition and it has to offer transactional support. They are met by using a relational database hosted in the cloud.

6.2.2 Policies Database

Together with the patients' identities, additional security policies and rights are defined. For example the list of doctors which have access to their data or the expiration interval for the data are stored in this database. Because the policies are often queried, it is important for this database to be searchable. It does not handle specialized content and there is also no need for high writability, so a relational database in the cloud will fit these requirements.

6.2.3 Descriptors Database

One patient has one or many sensors attached, with different characteristics and purposes. All this information about the sensors, like identifier, description, address, endpoint are stored in the Descriptors database, providing a syntactic description, used when a specific sensor needs to be discovered, the need for searchability arises. This database should be optimized mostly for reading, so a relational database hosted in the cloud fits very well with the requirements.

Table 2. Requirements for the databases involved in Scenario 2

Crt. Nr.	Database	Searchability	Transactional Support	Specialized Content
1	Identities	Yes	Yes	No
2	Policies	Yes	Yes	No
3	Descriptors	Yes	Yes	No
4	Semantic definitions	Yes	No	Yes
4	Collected data	No	No	No
5	Audit Policies	Yes	No	No
6	Logs	No	No	No

6.2.4 Semantic Definitions Database

The proposed IoT Governance architecture has a component that is mainly used by humans, for which the information should be presented in a high level manner. The simple description of a sensor's parameters is not enough; humans prefer information closely to their day-to-day language. During the setup of a new sensor in the system, high level information is also provided, consolidating the semantic of a registered sensor. This information is stored in a dedicated database which has to be searchable which contains dedicated content, usually written in XML format which can be queried with a SPARQL language, usually supported by a RDF database.

6.2.5 Collected Data Database

As per the first scenario, the data collected from the sensors has a simple structure but the streaming flow is usually extremely large. The need for searching is not pressing since this data is more likely designed to be analyzed through specialized visualisation tools. The most important requirements are in terms of high writability (lost data is not allowed) and scalability, due to the large amount of data. The NoSQL databases fit better depending on the type of the collected data. If the data is highly relational, graph databases are a good choice, otherwise key-value stores and time series databases can be successfully used.

6.2.6 Audit Policies Database

Various audit policies can be set for the data collected from patients, in order to detect dangerous thresholds for their physical health parameters. These parameters could be related, for example, to the level of glucose in their blood, the oxygen saturation, the blood pressure, or maybe values from bio-mechanical sensors, detecting if the patient has fallen in the house, or worst, outside. The audit policies must be read often and there is a need for them to be easy searchable. A relational database in the cloud fits to these requirements.

6.2.7 Logs Database

Collecting and storing data retrieved from the sensors in databases is not sufficient since we are interested in determining if the values exceed the established thresholds in order to be able to take the appropriate actions as soon as possible. These situations are logged in this specialized database. This is a good place to mine for the events associated with the registered patients. The need for a high writability leads to a NoSQL database of key-value or graph type.

7. CONCLUSION

Together with the emergence of the Internet of Things paradigm, other related domains like Pervasive Computing or Mobile Computing made significant progress towards bringing the smart devices and sensors much closer to humans, to improve the productivity and the quality of life. The e-Health field is not an exception for this rule and it is a domain in which many efforts have been made for many years to offer a better caring experience at the same time tackling cost savings.

In this chapter, we have presented an architecture for a scalable multi-agent system for Internet of Things governance with applications in home care monitoring. The usage of cloud computing enables this architecture to serve a big number of Home Care Systems in a safe and reliable way. Two possible scenarios have been presented, together with the relations between the things and the collected data. The storage layer was analyzed from the data structure and particular requirements and the database type for every datastore was identified.

We also envision that with the advance of technology in the future the ambient assisted living (AAL) will be perceived as an alternative for the in hospital treatment and the Internet of Things governance will play a crucial role in orchestrating the usage of the medical equipment embedded in an intelligent home.

ACKNOWLEDGMENT

This work was supported by the strategic grant POSDRU/159/1.5/S/137750, "Project Doctoral and Postdoctoral programs support for increased competitiveness in Exact Sciences research" cofinanced by the European Social Fund within the Sectoral Operational Programme Human Resources Development 2007-2013 and European Community's Seventh Framework Programme (FP7/2007-2013) under grant agreement no 318484 (FP7-ICT 2011-8-318484 MODAClouds). The views expressed in this paper do not necessarily reflect those of the corresponding projects' consortium members.

REFERENCES

Allouch, S. B., van Dijk, J. A., & Peters, O. (2009). The acceptance of domestic ambient intelligence appliances by prospective users. In *Pervasive computing* (pp. 77–94). Springer.

Ashraf, D., & Aboul, E. H. (2011). Wearable and implantable wireless sensor network solutions for healthcare monitoring. *Sensors (Basel, Switzerland), 11*(12), 5561–5595. doi:10.3390/s110605561 PMID:22163914

Chakravarthy, S., Krishnaprasad, V., Anwar, E. & Kim, S.-K. (1994). Composite events for active databases: Semantics, contexts and detection. *VLDB, 94*, 606-617.

Charu, C. A., Naveen, A., & Amit, S. (2013). The internet of things: A survey from the data-centric perspective. In Managing and mining sensor data (pp. 383-428). Springer US.

Chawla, V., & Dong, S. H. (2007). An overview of passive RFID. *IEEE Communications Magazine, 45*(9).

Chen, Y.-C., Peng, W.-C., & Lee, W.-C. (2013). A novel system for extracting useful correlation. In *Proceedings of Smart Home Environment Data Mining Workshops* (ICDMW) (pp. 357-364). ICDMW.

Cooper, J., & James, A. (2009). Challenges for database management in the internet of things. *IETE, 26*, 320–329. Retrieved May 20, 2014, from http://tr.ietejournals.org/text.asp?2009/26/5/320/55275

Copie, A., Fortis, T.-F., Munteanu, V. I., & Negru, V. (2013). From cloud governance to IoT governance. In *Proceedings of 2013 27th International Conference on Advanced Information Networking and Applications Workshops*. IEEE Computer Society.

DeCandia, G., Hastorun, D., Jampani, M., Kakulapati, G., Lakshman, A., Pilchin, A., & Vogels, W. et al. (2007). Dynamo: Amazon's highly available keyvalue store. *SIGOPS Oper. Syst. Rev., 41*(6), 205–220. doi:10.1145/1323293.1294281

European Commission. (2008). *Internet of things in 2020 - Roadmap for the future*. Information Society and Media.

Faloutsos, C., Ranganathan, M., & Manolopoulos, Y. (1994). Fast subsequence matching in time-series databases. *SIGMOD Record, 23*(2), 419–429. doi:10.1145/191843.191925

Gartner Says the Internet of Things Installed Base Will Grow to 26 Billion Units By 2020. (2013). Retrieved May 24, 2014, from http://www.gartner.com/newsroom/id/2636073

Gartner's 2013 Hype Cycle for Emerging Technologies Maps Out Evolving Relationship Between Humans and Machines. (2013). Retrieved May 24, 2014, from http://www.gartner.com/newsroom/id/ 2575515

Gilbert, S., & Lynch, N. (2002). Brewer's conjecture and the feasibility of consistent, available, partition-tolerant web services. *SIGACT News, 33*(2), 51–59. doi:10.1145/564585.564601

Graham, N., & Warner, J. (2009). Understanding Alzheimer's disease and other dementias. British Medical Association.

Gyllstrom, D., Wu, E., Chae, H.-J., Diao, Y., Stahlberg, P. & Anderson, G. (2006). *SASE: Complex event processing over streams*. arXiv preprint cs/0612128.

Hawley, M., Poor, R. D., & Tuteja, M. (1997). Things that think. *Personal Technologies, 1*(1), 13–20. doi:10.1007/BF01317884

Hinze, A., Sachs, K., & Buchmann, A. (2009). Event-based applications and enabling technologies. In *Proceedings of the Third ACM International Conference on Distributed Event-Based Systems*. ACM.

Internet of Things - Architecture (IoT-A). (n.d.). Retrieved May 19, 2014, from http://cocoa.ethz.ch/downloads/2014/01/1524_D1.3_Architectural_Reference_Model_update.pdf

Internet of Things - Erricson Report. (2013). Retrieved May 25, 2014, from https://labs.ericsson.com/research-topics/internet-of-things

Kinsella, K., & Phillips, D. R. (2005). Global aging: The challenge of success. *Population Bulletin*, *60*, 1–42.

Kleinberger, T., Becker, M., Ras, E., Holzinger, A., & Müller, P. (2007). Ambient intelligence in assisted living: Enable elderly people to handle future interfaces Universal access in human-computer interaction. Springer.

Kramp T., Kranenburg R. V., & Lange, S. (2013). Introduction to the internet of things. In *Enable things to talk*. Springer.

Leppanen, T., & Riekki, J. (2008). *A lightweight agent-based architecture for the internet of things*. Academic Press.

Network Society. (n.d.). Retrieved May 20, 2014, from http://www.ericsson.com/thinkingahead/n_s

Neumeyer, L., Robbins, B., Nair, A., & Kesari, A. (2010). S4: Distributed stream computing platform. In *Proceedings of Data Mining Workshops* (ICDMW). IEEE.

Ollero, A., Wolisz, A., & Banătre, M. (2008). An introduction to the concept of cooperating objects and sensor networks cooperating embedded systems and wireless sensor networks. Wiley Online Library.

Patel, S., Park, H., Bonato, H., Chan, L., & Rodgers, M. (2012). A review of wearable sensors and systems with application in rehabilitation. *Journal of Neuroengineering and Rehabilitation*, *9*(1), 21. doi:10.1186/1743-0003-9-21 PMID:22520559

Satyanarayanan, M. (2001). Pervasive computing: Vision and challenges. *IEEE Personal Communications*, *8*(4), 10–17. doi:10.1109/98.943998

Stankovic, J.A. (2014). Research directions for the internet of things. *IEEE Internet of Things Journal*, *1*(1), 3-9.

Storf, H., Kleinberger, T., Becker, M., Schmitt, M., Bomarius, F., & Prueckner, S. (2009). *An event-driven approach to activity recognition in ambient assisted living*. Springer Berlin Heidelberg. doi:10.1007/978-3-642-05408-2_16

Vogt, H. (2002). Efficient object identification with passive RFID tags. In *Pervasive computing* (pp. 98–113). Springer Berlin Heidelberg. doi:10.1007/3-540-45866-2_9

Weiser, M. (1991). The computer for the 21st century. *Scientific American*, *265*(3), 94–104. doi:10.1038/scientificamerican0991-94

Wooldridge, M. (1999). *Multiagent systems, a modern approach to distributed artificial intelligence* (G. Weiss, Ed.). Massachusetts Institute of Technology.

Wooldridge, M., & Jennings, N. R. (1995). Intelligent agents: Theory and practice. *The Knowledge Engineering Review*, *10*(02), 115–152. doi:10.1017/S0269888900008122

World Alzheimer Report. (2013). *Alzheimer's disease international, journey of caring*. Retrieved May 24, 2014, from http://www.alz.co.uk/research/WorldAlzheimerReport2013ExecutiveSummary.pdf

Xingyi, J., Xiaodong, L., Ning, K., & Baoping, Y. (2008).Efficient complex event processing over RFID data stream. In *Proceedings of Computer and Information Science*. IEEE.

Yu, H., Shen, Z., & Leung, C. (2013, August). From internet of things to internet of agents. In *Proceedings of Green Computing and Communications* (GreenCom) (pp. 1054-1057). IEEE. doi:10.1109/GreenCom-iThings-CPSCom.2013.179

Zang, C., & Fan, Y. (2007). Complex event processing in enterprise information systems based on RFID enterprise information systems. *Taylor & Francis Group*, *1*, 3–23.

KEY TERMS AND DEFINITIONS

Ambient Assisted Living: An intelligent system of assistance for a better, healthier and safer life in the preferred living environment.

Cloud Computing: Paradigm which offers computation, storage or networking on a service based approach, in a similar way in which other utilities like electricity, gas, water or telephony are provided to people.

Distributed Systems: A software system consisting in interconnected components that act together for accomplishing a common goal and communicate using message passing protocols.

Internet of Things: Interconnection of unique identifiable devices using the existing internet infrastructure and a variety of communication protocols in order to collect a wide spectrum of data for real time processing or for further analyse and storage.

IoT Governance: Essential activity reflected over the IoT systems to maintain the control over the increasingly complex components consisting in systems and services. Usually, the IoT Governance solves capital aspects like access control, keys and passwords management, logging and auditing or API integration.

NoSQL Databases: Databases that support a different model than the one used by the relational databases, usually represented by key-value dictionaries, documents of graphs, motivated by the design simplicity and higher availability level.

ENDNOTES

[1]   http://www.aal-europe.eu/
[2]   http://storm.incubator.apache.org/
[3]   http://twitter.github.io/finagle/
[4]   http://www.xeround.com
[5]   http://www.nuodb.com/
[6]   https://www.cleardb.com/
[7]   http://voltdb.com/
[8]   http://aws.amazon.com/s3/
[9]   http://www.project-voldemort.com/voldemort/
[10]   http://fallabs.com/tokyocabinet/

[11]   http://memcachedb.org/
[12]   http://code.google.com/p/scalaris
[13]   http://tempo-db.com
[14]   http://opentsdb.net
[15]   http://www-01.ibm.com/software/data/informix
[16]   http://www.neo4j.org
[17]   http://graphbase.net/
[18]   http://infogrid.org/trac/
[19]   http://jade.tilab.com/

APPENDIX: LIST OF ACRONYMS

AAL: Ambient Assisted Living

ACID: Atomicity, Consistency, Isolation, Durability

AI: Artificial Intelligence

API: Application Programming Interface

AmI: Ambient Intelligence

CAP: Consistency, Availability, Partition tolerance

CEP: Complex Event Processing

CO: Cooperating Objects

CPS: Cyber Physical System

CRUD: Create, Read, Update, Delete

EPC: Electronic Product Code

GPS: Global Positioning System

HCS: Home Care System

HTTP: Hypertext Transfer Protocol

IPv6: Internet Protocol version 6

IT: Information Technology

IoT: Internet of Things

MC: Mobile Computing

NoSQL: Not Only SQL

PC: Pervasive Computing

RDBMS: Relational Database Management System

RDF: Resource Description Framework

RFID: Radio Frequency Identification

SPARQL: Simple Protocol and RDF Query Language

SQL: Structured Query Language

TCP/IP: Transmission Control Protocol/Internet Protocol

TTT: Things That Think

WSN: Wireless Sensor Network

XML: Extensible Markup Language.

Chapter 7
Citizen Science, Air Quality, and the Internet of Things

Ilze Black
Queen Mary University of London, UK

Graham White
Queen Mary University of London, UK

ABSTRACT

This chapter discusses the emergence of the Internet of Things, using a case study of a citizen science initiative, focusing in particular on issues involved in measuring air quality. The core of the citizen science initiative was formed by a world-wide network of early adaptors of the Internet of Things who, motivated by public health issues, set out to create widely available tools for air quality measuring. With these tools, they established a global, citizen-led, air quality measurement network. Besides highlighting a number of social and technological issues which are involve any such enterprise, this chapter engages with the discourse surrounding the use of IoT in collective sensing projects. Two questions are salient here. Firstly, can IoT technology be used in a citizen science context to monitor air quality? And secondly, does the construction of these devices lead to a successful mobilisation around issues of air quality?

INTRODUCTION

The study of atmospheric pollution is admittedly an untidy science. (Meetham, 1952)

While there are many environmental factors that can affect our health and well being the air all around us is often perceived as a matter of lesser importance. It is only in the case of major incidents, such as leaks from chemical factories, the explosion at Bhopal, or radioactive fallout like that from Chernobyl or Fukushima that raise public concerns and demand action. This apparent contentedness might be due to two factors – as a major environmental matter air is seen as universal, shared and paramount. Invisible in its nature, it can be perceived as something that cannot be affected by ones individual actions. Second, despite the evidence and growing concerns over the effects of air quality, one could argue (even if incorrectly) that we are living in a much cleaner environment, when compared to the not so distant

DOI: 10.4018/978-1-5225-1832-7.ch007

past. In recent years, however, there has been a growing interest in and concern about air quality. As this research will argue, the conversation about air quality has been renewed by recent developments in technology and citizen science.

The data in this study is drawn from ethnographic research conducted in physical and virtual spaces, primarily between 2011 and 2013, of a group of early Internet of Things (IoT) developers and an evolving community of air quality activists. It uses theoretically informed analysis of data from interviews, mailing list exchanges and comments on online platforms. We augment the methods of traditionally qualitative approach, with its desire to understand the social world and its meaning for its participants, with elements of discourse analysis in order to uncover the ways in which this world is produced. It is from such a viewpoint that this chapter will address the relation between the citizen science, IoT and the complexities involved in measuring the air quality.

AIR POLLUTION AND SOCIAL AWARENESS

The discourse around air pollution is centuries old, while the legislative process is slow and most often ineffective. In Britain, the first recorded effort to combat air pollution dates back to the reign of King Edward I in the year 1272, when at the request of some noblemen and clergy, the king banned the use of sea-coal. "Anyone caught burning or selling the stuff was to be tortured or executed" (Urbinato, 1994). The ban seemed to have little effect, as in the 14th and 15th centuries, other measures to regulate the use of sea-coal were introduced by subsequent kings (Kotin & Falk, 1964). In 1661, John Evelyn, a notable diarist of the days of King Charles II, published the anti-coal pamphlet: *Fumifungium: or the Inconvenience of the Aer and Smoke of London Dissipated.* Pleading with the King and Parliament to do something about the burning of coal in London and its effect on the health of the citizens he wrote: "Aer, that her Inhabitants breathe nothing but an impure and thick Mist accompanied with a fuliginous and filthy vapour..." (Evelyn, 1661). However, his message did not have any effect, and the pamphlet was forgotten for more than a century (Staniforth, 2013). In the 19th century, the famous fogs were widely referred to as *pea soup*, or a *pea souper*, or as *black smog* and more frequent references to its effects on health and premature death were made (Stern, 1982; Urbinato, 1994).

In Britain, it was only after the Great Smog of 1952 that real reform was passed by the Parliament. At the time, it was thought that 4000 people had died from Great Smog. Later research placed the death toll around 12,000 (Bell & Davis, 2001). Parliament took action, passing the 1956 Clean Air Act (Davis, Bell, & Fletcher, 2002). Today, European air quality is managed by directives issued by the EU, set in place since 1980s with directive 80/779/EEC, which set air quality limit values (AQLVs) and guide values for SO_2 and suspended particulates (SP). Later directives set limit values for lead, nitrogen dioxide, and ozone (DNERI et al, 2004). In the Unites States, it was the investigation into the Donora Smog Disaster that led to the first federal clean-air act, passed in 1955. In 1948, the town of Donora, in the Monongahela River Valley, Pennsylvania, was covered in toxic smog caused by a weather inversion. It trapped a cocktail of sulphur dioxide, carbon monoxide, nitrogen oxides, fluoride chlorine and metal dust emitted from local coal burning plants and furnaces located in the valley and town. Over four days, 20 people died, and 7,000 were reported to be sick (Townsend, 1949). The clean air act forced the plants and furnaces to close down. It was in the late 1950s when the first links between air pollution and motor vehicle emissions were made, with the State of California enacting a legislation requiring its Department of Public Health to establish air quality standards for vehicle emissions. This led to the federal government's *The Motor Vehicle Exhaust Study Act of 1960* and subsequent legislation. Just like with air pollution in the previous century, some of legislative acts proposed later were seen more as a nuisance and never got passed or taken seriously (Stern, 1982).

Fifty years into their accelerative growth, the number of petroleum-fuelled motor vehicles on the roads, globally, has become a major source of air pollution (European Environmental Agency, 2015). In early 2016, the World Health Organisation issued a warning about deadly levels of pollution in many of the world's biggest cities. Pollutants not only exceed the currently set safe air quality values. They also kill millions across the globe (WHO, 2016). As the WHO has shown, air pollution has worsened since 2014 in hundreds of urban areas. The WHO warns there is now a global "public health emergency" that will have untold health and fiscal implications (Vidal & Helm, 2016). Only two weeks into 2016, and London had already exceeded its annual limit for nitrogen dioxide (Vaughan, 2016). As a study done by researchers at King's College London show, 9,500 Londoners die each year because of air pollution, twice as many as previously thought. "The premature deaths are mainly due to two key pollutants, fine particulates known as PM2.5s and the toxic gas nitrogen dioxide (NO_2)" (Walton et al., 2015).

Many have pondered why it has taken so long to recognise the deadly effects of air pollutants to human health and why there has been little action to combat this situation. In their very first attempt to encompass the analyses on correlations between air pollution and human health data, almost a decade after the Clean Air Acts were installed, Kotin and Falk (1964) pointed out the very problem with the concept of clean air in the *Annual Review of Medicine*. As they explained:

A major consideration in the recognition of potential adverse health effects of air pollution is the knowledge that pure urban air from a chemical viewpoint is virtually non-existent. Movement of air and dilution of pollutants in the large volume of the atmosphere are the two chief mechanisms of air purification. Interference with either, or, as most frequently occurs, with both simultaneously, results in the accumulation of progressively increasing levels of pollutants. (Kotin & Falk, 1964)

Bohm (1982), writing about the correlation between increased lung cancer and air pollution suggested that this inability to grasp the seriousness of the issue is rather a question of human perception: "Mankind accepts the risk of long-term and low-level exposure to carcinogens. As a rule, immediate benefits are sought and remote hazards ignored" (Bohm, 1982). Seaton, MacNee, Donaldson, and Godden (1995), reassessing the limited impact of studies correlating the effects of air quality and human health pointed out that there might be a problem with the scientific method of capturing this complex issue:

These findings have encountered some skepticism, partly because the concentrations of particles at which effects seem to occur are low by comparison with those to which many people are exposed in industrial workplaces without apparent harm; and partly because no plausible hypothesis has yet been advanced to explain the associations. (Seaton, MacNee, Donaldson, & Godden, 1995)

In response, by explaining how harmful particles behave in the environment and in the respiratory system, their study proposed the hypothesis that the "acidic ultra-fine characteristics of air pollution particles provoke alveolar inflammation, which causes both acute changes in blood coagulability and the release of mediators able to provoke attacks of acute respiratory illness in individuals."[1] They established the current leading theory on the mechanisms through which the particles harm human health – they cause an inflammatory response that weakens the immune system.

AIR QUALITY AND HUMAN HEALTH

It is widely accepted today that there are various air pollutants that differ, in their chemical composition, reaction properties, emissions, persistence in the environment, ability to be transported long distances, and eventual impact on human health. Yet, they share some similarities and can be grouped to four categories:

1. Gaseous pollutants (SO_2, NO_x, CO, ozone, volatile organic compounds);
2. Persistent organic pollutants (dioxins);
3. Heavy metals (lead, mercury); and
4. Particulate matter (Kampa & Castanas, 2008). Similarly, there is agreement in how each affect human health.

Indoor and outdoor air quality are linked. It is well established that "much of what is outdoors comes indoors. Estimates of the fraction of indoor fine particles that originated outdoors range from 46% to 84% depending on whether the house was air-conditioned and whether windows were left open" (Wilson, Mage, & Grant, 2000; Smith et al., 2014). Likewise, the rate at which outdoor air circulates through a house depends on the season and the weather. Indoor air pollution is not only affected by outdoor air quality, but also by furniture, cooking gas, chemicals used in the house, etc., all contributing pollutants to our environments (Spengler, Samet & McCarthy, 2000).

It is widely perceived that air pollution mainly affects the respiratory system and lungs. Short term exposure can lead to burning of the eyes and throat and difficulty breathing (Waldbott, 1978; Schell & Denham, 2003). It may also result in chronic lung disease (Kotin & Falk, 1964; Whittemore, 1981; Utell, Sawyer, & Warren, 1994), and trigger asthma attacks in adults (Schwartz, Slater, Larson, Pierson, & Koenig, 1993) and children (Wjst et al., 1993; Clark et al., 2010). Long-term exposure can reduce lung function and increase the risk of developing lung cancer (Nyberg, Gustavsson, Ja, Bellander, & Berglind, 2000; Smith et al., 2014).

As many epidemiological studies have shown, the effects of air pollution can impact other parts of the body (Utell, Sawyer, & Warren, 1994; Pope, Bates, & Raizenne, 1995; Schell, & Denham, 2003), causing heart attacks, irregular heart rhythms, and strokes (Seaton, MacNee, Donaldson, & Godden, 1995; Miller et al., 2007; Brook et al., 2004, 2010). The heavy metals such as lead, mercury and arsenic, as well as dioxins, can also affect the nervous system (Lasley & Gilbert, 2000; Kampa & Castanas, 2008), urinary system (Damek-Poprawa & Sawicka-Kapusta, 2003; Kampa & Castanas, 2008) and digestive system (Kimbrough, Carter, Liddle, & Cline, 1977; Kampa & Castanas, 2008).

A body of work has been carried out on the effects of air pollution on different social groups. For example, in infants and young children it can decrease nerve conduction velocity and impair mental development (Walkowiak et al., 2001), can be an indicator of poor health at birth (Chay & Greenstone, 2003; Currie & Neidell, 2004), and a reason for low birth weight (Almond, Chay, & Lee, 2005). It affects growth and development (Fogel, 1986) and leads to premature infant death (Currie & Neidell, 2005; Smith et al., 2014). Likewise, the effects of air quality have also been studied in the context of other consequences. It is a cause of multiple hospital admissions (Dockery & Pope III, 1994; Klot et al., 2002), absence from work and school (Park et al., 2002), restricting activity (Pope III, David, & Raizenne, 1995) and increasing medication use (Peters, Dockery, Heinrich, & Wichmann, 1997; Klot et al., 2002).

As many of these studies on the impact of air quality on human health have noted, the subject has often proven to be difficult due to the many complex factors involved in assessing the impact of one or other pollutant or due to the variety of health factors affecting test subjects. The relevant studies have also confirmed there is often some type of limitation involved, either due to the measurement of one or other pollutant and its effects over time, or with the variety of observed subjects and their individual circumstances. Likewise, studies have revealed their dependency on the research methods used, as there is often some element of prediction involved, either in the use of algorithms that correlate predictions and the actual levels of pollution, or with the quality of measurements conducted by AQ monitor stations. Thus any findings are often seen as estimates only (Currie & Neidell, 2004).

Writing at the turn of the century Gochfeld and Goldstein (1999) reassessed the lessons from environmental health from the 20th century in their article in the Annual Review of Public Health. There they acknowledged the rapid development of new technologies and new methods in the field of Public Health and in air quality discourse. Advances in analytics, data acquisition, modelling, toxicology and risk assessment, have all had immense impact on how studies can be conducted and how growing concerns over air quality could be addressed. They suggested three main areas lessons could be drawn from:

1. For science and technology to play lead roles in primary and secondary prevention, environmental-health scientists must participate in policy;
2. Environmental health problems and solutions are complex; interdisciplinary research is required; and,
3. Environmental health is a global issue. (Gochfeld & Goldstein, 1999),

With accumulated knowledge in this field of study and directives issued by air quality monitoring agencies, the impact of air pollution on human life is still perceived as gravely neglected. In the following analysis into the rise of Citizen Science and community-led air quality monitoring networks, this research will argue that the perceived failure of established science to deliver change and the quest to affect policy-making processes, have led to ordinary citizens adopting the technologies and organising themselves. A closer analysis of these desires and of the adopted methods and technologies used in research suggest the impact such a bottom up approach could have to increase awareness of the subject and subsequently lead to action in this field. Before that, the following section will address the technological advances that, as our research suggests, has empowered this popular movement.

TECHNOLOGICAL AND SOCIAL CHANGE: ARRIVAL OF THE INTERNET OF THINGS

Technological developments of the last decade have led to more advances in the application of sensor technologies and the rise of the phenomenon of the Internet of Things (IoT). Ubiquity of computing and an increasing number of electronic sensors applied to the diverse physical processes of the planet's environmental systems, body monitoring, and the augmentation of everyday objects, allow data capture, storage and analytics, now most often in realtime. The Internet of Things envisions a connected world of billions of smart things, devices, smartphones, smart cars, smart homes, and smart cities (Fleisch, 2010; Haller, 2010; Evans, 2011; Mitton & Simplot-Ryl, 2011; Stankovic, 2014; Behmann & Wu, 2015; Miller, 2015). Gartner Inc. forecasts that 6.4 billion connected things will be in use worldwide in 2016, and will reach 20.8 billion by 2020.[2] Cisco has estimated the number being even higher, with up to 50 billion devices being connected by 2020 (Evans, 2011).

The IoT has been presented as a way to make intelligent hardware more pervasive by reducing hardware size, cost, and power consumption. Another important factor was the development of open source software and hardware platforms, in particular, the microelectronic platforms with an easy to use Integrated Development Environment (IDE). The low cost platforms such as Arduino (2004), Zigbee (2006), Nanode (2011), Raspberry Pi (2012), and the like, have democratised access to, and use of, these technologies. This has led to a situation where increasing numbers of computing projects involving network sensing and other interactive digital urban intervention projects are today developed not only by large technology companies but also by a wide variety of individuals, groups and communities empowered by these technologies (Kuznetsov, 2010).

The other requirement of pervasive distributed sensor networks and the IoT is that of network architecture, with its need for devices to configure their own network configuration. Thus not only have devices became smaller, more numerous, and more pervasive, but also the networks in which they are located promise less hierarchical system approaches, and are thus also less susceptible to certain types of regulation. The latest developments in machine to machine learning (M2M) (Tan & Wang, 2010) and the development of autonomous IoT interconnected systems (S. Park, Crespi, H. Park, & Kim, 2014), in which machines and devices will be able to pass information and/or contexts between each other, will enable further machine autonomy in decision-making. It is this very idea of the interoperability of devices, networks and intranets - anytime, anyone, anything, any place, any service, and any network (Sundmaeker et al., 2010) - that is fostering the development in areas of IoT, such as standardisation, semantics, data platforms and management of interoperability both in technical and social terms.

CITIZEN SCIENCE AND COLLECTIVE SENSOR NETWORKS

The low cost of and open access technologies have given rise to two recent phenomena: Citizen Science (Riesch & Potter, 2014; Kullenberg & Kasperowski, 2016) and the Collaborative Economy (Bauwens, 2012). As Bauwens noted, "The players of this emerging collaborative economy are diverse: their objectives, attitudes towards collaboration and sharing, their methods of work as well as their business models are heterogeneous." Two major types of approaches can be distinguished in Citizen Science (CS). While many Citizen Science projects refer to an approach of science that mobilises crowds outside science to assists with observations and classifications, what we will discuss here is the other account, which refers to CS as a way of democratizing science - "aiding concerned communities in creating data to influence policy and as a way of promoting political decision processes involving environment and health" (Kullenberg & Kasperowski, 2016).

Alan Irwin (1995), in his seminal work *Citizen Science,* made explicit the link between the environmental challenges, global developments and rise of citizen-science initiatives. Irwin argued that these global challenges and in particular the environmental threats "can not be successfully tackled without a full consideration of *local* as well as global initiatives of *citizen-oriented* programmes". In 2010, Kera and Graham also introduced the term *Collective Sensor Networks* (CSN) to describe activities that involve sensor technologies and involve diverse groups of participants working to integrate sensor data from various environmental sources. Examples of such projects include citizen-led citizen science initiatives that often focus on solving environmental problems affecting people locally. In this respect, as acknowledged by the EU research policy study, "the questions that citizens – not just scientists – seek to answer can set the agenda for environmental research and policy debate" (Science Communication Unit, 2013).

There are a numerous examples of citizen-led initiatives that have tackled the local concerns of air pollution. For example the well documented struggle of African American residents of the Diamond subdivision in Norco, Louisiana, who through the late 1990s until 2002, "waged a heated campaign against the Shell Chemical plant adjacent to their community" (Ottinger, 2010). By use of analogue tools for air quality measurement such as buckets[3], "activists measured short-term spikes in air pollution levels and compared their data to arguably incommensurate regulatory standards to demonstrate that the air was unsafe" (Ottinger, 2010). However, retelling their story Ottinger argued that, despise the rhetoric of how citizen-science could influence the research directions and policies, there is a visible disparity between methods and data created by the citizens and scientists. As she pointed out it is standardized practices for measuring and evaluating air quality that determine to what extent and in what ways the nonscientists' knowledge production is assessed. Ottinger argued that "regulatory standards for air quality, combined with standardized practices for monitoring, provided regulators with a ready-made way to dismiss activists' data as irrelevant to air quality assessment" (Ottinger, 2010).

The advent of IoT has brought about a new opportunity not only for development of easy accessible set of new digital tools, but also their networked capabilities with its real-time data storage and analytics. It is, then, not surprising that the IoT was, early in its development, embraced by the CS movement, and used for intervention in the public health sphere and air quality monitoring. The following chapter will focus on discussing and analysing a case study based on one such citizen science initiative. The core of this initiative was formed by a global network of early adaptors of IoT who set out to create widely available tools for air quality measuring. With these tools, they established a global, citizen-led, air quality measurement network and subsequent sensing intranets.

Besides highlighting a number of social and technological issues that are involved in such an enterprise, such as a community approach to measurements and calibration, this chapter will foreground practical difficulties involved in such enterprise. While building tools and contributing to the spread of CS know-how is fundamental here, the difficulties this community faced is not accidental, but rather deeply routed in dichotomy of science versus CS discourse, already highlighted by Ottinger (2010). Thus we would argue for CS to be taken seriously and better organised it is important to evaluate the strength and weaknesses of past events, so that lessons can be learned for future causes.

CASE STUDY: PACHUBE AND THE AQE COMMUNITY

The community in question consisted (2011-2012) of developers and citizen science activists who associated themselves with one of the earliest IoT data platforms. It was formerly known as Pachube, Cosm, and, later, as Xively. In its Pachube incarnation, it was 'one of the first available Cloud-based services for managing sensor data, that provide[d] a light application programming interface (API) for sending data directly from sensors and its web environment allow[ed] the visualization of data in graphs' (Doukas, 2012). The London-based architect and designer Usman Haque initiated the Pachube project in 2006 as a monitoring system for his interactive art installations. Later it was opened up to other participants and by 2008, it provided a public platform and became a meeting ground for DIY sensor data enthusiasts. By mid-2011, Pachube accounted for an average of 6,000 users worldwide. At that time, it became a start-up company, as the Boston based cloud-service provider LogMeIn acquired it (Butcher, 2011).

Diverse interests motivated the users of Pachube. Initially, the largest group was enthusiasts engaging with their home energy monitoring systems (Dittus, 2012). In 2011, after the devastation caused by the tsunami in Japan and by the consequent meltdown at the Fukushima nuclear power plant, Pachube became network central for a citizen-run network of connected Geiger counters that measured nuclear radiation in real time. These sensors were set up by concerned citizens, in Japan, and later globally, as a response to the poor quality of the emission data released by the Japanese government. In less than 24 hours the interactive designer Haiyan Zhang created the first data map, visualising the Geiger counter data. The map pulled all of its real time data from the Pachube platform and showed the movement of radiation spills.[4]

The same year, Pachube's rather accidentally assembled user community gained a more coherent shape, as series of the earliest IoT meet-ups in New York, London, Madrid, and Amsterdam were set up. The broad and spontaneous public participation in the aftermath of the Fukushima disaster inspired a second citizen science interest group focused on air quality. It was during the January 2011 meetup in New York that the Pachube community organiser Ed Bordon and technologist Joe Savera suggested the development of a community driven air quality network. This led to the development of the Air Quality Egg (AQE) project, a sensor hardware device (Egg) and an air quality egg network. A year later, as a development of early prototypes of this affordable, open and easy to use measurement tool for air quality was underway, the group launched a Kickstarter campaign to drive up the interest of the wider public, to round up a group of supporters and to spread the great news of growing citizen concern about air quality.

In contrast to other existing projects the AQE project grow out not from a particular 'local community' concerned with a particular problem, but rather from a globally dispersed group interested in use of connected monitoring device. As people started to join the campaign, it was valuable to see what motivated these early adopters of technology and supporters of the AQE project. While the majority of Kickstarter supporters were often technologically aware enthusiasts interested in social tech, there were also many who were driven by common concern for the planet or for their own welfare and who were looking for technology that could support their struggles. When we analyse the responses to a question of what motivated them to join the campaign, we could distinguish three major themes. The first would be the already mentioned technologists involved with development of social technologies, as these examples illustrate:

E1: *I'm XXXX. I'm a London-based UX designer, who is interested in using pervasive technology to help improve people's lives. This seems like a very interesting experiment.*

E2: *I am a semi-retired instrumentation technician living in the high desert of N.M. I have a Pachube feed now just for hobby purposes. Interest in air quality is just concern with keeping the planet livable.*

As these comments show, such a community project seems to appeal to a skilled people who see the opportunity for their skills to be applied, even in retirement or in their free time. Similarly, it was attractive to technologists and activists involved in some already existing communities or to education projects, as illustrated by the following:

E3: *I am an architecture student working for a non-profit community design center called building community WORKSHOP. I am leading an energy education initiative, and we are working on a plan to implement home energy metering and feedback at community scale. I think air-quality goes hand in hand with efficient energy use and "healthy neighbourhoods". We are working on solutions to bring forward the benefits of sensor technology in making educated behavioral choices related to building energy performance in low-income communities.*

The second group are day-to-day activists who in general are interested in the common good, the health of common resources, and in activism as such. While expressing global concerns, this group is more concerned with local issues. Examples can be drawn from comments such as:

E4: *Hi, I live in London England and always wonder just what I'm breathing in, in this unnatural world we live in!*

E5: *I want to know what kind of air quality we have here in Valparaiso, IN, with Chicago being just upstream from us and all.*

E6: *Hey - I live in Atlanta, GA - Would like to monitor air quality. I'm about 2 miles from downtown and the junction of I20 and I75/I85.*

E7: *I am interested in the 'activist' angle - data that compliments or supersedes that provided by established power structures.*

The third group, and the one we are most interested in the context of this article, are people with existing health problems who are looking for the tools to explore their own environments and thus to tackle or self-manage concerns driven by their or their own or family's health.

E8: *Hi, my interest is in the levels of pollen, mold and humidity as I am asthmatic. Cheers from New Zealand.*

E9: *I am in Switzerland and they smoke so much here, they also use a lot of chemicals, from paint to the oils for heating..... I am sure this has affected my breathing these last years.*

E10: *My children have developed asthma symptoms, and I would like to know how the air quality is to see what correlation can be inferred from the data.*

E11: *My family lives several miles from the Rhode Island Central Landfill, which was never an issue until around September of this year, when foul gas odors began emanating from the landfill and spreading far beyond the landfill's boundaries. Sometimes the smell is so pronounced and gag-worthy as to induce headaches and nausea. I have a hard time believing that a gas so noxious could possibly be benign, and I'd love to contribute in any way to help measure and map air quality in our community.*

These examples corroborate the broader trends observable across responses received from 927 backers of the Kickstarter campaign. The growing community involved in supporting this project had a global character. Likewise, it seemed to engage citizens in both urban and rural settings interested in both indoor and outdoor air monitoring. Some of them had some other group affiliation, some didn't. As the community set off to develop the AQE device more direct references to overriding health concerns linked to air quality could be observed over time. Discussing the process of development or negotiating the thinking process, actors kept bringing up their motivational concerns. On the AQE group mailing list such cases appeared across time. As in following example after the launch of the AQE, one of the developers arguing for the validity of the chosen 'community approach' decided to tell a story to argue his point.

E12: *Years ago, I was interviewing a young woman in Chicago whose son had serious asthma. She checked the EPA website every morning to see what the air quality was that day. She made decisions about which streets to walk her son to school along and whether to ask teachers to keep her son indoors. The problem with this is that because the sensors were so expensive, the EPA data for*

Chicago came from six sensors, none of which were near her home. She didn't know which streets were better. She didn't know what the indoor air quality was like in her son's school. She needed the kind of data that can only be collected by many inexpensive sensors. She needed something just like Eggs and any of those three levels of data would have worked better than what she had.

While these are comments from only a few members, they illustrate well the three general themes, as well as how often overlapping their interests and motivations are. Likewise, they highlighted some other underlying concerns that echo across the community discussion we have observed on and offline. Example 3 touches upon the idea of behaviour change that such sensing technologies could encourage. The idea of behaviour change echoes across many other IoT projects today, suggesting technocratic framing for these developments and how well such citizen science network sits within the broader IoT discourse. Examples 7 and 12 similarly highlight the issue of concern that can be found across our study, that of power relations. Drawing parallels with established data sources, or criticising the shortcomings of existing air quality measurement stations or their network density, there seems to be a common distrust of government data. As we will see in discussion below, these underlying motives were also used to define more practical decision making processes and to negotiate the space for the community approach.

Community Approach: An Opportunity to Do It Differently

As community development of the Air Quality Egg device was underway, there were numerous discussions of what the distinct characteristics of this community-run network would be, of the device itself, and how to determine their unique properties. The slogan for the AQE Kickstarter campaign (launched March 2012) stated: "A community-led air quality sensing network that gives people a way to participate in the conversation about air quality." However, around that time there were a few other air quality measuring projects that sought to empower communities by providing tools and in a similar manner set about fostering conversation.

There have been a number of studies conducted on development of sensor devices, for example, measuring the pollution of motor vehicles such as diesel buses. In California the Dump Dirty Diesel Campaign commissioned 'The School Bus Monitoring Study' to highlight the health hazards posed to school children by daily exposure to diesel pollutants (Solomon et al., 2001). While this study focused specifically on bus emissions others use buses for broader citywide air pollution monitoring. The Swiss Scientific Initiative's project OpenSense, has installed sensors on the roofs of city buses and trams, to create public air quality monitoring resource (Aberer et al., 2010). Similar pollution sensing projects using buses have been trailed in the city of Sharjah, UAE (Zualkernan & Aloul, 2010).

Around the same time as AQE development took place there were other more citizen-oriented projects. In 2011, in New York, Google funded non-profit environmental health justice organization HabitatMap to develop an Air Casting application for mobile platforms. As part of this project Air Casting Air monitor was developed and later open-sourced as build-your-own hardware platform (Yap, 2012). In Europe, same year EU Seventh Framework Programme, funded consortium of European institutions to develop Everyware project. Part of this larger project, researchers developed an air quality monitoring kit – SensorBox for community-led air quality monitoring (Elen et al., 2012).

While AQE project developers were aware of these other explorations in the field, from the projects outset they tried to argue for a different approach. In the following examples, the authors have tried to distil the core difference this community chose to highlight. While various actors often repeat these themes in meetings and conversations, these particular examples are taken from the key developers of the project and thus best elaborate the underlying themes. As we can see in Example 13, key to this development was the idea of multiple developers and voices participating in decision-making, which was seen as a pedigree for the democratic nature of the project and the global characteristic of this community.

E13: *The most valuable part of it is the way it is extremely democratic and community driven project. Even from the concepts, to every part of development now: the hardware, the software, the productization of it. All those things are happening simultaneously from multiple communities.*

Example 13 talks primarily about the community of developers and the difference it makes in comparison to other similar projects that were seen as much more top down in the way they were executed. For example in case of Everyware project the developers of the air monitoring kit applied a scientific approach. As it was the established scientists and academics in field of air monitoring who developed this kit, there were only limited numbers of units built and used in trials by selected community members. In contrast the AQE community members were self-selected. Example 14 turns to the value of users/participants within AQE community and what they could bring to the interactivity and way the system operates and its supporting applications. This example is taken from the mailing list conversation at the conceptual development stage of the AQE development, and as such, well illustrates the aspirations of the project rather than the final outcomes.

E14: *We're not (i think) simply trying to build yet-another-air-quality sensing system that passively monitors the environment; or simply trying to replace an official network with a distributed/citizen-led initiative. we are (i think) trying to do something authentically participative that goes to the heart of why exactly people (i.e. citizens/normal people/everybody) would even want to *know about* and *do something about* air quality. by way of analogy, there's a difference between a security camera that continually streams footage in the hope of catching something significant; and a handheld still camera that encourages - actually *requires* - the bearer of the camera to think about the moment of taking a photo and then trying to recognise and capture something significant. there is a completely different participation with and interaction with the generated 'data'.*

This "requirement to think about" by providing a human feedback option to the otherwise passive observation system did not materialise in the AQE V1 and its system. However, the question about tools for user participation resonated across many discussions, and often provided a fertile ground for "thinking" further and conversing about such system applications, and in particular, the tagging mechanisms that could be employed. The third key argument about the uniqueness of such a community-driven approach to air quality measuring was that of network density. As Example 15 shows, the argument about the density of distribution of air quality measurement devices that such a network of everyday people could provide is what sets this project apart from "government" run networks or any other top-down infrastructure.

E15: *Even if our data is not validated scientifically or in that technical direction, I hope that we get the right information to say – there needs to be more study. The air quality sensors like this are really – it can be the go to for application real high-end sensors. I mean, the government has picked the places to put sensors, but what if we say, well, there are real pockets here that you need to be* *careful about. Or 'right around the school there is a traffic intersection that we have really, really weird readings and we changed our sensor three times and we still getting real weird readings', you know, further investigation! And that's a win right there. You know, weather or not data is great or not I don't really care.*

Like Examples 7 and 12, Example 15 hints of the power relations and how such tools in the hands of many could generate knowledge about very local issues that often are overlooked by a more centralised viewpoint. Opting for a development of a broadly available product rather than specific or experimental community solution, or release of just How To guide to monitor building was seen as only feasible way to reach mass user base. Likewise, Example 15 offers insight into the key, and the same time, most contested, value the project has created – that of data created by the device, system and community at large. The data will be discussed later on. However, it is important to note that it is this belief in data acquisition that is seen to empower the actors' agency.

Community Approach: AQE - A Measurement Tool and Its Calibration

One of the key components of the AQE project was the development of the air quality measuring device, the Egg, or AQE, that could enable popular access to the atmospheric data. It consists of a number of low cost sensors, mainly temperature, humidity, NO_2 and CO sensors[5], and a microelectronic board with an added Ethernet board for connectivity and on-board LED lights to indicate status. The components of the egg are modular, and all codes are open and published on GitHub. The device has an egg shape plastic closure and power adapter. Depending on their level of technological understanding, users can ether 'plug and play' the AQE or tweak it for specific case requirements.

In applying technology to any given natural phenomenon, there are two fundamental issues that are of concern. First is the question of measurement, i.e. what it is that is measured. The second is the question of the measurement tool's calibration. Within our given subject, both considerations encompass a complex set of issues. The most common way to measure air quality is perceived to be by measuring the presence of contaminants in the air. As already cited, the AQE V1 (2012) focused on two main pollutants, CO and NO_2 and on temperature and humidity. However, AQE was built as a modular unit thus other sensors could be added. (It should be noted here that today [2016] AQE V2 for $PM_{2.5}$ and PM_{10}, O_3 and SO_2 are also available).

While there is a standardised way of measuring pollutants, the approach much depends on measurement tools and approaches. Each pollutant can be measured in a variety of ways and units. The concentration of NO_2 is most commonly measured in micrograms per cubic metre of air ($\mu g/m^3$). The AQE device measures CO and NO_2 in ppb (parts per billion), the other possible way for measuring air pollutants. The measurement is defined by national standard, for example in the US EPA standard for NO_2 is based on ppm, while the European one are based on milligrams, however, there is a standard way to convert readings from $\mu g/m^3$ to ppb.

It was early on in a group's discussion when the decision to focus on the two main pollutants was made. As one of the main objectives was the creation of an easy to use and affordable device, the decision was made to apply low cost, off-the-shelf available sensors. The discussion regarding what sensors to incorporate into the device soon turned to the calibration of these sensors. It seemed clear from the start that off-the-shelf sensors might not provide the desired accuracy. On a mailing list, the conversation kicked off with suggestions of a number of ways that calibration could be developed. Example

16 presents one of the earliest suggestions that also illustrate the general stand of the community with regards to data reading.

E16: *The egg is hopefully going to tell us that "some of something" is there, but as useful as knowing there is 'some' there knowing _how much_ of it, and accurately, is going to be as important.... In the UK it is a legal requirement for cars to be tested annually. The equipment for that testing is available, at every MOT test centre. One possibility might be to take along one's egg to the MOT and use the test's data report as a means to at least know a single reference point.*

The DIY approach suggested in Example 16 soon received many responses. One of the predominant suggestions was that of *scale-free calibration* for which some high-end calibrated sensor used by a known source could be used to compare the data created by an AQE, as suggested in Example 17 by use of term 'official data':

E17: *I think we could calibrate the eggs using the official data... and perhaps it is not necessary to quantify that there are xxxx ppb NO2, but just qualify that NO2 level is low, medium, high or very high.*

Other methods suggested included that of 'Blind Calibration' and 'Network Calibration'. Blind Calibration, as discussed by Balzano and Nowak (2007), is one way of thinking how to make sense out of raw data read from sensors with no calibrated source. They applied the term *Blind Calibration* to "automatic methods for jointly calibrating sensor networks in the field, without dependence on controlled stimuli or high-fidelity ground-truth data". They propose an algorithmic solution a "novel automatic sensor calibration procedure that requires solving a linear system of constraints involving routine sensor measurements" (Balzano & Nowak, 2007). The group itself put the 'network calibration' approach forward. It is explained in the following Example 18:

E18: *"Network calibration" aspect: using the size and distribution of a large sensor network to improve on the sensing quality provided by its constituent devices. Picking up on a few discussion threads I suggest three phases/strands:*
- Collect known system limitations (how good/bad are our sensors really?).
- Collect recommendations for metadata to collect ("traceability").
- Review potential network calibration models, pick one.

However, soon into the discussion of both these methods the comment was made about the lack of supporting sources for these approaches:

E19: *There is no useful theory that anyone has put forward or a technical paper identified that supports the concept of "Blind Calibration" for a simple stationery sensor - that is making sense out of raw data read from sensors with no calibrated source. There appears to be a lot of wishful thinking.*

The problems with 'network calibration' similarly lacked technical papers to support this approach. Up until today, there has not been a network-wide calibration, and most of the AQE V1 observable on this network, use the sensor factory settings. As Examples 20 and 21 show people continued to contemplate and experiment with calibration, to draw the meaning from the raw sensor data, thus contributing to the community's shared knowledge pool.

E20: *Yes, I think in the long term calibration is very important to this project. While I am not an expert at calibration, I am involved with a project that will be testing some Sensaris Sensors against Alberta Environments reference method to see how the data compares for NOx. I had suggested that we test the AQegg sensors as well. I believe that we need to know what the sensor's data is saying, and how it correlates to a reference method. What is the variance, drift, etc.*

E21: *Based on the number of sensors (and data) that will be available and the fact that data will be 'raw' (uncalibrated, etc.) this looks like a very interesting project and challenge for applying pattern recognition techniques in order to either identify patterns (based on location of eggs, sensors used, etc.) and/or classify air quality (based on user estimation, correlation with other data, etc.).*

While the discussion about calibration is ongoing, the version 1 of the AQE was launched without specific method adopted and all sensors were not calibrated. The key argument to this approach, also reflected in statement on Kickstarter campaigns website, was made by a community organiser who wrote the following statement on campaigns discussion board:

E22: *A note on calibration: Impossible. We cannot build a consumer-focused product that requires regular maintenance/calibration of the sensors. Moreover, off-the-shelf sensors like we are using do not come calibrated, and so we would incur significant expenses to attempt to calibrate them after integration, only to still have the problem of re-calibration later on. Therefore, we can, and will, only look at trends in the data. Smart people, I'm sure, will find savvy ways to interpret this data for us, match it up with calibrated datasets (government or scientific institutions may be able to provide these), and /or learn things we never thought we would learn due to the sensor resolution, update frequency, and resolution we aim to achieve.*

However, this did not stop the community members from sharing their findings, thoughts and processes on this matter, and in the process create a resource of collective shared knowledge. In fact over 90% of all discussion on calibration took place after the Kickstarter statement was released. The discussion continued on mailing list and technical forums, and led the developers of AQE V2 to reconsider the importance of this matter. AQE V2 was launched later in that year with two additional AQE modalities, for PM, and for Ozone and SO_2. AQE V2 now uses fundamentally different sensor technology that is factory calibrated.

Furthermore, there have also been numerous community-led local AQE deployment projects that have published and shared reports on their findings and processes. The Citizens For Clean Air, in the Grand Valley in Northwestern Colorado run experiments with five eggs installed at different locations across valley. Not only they published and shared their findings with AQE community[6], but also made it to a local news channel[7]. In London, *Breathe Heathrow* project distributed AQE among residents of Heathrow airport area and as a result succeeded in informing broader policy debate and subsequent delaying of airport expansion in South East England[8]. Some members have developed AQE reading and geo tracking maps[9], and browser extensions[10]. Others have applied and perfected community-driven approaches to air measurements similar to the AQE community while using other types of devices.[11] These latest actions, recorded years later, show that processes started by such citizen science community group might not have immediate effect, but could deliver value as time goes on. Likewise, as authors would argue, such community-led developments can mobilise and connect citizens interested in air quality or other aspects of environmental research and public health.

CURRENT TECHNOLOGICAL LIMITATIONS

Sensors and Calibration

The complexity of issues involved in the calibration process goes beyond just the method of calibration. In any technological setting faults can occur frequently, at different levels. While it might appear that the device is still monitoring, the data it transmits, might be incorrect. Kingsly and Kaviyarasi (2014), analysing the fault detection techniques in Wireless Sensor Networks noted that:

In general, fault occurs in sensor network can be classified into two types. They are function faults and data faults. Function faults normally refer to abnormal behaviors of the sensor node, and this leads to network failure or breakdown of a node. Whereas in data faults, nodes behave as a normal nodes but they sense wrong information when compared to other nodes in the network. (Kingsly & Kaviyarasi, 2014)

AQE mailing list members similarly brought up the issues of faults, and numerous problems with 'any type of' calibration were identified. Those included not only technical i.e. those associated with hardware and software applications or processes, but also social and socio-economical ones, such as regulation standards in different countries. Here is a list of few problems identified:

- *The sensors will degrade over time.*
- *The devices don't always perform the method correctly. They get out of whack; they're technology.*
- *In developing software one sets up procedures.*
- *Calibration is only valid for a limited time.*
- *There are different definitions of calibration.*
- *I realized air quality limits differ from US to EU and elsewhere in the world.*

The issues of social context and its values were discussed within a broader Pachube community. The 'faulty node issues' were highlighted, for example, in a case of the radiation network in Japan, as they surfaced during the network data visualisation process[12]. In Japan, the members of community, alerted by the irregularity of readings from one such node, contacted the owner of the node to discover that it was affected by falling raindrops. Such power of many, as this example suggested, can have a positive impact for 'community network approach' argument and its practical values.

In a recent [2016] comparative sensor performance study, conducted by South Coast Air Quality Management District researchers, three Air Quality Egg V2 sensor devices were run side-by-side with Federal Reference Method (FRM; EPA approved) instruments measuring the same pollutants. Study found that overall, the three Air Quality Egg V2 sensor devices tested, each one measuring CO and NO_2, "were reliable (i.e. no down time over a period of about two months) with a high data recovery ~100%, but showed substantial intra-model variability". Furthermore, there seemed to be "a complete lack of correlation between the CO and NO_2 sensor data and the corresponding FRM data," noting that further "chamber testing under known target/interferent gas concentrations and controlled (temperature and relative humidity) conditions is necessary to fully evaluate the performance of the three Air Quality Egg V2 units."[13] However, the study conducted on $PM_{2.5}$ sensor showed that Air Quality Egg V2 not only correlates well with the FEM $PM_{2.5}$ data, but also outperforms other available sensor devices on market such as Dylos, AirBeam, and MetOne.[14]

Data Quality Reassurance

This study has only focused on one community and its contribution to the development of air quality measurement tools, and it has not analyse in-depth the other important aspect of this and similar projects. As it has been pointed out, the AQE sensor would not exist nor have any impact in isolation from the 'web or networked fabric of Pachube' (McCue, 2012), its online data repository. It is where the data stream graphs are updated every three minutes and data is displayed in human readable form. The Pachube data platform, and any other equivalent data hosting platform, is another important layer in the overall story. Not only it is at these online repositories where raw data get converted and displayed, it also where the data is archived and made available. Other important matters, such as data security, storing and service providing for data interoperability, are also conducted by these data hosting platforms, thus adding additional layer of complexity to the overall process, however seamless it might appear.

At the time of the early development of the Air Quality Egg (2011-2012), one Pachube/Cosm data corpus analysis noted: "Many Cosm feeds have not been annotated with a sufficient degree of detail. Even the scale and units of measurement can differ within groups of sensors that observe the same physical property." Likewise, the analysis of the study pointed to the lack of clarity and uniformity of metadata that supports the data streams. On the other hand, the study concluded: "This result does not put in question that there may be a potential ability of such community sensor activities to yield data suitable for building large-scale spatiotemporal models, but it clearly indicates that such data aggregation is only possible when the metadata supports it, and currently Cosm metadata is too heterogeneous" (Dittus, 2012).

Data platforms such as Pachube/Cosm and others, enables the access to data, and data aggregation from which further meanings could be derived, which, in turn, could present the data as an information or political tool. However, this part often presents itself as the most problematic. As Examples 23 and 24 reveals, seeing the patterns of change in data is not enough, and further discussion is needed about what can be done with such data, or what actions one could take in response to such data. What are the philosophical and ethical implications of data-empowered global citizens?

E23: *My question is how can I interpret these numbers. My family is mostly asthmatic and this would indicate to us that we should move right away... not trying to be alarmist but since we aren't totally sure what were looking at some info would be helpful. We want to know the meaning of the data over time. Especially anything we can do to calibrate things so we can see changes seasonal.*

E24: *After all with air pollution the origins are not always clear, your agency as an individual is very very little and CO2 is not to argue with on a local neighborhood scale. So you install an air pollution sensor and the air is consistently very bad (like it is and will be where I live). I know, now I can see it for it for myself. So what? What can I do? Move? Where to? Sell the house and not tell the new buyers why I move? How ethical is that? Having data in itself does not bring knowledge or change. Only agency to act on that data will bring information, knowledge or change. Without a*

*'how to do' kit that goes with the tech (is it not plain tech push otherwise?) about possible commu-
nity action, counter activities with plants, herbs and planting certain vegetation community garden
style, boycotts of products of companies that produce traceable pollution in an area, making pollution visible by putting up real blockades with wood and blocking intersections, cough consistently
within and with a whole street for a week... I don't see why it would makes sense to have this data.*

CONCLUSION

Assessing the effect of air quality is, as many studies have confirmed, not an easy task. Research in
health studies has shown dependency on the method used and, bias from predictions due to algorithms
that correlate between predictions and the actual levels of pollution. Thus any findings are seen as estimates (Currie & Neidell, 2004). Likewise, these studies would have been based on data measured by air
quality monitoring stations run by established government agency. As our study has indicated, the data
generated by these stations have limited scope (mainly due to their low distribution density), and have
thus stimulated a whole field of citizen community projects that aim to question government data by
the use of 'citizen sensor devices' that promise sensor access to very local environments. However, our
study also points out that data created by citizen-led initiative often lack accepted scientific standards.

Technically, air quality itself is a highly variable phenomenon: measurements of air quality can vary
greatly even at locations close to one another, and over a variety of timescales. Finding global, or average, figures can thus seem to be problematic. Politically, air quality is a difficult concept to mobilise
around: the pollutants are invisible, and their effects are usually widely separated, temporally and spatially, from the exposure. Nevertheless, as the authors argued, the rise of the IoT has fostered community
development of air measurement devices that in its turn have created space for discussion and practical
application. This can lead to a shared knowledge distribution base, from which empirical learning and
further initiatives can spring.

One aspect this chapter did not address is the socio-economics surrounding such citizen science
projects. Issues include necessary support systems and organisational structures. AQE development at
its outset was supported by the Pachube enterprise, financially and technically. Likewise, it was driven
by the enthusiasm of its key players. How can such structural forms be foster for future sustainability
so that such citizen-led air monitoring networks could be integrated into overall air quality monitoring
system or their data made interoperable, with relevant metadata and human feedback? Further research
and discussion would be an opportunity to address some of these issues.

While this chapter contributes to the field of collaborative sensing and of the collaborative IoT, it
also hopes to contribute to the discussions in the field of public health. As more and more devices get
employed to support human health and wellbeing, it is more important than ever to be aware of processes
and complexities involved in measuring and calibrating such devices and systems. While community-led
projects might not deliver the intended accuracy with of-the-shelf solutions, they can in some way foster
discussion, widen knowledge, educate and mobilise for common goals. Further explorations of how such
knowledge and abilities could be put to practical use and application are necessary to unveil the nature
and potentiality of IoT applications in the field of health science and public health.

REFERENCES

Aberer, K., Sathe, S., Chakraborty, D., Martinoli, A., Barrenetxea, G., Faltings, B., & Thiele, L. (2010). OpenSense: Open Community Driven Sensing of Environment. In *Proceedings of ACM SIGSPATIAL International Workshop on GeoStreaming*, (pp. 39–42). ACM. doi:10.1145/1878500.1878509

Almond, D., Chay, K., & Lee, D. (2005). The Costs of Low Birth Weight. *The Quarterly Journal of Economics, 102*(3), 1031–1083.

Balzano, L., & Nowak, R. (2007, April). Blind calibration of sensor networks. In *Proceedings of the 6th international conference on Information processing in sensor networks* (pp. 79-88). ACM.

Bauwens, M., Mendoza, N., & Iacomella, F. (2012). *Synthetic overview of the collaborative economy.* Chiang Mai: P2P Foundation. Retrieved August 14, 2014, from https://wiki.p2pfoundation.net/Synthetic_Overview_of_the_Collaborative_Economy

Behmann, F., & Wu, K. (2015). *Collaborative Internet of Things (C-IoT): For Future Smart Connected Life and Business.* John Wiley & Sons. doi:10.1002/9781118913734

Bell, M. L., & Davis, D. L. (2001). Reassessment of the lethal London fog of 1952: Novel indicators of acute and chronic consequences of acute exposure to air pollution. *Environmental Health Perspectives, 109*(s3), 389–394. doi:10.1289/ehp.01109s3389 PMID:11427388

Boehm, G. M. (1981). Air pollution and lung cancer. *Cancer Detection and Prevention, 5*(4), 371–374. PMID:7182064

Brook, R. D., Franklin, B., Cascio, W., Hong, Y., Howard, G., Lipsett, M., & Tager, I. (2004). Air pollution and cardiovascular disease - A statement for healthcare professionals from the expert panel on population and prevention science of the American Heart Association. *Circulation, 109*(21), 2655–2671. doi:10.1161/01.CIR.0000128587.30041.C8 PMID:15173049

Brook, R. D., Rajagopalan, S., Pope, C. A., Brook, J. R., Bhatnagar, A., Diez-Roux, A. V., & Peters, A. et al. (2010). Particulate matter air pollution and cardiovascular disease an update to the scientific statement from the American Heart Association. *Circulation, 121*(21), 2331–2378. doi:10.1161/CIR.0b013e3181dbece1 PMID:20458016

Butcher, M. (2011, July 20). LogMeIn acquires 'Internet of Things' Startup Pachube for $15m in Cash. *TechCrunch*. Retrieved on August 2, 2016, from http://techcrunch.com

Chay, K. Y., & Greenstone, M. (2003). The Impact of Air Pollution on Infant Mortality: Evidence from Geographic Variation in Pollution Shocks Induced by a Recession. *The Quarterly Journal of Economics, 118*(3), 1121–1167. doi:10.1162/00335530360698513

Clark, N. A., Demers, P. A., Karr, C. J., Koehoorn, M., Lencar, C., Tamburic, L., & Brauer, M. (2010). Effect of Early Life Exposure to Air Pollution on Development of Childhood Asthma. *Environmental Health Perspectives, 118*(2), 284–290. doi:10.1289/ehp.0900916 PMID:20123607

Currie, J., & Neidell, M. (2004). Air Pollution and infant health: What can we learn from California's recent experience? *The Quarterly Journal of Economics, 120*(3), 1003–1030.

Damek-Poprawa, M., & Sawicka-Kapusta, K. (2003). Damage to the liver, kidney, and testis with reference to burden of heavy metals in yellow-necked mice from areas around steelworks and zinc smelters in Poland. *Toxicology, 186*(1-2), 1–10. doi:10.1016/S0300-483X(02)00595-4 PMID:12604166

Danish National Environmental Research Institute, Center for Clear Air Policy, & Milieu Ltd. (2004). *Comparison of the EU and US Air Quality Standards & Planning Requirements*. Authors.

Davis, D. L., Bell, M. L., & Fletcher, T. (2002). A Look Back at the London Smog of 1952 and the Half Century Since. *Environmental Health Perspectives, 110*(12), 734–735. doi:10.1289/ehp.110-a734 PMID:12501843

Dittus, M. S. (2012). *The Cosm Sensor Data Set Data Integration of a Sensor Commons* (Dissertation). UCL, UK. Retrieved on August 14, 2014, from http://dekstop.de/temp/dissertation/Martin_Dittus-Cosm_Data-20120908.pdf

Dockery, D. W., & Pope, C. A. III. (1994). Acute respiratory effects of particulate air pollution. *Annual Review of Public Health, 15*(1), 107–132. doi:10.1146/annurev.pu.15.050194.000543 PMID:8054077

Doukas, C. (2012). *Building Internet of Things. Part 1*. CreateSpace Independent Publishing Platform.

Elen, B., Theunis, J., Ingarra, S., Molino, A., Van den Bossche, J., Reggente, M., & Loreto, V. (2012). *The EveryAware SensorBox: a tool for community-based air quality monitoring*. Paper presented at the Sensing a Changing World.

European Environmental Agency. (2015). *Air quality in Europe — 2015 report*. Retrieved on August 1, 2016, from http://www.eea.europa.eu/publications/air-quality-in-europe-2015

Evans, D. (2011). *The Internet of Things How the Next Evolution of the Internet* (White Paper). Cisco.

Evelyn, J. (1661). Fumifungium: or the Inconvenience of the Aer and Smoake of London Dissipated. In S. Staniforth (Eds.), Historical Perspectives on Preventive Conservation (pp. 262-269). Getty Conservation Institute.

Fleisch, E. (2010). *What is the Internet of Things? An Economic Perspective* (White Paper). Auto-ID Labs.

Fogel, R. W. (1986). Physical growth as a measure of the economic well-being of populations: the eighteenth and nineteenth centuries. In F. Falkner & J. M. Tanner (Eds.), *Human Growth: A Comprehensive Treatise* (pp. 263–281). New York: Plenum. doi:10.1007/978-1-4615-7198-8_13

Gasser, U., & Palfrey, J. (2007). *Breaking Down Digital Barriers: When and How ICT Interoperability Drives Innovation*. Berkman Publication Series.

Gochfeld, M., & Goldstein, B. D. (1999). Lesson in Environmental health in the twentieth century. *Annual Review of Public Health, 20*(1), 35–53. doi:10.1146/annurev.publhealth.20.1.35 PMID:10352848

Haller, S. (2010). *The Things in the Internet of Things*. Paper presented at Internet of Things Conference, Tokyo, Japan.

Helbing, D., Bishop, S., Conte, R., Lukowicz, P., & McCarthy, J. B. (2012). FuturICT: Participatory computing to understand and manage our complex world in a more sustainable and resilient way. *The European Physical Journal. Special Topics, 214*(1), 11–39. doi:10.1140/epjst/e2012-01686-y

Irwin, A. (1995). *Citizen Science: A study of People, Expertise and Sustainable Development*. London: Routledge.

Kampa, M., & Castanas, E. (2008). Human health effects of air pollution. *Science Direct, 151,* 362–367. PMID:17646040

Kampa, M., Nistikaki, A., Tsaousis, V., Maliaraki, N., Notas, G., & Castanas, E. (2002). A new automated method for the determination of the Total Antioxidant Capacity (TAC) of human plasma, based on the crocin bleaching assay. *BMC Clinical Pathology, 2,* 3. PMID:12197944

Kera, D., & Graham, C. (2010, November). Collective sensor networks and future communities: designing interaction across multiple scales. In *Proceedings of the 22nd Conference of the Computer-Human Interaction Special Interest Group of Australia on Computer-Human Interaction* (pp. 396-399). ACM. doi:10.1145/1952222.1952312

Kimbrough, R. D., Carter, C. D., Liddle, J. A., Cline, R. E., & Phillips, P. E. (1977). Epidemiology and pathology of a tetrachlorodibenzodioxin poisoning episode. *Archives of Environmental Health, 32*(2), 77–86. doi:10.1080/00039896.1977.10667259 PMID:557961

Kingsly, S. R., & Kaviyarasi, G. (2014). A survey of fault node identification. *Development Research, 4,* 898–901.

Kotin, P., & Falk, H. L. (1964). Atmosphere Pollutants. *Annual Review of Medicine, 15*(1), 233–254. doi:10.1146/annurev.me.15.020164.001313 PMID:14133847

Kullenberg, C., & Kasperowski, D. (2016). What Is Citizen Science? - A Scientometric Meta-Analysis. *PLoS ONE, 11*(1), 1–16. doi:10.1371/journal.pone.0147152 PMID:26766577

Kuznetsov, S. (2010). Rise of the expert amateur: DIY projects, communities, and cultures. In *Proceedings of the 6th Nordic Conference on Human-Computer Interaction: Extending Boundaries* (pp. 295–304). doi:10.1145/1868914.1868950

Lasley, S. M., & Gilbert, M. E. (2000). Glutamatergic components underlying lead-induced impairments in hippocampal synaptic plasticity. *Neurotoxicology, 21*(6), 1057–1067. PMID:11233752

McCue, T. J. (2012, April 4). 14 billion software as a service industry growth influences maker companies. *Forbes*. Retrieved on June 16, 2015, from http://www.forbes.com

Miller, K. A., Siscovick, D. S., Sheppard, L., Shepherd, K., Sullivan, J. H., Anderson, G. L., & Kaufman, J. D. (2007). Long-Term Exposure to Air Pollution and Incidence of Cardiovascular Events in Women. *The New England Journal of Medicine, 356*(5), 447–458. doi:10.1056/NEJMoa054409 PMID:17267905

Miller, M. (2015). *The Internet of things: How smart TVs, smart cars, smart homes, and smart cities are changing the world*. Pearson Education.

Mitton, N., & Simplot-Ryl, D. (2011). From the Internet of things to the Internet of the physical world. *Comptes Rendus Physique, 12*(7), 669–674. doi:10.1016/j.crhy.2011.06.006

Nyberg, F., Gustavsson, P., Ja, L., Bellander, T., & Berglind, N. (2000). Urban Air Pollution and Lung Cancer in Stockholm. *Epidemiology (Cambridge, Mass.), 11*(5), 487–495. doi:10.1097/00001648-200009000-00002 PMID:10955399

O'Rourke, D., & Macey, G. P. (2003). Community environmental policing: Assessing new strategies of public participation in environmental regulation. *Journal of Policy Analysis and Management, 22*(3), 383–414. doi:10.1002/pam.10138

Ottinger, G. (2010). Buckets of resistance: Standards and the effectiveness of citizen science. *Science, Technology & Human Values, 35*(2), 244–270. doi:10.1177/0162243909337121

Park, H., Lee, B., Ha, E., Lee, J., Kim, H., & Hong, Y. (2002). Association of Air Pollution With School Absenteeism Due to Illness. *Archives of Pediatrics & Adolescent Medicine, 156*(12), 1235–1239. doi:10.1001/archpedi.156.12.1235 PMID:12444836

Park, S., Crespi, N., Park, H., & Kim, S. H. (2014, March). IoT routing architecture with autonomous systems of things. In *Internet of Things (WF-IoT), 2014 IEEE World Forum on* (pp. 442-445). IEEE. doi:10.1109/WF-IoT.2014.6803207

Peters, A., Dockery, D. W., Heinrich, J., & Wichmann, H. E. (1997). Medication Use Modifies the Health Effects of Particulate Sulfate Air Pollution in Children with Asthma. *Environmental Health Perspectives, 105*(4), 430–435. doi:10.1289/ehp.97105430 PMID:9189709

Pope, C. A. III, Bates, D., & Raizenne, E. (1995). Health Effects of Particulate Air Pollution: Time for Reassessment? *Environmental Health Perspectives, 103*(5), 472–480. doi:10.1289/ehp.95103472 PMID:7656877

Riesch, H., & Potter, C. (2014). Citizen science as seen by scientists: Methodological, epistemological. *PUS, 23*(1), 107–120. PMID:23982281

Schell, L. M., & Denham, M. (2003). Environmental Pollution in Urban Environments and human Biology. *Annual Review of Anthropology, 32*(1), 111–134. doi:10.1146/annurev.anthro.32.061002.093218

Schwartz, J., Slater, D., Larson, T. V., Pierson, W. E., & Koenig, J. Q. (1993). Particulate air pollution and hospital emergency room visits for asthma in Seattle. *The American Review of Respiratory Disease, 147*(4), 826–831. doi:10.1164/ajrccm/147.4.826 PMID:8466116

Science Communication Unit, University of the West of England, Bristol. (2013). *Science for Environment Policy In-depth Report: Environmental Citizen Science*. Report produced for the European Commission DG Environment.

Seaton, A., MacNee, W., Donaldson, K., & Godden, D. (1995). Particulate air pollution and acute health effects. *Lancet, 345*(8943), 176–178. doi:10.1016/S0140-6736(95)90173-6 PMID:7741860

Smith, K. R., Bruce, N., Balakrishnan, K., Adair-Rohani, H., Balmes, J., Chafe, Z., & Rehfuess, E. (2014). Millions dead: How do we know and what does it mean? Methods used in the comparative risk assessment of household air pollution. *Annual Review of Public Health, 35*(1), 185–206. doi:10.1146/annurev-publhealth-032013-182356 PMID:24641558

Solomon, G. M., Campbell, T. R., Feuer, G. R., Masters, J., Samkian, A., & Paul, K. A. (2001). *No Breathing in The Aisles: Diesel Exhaust Inside School Buses*. Natural Resources Defense Council Coalition for Clean Air.

Spengler, J., Samet, J., & McCarthy, J. F. (2000). *Indoor Air Quality Handbook*. New York: McGraw Hill Book Co.

Staniforth, S. (2013). *Historical perspectives on preventive conservation* (Vol. 6). Getty Publications.

Stankovic, J. A. (2014). Research directions for the Internet of things. *IEEE Internet of Things Journal*, *1*(1), 3–9. doi:10.1109/JIOT.2014.2312291

Stern, A. C., & Professor, E. (1982). History of Air Pollution Legislation in the United States. *Journal of the Air Pollution Control Association*, *32*(1), 44–61. doi:10.1080/00022470.1982.10465369 PMID:7033323

Sundmaeker, H., Guillemin, P., Friess, P., & Woelfflé, S. (2010). *Vision and challenges for realising the Internet of Things. Cluster of European Research Projects on the Internet of Things*. European Commission.

Tan, L., & Wang, N. (2010, August). Future internet: The internet of things. In *2010 3rd International Conference on Advanced Computer Theory and Engineering (ICACTE)* (Vol. 5, pp. 376-380). IEEE.

Townsend, J. G. (1949). Investigation of the Smog. Incident in Donora, Pa., and Vicinity. *American Journal of Public Health*, *40*(2), 183–189. doi:10.2105/AJPH.40.2.183 PMID:15409515

Urbinato, D. (1994). *London's historic pea-soupers. EPA Journal*.

Utell, M. J., Warren, J., & Sawyer, R. F. (1994). Public health risks from motor vehicle emissions. *Annual Review of Public Health*, *15*(1), 157–178. doi:10.1146/annurev.pu.15.050194.001105 PMID:8054079

Vaughan, A. (2016, Jan 8). London takes just one week to breach annual air pollution limits. *The Guardian*. Retrieved on March 10, 2016, from http://www.theguardian.com

von Klot, S., Wölke, G., Tuch, T., Heinrich, J., Dockery, D. W., Schwartz, J., & Peters, A. et al. (2002). Increased asthma medication use in association with ambient fine and ultrafine particles. *European Research Journals*, *20*(3), 691–702. doi:10.1183/09031936.02.01402001 PMID:12358349

Yap, R. (2012). *How to Build an AirCasting Air Monitor*. Retrieved on June 16, 2016 from habitatmap. org/habitatmap_docs/HowToBuildAnAirCastingAirMonitor.pdf

Zualkernan, I., & Aloul, F. (2010). A Mobile GPRS-Sensors Array for Air Pollution Monitoring. *IEEE Sensors Journal*, *10*(10), 1666–1671.

Waldbott, G. L. (1978). *Health effects of environmental pollutants* (2nd ed.). The CV Mosby Company.

Walkowiak, J., Wiener, J. A., Fastabend, A., Heinzow, B., Kramer, U., Schmidt, E., & Winneke, G. et al. (2001). Environmental exposure to polychlorinated biphenyls and quality of the home environment: Effects on psychodevelopment in early childhood. *Lancet*, *358*(9293), 1602–1607. doi:10.1016/S0140-6736(01)06654-5 PMID:11716887

Walton, B. H., Dajnak, D., Beevers, S., Williams, M., Watkiss, P., & Hunt, A. (2015). *Understanding the Health Impacts of Air Pollution in London For: Transport for London and the Greater London Authority*. King's College London.

Whittemore, A. S. (1981). Air pollution and respiratory disease. *Annual Review of Public Health*, *1*(1), 397–429. doi:10.1146/annurev.pu.02.050181.002145 PMID:7348558

WHO. (2016). *Burden of disease from ambient and household air pollution*. Retrieved on June 16, 2016, from http://www.who.int

Wilson, W., Mage, D., & Grant, L. (2000). Estimating Separately Personal Exposure to Ambient and Non-ambient Particulate Matter for Epidemiology and Risk Assessment: Why and How. *Journal of the Air & Waste Management Association*, *50*(7), 1167–1183. doi:10.1080/10473289.2000.10464164 PMID:10939210

Wjst, M., Reitmeir, P., Dold, S., Wulff, A., Nicolai, T., von Loeffelholz-Colberg, E. F., & von Mutius, E. (1993). Road traffic and adverse effects on respiratory health in children. *British Medical Journal*, *307*(6904), 596–600. doi:10.1136/bmj.307.6904.596 PMID:7691304

KEY TERMS AND DEFINITIONS

Air Pollutants: Gasses, particles, organic pollutants and heavy metals in the air composition.

Air Quality: A popular term to describe a quality of air and its pollution.

Calibration: Process to determine the relations between two unknown quantities.

Citizen Science: Science research conducted by diverse group of people for perceived common good. Could include professional and nonprofessional scientists.

Collective Sensor Networks: Projects, groups and communities that use sensing technologies to create data from heterogeneous environmental sources.

Internet of Things: Internet of connected things, objects, vehicles, buildings, cities or any other entity in physical world that has been embedded with electronics for data collection and exchange.

Measurement: Depending from discipline, the value or number assigned to a property of an object or event.

Sensor Technologies: technologies with sensing capabilities to detect the events or changes in its immediate environment.

ENDNOTES

[1]   Slightly paraphrased for clarity

[2]   Gartner, Inc. forecasted that 6.4 billion connected things will be in use worldwide in 2016, up 30 present from 2015, and will reach 20.8 billion by 2020. In 2016, 5.5 million new things will get connected every day. Read more about this prediction here http://www.gartner.com/newsroom/id/3165317

[3]   Since their invention in early 1990s, buckets have become widely used by the environmental action groups, sometimes referred to as "Bucket Brigades". The air is collected in bucket that is lined with Tedlar bag. Air collected at regular intervals and samples sent to labs for analysis. For more details on Bucket Brigade see O'Rourke and Macey (2003).

[4]   The original Pachube blog post has been taken offline after Xively redesigned their site. The recorded snapshot can be traced via web.archive.org

[5]   The summery of AQE community discussion on hardware and sensor issues can be found on AQE wiki site. http://airqualityegg.wikispaces.com/Hardware-Sensors

[6]   Referencing here two documents published by Grand Valley community members: 'Frequently asked questions about the Air Quality Egg Project in the Grand Valley' and 'Monitoring Air Quality In The Grand Valley: Assessing The Usefulness Of The Air Quality Egg' by Nelson (2015).

[7]   TV episode is accessible online. Retrieved on August 10, 2016 from www.westernslopenow.com news website.

[8]   This was a temporary project developed by OpenSensors.org and postgraduate student Natalia Oskina. Read more on its impact on Open Data Institute's blog. Retrieved on August 10, 2016, from https://theodi.org/blog/a-year-in-open-data-breathe-heathrow-informs-policy-making

[9]   During the winter semester 2012/13 the bachelor students at the Institute for Geoinformatics developed modelling and visualisation of AQE network data. Their code can be found on GitHub

[10]   The founder of FTP software, John Romkey wrote a Chrome browser extension that can be downloadable from his personal blog. Retrieved on August 10, 2016, from https://romkey.com/code/air-quality-egg-helper-browser-extension/

[11]   Madrid based *The Data Citizen Driven City* project used AQE to set up *The Device Library,* citizen device *How To* database.

[12]   At 4th IoT London Meetup, designer Haiyan Zhang presented her work on radiation network visualisation. She described a case of such faulty node that was sending data 'off the beat', and how the data gave a 'clue' that there might be some problem with the node.

[13]   AQMD test preliminary results retrieved on August 1, 2016, from: http://www.aqmd.gov/docs/default-source/aq-spec/field-evaluations/air-quality-egg-v2_co-no2---field-evaluation.pdf?sfvrsn=0

[14]   Full list of AQMD tested devices and test results can be downloaded here: http://www.aqmd.gov/aq-spec/evaluations#&MainContent_C001_Col00=2

This work was previously published in Internet of Things and Advanced Application in Healthcare edited by Catarina I. Reis and Marisa da Silva Maximiano, pages 138-169, copyright year 2017 by Medical Information Science Reference (an imprint of IGI Global).

Chapter 8

The Internet of Things and Assistive Technologies for People with Disabilities:
Applications, Trends, and Issues

Hwa Lee
Bradley University, USA

ABSTRACT

With the Americans with Disabilities Act (ADA), the past two decades have seen a proliferation of Assistive Technology (AT) and its enabling impact on the lives of people with disabilities in the areas of accessing information, communication, and daily living activities. Due to recent emergence of the Internet of Things (IoT), the fields of rehabilitation, healthcare, and education are challenged to incorporate the IoT applications into current AT services. While IoT applications continue to be developed and integrated into AT, they are still at a primitive stage where clear guidelines are yet to be developed and benefits are yet to be substantiated to ensure the quality of lives of people with disabilities. This chapter provides an overview of the IoT and AT integrated applications based on the building blocks of the IoT, along with recent trends and issues relevant to accessing technology for people with disabilities.

INTRODUCTION

The IoT is reshaping our society by changing many aspects of everyday life of potential users (Bandyopadhyay & Sen, 2011). Smart health, assisted living, smart homes, and enhanced learning are only a few examples of possible application scenarios in which this new technology will play a leading role in the near future for people with disabilities (Atzori, Iera, & Morabito, 2010). The IoT for people with disabilities is likely to become more personalized to meet individual needs and user requirements. With large IT companies such as Intel, Cisco, Samsung, Google, and Apple developing the IoT ecosystems, newer and revolutionized IoT innovations for people with disabilities are emerging. The IoT allows medical devices and assistive devices to collect, store, send and receive patient and customer data and

DOI: 10.4018/978-1-5225-1832-7.ch008

is likely to become an important part of their lives. While the IoT is one of the hot technologies of this decade and a large number of studies focus on the technical aspects of the IoT such as management of resource constraint devices and mechanisms of interconnection mechanisms (Bui, Castellani, Casari, & Zorzi, 2012; Gluhak et al., 2011; Atzori et al., 2010; Sehgal, Perelman, Kuryla, & Schonwalder, 2012), a paucity of studies exists on the use of the IoT for people with disabilities.

There is little doubt that the IoT is highly likely to enhance the use of Assistive Technology (AT) by increasing the accessibility and functional capabilities for people with disabilities in the areas of communication, self-care, independent living, health care, mobility and transportation, and education and learning (Lee, 2009). While the IoT is at the early stage of making a positive impact on the lives of people with various disabilities, the potentials for the range of benefits are unlimited. According to Gartner (2013), people with disabilities make up 15% of the world's population. Assistive technology devices marketed to people with disabilities can also be sold to the other 85% of the population that is "situationally disabled" during some part of their day. With the growing population of elders, more attention needs to be given to the elderly citizens who require accommodations in the areas of cognitive, physical, and sensory abilities that are associated with aging (Morris, Mueller, & Jones, 2010). Hence, healthcare and related area professionals need to have a better understanding of how people with disabilities may interact with various IoT innovations to help researchers and AT developers to develop more user-friendly and effective IoT-based AT applications. In the following, basic building blocks of the IoT architecture are explored for AT integration.

BASIC BUILDING BLOCKS OF THE IoT ARCHITECTURE

A suitable architecture for the Internet of Things (IoT) requires the implementation of several and distinct technologies in computing, communications, and data mining (Lopes, Pinto, Furtado, & Silva, 2014). As architecture will have a significant bearing on the field itself and needs to be investigated (Gubbi, Buyya, Marusic, & Palaniswami, 2013), basic IoT architecture needs to be established and updated continuously to commission and decommission various IoT assets. Domingo (2012) suggests three layers of IoT architecture: perception, network, and application. This layer architecture represents a hierarchical structure of IoT systems. To complement this hierarchical view of the IoT systems, five technology building blocks of the IoT architecture can be examined: Radio Frequency Identification (RFID), sensors, sensor network, cloud computing, and applications. Recent IoT devices for people with disabilities represent at least three, if not all, of these building blocks. Figure 1 shows the five technology building blocks with various technological components. These building blocks become the basis for AT that support independence, freedom, and dignity of people with disabilities in various environments.

Radio Frequency Identification (RFID)

Radio Frequency Identification (RFID) refers to the system of electronic and computing devices which enables objects with an RFID tag embedded to be wirelessly identified and tracked. RFID use electromagnetic energy to wirelessly transmit data from the RFID tag to the RFID reader (Want, 2006). When the object embedded with the RFID tag passes near a reader, the electromagnetic energy emanated from the reader's antennas creates electric power for the tag to transmit stored data by radio wave to the reader. Major applications of RFID have been developed in the manufacturing, healthcare, and transportation

Figure 1. The five technology building blocks

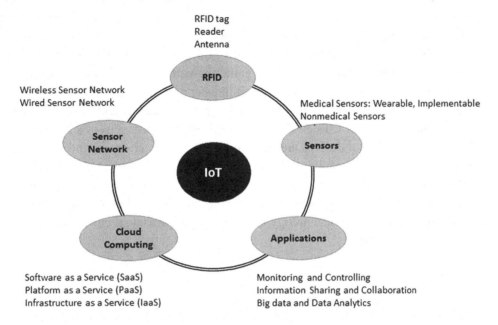

sectors. RFID has become an important building block for the IoT (Lee & Lee, 2015). RFID tags can provide much of the essential data that the IoT devices need to provide. When used in hospital or homecare settings for people with disabilities, RFID-enabled AT applications allow care givers to identify the exact location of the people inside the premises of care services and monitor their movements in real-time. El-Basioni, El-Kader, and Elissa (2014) proposed a smart home that presents a complete solution for a supportive environment that utilizes the RFID system with AT applications for elderly citizens with disabilities. Also, a smart home with an RFID system allows people with disabilities to make meaning-ful contributions by completing tasks without which would not be possible (Neßelrath, Haupert, Frey, & Brandherm, 2011; Mulfari, Celesti, Fazio, Villari, & Puliafito, 2014).

Sensors

One of the biggest drivers of the IoT revolution is the increasing number of low-cost sensors available for many different kinds of functionality (Swan, 2012). The sensor industry is accelerating technological innovations due to the market potential created by the advent of the IoT. Sensors can be either wired or wireless, and are used to monitor and alert change in environments such as temperature, weight, altitude, chemicals, moisture, light, sound, motion, etc. Sensors are often embedded in machines and devices. Smart sensor-based technology has enabled home automation utilizing various devices including light-ing and temperature control, home security management devices, and adaptive kitchens (Domingo, 2012). The application of sensors can be divided into two major categories: medical applications and non-medical applications (Ameen, Liu, & Kwak, 2012). The medical applications of sensors can be of two types: wearable and implanted. Wearable devices are those that can be used on the body surface of a human or just at close proximity of the user to measure temperature and monitor blood pressure, respiration, heart rate, etc. The implantable medical devices are those that are inserted inside human body to monitor cardiac arrhythmia, brain liquid pressure, etc. (Ameen et al., 2012). The sensor communicates with the other sensors to transmit collected data. A network of multiple sensors may be used to perform collaborative tasks. For example, a temperature sensor may work with a moisture sensor to keep the optimal level of the room condition for patients. Data generated by the sensor are used for data analysis and decision making. In another example, gathering patient medical data remotely helps provide emergency care, conduct diagnostics, and even administer preventive medical treatment. Accurate, automated, and real-time information reduce errors and improve quality and efficiency of medical services. Due to the miniaturization of IoT devices, sensors have the requirements of small size and energy efficiency. Various types of sensor devices are being utilized in smart environments for data gathering and management for people with disabilities (El-Basioni, et al., 2014; Joseph et al., 2015; Lambrinos & Dosis, 2013; Oniga & Sütö, 2014). Also, Busch et al. (2013) proposed a user-centered smart medicine cabinet with clear and self-explanatory interface elements along with AT features such as text-to-speech output. A noteworthy feature of this technology is the enhanced privacy, security, and trust of people with cognitive and motor disabilities.

Sensor Network

A sensor network connects sensors with one another, and transmits signals. While wired sensor networks are used for some IoT applications, they reduce the location independence of the sensors or sensor-embedded devices. A wireless sensor network (WSN) consists of a large number of tiny low-cost energy-efficient nodes that have small capacities of sensing, processing and communicating via radio medium (Demigha, Hidouci, & Ahmed, 2012). WSNs can be categorized into event-driven, time-driven, and query-driven (Barrenetxea, et al., 2008). While RFID is used for low-cost identification and tracking, WSNs bring IoT applications richer capabilities for both sensing and actuation (Lazarescu, 2013).

WSNs are gaining momentum in the IoT industry with the growth of IoT devices. Smart home, smart manufacturing, and smart city mostly depend on the WSN for the deployment of sensors and devices. Research in healthcare applications of sensor devices is currently under progress. Sensor networks applications in healthcare have potential for huge impacts. A wireless body sensor network (WBSN) with locally computational intelligence provides pervasive monitoring environment while at the same time guaranteeing the mobility of monitored patients (Aziz et al., 2008). These benefits can be realized through real-time, continuous vital monitoring to give immediate alerts to caregivers about patient status. As thousands of devices and sensors are connected, sensor networks need to be energy efficient, highly reliable, and secure.

Networking technologies in data collection allow users to control and monitor events in various settings. Sula, Spaho, Barolli, and Miho (2014) present an IoT based framework that utilizes a combination of robots, tablets, smart phones, laptops, and Playstation devices to help children with autism spectrum disorder accomplish various tasks. The integrated SmartBox device in this framework includes various sensors such as body sensor, chair or bed vibrator control, smell, sound, and remote control socket. This device is combined with various visual systems, such as objects, photographs, pictures, realistic drawings, line drawings, and written words for children who can readily comprehend the visual representation. Children with autism are highly interested and motivated by computers and touch screen tablets. Therefore, the integrated SmartBox device allows children with autism to interact, make choices, respond, gain new communication skills and create peer-to-peer (P2P) communication between children, caregivers and therapists. This assistive environment along with the use of heuristic diagnostic teaching process is expected to identify learning abilities and creative traits of students with autism (Sula et al., 2014).

An attempt to bring the IoT and AT together with the use of neural networks yielded a system that can contribute to the independence of people with disabilities (Oniga & Sütö, 2014). They propose a human activity and health monitoring system composed of micro-controller development board, a 3 axes accelerometer sensor, a heart rate belt sensor and communication modules, all of which is part of a smart environment with IoT and AT features. This proposed system is reported to have obtained positive recognition rates but researchers indicate that tests across settings and personnel are required for further utilization.

Cloud Computing

Cloud computing is a computing paradigm that relies on sharing computing resources such as servers, storage, bandwidth, and applications for an organization's computing needs. According to National Institute of Standards & Technology (Mell & Grance, 2011), "Cloud computing is a model for enabling ubiquitous, convenient, on-demand network access to a shared pool of configurable computing resources (e.g., networks, servers, storage, applications, and services) that can be rapidly provisioned and released with minimal management effort or service provider interaction." Cloud computing has five essential characteristics: on-demand self-service, broad network access, resource pooling, rapid elasticity, and measured service (Mell & Grance, 2011). The three main services are provided by the cloud computing architecture to meet the various needs of users: Software as a Service (SaaS), Platform as a Service (PaaS), and Infrastructure as a Service (IaaS) (Buyya, Yeo, Venugopal, Broberg, & Brandic, 2009; Cusumano, 2010). The IoT devices generate enormous amount of data, which have to be stored, processed and shared (Gubbi et al., 2013). Main deployment models include the public cloud, private cloud, community cloud, and hybrid. The community cloud is shared by multiple organizations with similar purposes of cloud deployment. The hybrid cloud is a cloud environment in which an organization owns and manages their private cloud and leverages a public cloud or a community cloud provided externally. Cloud computing has been recognized as a building block of the IoT architecture, since it can support gigantic data storage and processing needs of the individual sensors and devices. For example, the IoT devices can feed data to cloud datacenters for analysis and share data through the datacenter with other devices connected on the sensor network. Cloud datacenters possess the ability to increase and decrease computing capacity according to demand, while remaining accessible anywhere from any device. High performance data processing algorithms, control methods, and learning techniques can be installed and run at the centralized datacenters. The integration of cloud into IoT systems will accelerate the development of new IoT-based applications. With so much data generated by potentially billions of different sensors and devices, cloud computing will play the central role in filtering, analyzing, storing, and accessing data and applications in useful ways. Cloud computing can be one of the major potential enablers of the next generation smart environments for people with disabilities (Gubbi et al., 2013). Cloud-based IoT is considered a future trend (Dores, Reis, & Lopes, 2014). Cloud computing can decouple the AT devices from the computers by avoiding application installations on each available computer (Mulfari et al., 2015). IoT-based AT devices can make use of cloud computing to upgrade/expand functions without much of the user effort and time. Because cloud computing has such advantages as platform-independence, high reliability, high efficiency and scalability, the construction of cloud centers at hospitals and medical facilities can promote resource sharing and facilitate the development of highly reliable medical monitoring and management

Figure 2. A platform independent cloud-based IoT environment for ATs

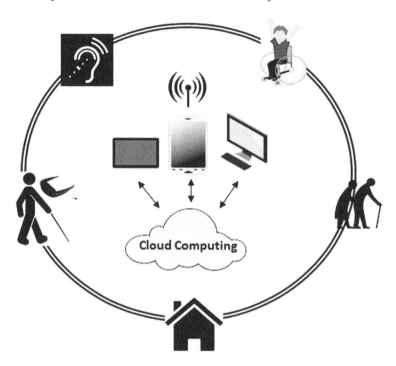

systems (Liu et al, 2015). Figure 2 shows a platform independent cloud-based IoT environment for AT devices for people with variety of disabilities.

Applications

The IoT can be classified into three major areas of applications: monitoring and controlling, information sharing and collaboration, and big data and data analytics (Lee & Lee, 2015). IoT applications are the most visible part to the users in the IoT system. IoT applications perform specific functions such as monitoring machines remotely, informing a caregiver of the real-time medical condition of a person with disability, and analyzing environmental data collected from sensors. Smart healthcare which monitors patients' living conditions and health status using small sensing devices and collecting their data over a network under daily life is expected as a new trend (Suzuki, Tanaka, Minami, Yamada, & Miyata, 2013). For example, IoT-based applications for fall detection will provide help and security for elderly or disabled people living independently. IoT applications for collaboration will require constant communications and interactions between devices and devices, and devices and humans.

Monitoring and control can be part of a much larger collaboration application. For example, Nest has more than a dozen other IoT devices from various external developers that will collaborate with its thermostat in home automation applications. While monitoring and control devices may work independently of each other, collaboration applications require multiple devices working in sync for common purposes. For example, various sensing devices in building and facilities can perform collaboration for a smart building operation (Yu, Kim, Bang, Bae, & Kim, 2015). Big data and data analytics is another promising area of IoT applications (Lee & Lee, 2015). IoT data can be very large when data is generated over a certain amount of time (Liu, Yang, Zhang, and Chen, 2015). These IoT data can also be put to cloud datacenters for processing (Ma et al., 2012). The capacity of cloud datacenters is growing exponentially and storage capacity is now less of a concern, and the proper use of it to add significant value to the users and organizations is a more concern. For example, analysis of the huge data stored at the datacenter may indicate certain patterns of when a person with disability is at health risk and may be able to alert health professionals of the impending problem. Busch et al. (2013) propose a user centered smart medicine cabinet that focuses on information sharing and collaboration. This technology provides a clear and self-explanatory interface elements along with AT features such as text-to-speech output function for communicating the system's trustworthiness state. A noteworthy feature of this technology is the enhanced privacy, security, and trust of people with cognitive and motor disabilities. While the above discussions are general and applicable for wide areas of the communities, the following section focuses on the AT applications in the context of people with disabilities.

THE IoT-INTEGRATED STATE-OF-THE-ART ASSISTIVE TECHNOLOGY

Assistive Technology (AT) has been developed to increase the quality of life of people with disabilities with improved services in education, rehabilitation, and healthcare (Alper & Raharinirina, 2006; Lee & Templeton, 2008; Scherer & Cushman, 2001). As the available features and options of AT have increased, their use has been more widely considered and recommended (Scherer & Cushman, 2001). According to the U.S. "Technology-Related Assistance of Individuals with Disabilities Act of 1988" (P.L. 100-407), Assistive Technology is defined as "any item, piece of equipment, or product system, whether acquired commercially off the shelf, modified, or customized, that is used to increase, maintain, or improve functional capabilities of individuals with disabilities." Types of AT include communication tools including text-voice converter, education aides for reading and writing, daily living devices such as robotics for household maintenance, mobility, and home automation such as smoke detectors, remote lighting, and water control. Since the advent of the IoT, some of the traditional ATs have been gradually integrated into IoT capabilities. Types of disabilities that are currently supported with IoT-integrated ATs include hearing, vision, mobility, cognition, and learning disabilities. This section explores what IoT-integrated ATs have been developed and are under development to empower the people with disabilities. In the following, we discuss IoT-integrated ATs for people with hearing impairment, visual impairments, and mobility disabilities.

IoT Applications for People Who Are Deaf or Hearing Impaired

The IoT is improving the lives of the hearing impaired and deaf. People who are hearing impaired can benefit from external or internal (implanted in the ear) AT devices and sensors that helps improve hearing. The three major design features of AT devices for the hearing impaired are: sound amplification, visual information output (e.g., flashing lights, sign language, and text output) and tactile output (e.g., vibrating alarm clock). In an IoT-based home automation setting, sensors monitor the surrounding environment and detect certain events such as heat, smoke or fire that triggers an alarm signal which in turn is sent to the control station. The control station forwards it to the AT device as an amplified alarm signal for the hearing impaired or flash signal for the deaf.

HandTalk is a low-cost, portable gesture-to-speech glove prototype designed to help the hearing impaired communicate with those who are not familiar with the American Sign Language (ASL) (Sarji, 2008). HandTalk has a simple mechanism to switch from standby to ready mode and back, and uses commercial-off-the-shelf applications compatible with standard cell phones and hand held devices. The glove is fitted with flex sensors which sense the position of the fingers and sends it to a monitoring station using Bluetooth. If the position data matches the set of values associated with an ASL sign of a stored database, the sign is converted into text and finally into speech.

The hearing aid market is one of the largest markets for the hearing impaired. A number of tech companies are competing to grab the hearing aid market with IoT integration. In the 2015 International Consumer Electronic Show, Siemens has introduced the EasyTek smart hearing aid system which adds functions and connectivity of each hearing-aid via Bluetooth to an EasyTek disc that people wear around their neck. The EasyTek disc is used to control the volume in the device, or turn the hearing aid on or off. The device also connects via Bluetooth to the Siemens EasyTek app on iOS or Android devices to control the parameters of the hearing aid (iTunes, 2016). The device has noise cancellation technology that removes noise and amplifies the voice of the person who is directly in front of the hearing aid wearer. This system exemplifies the idea of the IoT-integrated monitoring and control. Smart Hearing Aid, a Bluetooth ear set with a hearing aid feature is another example of using smartphones for hearing aids. While wirelessly connected to users' smartphones, Smart Hearing Aid provides basic ear set features such as hands-free voice calling and CD-quality music play and offers a four-channel hearing aid feature for people with hearing loss via a smartphone app (SK Telecom, 2015). Building on the existing Bluetooth standard that is widely supported in today's smartphones, tablets and personal computers, the IoT will give hearing-impaired users the same choice of products and opportunities as everyone else.

The individual hearing aid system collects data about device setting, age, gender, audio preferences and their everyday listening environments. These data can be uploaded to the cloud datacenter for further analysis. Big data analytics of hearing aids is another example of a paradigm shift in the hearing science. The IoT enables the recording of personalized hearing adjustment and linking the data for further remote analysis at the datacenters. In the near future, hearing aid users will get the opportunity to participate in hearing aid development. Results by hundreds of thousands of users will be submitted to big data analysis engines, aimed at algorithm optimization for audiologists (de Vries, 2014). The IoT-integrated hearing aids fully realize the application of monitoring and control, information sharing and collaboration, and big data and data analytics. One of the more recent medical technologies, cochlear implant (CI) (American Academy of Audiology, n.d.), has been widely implemented for infants as young as 3 months old. The effectiveness of CI has been well-received but not without resistance from the deaf community. Considering the critical language acquisition period hypothesis, CI is considered most effective when done as early as possible for the acquisition of speech sounds. Whether CI is the miracle ear as some consider it is yet to be witnessed with further efficacy studies. The good news for the deaf is that recent CI technology has shifted from auditory based only system to an IoT-integrated system with additional text and image based output.

Another application of the IoT-integrated ATs for the hearing impaired and a deaf is in the area of home networking. LIFX pioneered a smart light with the wifi-enabled, multi-colored LED that is controllable via a smart device (LIFX, n.d.). LIFX light bulbs flash red to let hearing impaired users know there might be danger from elevated smoke or carbon monoxide (CO) levels. The environment also has a multitude of Internet-connected displays, RFID, and other near field communication (NFC) scanners. The deaf person brings a tag which is continuously monitored by a scanner. As his identity and location and subsequent preferences are known to the LIFX systems, the connected displays in the person's vicinity can adapt their signage to the appropriate modality.

IoT Applications for People Who Are Blind or Visually Impaired

The three main common design features of AT applications for people who are blind or visually impaired are: magnification (e.g., zoom text, large fonts), auditory output (e.g., screen reader, text to speech output devices), and tactile information output (e.g., braille, raised maps). Individuals who are blind have been less dependent upon other individuals due to AT applications that enable them to complete tasks in daily living skills. These include color and pattern analyzer for dressing and speech output applications for accessing information on the web, books, and emails. As a navigation tool for people who are blind, the white cane, a tactile based device, has been used for several decades. Multiple IoT-integration projects will give more options for people who are blind, and the white cane may become a thing of the past. The Indoor Navigation Project at Curtin University will enable people who are blind to sense their surroundings using special multi-sensor array technology (Curtin University, 2013). The special multi-sensor array technology senses an entire room's features, builds a virtual map of it and communicates this to the user. Unlike a cane with limited range of sensing, the multi-sensor device covers a wide range and types of sensing and mapping including the change of velocity, images, or noise in an indoor environment.

A 3-D navigation system for the blind was developed at the Institute of Intelligent Systems and Robotics at the Pierre and Marie Curie University in Paris, France (Jablonski, 2012). It consists of a pair of glasses equipped with cameras and sensors utilizing sensing systems for robots, and a handheld electronic Braille device. The system produces a 3-D map of the wearer's environment and his/her position within it that is constantly updated and displayed in a simplified form on the handheld device and helps blind people to move about indoor and outdoor spaces independently. It uses a collection of accelerometers and gyroscopes that keeps track of the user's location and speed. This information is combined with the image to determine the user's position in relation to other objects, which are transmitted to the handheld Braille device to be displayed as a dynamic tactile map. Recently, a navigation system using a wearable sensor and social sensors to increase situational awareness for the blind utilizing real-time localization technologies was created (Joseph et al., 2013). This navigation system promotes independent traveling for the blind by utilizing the information of the events gathered from the Internet.

Another IoT-based new navigation system for the blind is MIT's EyeRing, which uses a small camera worn as a ring which was developed by a team from the Fluid Interfaces Group at MIT's Media Lab. This device translates images of objects captured through a camera into aural feedback to aid the blind. The ring takes a picture or a video that is then sent wirelessly to a mobile phone, where an application analyzes the content and reads out an answer. It consists of a 3D-printed ABS nylon outer housing containing a small VGA camera unit, a 16 MHz AVR processor, a Bluetooth radio module and a 3.7V Li-ion battery (Ridden, 2012).

Many IoT applications utilize wearable technology such as smart watches, smart wristbands, and smart glasses. Many wearable devices are used to track how many steps the user takes, or even how many miles the wearer traveled, but has not been used for the visually impaired. A startup company called Ducere Technologies is looking to use wearable technology along with the IoT to make the lives of the visually impaired much easier. The company is developing a touch-based interactive footwear called Lechal (Lechal, n.d.). A specialized shoe insole vibrates to alert users when they're supposed to make a turn, acting like a real-time GPS device for their feet, directing the wearer where he or she should go (Annear, 2014).

Like Bluetooth-based hearing aid, Bluetooth technology is also integrated to help people who are blind or visually impaired. An Austrian company called Indoo.rs and the San Francisco Airport (SFO) department are developing iOS assistive technologies with iBeacons sensors to create an indoor navigation system for the visually impaired at SFO Terminal 2 (Param, 2014). This innovative app uses a couple of hundred iBeacons installed throughout the terminal not only to facilitate physical movement through space, but also to provide intelligent navigation to people who are blind or visually impaired by speaking out various objects and locations in the terminal. The users download the indoo.rs app on their iPhone. iBeacons, which are placed near an object, use Bluetooth to transmit a unique identifier of an object to the user's iPhone to look up information related to the ID over the Internet.

IoT Applications for Mobility Disability

AT for mobility/ambulation can also be referred to as ambulatory aids. Ambulatory aids clean floors and items, water plants, control light and temperature, open and close garages and perform other functions to ensure safety, comfort, and convenience for the people with mobility disability. The IoT brings ambulatory aids new capabilities. A smart connected wheelchair is a concept designed by Intel interns as part of the Intel Collaborators program, and has been endorsed by the award-winning theoretical physicist, Stephen Hawking (del Castillo, 2014). This wheelchair is capable of monitoring vitals of the person sitting in the chair, including blood pressure, heart rate, and body temperature. The wheelchair is also equipped with an application that allows wheelchair users to rate accessibility of different locations, further enhancing the user experience. It even informs the users of the wheelchair's status, keeping them even more safe and comfortable wherever they may go. The IoT systems for the people with mobility disabilities need to collect, analyze, and apply recommendations autonomously and unobtrusively. This connected smart wheelchair enables monitoring and control, information sharing and collaboration, and big data and data analytics. An application called 'use-case' enables children with cerebral palsy to interact with their toys and their caregivers through a mobile device such as smart phone or tablet which has an installed learning game (Lopes, Pinto, Furtado, & Silva, 2014).

Brain-Computer Interfaces (BCI) systems help people with severe motor disabilities to regain independence to some extent (Leeb et al., 2015). BCI systems use brain signals as a communication and control channel to perform navigation tasks through a bidirectional audio/video connections to a telepresence mobile robot. BCI users are able to have interactions with family members and friends at different locations from the users. While BCI technology significantly improves the quality of human to human interaction to some extent, authors caution that controlling the robots is a complicated task and that shared control can better facilitate the BCI operation than direct control. Lambrinos and Dosis (2013) propose a parking space management system for people with disabilities utilizing monitoring technology which integrates sensor and smart phones, and wireless and mobile communications. This system can assist the parking authorities with usage monitoring to allow better parking space allocation used for people with mobility disabilities.

Cognitive info-communications (CogInfoCom) is used to help people with mobile disability. CogInfoCom is based on the research of virtual reality systems to create special three dimensional (3D) environments in the hope that through which people with disabilities can actively participate in the labor market (Juhasz, Juhasz, Steiner, & Kertesz, 2013). The use of 3D environments such as office environments with

IoT applications should be given to careful examination of individual differences such as preferences, interests, and cognitive abilities. Home automation and security applications also offer benefits to people with disabilities or older adults. Home automation applications allow people with mobility disability to change thermostat settings remotely, adjust lighting, activate security alarms and cameras, control appliances, and control door locks, typically via smartphones and online monitoring. Smart transportation and self-driving cars are also helpful new options for people with mobility disability (American Association of People with Disabilities, 2015). El-Basioni, El-Kader, & Eissa (2014) propose a smart home wireless sensor networks called E/D-WSH system suitable for elders and people with disabilities. E/D-WSH system offers a complete solution for the whole home environment with entering system, fall detection system, RFID system, lighting system, microphone/speech recognition system, proximity sensor/sound synthesizer system, gas leakage detection system, electrical devices monitoring and home structure health system. As shown in various applications, IoT consistently help improve the safety of the people with mobility disability by gathering information on user patterns, environmental dangers, assessing the individual's needs, and taking and proactive measures when a safety threshold has been breached. Table 1 summarizes various IoT studies reviewed.

TRENDS OF THE IOT TECHNOLOGIES FOR AT

A rapid advancement in the IoT technologies for AT has been made in network, software and algorithm, hardware, and data processing. Network technology is moving to unobtrusive wire-free communication technology and a context-aware autonomous network (Sundmaeker, Guillemin, Friess, & Woelfflé, 2010). While RFID tags and sensors have been the focus of hardware innovation, miniaturization of hardware and nanotechnology is leading the energy-efficient hardware evolution as shown in Smart Home technology for people with disabilities. Since processing a large amount of IoT data in real-time will increase workloads of data centers at an exponential rate, data processing will become more context-aware, optimized and cognitive. The challenge is to identify issues associated with data storage and processing as IoT technology is increasingly applied to AT.

Smart Sensors

Spencer, Ruiz-Sandoval, & Kurata (2004) define smart sensors with four features:

1. On-board computing capability,
2. Small size,
3. Wireless communication, and
4. Low cost.

According to WinterGreen (Kharif, 2013), the current size of the smart sensor market is about 65 million devices, but it is expected to reach 2.8 trillion devices by 2019. Advances in sensor technology have enabled miniature smart sensors to unobtrusively monitor physiological signals, body posture, type and level of physical activity, and environmental conditions (Milosevic, Milenkovic, & Jovanov, 2013). Due to the explosion of the data collected with the proliferation of the IoT devices, sensors need to monitor the data quality and perform preliminary data processing. A smart sensor includes a microproces-

Table 1. IoT for people with disabilities: roles, application category, benefits, and future works

Authors	IoT Roles	IoT Application Category	Benefits	Future Work
Busch et al. (2013)	• A user-centered smart medicine cabinet that informs about potential privacy and security risks along with helping users manage their life • Clear and self-explanatory interface elements, readable font size, and clear visual design • Acoustic reminder for taking medicine, haptic feedback for communicating the system's trustworthiness state, using text-to-speech functionalities	Information sharing and collaboration	Enhanced privacy, security, and trust of people with mental and physical disabilities	• Expansion of the cabinet to people with dyslexia or impaired vision to see how well they can use the cabinet and how trustworthy it is perceived by them • Publish guidelines about how best to present security information to people regardless of their disabilities. That way everyone can have a trustworthy experience in the IoT
Dores, Reis, & Lopes (2014)	Machine to machine instant messaging platform useful in Integrating the cloud Internet platform and diverse IoT devices	Information sharing and collaboration	Care system for people with disabilities for more independence through cloud-based communication systems	Various security technologies need to be tested and improved for quality of service
El-Basioni, El-Kader, & Eissa (2014)	Elders/Disabilities Wireless Smart Home for assistive independent living (E/D-WSH)	Monitoring and control	• The home automation system which can be controlled locally using a remote control or an application on a PC or laptop, or remotely through the Internet • A complete solution for the whole home environment for elders and disabilities by designing entering • system, fall detection system, RFID system, lighting system, microphone/ speech recognition system, proximity sensor	• Realizing energy saving of smart home technology by using alternative power especially the solar power • Continuous measuring of power consumption of different devices to help home owners manage their use of electrical devices
Jablonski, C. (2012).	Sensing systems for robots to help for people with visual impairment navigate unknown terrains	Monitoring and Control application	The system produces a 3-D map of the wearer's environment and his/her position within it that is constantly updated and displayed in a simplified form on the handheld device	Need to be integrated with mobile phones and voice-assisted devices
Joseph et al. (2015)	• Assistive navigation using wearable sensors and social sensors for people with visual impairment • Fusion of social media messages, wearable sensors, and real-time localization technologies	• Monitoring and control • Information sharing and collaboration	Enhanced situation awareness with crowdsourced social media data	• Need to improve the quality using more rules and patterns • Further research on obstacle objects recognition, such as recognizing chairs or stairs

continued on following page

Table 1. Continued

Authors	IoT Roles	IoT Application Category	Benefits	Future Work
Juhasz, Juhasz, Steiner, & Kertesz (2013)	• Personal 3D environments for people with special needs or disabilities • The physical surroundings of the subject is combined with representations of virtual reality	Information sharing and collaboration	Provide people with disabilities to join in the workflow of a company	Need to do further testing in real life situations
Lambrinos & Dosis (2013)	Parking space management for people with disabilities	• Monitoring and control • Information sharing and collaboration	• Better utilization and management of parking spaces allocated for use by people with disabilities • Assisting the authorities with usage monitoring for law enforcement as well as capacity planning purposes	Various improvements to the system concentrating on user verifications and reservation enforcement which will enable for reservations to be made for future time periods
Leeb et al. (2015)	Brain-computer interfaces (BCI) systems with a telepresence robot for people with severe motor disabilities	Information sharing and collaboration	• Use brain signals as a communication and control channel to complete navigation tasks of a mobile robot • Empower people with severe motor disabilities to regain a degree of independence	More extensive comparisons with alternative systems
Lopes, Pinto, Furtado, & Silva (2014)	Two use cases that are currently being deployed for people with visual impairment and people with neurologic impairment	• Monitoring and control • Information sharing and collaboration • Big Date and data analytics	Improving the independence of people with visual impairment and people with neurologic impairment for	Currently laboratory stage. Need to test the use cases with users and analyze their adaptation to the AT devices
Mulfari, Celesti, Fazio, Villari, & Puliafito (2014)	The usage of embedded systems able to interface sensors and existing AT software tools running on user's personal computing devices	Information sharing and collaboration	Decouple AT software tools from the accessed computer systems, allowing us to control various kinds of computer systems, in order to natively interact with many platforms	Integration of plugins with cloud computing platform is needed in order to natively interact with many computers
Neßelrath et al. (2011)	A fusion of several systems comprising the intelligent medicament blister and the task-based calendar	• Monitoring and control • Information sharing and collaboration	The intelligent medicament blister helps to increase a patient's compliance and the task-based calendar assists people with cognitive disabilities in their activities of daily living like cooking tea	Seamless integration of multiple vendor systems based on open standards and architectures
Oniga & Suto (2014)	An assistive assembly consisting of a smart and assistive environment, a human activity and health monitoring system, an assistive and telepresence robot, together with the related components and cloud services	• Monitoring and control • Information sharing and collaboration • Big Data and data analytics	Adaptive capability and learning behavior of AT devices for independent daily life assistance of elderly or persons with disabilities	• Further testing of the systems in different circumstances and with different people • Need for further simulation of more artificial neural networks types for activity/health status recognition

continued on following page

Table 1. Continued

Authors	IoT Roles	IoT Application Category	Benefits	Future Work
Sarji (2008)	"Smart glove" that can recognize basic hand gestures and convert them into written words	Information Sharing and Collaboration	A low-cost, portable gesture-to-speech glove prototype	• Currently the device can convert only few words, suggests that sensor gloves can be used for partial sign language recognition • More sensors need to be employed to recognize full sign language
Sula, Spaho, Barolli, & Miho (2014)	An AT system combined consisting of the IoT, peer to peer technology and heuristic diagnostic teaching principles	• Monitoring and control • Information sharing and collaboration	• Use of the smart environment to support students that are diagnosed within Autism Spectrum disorder (ASD) • Better support the students during their learning by actively engaging the students during their learning and creating and maintaining their calm alert state	Need to evaluate the assessment results to design learning objectives and lessons for students with autism spectrum disorder

sor that can be used for digital signal processing, data filtering, self-diagnosis, self-identification, and self-adaptation. Some smart sensors can be programmed to send alerts to users when predefined events take place. IBM is developing Secure Living project utilizing smart sensors (IBM, n.d.). The homes for senior citizens and people with disabilities equipped with remote sensors to monitor the environment in real time, checking for changes in temperature or potential dangers such as water leaks or high levels of carbon monoxide. Data is transmitted and displayed on a dashboard in an off-site central control room, and on an assigned operator's Android mobile device via e-mail, SMS or Twitter. When problems arise and immediate action is required, alerts are sent to family members, volunteer 'angels,' members of the social services department or local emergency staff, based on the individual's specific need. The smart sensors can also learn the user's preferences and adjust its behaviors accordingly.

Self-Powered Sensors

Because of the large number, small sizes and complicated surrounding environments, powering wireless sensors with conventional batteries creates challenges in replacement or on-site charging of the batteries (Gheibi, Latifi, Merati, & Bagherzadeh, 2012; Huang et al., 2010). Since batteries have a limited life and need to be maintained regularly, the consumption of electric power by the batteries of the wireless sensors limited the scope of the IoT applications for AT devices (e.g., patient monitoring). Self-powering of electronic devices has emerged as a viable solution by integrating a power generator that can scavenge and turn the surrounding local energy into electrical energy to drive the electronic devices sustainably without any other electrical input (Gheibi et al., 2014). Self-powering sensor technology offers advantages of location independence, minimum space, and zero wired-power requirements. Self-powering sensors use a variety of methods to generate or store electricity such as inductive switches, solar cells, and thermo-energy harvesters. Wireless Body Area Networks (WBANs) medical applications are actively utilizing smart and self-powered sensor devices that can be attached, or even implanted into, humans to monitor their physiological parameters (e.g., temperature, blood pressure, heart pulse rate, etc.), body motion as well as their surrounding environment. All the monitored parameters are then transmitted wirelessly, using short-range on-body or Intra-WBAN communications, from the on/in-body sensors to the monitoring centers for further data processing and analysis (Alam & Hamida, E2104).

Nanotechnology Sensors

Nanotechnology encompasses various technologies that cross sectors, such as nanomaterials (NMs), medicine, devices, fabrication, electronics, communications, and energy. There has been a phenomenal development in nanotechnology during the last two decades (Leary, 2010; Weiss, 2010). Nanotechnology will be driving a strong force in developing miniaturized sensors and related AT devices. Operating on the scale of atoms and molecules at the measure unit of 0.001 microns, nanotechnologies promise dramatic improvements in sensor designs and capabilities. Nano-size materials display different properties from bulk (or micrometric and larger) materials as a result of their size. These differences include physical strength, chemical reactivity, electrical conductance, magnetism, and optical effects (Rai & Ingle, 2012). Nanotechnology sensors are tiny, lower weight, and energy efficient. Nanosensors and nano-enabled smart sensors have applications in biosensors, diagnostics, environmental monitoring, drug delivery, therapeutic, healthcare, medicine, etc. Considerable efforts are made to reduce the cost of nano-size materials, improve reliability, and create useful sensors. Zhu et al. (2015) propose a clustered-sensor system through a project called SPHERE to provide analytics-driven, data gathering platforms for the field of healthcare management. This proposed system, currently being implemented in a real house, aims to bridge e-health and IoT by processing the sensor based data in real time for health monitoring.

Context-Aware Computing

Context-aware computing has the capacity to be aware of environments and their characteristics through sensors. In the IoT environment, a large number of devices are connected with each other and it is not feasible to process all the streaming data available to those devices. Understanding the context makes it easier to perform machine-to-machine and machine-to-human communication as it is a core element in the IoT vision (Perera, Zaslavsky, Christen, & Georgakopoulos, 2014). Context is classified into a low-level context involving time, location, identity, and activity, which are the most utilized contextual information, and a high-level context, which involves any other information that can be derived from the low-level types (Abowd et al., 1999). The success of context-aware information delivery requires an effective localization solution, as context-aware applications need to know the location of the user/object to determine and provide relevant information and services. Bradley and Dunlop (2008) discuss how contextual information such as location and personal preferences can be embedded into user-computer interactions and how these facilities and capabilities could be used to assist the visually impaired traveler on a long distance journey. Smart phones are a valuable platform that bears significant potential to support context-aware applications along with built in accessibility features (Li & Becerik-Gerber, 2012). Context-aware AT devices will possess a high level of intelligence in their control, actions and interactions with people with cognitive disabilities, offering them high level of comfort and functionality.

Interoperability of the IoT Systems

The IoT ecosystem needs to support interactions among many heterogeneous sources of data and many heterogeneous devices through the use of standard interfaces and data models to ensure mapping and cross-referencing among applications and services in order to exchange data. Interoperability is significantly more challenging for the IoT as it is not only about connecting people with people, but about a seamless interaction between devices and devices. Two types of interoperability are identified:

1. **Technological Interoperability:** The IoT devices can differ regarding their technological capabilities, and
2. **Semantic Interoperability:** For full interoperability, it is necessary that the devices interpret the shared information correctly and act accordingly (Gazis et al., 2015).

Standards play an important role to create collaborative technological solutions both within a single service provider and across multiple providers. Standards remove ambiguity about the interpretation of the information they exchange. Standards regarding communication, data sharing, and application interfaces will ensure that the IoT devices collaborate with each other. Standards for interoperability are a prerequisite for the integration of the multi-vendor AT devices for people with multiple disabilities who need comprehensive support services.

Other Trends

The principle of universal design, which promotes product development to reach the widest range of individuals with varying abilities, has been the basis for the development of various AT applications (www.cast.org). One such example is the built-in accessibility features in products such as computers, tablets, and mobile phones. These seamless features allow people with disabilities to access information, participate in social media, and IoT applications. These built-in accessibility features enable customization for people with disabilities at no extra cost. For example, keyboard functions can be manipulated to control the rate of typing and manner of pressing keys for people with limited motor abilities; sound input can be controlled via amplification and speech recognition; and screen display modes include visual notifications, magnifiers, and different text sizes (Apple, n.d.; Microsoft, n.d.). It is expected that the principle of universal design is widely applied to the design of IoT devices to allow people with disabilities to access services with high-levels of comfort and ease.

Another significant trend that has been getting increasing attention is the development of numerous smartphone-based applications for learning, mobility, communication, information sharing, and monitoring. For example, the iPad is utilized as a platform for applications in various areas of learning and communication (Catlett & Turan, 2013; More & Travers, 2013). Naturally, many pages of recent technology journals cover the studies that examined the effectiveness of iPad apps for reading, attention, communication, and cognitive support. Exhibits at technology conferences shift from small hardware devices to applications and software devices for learning, communication, and daily living. iPad-based applications are taking over other traditional AT devices, especially in the categories of education and communication.

ISSUES OF THE IOT-BASED ASSISTIVE TECHNOLOGY FOR PEOPLE WITH DISABILITIES

Barriers to accessing technology for people with disabilities have been addressed (Lee & Templeton, 2008). New issues arise when the IoT meets ATs. Based on the literature of AT practices, this section identifies several issues in the IoT-integrated AT development. There is an urgent need to address the issues in security, privacy, reliability, changing roles of health care professionals, and involvement of users and families to seamlessly integrate the IoT into the ATs.

Security

Security is defined as the subjective probability with which consumers believe that their personal information (private and monetary) will not be viewed, stored, and manipulated during transit and storage by inappropriate parties in a manner consistent with their confident expectations (Flavián, & Guinalíu, 2006). Kalakota & Whinston (1996) define security threat as a circumstance, condition, or event with the potential to cause economic hardship to data or network resources in the form of destruction, disclosure, modification of data, denial of service, and/or fraud, waste, and abuse. Security threats also include data theft, resource theft, fire, natural disasters, burglaries, virus, and cyber-terrorism. Connected IoT devices are likely to fall victims in unsecure networks. A survey conducted by PricewaterhouseCoopers has indicated that the total number of security incidents has increased 48% over 2013. According to a Hewlett-Packard (HP) report (Kovacs, 2014), a total of 250 security holes have been found in tested IoT devices - on average, 25 per device. The issues are related to privacy, insufficient authorization, lack of transport encryption, inadequate software protection, and insecure web interfaces. With HP reporting that up to 70% of devices developed for the IoT are vulnerable to cyber-attacks, the need to 'lock down' mission critical' data across multiple applications has never been greater. Vulnerabilities of the IoT will continue to arise as more and more devices are connected to the IoT world.

Privacy

Privacy is defined as a two-dimensional construct with physical space and information (Goodwin, 1991). Any application that collects data from users has to be clear about what it collects and how it is used in order to build trust. Ackerman, Cranor, and Reagle (1999) gave participants four scenarios in which they had to indicate whether they were comfortable providing various types of personal information. A majority of users were very comfortable with providing general information (e.g., favorite food) and somewhat comfortable with providing directory-type information (name, address, e-mail), but they were uncomfortable with providing financial and health information (e.g., credit card, health status). For questions relating to the users' general attitudes regarding providing personal information, Ackerman et al. (1999) concluded that users can be classified as:

1. Marginally concerned,
2. Privacy fundamentalists (users who are very concerned with privacy), or
3. Pragmatic (users whose concerns vary as a function of the type of transaction being performed).

People with disabilities show various levels of privacy concerns when it comes to using ATs. With connected IoT devices deployed around users' homes and bodies and potentially collecting data that government and other third parties can access, they may start to self-consciously protect their privacy. Government regulation of the IoT privacy is under way. The Article 29 Working Party, a European Union privacy body (Justice, n.d.), and the Article 5(3) of Directive 2002/58/EC as amended by Directive 2009/136/EC (the ePrivacy Directive) stipulates that Member States shall ensure that "the storing of information, or the gaining of access to information already stored, in the terminal equipment of a subscriber or user" is only allowed on the condition that the subscriber or user concerned has given his or her consent, having been provided with clear and comprehensive information in accordance with Directive 95/46/EC6 (the Data Protection Directive), inter alia, about the purposes of the information processing. These documents say consumers should remain in control of their personal data throughout the life of the product. In some parts of Europe, such as the U.K, the industry is working closely with the government which is a desirable way of developing guidelines.

Reliability

In industrial environments or in emergencies, even temporary failure of AT devices is unacceptable. Hence, resilience and reliability issues in the AT devices need to be addressed from an overall system point of view and include such dimensions as availability, robustness, and flexibility of the devices to changing environmental conditions, and the robustness of data processing to uncertain information (Gazis et al., 2015). The IoT devices have to be resilient to communication errors by providing efficient mechanisms for information distribution especially in the multi-hop scenario (Maalel, Natalizio, Bouabdallah, Roux, & Kellil, 2013). System reliability is the result of a combination of individual reliabilities and the weakest component dominates the reliability of the entire system. The failures of the entire IoT system are experienced more frequently when there is a large number of deployed devices and sensors. Mathematical models of failure analysis may provide greater insight into the probability and costs of failures and requirements for minimum acceptable performance. There are multiple components in any IoT system. A well-designed system requires understanding of exactly what is a dominant reliability-related component in the IoT system and therefore needs redundancy and backups. For example, a single sensor may cause the entire system to stop functioning, and therefore redundancy of the sensor can be warranted.

Changing Roles of Health Care Professionals

Implementing AT services in rehabilitation programs is a complex process. AT selection and services are influenced by the availability of AT options, knowledge and experience of professionals, and budget limitations (Okolo & Deidrich, 2014). While the effectiveness of AT on learning and daily lives for people with disabilities across ages has been well documented, professionals face multiple challenges in providing effective AT services, especially in compliance with federal laws, funding, training, and collaboration. Due to the recent technological advancements in AT devices along with the IoT, healthcare professionals are faced with new challenges. The paradigm shift to the IoT-integrated AT will change the roles of various healthcare professionals. People with disabilities will be more empowered with more personalized and user-centered services. Many healthcare professionals may have doubts about their future position as the self-service component of the IoT-integrated ATs accelerates. To remain most valuable in the value chain of the AT industry, they need to retrain themselves for new value added services and new technologies and need to be willing to adapt to all possible changes in their area.

Involvement of Users and Families

AT services are typically provided by a number of multidisciplinary professionals including occupational therapists, physical therapists, speech therapists, teachers, and rehabilitation technologists. Families of people with disabilities should be included as meaningful partners in the implementation of AT applications. Yet, the key elements of the existing literature on the IoT-integrated AT do not necessarily include family as an integral member of the technology application process. Developing cultural sensitivity in the selection and use of AT devices and services is critical for people with disabilities and their families with diverse backgrounds. In addition, the use of AT devices may require extensive training and collaboration between the family members and the service providers. AT users and their family members may feel overwhelmed and reluctant to go through the training even when they do not understand the benefits of a new AT device and are cognitively challenged due to a technical complexity. Kling, Campbell, & Wilcox (2010) shows parents do not feel knowledgeable enough to utilize AT devices even though they believe AT is beneficial for their children's physical development. Also, early intervention professionals do not feel confident enough to train parents for the utilization of AT devices at home. To prevent the abandonment of the acquired devices, professionals need to put family needs as a priority over their own agenda when considering the selection and utilization of a new IoT-integrated AT for individuals.

CONCLUSION

This chapter discussed various IoT applications which is a certainty of future technology that will makes positive differences in the lives of people with disabilities. Medical and technological advancement have made it possible for people with disabilities to enjoy the quality and longevity of their lives, which in turn has required healthcare and rehabilitation professionals to utilize various types of AT and IoT-integrated AT devices. Numerous IoT-integrated applications are being introduced into the AT market. However, the IoT being a relatively new development, has yet to see solid benefits of the IoT applications for people with disabilities. People with disabilities are a heterogeneous group and each individual case needs to be carefully examined when considering which applications should be utilized in under which circumstances. The field of special education has various AT service delivery models due to the AT federal legislation for children with disabilities. The healthcare field is faced with the following remaining tasks: including identifying or developing assessment instruments in order to identify which IoT-integrated AT applications will be used at which environment for which tasks, identifying funding sources and obtaining the devices, and securing qualified personnel for customization and implementation of the technology. The lack of valid information and unfamiliarity with the technology will make it difficult for professionals in healthcare and rehabilitation agencies to support people with disabilities in making informed decisions when adopting IoT-integrated AT applications. Research on the effectiveness of IoT-integrated AT applications that improve the quality of the lives of people with disabilities have a long way to go. However, the emergence of various IoT-integrated AT applications shed a promising light to the field; yet more attention should be given to security, trustworthiness, and reliability in the development and utilization of these applications. As noted by Busch et al. (2013), it is critical that technology-related disciplines promote enhanced privacy, security, and trust of people with various types of disabilities. User experience surveys involving all stakeholders - developers, users, family members, healthcare providers, and caregivers - is critical. Also, collaborative, coordinated, multidisciplinary efforts are a must to see the true intent of the above mentioned technological advancement in order to support people with disabilities as independent and productive citizens.

REFERENCES

Abowd, G. D., Dey, A. K., Brown, P. J., Davies, N., Smith, M., & Steggles, P. (1999). Towards a better understanding of context and context-awareness. In *HUC '99 Proceedings of the 1st international symposium on Handheld and Ubiquitous Computing*, (pp. 304-307).

Ackerman, M. S., Cranor, L. F., & Reagle, J. (1999). Privacy in e-commerce: examining user scenarios and privacy preferences. In *Proceedings of the 1st ACM conference on Electronic commerce* (pp. 1-8). New York: ACM. doi:10.1145/336992.336995

Alam, M. M., & Hamida, E. B. (2014, May). Surveying Wearable human assistive technology for life and safety critical applications: Standards, challenges and opportunities. *Sensors (Basel, Switzerland)*, *14*(5), 9153–9209. doi:10.3390/s140509153 PMID:24859024

Alper, S., & Raharinirina, S. (2006). Assistive technology for individuals with disabilities: A review and synthesis of the literature. *Journal of Special Education Technology*, *21*(2), 47–64.

Ameen, M. A., Liu, J., & Kwak, K. (2012). Security and Privacy Issues in Wireless Sensor Networks for Healthcare Applications. *Journal of Medical Systems*, *36*(1), 93–101. doi:10.1007/s10916-010-9449-4 PMID:20703745

American Academy of Audiology. (n.d.). *Cochlear Implants in Children*. American Academy of Audiology. Retrieved from: http://www.audiology.org/publications-resources/document-library/cochlear-implants-children

American Association of People with Disabilities. (2015). Retrieved January 23, 2016, http://www.aapd.com/resources/power-grid-blog/iot-innovations.html

Americans with Disabilities Act of 1990, Pub. L. No. 101-336, § 1, 104 Stat. 328 (1990).

Annear, S. (2014). *What the Tech? Lechal 'Smart Shoes' Help the Blind Get Around*. Retrieved August 10, 2015, http://www.bostonmagazine.com/news/blog/2014/03/05/lechal-insoles-mit-visually-impaired/

Apple. (n.d.). *Accessibility*. Retrieved from: http://www.apple.com/accessibility/

Atzori, L., Iera, A., & Morabito, G. (2010). The Internet of Things: A survey. *Computer Networks*, *54*(15), 2787–2805. doi:10.1016/j.comnet.2010.05.010

Aziz, O., Lo, B., Pansiot, J., Atallah, L., Yang, G.-Z., & Ara Darzim, A. (2008). From computers to ubiquitous computing by 2010: health care. *Philosophical Transactions* A: *Mathematical, Physical & Engineering Sciences, 366*(1881), 3805-3811.

Bandyopadhyay, D., & Sen, J. (2011). Internet of Things: Applications and challenges in technology and standardization. *Wireless Personal Communications*, *58*(1), 49–69. doi:10.1007/s11277-011-0288-5

Barrenetxea, G., Ingelrest, F., Schaefer, G., Vetterli, M., Couach, O., & Parlange, M. (2008). Sensor-Scope: Out-of-the-Box Environmental Monitoring. *Information Processing in Sensor Networks, 2008. IPSN '08. International Conference on*, (pp. 332–343).

Bradley, N., & Dunlop, M. (2008). Navigation AT: Context-aware computing. In M. A. Hersh & M. A. Johnson (Eds.), *Assistive Technology for Visually Impaired and Blind People* (pp. 231–260). Springer London. doi:10.1007/978-1-84628-867-8_7

Bui, N., Castellani, A. P., Casari, P. M., & Zorzi, M. (2012). The internet of energy: A web-enabled smart grid system. *IEEE Network*, *26*(4), 39–45. doi:10.1109/MNET.2012.6246751

Busch, M., Hochleitner, C., Lorenz, M., Schulz, T., Tscheligi, M., Wittstock, E. (2103). All in: Targeting trustworthiness for special needs user groups in the Internet of Things. *Lecture Notes in Computer Science, 7904*, 223-231. DOI: 10.1007/978-3-642-38908-5_17

Buyya, R., Yeo, C., Venugopal, S., Broberg, J., & Brandic, I. (2009). Cloud computing and emerging IT platforms: Vision, hype, and reality for delivering computing as the 5th utility. *Future Generation Computer Systems*, *25*(6), 599–616. doi:10.1016/j.future.2008.12.001

Catlett, C., & Turan, Y. (2013). Technology applications to support your work, Part 1& Part 2. *Young Exceptional Children*, *16*(1), 46–50. doi:10.1177/1096250612473130

Coetzee, L., & Olivrin, G. (2012). Inclusion through the internet of things. Inclusion Through the Internet of Things. In *Assistive Technologies*. InTech. Available from: http://www.intechopen.com/books/assistive-technologies/inclusion-through-the-internet-of-things

Curtin University. (2013). *New navigation gadget for people who are blind.* Curtin University. Retrieved from: http://news.curtin.edu.au/media-releases/new-navigation-gadget-for-people-who-are-blind/

de Vries, B. (2014). Introducing data science: Hearing aids on the brink of a paradigm shift. *Audiology Worldnews*. Retrieved on 11/13/15 from http://www.audiology-worldnews.com/focus-on/1215-introducing-data-science-hearing-aids-on-the-brink-of-a-paradigm-shift

del Castillo, M. (2014). *Stephen Hawking endorses Intel's souped up smart wheelchair.* Retrieved July 28, 2015, http://upstart.bizjournals.com/multimedia/interactives/2014/09/stephen-hawking-endorses-intel-s-souped-up-smart.html

Demigha, O., Hidouci, W., & Ahmed, T. (2012). On Energy Efficiency in Collaborative Target Tracking in Wireless Sensor Network: A Review. *IEEE Communications Surveys and Tutorials*, *15*(3), 1210–1222. doi:10.1109/SURV.2012.042512.00030

Domingo, M. C. (2012). An overview of the Internet of Things for people with disabilities. *Journal of Network and Computer Applications*, *35*(2), 584–596. doi:10.1016/j.jnca.2011.10.015

Dores, C., Reis, L. P., & Lopes, N. V. (2014). Internet of Things and Cloud Computing.*Iberian Conference on Information Systems & Technologie (CISTI)*.

El-Basioni, B. M., El-Kader, S. M., & Eissa, S. E. (2014). Independent living for persons with disabilities and elderly people using smart home technology. *International Journal of Application or Innovation in Engineering and Management*, *3*(4), 11–28.

Flavián, C., & Guinalíu, M. (2006). Consumer trust, perceived security and privacy policy: Three basic elements of loyalty to a web site. *Industrial Management & Data Systems*, *106*(5), 601–620. doi:10.1108/02635570610666403

Gartner. (2013). *Market Trends: New Technologies Benefit Employees and People With Disabilities*. Retrieved August 1, 2015 from https://www.gartner.com/doc/2593617/market-trends-new-technologies-benefit

Gazis, V., Goertz, M., Huber, M., Leonardi, A., Mathioudakis, K., Wiesmaier, A., & Zeiger, F. (2015). Short Paper: IoT: Challenges, projects, architectures. *2015 18th International Conference on Intelligence in Next Generation Networks (ICIN)*, (pp. 145-147).

Gheibi, A., Latifi, M., Merati, A. A., & Bagherzadeh, R. (2014). Piezoelectric electrospun nanofibrous materials for self-powering wearable electronic textiles applications. *Journal of Polymer Research*, *21*(7), 469. doi:10.1007/s10965-014-0469-5

Gluhak, A., Krco, S., Nati, M., Pfisterer, D., Mitton, N., & Razafindralambo, T. (2011). A survey on facilities for experimental internet of things research. *IEEE Communications Magazine*, *49*(11), 58–67. doi:10.1109/MCOM.2011.6069710

Goodwin, C. (1991). Privacy: Recognition of a consumer right. *Journal of Public Policy & Marketing*, *10*(1), 149–166.

Gubbi, J., Buyya, R., Marusic, S., & Palaniswami, M. (2013). Internet of Things (IoT): A vision, architectural elements, and future directions. *Future Generation Computer Systems*, *29*(7), 1645–1660. doi:10.1016/j.future.2013.01.010

Huang, J. (2013). Research on application of internet of things in nursing home. Applied Mechanics and Materials, 303-306, 2153-2156. DOI: 10.4028/www.scientific.net/AMM.303-306.2153

IBM. (n.d.). *A New vision for 'social security': Home healthcare smart sensors help keep Italian seniors living in place*. IBM. Retrieved from: http://www-03.ibm.com/able/news/homehealthcare.html

iTunes. (2016). *easyTek*. Apple. Retrieved from: https://itunes.apple.com/us/app/siemens-easytek/id893105249?mt=8

Jablonski, C. (2012). *Sensing systems for robots could help blind navigate*. Retrieved August 9, 2015, http://www.zdnet.com/article/sensing-systems-for-robots-could-help-blind-navigate/

Joseph, S. L., Xiao, J., Zhang, X., Chawda, B., Narang, K., Rajput, N., & Subramaniam, L. V. et al. (2015). Being aware of the world: Toward using social media to support the blind with navigation. *IEEE Transactions on Human-Machine Systems*, *45*(3), 399–405. doi:10.1109/THMS.2014.2382582

Juhasz, B., Juhasz, N., Steiner, H., & Kertesz, Z. (2013). Coginfocom in collaborative virtual working environments. In *4th IEEE International Conference on Cognitive Infocommunications, CogInfoCom 2013 - Proceedings*, (pp. 475-480). doi:10.1109/CogInfoCom.2013.6719294

Justice. (n.d.). *Article 29: Working Party. Justice: Building a European Area of Justice*. Retrieved from: http://ec.europa.eu/justice/data-protection/article-29/index_en.htm

Kalakota, R., & Whinston, A. B. (1996). *Frontiers of electronic commerce*. Addison-Wesley.

Kharif, O. (2013). *Trillions of Smart Sensors Will Change Life*. Retrieved July 26, 2015, http://www.bloomberg.com/news/articles/2013-08-05/trillions-of-smart-sensors-will-change-life-as-apps-have

Kling, A., Campbell, P. H., & Wilcox, J. (2010). Young children with phyical disabilities: Caregiver perspectives about assistive technology. *Infants and Young Children, 23*(3), 169–183. doi:10.1097/IYC.0b013e3181e1a873

Kovacs, E. (2014). *70 Percent of IoT Devices Vulnerable to Cyberattacks: HP*. Retrieved on July 28, 2015, http://www.securityweek.com/70-iot-devices-vulnerable-cyberattacks-hp

Lambrinos, L., & Dosis, A. (2013). *UbiComp 2013 Adjunct - Adjunct Publication of the 2013 ACM Conference on Ubiquitous Computing*. Doi:10.1145/2494091.2494162

Lazarescu, M. T. (2013). Design of a WSN Platform for Long-Term Environmental Monitoring for IoT Applications. *IEEE Journal of Emerging and Selected Topics in Circuits and Systems, 3*(1), 45–54. doi:10.1109/JETCAS.2013.2243032

Leary, J. F. (2010). Nanotechnology: What is it and why is small so big? *Canadian Journal of Ophthalmology, 45*(5), 449–456. doi:10.3129/i10-089 PMID:20856270

Lechal. (n.d.). *Lechal*. Retrieved from: http://lechal.com/

Lee, H. (2009). Using assistive technology to ensure access to E-Learning for individuals with disabilities. In I. Lee (Ed.), *Encyclopedia of E-Business development and management in the digital economy*. Hershey, PA: IGI Publishing.

Lee, H., & Templeton, R. (2008). Ensuring equal access to technology: An overview of providing assistive technology services to students with disabilities. *Theory into Practice, 47*(3), 212–219. doi:10.1080/00405840802153874

Lee, I., & Lee, K. (2015). The Internet of things (IoT): Applications, investments and challenges for enterprises. *Business Horizons, 58*(4), 431–440. doi:10.1016/j.bushor.2015.03.008

Leeb, R., Tonin, L., Rohm, M., Desideri, L., Carlson, T., & Millán, J. D. R. (2015). Towards independence: A BCI telepresence robot for people with severe motor disabilities. *Proceedings of the IEEE, 103*(6), 969–982. doi:10.1109/JPROC.2015.2419736

Li, N., & Becerik-Gerber, B. (2012). Assessment of a Smart Phone-Based Indoor Localization Solution for Improving Context Awareness in the Construction Industry. *Computing in Civil Engineering*, 561-568.

LIFX. (n.d.). *LIFX*. Retrieved from: http://www.lifx.com

Liu, C., Yang, C., Zhang, X., & Chen, J. (2015). External integrity verification for outsourced big data in cloud and IoT: A big picture. *Future Generation Computer Systems, 49*, 58–67. doi:10.1016/j.future.2014.08.007

Liu, Y., Dong, B., Guo, B., Yang, J., & Peng, W. (2015). Combination of cloud computing and Internet of Things (IOT) in medical monitoring systems. *International Journal of Hybrid Information Technology, 8*(12), 367–376. doi:10.14257/ijhit.2015.8.12.28

Lopes, N. V., Pinto, F., Furtado, P., & Silva, J. (2014). IoT architecture proposal for disabled people. *2014 IEEE 10th International Conference on Wireless and Mobile Computing, Networking and Communications*, (pp. 152-158).

Ma, Y., Rao, J., Hu, W., Meng, X., Han, X., Zhang, Y., & Liu, C. et al. (2012). An efficient index for massive IoT data in cloud environment. In *Proceedings of the 21st ACM International Conference on Information and Knowledge Management*. doi:10.1145/2396761.2398587

Maalel, N., Natalizio, E., Bouabdallah, A., Roux, P., & Kellil, M. (2013). Reliability for Emergency Applications in Internet of Things.*2013 IEEE International Conference on Distributed Computing in Sensor Systems (DCOSS)*, (pp. 361-366). doi:10.1109/DCOSS.2013.40

Mell, P., & Grance, T. (2011). *The NIST Definition of Cloud Computing*. NIST Special Publication 800-145, National Institute of Standards and Technology. Retrieved on January 26, 2016 from http://csrc.nist.gov/publications/nistpubs/800-145/SP800-145.pdf

Microsoft. (n.d.). *Microsoft Accessibility*. Microsoft. Retrieved from: https://www.microsoft.com/enable/

Milosevic, M., Milenkovic, A., & Jovanov, E. (2013). mHealth @ UAH: computing infrastructure for mobile health and wellness monitoring. *XRDS: Crossroads. The ACM Magazine for Students, 20*(2), 43–49. doi:10.1145/2539269

More, C. M., & Travers, J. C. (2013). What's App with that? Selecting educational apps for young children with disabilities. *Young Exceptional Children, 16*(2), 15–32. doi:10.1177/1096250612464763

Morris, J., Mueller, J., & Jones, M. (2010). Tomorrow's elders with disabilities: What the wireless industry needs to know. *Journal of Engineering Design, 21*(2/3), 131–146. doi:10.1080/09544820903303431

Mulfari, D., Celesti, A., Fazio, M., Villari, M., & Puliafito, A. (2014). Using embedded systems to spread assistive technology on multiple devices in smart environments. In *Proceedings - 2014 IEEE International Conference on Bioinformatics and Biomedicine*. doi:10.1109/BIBM.2014.6999234

Mulfari, D., Celesti, A., Fazio, M., Villari, M., & Puliafito, A. (2015). Achieving assistive technology systems based on IoT devices in cloud computing. *EAI Endorsed Transactions on Cloud Systems, 1*(1), e4. doi:10.4108/cs.1.1.e4

Neßelrath, R., Haupert, J., Frey, J., & Brandherm, B. (2011). Supporting persons with special needs in their daily life in a smart home. In *Proceedings - 2011 7th International Conference on Intelligent Environments*. doi:10.1109/IE.2011.75

Okolo, C. M., & Diedrich, J. (2014). Twenty-Five Years Later: How is technology used in the Education of students with disabilities? Results of a statewide study. *Journal of Special Education Technology, 29*(1), 1–20. doi:10.1177/016264341402900101

Oniga, S., & Süto, J. (2014). Human activity recognition using neural networks. In *Proceedings of the 2014 15th International Carpathian Control Conference, ICCC 2014*. doi:10.1109/CarpathianCC.2014.6843636

Papetti, A., Iualé, M., Ceccacci, S., Bevilacqua, R., Germani, M., & Mengoni, M. (2014). *Smart objects: An evaluation of the present state based on user needs.* doi:10.1007/978-3-319-07788-8_34

Param. (2014). IoT iBeacons for the Visually Impaired at SFO. *LyfeArts Blog.* Retrieved from: http://www.lyfearts.com/iot-assistive-tech-and-living/

Perera, C., Zaslavsky, A., Christen, P., & Georgakopoulos, D. (2014). Context Aware Computing for the Internet of Things: A Survey. *IEEE Communications Surveys and Tutorials, 16*(1), 414–454. doi:10.1109/SURV.2013.042313.00197

Rai, M., & Ingle, A. (2012). Role of nanotechnology in agriculture with special reference to management of insect pests. *Applied Microbiology and Biotechnology, 94*(2), 287–293. doi:10.1007/s00253-012-3969-4 PMID:22388570

Ridden, P. (2012). *Camera-toting EyeRing could help blind people to "see" objects.* Retrieved August 9, 2015, http://www.gizmag.com/eyering-object-recognition-aural-feedback-mit/23677/

Sarji, D. K. (2008). HandTalk: Assistive technology for the deaf. *Computer, 41*(7), 84–86. doi:10.1109/MC.2008.226

Scherer, M. J., & Cushman, L. A. (2001). Measuring subjective quality of life following spinal cord injury: A validation study of the assistive technology device predisposition assessment. *Disability and Rehabilitation, 23*(9), 387–393. doi:10.1080/09638280010006665 PMID:11394589

Schulz, T., Fuglerud, K. S., Arfwedson, H., & Busch, M. (2014). A case study for universal design in the internet of things. *Assistive Technology Research Series, 35*, 45–54. doi:10.3233/978-1-61499-403-9-45

Sehgal, A., Perelman, V., Kuryla, S., & Schonwalder, J. (2012). Management of resource constrained devices in the internet of things. *IEEE Communications Magazine, 50*(12), 144–149. doi:10.1109/MCOM.2012.6384464

Spencer, B. F. Jr, Ruiz-Sandoval, M. E., & Kurata, N. (2004). Smart sensing technology: Opportunities and challenges. *Journal of Structural Control and Health Monitoring, 11*(4), 349–368. doi:10.1002/stc.48

Sula, A., Spaho, E., Barolli, L., & Miho, R. (2014). A proposed framework for combining smart environment and heuristic diagnostic teaching principles in order to assess students' abilities in math and supporting them during learning. *Mediterranean Journal of Social Sciences, 5*(2), 187–196. doi:10.5901/mjss.2014.v5n2p187

Sundmaeker, H., Guillemin, P., Friess, P., & Woelfflé, S. (2010). *Vision and challenges for realising the Internet of Things, CERP-IoT – Cluster of European Research Projects on the Internet of Things.* Retrieved August 16, 2014 from http://www.researchgate.net/publication/228664767_Vision_and_challenges_for_realising_the_Internet_of_Things

Suzuki, T., Tanaka, H., Minami, S., Yamada, H., & Miyata, T. (2013). Wearable wireless vital monitoring technology for smart health care. *Medical Information and Communication Technology (ISMICT), 2013 7th International Symposium on,* (pp. 1-4).

Swan, M. (2012). Sensor Mania! The Internet of Things, Wearable Computing, Objective Metrics, and the Quantified Self 2.0. *Journal of Sensor and Actuator Networks, 1*(3), 217–253. doi:10.3390/jsan1030217

Technology-Related Assistance for Individuals with Disabilities Act (Tech Act), P.L., 100-407 (1988, 1998, 2004).

Telecom, S. K. (2015). SK Telecom Rargets Global IoT Market with Lifeware. *PRNewswire*. Retrieved from: http://www.prnewswire.com/news-releases/sk-telecom-targets-global-iot-market-with-lifeware-300043278.html

Turcu, C., Turcu, C., & Gaitan, V. (2012). Integrating robots into the internet of things. *International Journal of Circuits, Systems and Signal Processing, 6*(6), 430-437. Retrieved from www.scopus.com

Vilarinho, T., Farshchian, B. A., Floch, J., & Mathisen, B. M. (2013). A communication framework for the internet of people and things based on the concept of activity feeds in social computing. In *Proceedings - 9th International Conference on Intelligent Environments*. doi:10.1109/IE.2013.24

Want, R. (2006). An introduction to RFID technology. *Pervasive Computing, IEEE, 5*(1), 25–33. doi:10.1109/MPRV.2006.2

Weiss, P. S. (2010). Nanoscience and nanotechnology: Present and future. *ACS Nano, 4*(4), 1771–1772. doi:10.1021/nn100710n PMID:20420466

Yu, J., Kim, M., Bang, H. C., Bae, S. H., & Kim, S. J. (2015). IoT as a applications: Cloud-based building management systems for the internet of things. *Multimedia Tools and Applications*. doi:10.1007/s11042-015-2785-0

Zhu, N., Diethe, T., Camplani, M., Tao, L., Burrows, A., Twomey, N., & Craddock, I. (2015). Bridging e-health and the internet of things: The SPHERE project. *IEEE Intelligent Systems, 30*(4), 39–46. doi:10.1109/MIS.2015.57

KEY TERMS AND DEFINITIONS

Assistive Technology (AT): Technologies that assist individuals with disabilities in learning, communication, daily living, and accessing information.

Cloud Computing: A computing paradigm that relies on sharing computing resources such as servers, storage, bandwidth, and applications for an organization's computing needs.

Context-Aware Computing: Computing with the capacity to be aware of environments and their characteristics through sensor.

IoT Applications: Various IoT-based technologies developed to perform specific functions such as monitoring machines remotely, informing a caregiver of the real-time medical condition of a person with disability, etc.

Radio Frequency Identification (RFID): A system of electronic and computing devices which enables objects with embedded tag to be wirelessly identified and tracked.

Sensors: Wired or wireless devices used to monitor and alert change in environments such as temperature, light, sound, motion, etc.

Sensor Network: Sensors that are connected to one another to transmit signals to use for sensing, processing, and communicating via radio medium.

Smart Homes: Homes with various features of ambient assisted living along with surveillance systems and control and optimization devices including lighting, window blinds, heating or alarm installations for people with disabilities.

Smart Sensors: Sensors with microprocessor that can be used for digital signal processing, data filtering, self-diagnosis, self-identification, and self-adaptation.

Section 3
Security, Privacy, and Forensics

Chapter 9
Security Issues and Challenges in Internet of Things

Sudhosil Panda
Silicon Institute of Technology, India

ABSTRACT

The Internet of Things (IoT) aims at connecting a large number of communication and information systems. With the further development of pervasive computing, these systems can be integrated into everyday objects, such as household devices and tools. When complex systems are interconnected, it is complicated to keep track of how secure a system or connection is and to distinguish which devices are connected within the IoT and which devices are not. As to the security, the IoT will be faced with more severe challenges. There are the following reasons: 1) the IoT extends the 'internet' through the traditional internet, mobile network and sensor network and so on, 2) every 'thing' will be connected to this 'internet' and 3) these 'things' will communicate with each other. Therefore, the new security and privacy problems will arise out of which authentication and access control are the most vital security issues that need to be taken care of. Therefore, we should pay more attention to the issues for confidentiality, authenticity and integrity of data in the IoT.

1. INTRODUCTION

Day-by-day the Internet of Things is gaining success in the field of wireless telecommunications. (Atzori, Iera, & Morabito (2010)) Around two billion people are using internet for different purposes. This concept is based on the interaction of various "things" to minimize human effort and start a new technology. The effects of advancements in IoT can be seen in many fields such as e-health, e-traffic etc. The things are connected to the network with the help of Radio Frequency IDentification (RFID) tags, sensor nodes, addressing schemes, data storage mechanisms and visualization processes. This paradigm is slowly becoming the center of all the things or devices that involve human intervention. The interoperability of interconnected devices is the most highlighted issue in case of IoT.

The Internet of Things is a vast arena which is mostly unexplored where all the current technologies can play a role. (Zorzi, Gluhak, Lange, & Bassi (2010)) IoT can be the pillar of future internet and recent

DOI: 10.4018/978-1-5225-1832-7.ch009

advances in reduction of energy consumption, miniaturization of devices and increase in computational power are bringing this concept closer to reality. Because of IoT, it is possible not only to actively interconnect things in physical world, but also to enable them to exchange and make use of their information. In the past decade, the applications of Internet of Things have been more advanced involving applications in healthcare, utilities, transport etc. Based on the use of Radio Frequency IDentification (RFID), Wi-Fi and wireless sensor nodes, IoT has become the center of every activity connected to internet these days.

One of the most challenging topics (Mayer (2009)) in such an interconnected world of miniaturized devices and sensors are its security and privacy aspects i.e. users will be unwilling to adopt this new technology if the privacy of the shared information and data is not ensured as this technology will be invisibly integrated with their environment and life. Having every "thing" connected to a network and making these "things" interact with each other, new security and privacy issues such as: confidentiality, authenticity and integrity of data exchanged by "things". Unauthorized access and tracking of devices should be prevented to make the Internet of Things more secure.

The main challenges (Mahalle, Anggorojati, Prasad, & Prasad (2013)) are to ensure access to data and services to authorized entities, mutual authentication, authorization, identity management and prevention from threats and attacks. Security and privacy are the key issues that determine the future of this web of things.

The rest of the chapter is structured as follows: Section 2 presents the background details, architecture as well as applications of IoT. Section 3 describes why Internet of Things is vulnerable to different security issues and attacks. Section 4 shows the different challenges faced. Section 5 shows the different risks that IoT possesses due to security vulnerabilities. Section 6 describes the central elements to address the security and privacy issues i.e. authentication and access control. The different threats and attacks are described in section 7 and the privacy of network of "things" is given in section 8. The features of IoT that needs to be taken care of are shown in section 9 and the related work done for addressing these security and privacy issues are presented in section 10 before concluding in section 11.

2. BACKGROUND AND RELATED WORK

Converting the concept of IoT into reality is possible by the integration of certain technologies such as: Identification, sensing and communication technologies and other middleware technologies.

The communication technology needs to be advanced to make the technology "anytime, anywhere, anymedia" form. (Atzori, Iera, & Morabito (2010)) Wireless technologies play a vital role for this advancement. Radio can be integrated in any "thing" or "device" that need to be connected to the network. RFID systems are the key elements in this context. This system allows us to integrate radio to the devices for them to be identified. RFID systems consist of a reader and one or more RFID tags. These tags can be uniquely identified and applied to the objects. The reader reads the signal transmitted by RFID tags and these tags respond only to the commands of the reader. Thus real objects can be connected through virtual world through this object recognition mechanism by RFID tags. A RFID tag is a microchip attached to the antenna that is used both for receiving reader signal as well as for transmitting the tag ID. These RFID tags are passive as they do not need direct current supply rather some RFID tags get power supply by batteries.

Figure 1. Internet of Things
Source: www.IoT-A.eu.

Wireless sensor networks also play a vital role in case of IoT. These sensors can get connected to the RFID systems to keep track of the locations and movements of the devices. Sensor networks consist of certain number of sensor nodes that communicate with each other. Recent technological advances in low power integrated circuits and wireless communications have made available efficient, low cost, low power miniature devices for use in remote sensing applications. Sensor data are shared among sensor nodes and sent to a distributed or centralized system for analytics. The sensor nodes report the results of their sensing to a small number of special nodes known as sinks. However, if sensing RFID systems can be implemented in IoT, the applications of IoT may get increased.

The ability to uniquely identify 'Things' is critical for the success of IoT. (Gubbi, Buyya, Marusic, & Palaniswami, 2013) This will not only allow us to uniquely identify billions of devices but also to control remote devices through the Internet. The few most critical features of creating a unique address are: uniqueness, reliability, persistence and scalability. Every element that is already connected and those that are going to be connected, must be identified by their unique identification, location and functionalities. The current IPv4 may support to an extent where a group of cohabiting sensor devices can be identified geographically, but not individually. To address these issues, the Uniform Resource Name (URN) system is considered fundamental for the development of IoT. The things and devices are

Figure 2. Architecture of Internet of Things

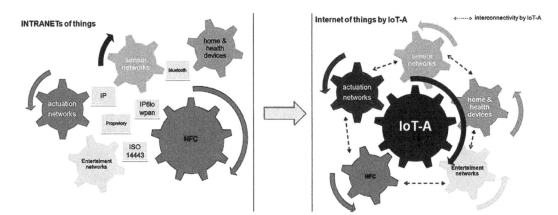

made addressable through URN, accessible through URL (Uniform Resource Locator) and controllable through URC (Uniform Resource Controller).

Due to the recent advances in touch screen technologies, modern world has been moved from 2D to 3D era. Thus more information can be provided through useful ways to the consumer. Hence visualization is critical in IoT as the advances in technologies must be implemented in the root of the devices.

Applications of IoT can be seen in different domains such as transportation, healthcare, personal and social domain. Smart cars, buses, trains are becoming more advanced by sensors and actuators. Roads and other goods are also becoming smarter for sending important information to traffic control sites and for providing appropriate transportation information. The sensors, actuators and processing power

Figure 3. Model for Internet of Things
Source: IBM X-Force Research and Development.

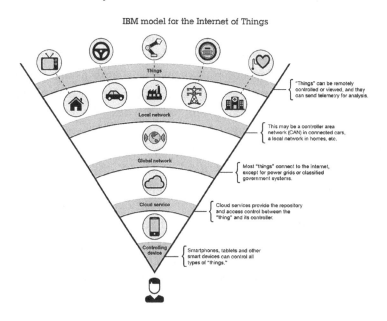

deployed in smart vehicles can also provide information to the driver regarding safety and navigation thus providing assisted driving.

Tracking of objects and people, identification and authentication of staffs and patients and automatic data collection and sensing: these advancements in healthcare domain can only be possible because of IoT. In healthcare domain, there is important usage of smart devices. Tracking enables keeping track of motion of patients and also localization of smart devices. Identification and authentication is required to reduce incidents harmful to patients.

Environment is being smarter due to use of Internet of Things on a daily basis. Sensors and actuators distributed in homes and offices make the day-to-day life more comfortable. Automation in industrial plants is another application of smart environment provided by IoT. Smart museum and gym give more advanced facilities than the normal ones.

Applications of IoT in personal and social domain can be shown by enabling the users to interact with other people to maintain social relationships. This application involves the automatic updation of information about our social activities in social networking sites. Search engine for tools help in finding objects that we have lost or forgotten.

Although the enabling technologies make IoT more feasible and advanced, a research is still required for different open challenges that IoT will face. Privacy involves security of personal information as well as the ability of controlling what happens to this information. Authentication is difficult in IoT as it requires appropriate infrastructures for implementing authentication which may not be available in case of IoT. Integrity of data is provided by enabling the security of data by using passwords but in case of IoT, the passwords used are too short to provide strong protection. A lot of private information can be collected from the smart devices. Control on this information is weak in current IoT techniques. As most of the communications are wireless in IoT, eavesdropping is more daunting and thus different attacks are also possible for smart devices. Most of the IoT components have low energy and computational power. The system also has to be resilient to all kinds of security attacks that it can face. Hence technologies

Figure 4. Applications of Internet of Things
Source: Atzori, Iera, & Morabito (2010).

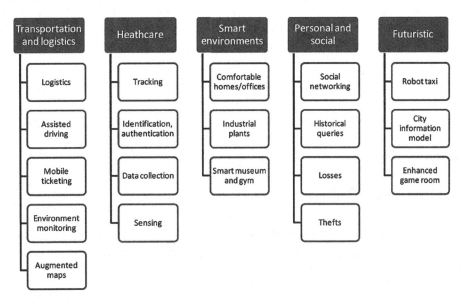

involving security and privacy may not be supported in IoT. The problem becomes nearly impossible to be solved in case of wireless sensor networks.

Though the fulfilment of customer privacy requirements is nearly impossible, still there are some privacy enhancing technologies (PET) (Weber (2010)) that are deployed to secure IoT. *Virtual Private Networks (VPN)* are used by close groups of business partners as they promise to have integrity. But this technique is impractical in case of third parties. *Transport Layer Security (TLS)* can also have confidentiality and integrity of IoT, but it can also be affected negatively by the other layers. *DNS Security Extensions (DNSSEC)* use public key cryptography to guarantee authenticity and integrity of data and information, but it can only assure global information authenticity. *Onion Routing* mixes internet traffic from different from different sources i.e. data is encapsulated in multiple layers of encryption, but as this increases waiting time, there are performance issues. *Private Information Retrieval (PIR)* is a system in which the customer only sees the information that he/she is interested in, but it also becomes impractical in a globally accessible system. Hence, as all the techniques deployed till now are inappropriate and impractical, the Internet of Things system becomes vulnerable to all kinds of security and privacy issues.

It's not that no work is done for securing this unsecure Internet of Things. Previously, any techniques have been proposed. The proposed work has been discussed below.

2.1. Key Establishment

Key establishment protocols or key exchange protocols (Saied, Olivereau, Zeghlache, Laurent (2014)) are used for to provide sharing secrets between two or more parties for cryptographic purposes. These protocols use message authentication codes as security primitives for enabling authentication, integrity protection and confidentiality.

Two party key transfer protocol is used in which one or more secret value(s) are generated at one peer and are secretly transferred to the other. These keys are generated from public information exchanged between the peers. A resulting key is derived at both peers as a function of transferred secret values and other parameters that may have been exchanged during key transport.

Key transport and key agreement rely on either symmetric or asymmetric cryptography. Key transport with symmetric cryptographic primitives, involves algorithms in which two peer, already owning a shared key, derive another one. Key transport with asymmetric cryptographic primitives, involves protocols in which one pass encryption of secret key with public key as well as more complex encryption methods are used.

Authentication for a pair-wise key establishment protocol refers to binding the keying material with the identity of its peer. Commonly, only one peer is authenticated to the other.

The existing key establishment protocols are mainly based on asymmetric cryptography. However, symmetric cryptography based key establishment protocols do exist but they consist key refresh or key derivation protocols which do not qualify key establishment protocol requirements.

2.2. Trust in Internet of Things

Users need to know the technology's intentions, in order to make right decisions for protecting their data. (Yan, Zhang, Vasilakos (2014)) Awareness of technology's intent is a prerequisite for trust management of a system.

Legal data protection mechanisms need to be established. Currently available legal measures are insufficient for security of smart devices. Design should be used to create trustworthy interfaces and communicate real trustworthiness to the user. Security, design and technology need to be built around the user's needs. The technology should make the devices more efficient.

To provide a good communication between the user and the system, the users should be provided with information about consequences for connecting to an unsecure network and other security issues.

2.3. Identity Authentication and Capability Based Access Control (IACAC)

Wireless Internet Service Provider roaming (WISPr) is the existing solution to provide centralized authentication and authorization in Wi-Fi. IACAC is compatible with underline access technologies like Bluetooth, 4G, WiMax and Wi-Fi. This algorithm involves secret key generation, identity establishment and capability creation for access control.

Secret key is established using key establishment protocol. Identity establishment or authentication can be one-way authentication or mutual authentication. For capability creation, a token can be used that gives permission for accessing devices.

The IACAC protocol (Mahalle, Anggorojati, Prasad, & Prasad (2013)) for mutual authentication and access control for IoT devices takes less time as compared to other models proposed for authentication and access control.

2.4. Rapid Identification Authentication Protocol

It is a convenient protocol in the environment of Internet of Things with privacy protection where the mobile nodes are required to be authenticated by a cluster to perform communication. This method involves a valid request message and an answer authentication message which implements identification authentication and privacy protection. As compared to other privacy mechanisms, this protocol is proven to be more efficient and privacy preserving having less communication overhead. The purpose of this authentication protocol is to provide access of IoT to legitimate users. Role-Based Access Control mechanism is used for controlling unauthorized access.

2.5. Protocol and Network Security

It is important to provide support for existing security protocols. Some protocols can be implemented without any major changes but some other need to be adapted due to complexity of their design. Such protocols need to have a tradeoff between simplicity and adaptability. However, beyond the optimization of security protocols there is also implementation of compact cryptographic algorithms.

2.6. Distributed Secret Sharing

In secret sharing, a trusted central authority shares a single secret for many users. In distributed secret sharing, unconditional secrecy is achieved through the server's use of hash functions for share generation that are known only to the server; not even the users can access the share.

Traditional secret sharing creates shares from a single unique secret where as in case of distributed secret sharing, each sensor has a correlated reading of the others representing a composite secret. In traditional secret sharing, an attacker just needs to physically compromise the server to eavesdrop but in distributed secret sharing, a general security solution is provided for all the sensors in IoT. A visual secrecy measure is employed which degrades proportional to the number of shares in possession of an eavesdropper. Hence, this scheme is proposed for multimedia traffic security for IoT.

2.7. Public Key Cryptography and Pre-Shared Keys

Digital signature schemes, key exchange protocols and public key encryption schemes can be used for implementation of public key cryptography (PKC) (Roman, Alcaraz, Lopez, Sklavos (2011)). The distribution of secret key can be done both online and offline and the public key certificates can be preloaded in the devices or transmitted upon request. Also, both clients and servers can be authenticated. As the device stores its public key and private key, an attacker can only have control over that particular device. The performance of PKC in client nodes can be too low to be used in web server.

In the pre-shared key strategy, the clients and servers share some pre-established keying material that can be used to derive a shared key between peers. Actually, in a WSN scenario, there are multiple approaches to implement this particular strategy. For example, for external connections, a group of sensor nodes can have the same pre-shared secret, or every sensor node can have its own pre-shared secret.

One of the major drawbacks of these approaches is that, it is possible to connect clients and servers that already know each other and another drawback is the overall resilience of these approaches. As one element stores the security key, that element becomes the weakest link of the security chain.

3. SECURITY VULNERABILITIES

As we talk about IoT being used in every field, we should also consider its security and privacy aspect. Last year, an unknown attacker used a known vulnerability in a popular web connected baby monitor to spy on a two-year-old. This eye opening incident shows what a high risk IoT poses to enterprises as well as people. According to a study from HP security research, 70% of the most commonly used IoT devices had security vulnerabilities. Thus, the security vulnerabilities in IoT can be discussed in different areas or fields that are used for data exchange as well as device accessing. (Mayer (2009))

- **Communication:** Mechanisms for securing communication in Internet of Things are well established but seldom applied. And in small devices with weak processing power, communication security is often missing.
- **Sensors:** Privacy is a major problem in case of sensors. The main cause of this is people unaware of being sensed. This is happening because users are unable to opt out of being sensed.
- **Devices:** Integrity of devices is an issue that needs to be taken care of at the earliest. This is an issue that still is unresolved and is the main reason of security vulnerabilities.
- **Storage:** Mechanisms for integrity of stored data are unfortunately complex to employ. Hence the information sensitive to privacy should be ensured not to be contained in stored data.
- **Data Processing:** Mechanisms for data processing must ensure that no private data is being sent to untrusted devices or storage. Mechanisms for preserving privacy of data are seldom applied.
- **Localization and Tracking:** Tracking of smart devices mechanism is poorly applied in case of IoT. The users should be able to track their smart devices in case of data theft or loss.

Figure 5. Challenges faced by Internet of Things
Source: www.ejanco.com/Article/2014.

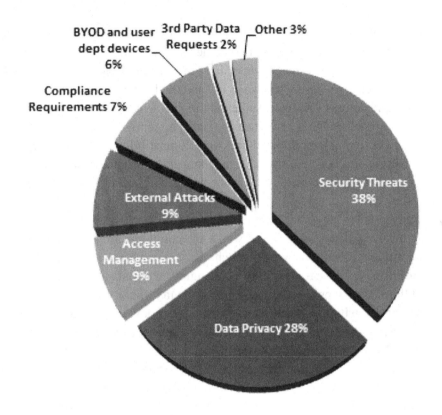

4. CHALLENGES

In order to make the IoT services available at low cost with a large number of devices communicating to each other, there are many challenges to overcome. These challenges are divided into two categories as: Technical challenges and Security challenges. (Mahalle, Anggorojati, Prasad, & Prasad (2013))

Here, the security challenges faced by IoT are briefly discussed.

- **Heterogeneity:** IoT should be able to integrate many types of devices, technologies and services. (Zorzi, Gluhak, Lange, & Bassi (2010)) It includes different types of features for data communication capabilities, energy availability, storage power of different devices. The system should be able to support varieties of different applications in terms of characteristics and requirements. These qualities of the system make data communication more challenging especially, due to wireless communications among devices of varying capabilities and performance leading to degradation of performance of the whole system.
- **Scalability:** Unbounded number of devices create larger scope and scalability. Presence of large number of nodes cannot be expected to be well-coordinated making the performance of most communication systems suffer. In wireless context, these problems become more daunting. Management of a large network becomes too difficult in a distributed environment and solutions for this problem need to be found.

- **Connectivity:** In wireless communications, connecting various devices of different capabilities is another challenge to be taken care of. Issues such as interoperability of various devices, energy consumption will have to be addressed.

- **End-to-End Security:** End-to-end security measures between IoT devices and Internet hosts are equally important. Applying cryptographic schemes for encryption and authentication codes to a packet is not sufficient for the resource constrained IoT. Hence future research is required into efficient end-to-end security measures between IoT and the Internet.

- **Authentication and Access Control:** Authentication is identity establishment between communicating parties. Authentication is important to establish secure communication between multiple devices and services. Interoperability and backward compatibility are the two key issues to be addressed. Another important aspect related to authentication, is authorization. If there is no access control, everything will be accessed by everyone which will lead to all kinds of different security issues.

- **Identity Management:** Due to the scale of economics in the IoT, unbounded numbers of things or objects are involved in accessing IoT networks and communicating with each other. Hence, efficient and lightweight identity management schemes are required. In addition to this, the distributed nature of IoT makes this problem more challenging. Without authentication, it is not possible to assure that the data flow produced by an entity contains what it is supposed to contain.

- **Attack Resistant Security Solutions:** Due to diversity of devices and end users, there should be attack resistant and lightweight security solutions. All the devices in IoT have low memory and limited computation resources, thus they are vulnerable to resource enervation attack. When the devices join and commissioned into the network, keying material, security and domain parameters could be eavesdropped. Possible external attacks like denial of service attack, flood attack, etc., on device and mitigation plan to address these attacks is another big challenge.

5. SECURITY RISKS

IoT possibilities are limitless and so are the number of devices that could manifest. Any device that can connect to internet has an embedded operating system deployed in its firmware. As embedded operating systems are often not designed with security as its primary consideration, there are vulnerabilities and these vulnerabilities are discussed in section 3. However, in this section, the risks that IoT poses due to security and privacy issues are discussed.

- Paralyzing a service is more serious if all devices are connected.
- Malicious codes can be used to infect hundreds of computers to control a network of smart devices or to put their software in danger.
- Spying on communications and gathering data on these smart devices can compromise our privacy.
- Our confidential data can be lost or accidentally disclosed if the devices do not protect privacy.
- Cyber attackers could potentially hijack sensitive information recorded by the devices, their mobile apps and cloud services.
- These cyber-attacks can be a risk for physical safety of consumers.

Figure 6. Security challenges in Internet of Things
Source: Miorandi, Sicari, Pellegrini, & Chlamtac (2012).

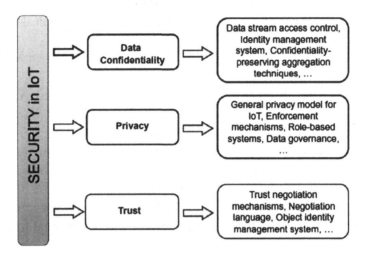

6. AUTHENTICATION AND ACCESS CONTROL

Authentication and access control technologies (Sandhu & Samarati (1996)) are known as the central elements to address security and privacy problems in computer networks. They help in preventing unauthorized users from accessing to resources, preventing legitimate users from accessing resources in an unauthorized manner, and enabling legitimate users to access resources in an authorized manner. When building an IoT infrastructure, the efficiency, security scalability and market oriented computing, power resource and storage features should always be taken into consideration for the best quality of services to be provided to the costumers or users.

6.1. Authentication

Authentication can be of three types:

1. **Password-Based Authentication:** Password-based authentication is the most common technique but it has significant problems. It is based on something that the user knows, such as a password. Passwords can be observed or guessed. Password management should allow the users to change their passwords regularly and to protect them. Users can share the passwords with other users, which breaks down accountability; this is the major problem for password-based authentication. However, as passwords are effective and cheap, they are likely to remain in use.
2. **Token-Based Authentication:** It is based on something that the user has, such as a cryptographic token or a smart card. However, this method does not authenticates the user rather it authenticates the token. Each token contains a secret key which should not be revealed at any cost and attempts to break the token to know the secret key should cause the key to be lost. User-to-token authentication should be based on passwords in the form of PIN.
3. **Biometric Authentication:** It is based on something that the user is, such as a biometric signature in the form of a finger print or voice print. This method is used for high-end application.

Technically, the best combination would be user-to-token biometric authentication, followed by mutual cryptographic authentication between the token and system services. This combination may emerge sooner than we imagine, although there are social issues in addition to technical ones.

6.2. Access Control

Access control schemes are usually applied after authentication is established. Access control can take several forms such as:

- **Discretionary Access Control (DAC):** It is based on the idea that owner of the data decides who has access to it, but DAC allows the data to be copied from object to object, so even if access to the original data is denied, access to copy can be obtained.
- **Lattice-Based or Mandatory Access Control (MAC):** This method confines the transfer of information to one direction in a lattice of security labels. It has emerged from confidentiality requirements of military.
- **Role-Based Access Control (RBAC):** It requires that access rights should be assigned to roles rather than individual users as in DAC. Users obtain these rights by being assigned membership in appropriate roles.

Existing systems take a feature based approach for access control in which multiple facilities are configured. Unfortunately, access control features are poorly implemented.

7. THREATS AND ATTACKS

An important aspect is to note down the activities of IoT attacks to understand the sequence of actions taking place when the attacks are happening. The modelling of the security attacks (Roman, Alcaraz, Lopez, & Sklavos (2011)) helps to understand an actual view of the IoT networks and enables us to decide the mitigation plans.

- **Man-in-the-Middle Attack:** When the devices are commissioned into a network, keying material, security and domain parameters could be eavesdropped. (Mahalle, Anggorojati, Prasad, & Prasad (2013)) Keying material can reveal the secret key between devices and authenticity of the communication channel could be compromised. Man-in-the-middle attack is one type of the eavesdropping possible in the IoT. Passive attackers can target various communication channels to extract data from information flow. As device authentication involves exchange of device identities, identity theft is possible due to man-in-the-middle attack.
- **Denial of Service Attack:** All the devices in IoT have low memory and limited resources, thus they are vulnerable to resource usage attack. Attackers can send messages or requests to specific device so as to consume their resources. This attack is more serious in IoT since attacker might be single in number and resource constrained devices are large in numbers. Wide range of DoS attacks can be launched against IoT. The actual wireless communication infrastructure can be targeted and malicious internal attackers can take control of a part of the infrastructure.

- **Replay Attack:** During the exchange of identity related information or other credentials in IoT, this information can be spoofed, altered or replayed to repel network traffic. This causes a very serious replay attack. Replay attack is essentially one form of active man-in-the-middle attack. Our solution prevents replay attacks by maintaining the freshness of random number, for example by using time stamp or nonce by including Message Authentication Code (MAC) as well.
- **Node Capture:** Things are located in certain environment. An active attacker cam extracts the information that the devices contain instead of destroying them. The attackers can also target the infrastructures that store information for data processing or data storage.
- **Physical Damage:** Active attackers usually lack technical knowledge and can only affect IoT system by destroying the things and devices that are commissioned into a network. This attack is daunting in IoT as the 'things' might be easily accessible to everyone.
- **Controlling:** As long as there is an attack path, active attackers can gain partial or full control over IoT entities. The damage that can be caused by this kind of attacker depends upon the importance of data managed by that particular entity and the services provided by that entity.

8. PRIVACY OF NETWORK OF "THINGS"

Whenever networks are deployed in a large scale, security becomes a major concern. There are many ways a network can be attacked; it may be weakening of RFID system or cloud of things, networks have always been vulnerable for security and privacy issues.

As RFID includes tracking and identification of object, it is the most vulnerable entity of IoT in case of security attacks. Also the things and objects are not intelligence enabled. Cryptographic methods can be used for this purpose. High level encryption techniques can be used to ensure data confidentiality and as discussed earlier, authentication methods are used to ensure data authenticity. Sensor nodes also need to be reprogrammed for updating sensor applications. A secure programming technique can be used to authenticate the code updates and prevent malicious installation.

Security of cloud of things is also a security challenge that needs to be taken care of. Security and identity protection becomes critical in network of things. Wireless channel increases the risk of security attacks due to remote access capabilities which exposes the system to different security and privacy attacks.

9. FEATURES THAT IoT NEEDS TO SUPPORT

- **Devices heterogeneity:** IoT will be characterized by a large heterogeneity in terms of devices taking part in the system, which are expected to present very different capabilities from the computational and communication standpoints. The management of such a high level of heterogeneity shall be supported at both architectural and protocol levels. In particular, this may question the ''thin waist'' approach at the basis of IP networking.
- **Scalability:** As everyday objects get connected to a global information infrastructure, scalability issues arise at different levels, including:
  - **Naming and Addressing:** Due to the sheer size of the resulting system,
  - **Data Communication and Networking:** Due to the high level of interconnection among a large number of entities,

- ○ **Information and Knowledge Management:** Due to the possibility of building a digital counterpart to any entity and/or phenomena in the physical realm and
- ○ **Service Provisioning and Management:** Due to the massive number of services/service execution options that could be available and the need to handle heterogeneous resources.
- **Ubiquitous Data Exchange through Proximity Wireless Technologies:** In IoT, a prominent role will be played by wireless communications technologies, which will enable smart objects to become networked. The ubiquitous adoption of the wireless medium for exchanging data may pose issues in terms of spectrum availability, pushing towards the adoption of cognitive/dynamic radio systems.
- **Energy-Optimized Solutions:** For a variety of IoT entities, minimizing the energy to be spent for communication/computing purposes will be a primary constraint. While techniques related to energy harvesting (by means, e.g., of piezoelectric materials or micro solar panels) will relieve devices from the constraints imposed by battery operations, energy will always be a scarce resource to be handled with care. Thereby the need to devise solutions that tend to optimize energy usage (even at the expenses of performance) will become more and more attractive.
- **Localization and Tracking Capabilities:** As entities in IoT can be identified and are provided with short-range wireless communications capabilities, it becomes possible to track the location (and the movement) of smart objects in the physical realm. This is particularly important for application in logistics and product life-cycle management, which are already extensively adopting RFID technologies.
- **Self-Organization Capabilities:** In order to support the expected scale of the IoT, devices will need to self-manage without external intervention. Smart objects should be able to react to wide range of situations to minimize human intervention. Objects should be able to perform device and service recovery without external trigger.
- **Embedded Security and Privacy-Preserving Mechanisms:** Due to the tight entanglement with the physical realm, IoT technology should be secure and privacy-preserving by design. This means that security should be considered a key system-level property, and be taken into account in the design of architectures and methods for IoT solutions. This is expected to represent a key requirement for ensuring acceptance by users and the wide adoption of the technology.

10. MEASURES FOR SECURING NETWORK OF THINGS

- Security should be built into devices at the design stage; access risks, collect the necessary minimum information.
- Authentication methods must be adequate adopting stronger passwords so that the data is correctly encrypted.
- Many devices are connected via wireless network. So strong encryption methods must be adopted.
- Special care should be taken with software and firmware of the smart devices i.e. they should be able to update and each update must incorporate security mechanisms.
- Smart devices should be provided with right set of tools and mechanisms required to provide security preserving capabilities.
- Any project involving IoT must be designed with security in mind and incorporate security controls.

- Extra measures should be considered to keep unauthorized users away from accessing personal data stored by devices.
- Connected devices should be carefully monitored throughout their expected life cycle and security patches should be provided for all known risks.

11. CONCLUSION

Heterogeneous wireless networks possess a lot of security risks. Internet of Things is becoming the technical reality today. The day when virtually everything will be connected to internet is not far away. The use of this mechanism will be further more if it will be more secure.

In this chapter, we have discussed the architecture and central elements of Internet of Things. The different security and privacy issues that need to be taken care of are identified. The features of IoT that need to be supported are described. Some proposed models for improving the security and privacy feature of IoT are also shown.

REFERENCES

Atzori, L., Iera, A., & Morabito, G. (2010). Internet of Things: A Survey. *Computer Networks*, 54.

Gubbi, J., Buyya, R., Marusic, S., & Palaniswami, M. (2013). Internet of Things (IoT): A vision, architectural elements, and future directions. *Future Generation Computer Systems*, 29.

Hochleitner, C., Graf, C., Unger, D., & Tscheligi, M. (2012). Making Devices Trustworthy: Security and Trust Feedback in the Internet of Things.*Fourth International Workshop on Security and Privacy in Spontaneous Interaction and Mobile Phone Use (IWSSI/SPMU)*.

Kai, K., Zhi-bo, P., & Cong, W. (2013). Security and privacy mechanism for health Internet of Things. *The Journal of China Universities of Posts and Telecommunications, 20*(Suppl. 2).

Kumar, J. S., & Patel, D. R. (2014). A Survey on Internet of Things: Security and Privacy Issues. *International Journal of Computer Applications, 90*(11).

Liu, C. H., Yang, B., & Liu, T. (2014). Efficient naming, addressing and profile services in Internet-of-Things sensory environments. *Ad Hoc Networks*, 18.

Mahalle, P. N., Anggorojati, B., Prasad, N. R., & Prasad, R. (2013). Identity Authentication and Capability based Access Control (IACAC) for the Internet of Things. *Journal of Cyber Security and Mobility, 1*.

Mayer, C. P. (2009). *Security and Privacy Challenges in the Internet of Things* (Vol. 17). Electronic Communications of the EASST.

Miorandi, D., Sicari, S., Pellegrini, F. D., & Chlamtac, I. (2012). Internet of things: Vision, applications and research challenges. *Ad Hoc Networks*, 10.

Ndibanje, B., Lee, H., & Lee, S. (2014). Security Analysis and Improvements of Authentication and Access Control in the Internet of Things. *Sensors (Basel, Switzerland)*, 14. PMID:25123464

Qiang, C., Quan, G., Yu, B., & Yang, L. (2013). Research on Security Issues of the Internet of Things. *International Journal of Future Generation Communication and Networking, 6*(6).

Ray, B. R., Abawajy, J., & Chowdhury, M. (2014). Scalable RFID security framework and protocol supporting Internet of Things. *Computer Networks*, 67.

Roman, R., Alcaraz, C., Lopez, J., & Sklavos, N. (2011). Key management systems for sensor networks in the context of te Internet of Things. *Computers & Electrical Engineering*, 37.

Roman, R., Zhou, J., & Lopez, J. (2013). On the features and challenges of security and privacy in distributed internet of things. *Computer Networks*, 57.

Saied, Y. B., Olivereau, A., Zeghlache, D., & Laurent, M. (2014). Lightweight collaborative key establishment scheme for the Internet of Things. *Computer Networks*, 64.

Sandhu, R., & Samarati, P. (1996). Authentication, access control, and audit. *ACM Computing Surveys, 28*(1), 241–243. doi:10.1145/234313.234412

Suo, H., Wan, J., Zou, C., & Liu, J. (2012). Security in the Internet of Things: A Review.*International Conference on Computer Science and Electronics Engineering*. doi:10.1109/ICCSEE.2012.373

Weber, R. H. (2010). Internet of Things – New security and privacy challenges. *Computer Law and Security Review, 26*.

Yan, Z., Zhang, P., & Vasilakos, A. V. (2014). A survey on trust management for Internet of Things. *Journal of Network and Computer Applications*, 42.

Zhou, L., & Chao, H. (2011). Multimedia Traffic Security Architecture for the Internet of Things. *IEEE Network, 25*(3), 35–40. doi:10.1109/MNET.2011.5772059

Zorzi, M., Gluhak, A., Lange, S., & Bassi, A. (2010). From Today's INTRAnet of Things to Future INTERnet of Things- and Mobility- Related View. *IEEE Wireless Communications*.

This work was previously published in the Handbook of Research on Advanced Wireless Sensor Network Applications, Protocols, and Architectures edited by Niranjan K. Ray and Ashok Kumar Turuk, pages 369-385, copyright year 2017 by Information Science Reference (an imprint of IGI Global).

Chapter 10

A Study on M2M (Machine to Machine) System and Communication:
Its Security, Threats, and Intrusion Detection System

Rami Haidar Ahmad
Technische Universität Berlin (TU Berlin), Lebanon

Al-Sakib Khan Pathan
Southeast University, Bangladesh

ABSTRACT

The increase of the applications of numerous innovative technologies and associated devices has brought forward various new concepts like Cyber-Physical System (CPS), Internet of Things (IoT), Smart environment, Smart cities, and so on. While the boundary lines between these concepts and technologies are often kind of blur and perhaps, each one's development is helping the development of the other, M2M (Machine to Machine) communication would surely play a great role as a key enabler of all these emerging scenarios. When we see the same smart concept from different angles; for instance, from the participating device, or human being's angle, we get different definitions and concept-specific standards. In this chapter, our objective is to study M2M system and communication along with its security issues and intrusion detection systems. We have also proposed our framework in line with the standardization efforts for tackling security issues of M2M.

INTRODUCTION

According to a prediction by Ericsson, by the year 2020, 50 billion devices will be connected to the Internet ("More than,", 2011). We have already started seeing the effects of Internet-based communications in a massive scale. A key aspect of this kind of communication is the underlying technology

DOI: 10.4018/978-1-5225-1832-7.ch010

of Machine to Machine (M2M) communication. M2M basically refers to technologies that allow both wireless and wired systems to communicate with other devices of the same type. In practice, Machine to machine (M2M) is a broad label which is applied to describe any technology that enables networked devices to exchange information and perform actions without the manual assistance of human beings. M2M is considered an integral part of the Internet of Things (IoT) and its nervous system (Duquet, 2015), which brings several benefits to industry and business. It is expected that in the coming years, both of our personal life and business life would be heavily influenced by M2M communication technologies. Usually, M2M systems allow a large number of diverse devices to communicate with each other over converged networks without human intervention. Recent studies (Duquet, 2015; Świątek, Tarasiuk, & Natkaniec, 2015; Hakiri & Berthou, 2015; Pathan, Khanam, Saleem, & Abduallah, 2013) mention a significant increase in the number of connected devices in various application domains such as eHealth, city automation, and smart metering, which will make a significant impact in the way we live today.

To get a better picture of M2M, we need to know that for quite a long time, it has been a real challenge to connect smart devices, sensors, meters to a network or to the Internet and to enable all these devices to share an application (bidirectional: sending and receiving information) without any manual effort of humans. After years of research works, with the advancements of various technologies, this objective has been somewhat achieved today. The enhancements of the capabilities of the end devices have truly started changing our daily life and more innovating business opportunities are expected from these in near future ("The Global," 2009; W. Ren, Yu, Ma, & Y. Ren, 2013). This scenario is what we call as M2M, i.e., Machine to Machine communication. Figure 1 shows a conceptual diagram.

A representative example of practical usage of M2M is in smart grid networks. The smart grid is an electronically controlled electrical grid that connects power generation, transmission, distribution, and consumers using Information and Communication Technologies (Zeadally, Pathan, Alcaraz, & Badra, 2013). Smart grid needs the support for bi-directional information flow between the consumer of electricity and the utility provider. To implement such an intelligent electricity network, smart metering system in M2M can facilitate flexible demand management in which case, a smart meter (SM) would be a two-way communicating device that would measure energy (e.g., electricity, gas, water, heat) consumption and communicate that information via some communications channels back to the local utility (Tan, Sooriyabandara, & Fan, 2011). In addition to that, there are models of M2M based sensor communications or mobile networks (Dohler, Boswarthick, & Alonso-Zárate, 2012) which could add more functionalities to the smart grid environment.

The European Telecommunications Standards Institute (ETSI) is now working as one of the leading standardization organizations producing globally-applicable standards for M2M sector (the readers are encouraged to see various M2M standards available at (W. Ren et al., 2013; "Machine-to-Machine communications," 2015; Chang, Soong, Tseng, & Xiang, 2011). The fundamental idea is to develop the existing vertical M2M applications, which use a multitude of technical solutions and diverse standards, into a fully interoperable M2M service platform that would permit horizontal business models (as shown in Figure 2 (diagram generated based on (Koss, 2014)). To clarify a bit, a vertical application basically refers to any software or other application that can support a specific business-process and targets a relatively smaller number of users with specific skill sets and job responsibilities within an organization. The horizontal M2M architecture would allow applications to share common data, infrastructure and network elements.

Security in Machine to Machine communication is addressed especially in the later ETSI specifications releases ("Machine-to-Machine communications (M2M)," 2011). Bootstrapping (e.g., Generic

Figure 1. Basic M2M concept

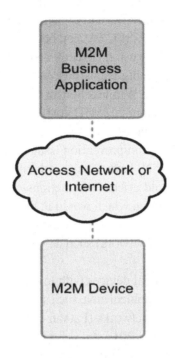

Figure 2. From vertical applications to horizontal business model

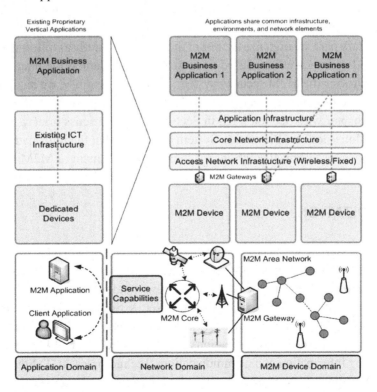

Bootstrapping Architecture (GBA), Extensible Authentication Protocol (EAP) based) key provisioning and hierarchy derivation, service connection and registration are well defined in the specifications alongside the Security Service Capability, xSEC ('*x*' can be the device gateway or the network).

While research in the field of M2M Intrusion Detection System (IDS) or Intrusion Prevention System (IPS) is still in its infancy stage and a big gap still exists, M2M systems have inherited many new challenges and security threats either from Wireless Sensor Networks (WSNs) or from other emerging computer networking technologies. Therefore, M2M IDS (MIDS) system has to combine the two features; first, of the IDS for computer networks and second, of the IDS for the WSNs or similar low-resource networks. This makes the intrusion detection/prevention issue even more complicated in this case. For instance, Wireless Sensor Networks (WSN) have a major vulnerability like the Denial of Service (DoS) (Wood & Stankovic, 2002), which would affect the functions of this network by causing the stop of transmission of valuable sensed information which would in turn cause the collapse of the whole decision making system that is based on the sensors (i.e., tiny physical device). Again, M2M can be affected by many others threats (as in a computer network) such as virus, unauthorized access of services, and so on (Lee, 2013; Qiu & Ma, 2015).

As M2M systems often have many small devices with low computational power and battery power, and they are implemented in a wide geographical area, such systems face relatively more security threats than the usual computer communication networks (Pathan et al., 2013; Aboelaze & Aloul, 2005; Abduvaliyev, Pathan, Zhou, Roman, & Wong, 2013; Lu, Li, Liang, Shen, & Lin, 2011; Shih et al., 2013; Cha, Shah, Schmidt, Leicher, & Meyerstein, 2009). The usual security procedure of key generation, distribution, authentication, encryption and so on, are not anyway alone capable of affording security for a widely distributed hybrid system or environment (like that is between WSN and computerized systems). Therefore, IDS or IPS would play a major role here, and any pragmatic IDS/IPS has to take all these details into consideration.

With this introductory part, we organize the rest of the part of this study as follows: Section II discusses the ETSI's M2M standardization effort. Based on that, Section III depicts the functional architecture of M2M, Section IV addresses the M2M security system. Then, in Section V, we analyze various security threats against M2M. We propose our generally applicable framework for M2M IDS in Section VI. Before concluding the chapter with Section VIII, in Section VII, we discuss briefly some supplementary issues about wireless Intrusion and Prevention System (IDPS) so that the information could be used for future works while devising technical solutions for the wireless segment of M2M IDS.

M2M STANDARDIZATION

As mentioned before, the European Telecommunications Standards Institute (ETSI) has been generating the common standardization of M2M technology with the objective of achieving global applicability. Another related organization, oneM2M, is supposed to be also a new standardization body for M2M technology. oneM2M ([oneM2M], 2015; Swetina, Lu, Jacobs, Ennesser, & Song, 2014) was launched in 2012 as a global initiative to ensure the most efficient worldwide deployment of M2M communications systems and the Internet of Things (IoT). This organization comprises of fourteen (14) partners including ETSI and seven other leading Information and Communications Technologies (ICT) Standards Development Organizations (SDOs) representatives of different industry sectors. Existing vertical M2M applications use a multitude of technical solutions and diverse standards; hence, these formally established bodies are working towards developing fully interoperable M2M service platform to support various horizontal business models. The high level architecture of M2M is shown in Figure 3.

Based on such M2M architecture, the M2M system can be divided into different components which will be presented in the following subsections.

Device and Gateway Domain

- **M2M Device:** This is the end-user device, which can be either mobile or a static one. It can be a device with M2M application and M2M service capabilities (ETSI standardized device) or any other device such as Zigbee device, android or others (Non-ETSI standardized device).
- **M2M Gateway:** It is a device that acts as a proxy between the M2M devices and the network domain. It would run M2M application and use M2M service capabilities.
- **M2M Area Network:** It is any network that facilitates the connectivity between the M2M device and the M2M Gateway.

Network Domain

- **Access Network:** Allows M2M Device and Gateway domain to communicate with the Network domain, Access network may be but not limited to xDSL (Digital Subscriber Line - the '*x*' in xDSL is a variable that can change depending upon the speed and application of the xDSL technology like for instance, ADSL, VDSL, etc.), HFC (Hybrid Fiber-Coaxial), satellite, GERAN (GSM/EDGE Radio Access Network), UTRAN (Universal Terrestrial Radio Access Network), W-LAN (Wireless Local Area Network) and WiMAX (Worldwide Interoperability for Microwave Access).
- **Core Network:** It can provide the IP (Internet Protocol) connectivity, the service and network control functions, Interconnection (with other networks), Roaming and other services. Access network and the core network can be assumed together as a mobile operator providing the M2M services.
- **M2M Service Capabilities:** Provide M2M functions that are to be shared by different applications by exposing them through a set of open interfaces. M2M service capabilities use Core Network functionalities.
- **M2M Applications:** These applications run using M2M service capabilities so they are accessible through open interfaces.
- **M2M Management Functions:** These are the functions required for managing M2M Service Capabilities in the Network Domain. MSBF (M2M Service Bootstrap Function) is the first function and is realized within an appropriate server. It is responsible of facilitating the bootstrapping of M2M service layer security credentials in the M2M Device (or M2M Gateway) and the M2M Service Capabilities in the Network Domain. Permanent security credentials that are bootstrapped using MSBF are stored in MAS (M2M Authentication Server), a safe location, which can be an AAA (Authentication, Authorization, and Accounting) server. MSBF can be included within MAS, or it may communicate the bootstrapped security credentials to MAS, through an appropriate interface (e.g., Diameter (Calhoun, Zorn, Pan, & Akhtar, 2001) for the case where MAS is an AAA server).

Figure 3. M2M architecture
Adopted from ("Machine-to-Machine communications (M2M)," 2011)

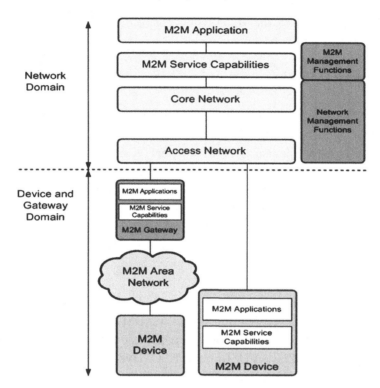

- **Network Management Functions:** Functions that are required to manage the Access and Core Networks: Provisioning, Supervision, Fault Management, etc.

FUNCTIONAL ARCHITECTURE OF M2M

After knowing the overview of M2M system architecture as mentioned in the previous section, it is necessary to get some knowledge about the functional architecture of M2M, including the service capabilities and the reference points.

The main strength of M2M system is in the Service Capabilities Layer (SCL) which provides M2M functions that are to be exposed to different M2M applications through a set of interfaces. In this section, we will mention all these service capabilities in the Device, Gateway and Network sides. Also, we will learn about various types of interfaces (just to note here, Security Service Capability will be mentioned in the security system part later).

M2M Service Capabilities List

Service Capabilities ("Machine-to-Machine communications (M2M)," 2011) are in the three main parts of an M2M system, i.e., in the device, gateway and network (see Figure 4). Therefore, 'x' here (as noted below) can be gateway, device, or network.

- Application Enablement (xAE)
- Generic Communication (xGC)
- Reachability, Addressing and Repository (xRAR)
- Communication Selection (xCS)
- Remote Entity Management (xREM)
- SECurity (xSEC)
- History and Data Retention (xHDR)
- Transaction Management (xTM)
- Compensation Broker (xCB)
- Telco Operator Exposure (xTOE)
- Interworking Proxy (xIP)

It should be noted here that, not all M2M Service Capabilities are needed to be instantiated in different parts of the system, but rather the interfaces are considered obligatory.

M2M Reference Points

- **mIa:** The *mIa* reference point ("Machine-to-Machine communications (M2M)," 2015) offers generic and extendable mechanism for Network Applications (NA) interactions with the NSCL (Network Service Capability Layer). The *mIa* reference point, between NA and NSCL, supports the following functions:
  - Registration of NA to the NSCL.

Figure 4. M2M functional architecture

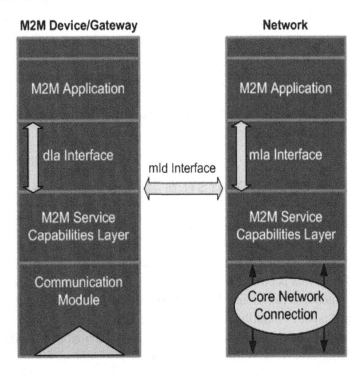

- Requesting to Read/Write, subject to proper authorization, information in the NSCL, GSCL (Gateway Service Capabilities Layer), or DSCL (Device Service Capabilities Layer).
  - Requesting device management actions (e.g., software upgrade, configuration management).
  - Subscription and notification to specific events.
- **dIa:** The *dIa* reference point ("Machine-to-Machine communications (M2M)," 2015) offers generic and extendable mechanism for Device Application (DA)/Gateway Application (GA) interactions with the DSCL/GSCL. The *dIa* reference point supports the following functions:
  - Registration of DA/GA to GSCL.
  - Registration of DA to DSCL.
  - Requesting to Read/Write, subject to proper authorization, information in the NSCL (Network Service Capabilities Layer), GSCL, or DSCL.
  - Subscription and notification to specific events.
  - Requesting the creation, deletion and listing of group(s).
- **mId:** The *mId* reference point offers generic and extendable mechanism for SCL interactions. *mId* reference point usually exists between SCLs and supports the following:
  - Registration of a DSCL/GSCL to NSCL.
  - Requesting to Read/Write, subject to proper authorization, information in the NSCL, GSCL, or DSCL.
  - Requesting device management actions (e.g., software upgrade, configuration management).
  - Subscription and notification to specific events.
  - Requesting the creation, deletion and listing of group(s).
  - Providing security related features.

These reference points are mapped in the system overall as follows:

- **The Gateway:** It provides M2M Gateway Service Capability Layer (GSCL), communicates through the *mId* to the Network Service Capability Layer (NSCL) and it should communicate with the Gateway Application (GA) or the Device Application (DA) through the *dIa* interface.
- **The Device (with M2M service capabilities):** Communicates with an NSCL using the *mId* reference point and to DA using the *dIa* reference point.
- **The Device (not implementing an M2M service capability):** Communicates with the Gateway (GSCL) through the *dIa* interface.

ETSI-SPECIFIED M2M SECURITY SYSTEM

Given the status quo, Machine to Machine (M2M) is still a growing field, hence various studies and research works (Suo, Wan, Zou, & Liu, 2012; Roman, Zhou, & Lopez, 2013; Chen & Chang, 2012) insisted on the security issues of M2M, noting that we do not like to repeat the same mistake of the Internet - that the *Internet-boom* occurred first and afterwards, everyone began searching for solutions to the security threats (such as viruses and hackers). So, our take from this is that it is better to take security issues into practical consideration when first building a system.

While M2M is still being standardized, in parallel, some research works (Chang et al, 2011; Hongsong, Zhongchuan, & Dongyan, 2011; Barnhart & Bokath, 2011; Lai, Li, Zhang, & Cao, 2012; Bojic et al, 2014) are studying the security aspects of M2M. These studies are mainly concerned about how it is formed (Maras, 2015; Jover, 2015; Granjal, Monteiro, & Silva, 2013), its functional architecture, different mechanisms and topologies. Also, some other studies focus on the implementation of M2M in different domains and the tailoring of the security mechanism to fit in the new sectors where the M2M technology is expected to be implemented (Jover, 2015; Bartoli, 2013; Demblewski, 2015; Cimler, Matyska, Balik, Horalek, & Sobeslav, 2015; Arnoys, 2015; Satyadevan, Kalarickal, & Jinesh, 2014; John-Green & Watson, 2014; Sicari, Rizzardi, Coen-Porisini, Grieco, & Monteil, 2015; Jaber, Kouzayha, Dawy, & Kayssi, 2014). ETSI, by its turn, worked on the specification for standardization of M2M security system in most of its aspects, as a mechanism or as technical details. In this section, we will focus mainly on the different security mechanisms presented by ETSI without going into deep technical details of every mechanism since that is out of the scope of this chapter.

First, we will present the key hierarchy and realization, then the bootstrapping and service provisioning, security procedures for service connection between M2M Device/Gateway and the network, mId security, and finally, the security service capability in the device/gateway and in the network which governs all these procedures.

Second, we will present the supposed overall security mechanism; in other words, all the above mentioned functions and procedures - how they are supposed to work together so that the connection between the M2M device and the network is secured.

Key Hierarchy and Realization

In M2M, we have three types of keys: *Kmr*, *Kmc*, and *Kma* (see Figure 5). *Kmr* is the M2M root key, *Kmc* is the M2M connection key, and *Kma* is the M2M application key. *Kmc* is derived from *Kmr*, while *Kma* is derived from Kmc ("Machine-to-Machine communications (M2M)," 2011; "Machine-to-Machine communications (M2M)," 2015).

- **M2M Root Key (*Kmr*):** This key is used for mutual authentication and key agreement between the Device/Gateway M2M node and the M2M Service Provider. *Kmr* is also used for deriving an M2M Connection Key (*Kmc*). At the Network side, *Kmr* is stored in a Secured Environment within MAS (M2M Authentication Server). The Secured Environment should protect the information within (e.g., *Kmr* and the *Kmc* derivation process) from access or manipulation by unauthorized entities; also, in the device gateway side, *Kmr* must be stored within a Secured Environment Domain controlled by the M2M Service Provider ("Machine-to-Machine communications (M2M)," 2011; "Machine-to-Machine communications (M2M)," 2015).

- **M2M Connection Key (*Kmc*):** This key is derived from *Kmr*, after successful mutual authentication of the Device/Gateway M2M node. Upon derivation, *Kmc* is delivered from MAS (wherein, it is derived within the same Secured Environment as *Kmr*) to NSEC (Network Security Capability Service), where it is stored in a local Secured Environment. *Kmc* expires upon termination of the corresponding M2M Service connection. Lifetime of *Kmc* is less than or equal to the lifetime of *Kmr*. A different *Kmc* is generated for every new M2M Service connection procedure of the Device/Gateway (D/G) M2M node with the same or a different Network M2M node ("Machine-to-Machine communications (M2M)," 2011; "Machine-to-Machine communications (M2M)," 2015).

Figure 5. Different types of keys of M2M system
Based on ("Machine-to-Machine communications (M2M)," 2011)

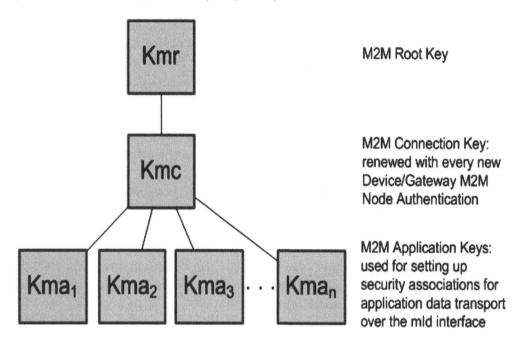

- **M2M Application Key (*Kma*):** This optional key is used as symmetric shared secret for setting up secure application data sessions between NGC (Network Generic Communication) and DGC (Device Generic Communication) and/or between NGC and GGC, for authorized applications. *Kma* keys are derived from *Kmc*, after successful mutual authentication between D/G M2M node and M2M Service Provider. *Kma* is shared between D/G M2M node and NGC. *Kma* is used for authentication and authorization of M2M applications at the M2M Device/Gateway and for protection of application data traffic ("Machine-to-Machine communications (M2M)," 2011; "Machine-to-Machine communications (M2M)," 2015).

Bootstrapping

In M2M system, the main task of bootstrapping and especially, what is called *service bootstrapping* is provisioning the keys (M2M root keys) into the device or gateway from one side, and in the M2M Authentication server (MAS) from the other side and many other parameters as M2M node ID, SCL (Service Capability layer) ID and a list of NSCL identifiers to the M2M D/G node.

In ETSI M2M specifications, all the available Bootstrapping procedures have been explained in details, from the GBA (Generic Bootstrapping architecture) to EAP (Extensible Authentication Protocol) way of bootstrapping. In this chapter, we opt not to write in details about those procedures (like, Service Bootstrapping), neither about GBA and EAP. Instead, they will be only mentioned as we have done so far, with two figures explaining the bootstrapping (GBA or EAP) as a part of the overall M2M service connection. Figure 6 and Figure 7 are generated based on the standardization drafts presented in ("Machine-to-Machine communications (M2M)," 2011; "Machine-to-Machine communications (M2M)," 2015).

Figure 6. M2M service bootstrap based on the Generic Bootstrapping Architecture. Here, NAF stands for "Network Application Function", BSF stands for "Bootstrapping Server Function", HSS stands for "Home Subscriber Server" and AV means "Authentication Vector"

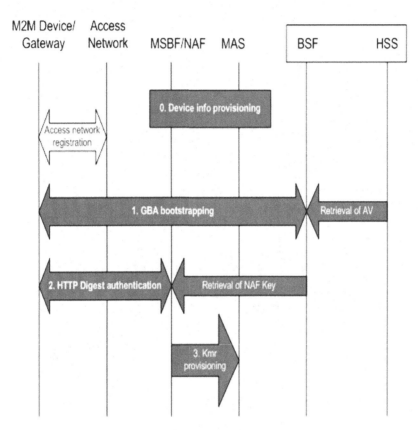

Security of Service Connection

After provisioning the M2M root key to the D/G M2M node, the service connection procedure can take place. The Service connection, as the bootstrap procedure, can have many mechanisms and that depends on the business relation between the mobile operator and the M2M service provider. With business relation between the mobile operator and the M2M operator, "*access network assisted*" bootstrap or service connection is used and this is different than the case when no business relation exists between the mobile operator and the M2M service provider. Service connection procedure is fulfilled through specific steps:

- The mutual authentication of the **mId** end points.
- Agreement of "*Intended to be used*" Keys.
- Establishment of secure session using encryption over **mId**.

Figure 7. M2M Service Bootstrap based on EAP/PANA (Protocol for Carrying Authentication for Network Access)

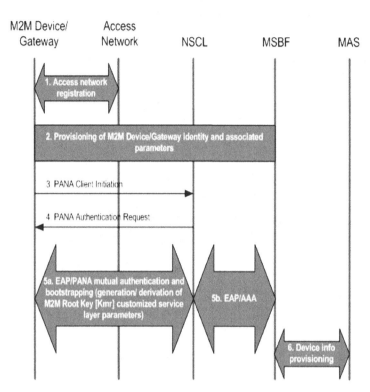

mId Interface

There are many levels of security for the mId interface. In some cases, we can rely on the access network security since in this case, a trust relation exists between the M2M service provider and the Mobile operator, and an encryption will be on the access network. From another hand, a secure communication can be established between the D/GSCL and the NSCL using TLS (Transport Layer Security) or IPsec (Internet Protocol Security). *Kmc* or *Kma* shall be used as a shared secret key between the two end-points for performing the end-point authentication. Once a secure channel is established (e.g., a TLS or IPsec tunnel), mId protocols shall be carried over that channel for achieving security. Secure channel can be built only after the M2M Service Connection procedure takes place.

An *object security* level can also be used by securing data at the object (i.e., protocol payload) level. *Channel security* encrypts all the traffic and this is kind of inefficient. This potential inefficiency could be minimized by using security at the same layer as data are transmitted; hence, gaining finer-granularity security over the data. Each data element could be individually integrity-protected and encrypted without any regard to how other data are treated ("Machine-to-Machine communications (M2M)," 2015).

M2M Security Capability (xSEC)

- **Network Security Capability (NSEC):** The NSEC Capability in the NSCL provides the following functionalities:

- Supporting M2M Service Bootstrap.
- Supporting key hierarchy realization for authentication and authorization.
- Performing mutual authentication and key agreement.
- Verifying the integrity validation status reported by the M2M Device/Gateway and triggering appropriate post validation actions.

- **Gateway SECurity (GSEC) Capability:** In addition to supporting M2M bootstrapping process and key hierarchy realization for authentication and authorization, the other functionalities provided by the GSEC Capability in the GSCL are:
  - Initiating mutual authentication and key agreement.
  - If supported by the M2M Gateway, it should report the integrity validation status to the NSEC and react to post validation actions triggered by NSEC.
  - The GSEC is responsible for the storage and handling of M2M Connection Keys.

- **Device *SECurity (DSEC) Capability*:** In addition to supporting M2M Bootstrap and key hierarchy realization for authentication and authorization, the DSEC Capability in the DSCL provides the following functionalities:
  - Initiating mutual authentication and key agreement.
  - If supported by the M2M Device, it can report the integrity validation status to the NSEC and react to post validation actions triggered by NSEC.
  - The DSEC is responsible for the storage and handling of M2M Connection Keys.

Security Mechanisms at a Glance

All the ETSI-specified security mechanisms could be put together as a part of the overall M2M communication establishment as follows:

- **Application registration:** is the registration of an Application with the SCL that can be on the Device, Gateway or Network side, which will allow the application to use the functions offered by the local M2M SCL.
- **Network bootstrap:** will configure the M2M Device/Gateway with the necessary configuration data to connect and register to the access network (example: from UICC (Universal Integrated Circuit Card))
- **Network registration:** Registration of the Device Gateway with the access network.
- **M2M service bootstrap procedure & M2M service connection:** as were noted before.
- **SCL registration of D/G SCL with NSCL:** After successful M2M Service connection between D/G M2M node and Network node, it is the registration of the SCL of the D/G SCL with the Service Capability Layer on the Network side.

SECURITY THREATS AGAINST M2M

M2M communication will be mainly involved in eHealth applications, intelligent transportation, power generation and distribution, tracking systems, rural area monitoring and many other sectors; therefore, the M2M devices or what is called as the *low-level* of M2M stack, is the main part affected by the posed

Figure 8. Denial of Service (DoS) attack scenario

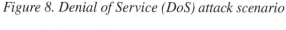

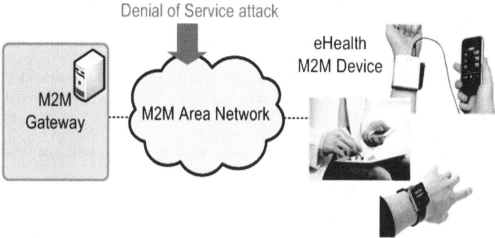

challenges. On the other hand, the M2M platform, as a core, is also a major target for many security threats and challenges such as viruses or unauthorized access to the offered services and so on.

Since M2M technology still remains as a field of research on various facets of it, we could get increasingly large number of innovative business applications in the coming days. Thus, making a complete list of all the security challenges and threats would be an extremely difficult task, if not impossible.

Security threats and challenges have been indeed studied in some previous works like (John-Green & Watson, 2014; Atamli & Martin, 2014; Rubertis et al., 2013; Singh, Pasquier, Bacon, Ko, & Eyers, 2015; Aris, Oktug, & Yalcin, 2015; Fink, Zarzhitsky, Carroll, & Farquhar, 2015; Nie & Zhai, 2013; Genge, Haller, Gligor, & Beres, 2014; Hossain, Fotouhi, & Hasan, 2015; Schurgot & Shinberg, 2015; Fremantle & Scott, 2015). In a continuous effort, some other works have tried to find enhancements and solutions to the weaknesses in the M2M security systems and proposed various mechanisms and techniques, as security management approach (Jung & Kim, 2013; Huang, Craig, and Yan, 2015), key generation (Granjal, Monteiro, & Silva,, 2013; Qiu & Ma, 2015; Lake, Milito, Morrow, & Vargheese, 2014; Liu, Gu, & Ma, 2015; Hussen et al., 2013), and distribution (Jung, Ahn, Hwang, & Kim, 2012; Shafagh & Hithnawi, 2014; N. Park, J.S. Park, & Kim,, 2014; Inshil, Jiyoung, Shi, & Kijoon, 2014), authentication (Qiu & Ma, 2015; N. Park, J.S. Park, & Kim, 2014; Hu et al., 2012; Kim, Jeong, & Hong, 2014; Doh, Chae, Lim, & Chung, 2015; N. Park, J.S. Park, & Kim, 2015; Jin & Hahm, 2013; Jin, Park, Lee, & Jun, 2013; Sun, Men, Zhao, & Zhou, 2015; Ukil, Bandyopadhyay, Bhattacharyya, Pal, and Bose, 2014; Kim, Jeong, & Hong, 2011) encryption technique (N. Park, J.S. Park, & Kim, 2015). In addition, some works proposed security mechanisms for M2M security, for end-to-end security (Chen, You, Weng, Cheng, & Huang, 2016; Lai, Li, Lu, Shen, & Cao, 2013; W. Zhang, Y. Zhang, Chen, Li, & Wang, 2013; Kothmayr, Hu, Brunig, & Carle, 2012), and other security models related to context awareness (Hu et al., 2012; Lee & Chung, 2012), or related to other techniques as cooperative security (Jung, Kim, & Seoksoo, 2013), distributed approach (Ben, Olivereau, & Laurent, 2012; Karim, Anpalagan, Nasser, Almhana, & Woungang, 2013) and in relation to device cloud (Moon, Lee, Kim, & Choi, 2014; Cagalaban, Ahn, & Kim, 2012; (Sicari, Rizzardi, Coen-Porisini, Grieco, & Monteil, 2015; Anggorojati & Prasad, 2014). Lately, as M2M is being used in different sectors, some works proposed specific security frameworks for different M2M implementation scenarios, as in eHealth (Granjal, Monteiro, & Silva, 2013; Lake, Milito, Morrow, & Vargheese, 2014; Saleem, Derhab, Al-Muhtadi, & Shahzad,, 2015; Choi, Doh, Park, & Chae, 2012), or in transportation (Lee & Kim, 2015; Masek, Muthanna, & Hosek, 2015), metering (Riker et al., 2014), mobile networks (Choi, Han, & Choi, 2015) and many other security frameworks (Mahkonen et al., 2013; Neisse, Steri, Fovino, & Baldini, 2015; Boubakri, Abdallah, & Boudriga, 2014) and mechanisms (Ben, Olivereau, & Laurent, 2012; Anggorojati & Prasad, 2014; Neisse et al., 2014; Gyrard, Bonnet, & Boudaoud, 2014; Farooqi, Khan, Wang, & Lee, 2013).

What we will be doing here is, we will mention all the known security threats and try to clarify the full picture of what M2M communication is facing as security threats. From the next subsection, let us know about the security challenges to the M2M system on the device and gateway level, and then, how those also affect the core or platform level.

Security Threats at the Device Level

Device Compromising

The wide implementation of the devices in different places and the overall system environment make compromising an M2M device an easy task which is not the case in the usual H2H (Human to Human) communication since human is holding the device. One of the general scenarios that we can imagine is some devices are deployed for rural observation and monitoring, so it will take just a little effort by an attacker to get to the physical device and then compromise it. From other hand, many devices will be deployed in indoor environment; therefore, the house owner or others in the house would have the full time to get access to the device.

What would happen if the device is compromised? The list of answers would be very long, which begins with the unauthorized use of the device. A famous case would be what happened in South Africa, as mentioned in ("No stopping," 2015):

As its high walls, electric fences and armed security patrols demonstrate, Johannesburg is well prepared for thwarting the ingenuity of burglars in most situations. But no one thought about traffic lights. Hundreds of lights have been damaged by thieves targeting the machines' SIM cards, which are then used to make mobile phone calls worth millions of South African rand.

In this case, SIM (Subscriber Identity Module) cards were stolen from the implemented smart traffic light devices! As a result, it caused many car crashes and cost thousands of money to fix the whole system. Hence, we learn that there is never an end to the capability of launching an internal attack on the system from the compromised node. This issue then enters into the domain of physical security which becomes more complicated and goes out of the general security issues of M2M or its applications.

Usually, the internal attacks are more dangerous since the other nodes and the system would behave normally with the compromised node as a trusted node and this could cause a significant damage (V.B. Misic & J. Misic, 2014) to the M2M system - even to the M2M area network and to the participating device (especially, in mesh network topology). Different kinds of viruses can also take the compromised node as a bridge to the core platform.

Denial of Service (DoS) Attack

In practicality, a DoS situation can occur due to any kind of incident that diminishes, eliminates, or hinders the normal activities of the network. Say for example, any kind of hardware failure, software bug, resource exhaustion, environmental condition, or any type of complicated interaction of these factors can create *denial of service*. It should be noted that the term 'DoS' indicates to a particular situation in the network and when DoS situation occurs due to an intentional attempt of an adversary, it is called DoS attack (Pathan, 2010a). Although attackers commonly use the Internet to exploit software bugs when making DoS attacks, here we consider primarily protocol- or design-level vulnerabilities (Wood & Stankovic, 2002).

An M2M system can be significantly affected by the DoS attack since such a system depends heavily on the M2M area network. We can imagine a scenario where M2M technology is used for the eHealth application (shown in Figure 8). Let us consider that there are thousands of smart metering devices (M2M devices) implemented and connected to gateways through an M2M area network. Any jamming on the channel can break the circle and cause DoS; therefore, no information would be transmitted from or to the M2M device and this may threaten a patient's life. In this case and many other similar cases, M2M security challenges could affect human lives directly, not only the security of data or just the privacy issue.

In other situations, depending on the M2M area network topology (where the DoS attack is expected to happen), DoS attack can be much easier to launch. For instance, an access M2M area network based on mesh topology is very susceptible to such attacks ("Denial-of-Service Developments," 2000). Here, any compromised device can launch an internal DoS attack, potentially putting many nodes *out of the service* at the same time.

Viruses

The M2M Platform will be the target of different kinds of computer viruses and malwares (Dagon, Martin, & Starner, 2004) since it holds information as personal information and the most important fact is that it offers services which have good monetary value. Hence, the goal of the attackers can vary, from destroying the platform and putting it *out of service* by manipulating databases to control various functions and services, or by partly controlling the platform, snatching specific information about customers, locations and many other sensitive establishments - even partly controlling the platform to have unauthorized access to various services. This kind of threat (i.e., virus, malware) falls under the category of computer or computing device security (Wang, Streff, & Raman, 2012; Mohammed & Pathan, 2013) and it could really harm any computerized system involved in the M2M system.

M2M INTRUSION DETECTION SYSTEM: MIDS

So far, we have known that the M2M security system standardized by ETSI addresses a big part of the security area and manages many mechanisms for authentication, key provisioning, and other issues. As we have mentioned before, all these mechanisms are still insufficient to protect M2M systems from intrusion attacks. As per our detailed investigation in the area, we have found that though there are some other efforts to device specific IDS for M2M systems (Aris, Oktug, & Yalcin, 2015; Jung & Kim, 2013; Anggorojati & Prasad, 2013), there still remains enough scope of research on M2M security and especially, in the area of Intrusion Detection System (IDS). The way the intrusions are tackled or prevented or detected is not really clear in the ETSI specifications – in fact, we do not have any common scenario yet. Hence, we will address here the IDS for M2M.

After the overview of the M2M system, security system, and security threats for the M2M, in this section, we will try to draw the principle lines of an M2M Intrusion Detection System (MIDS). But, before that, let us have a look at the capabilities and limitations of the M2M devices since any IDS will rely heavily on those participating devices.

Challenges for Security System and for M2M IDS

Due to the heterogeneity and great number of the devices in an M2M system, designing a common platform for intrusion detection system would be very complex. There would be a wide range of devices ranging from the devices with low computational and battery power (Khan, Pathan, & Alrajeh, 2012) to smartphones and handheld or static devices that can have advanced technologies with high computational resources and battery power. The capacity of these devices is a very critical issue because the Device Level will be the actual basis of any kind of security mechanism:

- **Device Battery Power:** Battery power is a very important matter especially for security. First of all, battery power forms the most challenging issue since most of the DoS attacks focus mainly on exhausting the battery power so the device will be off and *out of service*. Second, battery power is related to the computational power or in other words, to the processor capabilities. When the processor is used heavily as in encryption and decryption tasks, the processor would consume more power and therefore, the device battery will run out fast. In the end, designing an M2M Intrusion Detection System must take into consideration the device battery power capability (Pirretti et al., 2006) because the battery power limits the overall available processing time of the device and the computational power of the processor (which is used in encryption and other security related tasks).
- **Computational Power:** The device computational power is a great challenge for the development and practical implementation of a security mechanism/system since the processor at the end would be doing all the ciphering/deciphering and calculations for generating/using keys or running the security codes. Most of the M2M devices except the latest smartphones are either sensors or other similar types of devices with low computational power, often incapable of performing huge and complex cryptographic operations (Azad & Pathan, 2014; Pathan, 2010b) for all the transmitted data.
- **Physical Security of the Device and Security of the Keys:** If someone can access the security keys in the M2M devices, it will be easy for him first to decrypt all the traffic from and to the device and he can send arbitrary data (malicious data) from this device. Hence, physical security of the device plays a role in keeping the implemented keys safe in the device. In addition to thinking about the physical security, the security keys should also be stored in the device in a secure way so that it would be difficult for any attacker to extract the keys, even if he gains physical access to the device (which will be very likely due to the uncontrollable wide implementation of M2M devices). A possible mechanism to ensure this kind of security could be using *tamper-proof* device that would run self-destruction or erasing operation of memory if opened or touched or broken

after deployment or the keys should be stored in a distributed fashion in different separate devices or so. Readers are referred to (Mo et al., 2012; Pathan, 2015) for further reading in this area.

- **Different Kinds of Devices with Different Protocols:** In M2M systems, we will have different kinds of devices and protocols (RFID (Radio-Frequency IDentification), Zigbee, Wi-Fi, etc.) and what is common among them is only the M2M network. Hence, this kind of heterogeneity is also a challenge for designing a common security platform for M2M since every technology has its own security standards and associated mechanisms. Figure 9 shows the pictorial view of the presence of different kinds of technologies (devices and protocols) in the M2M system.

More About MIDS

As we can see in the Figure 10, the supposed M2M security stack is formed from base to top. The Device Level physical security forms the solid ground of the security system since any kind of security system will be weak and vulnerable if the device level is exposed to manipulation and compromise. Hence, the first step would be to find solutions for all the security threats on the device level.

- **Device Compromising and the Physical Security of Implemented Keys:** Many existing solutions for such situations can be used to defend against device compromising, however the issue is that every solution is compatible with the devices of specific configurations and often, the specific way they are used. While many, if not most of those solutions are mainly implementable for the static (i.e., which does not move) devices, only a few may really work in the devices with frequent mobility.

Figure 9. Different technologies in an M2M system at the Device Level

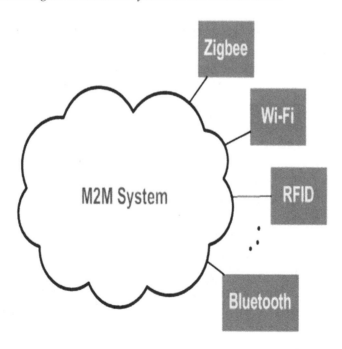

- ○ **Hardware Security:** There should be strong mechanisms to safeguard and manage digital keys for strong authentication and to provide crypto-processing. M2M device should also have strong password system which would be capable of protecting the device's secret keys from the well-defined attack/breaking attempts (Mo et al., 2012; Pathan, 2015).
- ○ **Neighbor Watch Theory:** This method is very effective in case of devices (sensors, actuators or the like) used in a close geographic proximity (e.g., rural regions monitoring, Intelligent transportation devices on roads). These devices can be implemented in an intelligent way in a cluster of 3 devices, where each device will have the responsibility of watching its neighbor by a *Beacon* message and whenever this message is off for a certain time (perhaps, due to the device compromising), a message can be sent to the gateway and then to the IDS server (Song, Xie, Zhu, and Cao, 2007).

- **Remote Device Wiping:** In many cases, the capability of remote wiping of the device can be an acceptable solution for protecting some sensitive information on it. Remote device wiping ("Remote wipe," 2015) refers to a security feature that allows a network administrator (or, device owner) to send a command to a computing device and delete data. It is very useful when a device is lost or stolen to erase all its data and to do a factory reset. Combining this capability with the other mechanisms (mentioned before), we can make it one additional component of the first level of the M2M security stack (see Figure 10).
  - ○ **Devices Locator:** When the neighbor watch theory does not work (for instance, due to the geographical barriers or the way M2M devices are deployed/implemented), *Device locator* through the GPS (Global Positioning System) or through a local station (for tracking system) can protect the device from being manipulated or moved. In case of any unexpected move, the IDS will be alerted through the gateway (Pei, 2012). The majority of the M2M devices are supposed to be static devices and the ones that are mobile can be related to handheld devices or smartphones or such devices. Even so, many M2M devices could afford M2M security services while on the move allowing the location finding algorithms to work properly on the devices.

- **Different Approaches for the IDS:** Intrusion Detection System (IDS) basically refers to any system that detects and warns about illegal breaking into the system and misuse of it, or tries to prevent the entities having legal access from not abusing their privileges (Heady, Luger, Maccabe, & Servilla, 1990; Pathan, 2014). For this reason, the mechanisms in an IDS monitor everything (traffic) to find any potential intrusion. IDSs are mainly based on two types of underlying technologies: the *Misuse based* detection and the *Anomaly based* detection.
  - ○ **Misuse based Detection:** Virus patterns and known threats are recorded in the IDS database, and the IDS searches and scans all the data traffic for a matching of pattern with the database. Once any suspicious data is discovered, an alarm is triggered. The main disadvantage of the misuse based detection is its weakness in discovering new threats (Abduvaliyev et al., 2013; Pathan, 2014; Roesch, 1990; Paxson, 1990).
  - ○ **Anomaly based detection:** In this method, the IDS creates a normal profile for users based on their history of use and then, compare any activity with the usual behavior. Any unexpected change is considered suspicious. This way is very efficient in discovering new attacks and threats but the main disadvantage is that the system needs more computational power, often extra human efforts as well (Paxson, 1990; Chan, Mahoney, & Arshad, 2003).

Figure 10. M2M security stack

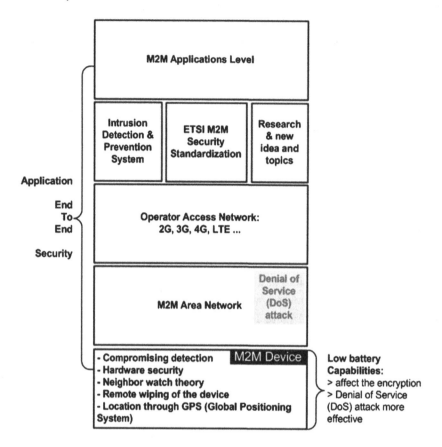

There can be a third kind of approach, which is called the *Specification based* detection. This is basically a combination of the two major ways of detection, by using manually developed specifications to characterize *normal system behavior*. Table 1 shows a list of IDS frameworks that are somewhat related to the M2M applications and systems. A wide range of techniques are noted for the readers to get relevant references.

The Operational Concept of MIDS

Given the M2M device capabilities or the expected ways the devices will be implemented or deployment, or the different policies of intrusion detection systems that would be employed, the best idea of a standard M2M Intrusion Detection System (MIDS) would be what is close to the reality and could be adapted or adjusted based on the need for specific application scenarios. Hence, what we propose is formulating a general concept of IDS which can combine many other schemes related to intrusion detection or prevention activities. Therefore, hybrid intrusion detection systems (Pathan, 2014; Huh & Hai, 2011) are the best candidates in this direction.

There are a few practical implementation issues here that should be mentioned. First, due to the limited capacities, M2M devices would be incapable of saving the entire malicious data signature (viruses,

Table 1. Different relevant IDS frameworks at a glance

IDS Title	Used Detection Policy
Hybrid intrusion detection system (Hai, Khan, & Huh,, 2007)	Misuse and anomaly based
Spontaneous Watchdog (Roman, Zhou, & Lopez, 2006)	Based on local-, regional- and central agents in nodes
Cooperative local auditing (Krontiris & Dimitriou, 2007)	Specification based
LIDeA (Krontiris, Dimitriou, & Giannetsos, 2008)	Specification based
Decentralized intrusion detection model (Da Silva et al. 2008)	Specification based
Neighbor-based intrusion detection (Stetsko, Folkman, & Vashek, 2010)	Specification based
Fixed-width clustering (Loo, Ng, Leckie, & Palaniswami, 2010)	Anomaly based
Artificial immune system (Drozda, Schaust, & Szczerbicka, 2010)	Anomaly based
Intrusion aware validation algorithm (Shaikh, Jameel, Auriol, Lee, & Song, 2008)	Anomaly based
Group-based detection scheme (Li, He, & Fu, 2008)	Anomaly based
ANDES algorithm (Gupta, Zheng, & Cheng, 2007)	Anomaly based
Application-independent framework (Zhang, Yu, & Ning, 2008)	Anomaly based
Cumulative summation (Phuong, Hung, Cho, Lee, & Lee, 2006)	Anomaly based
Hierarchical intrusion detection model (Phuong, Hung, Cho, Lee, & Lee, 2006)	Anomaly based
Pair-based approach (K.R. Ahmed, K. Ahmed, S. Munir, & Asad, 2008)	Misuse and Anomaly based
SVELTE (De Almeida, Ribeiro, & Moreno, 2015)	Real time IDS, Misuse and Anomaly based
New IoT IDS (W. Li, Ping, Wu, Pan, & J. Li, 2014)	*K*-nearest neighbor, Misuse and Anomaly based
NAN IDS (Beigi-Mohammadi, J., Misic, H., Khazaei, & V.B. Misic, 2014)	signature and anomaly-based detection systems
Novel IDS for WSN (Karuppiah, Dalfiah, Yuvashri, Rajaram, & Pathan, 2014)	Based on Energy-Efficient Sybil Node Detection Algorithm and Misuse and Anomaly based.
IT-OCSVM, IDS for SCADA (Maglaras, Jiang, & Cruz, 2015)	Combining ensemble methods and social network metrics
IL-IDS (Ren & Gu, 2015)	AI (instance learning) based IDS
IDS for WSN (Wang, Wu, & Chen, 2015)	mathematical morphology

malware, etc.) neither all the suspicious nodes' IDs (Identities) (to accomplish misuse detection policy on the low device level). Also, it would be impossible for such a device to scan all the transmitted data, from and to it (to run anomaly detection mechanism). From this point, we can think of defining the role of some kind of local detection agent as mentioned in (Huang, Jasper, & Wicks, 1999) that could be implemented on the M2M device by only affording the low level device security (as we see in the Figure 10, first level). Device compromise detection, neighbor watch, device localization, device wiping, and hardware security will form the main job of this LDA (Local Detection Agent). The local agent will refer to a regional agent (which could be mainly the gateway), and on the network side, the central detection agent will be a *multi-level* priority system.

- Let's begin with the multi-level of priority. The threats or intrusion events/attempts can be disposed on many levels of priorities. Hence, the IDS system will assign to every M2M device or node an ID, and a table containing a combination of the IDs and the current situation.
- The local agent will have various functions like the device compromise detection function, device localization function, hardware security detection function, and many others that can be defined by the operator/administrator. For instance, if device compromise function sends an alert, this will be assigned a high level of priority. Again, if the localization function sends an alert about an unexpected movement of a device, this will be considered a second level priority incident. The levels of priorities can be assigned also by the operator and that depends on the specific M2M system. Those alerts will play a major role in the MIDS decision making process.

Coming back to the hybrid (Pathan, 2014; Huh & Hai, 2011) aspect of MIDS, the system will work on the specification based detection policy. MIDS will be formed by a part working on the anomaly based detection policy which will first build normal profiles for users based on their activity history and daily usage behavior, and when any change in this usual behavior is observed, the distributed local detection agent and regional agent would generate alert and set its priority level. The IDS verification system will then scan the transmitted data from the suspected node or user by applying 2 criteria:

- The amount of transmitted data and comparing it to the usual volume.
- By applying the misuse based policy function for searching about suspicious data (according to the saved malicious and virus patterns)

IDS needs to be also combined with many other procedures that intend to protect the M2M area network from Denial of Service (DoS) attacks and all kinds of *over-the-air* attacks (some issues are mentioned in Section VII), which can be the field of study in others future works. Here, our suggestion is to design a common IDS platform by combining the low level device security based on the M2M security stack presented in this chapter. While this is in essence a foundation step, the concept would have enough scope for expansion by adding new parts and functionalities (as in section VII) and practical implementation.

Now, let us take a look at the way an MIDS (M2M IDS) would work. The MIDS functional blocks are shown in Figure 11. As understood, it's a combination of various sub-blocks and functionalities, including the entities like the local and regional detection agents, the central detection agent, the *"Anomaly Policy"* detection function, the *"Misuse Policy"* detection function, and the MIDS decision function. The Local detection agent discovers an event, as device compromising event or movement of a device, etc. Those events should be defined by the operator/administrator in a way compatible with the nature of M2M system. The local detection agent will generate an alert.

1. This alert with the user ID will be forwarded to the Regional agent (in the gateway).
2. The regional agent then will forward the alert with the user ID to the Central Detection agent.
3. The central detection agent will process the alert and assign to it a certain level of priority and forward it to the MIDS decision function.
4. The MIDS decision function will forward the User ID to the *"Anomaly policy"* detection function which will check up for any change in the user behavior in comparison to its usual activity profile.

5. In case of a change in the user profile, The *"Anomaly Policy"* function will forward then the user ID to the *"Misuse Policy"* detection function. This function will scan all the traffic coming from this node based on 2 criteria:
6. the usual generated amount of data generated by this node and
7. by searching on any matching with the known stored virus patterns and signatures.
8. The *"Misuse Policy"* detection function will forward the scan result to the MIDS decision function for further action. The intruder would be then purged our locked within the network based on the employed strategy of tackling with intrusion.

Hence, MIDS decision function will take the decision of allowing the traffic or discarding it.

WIRELESS IDPS: SUPPORTING MIDS AS A LOCAL AGENT

M2M communication will include many kinds of wireless devices and technologies for which we need to talk a bit about the wireless IDPS supporting the MIDS framework. A significant portion of the M2M system may be wireless sensor network or the like. Hence, MIDS framework could work with any wireless IDPS (Intrusion Detection and Prevention System) as well. An IDPS is basically a combination of both *"Intrusion detection"* and *"Intrusion prevention"* mechanisms (W. Ren et al., 2013; Mohammed & Pathan, 2013).

A wireless IDPS (Pathan et al., 2013) monitors wireless network traffic and analyzes wireless networking protocols for identifying malicious behavior. However, it has a limitation that it cannot identify suspicious activity/data in the application or higher-layer network protocols (e.g., TCP, UDP) that the wireless network traffic is transferring. It is most commonly deployed within the range of an organization's wireless network to monitor it, but it can also be deployed to locations where unauthorized wireless networking could occur.

Though due to the transmission methods, wireless network attacks differ often from those on the wired networks, the basic components involved in a wireless IDPS are the same as the network-based IDPS (for example, consoles, database servers, management servers and sensors). A wireless IDPS monitors the network by sampling the traffic. There are two frequency bands to monitor (2.4 GHz and 5 GHz), and each band includes many channels. A software sensor (here, we mean, any kind of sensing mechanism – mainly software or programming application running on a computing device) is used to monitor a channel at a time and it can switch to other channels as needed.

We should mention that most of the WLANs (Wireless LANs) use the Institute of Electrical and Electronics Engineers (IEEE) 802.11 family of WLAN standards. IEEE 802.11 WLANs have two main architectural components:

- A station, which is a wireless end-point device (e.g., laptop computer, personal digital assistant).
- An access point, which logically connects stations with an organization's wired network infrastructure or other network.

Some WLANs also use wireless switches, which act as intermediaries between access points and the wired network. A network based on stations and access points is configured in infrastructure mode; a network that does not use an access point, in which stations connect directly to each other, is configured in ad hoc mode. Nearly all organizational WLANs use infrastructure mode. Each access point in a WLAN has a name assigned to it called a service set identifier (SSID). The SSID allows stations to distinguish one WLAN from another.

Wireless *security sensors* (here, we mean the *software sensor* – i.e., code that senses intrusion or malicious activity) have several available forms. A dedicated sensor of this type is usually passive, performing wireless IDPS functions but not passing traffic from source to destination. Dedicated sensors may be designed for fixed or mobile deployment, with mobile sensors (similar to mobile software robot or so) used primarily for auditing and incident handling purposes (e.g., to locate rogue wireless devices). Sensor software is also available bundled with access points and wireless switches. Some vendors also have host-based wireless IDPS sensor software that can be installed on stations, such as laptops. The sensor software detects station misconfigurations and attacks within range of the stations. This kind of software/application may also be able to enforce security policies on the stations, such as limiting access to wireless interfaces.

If an organization uses WLANs, it most often deploys wireless sensors to monitor the radiofrequency range of the organization's WLANs, which often includes mobile components such as laptops and personal digital assistants (PDAs). Many organizations also use software sensors to monitor areas of their facilities where there should be no WLAN activity, as well as channels and bands that the organization's WLANs should not use, as a way of detecting rogue devices.

Wireless IDPS Security Capabilities

The main advantages of Wireless IDPSs include detection of attacks, misconfigurations, and policy violations at the WLAN protocol level, primarily examining IEEE 802.11 protocol communication. The major limitation of a Wireless IDPS is that it does not examine communications at higher levels (e.g., IP addresses, application payloads). Some products perform only simple signature-based detection, whereas others use a combination of signature-based, anomaly based, and stateful protocol analysis detection techniques. Most of the types of events commonly detected by wireless IDPS sensor software include unauthorized WLANs and WLAN devices and poorly secured WLAN devices (e.g., misconfigured WLAN settings). Additionally, the Wireless IDPSs can detect unusual WLAN usage patterns, which could indicate a device compromise or unauthorized use of the WLAN, and the use of wireless network scanners.

Other types of attacks such as Denial of Service (DoS) conditions, including logical attacks (e.g., overloading access points with large number of messages) and physical attacks (e.g., emitting electromagnetic energy on the WLAN's frequencies to make the WLAN unusable), can also be detected by wireless IDPSs. Some wireless IDPSs can also detect a WLAN device that attempts to spoof the identity of another device.

Another significant advantage is that most wireless IDPS sensors (software) can identify the physical location of a wireless device by using triangulation – estimating the device's approximate distance from multiple sensors from the strength of the device's signal received by each sensor, then calculating the physical location at which the device would be, the estimated distance from each sensor. Handheld IDPS sensors can also be used to pinpoint a device's location, particularly if fixed sensors do not offer triangulation capabilities or if the device is moving.

Wireless IDPS overcome the other types of IDPS by providing more accurate prevention; this is largely due to its narrow focus. Anomaly-based detection methods often generate high false positives, especially

Figure 11. MIDS functional blocks

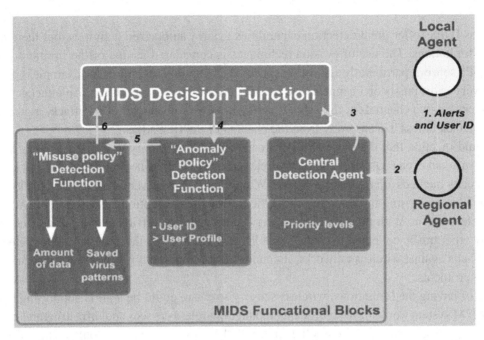

if threshold values are not properly maintained. Although many alerts based on benign activities might occur, such as another organization's WLAN being within range of the organization's WLANs, these alerts are not truly false positives because they are accurately detecting an unknown WLAN.

Some tuning and customization are required for the Wireless IDPS technologies to improve their detection accuracy. The main effort required in the Wireless IDPS is in specifying which WLANs, access points, and stations are authorized, and in entering the policy characteristics into the wireless IDPS software. As wireless IDPSs only examine wireless network protocols, not the higher-level protocols (e.g., applications), generally there is not a large number of alert types, and consequently, not many customizations or tunings that are available.

Wireless IDPS sensors provide two types of intrusion prevention capabilities:

- Some sensor software can terminate connections through the air, typically by sending messages to the end points telling them to dissociate the current session and then refusing to permit a new connection to be established.
- Another prevention method is for a sensor to instruct a switch on the wired network to block network activity involving a particular device on the basis of the device's media access control (MAC) address or switch port. However, this technique is only effective for blocking the device's communications on the wired network, not the wireless network.

An important consideration when choosing prevention capabilities is the effect that prevention actions can have on sensor monitoring. For example, if a sensor is transmitting signals to terminate connections, it may not be able to perform channel scanning to monitor other communications until it has completed the prevention action. To mitigate this, some sensors have two radios – one for monitoring and detection, and another for performing prevention actions.

Wireless IDPS Limitations

The wireless IDPSs offer great detection capabilities against authorized activities, but there are some significant limitations. The use of evasion techniques is considered as one of the limitations of some wireless IDPS sensors, particularly against sensor channel scanning schemes. One example is performing attacks in very short bursts on channels that are not currently being monitored. An attacker could also launch attacks on two channels at the same time. If the sensor detects the first attack, it cannot detect the second attack unless it scans away from the channel of the first attack.

We should mention that the wireless IDPSs cannot detect certain types of attacks against wireless networks. An attacker can passively monitor wireless traffic, which is not detectable by wireless IDPSs. If weak security methods are used, for example, Wired Equivalent Privacy (WEP), the attacker can then perform *off-line* processing of the collected traffic to find the encryption key used to provide security for the wireless traffic. With this key, the attacker can decrypt the traffic that was already collected, as well as any other traffic collected from the same WLAN. As the Wireless IDPSs cannot detect certain types of attacks against wireless networks, it cannot fully compensate for the use of insecure wireless networking protocols.

In spite of having the limitations, wireless sensory software could be a good supporting part of the MIDS as M2M system would have significant amount of wireless devices and infrastructure in it. In fact, a wireless sensor software (i.e., wireless IDPS) installed on a wireless device could be the local agent in the MIDS framework combined with other functionalities. Further thoughts and research studies could be performed in this direction in future, for which we have opted to put this section in this chapter. We believe that this area will prosper as fast as the implementation of new M2M-enabled innovations in different sectors of life begins to materialize accompanied by different new security threats in addition to the ones mentioned before.

CONCLUSION

In this chapter, we explained the M2M system and its security challenges. We discussed the security threats that the M2M communication faces and then, highlighted the M2M capabilities to support an Intrusion Detection System. After studying various relevant IDS technologies, we designed a common platform for IDS for M2M system; we suggested an M2M IDS framework combining the device level and wireless IDPS, that may be worked on further towards practical implementation based on various applications and design scenarios emerging for the M2M systems.

REFERENCES

Abduvaliyev, A. Pathan, A.-S.K., Zhou, J., Roman, R., & Wong, W.-C. (2013). On the Vital Areas of Intrusion Detection Systems in Wireless Sensor Networks. *IEEE Communications Surveys & Tutorials*, *15*(3), 1223-1237.

Aboelaze, M., & Aloul, F. (2005). Current and future trends in sensor networks: a survey.*Second IFIP International Conference on Wireless and Optical Communications Networks 2005 (WOCN 2005)*, (pp. 551-555). doi:10.1109/WOCN.2005.1436087

Ahmed, K. R., Ahmed, K., Munir, S., & Asad, A. (2008). Abnormal node detection in wireless sensor network by pair based approach using IDS secure routing methodology. *Int J Comput Sci Netw. Sec*, 8(12), 339–342.

Anggorojati, B., & Prasad, N. R. (2013). An Intrusion Detection game in access control system for the M2M local cloud platform. *2013 19th Asia-Pacific Conference on Communications (APCC)*.

Anggorojati, B., & Prasad, N. R. (2014). Secure capability-based access control in the M2M local cloud platform. *2014-4th International Conference on Wireless Communications, Vehicular Technology, Information Theory and Aerospace & Electronic Systems (VITAE'14)*.

Aris, A., Oktug, S. F., & Yalcin, S. B. O. (2015). Internet-of-Things security: Denial of service attacks.*2015 Signal Processing and Communications Applications Conference (SIU'15)*, (pp. 903-906). doi:10.1109/SIU.2015.7129976

Arnoys, L. (2015). The internet of things: communicating with the cloud, the protocols, security and big data. *NMCT 2015*. Available at: http://hdl.handle.net/10046/1184

Atamli, A. W., & Martin, A. (2014). Threat-Based Security Analysis for the Internet of Things.*2014 International Workshop on Secure Internet of Things (SIoT'14)*. doi:10.1109/SIoT.2014.10

Azad, S., & Pathan, A.-S. K. (Eds.). (2014). Practical Cryptography: Algorithms and Implementations using C++. CRC Press, Taylor & Francis Group.

Barnhart, E. N., & Bokath, C. A. (2011). Considerations for Machine-to-Machine communications architecture and security standardization. *2011 IEEE 5th International Conference on Internet Multimedia Systems Architecture and Application (IMSAA'11)*.

Bartoli, A. (2013). *Security protocols suite for machine-to-machine systems* (Ph.D. Thesis). Universitat Politècnica de Catalunya, Departament d'Enginyeria Telemàtica.

Beigi-Mohammadi, N., Misic, J., Khazaei, H., & Misic, V. B. (2014). An intrusion detection system for smart grid neighborhood area network.*2014 IEEE International Conference on Communications (ICC'14)*. doi:10.1109/ICC.2014.6883967

Ben, S. Y., Olivereau, A., & Laurent, M. (2012). A Distributed Approach for Secure M2M Communications. *2012-5th International Conference on New Technologies, Mobility and Security (NTMS'12)*.

Bojic, I., Granjal, J., Monteiro, E., Katusic, D., Skocir, P., Kusek, M., & Jezic, G. (2014). *Communication and Security in Machine-to-Machine Systems.*Lecture Notes in Computer Science, 8611, 255–281.

Boubakri, W., Abdallah, W., & Boudriga, N. (2014). A chaos-based authentication and key management scheme for M2M communication. *2014 9th International Conference for Internet Technology and Secured Transactions (ICITST'14)*.

Cagalaban, G., Ahn, J. Y., & Kim, S. (2012). A Secure Machine to Machine-Based Framework for Service Provisioning in Cloud Computing Infrastructures. Business, Economics, Financial Sciences, and Management. Springer.

Calhoun, P. R., Zorn, G., Pan, P., & Akhtar, H. (2001). *Diameter Framework Document.* IETF Draft. Retrieved 5 Dec. 2015 from: http://tools.ietf.org/html/draft-calhoun-diameter-framework-09

Cha, I., Shah, Y., Schmidt, A. U., Leicher, A., & Meyerstein, M. V. (2009). Trust in M2M communication. *IEEE Vehicular Technology Magazine, Volume, 4*(3), 69–75. doi:10.1109/MVT.2009.933478

Chan, P. K., Mahoney, M., & Arshad, M. (2003). Learning Rules and Clusters for Anomaly Detection in Network Traffic. In *Managing Cyber Threats*, (pp. 81-99). Academic Press.

Chang, K., Soong, A., Tseng, M., & Xiang, Z. (2011). Global Wireless Machine-to-Machine Standardization. *IEEE Internet Computing, Volume, 15*(2), 64–69. doi:10.1109/MIC.2011.41

Chen, D., & Chang, G. (2012). A Survey on Security Issues of M2M Communications in Cyber-Physical Systems. *Transactions on Internet and Information Systems (Seoul), 6*(1), 24–45.

Chen, H.-C., You, I., Weng, C.-E., Cheng, C. H., & Huang, Y.-F. (2016). A security gateway application for End-to-End M2M communications. *Computer Standards & Interfaces, 44*, 85–93. doi:10.1016/j.csi.2015.09.001

Choi, H. K., Han, C. K., & Choi, D. S. (2015). Improvement of security protocol for Machine Type Communications in LTE-advanced.*Wireless Communications and Mobile Computing Conference 2015 (IWCMC'15).* doi:10.1109/IWCMC.2015.7289270

Choi, Y., Doh, I., Park, S. S., & Chae, K. J. (2012). Security Based Semantic Context Awareness System for M2M Ubiquitous Healthcare Service. In Ubiquitous Information Technologies and Applications. (LNCS), (vol. 214, pp. 187-196). Springer.

Cimler, R., Matyska, J., Balik, L., Horalek, J., & Sobeslav, V. (2015). Security Aspects of Cloud Based Mobile Health Care Application. In *Nature of Computation and Communication.* Springer.

Da Silva, A. P. R., Martins, M. H. T., Rocha, B. P. S., Loureiro, A. A. F., Ruiz, L. B., & Wong, H. C. (2008). Decentralized intrusion detection in wireless sensor networks.*Proceedings of the 1st ACM international workshop on quality of service and security in wireless and mobile networks.*

Dagon, D., Martin, T., & Starner, T. (2004). Mobile phones as computing devices: The viruses are coming! *IEEE Pervasive Computing, Volume, 3*(4), 11–15. doi:10.1109/MPRV.2004.21

De Almeida, F. M., Ribeiro, A. R. L., & Moreno, E. D. (2015). An Architecture for Self-healing in Internet of Things.*UBICOMM 2015: The Ninth International Conference on Mobile Ubiquitous Computing, Systems, Services and Technologies.*

Demblewski, M. (2015). *Security Frameworks for Machine-to-Machine Devices and Networks* (Doctoral dissertation). Nova Southeastern University. Retrieved from: NSUWorks, College of Engineering and Computing.

Denial-of-Service Developments. (2000). *CERT Advisory CA-2000-01*. Retrieved 6 Dec. 2015, from: http://www.cert.org/advisories/CA-2000-01.html

Doh, I., Chae, K., Lim, J., & Chung, M. Y. (2015). *Authentication and Key Management Based on Kerberos for M2M Mobile Open IPTV Security. In Intelligent Automation & Soft Computing* (Vol. 21, pp. 543–558). Taylor & Francis Group.

Dohler, M., Boswarthick, D., & Alonso-Zárate, J. (2012). Machine-to-Machine in Smart Grids & Smart Cities. Technologies, Standards, and Applications. Tutorial Globecom 2012, Anaheim, CA.

Drozda, M., Schaust, S., & Szczerbicka, H. (2010). AIS for misbehaviour detection in wireless sensor networks: performance and design principles. In Congress on evolutionary computation, (pp. 3719-3726).

Duquet, S. (2015). *Smart Sensors: Enabling Detection and Ranging for the Internet of Things and Beyond*. LeddarTech, White paper.

Farooqi, A.H., Khan, F.A., Wang, J., & Lee, S. (2013). A novel intrusion detection framework for wireless sensor networks. *Personal and Ubiquitous Computing, 17*(5), 907-919.

Fink, G. A., Zarzhitsky, D. V., Carroll, T. E., & Farquhar, E. D. (2015). Security and privacy grand challenges for the Internet of Things. *2015 International Conference on Collaboration Technologies and Systems (CTS'15)*. doi:10.1109/CTS.2015.7210391

Fremantle, P., & Scott, P. (2015). A security survey of middleware for the Internet of Things. *PeerJ PrePrints* 3:e1521. Retrieved 6 Dec. 2015 from: https://peerj.com/preprints/1241/

Genge, B., Haller, P., Gligor, A., & Beres, A. (2014). An Approach for Cyber Security Experimentation Supporting Sensei/IoT for Smart Grid. *2nd International Symposium on Digital Forensics and Security (ISDFS'14)*.

Granjal, J., Monteiro, E., & Silva, J. S. (2013). *Security Issues and Approaches on Wireless M2M Systems. In Wireless Networks and Security Part of the series Signals and Communication Technology* (pp. 133–164). Springer Berlin Heidelberg.

Gupta, S., Zheng, R., & Cheng, A. M. K. (2007). ANDES: an anomaly detection system for wireless sensor networks. *International conference on mobile ad hoc and sensor systems*, (pp. 1–9). doi:10.1109/MOBHOC.2007.4428636

Gyrard, A., Bonnet, C., & Boudaoud, K. (2014). An Ontology-Based Approach for Helping to Secure the ETSI Machine-to-Machine Architecture. *2014 IEEE International Conference on Internet of Things (iThings), Green Computing and Communications (GreenCom), IEEE and Cyber, and Physical and Social Computing(CPSCom)*. IEEE. doi:10.1109/iThings.2014.25

Hai, T. H., Khan, F., & Huh, E.-N. (2007). Hybrid intrusion detection system for wireless sensor networks. Springer. doi:10.1007/978-3-540-74477-1_36

Hakiri, A., & Berthou, P. (2015). *Leveraging SDN for the 5G Networks. Software Defined Mobile Networks (SDMN): Beyond LTE Network Architecture* (M. Liyanage, A. Gurtov, & M. Ylianttila, Eds.). Chichester, UK: John Wiley & Sons, Ltd. doi:10.1002/9781118900253.ch5

Heady, R., Luger, G., Maccabe, A., & Servilla, M. (1990). *The Architecture of a Network Level Intrusion Detection System. Technical report.* University of New Mexico. doi:10.2172/425295

Hongsong, C., Zhongchuan, F., & Dongyan, Z. (2011). Security and trust research in M2M system.*2011 IEEE International Conference on Vehicular Electronics and Safety (ICVES'11)*. doi:10.1109/ICVES.2011.5983830

Hossain, M. M., Fotouhi, M., & Hasan, R. (2015). Towards an Analysis of Security Issues, Challenges, and Open Problems in the Internet of Things.*2015 IEEE World Congress on Services (SERVICES'15)*. doi:10.1109/SERVICES.2015.12

Hu, L., Chi, L., Li, H. T., Yuan, W., Sun, Y., & Chu, J. F. (2012). The classic security application in M2M- the authentication scheme of Mobile Payment. *Transactions on Internet and Information Systems (Seoul)*, *6*(1), 131–146.

Huang, M.-Y., Jasper, R. J., & Wicks, T. M. (1999). A large scale distributed intrusion detection framework based on attack strategy analysis. *Computer Networks*, *31*(23–24), 2465–2475. doi:10.1016/S1389-1286(99)00114-0

Huang, X., Craig, P., & Yan, H.L.Z (2015). SecIoT: a security framework for the Internet of Things. *Security and Communication Networks*. DOI: 10.1002/sec.1259

Huh, E.-N., & Hai, T. H. (2011). Lightweight Intrusion Detection for Wireless Sensor Networks. In Intrusion Detection Systems. Academic Press.

Hussen, H. R., Tizazu, G. A., Ting, M., Lee, T., Choi, Y., & Kim, K. H. (2013). SAKES: Secure authentication and key establishment scheme for M2M communication in the IP-based wireless sensor network (6L0WPAN).*2013 Fifth International Conference on Ubiquitous and Future Networks (ICUFN'13)*, (pp. 246-251). doi:10.1109/ICUFN.2013.6614820

Inshil, D., Jiyoung, L., Shi, L., & Kijoon, C. (2014). Pairwise and group key setup mechanism for secure machine-to-machine communication. *Science and Information Systems*, *11*(3), 1071–1090. doi:10.2298/CSIS130922065D

Jaber, M., Kouzayha, N., Dawy, Z., & Kayssi, A. (2014). On cellular network planning and operation with M2M signalling and security considerations.*2014 IEEE International Conference on Communications Workshops (ICC'14)*. doi:10.1109/ICCW.2014.6881236

Jin, B. W., & Hahm, H. (2013). A Design of Advanced Authentication Method for Protection of Privacy in M2M Environment. *International Journal of Smart Home*, *7*(5), 145–154. doi:10.14257/ijsh.2013.7.5.15

Jin, B. W., Park, J. P., Lee, K. W., & Jun, M. S. (2013). A Study of Authentication Method for Id-Based Encryption Using In M2M Environment. *Journal of the Korea Academia-Industrial Cooperation Society*, *14*(4), 1926–1934.

Jover, R. P. (2015). Security and impact of the IoT on LTE mobile networks. In *Security and Privacy in the Internet of Things (IoT): Models, Algorithms, and Implementations*. CRC Press, Taylor & Francis. Retrieved 6 Dec., 2015 from: http://www.ee.columbia.edu/~roger/LTE_IoT.pdf

Jung, S., Ahn, J. Y., Hwang, D. J., & Kim, S. (2012). A Study on Key Distribution Protocol with Mutual Authentication for M2M Sensor Network. Information, 15, 1229-1240.

Jung, S., Kim, D., & Seoksoo, S. (2013). *Cooperative Architecture for Secure M2M Communication. In Advanced Science and Technology Letters* (Vol. 29, pp. 37–40). SecTech.

Jung, S., & Kim, S. (2013). Hierarchical Security Management for M2M Wireless Sensor Networks. *International Journal of Advancements in Computing Technology, 5*(11), 238–244. doi:10.4156/ijact. vol5.issue11.26

Karim, L., Anpalagan, A., Nasser, N., Almhana, J. N., & Woungang, I. (2013). *An energy efficient, fault tolerant and secure clustering scheme for M2M communication networks. In 2013 IEEE Globecom Workshops* (pp. 677–682). Atlanta, GA: GC Wkshps.

Karuppiah, A. B., Dalfiah, J., Yuvashri, K., Rajaram, S., & Pathan, A.-S. K. (2014). Energy-Efficient Sybil Node Detection Algorithm for Wireless Sensor Networks.*3rd International Conference on Eco-Friendly Computing and Communication Systems (ICECCS 2014).*

Khan, S., Pathan, A.-S. K., & Alrajeh, N. A. (2012). Wireless Sensor Networks: Current Status and Future Trends. Auerbach Publications, CRC Press, Taylor & Francis Group. doi:10.1201/b13092

Kim, J.M., Jeong, H.Y., & Hong, B.H. (2011). A User Authentication Method for M2M Environments. Computer Science and Convergence, *Lecture Notes in Electrical Engineering, 114,* 589-595.

Kim, J.M., Jeong, H.Y., & Hong, B.H. (2014) A study of privacy problem solving using device and user authentication for M2M environments. *Security and Communication Networks, 7*(10, 1528–1535.

Koss, J. (2014). *ETSI Standardizes M2M Communications*. Retrieved 28 Nov. 2015 from: http://www. telit2market.com/wp-content/uploads/2014/10/t2m0510_p038-p039.pdf

Kothmayr, T. D., Hu, W., Brunig, M., & Carle, G. (2012). A DTLS based end-to-end security architecture for the Internet of Things with two-way authentication. *2012 IEEE 37th Conference on Local Computer Networks Workshops (LCN Workshops).*

Krontiris, I., & Dimitriou, T. (2007). Towards intrusion detection in wireless sensor networks. *13th European wireless conference.*

Krontiris, I., Dimitriou, T., & Giannetsos, T. (2008). LIDeA: A distributed lightweight intrusion detection architecture for sensor networks. ACM secure communication.

Lai, C., Li, H., Lu, R., Shen, X. S., & Cao, J. (2013). A unified end-to-end security scheme for machine-type communication in LTE networks.*2013 IEEE/CIC International Conference on Communications in China (ICCC).* doi:10.1109/ICCChina.2013.6671201

Lai, C., Li, H., Zhang, Y., & Cao, J. (2012). Security Issues on Machine to Machine Communications. *Transactions on Internet and Information Systems (Seoul), 6*(2), 498–514.

Lake, D., Milito, R., Morrow, M., & Vargheese, R. (2014). Internet of Things: Architectural Framework for eHealth Security. *Journal of ICT Standardization, 3-4,* 301–328.

Lee, H., & Chung, M. (2012). Context-Aware Security System for the Smart Phone-based M2M Service Environment. *Transactions on Internet and Information Systems (Seoul)*, *6*(1), 64–83.

Lee, K.L. & Kim, S.K. (2015). Authentication Scheme based on Biometric Key for VANET Information System in M2M Application Service. *Applied Math and Information Science Journal*, *9*(2L), 645-651.

Lee, M. (2013). *M2M and the Internet of Things: How secure is it?* Retrieved 29 Nov. 2015 from: http://www.zdnet.com/article/disgruntled-over-big-data-maybe-its-that-visualization-magic-box-dependence

Li, G., He, J., & Fu, Y. (2008). A group based intrusion detection scheme in wireless sensor networks. *The 3rd international conference on grid and pervasive computing—workshop*, (pp. 286-291).

Li, W., Yi, Wu, Y., Pan, L., & Li, J. (2014). A New Intrusion Detection System Based on KNN Classification Algorithm in Wireless Sensor Network. Journal of Electrical and Computer Engineering.

Liu, L., Gu, M., & Ma, Y. (2015). *Research on the Key Technology of M2M Gateway.*Lecture Notes in Computer Science, 8944, 837–843. doi:10.1007/978-3-319-15554-8_76

Loo, C. E., Ng, M. Y., Leckie, C., & Palaniswami, M. (2010). Intrusion detection for routing attacks in sensor networks. *International Journal of Distributed Sensor Networks*, *2*(4), 313–332. doi:10.1080/15501320600692044

Lu, R., Li, X., Liang, X., Shen, X., & Lin, X. (2011). GRS: The green, reliability, and security of emerging machine to machine communications. *IEEE Communications Magazine, Volume*, *49*(4), 28–35. doi:10.1109/MCOM.2011.5741143

Machine-to-Machine Communications (M2M) Functional Architecture. (2011). *The European Telecommunications Standards Institute (ETSI), TS 102 690 V1.1.1 (2011-10), 2011*. Retrieved 28 Nov. 2015 from: http://www.etsi.org/deliver/etsi_ts/102600_102699/102690/01.01.01_60/ts_102690v010101p.pdf

Machine-to-Machine Communications (M2M) mIa, dIa and mId Interfaces. (2015). *ETSI TS 102 921 V1.3.1 (2014-09)*. Retrieved 29 Nov., 2015 from: http://www.etsi.org/deliver/etsi_ts/102900_102999/102921/01.03.01_60/ts_102921v010301p.pdf

Machine to Machine Communications. The European Telecommunications Standards Institute (ETSI) standards. (n.d.). Retrieved 28 Nov., 2015 from: http://www.etsi.org/technologies-clusters/technologies/m2m

Maglaras, L. A., Jiang, J., & Cruz, T. G. (2015). Combining ensemble methods and social network metrics for improving accuracy of OCSVM on intrusion detection in SCADA systems. Journal of Information Security and Applications.

Mahkonen, H., Rinta-aho, T., Kauppinen, T., Sethi, M., Kjällman, J., & Salmela, P. (2013). Secure M2M cloud testbed.*Proceedings of the 19th annual international conference on Mobile computing & networking (MobiCom '13)*. ACM. doi:10.1145/2500423.2505294

Maras, M. H. (2015). Internet of Things: security and privacy implications. *International Data Privacy Law*. Retrieved 6 Dec., 2015 from: http://idpl.oxfordjournals.org/content/5/2/99

Masek, P., Muthanna, A., & Hosek, J. (2015). Suitability of MANET Routing Protocols for the Next-Generation National Security and Public Safety Systems. Internet of Things, Smart Spaces, and Next Generation Networks and Systems, Volume 9247 of the series. *Lecture Notes in Computer Science, 9247,* 242–253. doi:10.1007/978-3-319-23126-6_22

Misic, V. B., & Misic, J. (2014). *Machine-to-Machine Communications: Architectures, Technology, Standards, and Applications.* CRC Press.

Mo, Y., Kim, T. H.-H., Brancik, K., Dickinson, D., Lee, H., Perrig, A., & Sinopoli, B. (2012). Cyber–Physical Security of a Smart Grid Infrastructure. *Proceedings of the IEEE, 100*(1), 195-209.

Mohammed, M., & Pathan, A.-S. K. (2013). Automatic Defense against Zero-day Polymorphic Worms in Communication Networks. CRC Press, Taylor & Francis Group. doi:10.1201/b14912

Moon, Y. k., Lee, E. K., Kim, J. J., & Choi, H. R. (2014). *Study on the Container Security Device based on IoT. In Information* (pp. 5425–5433). Tokyo: International Information Institute.

More than 50 billion connected devices. (2011). Ericsson white paper, 28423-3149Uen.

Neisse, R., Fovino, I. N., Baldini, G., Stavroulaki, V., Vlacheas, P., & Giaffreda, R. (2014). A Model-Based Security Toolkit for the Internet of Things. *Availability, Reliability and Security (ARES),2014 Ninth International Conference on Availability, Reliability and Security (ARES'14),* (pp. 78 – 87). doi:10.1109/ARES.2014.17

Neisse, R., Steri, G., Fovino, I.N., & Baldini, G. (2015). SecKit: A Model-based Security Toolkit for the Internet of Things. *Computers & Security, 54,* 60–76.

Nie, X., & Zhai, X. (2013) M2M security threat and security mechanism research. *3rd International Conference on Computer Science and Network Technology (ICCSNT 2013),* (pp. 906-909). doi:10.1109/ICCSNT.2013.6967252

No stopping Johannesburg's traffic light thieves. (2015). Retrieved 30 November, 2015 from: http://www.theguardian.com/world/2011/jan/06/johannesburg-traffic-light-thieves-sim

oneM2M. (2015). Retrieved 29 Nov. 2015 from: http://www.etsi.org/about/what-we-do/global-collaboration/onem2m

Park, N., Park, J. S., & Kim, H. J. (2015). *Inter-Authentication and Session Key Sharing Procedure for Secure M2M/IoT Environment. In Information* (pp. 261–266). Tokyo: International Information Institute.

Park, N., Park, J. S., & Kim, H. K. (2014). *Hash-based authentication and session key agreement Scheme in Internet of Things Environment. In Advanced Science and Technology Letters* (Vol. 62, pp. 9–12). Sensor.

Pathan, A.-S. K. (2015). Securing Cyber Physical Systems. CRC Press, Taylor & Francis Group.

Pathan, A.-S. K. (2010). Denial of Service in Wireless Sensor Networks: Issues and Challenges. In A. V. Stavros (Ed.), *Advances in Communications and Media Research* (Vol. 6). Nova Science Publishers, Inc.

Pathan, A.-S. K. (2010). Major Works on the Necessity and Implementations of PKC in WSN A Beginner's Note. Security of Self-Organizing Networks: MANET, WSN, WMN, VANET. Auerbach Publications, CRC Press, Taylor & Francis Group.

Pathan, A.-S. K. (2014). The State of the Art in Intrusion Prevention and Detection. CRC Press, Taylor & Francis Group. doi:10.1201/b16390

Pathan, A.-S. K., Khanam, S., Saleem, H. Y., & Abduallah, W. M. (2013). Tackling Intruders in Wireless Mesh Networks. In Distributed Network Intelligence, Security and Applications. CRC Press, Taylor & Francis Group.

Pathan, A.-S. K., Monowar, M. M., & Fadlullah, Z. M. (2013). Building Next-Generation Converged Networks: Theory and Practice. CRC Press, Taylor & Francis Group. doi:10.1201/b14574

Paxson, V. (1990). Bro: A system for detecting network intruders in real-time. Computer Networks. *The International Journal of Computer and Telecommunications Networking*, *31*(23-24), 2435–2463.

Pei, Y. (2012). A Survey on Localization Algorithms for Wireless Ad Hoc Networks. In Communications and Information Processing. Springer.

Phuong, T. V., Hung, L. X., Cho, S. J., Lee, Y. K., & Lee, S. (2006). An anomaly detection algorithm for detecting attacks in wireless sensor networks. Intelligent and Security Informatics, 735–736.

Pirretti, M., Zhu, S., Vijaykrishnan, N., McDaniel, P., Kandemir, M., & Brooks, R. (2006). The Sleep Deprivation Attack in Sensor Networks: Analysis and Methods of Defense. *International Journal of Distributed Sensor Networks*, *2*(3), 267–287. doi:10.1080/15501320600642718

Qiu, Y., & Ma, M. (2015). Security Issues and Approaches in M2M Communications. In Securing Cyber Physical Systems. CRC Press, Taylor & Francis Group.

Remote wipe definition. (2015). *TechTarget*. Retrieved 6 Dec., 2015 from: http://searchmobilecomputing.techtarget.com/definition/remote-wipe

Ren, F., & Gu, Y. (2015). Using Artificial Intelligence in the Internet of Things.ZTE Communications, 13(2).

Ren, W., Yu, L., Ma, L., & Ren, Y. (2013). RISE: A ReIIable and SEcure Scheme for Wireless Machine to Machine Communications. *Tsinghua Science and Technology*, *18*(1), 100–117. doi:10.1109/TST.2013.6449413

Riker, A., Cruz, T., Marques, B., Curado, M., Simoes, P., & Monteiro, E. (2014). *Efficient and secure M2M communications for smart metering. In 2014 IEEE Emerging Technology and Factory Automation* (pp. 1–7). Barcelona: ETFA. doi:10.1109/ETFA.2014.7005176

Roesch, M. (1999). Snort - Lightweight Intrusion Detection for Networks.*Proceedings of the 13th USENIX conference on System administration (LISA'99)*, (pp. 229-238).

Roman, R., Zhou, J., & Lopez, J. (2006). Applying intrusion detection systems to wireless sensor networks. *3rd IEEE consumer communications and networking conference*, (pp. 640–644).

Roman, R., Zhou, J., & Lopez, J. (2013). On the features and challenges of security and privacy in distributed internet of things. *Computer Networks*, *57*(10), 2266–2279. doi:10.1016/j.comnet.2012.12.018

Rubertis, D. A., Mainetti, L., Mighali, V., Patrono, L., Sergi, I., Stefanizzi, M. L., & Pascali, S. (2013). Performance evaluation of end-to-end security protocols in an Internet of Things. *2013 21st International Conference on Software, Telecommunications and Computer Networks (SoftCOM'13)*.

Saleem, K., Derhab, A., Al-Muhtadi, J., & Shahzad, B. (2015). *Human-oriented design of secure Machine-to-Machine communication system for e-Healthcare society. In Computers in Human Behavior* (Vol. 51, pp. 977–985). Elsevier.

Satyadevan, S., Kalarickal, B. S., & Jinesh, M. K. (2014). Security, Trust and Implementation Limitations of Prominent IoT Platforms.*Proceedings of the 3rd International Conference on Frontiers of Intelligent Computing: Theory and Applications (FICTA) 2014*.

Schurgot, M. R., & Shinberg, D. A. (2015). Experiments with security and privacy in IoT networks. *2015 IEEE 16th International Symposium on a World of Wireless on Mobile and Multimedia Networks (WoWMoM)*.

Shafagh, H., & Hithnawi, A. (2014). Poster Abstract: Security Comes First, a Public-key Cryptography Framework for the Internet of Things.*2014 IEEE International Conference on Distributed Computing in Sensor Systems (DCOSS)*. doi:10.1109/DCOSS.2014.62

Shaikh, R. A., Jameel, H., Auriol, B. J., Lee, S., & Song, Y. J. (2008). Trusting anomaly and intrusion claims for cooperative distributed intrusion detection schemes of wireless sensor networks. *The 9th international conference for young computer scientists*, (pp. 2038-2043).

Shih, J.-R., Hu, Y., Hsiao, M.-C., Chen, M.-S., Shen, W.-C., Yang, B.-Y., & Cheng, C.-M. et al. (2013). Securing M2M With Post-Quantum Public-Key Cryptography. *IEEE Journal on Emerging and Selected Topics in Circuits and Systems, Volume, 3*(1), 106–116. doi:10.1109/JETCAS.2013.2244772

Sicari, S., Rizzardi, A., Coen-Porisini, A., Grieco, L. A., & Monteil, T. (2015). Secure OM2M Service Platform. Autonomic Computing (ICAC). *2015 IEEE International Conference on Autonomic Computing (ICAC)*. doi:10.1109/ICAC.2015.59

Sicari, S., Rizzardi, A., Grieco, L. A., & Coen-Porisini, A. (2015). Security, privacy and trust in Internet of Things: The road ahead. *Computer Networks*.

Singh, J., Pasquier, T., Bacon, J, Ko, H., & Eyers, D. (2015). Twenty security considerations for cloud-supported Internet of Things. *IEEE Internet of Things Journal*.

Song, H., Xie, L., Zhu, S., & Cao, G. (2007). Sensor node compromise detection: the location perspective. *Proceedings of the 2007 international conference on Wireless communications and mobile computing (IWCMC '07)*. doi:10.1145/1280940.1280993

St. John-Green, M., & Watson, T. (2014). Safety and Security of the Smart City - when our infrastructure goes online.*9th IET International Conference on System Safety and Cyber Security*. doi:10.1049/cp.2014.0981

Stetsko, A., Folkman, L., & Vashek, M. (2010). Neighbor-based intrusion detection for wireless sensor networks. *6th IEEE international conference on wireless and mobile communications*.

Sun, X., Men, S., Zhao, C., & Zhou, Z. (2015). A security authentication scheme in machine-to-machine home network service. Security and Communication Networks, 8(16), 2678–2686. doi:10.1002/sec.551

Suo, H., Wan, J., Zou, C., & Liu, J. (2012). Security in the Internet of Things: A Review.*2012 International Conference on Computer Science and Electronics Engineering (ICCSEE)*, (vol. 3, pp. 648-651). doi:10.1109/ICCSEE.2012.373

Swetina, J., Lu, G., Jacobs, P., Ennesser, F., & Song, J. (2014). Toward a standardized common M2M service layer platform: Introduction to oneM2M. *IEEE Wireless Communications, 21*(3), 1536–1284. doi:10.1109/MWC.2014.6845045

Świątek, P., Tarasiuk, H., & Natkaniec, M. (2015). *Delivery of e-Health Services in Next Generation Networks.*Lecture Notes in Computer Science, 9012, 453–462.

Tan, S.K., Sooriyabandara, M., & Fan, Z. (2011). M2M Communications in the Smart Grid: Applications, Standards, Enabling Technologies, and Research Challenges. *International Journal of Digital Multimedia Broadcasting.* doi:10.1155/2011/289015

The Global Wireless M2M Market. (2009). *Berg Insight.* Retrieved 6 Dec. 2015 from: http://www.berginsight.com/ShowReport.aspx?m_m=3&id=95

Ukil, A., Bandyopadhyay, S., Bhattacharyya, A., Pal, A., & Bose, T. (2014). Auth-Lite: Lightweight M2M Authentication reinforcing DTLS for CoAP.*2014 IEEE International Conference on Pervasive Computing and Communications Workshops (PERCOM Workshops).* doi:10.1109/PerComW.2014.6815204

Wang, Y., Streff, K., & Raman, S. (2012). Smartphone Security Challenges. *IEEE Computer, Volume, 45*(Issue: 12), 52–58. doi:10.1109/MC.2012.288

Wang, Y., Wu, X., & Chen, H. (2015). *An intrusion detection method for wireless sensor network based on mathematical morphology. In Security and Communication Networks.* John Wiley & Sons, Ltd.

Wood, A., & Stankovic, J. A. (2002). Denial of service in sensor networks. *Computer, Volume, 35*(10), 54–62.

Zeadally, S., Pathan, A.-S. K., Alcaraz, C., & Badra, M. (2013). Towards Privacy Protection in Smart Grid. *Wireless Personal Communications, Springer, 73*(1), 23–50. doi:10.1007/s11277-012-0939-1

Zhang, Q., Yu, T., & Ning, P. (2008). A framework for identifying compromised nodes in wireless sensor networks. *ACM Transactions on Information and System Security, XI*(3), 1–37.

Zhang, W., Zhang, Y., Chen, J., Li, H., & Wang, Y. (2013). End-to-end security scheme for Machine Type Communication based on Generic Authentication Architecture. *Cluster Computing, Springer, 16*(4), 861–871. doi:10.1007/s10586-013-0259-6

This work was previously published in Security Solutions and Applied Cryptography in Smart Grid Communications edited by Mohamed Amine Ferrag and Ahmed Ahmim, pages 179-214, copyright year 2017 by Information Science Reference (an imprint of IGI Global).

Chapter 11

Internet of Things:
The Argument for Smart Forensics

Edewede Oriwoh
University of Bedfordshire, UK

Geraint Williams
IT Governance Limited, UK

ABSTRACT

The Internet of Things (IoT), a metaphor for smart, functional Cyberphysical Environments (CPE), is finding some usefulness in various sectors including healthcare, security, transportation, and the Smart Home (SH). Within the IoT, objects potentially operate autonomously to provide specified services and complete assigned tasks. However, the introduction of new technologies and/or the novel application of existing ones usually herald the discovery of unfamiliar security vulnerabilities, which lead to exploits and sometimes to security breaches. There is existing research that identifies IoT-related security concerns and breaches. This chapter discusses existing Digital Forensics (DF) models and methodologies for their applicability (or not) within the IoT domain using the SH as a case in point. The chapter also makes the argument for smart forensics, the use of a smart autonomous system (tagged the Forensics Edge Management System [FEMS]) to provide forensic services within the self-managed CPE of the SH.

INTRODUCTION: THE INTERNET OF THINGS

The Internet of Things (IoT) (Lu Tan & Neng Wang, 2010; Uckelmann, 2011) is also referred to variously as the Internet of Objects (Xia, Yang, Wang, & Vinel, 2012), Future Internet (FI) (Hernández-Muñoz et al., 2011), Machine to Machine (M2M) communications (Y. Chen, 2012; Igarashi, Ueno, & Fujisaki, 2012), and the Internet of Everything (IoE) (Castro, Jara, & Skarmeta, 2012; Lin, Leu, Li, & Wu, 2012; Ning & Hu, 2011). It is an extension of traditional networks such as the Internet and social networks. It is the true Network of networks because it describes the potential for the interconnection of every (feasible) object to every other (feasible) object and all the underlying processes and protocols that enable and support these interconnections (Figure 1).

DOI: 10.4018/978-1-5225-1832-7.ch011

Figure 1. Key interconnected elements that make up the IoT

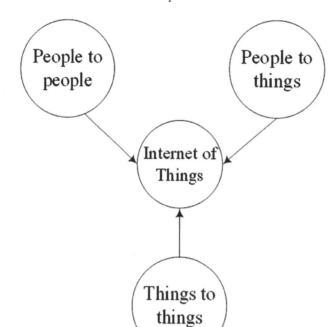

Ericsson estimates that more than 50 billion devices will be connected by 2020 (Ericsson White paper, 2011) while Morgan Stanley suggests that by the same date there will be 75 billion devices connected to the IoT (Proffitt, 2013).These connected items will be of a variety of types and shapes and will vary from traditional computing devices to ordinary everyday objects. For instance within the Smart Home (SH), Things (also known as *Blogjects* (Nova & Bleecker, 2006), *Spimes* (McFedries, 2010) or *IoT-ware* (Oriwoh, Jazani, Epiphaniou, & Sant, 2013)) may include kettles, cars, fridges, Personal Computers, smart phones and washing machines. Various sectors and industries currently benefit from having these interconnections including the transportation, communication, healthcare, smart houses and leisure industries (Fleisch, 2010; Juels, 2006; Kozlov, Veijalainen, & Ali, 2012; Laranjo, Macedo, & Santos, 2012). In the SH, these objects will be interconnected for the purpose of improving people's lives and making things more convenient for them (Alam, Reaz, & Ali, 2012; Hyungkyu Lee, Jooyoung Lee, & Jongwook Han, 2007). The IoT is enabled by technologies including sensors, Machine to Machine communications (M2M), Radio Frequency Identification (RFID) and so on. See Figure 2 for a summary of some cardinal elements of the IoT including the enabling technologies.

However, although the application domains and benefits of the IoT are numerous, a growing number of security concerns have been recognised in relation to the IoT (Juels, 2006). These concerns include *logical* threats (e.g. Denial of Service or DoS) and *physical* threats (e.g. tampering and theft). The discussion in this chapter is particularly focused on one of the many manifestations of the IoT - the SH, which is described by Ding et al. as "a residence equipped with technology that observes the residents and provides proactive services" (Ding, Cooper, Pasquina, & Fici-Pasquina, 2011). Some example SH projects are described in (Chan, Estève, Escriba, & Campo, 2008).

Figure 2. The Internet of things' cardinal elements

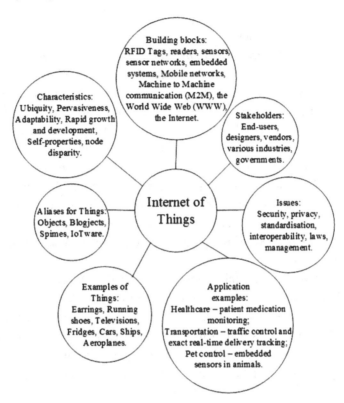

SH environments are susceptible to both traditional attacks such as burglary, theft, DoS as well as tailored attacks e.g. a fridge used as part of a botnet to propagate malware. There is already research that discusses providing security in home-based IoT applications (Chan et al., 2008; D. Chen et al., 2011; Ding et al., 2011; Ning & Liu, 2012; Seigneur, Jensen, Farrell, Gray, & Chen, 2003). However, there is no guarantee that every single logical and physical security measures will be completely attack-proof. Any breaches within SH environments will therefore have to be investigated both from the physical and the digital perspectives. In this light, some DF models and methodologies have been developed that propose to be applicable to CPE (Ademu, Imafidon, & Preston, 2011; Vlachopoulos, Magkos, & Chrissikopoulos, 2013).

This chapter, for its own part, proposes that as part of addressing security issues within SH environments, DF should become *smart* - i.e. through the use of automated smart devices to provide DF services within homes without the requirement for commercial (human) investigators except when absolutely necessary. As part of this contribution, the Forensics Edge Management System (FEMS) is introduced. Prior to this, a methodology for approaching IoT-based crime scenes is proposed. The aim of the methodology is to answer the following question: what is the best way to approach DF within the IoT context to ensure effective and maximum evidence acquisition and avoid time wastage?

BACKGROUND

De Silva et al. suggest that future homes will evolve in a similar way to phones (i.e. in their function). They also suggest that homes will play a role in *protecting* owners and occupants from unforeseen and unavoidable dangers. They describe a SH as having capabilities that allow it to provide home owners with "various facilities" (De Silva, Morikawa, & Petra, 2012). These facilities currently include comfort, location, energy-savings, and security services, among others. Unfortunately, security concerns have been identified as a factor that threaten the adoption of SH solutions by end users (Brush et al., 2011).

This chapter argues that these security concerns should not be allowed to stifle progress in IoT research and development. It suggests that since total freedom from even *attempted* breaches cannot be guaranteed, pro-active methods and approaches to dealing with potential security challenges should be the position taken by academia, policy-makers and other IoT stakeholders. This can be in the form of well-structured DF investigations the results of which, can lead to the identification of sources of security breaches. In addition, lessons learned from DF investigations can be useful during the development of future security measures and tools.

As a contribution towards this solution this chapter recommends a two-pronged approach: a triage-based Incident Response (IR) and DF methodology and the use of a smart device that can be installed within SH networks to provide real-time monitoring and forensics services. However, certain IoT characteristics may pose challenges to DF processes within IoT (SH) scenarios. The following discussion describes these characteristics and how they might influence future approaches to DF. IoT-ware is the term used to describe all end nodes, devices, objects, things, and so on within the IoT domain including the SH.

The IoT Characteristics

Ubiquity and Mobility

Atzori et al. contend that within the IoT current security risks have the potential to be more widely distributed (Atzori, Iera, & Morabito, 2010). Part of the reason for this is that within the IoT, IoT-ware such as sensor-tagged vehicles are as distributed as the homes of citizens (static vehicles) and other locations such as roads (moving vehicles) therefore the impact of any propagated attack is more widely spread. As a result, from the perspective of forensics Incident Response Teams (IRT), locating and gaining access to such widely dispersed potential Objects of Forensic Interest (OOFI) (Oriwoh et al., 2013) may be a challenge.

Autonomy

IoT-ware are able to operate on their own as described by the self-* properties - self-awareness, self-configuration, self-maintenance and self-destruction among others (Dobson, Sterritt, Nixon, & Hinchey, 2010; Gurgen, Gunalp, Benazzouz, & Gallissot, 2013). One of the goals of DF is to identify sources of breaches. Autonomy as encouraged by the IoT affects the achievement of this goal because with autonomous systems there is a question of *control* (who/what did it) and *responsibility* (who/what is at fault?). The subject of responsibility assignment and modelling in *socio-technical systems* - which arguably includes the IoT - is discussed extensively in (Sommerville, 2007).

Adaptability

This stems from the self-management property. Since IoT-ware can learn and adjust/adapt independently as situations call for it, they can be deemed unreliable sources of forensics evidence since any evidence stored on them can be changed without any human input and possibly before DF teams are able to acquire any evidence from them.

Heterogeneity and Disparity

From the SH perspective potential sources of evidence will be even more (physically) diverse than in traditional networks. This diversity presents challenges to investigators (Turnbull, 2008). There is a possibility that during investigations, some non-traditional OOFI e.g. fridges might unwittingly be missed simply because they do not fall under the group of items that *digital* IRT are used to accessing or querying for evidence. Another factor is the logical disparity between evidence sources such as sensor (tag) manufacturer ID conventions, timestamp formats and packet headers. In this light, captured sensor logs may rather than assist DF investigations, lead to confusion unless they are effectively sanitized and unified in order to achieve some form of correlation and therefore some usefulness.

Dual Presence

Within the IoT domain, IoT-ware may have both physical and virtual manifestations. There is on-going research into the development of methods of establishing these manifestations (Kindberg et al., 2002). This dual presence means that they can be accessed, queried and controlled by their owners both locally and via the World Wide Web (WWW). However, from a DF perspective, it means that sources of evidence will be distributed between these two domains posing interesting questions about how best to access both and obtain best evidence bearing in mind the dual access that users have to them. The use of timestamps will be very useful as one way of countering this challenge since all evidence obtained can be correlated based on their timestamps however this will only be helpful if the evidence needed is acquired before it is tampered with.

Size

With respect to DF, the size of end devices is not so much a problem as it is a challenge. Accessing certain IoT-ware may prove difficult. Moore's Law still holds true and processors and storage components will be progressively physically smaller (Mattern, 2003). The access to these devices may therefore be a challenge and DF will require a method of acquiring evidence from them without damaging them physically. An alternative may be for courts to be prepared in certain identified circumstances to always accept evidence from alternative sources, a concept discussed in (Oriwoh et al., 2013) where the Next Best Thing (NBT) serves as the source of *best* evidence. However, within the IoT, the miniturisation of objects is not the singular challenge presented to DF and IRTs. During investigations there is sometimes a need to contain, seize and remove physical evidence from crime scenes. Removing IoT-ware (e.g. fridges) may pose challenge to DF as it currently operates - although probably not so much for physical forensics which already deals with the removal of large objects from crime scenes. This can be resolved by cooperation between the physical and digital forensics teams - which in some instances may be even be one and the same. Alternatively, to counter this IRT may have to increasingly rely on data from central home control servers, external service providers, other end user portable devices and network logs for relevant evidence. Essentially, the best way to approach crime scenes with such irregular evidence sources will have to be agreed during the planning stage.

Invisibility

The nature of IoT-ware as technology that is enmeshed into our lives (Weiser, 1991) and is hence 'invisible' makes any and all potential IoT security challenges pose even greater risks than more familiar, well-known attacks. This embedded and sometimes non-apparent nature of IoT-ware may, in some instances, lead to loss of useful evidence. A potential solution to this would be the assignment of experienced investigators to these kinds of cases as well as diligence during the investigations. In addition, during IoT-ware deployment - in preparation for possible future DF investigations - *potential* OOFI can be identification. This effective and detailed pre-attack triage should be encouraged even in SH environments.

Jurisdiction

The wide distribution of OOFI within IoT domains can be across networks in different jurisdictions with different laws and policies. This is already the case with traditional networks such as the Internet however, within the IoT environment, the added dimension of networks such as Personal Area Networks (PAN) (Franklin & Rajan, 2010) and Body Area Networks (BAN) (Khan & Yuce, 2010) and the on-going discussion about user privacy concerns may lead to even more challenging legal wrangling. In addition, *moral* questions and decisions may have to be made. If gaining access to a device may endanger a patient, the moral decision may be to avoid doing so; this means that an alternative way to proceed with the investigation will have to be taken. Again, this can be achieved by identifying and locating alternative sources (i.e. NBT).

Dynamism

Wireless Sensor Networks (another manifestation of the IoT), as part of their self-management capability, can be configured to continually 'adjust and change' their form. This can be due to various factors such as device migration or even retirement (i.e. self-destruction). Also, there is existing research (Islam, Schmidt, Kolbe, & Andersson, 2012) to support random connection of (trusted) end user devices to Home Area Networks (HAN) (Bouhafs, Mackay, & Merabti, 2012) thereby continually changing the network topologies and router or home server configurations. This potential for networks to be created and broken up without any human input or involvement may pose an interesting challenge when it comes to the basic DF procedure of *locating* OOFI. This becomes even more of a challenge where there is a potential for the break-up (or self-destruction) to be triggered deliberately. This can be used by IoT botnet creators so that the botnets are broken up as soon as there is a chance they are being observed.

Standards (or the Present Lack There-of)

As the IoT develops, different vendors from small start-ups to large companies, industrial bodies, to governments develop their own 'solutions' to enable communication and interaction between IoT-ware. The absence of industry-wide standards for data protocols, platforms, connectors, etc. may become an issue for DF.

Based on the identified characteristics of the IoT there is a need to consider the applicability of the available tools and approaches to DF. The requirement for new tools is identified by Mohay in (Mohay, 2005). He explains that the possibility that data of evidentiary value may exist in new consumer products which have embedded logic creates a need for investigators to be able to access that data hence the requirement for new tools. The need for new methodologies is also acknowledged in research. Selamat at al. explain that the change in technology being encountered during investigations means a need for new methodologies to approach DF investigations (Selamat, Yusof, & Sahib, 2008). Lempereur et al., explain that "traditional and live forensic analysis techniques are maturing, but as the technologies subject to analysis change, research needs to keep pace and preempt emerging trends" (Lempereur, Merabti, & Shi, 2009).

Current Digital Forensics (DF) Approaches

This section discusses selected approaches to DF investigations and their applicability or otherwise within the IoT context.

The Digital Forensics Investigation Model (DFIM)

The DFIM (Ademu et al., 2011) is a four-tier model with an emphasis on iteration of its phases. The phases are Inception phase (this occurs iteratively throughout the entire forensics process), Interaction, Reconstruction and Protection phases. Their work recognises the diversity of devices that are encountered in digital forensics investigations (this is something that the 3-stage framework in (M. Kohn, Eloff, & Olivier, 2006) fails to do when it focusses on only the 'computer' as the source of evidence). However, although according to the authors, the aim of developing the DFIM is as a tool to bring about an improvement of the entire investigation process, their work focuses on digital evidence, describing its characteristics, and defining it as evidence that is "hidden". The DFIM model is limited in its focus in that it does not consider evidence sources that are physically present but which are not *obvious* as sources of digital evidence i.e. cyberphysical evidence.

The Hybrid Model (Vlachopoulos et al., 2013)

This model introduces the term Hybrid evidence to describe evidence which is not purely physical or digital but having a dual nature. This is similar to the view taken in this chapter although the preferred term is cyberphysical evidence. The hybrid model consists of the preparation, crime scene investigation, and laboratory examination and conclusion phases. The model is proposed for the investigation of crime scenes with either physical-only evidence, digital-only evidence or hybrid evidence. Its developer expounds it as one that "examines the whole process of crime investigations, starting from the notification that a crime has been committed, ending to the findings of the research". This model, although clearly recognising that the focus of DF investigations is becoming more varied and the scope is widening, does not appear to recognise that within the IoT there is a need for very quick responses to attacks else evidence can easily be lost or that a pre-attack triage may be useful to ensure that OOFI are identified quicker during IR. Under certain circumstances in the IoT the Hybrid model will be too slow however it can be applied during investigations *after* the initial response to the crime.

The Common Process Model for Incident Response (IR) and Computer Forensics

Freiling and Schwittway propose the Common Process Model for Incident Response and Computer Forensics (Freiling & Schwittay, 2007), an amalgamation of the concepts of IR and Computer Forensics (CF). The model is composed of the pre-analysis, analysis and post-analysis phases. The pre-analysis phase comprises detection of the incident(s) as well as all the steps that take place before actual analysis of available evidence. This step is carried out to identify available evidence that may need to be acquired for further analysis. The step can almost be described as a full IR model on its own. The model encapsulates what this chapter proposes - a need to prepare for incidents before they occur so that forensics processes are efficient and so yield relevant results. However, the authors discuss *Computer Forensics* thereby limiting the scope of the model.

The Abstract Digital Forensics Model (ADFM) (Reith, Carr, & Gunsch, 2002)

According to its proponents, the ADFM model is designed to be applicable to both currently known and future digital crime. The authors argue that some currently available models are too technology-specific and that the ADFM, though drawn from pre-existing models, is proposed to improve upon them and avoid their "shortfalls". Their work recognises a need to develop a more applicable framework and supports the argument made in that this chapter.

Generic Process Model for Network Forensics (GPMNF) (Pilli, Joshi, & Niyogi, 2010)

This model correctly states that as part of the preparation phase for forensics investigations, it is essential to have sensors deployed on the network to detect intrusions and monitor the network. This research meets this requirement through the use of the FEMS system.

Integrated Digital Forensics Process Model (IDFPM) (M. D. Kohn, Eloff, & Eloff)

The IDFPM is described by Kohn et al. as a "standardized" model for forensics investigations. Just as with the Hybrid and Integrated Digital Investigation model, the IDFPM recognises the need for the physical forensics and digital forensics to occur simultaneously. It also has as part of the Preparation Phase, an "Infrastructure Readiness" stage. These two points make the IDFPM more suitable to CPE than some of the other existing models and methodologies.

Automated Forensics

Cohen contends that automation on a large-scale leads to long-term cost reduction. He argues that for some crimes, automation that handles evidence collection and analysis with possibility of presentation of the case outcome for human players is a future vision of forensics (Cohen, 2012). Automated forensics also has the potential to save investigators' time as well as provide repeatable processes which are valuable to forensic investigations. Garfinkel argues that with the increasing complexity of networks and the increasing amounts of data being generated, effective DF automated tools are a necessity (Garfinkel, 2010). Other research (Cantrell, Dampier, Dandass, Niu, & Bogen, 2012; Case, Cristina, Marziale, Richard, & Roussev, 2008; Chen Lin, Li Zhitang, & Gao Cuixia, 2009) shows the inclination towards automating various parts of - or the entire – forensic process with special emphasis on obtaining cogent, relevant information quickly and efficiently without compromising the reliability of the evidence obtained. With the introduction of autonomous, pervasive, and ubiquitous interconnectivity to the home, users who live in smart houses will do so because they expect to be able to rely on the available technology for various tasks such as remembering when to switch their home heating on and off leaving them free to take care of other preferred duties. The FEMS is a contribution towards realizing this vision of the SH. In addition, the FEMS eliminates the requirement for a skilled examiner to turn up continually at users' homes. This in turn leaves examiners free and available to apply their skills to more specialist crimes.

Shortcomings of Examined Models

Extensive research has not yet uncovered a forensics model which takes into account the properties of the SH as a dynamic, largely automated and self-managed CPE. None of the models discussed in this chapter consider the benefits of registration of smart devices in a SH as part of the forensics preparation process. In addition, some of the models claim to be applicable to 'future' environments such as the SH however they fail to discuss their plan for approaching such environments in any appreciable detail. There is no real evidence to suggest they have been tested or validated within an IoT-based environment with its peculiar characteristics. Some existing frameworks (Baryamureeba & Tushabe, 2004) appear to assume that there will be luxury of time during investigations and that in these highly dynamic environments OOFI will be readily accessible during and, throughout investigations. The reality is that because of the autonomy of CPE, when a crime is committed the delay between its detection, reporting, arrival of the IRT, and commencement of the investigation, may prove too lengthy for any investigation to find any useful evidence or at the very least, it may mean that vital evidence is lost.

DF Triage

According to Roussev et al. "DF triage is a partial forensic examination conducted under (significant) time and resource constraints" (Roussev, Quates, & Martell, 2013). This practice is going to be essential for responses to crimes within the IoT, taking the CPE of the SH as an example. As noted before, some of the existing DF models erroneously assume that sources of evidence in crime scenes will be persistent. However, since there is no guarantee of this, it is essential that a form of triage is carried out as soon as a crime scene is approached in order to identify and secure potential sources of evidence. If a pre-preparedness/readiness list that identifies potential OOFIs is readily available this can be used to assist the triage process. In addition, if the FEMS (described later) has identified the sources of suspicious activity - even if not the actual source of the crime - the FEMS output could be useful by helping assisting investigators focus their investigation.

Digital Forensics Readiness

Evidence from DF investigations can be crucial to decision-making in legal or disciplinary proceedings. A key practice for ensuring that when DF investigations are carried out, investigators can find relevant results in timely manner is the practice of forensics *preparedness*. An extensive discussion of the topic of DF preparedness has been carried out (Rowlingson, 2004) where it is described by the author as "the ability of an organisation to maximize its potential to use digital evidence when required". Effective DF preparedness involves planning for any unanticipated or unwanted activity within digitized environments and this practice will be crucial to investigations in the IoT. Within the SH the need for forensics readiness is essential especially since some SH may be required to be able to self-manage. SH owners might therefore also expect to be able to rely on their homes to manage any (physical, logical and hybrid) security breaches that may arise without the continual requirement for a human involvement. One way to assist with this process can be through the use of a dedicated device that continually monitors network traffic, acquires logs, responds to and investigates detected anomalies and attacks as they happen.

THE PROPOSED INCIDENT RESPONSE AND DIGITAL FORENSICS APPROACH

DF would play an important role within the IoT however, in order for DF to remain an effective service it would have to evolve and become *smart* in its methods and tools whilst maintaining forensics principles so that any evidence produced is legally acceptable. Smart forensics encompasses the approaches to forensics that fit into the lifestyle of users in smart CPE - which in the near future would probably be a considerable proportion of the human population. The SANS 2013 *Survey of Forensics and Incident Response* (Henry, Williams, & Wright, 2013) of 450 DF-related companies indicated that some of the respondents consider the "lack of skills, training and/or certification on *proper methodology*" to be a main challenge when it comes to approaching DF in situations that involve 'atypical' evidence sources. It is hoped that the approach introduced in this chapter can provide a solution to this dilemma.

The approach to DF introduced in this chapter has the following aims:

- Ensure that relevant evidence is not lost due to delays and unnecessary activities by IRTs;
- Ensure that relevant evidence is acquired that can be used to support a court case;
- Encourage a minimum standard of forensics preparedness within smart CPE.

The flowchart of the proposed model is shown in Figure 3.

Establish Context (Commercial or Private)

Due to the scale (amount of data), location of OOFI, as well as privacy and moral concerns, IRTs should begin their approach to investigations by establishing the context of their investigation and identifying any legal or privacy issues and access constraints that may apply.

Determine Perimeter

The next point of focus for investigators should be to determine the perimeter of the network(s) that they are approaching, its potential size and type. The terms that can be used to illustrate the breadth of a network include Home Area Network (HAN) made up of several Body Area Networks (BAN), while the type can be mobile, fixed, wired, wireless (Wi-Fi, Bluetooth, etc.) and so on.

Split into Deterministic Sectors Using the 1-2-3 Zones Approach (Oriwoh et al., 2013)

The next step would be to split the crime scene as much as possible into deterministic zones. This can be done by labelling them as internal network, middle zone and external zone (Figure 4). This will aid investigators in gaining an overall picture of the situation that they are faced with.

Identify 'Best' Sources of Evidence

Applying the Next Best Thing (NBT) approach, any OOFI that cannot be accessed directly for evidence (e.g. a patient's pacemaker) can be listed as relevant whilst a closely related item that may hold relevant evidence (e.g. a hospital server) may be accessed for evidence instead. This way, no matter how remote or inaccessible OOFI are, some evidence can still be extracted and analysed.

Escalate

Investigators will have to make decisions about what investigations to escalate. For example in a situation where a human subject is refusing to grant investigators access to their property, there has to be a well-defined alternative course of action to be taken so that the investigation can proceed both from a physical investigation perspective as well as a digital one.

Acquire Relevant Evidence

Forensic readiness involves the steps taken in preparation for anticipated incidents and it is key to successful forensics investigations. In the SH scenario, one way to ensure that relevant evidence is secured and collected in preparation for an investigation will be to employ the services of the FEMS because as part of its setup, devices in the SH are registered with it after which it monitors, acquires and periodically stores network logs. Alternatively, evidence can be acquired using available forensics tools. As part of hardware evidence acquisition, the best procedure to follow has to be made at this point e.g. to seize evidence or operate in situ, to image wholly or selectively.

Select and Apply Preferred Tools

During this stage, the responding IRTs can make use of any selected appropriate tools and methodologies to acquire and analyse any identified evidence. The particular tools and methodologies chosen can be expected to vary depending on the type of investigation: mobile or fixed, wireless or wired, etc.

Figure 3. The SH incident response model

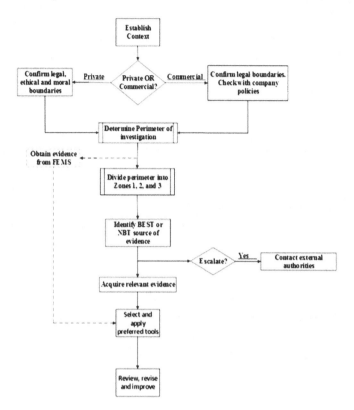

Figure 4. The 1-2-3 zones in a SH

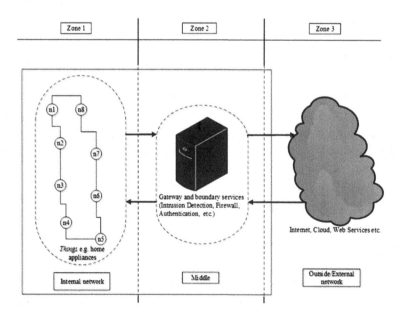

Review, Revise, and Improve

At this point the steps taken so far are reviewed to ensure that after following these steps, as much relevant evidence as possible has been obtained.

The Forensics Edge Management Server (FEMS)

When people go to work and lock the doors of their (non-smart) homes, they typically trust that their locked doors to keep out unwanted elements and keep their belongings in. They install locks they can trust and so have an understandable expectation of security and privacy. They trust these locks and other systems even if they may not know anything about their design or their inner workings. When homes become self-managing - and more susceptible to cyber-style attacks - end users can neither be expected to understand nor have the capability to investigate cyber security attacks such as DoS attacks on their fridges or man-in-the-middle attacks on their X-box consoles.

According to Sang-Hyun et al., the SH can and should be configurable to provide convenience and comfort, entertainment, communication, information and security systems (Sang-Hyun, Lee, & Kyung-Il, 2013). This chapter contends that the SH should be designed to support DF services as well. It should be equipped to withstand cyber-attacks, to investigate them if they are successful and to escalate issues where necessary (e.g. to the police or to external forensics response teams) all without disruption to the user. A forensics device can be deployed to perform these functions in the home. Without such a system to detect and investigate attacks, end users will either have to (attempt to) investigate attacks themselves – assuming they know what they are doing - or invite the vendors of each of the services, with each one required to investigate their own area of specialty e.g. automated lighting, the sprinkler systems and so on.

The FEMS (Figure 5and 6) is proposed in this chapter to perform these services. The FEMS can be deployed to monitor SH networks, acquire logs and detect sources of anomalies in real-time. It can be configured to receive input from any other available security systems around the house e.g. burglar alarms, fire and smoke detectors, baby monitors, and firewalls. Also, depending on the home network setup, these other security systems can still be allowed to function individually so that the fire alarm can directly send alerts to fire services and so on. The function of the FEMS would be to determine the causes and sources of attacks (Oriwoh & Sant, 2013)

Requirements for the FEMS. It must:

- Maintain integrity of evidence and provide proof of maintenance of Chain of Custody (CoC) throughout its operation;
- Not expose private data or information during its operation;
- Be fast and efficient and not cause (significant) delays on networks;
- Have a user friendly interface;
- Be vendor independent;
- Must make a backup copy of the original evidence.

Once installed on the home network, the FEMS will continually monitor network traffic and capture network logs (the logs are stored for a specified time period with a minimum storage period of 28 days or one month). Whilst setting up the FEMS, the user can specify acceptable thresholds ranges for certain parameters. Example parameters are minimum living room temperature/time of day, hour to lock front

Figure 5. The forensics edge management system: a high-level overview

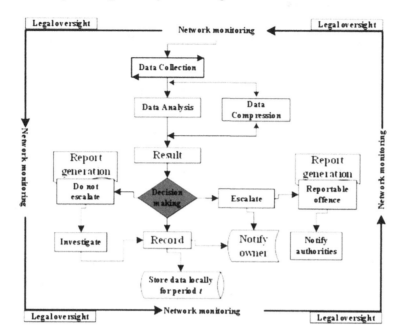

gate, volume of central Bluetooth speaker, week of month and day of week to send grocery shopping list to remote store, among others.

The FEMS forensics operation is triggered when an *event* is detected. An event occurs when a set threshold is exceeded e.g. the lights are switched on too early or too late in the day. All logs captured just before and after the incident was detected are labelled and stored as possibly relevant. Whilst the network monitoring and log acquisition continues online, the decision-making (indicated by the red-coloured rhombus in Figure 5.), investigation and report preparation phases take place offline. The investigation to find out the cause of the light scheduling problem (i.e. the attack) begins with a parse of the logs to identify and extract forensically relevant information such as source and destination IP addresses and (e.g. device IDs, source of control commands. If successful in identifying the source of the 'attack' the FEMS then prepares a report and notifies the user of the outcome. It also makes suggestions to the user about what they might wish to do next. If the investigation is unsuccessful, it escalates the issue to a designated external party.

Some tools that can be used to realize the FEMS include monitoring tools like *Microsoft Network Monitor* or the Linux *Top* program; *gzip* can be used to compress captured logs; *postfix* can be used to send notifications using email messages.

FUTURE RESEARCH DIRECTIONS

The next stage of this work will involve developing the decision-making algorithm (red rhombus in Figure 5) that the FEMS will apply to determine what constitutes forensically *relevant* evidence in the acquired logs. This algorithm will be tested on publically-available SH logs as well as logs generated specifically for this research. The outcome of the decision process of the algorithm and time taken to complete the operations will be compared with the expected outcome and time taken during from a manual investigation. This will be done so as to measure the accuracy and efficiency of the FEMS. Planned as part of the FEMS package is a mobile app that will show users the security status of their SH and present forensics reports to them.

CONCLUSION

This chapter discussed the characteristics of the Internet of Things that may make it a challenging domain to navigate from a DF perspective. The chapter provided an analysis of some current DF approaches and models and highlighted the deficiencies of these approaches with respect to the IoT. Considering the IoT characteristics identified, the chapter introduced an Internet of Things Incident Response and Forensics Methodology that should ensure that during IoT-related investigations, IRT and DF investigations can still be carried with as much relevant evidence as possible acquired and in a timely fashion. The chapter also introduced the Forensics Edge Management System as part of the holistic approach to DF in CPE with particular focus on the SH.

REFERENCES

Ademu, I. O., Imafidon, C. O., & Preston, D. S. (2011). A new approach of digital forensic model for digital forensic investigation. *International Journal of Advanced Computer Science and Applications, 2*(12).

Alam, M. R., Reaz, M. B. I., & Ali, M. A. M. (2012). A review of smart Homes—Past, present, and future. *IEEE Transactions on* Systems, Man, and Cybernetics, Part C: Applications and Reviews, *42*(6), 1190–1203.

Baryamureeba, V., & Tushabe, F. (2004). The enhanced digital investigation process model. *IEEE Power and Energy Magazine, 10*, 24-32.

Brush, A. J. B., Lee, B., Mahajan, R., Agarwal, S., Saroiu, S., & Dixon, C. (2011). Home automation in the wild: Challenges and opportunities. In *Proceedings of the SIGCHI Conference on Human Factors in Computing Systems*. Vancouver, Canada: ACM.

Cantrell, G., Dampier, D., Dandass, Y. S., Niu, N., & Bogen, C. (2012). Research toward a partially-automated, and crime specific digital triage process model. *Computer and Information Science, 5*(2), 29. doi:10.5539/cis.v5n2p29

Case, A., Cristina, A., Marziale, L., Richard, G. G., & Roussev, V. (2008). FACE: Automated digital evidence discovery and correlation. *Digital Investigation, 5, Supplement*(0), S65-S75.

Castro, M., Jara, A. J., & Skarmeta, A. F. (2012). An analysis of M2M platforms: Challenges and opportunities for the internet of things. In *Proceedings of Innovative Mobile and Internet Services in Ubiquitous Computing (IMIS)*, (pp. 757-762). IMIS.

Chan, M., Estève, D., Escriba, C., & Campo, E. (2008). A review of smart homes—Present state and future challenges. *Computer Methods and Programs in Biomedicine, 91*(1), 55–81. doi:10.1016/j.cmpb.2008.02.001 PMID:18367286

Chen, D., Chang, G., Sun, D., Li, J., Jia, J., & Wang, X. (2011). TRM-IoT: A trust management model based on fuzzy reputation for internet of things. *Computer Science and Information Systems, 8*(4), 1207–1228. doi:10.2298/CSIS110303056C

Chen, Y. (2012). Challenges and opportunities of internet of things. In *Proceedings of Design Automation Conference (ASP-DAC),* (pp. 383-388). ASP-DAC.

Cohen, F. (2012). *The future of digital forensics.* Unpublished manuscript. Retrieved 21st June 2013, from http://www.all.net/Talks/2012-09-21-Beijing-Keynote.pdf

De Silva, L. C., Morikawa, C., & Petra, I. M. (2012). State of the art of smart homes. *Engineering Applications of Artificial Intelligence, 25*(7), 1313–1321. doi:10.1016/j.engappai.2012.05.002

Ding, D., Cooper, R. A., Pasquina, P. F., & Fici-Pasquina, L. (2011). Sensor technology for smart homes. *Maturitas, 69*(2), 131–136. doi:10.1016/j.maturitas.2011.03.016 PMID:21531517

Dobson, S., Sterritt, R., Nixon, P., & Hinchey, M. (2010). Fulfilling the vision of autonomic computing. *Computer (New York), 43*(1), 35–41.

Ericsson White paper. (2011). *More than 50 billion connected devices.* Unpublished manuscript. Retrieved from http://www.ericsson.com/res/docs/whitepapers/wp-50-billions.pdf

Fleisch, E. (2010). What is the internet of things? An economic perspective. *Economics, Management, and Financial Markets,* (2), 125-157.

Franklin, S. W., & Rajan, S. E. (2010). Personal area network for biomedical monitoring systems using human body as a transmission medium. *International Journal of Bio-Science & Bio-Technology, 2*(2).

Freiling, F. C., & Schwittay, B. (2007). A common process model for incident response and computer forensics. *IMF, 7,* 19–40.

Garfinkel, S. (2010). *Automated computer forensics: Current research areas.* Retrieved June/26, 2013, from http://simson.net/page/Automated_Computer_Forensics

Gurgen, L., Gunalp, O., Benazzouz, Y., & Gallissot, M. (2013). Self-aware cyber-physical systems and applications in smart buildings and cities. In *Proceedings of the Conference on Design, Automation and Test in Europe,* (pp. 1149-1154). Academic Press.

Henry, P., Williams, J., & Wright, B. (2013). *The SANS survey of digital forensics and incident response: A SANS whitepaper* Retrieved from https://blogs.sans.org/computer-forensics/files/2013/07/sans_dfir_survey_2013.pdf

Hernández-Muñoz, J. M., Vercher, J. B., Muñoz, L., Galache, J. A., Presser, M., & Gómez, L. A. H. et al. (2011). *Smart cities at the forefront of the future internet. In The future internet* (pp. 447–462). Springer.

Igarashi, Y., Ueno, M., & Fujisaki, T. (2012). Proposed node and network models for an M2M internet. In *Proceedings of World Telecommunications Congress (WTC),* (pp. 1-6). WTC.

Islam, R. U., Schmidt, M., Kolbe, H., & Andersson, K. (2012). Nomadic mobility between smart homes. In *Proceedings of Globecom Workshops (GC Wkshps)*, (pp. 1062-1067). IEEE.

Juels, A. (2006). RFID security and privacy: A research survey. *IEEE Journal on* Selected Areas in Communications, *24*(2), 381–394.

Khan, J. Y., & Yuce, M. R. (2010). Wireless body area network (WBAN) for medical applications. *Mobile Networks and Applications, 7*(5), 365-376.

Kohn, M., Eloff, J., & Olivier, M. (2006). Framework for a digital forensic investigation. In *Proceedings of the ISSA 2006 from Insight to Foresight Conference, Sandton, South Africa.* ISSA.

Kozlov, D., Veijalainen, J., & Ali, Y. (2012). Security and privacy threats in IoT architectures. In *Proceedings of the 7th International Conference on Body Area Networks,* (pp. 256-262). Academic Press.

Laranjo, I., Macedo, J., & Santos, A. (2012). Internet of things for medication control: Service implementation and testing. *Procedia Technology, 5*(0), 777–786. doi:10.1016/j.protcy.2012.09.086

Lee, H., Lee, J., & Han, J. (2007). The efficient security architecture for authentication and authorization in the home network. In *Proceedings of Natural Computation,* (vol. 5, pp. 713-717). Academic Press.

Lempereur, B., Merabti, M., & Shi, Q. (2009). *Automating evidence extraction and analysis for digital forensics.* Academic Press.

Lin, C., Zhitang, L., & Cuixia, G. (2009). Automated analysis of multi-source logs for network forensics. In *Proceedings of Education Technology and Computer Science,* (pp. 660-664). Academic Press.

Lin, M., Leu, J., Li, K., & Wu, J. C. (2012). Zigbee-based internet of things in 3D terrains. In *Proceedings of Advanced Computer Theory and Engineering (ICACTE),* (vol. 5, pp. 376-380). ICACTE.

Mattern, F. (2003). From smart devices to smart everyday objects. *IEEE Spectrum, 47*(10), 25.

Mohay, G. (2005). Technical challenges and directions for digital forensics. In *Proceedings of Systematic Approaches to Digital Forensic Engineering,* (pp. 155-161). Academic Press.

Ning, H., & Hu, S. (2011). Internet of things: An emerging industrial or a new major? In *Proceedings of Internet of Things (iThings/CPSCom),* (pp. 178-183). iThings.

Ning, H., & Liu, H. (2012). Cyber-physical-social based security architecture for future internet of things. *Advanced in Internet of Things, 2*(1), 1–7. doi:10.4236/ait.2012.21001

Nova, N., & Bleecker, J. (2006). Blogjects and the new ecology of things. In *Proceedings of Lift06 Workshop.* Lift.

Oriwoh, E., & Sant, P. (2013). The forensics edge management system: A concept and design. In *Proceedings of Ubiquitous Intelligence and Computing, (UIC/ATC),* (pp. 544-550). UIC/ATC.

Oriwoh, E., Jazani, D., Epiphaniou, G., & Sant, P. (2013). Internet of things forensics: Challenges and approaches. In *Proceedings of Collaborative Computing: Networking, Applications and Worksharing* (Collaboratecom), (pp. 608-615). Collaboratecom.

Pilli, E. S., Joshi, R. C., & Niyogi, R. (2010). Network forensic frameworks: Survey and research challenges. *Digital Investigation*, 7(1–2), 14–27. doi:10.1016/j.diin.2010.02.003

Proffitt, B. (2013). *How big the internet of things could become: The potential size of the internet things sector could be a multi-trillion dollar market by the end of the decade.* Retrieved November/20, 2013, from http://readwrite.com/2013/09/30/how-big-the-internet-of-things-could-become#feed=/infrastruct ure&awesm=~oj3jHsZI8rJE6c

Reith, M., Carr, C., & Gunsch, G. (2002). An examination of digital forensic models. *International Journal of Digital Evidence*, 1(3), 1–12.

Rowlingson, R. (2004). A ten step process for forensic readiness. *International Journal of Digital Evidence*, 2(3), 1–28.

Sang-Hyun, L., Lee, J., & Kyung-Il, M. (2013). Smart home security system using multiple ANFIS. *International Journal of Smart Home*, 7(3), 121.

Seigneur, J., Jensen, C. D., Farrell, S., Gray, E., & Chen, Y. (2003). Towards security auto-configuration for smart appliances. In *Proceedings of the Smart Objects Conference.* Academic Press.

Selamat, S. R., Yusof, R., & Sahib, S. (2008). Mapping process of digital forensic investigation framework. *International Journal of Computer Science and Network Security*, 8(10), 163–169.

Sommerville, I. (2007). *Models for responsibility assignment. In Responsibility and dependable systems* (pp. 165–186). Springer. doi:10.1007/978-1-84628-626-1_8

Turnbull, B. (2008). The adaptability of electronic evidence acquisition guides for new technologies. In *Proceedings of the 1st International Conference on Forensic Applications and Techniques in Telecommunications, Information, and Multimedia and Workshop,* (pp. 1:1-1:6). Academic Press.

Uckelmann, D. (Ed.). (2011). *Architecting the internet of things.* Springerverlag. doi:10.1007/978-3-642-19157-2

Vlachopoulos, K., Magkos, E., & Chrissikopoulos, V. (2013). A model for hybrid evidence investigation. *Emerging Digital Forensics Applications for Crime Detection, Prevention, and Security,* 150.

Weiser, M. (1991). The computer for the 21st century. *Scientific American*, 265(3), 94–104. doi:10.1038/scientificamerican0991-94

Xia, F., Yang, L. T., Wang, L., & Vinel, A. (2012). Internet of things. *International Journal of Communication Systems*, 25(9), 1101–1102. doi:10.1002/dac.2417

KEY TERMS AND DEFINITIONS

Blogjects: These are objects with the capability to blog their status and activities.

Cyberphysical Environments (CPE): The combination of cyber and physical environments where cyber environments are the non-tangible and tangible technology-based aspects of our existence. Physical environments on the other hand are the natural and non-technology-based aspects of our existence.

IoT-Ware: This describes all the objects that are part of a home network including those with embedded intelligence e.g. smart meters and those with attached intelligence e.g. by RFID tagging.

Objects of Forensics Interest (OOFI): This refers to all IoT-ware within the IoT landscape with *digital* evidentiary value.

Smart Forensics: The use of smart devices and methods that apply scientific techniques to automatically and autonomously perform digital forensics investigations within Smart Home and similar environments in order to produce forensically relevant and acceptable evidence which can be used to aid private/corporate legal, disciplinary or other such proceedings.

Spimes: A combination of the words *sp*ace and t*ime*, it describes products that have identifiable and retrievable lifecycles that describe them from their production to retirement and/or destruction.

This work was previously published in the Handbook of Research on Digital Crime, Cyberspace Security, and Information Assurance edited by Maria Manuela Cruz-Cunha and Irene Maria Portela, pages 407-423, copyright year 2015 by Information Science Reference (an imprint of IGI Global).

Chapter 12
Internet of Things Research Challenges

Mahmoud Elkhodr
Western Sydney University, Australia

Seyed Shahrestani
Western Sydney University, Australia

Hon Cheung
Western Sydney University, Australia

ABSTRACT

The Internet of Things (IoT) promises to revolute communications on the Internet. The IoT enables numerous business opportunities in fields as diverse as e-health, smart cities, smart homes, among many others. It incorporates multiple long-range, short-range, and personal area wireless networks and technologies into the designs of IoT applications. This will result in the IoT being pervasive in many areas which raise many challenges. This chapter reviews the major research issues challenging the IoT with regard to security, privacy, and management.

INTRODUCTION

The Internet of Things (IoT) foresees the interconnection of billions of things by extending the interactions between humans and applications to a new dimension of communications via things. Rather than always interacting with the users, things will be interacting with each other autonomously by performing actions on behalf of the users. Consequently, the availability of information coming from non-traditional computer devices in the digital world will, in great parts, lead to improving the quality of life. Over the next couple of years, it is predicted that the industrial value of the IoT will surpass that of the Internet 30 times over, and to be a market that is worth more than $100 billion dollars (Clendenin, 2010). On the other hand, it is estimated that there will be more than 20 billion devices connected to the Internet by 2020 (Lomas, 2009). While Cisco predicts that the number of connected devices will exceed 50 billion in 2020 (Evans, 2012). The IoT will revolute many industries and elevate communications on the Inter-

DOI: 10.4018/978-1-5225-1832-7.ch012

net. The IoT provides the user with numerous services and capabilities. The obvious ones are the ability to control and monitor the physical environment remotely over the communication networks. Typical examples are the ability to close a door or receiving smoke alert notifications, and the likes, remotely over the Internet. However, the true vision of the IoT revolves around connecting networks and a group of sensors together in an intelligent and ubiquitous fashion. Thus, the IoT promises to enable numerous business opportunities in fields as diverse as e-health, smart cities, farming among many others.

The interconnection of things allows not only things to communicate with each other but also offers the opportunities of building intelligence and pervasiveness into the IoT. For instance, by connecting home appliances to the smart grid, the IoT will enable better energy consumption and water conservation. In addition to helping users in monitoring their own usage, the IoT will optimize energy demand distribution across a city and regulate the automatic consumptions of electricity and other resources. For that to happen, the IoT will need to access a vast array of data and devices, analyze the users' behaviors, and monitor occupancy and lighting conditions. It also needs to collect various sensitive information about the users, their activities and environment. This will result in the IoT being pervasive in many areas. Hence, the potentially massive number of things, their diversity, and the seamless and heterogeneous nature of communications encountered in the IoT raises many research challenges.

Many envisioned IoT applications will require the automated sharing of the users' information collected by things. This requires agreements on many applications and networks levels. How things will be identified and accessed on the Internet remains unclear. The integration of smart devices, Wireless Sensor Networks and IoT applications in one network pose numerous challenges to the traditional network and managements approaches. Additionally, the autonomous aggregation of users' information gathered by a large number of things and exchanged over various heterogeneous networks impinge on the security and privacy of the users. For this reason, the development of solutions to support security protection, management, and privacy preservations are key factors for the proliferation of the IoT. Towards this aim, this Chapter reviews some of the significant research issues challenging the IoT. The remainder of this chapter provides examples of Wireless Sensor Networks (WSN) applications in the IoT. It then moves to analyze the major research issues challenging the IoT with regard to security, privacy, interoperability and management. The chapter then concludes by outlining the key research issues pertaining to the advancement of the IoT.

IoT-WSN APPLICATIONS

The IoT promises to revolute communications on the Internet by incorporating multiple long-range, short-range, and personal area wireless networks and technologies into the designs of IoT applications. In environmental monitoring applications, IoT-WSN can be deployed over a wide area where some phenomenon can be monitored. Such applications can be used to sense and monitor volcanoes, earthquake, and oceans movement. They can also be used to detect bushfires, wild animals' movement and many others. Other environmental applications of WSN include monitoring of mountains' climate, such as in (Beutel et al., 2009), water flow such as in (Lin, Wu, & Wassell, 2008), and floods such as in (*HealthCast 2020: Creating a Sustainable Future*, 2005). For example, a WSN can be deployed in a forest to monitor the dramatic rise in temperature, humidity and detect gasses that could be produced by fires. This obviously helps in the early detection of fires. Furthermore, the IoT merges communications between WSNs and other areas of the IoT. Automation can then be built into IoT systems to better manage and respond to these natural disasters. For instance, embedding intelligence and automation into the fire detection system can assist in alerting the authorities, fire-freighter, medical teams and neighborhood in danger.

In mechanical monitoring applications, IoT-WSN can be deployed to monitor physical objects and structures. Such applications use a network of sensors and devices to sense modes of vibrations, structural modifications or breakages in physical structures. Examples of these applications can be found in systems designed to monitor bridges (*HealthCast 2020: Creating a Sustainable Future*, 2005), underground mines (Li & Liu, 2009), and in several other industrial environments (Low, Win, & Er, 2005). Connecting these WSNs applications with the IoT, would revolutionize communications on the Internet. For instance, in bridge monitoring systems, the IoT can leverage the communication capabilities of the network to communicate in real-time with the drivers of smart cars approaching the bridge; and to act upon or even prevent an event from occurring. By connecting the bridge monitoring system with the transport systems, the IoT can enhance the management of traffics in real-time as another example.

In e-health applications, many researchers have focused on the development of a body wireless sensor network (B-WSN) to monitor the health of patients remotely at homes. An example of these applications is the system proposed in (Lo, Thiemjarus, King, & Yang, 2005). It consists of a number of wearable sensors with an integrated wireless transmission that communicates with a base station providing constant monitoring of the patients' health. Furthermore, the IoT offers the opportunities of connecting the B-WSN with other IoT applications. That is, apart from communicating with healthcare providers' systems, a B-WSN can connect autonomously with emergency services, medical insurance companies, and the patients' relatives. In other applications such as in smart home applications, the IoT allows the user to keep track of his or her everyday objects by attaching small and low-cost devices to them. An example of this applications is presented in (Surie, Laguionie, & Pederson, 2008).

IoT IDENTIFICATION CHALLENGES

The IoT will indeed encompass devices that produce contents that need to be accessed only by authorized users or things. Thus, searching, finding and accessing things on the IoT require efficient addressing schemes. Currently, Domain Name service (DNS) is the Internet naming service that translates IP addresses into human-readable names. In the IoT, things will be connected using different technologies and protocols. Some of these protocols are non-HTTP, and some might not even be based on the IP protocol. Therefore, not all type of devices in the IoT would necessarily have an IP-address. As a result, there is a need for new solutions that uniquely identify things on the IoT.

Additionally, the characteristics of the traffic exchanged by things, in the IoT, could be periodic and very small. Further contributions are needed to determine if the TCP protocol is adequate to use in the IoT or if a new concept of a transport layer is required. This is due to the fact that the TCP is a connection-oriented protocol, in which sessions always starts with a connection setup procedure known as the three-way handshakes. Given that some of the communications within the IoT will involve the exchange of an only small amount of data generated by constrained devices, the TCP protocol cannot be used efficiently for transmission control. For example, consider a case where an IoT sensor is exchanging a small amount of data in a single session with another device or application. The TCP congestion control mechanism will add too much overhead to the communications if TCP is used. This is because the whole TCP session will be concluded with the transmission of the first segment and the consequent reception of the corresponding acknowledgment (Atzori, Iera, & Morabito, 2010). There is a need to support interoperable communications between TCP and future non-TCP enabled devices on the IoT as well.

On the other hand, the research into devices' naming or identity management is an active area as well. For instance, the work in (Liu, Yang, & Liu, 2014) points out that a device naming scheme should contain key elements of device meta-data, such as the device type and domain information. For addressing purposes, the format of the identifier should allow accessibility and addressability to the physical world in a granule and efficient way as well. Profile services are also needed to aid the application query and system configurations, such as the device status and presence in a location or network (Liu et al., 2014).

Other works on identity management in the IoT are based on the Service Oriented Architecture (SOA), such as OpenID. OpenID describes how users can be authenticated in a decentralized manner. This eliminates the need for services to provide their own ad-hoc systems. It also allows the users to consolidate their digital identities. Hence, these and similar authentication solutions are necessary for preserving the privacy of users in IoT. Preserving privacy has to take into account not only the privacy of services and data but also the discovery through user devices. The work in (Madsen, 2013) discusses the need to distinguish between connected things and their identities. The work proposes the use of tokens. A token is used by a device in an API call when engaging in communication. The users control the process of issuing tokens. This approach allows them to impose policies on the disclosure of data as to when that token can be used and how their information is shared (Madsen, 2013).

Physical and Virtual Things Identities

A physical thing can be any sort of object found in the physical world such as a mobile phone, sensor, actuator, table, door, meter, lock, medical device, network device, camera or even a network component. All of these examples of physical things should be referenced and identified by an identifier. In traditional network management systems, a node or a component is referenced by an ID which is associated with additional identifying information that reflects on the relationship with other objects. For example, a networking device (e.g. a router) may have a unique hostname, but each of its physical network interfaces is assigned an IP address. Furthermore, each of the router's components might have an identifier as well. As such the hostname of the device in combination with the IP address of a particular network interface can be used for identification purposes. Thus, this identification scheme defines the association between the router, in our example, and its network interfaces. The hostname and IP address are stored in a Management Information Base (MIBs) which is used by the Simple Network Management Protocol (SNMP) for management. Thus, similar addressing schemes for WSNs and group of things in the IoT should be explored.

Virtual things can be in the form of software, multimedia items, documents, services, among other examples of digital items. The ITU-T Object IDs (OIDs) can be used to refer to a number of virtual things ("The Internet of Things," 2005). The URL can be used to identify the web services and access them. Alternatively, the Digital Object Identifier (DOI) standard can be used to reference digital objects directly. It can also indicate how to access digital documents (Friese et al., 2010).

SECURITY AND PRIVACY CHALLENGES

Security Challenges

The evolution of wireless technologies and M2M communications is driving the growth of the IoT. New devices are increasingly getting connected to the Internet, from connected vehicles to connected homes and cities. This growth in connected devices to the communication networks translates into increased security risks and poses new challenges to security. A device which connects to the Internet, whether it is a constraint or smart device, inherits the security risks of today's computer devices. Almost all security challenges are inherent to the IoT. Hence, some fundamental security requirements in the IoT such as authorization, authentication, confidentiality, trust, and data security need to be considered.

Things should be securely connected to their designated network(s), securely controlled and accessed by authorized entities. Data generated by things need to be collected, analyzed, stored, dispatched and always presented in a secure manner. Notwithstanding, there are security risks associated with things-to-things communications as well. This is in addition to the risks relating to things-to-person communications. For instance, if things are to be accessed by things independently from the human users, then there are security measures that need to be enforced. These security measures are necessary to ensure that things are accessed only by authorized entities in a secure manner. Also, they need to ensure that things are not leaking information or disclosing private information to unauthorized things and users, or used miscellaneously. The security issues challenging the IoT can be summarized to as follows:

End-to-End Security

End-to-end security is concerned with protecting the communications and data exchanged between things and IoT applications without being read, eavesdropped, intercepted, modified, or tampered. Cisco defines end-to-end security as an absolute requirement for secure communications which encompasses five components: identity verification, protocols, algorithms, secure implementations, and, secure operations (Behringer, 2009). In the IoT, end-to-end security remains an open challenge for many IoT devices and applications. The nature of the IoT with its heterogeneous architecture and devices involve the sharing of information and collaboration between things across many networks. This poses serious challenges to the end-to-end security of things. When devices have different characteristics and operate using a variety of communication technologies (802.11 vs 802.15.4), establishing secure sessions and secure communications become a complex task to achieve. Additionally, not all devices in the IoT are equal. Normally, computer, mobile phones and other computerized devices connect to the Internet via HTTP, SMTP and the like for most of their activities. As such TLS and IPsec protocols are usually used to dynamically negotiate the session keys, and to provide the required security functions. However, some of the devices in the IoT does not possess the ability to run TLS and IPsec protocols due to their limited computation and power capabilities. Additionally, most embedded devices in the IoT are designed for low power consumption. They often have limited connectivity as such they might not necessarily use HTTP or even IP for the communication. Table 1 shows the relevant IoT end-to-end security requirements.

Table 1. End-to-end security requirements

Identity verification	This requirement demands that entities at both ends of the communications to have known and verifiable identities. As discussed earlier, this still unresolved in the IoT.
Protocols	Protocols are needed to negotiate session keys, and to provide the required security functions across several heterogeneous networks. This requires interoperability among things and their applications.
Algorithms	Protocols use algorithms to implement security functions e.g. encryption as in Secure Hash Algorithm (SHA-1). Simple, optimized and lightweight algorithms are needed in the IoT.
Secure implementations	The implementation of the security protocols and algorithms should be free of bugs and security holes that could compromise security.
Secure operations	Users and operators should understand security operations, which can be complex in the IoT given the diversity of things and the heterogeneous nature of IoT communications.

Data Security

This involves the protection of data during communications and storages. In (Summers, 2004), data security is defined as the process of protecting data from destructive forces or from unauthorized access. Examples of data security technologies include software and hardware disk encryption, and backups. Data security, also can be referred to as information security, is vital to the IoT security. Significantly, data security in the IoT is directly associated with safety. Usually, the impact of data security breaches on the human life remained within the scope of hacking personal information about an individual or more sensitive information such as financial data. However, data security breaches in the IoT could pose a serious threat to human safety. For instance, the accidental intrusion or malicious access that could interfere or interrupt the operations of a driverless car or a heart pacemaker will threaten the safety of the relevant user. Security breaches in an IoT forest fire detection system could lead to catastrophic results.

Identity and Access Management

Identity theft, forgery, and masquerading among other security attacks are some of the security issues challenging the protection of identity in the IoT. Typically, computer devices employ a secure mechanism that relies on complex algorithms in detecting suspicious access to data and the detection of imposters. The IoT is vulnerable to several identity attacks including Spoofing, Masquerade, MiM and Smurf attacks. The physical protection of the actual device from damage and unauthorized access is also important in the IoT. Consequently, several existing traditional security solutions need to be studied and examined to determine their feasibility and applicability in the IoT.

Regulations

Complying with government laws and industry regulations play a major role in preserving the security of IoT systems. Things in the IoT need to adhere to several data protection laws and privacy acts which vary from country to another. This is can be problematic in the IoT given that the IoT is built around autonomous communications between things. Therefore, there is a need to ensure the privacy of the users at all time. The privacy requirements can be summarized in three key concepts:

1. **User Consent**: Users need to be able to provide their informed consent on the data disclosed by things.
2. **Freedom of Choice**: Users should have the freedom of opting in and out from being involved or being part of a communication. This can be challenging in things-to-things communications.
3. **Anonymity**: Users have the right to remain anonymous when obtaining services that do not require identity verification. Data mining in the IoT is one of the major challenges to privacy protection in the IoT as identified in (Elkhodr, Shahrestani, & Cheung, 2013a).

Access Control

Access Control is the process of granting, limiting or restricting access to a resource. It regulates who or what can view or use resources. Role based access control (RBAC) is an example of a widely used access control model. Research should explore the traditional access control models and investigate their suitability for implementation in the IoT.

Significantly, these security issues cannot be solved with traditional Internet security solutions. This is due to the fact that IoT communications' architectures differ from those of the traditional Internet. As the IoT evolves and becomes more complex, the security issues increase in complexity as well. This growth in complexity can be attributed to two fundamental IoT factors: low-cost and heterogeneity. Some IoT devices should be available at relatively low prices. Low-cost is a significant characteristic that drives the support for large-scale deployment of things in the IoT. This low-cost requirement dictates that things are mostly resource constrained. This translates into devices with lower computational capabilities, a limited amount of memory and power supply. This is, in fact, constitute an obstacle to the application of many traditional cryptographic-based solutions. Given that traditional public-key infrastructures cannot accommodate the IoT (Roman, Najera, & Lopez, 2011). For instance, the implementation of many conventional and basic Internet security solutions such as PKI and CA demands to increase the computation capabilities of things which in turn increase their cost. Therefore, conventional Internet security technologies cannot provide a complete security solution for the IoT. The heterogeneity of devices, the multi-networks integration characteristic of the IoT, and the limited capabilities and low-cost requirement of some IoT devices require new and optimized security solutions.

Privacy Challenges

In the smartphone ecosystem, many mobile applications collect the location information of the users without their consent. For example, TaintDroid project (Enck et al., 2010), has identified that some Android's applications are releasing users' private information to online advertisers. TaintDroid is a joint study by Intel Labs, Penn State, and Duke University. The project is developed as a mobile application. It provides real-time monitoring services that precisely monitor the traffics exchanged by other applications installed on the same device. It detects when the user's private information are released by an application to a third party. TaintDroid revealed that 15 applications out of the 30 selected for the study were sending users' geographic location to remote advertisement servers. Another study found that 7.5% of the total applications on the Android market have the capability of accessing the user's stored contacts; while 28% of them had access to the user's location ("App Genome Project," 2011). The study in (THURM & KANE, 2010) analyzed the 101 most popular smartphone applications running on various mobile operating systems, including Windows Phone, iPhone, and Android. It was reported that out of the 101 applications, fifty-six were transmitting the unique phone ID to other companies without the user's permission. Forty-seven applications were caught transmitting location information to third parties as well. The other five applications were found to be leaking other specific information like gender and age.

The study conducted in (Gupta, 2012) pointed out that some applications running on the Window Mobile platform had the capability to access the user's picture library, video library, webcam's video feed, microphone's audio feed, location, and other parameters related to the Internet connection. Some of these applications also had the ability to add, change or delete files from both the picture and video libraries. Another study detailed the vulnerability of the RIM BlackBerry device (Fredrik, 2011). The author developed a spyware targeted to Blackberry devices. The spyware was able to access and transfer sensitive data to a remote server without being noticed by the user. The study in (Hoh, Gruteser, Xiong, & Alrabady, 2006) showed that a driver's home location can be inferred from the GPS data collected from his vehicle even if the location information was anonymized. The study conducted in (Elkhodr, Shahrestani, & Cheung, 2012) also reported on various privacy incidents associated with the use of mobile applications on the Android, Blackberry, iPhone, and Windows Phone platforms. It is concluded that the proliferation of mobile devices, GPS systems and other evolving technologies into our lives has introduced a new set of privacy threats.

Henceforth, given the impact smartphones have on the users' privacy, it is anticipated that the amount of personal data that would be occasionally collected in an IoT environment will be extremely larger than what we have ever experienced before. The IoT highly distributed nature of technologies, such as embedded devices in public areas, creates weak links that malicious entities can exploit and can as well open the door for a mass surveillance, tracing, tracking, and profiling of the users' movements and activities (Elkhodr, Shahrestani, & Cheung, 2013b). Moreover, the collection of sensitive data, the tracking of people's movement, data mining, and services provisioning can become automated and unpredictable in the IoT. With the pervasive growth of IoT-connected devices and applications, privacy threats are more likely to increase rapidly.

In addition, the foundations, laws and regulations for digital privacy were established some years ago when the Internet was centralized. These regulations deal, usually, with the collection of personal information, access rights, and ensure their correct handling. That's no longer considered enough in the IoT. At its simplest definition, privacy means, giving users the option to control how their collected personal information might be used; specifically for secondary usage and third party access. As an example, in the online environment, privacy choices can be exercised by simply clicking a box on the browser screen that indicates a user's decision with respect to the use of the information being collected. The concept remained the same in the evolution of social networking, where users in Facebook indicate to whom and to which extent their information can be revealed. These are known as the principles of notice and choice.

Privacy Middleware for the IoT

Developing new middleware solutions for the IoT is an active area of research (Satyanarayanan, 2001). Initially, these solutions were designed to support privacy protections in pervasive computing. They are also intended to guide the development and implementation of pervasive systems (Ranganathan et al., 2005). In regards to privacy, the physical outreach of IoT makes preserving the users' privacy a difficult task (Ranganathan et al., 2005). Typically, privacy is of three types: content, identity, and location (Cooper & Birman, 1995). Content privacy is concerned with keeping data or content private. The second type relates to hiding the identity of the user; while, location privacy is concerned with hiding the location of the user. Based on these types of privacy, Ranganathan et al. (Ranganathan et al., 2005) proposed a benchmark for pervasive computing systems which considered two characteristics for privacy models. The first is the user control over private information which is the model ability to provide content, identity, and location privacy. The second related to the unobtrusiveness of privacy mechanisms. Pervasive systems in the IoT attempt to provide a seamless user-centric environment, where users no longer need to spend much of their attention to computing machinery. Therefore, unobtrusiveness can be measured by the percentage of time a user consumes on interacting with privacy settings (Conti et al., 2012).

There is also a challenge of balancing privacy with usability (Bhaskar & Ahamed, 2007). Traditional models requiring explicit users' input have to be replaced with models that can sense information securely and automatically from the context and environment, and exchange it seamlessly with communicating devices and users. Dehghantanha et al. in (Dehghantanha, Mahmod, & Udzir, 2009) proposed an XML-based User-centered Privacy Model (UPM) for pervasive computing systems which provide content, identity, location, and time privacy with low unobtrusiveness. The model consists of three layers: User context layer, Service layer, and Owner layer. The model functions as follows: a user sends data to a portal without revealing the user's identity (portals are wireless nodes managing the users' context). Then the portal hides the user's location and forwards the data to an intermediate entity referred to as a lighthouse. A lighthouse is a trusted entity that holds the user's identity information; but it does not have access to user's location, content, and time of the interaction. By doing so, the user portal only knows the user's location and the lighthouse only know the user's identity. The lighthouse is responsible for communicating with the service provider. The service provider receives the needed contents from the owners. The authors claim that their UPM model provides the user with control over the content of the information disclosed and the disclosure settings of their identity, location, and time. In (Dehghantanha, Udzir, & Mahmod, 2011), the UPM model was evaluated based on the benchmark proposed in (Ranganathan et al., 2005) as follows: To assess the unobtrusiveness of the privacy policies, the percentage of time the user spends dealing with the privacy subsystem to make a decision was measured. An experiment was designed to show how to measure the model unobtrusiveness. Three tasks with different privacy levels were implemented. The aim is to demonstrate that the privacy files support mandatory and discretionary rules, reflect context sensitivity, handle uncertain situations and resolve conflicts (Dehghantanha et al., 2011).

In Lioudakis et al. (2007), a middleware architecture for privacy protection on the Internet is proposed. The middleware mediates between service providers and users and constitutes a distributed unit of trust that enforces the legal requirements. Before the development of the middleware, the authors classified the data into three types: active data (which are in direct control by the user), semi-active data (users have partial control over them such as RFIDs generated data) and passive data (these data are disclosed without any user's action). Next, the authors proposed a policy framework which incorporated a large set of rules. This framework is used to formalize how users express their privacy preferences. To model the rules, a relevant XML-based language was defined called the Discreet Privacy Language (DPL). To limit the control from the service provider over the user's personal data, a discreet Box was proposed. The Box incorporates the personal data repository that cashes personal data and a policy framework that is responsible for the decisions of personal data disclosure. It serves as the entry point for a service and its operation is similar to a proxy server. While the authors claim that the proposed architecture has numerous benefits, no evaluation has been performed.

Table 2. IoT privacy requirements

Collection Announcement	There is a need to find efficient ways to communicate and inform the user about collection procedures of his or her personal data in the IoT. There is a challenge in delivering the so-called the "data collection declaration" to the user who does not necessarily sit on any side of the communication. Communications in the IoT, as previously discussed, can be automated between various things.
Choice and Consent	The concept of choice and consent is to give users a selection mechanism so they can indicate which service they which to use. This is a challenging task to adopt in the IoT especially in an automated communication that may involve things that do not necessarily involve the human user directly. There is a need to provide the choice and consent right to users or things that represent them, and at the same time to allow an automated communication to be established.
Usage Logs	The users should be able to check the logs of their devices and the data they collect. This is necessary for accountability and audibility. There is also a need for digital forgetting.
Control over Contextual Data Disclosure	Given that interactions in the IoT are multi-dimensional, contextual data can reveal sensitive information about the users such as location information.

Other solutions such as the mix zone technique (Beresford & Stajano, 2004a) were designed to protect the privacy of users in location-aware pervasive computing applications. The mix zone is a middleware which enables an application to receive and reply to anonymous requests. It passes users' input and output between the application and the user. The mix zone is analogous to a mix node in a communication network (Danezis, 2003). A mix network provides anonymity using a store and forward network. The proposed technique was applied to location data collected from the Active Bat system installed at At&T Labs Cambridge (Hightower & Borriello, 2001). The results demonstrated that privacy is low even with a relatively large mix zone. However, the techniques could lead to a better privacy if applied over a larger and more populated area. While the mix zone technique provides a way of hiding the location of users, it does hide their identities. The choices are also restricted to two: anonymized or real location.

Therefore, solutions based on the mix networks, mix nodes model, pseudonyms, and those presented in (Beresford & Stajano, 2003, 2004b), provides location privacy without addressing the need to provide the user with granule control over the disclosure settings. Other alternative solutions, such as the LocServ model, support location privacy policies that can be checked automatically on behalf of the user (Myles, Friday, & Davies, 2003). However, LocServe suffers from considerable flexibility and arrangement limitations and cannot be reliably used in IoT. Table 2 summarizes the requirements for privacy in the IoT.

INTEROPERABILITY CHALLENGES

Interoperability in information technology is as old as the Internet is, if not older. Solutions considering the issues associated with information systems' interoperability can be traced back to 1988 (Science, Eliassen, & Veijalainen, 1988); and perhaps even earlier. Thus, interoperability is not new and it does not have a standard definition. For instance, Wikipedia defines Interoperability as "the ability of making systems and organizations work together" (Wikipedia). The IEEE defines interoperability as "the ability of two or more systems or components to exchange information and to use the information that has been exchanged" ("IEEE Standard Computer Dictionary: A Compilation of IEEE Standard Computer Glossaries," 1991). Other definitions of interoperability are further tailored according to the particular application's requirements or needs. As a result, different categories of interoperability have been emerging. Technical interoperability, Semantic interoperability, Syntactic interoperability, and Cross-domain interoperability are examples of these categories. To differentiate between these different types of interoperability, the following descriptions are provided:

- **Technical Interoperability:** *"is usually associated with hardware/software components, systems and platforms that enable machine-to-machine communication to take place. This kind of interoperability is often centered on (communication) protocols and the infrastructure needed for those protocols to operate" (van der Veer & Wiles, 2008).*
- **Syntactic Interoperability:** Deals with interoperable structures such as the format and syntax of the message exchanged between communication protocols. HTML, XML, SQL, ASN standards are among the tools of syntactic interoperability. Syntactic interoperability refers to the packaging and transmission mechanisms for data over a network.
- **Semantic Interoperability**: *In contrast with Syntactic Interoperability, which is concerned with the syntax of data, Semantic interoperability deals with the meaning of the data? "Semantic interoperability is the ability to interpret automatically the information exchanged meaningfully and accurately in order to produce useful results as defined by the end users of both systems" ("Semantic interoperability of health information ", 2011).*
- **Cross-Domain Interoperability** *"Exists when organizations or systems from different domains interact in information exchange, services and/or goods to achieve their own or common goals". When cross-domain interoperability exists, it means that users can seamlessly communicate and conduct activities, despite their reliance on different technical environments or frameworks ("Cross-Domain Interoperability," 2015).*

In regards to the IoT, every type and category of interoperability is needed to achieve seamless and heterogeneous communications in the IoT. Achieving interoperability is vital for interconnecting multiple things together across different communication networks. It defeats the purpose to have billions of sensors, actuators, tiny and smart devices connected to the Internet if these devices can't actually communicate with each other in a way or another. In fact, for the IoT to flourish, things connecting to the communication networks, which are heterogeneous, need to be able to communicate, share and receive information and/or instructions with other things or applications (Elkhodr, Shahrestani, & Cheung, 2016a).

Moreover, in traditional computer environments, computer devices are treated equally when connected to the Internet. Their functionalities vary depending on how the users use them. However, in the IoT, each device would be subject to different conditions such as power energy consumption restrictions, communication bandwidth requirements, and computation and security capabilities. Additionally, things might be made by different manufacturers that do not necessarily comply with a common standard. Things might also operate using a variety of communication technologies. These technologies might not necessarily connect things to the Internet in the same way a typical computer device usually do. For instance 6LoWPAN offers interoperability with other wireless 802.15.4 devices as well as with any IP-based devices using a simple bridging device (Elkhodr, Shahrestani, & Cheung, 2016b). However, bridging between ZigBee and non-ZigBee networks requires a more complex application layer gateway.

The highly competitive nature of the IoT makes interoperability between things even a more difficult task to achieve. Besides, wireless communication technologies are evolving and changing rapidly. This adds to the complexity of creating interoperable communications in the IoT as well. This inevitability results in heterogeneous devices that might not be able to communicate directly with each other on the IoT, raising integration issues. Service descriptions, common practices, standards and discovery mechanisms are among the many other challenges that also need to be considered before enabling an interoperable interaction between things (Elkhodr et al., 2016a).

MANAGEMENT CHALLENGES

Traditionally, network management solutions are needed to manage network equipment, devices, and services. However, with the IoT, there is a need to manage not only the traditional networked devices and their services, but also an entirely new range of things. The enormous number of things and their diversity create many management requirements. Thus, traditional management functionalities such as remote control, monitoring and maintenance are considered of paramount significance for the operation of things in the IoT. However, these management capabilities need to evolve to cater for the unique characteristics of the IoT. This is because the IoT is of a diverse nature supporting heterogeneous communications and seamless machine to machine interactions. This is in addition to the specific management capabilities required for managing things in the IoT. For example, self-configuration and network reconfiguration are essential management requirements in the IoT. On the other hand, traditionally, network management solutions aims at providing management information with a minimal response time. However, in some IoT scenarios which might involve lightweight devices, management solutions should provide comprehensive management information with minimal energy use (Welsh & Mainland, 2004).

Management Protocols

The purpose of a network management protocol is to transport management information from a device (e.g. a computer or a networked node) referred to as a managed device or object to an application referred to as the manager. Network management protocols are also used to transport control information from the manager to the managed devices. Traditionally, in a client-server scheme, a management protocol is used to transport messages between the manager and the network components. A network component can be a typical network device such as a server, router or a specific network interface on a router. Generally, network management protocols define a static protocol message format and a small set of predefined messages for gathering and posting managed information to and from the managed devices. Emerging standards, which are based on the distributed object-oriented approach, define more complex network management architecture. In this approach, the management protocol is tightly coupled with the management application; thereby facilitating code-on-demand (COD) object transmission, plug-and-play component management, and also defining a rich set of communication primitives between managers and managed devices (Elkhodr et al., 2016a).

The two most widely adopted management protocols are the Simple Network Management Protocol (SNMP), developed by the Internet Engineering Task Force (IETF), and the Common Management Information Protocol (CMIP), proposed by the International Standards Organization (ISO). Although these two protocols are similar in architecture, they vary slightly in operations. Both SNMP and CMIP define a single management device that assumes complete control over all management functions. The manager is an application that interacts with network agents embedded in each managed device using the network management protocol. In the context of SNMP and CMIP, agents are simple computational entities that provide mechanisms for accessing managed information stored on the managed devices (Sehgal, Perelman, Kuryla, & Schonwalder, 2012). SNMP's agents store device-specific information in managed information bases (MIB). On the other hand, the CMIP protocol defines a managed information tree (MIT) in order to store and access configuration information.

SNMP

Although SNMP was designed specifically for managing IP-based data networks, it has become the de facto standard for telecommunication network management. The popularity of SNMP is mainly due to its simplicity that allows manufacturers to enhance their products with network management functionality with a minimal effort. This protocol also provides simple, hierarchical management architecture with multi-vendor support.

SNMP aims to unify and minimize the complexity of management functions between various networked and hardware devices. The use of SNMP reduces the cost of management. Significantly, the SNMP's architecture enables the efficient integration of devices across a network. It facilitates seamless integration and management of existing and newly added hardware devices on a network. Additionally, SNMP implementations define a set of management functions that can be easily adopted by network managers and developers of network management systems. Another characteristic of SNMP is extensibility. SNMP's design allows the addition of newly developed extensions with less complexity. The SNMP protocol is a platform independent as well. It supports an array of various network technologies.

CMIP

Almost in parallel with the development of SNMP, the International Standards Organization (ISO) defined the specifications for the Common Management Information Protocol (CMIP). Unlike SNMP, CMIP is designed to provide network management operations for a wide variety of network architectures. In the open systems interconnection (OSI) architecture, the fundamental function of network management solutions is to assist with the exchange of management information between the manager and managed devices. This functionality is referred to as the common management information service element (CMISE) and is composed of two parts. The first specifies the services provided by the network management, and it is termed as the common management information service (CMIS). The second part is referred to as the common management information protocol (CMIP). It specifies the mechanisms and message format by which the management information is exchanged between the manager and managed devices.

The CMIP framework is broken down into three interacting components. These components consist of the layer management entity (LME), the system management application entity (SMAE), and the common management information protocol (CMIP); which facilitates the communication of managed information among the management layer and management devices.

The CMIP implements a much richer set of management functions when compared to SNMP. It organizes the managed entities and manager using a hierarchical approach. This allows managed information to be accessed within the scope of the manager. This hierarchical approach significantly increases the protocol's scalability. However, because the services offered by the CMIS entities are considerably more sophisticated than the management functions of SNMP, CMIP protocol is considered harder to implement. For this reason, CMIP has not gained as much popularity as SNMP.

Even though SNMP has gained major popularity in network management systems, the IETF designed this protocol to manage TCP/IP-based local area networks. Therefore, the challenges posed by emerging communication standards require a more sophisticated network management approach. CMIP was designed to provide a generic solution for overall network management; however it failed to gain global acceptance. Facing new technologies in the era of the IoT, network management approaches must implement scalable, flexible, robust, adaptive, and automated management architectures. This is because the IoT encompasses several heterogeneous networks consisting of a diversity of lightweight and more capable devices. This heterogeneity of devices and networks raises some novel management challenges. To target this challenge, studies such as the one reported in (Sehgal et al., 2012), examined the possibility of adopting existing network management protocols for the management of constrained networks and devices in the IoT. It is found, through simulation studies, that SNMP makes efficient use of resources on constrained devices (Sehgal et al., 2012). Future contributions are required to investigate the applicability and performance of traditional network management protocols such as the SNMP in physical IoT setups.

CONCLUSION

The Internet of things (IoT) is a heterogeneous network that encompasses sensors, actuators, smart devices, mobile and computer devices, and other physical objects embedded with electronics. The potentially huge number and the diversity of things that may be part of such an infrastructure bring tremendous amounts of complexity. Even though it is hard to predict exactly how the IoT will evolve, it is almost certain that the IoT will have significant impacts on the security and privacy of users, and on machine-to-machine communications throughout the Internet. The unique characteristics of things, specifically their low-power and low-cost requirements demand the optimization of many traditional solutions and the introduction of entirely new ones. Significantly, the connectivity of low-cost devices to the Internet create more complexity and new security risks. It also makes the implementation of privacy preservation solutions a challenging task. Compliance with regulations and privacy laws will continue to be a major issue in the IoT, specifically in health and public domains where the operation of things could have life and death implications. Additionally, interoperability is one of the major obstacles to the advancement of the IoT. If things and groups of things, operating using various wireless and LAN technologies, cannot communicate effectively with each other, we risk creating a very fragmented IoT. Other key challenges for the future of IoT include the design of security, management and privacy-focused solutions. Such solution should provide the users with options to opt in and opt out and increase transparency. To this end, future research on IoT should aim to develop lightweight cryptographic protocols, intelligent algorithms and Application Programing Interfaces (APIs), and new self-manageable network paradigms.

REFERENCES

App Genome Project. (2011). Retrieved from https://www.mylookout.com/appgenome

Atzori, L., Iera, A., & Morabito, G. (2010). The internet of things: A survey. *Computer Networks*, *54*(15), 2787–2805. doi:10.1016/j.comnet.2010.05.010

Behringer, M. H. (2009). End-to-End Security. *The Internet Protocol Journal, 12*(3), 20.

Beresford, A. R., & Stajano, F. (2003). Location privacy in pervasive computing. *Pervasive Computing, IEEE, 2*(1), 46–55. doi:10.1109/MPRV.2003.1186725

Beresford, A. R., & Stajano, F. (2004a). *Mix Zones: User Privacy in Location-aware Services.* Paper presented at the The Second IEEE Annual Conference on Pervasive Computing and Communications Workshops, Orlando, FL.

Beresford, A. R., & Stajano, F. (2004b). *Mix zones: user privacy in location-aware services.* Paper presented at the Pervasive Computing and Communications Workshops, 2004.

Beutel, J., Gruber, S., Hasler, A., Lim, R., Meier, A., Plessl, C.,... Woehrle, M. (2009). *PermaDAQ: A scientific instrument for precision sensing and data recovery in environmental extremes.* Paper presented at the 2009 International Conference on Information Processing in Sensor Networks.

Bhaskar, P., & Ahamed, S. I. (2007). *Privacy in Pervasive Computing and Open Issues.* Paper presented at the Availability, Reliability and Security, 2007. ARES 2007. The Second International Conference on.

Clendenin, M. (2010). *China's 'Internet Of Things' Overblown, Says Exec.* Retrieved from http://www.informationweek.com/news/storage/virtualization/225700966?subSection=News

Conti, M., Das, S. K., Bisdikian, C., Kumar, M., Ni, L. M., Passarella, A., & Zambonelli, F. et al. (2012). Looking ahead in Pervasive Computing: Challenges, Opportunities in the era of Cyber Physical Convergence. *Pervasive and Mobile Computing, 8*(1), 2–21. doi:10.1016/j.pmcj.2011.10.001

Cooper, D. A., & Birman, K. P. (1995). *Preserving privacy in a network of mobile computers.* Paper presented at the Security and Privacy, 1995.

Cross-Domain Interoperability. (2015). Retrieved from https://www.ncoic.org/cross-domain-interoperability

Danezis, G. (2003). *Mix-networks with restricted routes.* Paper presented at the Privacy Enhancing Technologies. doi:10.1007/978-3-540-40956-4_1

Dehghantanha, A., Mahmod, R., & Udzir, N. I. (2009). A XML based, User-centered Privacy Model in Pervasive Computing Systems. *International Journal of Computer Science and Network Security, 9*(10), 167–173.

Dehghantanha, A., Udzir, N., & Mahmod, R. (2011). Evaluating User-Centered Privacy Model (UPM) in Pervasive Computing Systems Computational Intelligence in Security for Information Systems. Springer Berlin / Heidelberg.

Elkhodr, M., Shahrestani, S., & Cheung, H. (2012). *A Review of Mobile Location Privacy in the Internet of Things.* Paper presented at the 2012 Tenth International Conference on ICT and Knowledge Engineering, Bangkok, Thailand. doi:10.1109/ICTKE.2012.6408566

Elkhodr, M., Shahrestani, S., & Cheung, H. (2013a). *The Internet of Things: Vision & Challenges.* Paper presented at the IEEE Tencon Spring 2013, Sydney, Australia.

Elkhodr, M., Shahrestani, S., & Cheung, H. (2013b). *Preserving the Privacy of Patient Records in Health Monitoring Systems. In Theory and Practice of Cryptography Solutions for Secure Information Systems* (pp. 499–529). IGI Global. doi:10.4018/978-1-4666-4030-6.ch019

Elkhodr, M., Shahrestani, S., & Cheung, H. (2016a). The Internet of Things: New Interoperability, Management and Security Challenges. *The International Journal of Network Security & Its Applications, 8*(2), 85–102. doi:10.5121/ijnsa.2016.8206

Elkhodr, M., Shahrestani, S., & Cheung, H. (2016b). *Wireless Enabling Technologies for the Internet of Things. In Handbook of Research on Next-Generation High Performance Computing.* Hershey, PA: IGI Global.

Enck, W., Gilbert, P., Chun, B.-G., Cox, L. P., Jung, J., McDaniel, P., & Sheth, A. N. (2010). *TaintDroid: an information-flow tracking system for realtime privacy monitoring on smartphones.* Paper presented at the 9th USENIX conference on Operating systems design and implementation, Vancouver, Canada.

Evans, D. (2012). The Internet of Everything. How More Relevant and Valuable Connections. Will Change the World. *Cisco IBSG*, 1-9.

Fredrik, H. (2011). *System Integrity for Smartphones: A security evaluation of iOS and BlackBerry OS. (Master).* Linkoping University.

Friese, I., Hogberg, J., Foll, F. A., Gourmelen, G., Lischka, M., Brennan, J.,... Lampe, S. (2010). *Bridging IMS and Internet Identity.* Paper presented at the 2010 14th International Conference on Intelligence in Next Generation Networks (ICIN). doi:10.1109/ICIN.2010.5640948

Gupta, P. (2012). *Metro Interface Improves Windows 8 While Increasing Some Risks.* Retrieved from http://blogs.mcafee.com/mcafee-labs/metro-interface-improves-windows-8-while-increasing-some-risks

HealthCast 2020: Creating a Sustainable Future. (2005). Retrieved from http://www.pwc.com/il/he/publications/assets/2healthcast_2020.pdf

Hightower, J., & Borriello, G. (2001). Location systems for ubiquitous computing. *Computer, 34*(8), 57–66. doi:10.1109/2.940014

Hoh, B., Gruteser, M., Xiong, H., & Alrabady, A. (2006). Enhancing security and privacy in traffic-monitoring systems. *IEEE Pervasive Computing / IEEE Computer Society [and] IEEE Communications Society, 5*(4), 38–46. doi:10.1109/MPRV.2006.69

Li, M., & Liu, Y. (2009). Underground coal mine monitoring with wireless sensor networks. *ACM Transactions on Sensor Networks, 5*(2), 10. doi:10.1145/1498915.1498916

Lin, M., Wu, Y., & Wassell, I. (2008). *Wireless sensor network: Water distribution monitoring system.* Paper presented at the Radio and Wireless Symposium. doi:10.1109/RWS.2008.4463607

Lioudakis, G. V., Koutsoloukas, E. A., Dellas, N. L., Tselikas, N., Kapellaki, S., Prezerakos, G. N., & Venieris, I. S. et al. (2007). A middleware architecture for privacy protection. *Computer Networks, 51*(16), 4679–4696. doi:10.1016/j.comnet.2007.06.010

Liu, C. H., Yang, B., & Liu, T. (2014). Efficient naming, addressing and profile services in Internet-of-Things sensory environments. *Ad Hoc Networks, 18*(0), 85–101. doi:10.1016/j.adhoc.2013.02.008

Lo, B., Thiemjarus, S., King, R., & Yang, G.-Z. (2005). *Body sensor network-a wireless sensor platform for pervasive healthcare monitoring*. Paper presented at the The 3rd International Conference on Pervasive Computing.

Lomas, N. (2009). *Online gizmos could top 50 billion in 2020*. Retrieved from http://www.businessweek.com/globalbiz/content/jun2009/gb20090629_492027.htm

Low, K. S., Win, W. N. N., & Er, M. J. (2005). *Wireless sensor networks for industrial environments*. Paper presented at the Computational Intelligence for Modelling, Control and Automation, 2005 and International Conference on Intelligent Agents, Web Technologies and Internet Commerce, International Conference on.

Madsen, P. (Producer). (2013). *OpenID Connect and its role in Native SSO*. Retrieved from https://www.youtube.com/watch?v=mTZ0bcNphVg

Myles, G., Friday, A., & Davies, N. (2003). Preserving privacy in environments with location-based applications. *Pervasive Computing, IEEE, 2*(1), 56–64. doi:10.1109/MPRV.2003.1186726

Ranganathan, A., Al-Muhtadi, J., Biehl, J., Ziebart, B., Campbell, R. H., & Bailey, B. (2005). *Towards a pervasive computing benchmark*. Paper presented at the Pervasive Computing and Communications Workshops, 2005. PerCom 2005 Workshops. Third IEEE International Conference on.

Roman, R., Najera, P., & Lopez, J. (2011). Securing the Internet of Things. *Computer, 44*(9), 51–58. doi:10.1109/MC.2011.291

Satyanarayanan, M. (2001). Pervasive computing: Vision and challenges. *Personal Communications, IEEE, 8*(4), 10–17. doi:10.1109/98.943998

Science, H. y. D. o. C., Eliassen, F., & Veijalainen, J. (1988). *A functional approach to information system interoperability*. Academic Press.

Sehgal, A., Perelman, V., Kuryla, S., & Schonwalder, J. (2012). Management of resource constrained devices in the internet of things. *Communications Magazine, IEEE, 50*(12), 144–149. doi:10.1109/MCOM.2012.6384464

Semantic interoperability of health information. (2011). Retrieved from http://www.en13606.org/the-ceniso-en13606-standard/semantic-interoperability

IEEE Standard Computer Dictionary: A Compilation of IEEE Standard Computer Glossaries. (1991). *IEEE Std 610*. doi:10.1109/IEEESTD.1991.106963

Summers, G. (2004). Data and databases. In *Developing Databases with Access*. Nelson Australia Pty Limited.

Surie, D., Laguionie, O., & Pederson, T. (2008). *Wireless sensor networking of everyday objects in a smart home environment*. Paper presented at the Intelligent Sensors, Sensor Networks and Information Processing, 2008. ISSNIP 2008. International Conference on. doi:10.1109/ISSNIP.2008.4761985

The Internet of Things. (2005). Retrieved from http://www.itu.int/osg/spu/publications/internetofthings/

Thurm, S., & Kane, Y. I. (2010). *Your Apps Are Watching You*. Retrieved from http://online.wsj.com/article/SB10001424052748704368004576027751867039730.html

van der Veer, H., & Wiles, A. (2008). *Achieving technical interoperability*. European Telecommunications Standards Institute.

Welsh, M., & Mainland, G. (2004). *Programming Sensor Networks Using Abstract Regions*. Paper presented at the NSDI.

Wikipedia. (n.d.). *Interoperability*. Retrieved from https://en.wikipedia.org/wiki/Interoperability

KEY TERMS AND DEFINITIONS

Actuators: Actuators are devices responsible for moving or controlling a mechanism or system.

Anonymization: Data anonymization is the process of either encrypting or removing identifiable information from personal data.

Internet of Things: The Internet of things is a technology that connects physical objects and not only computer devices to the Internet, making it possible to access data/services remotely and to control a physical object from a remote location.

IEEE 802.11ah: A wireless networking protocol that is an amendment of the IEEE 802.11-2007 wireless networking standard. It is intended to work with low-power devices.

Network Management: Network management refers to the activities and tools that pertain to the operation, administration, maintenance, and provisioning of networked systems.

Chapter 13
SONATA:
Social Network Assisted Trustworthiness Assurance in Smart City Crowdsensing

Burak Kantarci
Clarkson University, USA

Kevin G. Carr
Clarkson University, USA

Connor D. Pearsall
Clarkson University, USA

ABSTRACT

With the advent of mobile cloud computing paradigm, mobile social networks (MSNs) have become attractive tools to share, publish and analyze data regarding everyday behavior of mobile users. Besides revealing information about social interactions between individuals, MSNs can assist smart city applications through crowdsensing services. In presence of malicious users who aim at misinformation through manipulation of their sensing data, trustworthiness arises as a crucial issue for the users who receive service from smart city applications. In this paper, the authors propose a new crowdsensing framework, namely Social Network Assisted Trustworthiness Assurance (SONATA) which aims at maximizing crowdsensing platform utility and minimizing the manipulation probability through vote-based trustworthiness analysis in dynamic social network architecture. SONATA adopts existing Sybil detection techniques to identify malicious users who aim at misinformation/disinformation at the crowdsensing platform. The authors present performance evaluation of SONATA under various crowdsensing scenarios in a smart city setting. Performance results show that SONATA improves crowdsensing utility under light and moderate arrival rates of sensing task requests when less than 7% of the users are malicious whereas crowdsensing utility is significantly improved under all task arrival rates if the ratio of malicious users to the entire population is at least 7%. Furthermore, under each scenario, manipulation ratio is close to zero under SONATA while trustworthiness unaware recruitment of social network users leads to a manipulation probability of 2.5% which cannot be tolerated in critical smart city applications such as disaster management or public safety.

DOI: 10.4018/978-1-5225-1832-7.ch013

INTRODUCTION

The smart city concept denotes an intelligent platform consisting of interconnected sensors, embedded devices, decision making systems that process real time data (Chourabi, et al., 2012) (Meier & Lee, 2011) (Batty, 2014). Innovations in smart city design and applications can be accelerated by the integration of cloud computing into several smart city services such as transport, education, energy and water monitoring, healthcare, public safety and other ICT-based applications (Clohessy, Acton, & Morgan, 2014).A promising solution that would improve the benefits of smart city applications can be the integration of built-in sensors in mobile devices and providing the sensing resources as a service to particular smart city applications when needed (Kantarci & Mouftah, Trustworthy Sensing for Public Safety in Cloud-Centric Internet of Things, 2014). This concept is defined as Sensing as a Service (S^2aaS) in the literature (Sheng, Xiao, Tang, & Xue, 2013). In S^2aaS, distributed smart mobile devices participate in crowdsensing tasks that are requested by end users that are using either fixed computers or smart mobile devices.A comprehensive survey of S^2aaS in the context of cloud-centric Internet of Things has been presented in (Kantarci & Mouftah, Sensing as a Service in Cloud-Centric Internet of Things Architecture, 2015).

Trustworthiness of crowdsensed data is a crucial challenge in S^2aaS applications (French, Bessis, Maple, & Asimakopoulou, 2012). Kantarci and Mouftah have raised the trustworthiness issue in the recruitment process trough user centric incentives (Kantarci & Mouftah, Trustworthy Sensing for Public Safety in Cloud-Centric Internet of Things, 2014). Trustworthiness of crowdsensed data has been improved by applying a user reputation system that uses statistical accuracy of the crowdsensed data per mobile device. This approach has later been improved by incorporating mobility-awareness (Kantarci & Mouftah, Mobility-aware trustworthy crowdsourcing in cloud-centric Internet of Things, 2014) and social interaction-awareness (Kantarci & Mouftah, Trustworthy crowdsourcing via mobile social networks, 2014). In order to address trustworthiness issue, there have been studies which take social ties into consideration, and some mobile devices are defined as social sensors denoting the trusted crowdsensing nodes (Hao, Mingjie, Geyong, & Yang, 2014). Furthermore, social trust and reciprocity have been combined to maximize the crowdsensing utility by modeling the problem as maximizing utility of a circulation flow (Gong, Chen, Zhang, & Poor, 2014).

As known by everyone, social networks have become inseparable part of every life (Dingli & Seychell, 2012). Related works point out mobile social networks as a smart ecosystem to harvest data from smart mobile devices in a participatory manner (Hu, Li, Ngai, Leung, & Kruchten, 2014). In (Sheng, Xiao, Tang, & Xue, 2013), integration of mobile social network into mobile S2aaS has been pointed as an important challenge. Mobile social network denotes a geo-social model that connects all users based on interests, location, context and interaction (Cardone, et al., 2013). Mobile social network-aware crowdsensing has been shown to improve the platform utility as mobile device trajectories can be estimated based on user interaction (Kantarci & Mouftah, Trustworthy crowdsourcing via mobile social networks, 2014). Research findings of the same study report that trustworthiness-aware recruitment of mobile devices is crucial since in presence of malicious activity, recruitment of mobile devices with high reputation can avoid degradation in crowdsensing utility due to the payments made to malicious users and manipulation probability in the harvested data.Incorporating social behavior and social trust dimensions into S^2aaS by assigning social credits to users has been shown toimprove the effectiveness of crowdsensing(Gong, Chen, Zhang, & Poor, 2014).

In this paper, we aim at addressing the trustworthiness challenge in smart city cowdsensing by combining social network theory and S^2aaS. A minimalist illustration of the scenario is seen in Figure 1.a where crowdsensing for crisis management is depicted in the context of a smart city. The information is collected at the cloud platform, aggregated, analyzed and visualized for the end user. We adopt a Sybil detection approach (Yhang, Xue, Yang, Wang, & Dai, 2015) to detect the users who are in malicious activity. We propose Social Network-Assisted Trustworthiness Assurance (SONATA) as an effective and trustworthy recruitment framework for mobile devices sharing their built-in sensors for S²aaS applications. SONATA dynamically forms a social network by defining connections between the mobile devices that have common sensing tasks, and it further runs an auction which allows mobile devices (i.e., users) to join the auction and participate in crowdsensing. SONATA adopts the auction procedure that was previously proposed in (Kantarci & Mouftah, Trustworthy Sensing for Public Safety in Cloud-Centric Internet of Things, 2014). According to the auction, the value of sensing task is scaled by the average trustworthiness of the participant mobile devices. SONATA assesses the trustworthiness of a mobile device via recommendation (i.e., votes) of its neighbors in the dynamically formed social network. We evaluate our proposed scheme, SONATA, through simulations and show that the utility of the crowdsensing platform can be improved significantly via SONATA in presence of malicious activity and moderate load of sensing task requests (i.e., load level). Furthermore, as the ratio of malicious users increases, SONATA outperforms reputation unaware mobile device recruitment under any load level in terms of crowdsensing platform utility. Moreover, payment to malicious users and manipulation probability in the platform are significantly reduced by SONATA.

The paper is organized as follows. In Section 2, related work and motivation are presented while Section 3 presents the proposed framework in detail. Numerical results are presented and discussed in Section 4 while Section 5 concludes the paper and gives future directions.

SMART CITIES AND CROWDSENSING

There is a general consensus that the growing popularity and amount of smartphones in highly populated areas allows for the mass collection of sensing data. The applications on smartphones have the capability of collecting and sending sensing data with GPS coordinates. This data could be valuable given the right context to public safety, transportation, and environmental authorities.

There are several challenges in S²aaS-based crowdsensing systems as reported by Sheng et al. (2013). The most crucial ones among those challenges are sensing reliability, truthfulness, trustworthiness, and energy efficiency. Sensing reliability can lead to outliers in harvested data, and it is possible to address this challenge via outlier detection techniques (Zhang, Meratnia, & Havinga, 2010). Recently, GPS-less sensing has been proposed to allow the mobile devices to participate in the crowdsensing tasks when users place phone calls, write text messages via SMS services or browse on the web (Sheng, Tang, Xiao, & Xue, 2014).

As mentioned by Sheng et al (2013), incentivizing mobile smart device users is one of the most crucial challenges to help S²aaS-based crowdsensing become widely adopted. Related work presents two types of incentives as user-centric and platform-centric. When users are incentivized in a platform-centric manner, mobile devices that are to participate in crowdsensing activities are recruited and assigned their sensing tasks along with corresponding sensing plans. On the other hand, while recruitment is done in a user-centric manner, users make their own sensing plans and participate in a selection process which is based on an auction. User and platform-centric incentives have been studied thoroughly in (Yang, Xue, Fang, & Tang, 2012). The authors define the problem of truthfulness as users exploiting the benefits of incentive mechanism through reporting their sensing costs higher than the actual value so that they are compensated by being paid more than they were actually supposed to be. This type of situation may occur especially when users are recruited and compensated through a Local Search-Based (LSB) auction. The authors have addressed this issue through a monotonously decreasing marginal income of the crowdsensing platform, and called this the MSensing auction (Yang, Xue, Fang, & Tang, 2012).

We have looked at studiesthat propose crowdsensing applications for smart city management. Amongst these applications, the vCity Map system proposes collecting the sound of the city and analyzing that sound for passing-cars. The vCity Map system also proposes using vibration sensing of bicyclists to determine road conditions(Tobe, Usami, Kobana, Takahashi, Lopez, & Thepvilojanapong, 2014). Aiharaet al. propose numerous ideas on how we can use crowdsourced mobile sensing including frameworks to improve road conditions during winter and gathering location-specific information(Aihara, Imura, Takasu, Tanaka, & Adachi, 2014).

One of the larger holes in the crowdsensing platform comes from the lack of human incentive driving it. It is commonly believed the average consumers would prefer not to participate in these research instances without being compensated in some form. This is the exact issue that RasteyRishtey addresses. RasteyRishtey proposes the implementation of a GPS intensive social meeting media application. With this application, user incentivization comes from the typical desires that arise from social media and, subsequently, users agree to submit GPS data to the city's cloud during use(Rijurekha, 2014). However this is not the only proposed avenue of solution. Rather than using social media as a rewarding tool, it is argued to couple a trust based network, similar to what is addressed in this paper, with a user reciprocity program. Thus, when a user joins a network an agreement is met, that in order to request help a user needs to volunteer help when requested. This effectively creates a symbiotic relationship between users(Gong, Chen, Zhang, & Poor, 2014).

There are also works discussing how to make it easier for mobile application developers to integrate crowdsensing into their application. Creating a library that could take raw sensing data and turn that data into something meaningful would help bridge this gap. An open source library called Mobile Sensing Technology aims to achieve this goal(Cardone, Cirri, Corradi, Foschini, Ianniello, & Montanari, 2014). This technology is further expanded upon with development of Vita. Vita is a proposed universal architecture for communication between mobile "cyber-phyiscal" systems (CPS) and cloud systems. This technology is designed to create an easier and more structured foundation for mobile-cloud application developers while maintaining low mobile computation and communication overhead (Hu, Chu, Chan, & Leung, 2013).

The development of crowdsensing framework has been primarily designed to address mobile platforms. This framework could also encompass sensing data produced via the Internet of Things (IoT). ClouT is a proposed solution to this information gap. ClouT allows for the collection of sensing data from typical smart appliances (i.e. refrigerator, lights, thermostat, etc). This allows for the development of a much larger information network to better address a smart city's need (Benazzouz, Munilla, Gunalp, Gallissot, & Gurgen, 2014).

All these applications discussed use geographical coordinates as an element of their project. Geographical coordinates is useful data for computers to use, but when a human is trying to interpret the data it would be easier if a name was associated with the geographical coordinates(Chon, Kim, & Cha, 2013).Using the context of the user's social media when the data is collected could also enrich the data; i.e. an application designed for sharingphotos of foodfrom different restaurants in a city. Looking at the users social media during the time frame of that photo might give us more information about the food portrayed(Cardone, Cirri, Corradi, Foschini, Ianniello, & Montanari, 2014).These geo-social concepts are further expanded on and engrained in McSense. This system allows for the overall modelling of clusters of users based on multiple dimensions of collected information for use in a smart city setting(Cardone, et al., 2013).

There are definite benefits of smartphone sensing in areas of public safety, transportation, environmental protection, and end-user satisfaction. We need to consider the future of these benefits. As this data becomes more popular and our reliance increasesthere becomes a greater risk of an attack. A nefarious user may possibly to send the wrong interpretation of what his/her surrounding is. For the systems addressed above, there are reasons why a user might send forged data to an application.It is also possible that no user intention is the cause of the false information but instead a sensor is malfunctioning and to keep the data as clean as possible the system would want to identify it. This is where SONATA comes in and assists in determining how reliable the data we are receiving is.

SOCIAL NETWORK ASSISTED TRUSTWORTHINESS ASSURANCE (SONATA)

System Architecture

The system architecture is illustrated in Figure 1.b, and it consists of the following four layers as proposed in (Perera, Zaslavsky, Christen, & Georgapoulos, 2014) and applied in (Kantarci & Mouftah, Trustworthy Sensing for Public Safety in Cloud-Centric Internet of Things, 2014). The players in the four layer business model can be explained as follows:

- **Mobile Device Users-Service Providers:** A mobile device user serves as the service provider as soon as (s)he installs the mobile application that uses SONATA framework. Installation of the mobile app that uses SONATA framework grants the cloud platform access to the built-in sensors in his/her mobile device. Furthermore, a user who installs the mobile app is granted the privilege to vote for the trustworthiness of other users as long as they have common sensing tasks to report.
- **Data Publishers:** Having a data publishing layer helps retrieving data more easily through third party services. As most mobile device users have at least one social media account which is accessed via mobile app installed on their phones, using social media add-ons will enable flexibility and address the interoperability issue as end users may switch between cloud service providers.
- **The Cloud Platform:** SaaS/PaaS providers are named as the cloud platform, and their role is obtaining sensing data of the mobile device users through data publishers (i.e., social network services), and placing their rewards on their social media accounts. Furthermore, SaaS/PaaS providers implement data analytics software on the cloud platform, and run visualization algorithms to present the aggregated sensing data to the end user.
- **Mobile Device Users-Service Requesters:** As mentioned above, mobile device users can provide their built-in sensors as services while requesting sensing service from other mobile device users. Mobile device users, as the service requesters interact with the cloud platform via mobile application where they can submit sensing service requests and query historical data. In a smart city scenario, sensing service requester can be either a mobile device user who attempts to retrieve information for a particular event or smart city authority who aims at continuously monitoring the

Figure 1. Overview of the system architecture (a) Incident report collection and vote-based reputation maintenance, (b) Layered architecture (Kantarci & Mouftah, Sensing as a Service in Cloud-Centric Internet of Things Architecture, 2015)

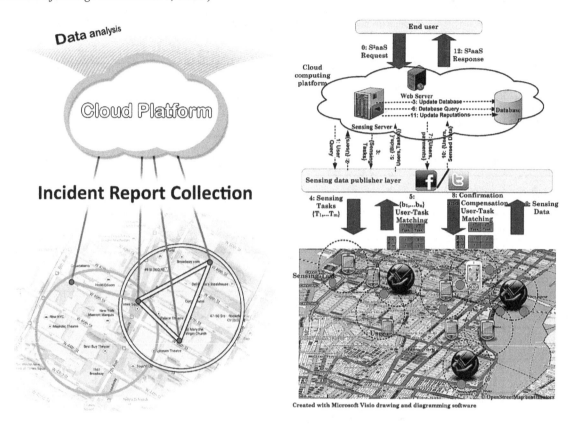

smart city ecosystem. In the figure, the end user is illustrated as the smart city authority (i.e., fixed user) that continuously monitors the responsiveness against an emergency situation.

The idea behind having a layered architecture is that the proposed concept is built on a cloud-inspired business model. Hence, the players in each layer act as service provider for the upper layer and service requester for the lower layer. For instance, the end user can switch between SaaS/PaaS providers (i.e., the cloud platform) while the cloud platform can switch between different social network services (e.g., Facebook or Twitter) to retrieve sensing data.

It is worthwhile mentioning that the social network in which the recommendations will be made is a hypothetical social network infrastructure that is dynamically formed at the platform site as the mobile devices have common tasks to sense. For two mobile devices having common sensing tasks leads to being connected over the hypothetical social network. The details of the social network reconfiguration are explained in the next subsection.

Before we proceed with the details of the proposed framework, it is worthwhile presenting the notation used in the description of the model. The reader is referred to Table 1 for the details of the notation.

Table 1. Notation used in the description of SONATA framework

Notation	Explanation
P	Set of mobile devices participating in the auction, i.e., participants
W	Set of winners in the auction
$\hat{W}$	Set of previously recruited mobile devices
$\mathfrak{R}_i(t)$	Trustworthiness of mobile device-i at time period t
$\vartheta(W)$	Total value of the sensing tasks in set-W
$\vartheta^{\mathfrak{R}}(W)$	Reputation-based total values of the tasks in the
$\vartheta_i^{\mathfrak{R}}(W)$	Reputation-based marginal value of mobile device-i on set-W
$b_i(c_i)$	Bid (sensing cost) of mobile device-i
ρ_i	Payment to the user/mobile device-i
T	Set of sensing tasks
$T_{\{S\}}$	Set of sensing tasks handled by the mobile devices in set-S
T_i	Set of sensing tasks handled by user/mobile device-i
ϑ_t	Value of the sensing task-t
Γ_t	Set of users handling task-t
ω_i	Vote capacity of user-i
C_{ij}	Binary value is one if user-i and user-j are connected over a social network
χ_j^i	Vote of mobile device-j for mobile device-i
$\mathfrak{R}_i^{ins}$	Instantaneous reputation of mobile device-i
$\mathfrak{R}_i(t)$	Trustworthiness of mobile device-i at the end of the auction-t
$\mathfrak{R}_i(t^-)$	Trustworthiness of mobile device-i prior to auction-t

Sonata Framework

The proposed scheme SONATA adopts the MSensing auction in (Yang, Xue, Fang, & Tang, 2012), and introduces user recommendation to the MSensing auction. As mentioned before, MSensing can be improved by incorporating user/mobile device reputation/trustworthiness-awareness. The main difference between SONATA and the previous work by Kantarci and Moufah(Kantarci & Mouftah, Trustworthy Sensing for Public Safety in Cloud-Centric Internet of Things, 2014) (Kantarci & Mouftah, Mobility-aware trustworthy crowdsourcing in cloud-centric Internet of Things, 2014) (Kantarci & Mouftah, Trustworthy crowdsourcing via mobile social networks, 2014) is that SONATA framework assumes that the mobile device users that are in adverse behavior are analogous to the Sybil-like attacks in social networks. Furthermore, SONATA models the crowdsensing network as a social network community the members of which are linked via common sensing tasks. Besides modeling of the crowdsensing community as a social network, recommendation-based trustworthiness assessment is another contribution of SONATA to the crowdsensing literature. To the best of our knowledge, Sybil-like behavior in crowdsensing environments has not been considered in S^2aaS studies so far.

As proposed in (Yhang, Xue, Yang, Wang, & Dai, 2015), a user can detect a malicious neighbor with a certain probability, and if each node in the social network is allowed to vote for the reputation of its neighbors, the trustworthiness of malicious users can be obtained. In network theory, which is later on applied to social networks as well, Sybil attacks occur when nodes with fake identities attempt joining the network. This can occur in the form of a wireless sensor node with a fake ID (Zhan, Shi, & Deng, 2012) or a social network user who sends friend requests to various users with a fake ID (Yhang, Xue, Yang, Wang, & Dai, 2015). By SONATA framework, we hypothesize that integration of a collaborative recommendation mechanism into MSensing reduces the probability of recruiting adversaries in crowdsensing, and in turn, experiencing better crowdsensing utility especially when the ratio of malicious users is not negligible. We further hypothesize that SONATA will improve the manipulation probability for having significant amount of malicious users eliminated before recruitment.

Voting in SONATA works as follows. Given a social network of four users, namely Alice, Bob, Carol, Dan; the users have the following reputation and vote capacity tuples respectively (0.9, 1), (0.8, 0.7), (0.7, 0.7), and (0.8, 0.9), respectively. As illustrated in Figure 2, Erin joins the network with no previous reputation or vote capacity. Each of these four users vote for Erin, and the value of each vote can be either positive or negative. Alice's, Carol's and Dan's votes are positive for Erin whereas Bob's vote is negative. A negative vote is counted as -1 while a positive vote is counted as 1. As seen in the example, Erin's reputation is calculated as the sum of all votes weighted by corresponding user reputations and vote capacities normalized by the total vote capacity. Thus, once Erin joins the network, her reputation is 0.58 with a vote capacity of 0.73. Upon joining the network, Erin inherits the average vote capacity of all users who have already voted for her. This approach was initially presented in (Yhang, Xue, Yang, Wang, & Dai, 2015). Here, SONATA re-visits the friend relationship in conventional social networks by defining connections between mobile devices based on them having common tasks to sense either in the current auction or in the past auctions.

As SONATA adopts the MSensing auction (Yang, Xue, Fang, & Tang, 2012), user recruitment consists of two steps, namely winner selection and payment determination. Figure 3 illustrates the flowchart of the winner selection step. SONATA starts with an empty set of winners, and runs subsequent iterations. At eachiteration, the algorithm aims at selecting the mobile device that will maximize the mar-

Figure 2. An illustrative example of voting mechanism adopted by SONATA

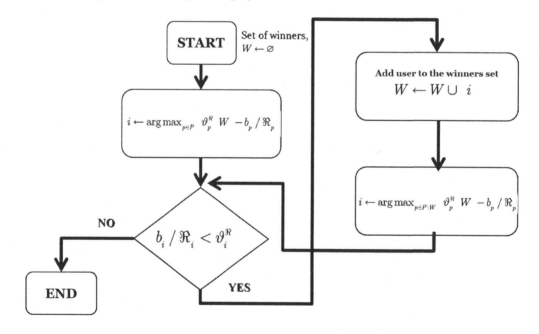

Name	Reputation	Vote Capacity
Alice	0.9	1
Bob	0.8	0.7
Carol	0.7	0.7
Dave	0.8	0.9

Vote for Erin
1
-1
1
1

Connect **Erin**

Erin's reputation: (0.9-0.8X0.7+0.7X0.7+0.9X0.8 / (0.9+0.8X0.7+0.7X0.7+0.9X0.8) = 0.58

Erin's vote capacity: (1+0.7+0.7+0.5)/4= 0.73

Figure 3. Selection of winners in the first step of user recruitment in SONATA

ginal contribution to the crowdsensing platform utility which is shown as $\vartheta_P^{\mathfrak{R}}(W) - b_p / \mathfrak{R}_p$ in the figure where $p \in P$. It is worthwhile noting that the reputation-based marginal contribution of user-p to the set W is defined as the difference between the values of the set, P, before and after adding the user-p to the set, W, as formulated in (1).

$$\vartheta_p^{\mathfrak{R}}(W) = \vartheta_p^{\mathfrak{R}}(W' \cup \{p\}) - \vartheta_p^{\mathfrak{R}}(W') \mid W' = W\{p\} \tag{1}$$

As seen in Figure 3, the bid (sensing cost) of a mobile device is scaled by its trustworthiness while calculating the marginal contribution. This value is called the modified bid, and the reason behind using modified bid is that the marginal contribution of mobile device with lower trustworthiness will be lower than a mobile device with the same sensing cost but higher trustworthiness.

Value of a set of mobile devices, W, is defined as the sum of the value of the tasks collaboratively sensed by the users in the corresponding set. However, since SONATA runs a reputation/trustworthiness-based recruitment procedure, the value of the set is the sum of the tasks that are collaboratively sensed by the mobile devices in the set scaled by the average reputation of the set as formulated by (2).

$$\vartheta^{\Re}(W) = \sum_{t \in T_w} \sum_{j \in \mathbb{G}_t} \vartheta_t . \Re_j / |\Gamma_t| \tag{2}$$

The crowdsensing platform keeps adding mobile devices as long as the maximum marginal contribution $(\vartheta_P^R(W) - b_p / R_p)$ to the platform utility is positive. Once the winners are selected, the second step is the payment determination (i.e., compensation) for the winners. To this end, for each selected mobile device, w, the platform first constructs a temporary set, Δ of non-winner mobile devices/users where each mobile device has a positive reputation-based contribution to the value of Δ. Then the platform searches for the maximum possible sensing cost for mobile device-w that will still make it preferable over any other mobile device in the set, Δ. The corresponding value is assigned as the payment to the mobile device user-w. The details of the payment decision procedure are illustrated in Figure 4.

As mentioned above, trustworthiness of a mobile device is assessed by using a recommendation technique which adopts the Sybil detection mechanism in (Yhang, Xue, Yang, Wang, & Dai, 2015) for online social networks. SONATA maintains a social network infrastructurewhich is re-configured as new mobile devices are recruited for participatory sensing. Every node in the social network votes for

Figure 4. Payment determination in SONATA. The framework adopts the payment determination phase in (Kantarci & Mouftah, Trustworthy Sensing for Public Safety in Cloud-Centric Internet of Things, 2014)

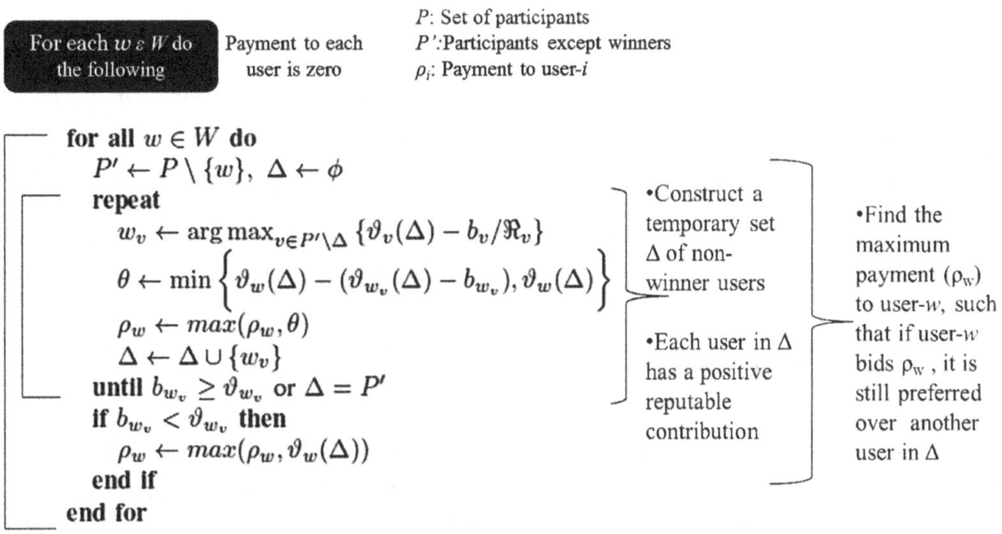

its neighbors where neighboring relation is defined as having at least one common sensing task in the current stream of sensing requests or having been recruited at least once before. $\hat{W}$ denoting the set of previously recruited mobile devices, connectivity of mobile device-i and mobile device-j is formulated as in (3).

$$C_{ij} = \begin{cases} 1 & (i,j \in \widehat{W}) \vee T_{\{i\}} \cap T_{\{j\}} \neq \varnothing \\ 0 & else \end{cases} \tag{3}$$

According to SONATA, each node in the social network votes for its neighbors to contribute to its trustworthiness assessment with its vote capacity. Vote capacity of a user is updated at each auction period as the weighted sum of its previous and current values as seen in. Υ is the weight factor which takes value in (0, 1). Thus, the higher the value is, the higher the impact of the previous vote capacities. Second component of the vote capacity in (4) is the current vote capacity of mobile device-i which is the aggregated vote capacity of its connections normalized by the size of the set of mobile devices that have been selected in the auction.

$$\omega_i = \Upsilon.\omega_i^- + (1-Y). \sum_{j|T_{\{i\}} \cap T_{\{j\}} \neq \varnothing} \frac{\omega_j}{\left\| \widehat{W} \right\|} \tag{4}$$

Once the vote capacity is updated, trustworthiness of mobile device-i is calculated as the total vote from the neighbors averaged by their total voting capacities. Equation 5 formulates this expression.

$$\mathfrak{R}_i^{ins} = \frac{\sum_{j|C_{ij}=1} \omega_j \chi_j^i \mathfrak{R}_j}{\sum_{j|C_{ij}=1} \omega_j \mathfrak{R}_j} \tag{5}$$

As sensing tasks arrive in bunches, mobile device recruitment is pursued via a series of auctions. Therefore, trustworthiness of a device varies between the auctions, and we denote the trustworthiness of a mobile device at auction-t as $\mathfrak{R}_i(t)$. Indeed the trustworthiness of user-i in (5) is instantaneous but a running average of trustworthiness should be applied to the recruitment steps. Thus, $\mathfrak{R}_i^{ins}(t)$ denoting instantaneous trustworthiness of the mobile device, $\mathfrak{R}_i(t-)$ standing for the previous trustworthiness of the mobile device, Equation 6 formulates the update procedure for mobile device trustworthiness.

$$\mathfrak{R}_i(t) = \sigma.\mathfrak{R}_i(t^-) + (1-\sigma).\mathfrak{R}_i^{ins}(t) \tag{6}$$

At the end of each auction, mobile device users are rewarded, trustworthiness of mobile devices is updated, and the crowdsensing platform proceeds with the next stream of sensing requests. As seen above, SONATA does not lead to a computational burden on the recruitment procedure. It requires $O(n^2)$ storage space due to keeping track of connectivity. On the other hand, all recommendation based calculations require $O(n^2)$ runtime overhead.

NUMERICAL RESULTS

Simulation Settings

We evaluate the performance of our proposal through simulations, and adopt the simulation settings in(Kantarci & Mouftah, Trustworthy Sensing for Public Safety in Cloud-Centric Internet of Things, 2014). We have built a Java-based tool to simulate the crowdsensing environment. A 1000x1000terrain is considered with 1000 users where 5% or 7% of them areset to be malicious in different scenarios. Sensing tasks are uniformly distributed over the terrain, and a mobile device shows interest in a sensing task if the phenomenon is within 30 units range of the mobile device. The mobile devices have no neighbors but have an initial reputation value that is assumed to have been carried out from previous event. Hence, the platform assumes three different scenarios for initial reputation of the users such that the users are trustworthy by 50%, 70% or 90% at the beginning of themonitoring event.

The crowdsensing platform generates sensing tasks requests varying between 20 tasks/min and 100 tasks/min. The entire event lasts for 30 minutes while sensing tasks arrivefollowing a Poisson distribution. The vote of a mobile devicefor its neighbor is either 1 or -1. We make an analogy betweenthe adversary behavior in this study (i.e., altered sensorreadings) and the Sybil attacks in social networks. Hence onefundamental assumption in this study is that there is a 20%chance that the recommendation of a mobile device for amalicious mobile device is -1. The value of a task is uniformlydistributed in [1,5] whereas sensing cost of a mobile device isdistributed between [1,10]. Furthermore, built-in sensors canprovide accurate readings with a probability between 0.97 and0.98(He & Li, 2013).The behavior of malicious users is adopted from (Kantarci & Mouftah, Trustworthy Sensing for Public Safety in Cloud-Centric Internet of Things, 2014). A malicious user joins the auction with one tenth of the actual sensing cost in order to be selected. For each sensing task arrival rate value, simulations have been run with five different seeds, and the average of five runs is presented in the results section. The simulation settings are summarized in Table 2.

For the assessment of the SONATA framework, the following metrics are used:

- **Crowdsensing Platform Utility:** As shown in Equation 7, utility of the end user is the difference between the total reputation-based value of the sensing tasks and the total payments made to the winners in the auction (ρ_i^τ). In the equation τ denotes the index of the period in which the cloud platform requests a new set of sensing tasks from the mobile devices.

$$U_{platform} = \sum_\tau \left(\sum_{t \in T_{W_t}} \vartheta^{\Re}\left(W_\tau\right) - \sum_i \rho_i^\tau \right) \tag{7}$$

Table 2. Overview of simulation settings

Terrain size	1000x1000
Number of mobile devices	1000
Sensing range	30 units
Initial reputation	0.50, 0.70, 0.90
Value of tasks	[1, 2, 3, 4, 5]
Value of sensing costs	[1,...,10]
Sensing task arrival rate [1/min]	{20, 40, 60, 80, 100}
Event duration	30 min
Malicious users ratio	{0.05, 0.07}
Probability of Sybil detection	0.20
Sensing accuracy	[0.97,0.98]
Vote	{-1,1}
σ	0.5
Υ	0.5
Initial vote capacity	1

$$U_{mobile} = \left(\sum_{\tau}((\sum_{i}\rho_i^{\tau} - \sum_{i}c_i^{\tau}) / |W_{\tau}|)) / \tau_{end} \right) \quad (8)$$

- **Utility of the Mobile Devices:** Equation 8 formulates the average utility of a mobile device as the difference between total payments made to the winners and the total sensing cost of the winners. The resulting value is averaged by which is the index of the last auction that has been run upon the arrival of last bunch of sensing tasks.
- **Manipulation Probability:** Manipulation probability is formulated as the ratio of the tasks for which at least one malicious user has been paid, to the total number of tasks.

It is worthwhile noting that the adversaries do not continuously attack but first aim to build reputation by sending accurate sensing data, and after reaching a certain threshold, they start sending altered data to the crowdsensing platform. This type of behavior increases the challenges and risks in such a system.

Simuation Results

The first set of results is collected by setting the ratio of malicious users at 5% under varying the initial reputation value for each mobile device user. As seen in Figure 5, SONATA increases the platform utility until 80 tasks/min arrival rate. Beyond arrival of 80 tasks/min, reputation unaware approach leads to

Figure 5. Crowdsensing utility when 5% of the mobile device users are malicious

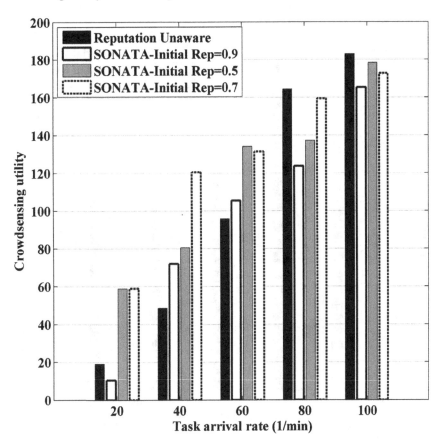

slightly higher utility. The reason of this behavior is that SONATA does not give a significant chance to a low reputation mobile device as the user reputation is derived based on the neighbor recommendation. Therefore when the number of tasks is higher, reputation unaware approach may capture more tasks. On the other hand, it is worthwhilementioning that the crowdsensing utility function uses reputation-based values of the set of tasks whereas user reputation is based on recommendation here while in reputation unaware approach outliers are eliminated and the total value gives the crowdsensing platform utility. As the utility functions are formed differently, reputation unaware approach's slightly higher crowdsensing platform utility does not guarantee efficiency in terms of platform utility.

Figure 6 depicts the manipulation probability. As seen in the figure, performance of SONATA is related to the initial reputation value assigned to mobile devices. If the initial reputation is too high (e.g., 0.9), manipulation probability is higher. This is an expected phenomenon since higher reputation will converge to a minimum in a longer time in case of a malicious user activity. As time elapses, the mobile device will be assigned new tasks that will lead to additional neighboring relations and possibly negative votes from the neighbors. On the other hand, a low reputation value will converge to zero faster as soon as the mobile device is assigned a sensing task and is identified as an adversary by the neighbors.

Figure 6. Manipulation probability when 5% of the mobile device users are malicious

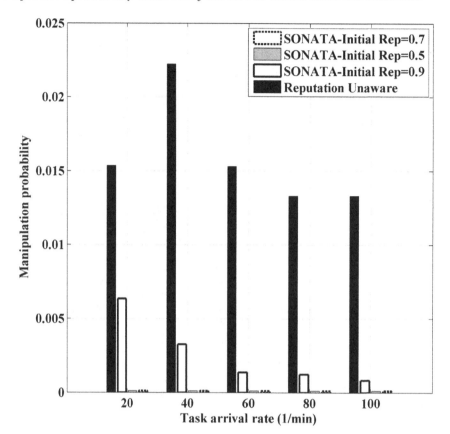

Figure 7 is a complement for Figure 6. As manipulation probability is defined as the ratio of the tasks for which at least one malicious user has been paid, total payments to malicious users is expected to have a similar behavior to that of the manipulation probability. Thus, the higher the manipulation probability, the higher the amount of payment made to the adversaries. Indeed, the direct relation between the two metrics also implies that the initial reputation of the mobile device users should not be set as high as 0.9 which is clearly seen in Figure 7.

The results in Figures 5-7 were limited to a specific scenario where the malicious mobile device users form 5% of the entire participant population. In order to investigate the relation between the malicious user percentage and the performance parameters defined above, in the next step, we increase set the ratio of the malicious users, and set at7%. All simulations are run, and the corresponding results are collected accordingly. Figure 8 illustrates the results for crowdsensing platform utility. As seen in the figure, as the malicious users increase, SONATA outperforms reputation unaware mobile device recruitment approach. The reason of this behavior can be explained as follows. As the number of malicious users increase, reputation unaware approach cannot be selective unlike SONATA.

Figure 7. Total payment to malicious users when 5% of the mobile device users are malicious

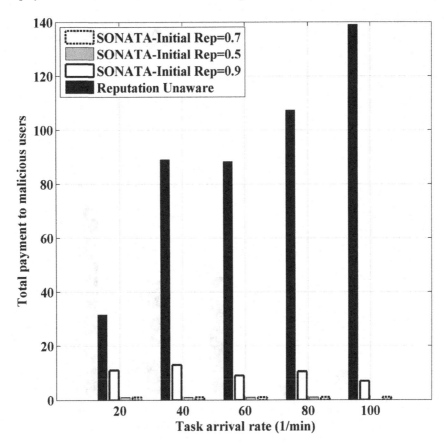

Figure 9 depicts the manipulation probability at the crowdsensing platform when 7% of the participating mobile device user population is malicious. Due to the same reason explained for the results in Figure 6, at some auction steps, reputation unaware approach ends up recruiting malicious users leading to manipulation as seen in Figure 9.

Furthermore, malicious users that are recruited are also compensated as seen in Figure 10. In both figures, SONATA achieves significantly low manipulation probability which results in almost zero payments to adversaries. This is due to SONATA's relying on the recommendation capabilities of the participating mobile devices.

In the last part of this study, we set the ratio of the malicious to three different values as follows: 0.03, 0.05 and 0.07. As SONATA leads to significantly lower manipulation probability (and corresponding payments to malicious users), we have tested the possible improvement if statistical trustworthiness scheme in (Kantarci & Mouftah, Trustworthy Sensing for Public Safety in Cloud-Centric Internet of Things, 2014) were used instead of SONATA. The results are presented in Table 3 for all three malicious mobile device ratios and sensing task arrival rates. As seen in the table, as the sensing task arrival rate increases, the payments made to malicious users increases as well. On the other hand, manipulation probability does not change significantly. Nevertheless, both manipulation probability and payments to malicious users have been remarkably decreased by SONATA.

Figure 8. Crowdsensing utility when 7% of the mobile device users are malicious

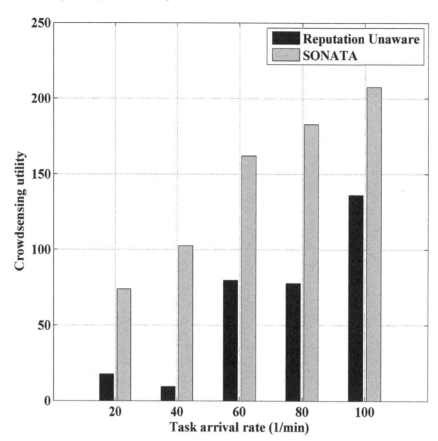

Table 3.Statistical trustworthiness in (Kantarci&Mouftah, 2014)

		20	40	60	80	100
Malicious users 3%	Manipulation Probability	4.8e-03	2.4e-03	4.1e-03	2.5e-03	3.5e-03
	Payment to malicious users	11	9.5	25	19.5	32.18
Malicious users 5%	Manipulation Probability	6.4e-03	7.6e-03	6.8e-03	5.5e-03	5.2e-03
	Payment to malicious users	13.33	29.75	39.64	38.66	54.12
Malicious users 7%	Manipulation Probability	8.5e-03	11e-02	8.5e-03	8.1e-03	8.6e-03
	Payment to malicious users	17	40.55	51.57	69.71	84.76

It is worthwhile mentioning that we are currently working on dynamically changing task arrival rates in the extension of this study. Under dynamic sensing task arrival rates, one of the most crucial challenges is the time for the user trustworthiness to converge. The trustworthiness of a malicious mobile device is expected to drop dramatically as soon as the mobile device reports altered sensing data since

Figure 9. Manipulation probability when 7% of the mobile device users are malicious

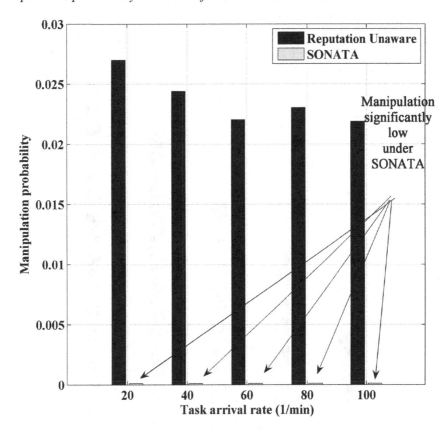

the number of connections who would detect malicious activity will increase as the sensing tasks and the size of the social network of the mobile device increase. Therefore, the mobile device will not be recruited anymore once its trustworthiness falls below a certain threshold. Thus, convergence of malicious users' trustworthiness values is expected to be faster than regular users.

CONCLUSION

Sensing-as-a-Service (S²aaS) has appeared as a promising solution with the advent of cloud computing and Internetof Things (IoT) paradigms. Smart cities can take advantage of crowdsensed datacollected, aggregated and analyzed through a cloud inspired model. Crowdsensing systems enable forming connected communities of mobile devices that provide their built-in sensors as a service for sensing several phenomena. Trustworthiness has been pointed out as an important challenge in crowdsensing systems since adversaries may lead to disinformation at the service requester site through manipulation of sensor readings. In this paper, we have proposed a crowdsensing framework in which trustworthiness assessment is based on negative and positive votes collected from dynamically formed social communities of mobile devices. We improve the reputation unaware mobile device recruitment by incorporating vote-based trustworthiness assessments via a dynamic social network structure. We have made an analogy between the adversary detection in crowdsensing systems and Sybil detection in social networks,

Figure 10. Payment to malicious users when 7% of the mobile device users are malicious

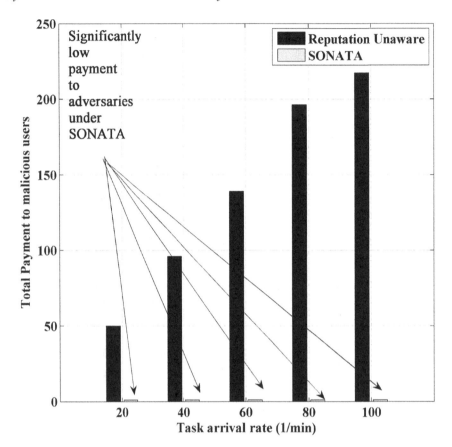

and have defined a dynamic social network topology upon the arrival of new sensing task requests. According to our proposal, mobile devices that have at least one common sensing task are connected over the social network topology, and those who are connected can vote for the trustworthiness of their neighbors. The proposed scheme recruits mobile devices based on an auction procedure where mobile devices join with their sensing costs. We have evaluated the performance of our proposed scheme via simulations, and through simulations we have shown that social network-aided trustworthiness assurance (SONATA) improves platform utility as the ratio of the malicious users increases. Furthermore, the proposed scheme SONATA significantly reduces the manipulation probability, as well as the payments made to the malicious users.

The extension of this work aims at addressing the scenarios where malicious users collaborate to mislead the end users during the monitored event in the region of interest. Furthermore, ongoing work also includes incorporation of other trustworthiness schemes and mobility-awareness into SONATA.

ACKNOWLEDGEMENT

This material is based upon work supported by the National Science Foundation (NSF) under Grant No. CNS1464273.

REFERENCES

Aihara, K., Imura, H., Takasu, A., Tanaka, Y., & Adachi, J. (2014). Crowdsourced Mobile Sensing for Smarter City Life. *IEEE 7th International Conference on Service-Oriented Computing and Applications (SOCA)*, (pp. 334--337).

Batty, M. (2014). Technologies for Urban and Spatial Planning: Virtual Cities and Territories. In N. Pinto, J. A. Tenedório, A. P. Antunes, & J. R. Cladera (Eds.), *Technologies for Urban and Spatial Planning: Virtual Cities and Territories* (pp. 1–13). Hershey, PA: IGI Global.

Benazzouz, Y., Munilla, C., Gunalp, O., Gallissot, M., & Gurgen, L. (2014). Sharing user IoT devices in the cloud. *IEEE World Forum on Internet of Things (WF-IoT)*, (pp. 373--374).

Cardone, G., Cirri, A., Corradi, A., Foschini, L., Ianniello, R., & Montanari, R. (2014, December). Crowdsensing in Urban Areas for City-Scale Mass Gathering Management: Geofencing and Activity Recognition. *IEEE Sensors Journal, 14*(12), 4185–4195. doi:10.1109/JSEN.2014.2344023

Cardone, G., Foschini, L., Bellavista, P., Corradi, A., Borcea, C., Talasila, M., & Curtmola, R. (2013, June). Fostering participaction in smart cities: A geo-social crowdsensing platform. *IEEE Communications Magazine, 51*(6), 112–119. doi:10.1109/MCOM.2013.6525603

Chon, Y., Kim, Y., & Cha, H. (2013). *Autonomous place naming system using opportunistic crowdsensing and knowledge from crowdsourcing. IEEE/ACM Information Processing in Sensor Networks* (pp. 19–30). IPSN.

Chourabi, H., Taewoo, N., Walker, S., Gil-Garcia, J. R., Mellouli, S., & Nahon, K. et al.. (2012). Understanding Smart Cities: An Integrative Framework.*45th Hawaii International Conference on System Sciences* (pp. 2289--2297). IEEE.

Clohessy, T., Acton, T., & Morgan, L. (2014). Smart City as a Service (SCaaS) - A Future Roadmap for E-Government Smart City Cloud Computing Initiatives. *IEEE/ACM 7th International Conference on Utility and Cloud Computing*, (pp. 836--842).

Dingli, A., & Seychell, D. (2012). Taking Social Networks to the Next Level.[IJDST]. *International Journal of Distributed Systems and Technologies, 3*(4), 24–33. doi:10.4018/jdst.2012100103

French, T., Bessis, N., Maple, C., & Asimakopoulou, E. (2012). Trust Issues on Crowd-Sourcing Methods for Urban Environmental Monitoring.[IJDST]. *International Journal of Distributed Systems and Technologies, 3*(1), 35–47. doi:10.4018/jdst.2012010103

Gong, X., Chen, X., Zhang, J., & Poor, V. H. (2014). From social trust assisted reciprocity (STAR) to utility-optimal mobile crowdsensing.*IEEE Global Conference on Signal and Information Processing (GlobalSIP)*, (pp. 742--745). doi:10.1109/GlobalSIP.2014.7032217

Hao, F., Mingjie, J., Geyong, M., & Yang, L. T. (2014). A trajectory-based recruitment strategy of social sensors for participatory sensing. *IEEE Network, 52*(12), 41–47.

He, Y., & Li, Y. (2013). Physical Activity Recognition Utilizing the Built-In Kinematic Sensors of a Smartphone. *International Journal of Distributed Sensor Networks, 2013*, 1–10.

Hu, X., Chu, T. H., Chan, H. C., & Leung, V. C. (2013). Vita: A Crowdsensing-Oriented Mobile Cyber-Physical System. *IEEE Transactions on Emerging Topics in Computing, 1*(1), 148–165. doi:10.1109/TETC.2013.2273359

Hu, X., Li, X., Ngai, E.-H., Leung, V. C., & Kruchten, P. (2014, June). Multidimensional context-aware social network architecture for mobile crowdsensing. *IEEE Communications Magazine, 52*(6), 78–87. doi:10.1109/MCOM.2014.6829948

Kantarci, B., & Mouftah, H. T. (2014). Mobility-aware trustworthy crowdsourcing in cloud-centric Internet of Things.*IEEE Symposium on Computers and Communications*, (pp. 1--6). doi:10.1109/ISCC.2014.6912581

Kantarci, B., & Mouftah, H. T. (2014). Trustworthy crowdsourcing via mobile social networks.*IEEE Global Communications Conference (GLOBECOM)*, (pp. 2905-2910).

Kantarci, B., & Mouftah, H. T. (2014, August). Trustworthy Sensing for Public Safety in Cloud-Centric Internet of Things. *IEEE Internet of Things Journal, 1*(4), 360–368. doi:10.1109/JIOT.2014.2337886

Kantarci, B., & Mouftah, H. T. (2015). Sensing as a Service in Cloud-Centric Internet of Things Architecture. In T. Soyata, Enabling Real-Time Mobile Cloud Computing through Emerging Technologies (p. (in press)). Hershey, PA: IGI Global. doi:10.4018/978-1-4666-8662-5.ch003

Meier, R., & Lee, D. (2011). Context-Aware Pervasive Services for Smart Cities. In K. Curran (Ed.), *Ubiquitous Developments in Ambient Computing and Intelligence: Human-Centered Applications* (pp. 1–16). Hershey: IGI Global. doi:10.4018/978-1-60960-549-0.ch001

Perera, C., Zaslavsky, A., Christen, P., & Georgapoulos, D. (2014). Sensing as a service model for smart cities supported by internet of things. *Transactions on Emerging Telecommunications Technologies, 25*(1), 81–93. doi:10.1002/ett.2704

Rijurekha, S. (2014). RasteyRishtey: A Social Incentive System to Crowdsource Road Traffic Information.*7th International Conference on Mobile Computing and Ubiquitous Networking (ICMU)*, (pp. 171--176).

Sheng, X., Tang, J., Xiao, X., & Xue, G. (2014, August). Leveraging GPS-Less Sensing Scheduling for Green Mobile Crowd Sensing. *IEEE Internet of Things Journal, 1*(4), 328–336. doi:10.1109/JIOT.2014.2334271

Sheng, X., Xiao, X., Tang, J., & Xue, G. (2013, October). Sensing as a Service: Challenges, Solutions and Future Directions. *IEEE Sensors Journal, 13*(10), 3733–3741. doi:10.1109/JSEN.2013.2262677

Tobe, Y., Usami, I., Kobana, Y., Takahashi, J., Lopez, G., & Thepvilojanapong, N. (2014). vCity Map: Crowdsensing Towards Visible Cities.*IEEE Sensors Conference*, (pp. 17--20).

Yang, D., Xue, G., Fang, X., & Tang, J. (2012). Crowdsourcing to Smartphones: Incentive Mechanism Design for Mobile Phone Sensing. *18th annual international conference on Mobile computing and networking (Mobicom)* (pp. 173--184). ACM.

Yhang, Z., Xue, J., Yang, X., Wang, X., & Dai, Y. (2015). VoteTrust: Leveraging Friend Invitation Graph to Defend against Social Network Sybils. *IEEE Transactions on Dependable and SecureComputing*(VoteTrust: Leveraging Friend Invitation Graph to Defend against Social Network Sybils), accepted.

Zhan, G., Shi, W., & Deng, J. (2012, March-April). Design and Implementation of TARF: A Trust-Aware Routing Framework for WSNs. *IEEE Transactions on Dependable and Secure Computing*, *9*(2), 184–197. doi:10.1109/TDSC.2011.58

Zhang, Y., Meratnia, N., & Havinga, P. (2010). 2nd Quarter). Outlier Detection Techniques for Wireless Sensor. *IEEE Communications Surveys and Tutorials*, *12*(2), 159–170. doi:10.1109/SURV.2010.021510.00088

This work was previously published in the International Journal of Distributed Systems and Technologies (IJDST), 7(1); edited by Nik Bessis, pages 59-78, copyright year 2016 by IGI Publishing (an imprint of IGI Global).

Section 4
Strategic Innovation and Data Management

Chapter 14
A Key to 5G Networks of Tomorrow

Aqeel ur Rehman
Hamdard University, Pakistan

Ahmar Murtaza
Hamdard University, Pakistan

Syed Muhammad Kashif Alam
Hamdard University, Pakistan

Iqbal Uddin Khan
Hamdard University, Pakistan

ABSTRACT

The emergence of mobile telephony increases the options of its deployment and utilization. As the research goes further, it also delivered Generations of Mobile Communication to us after rapid intervals of time. Each advancement is considers as the generation. Till now Forth Generation (4G) is in its maturity phase and researchers are planning to see 5G commercially around 2020. In upcoming Fifth Generation (5G), vision is to reduce latency typically it will be of less than 1ms, as the latency decrease one more thing will be achieved which can be named as Virtually Zero Distance. As the world is becoming the connected world, the availability of data on global network is going to be huge in size. In addition to that the new emerging concepts like Internet of Things (IoT) are giving boost to the requirement of big data storage and analysis. Internet of Things (IoT) is a concept of providing uniquely identifiable objects connectivity to Internet. This chapter is proposed to highlight the IoT concept and its requirements that are directly linked with the 5G Network technology services.

INTRODUCTION

What is IoT?

Nowadays, "Internet of Thing" (IoT) is one of the most famous topic in researcher's, business developers and IT industries because they are expecting more than 20 billion devices will be on internet by 2020 and their aim is to enable the interconnection between peoples as well as their environment things based on standardized communication protocols under the name of "Internet of Thing" (IoT). In other word, the monitoring of critical situations, remote management and the wish of keep in touch pushes multiple fields to adopt the terminology called IoT. The Internet of Things (IoT) is the emerging area for the interest of

DOI: 10.4018/978-1-5225-1832-7.ch014

researchers which provides a unique communication and remote control capabilities of monitoring and controlling to any physical or virtual objects having any shape and any size, anywhere, anytime and by any one via secured infrastructure of internet with evolving of existing and future technologies. The key of the IoT is that each and every thing which is laid under the term Electronics and can controlled may be connected to the cloud of network and can or may continuously transmit its status or data or receive the date to store or any instruction to be followed. As the above said lines reflects not only the vast area to be considered for development and advancement.

As the technology advances, many different platforms started to evolve with communication features. As we can observed on graph, that in past decade internet started to grow like an impulse. Integration of device sizes, appreciation of Wireless technologies, and growth in demand of palm top or hand held devices led us towards a though that we can have control of each and every electronic device if it can be connected to internet. Evolution of the Internet has occurred five tiers. As the internet is the network of networks, it begins from the connection of two computers and then with help of research and development advanced towards World Wide Web, i.e. huge numbers of computers are connected all together. Mobile-Internet is also a thick branch of internet providing platform to mobile devices to become the part of Internet. Then, via internet social networks emerged. And now, it is rapidly moving towards IoT, means connecting each and everyday objects to the Internet (Perera, Zaslavsky, Christen, & Georgakopoulos, 2014).

Available Wireless Technologies

As every field has its own requirements which may be of high data rate, every field has its own accessing techniques over RF, which may be WiFi, WiMax or any other guided and unguided standard. Similarly, there are numerous technologies and protocol standards will be unified in macro IoT and maximum adoption will be done via unified infrastructure of internet mobility, sensing network and medical field and many more, as all of them could has to transmit bulk amount of data in real time.

Furthermore, the emergence of mobile telephony increases the options of its deployment and utilizations, which pushes researches to increase the options and facilitates over the platform of communication and under the word mobility. As the research goes further, it also delivered Generations of Mobile Communications to us after rapid shit of time intervals. Starting from few character texting services towards the sharing and downloading of bulk data in Gigabytes has come to us. Each advancement is considers as the generation. Till now Forth Generation (4G) is in its maturity phase and researchers are planning to see 5G commercially around 2020.

Evolution of 5G

The sharing of information exhibits more constrains as the distance between communicating entities changes from far too far-off. These constrains includes the increase of latency per hop using single technology as well as the use of multiple technologies per transfer over RF platform.

5G technology, known as the 5th generation mobile technology, is the upcoming mobile communication technology standard. 5G is expected to be rollout in 2020. In upcoming Fifth generation (5G), vision is to reduce latency typically it will be of less than 1mSec, as the latency decrease one more thing will be achieved which can be named as Virtually Zero Distance. Along with the before points, high data rate will also available with RF platform independency. RF platform independency can be elaborated as the higher data rate will be available over any spectrum and any access technology.

Flat IP network will be the key for 5G network to be acceptable for all kind of technologies. Flat IP architecture provides a way to identify the devices using symbolic name instead of hierarchal addressing scheme used in traditional IP networks.

5G Network Architecture

5G Network is known as the Nanocore architecture (Patil, Patil, & Bhat, 2012) that is the convergence of i) Nano Technology, ii) Cloud Computing, and iii) All IP network. Figure 1 is showing the 5G network architecture.

5G mobile communication technology will enable mobile phones to access different wireless technology at the same time and the terminal will be able to combine different data flows from different technologies. Figure 2 is mentioning the 5G mobile network architecture.

Benefits of 5G Technology

Following are the key benefits of 5G technologies (VIPIN, July 20, 2014):

Figure 1. 5G Architecture: the nano core

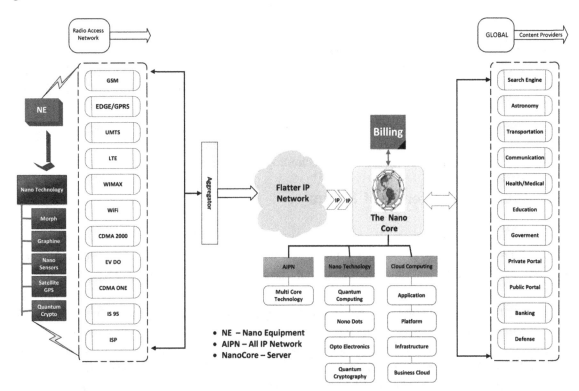

Figure 2. 5G Mobile Network Architecture

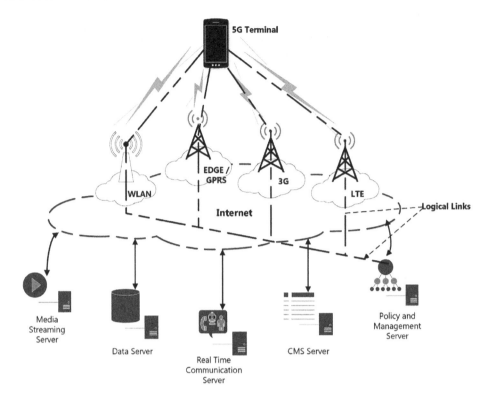

- High speed, high capacity, and low cost per bit
- Support interactive multimedia, voice, streaming video, Internet, and other broadband services
- Global access, service portability, and scalable mobile services
- Bi directional, accurate traffic statistics.
- Large broadcasting of data in Gigabit, supporting almost 65,000 connections
- Remote management for a user to get better and fast solution
- Policy based high quality services of 5G technology to avoid error

5th Generation and Internet of Things

As 5G is in the discussion phase, the concept of each and every device connected to internet, also known as Internet of Things is in research phase and will be granted a standard very soon. Under the roof of IoT, it is predicted that more than 20 billion devices will be the subset of the internet up to the year 2020 (Bassi et al., 2013). The internet enabled devices will be mostly from the field of medical and sensing networks as they are deployed in critical situations and areas. Just imagine the amount of traffic which will be generated by the predicted amount of devices connected to internet, which increases the importance of data collection in minimum latency, as data could be sensitive as well critical if it is transmitted from and patient or sensing network. The size of data bunch generated by any medical or sensing network node can vary and can be of large size with the condition of real time delivery. So all these predicted situations are promised to be solved and will be well entertained in 5G.

IoT VISION AND ARCHITECTURES

IoT Vision

In 1998 Kevin Ashton names the concept of connecting everything to internet, The Internet of Things. The scope of internet of things can be as vaster as much as we think about it (Bassi et al., 2013). As it is understood that the wider the scope of technology the more sophisticated and complex solutions required to heading problems, Which elaborated that each and every thing can and will be connected to internet. Internet of Things (IoT) is a huge domain, which connects any smart device with Internet using a dependable protocol and numerous information sensing equipment such as simple wireless senor may be including RFID, other infrared sensors, global positioning system (GPS), mobility and a huge data center or a web server or anything that can come under any processing limit and size that can be communicated to each other or to a specific device/thing or user by using any path/network or service (Zhang & Zhu, 2011). The larger the scale of Internet of thing the more vulnerable it becomes. The equipment, nodes or things in *IoT* may have many features to be considered and many core requirements shall be considered to develop a mature architecture of *IoT* platform (Bassi et al., 2013). The general view of Internet of things is illustrated in Figure 3.

We have a vision of IoT, referring ubiquitous computing that how and where it can be deployed. In the Figure 4 we have illustrated three broad areas under IoT Vision.

Figure 3. A General View of Internet of Things

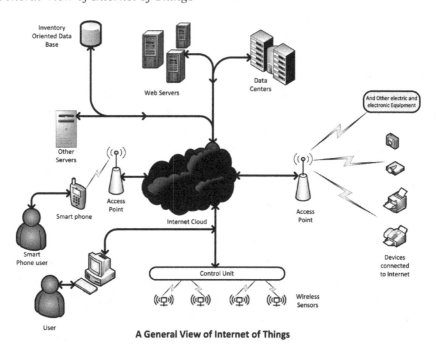

A General View of Internet of Things

Figure 4. Application Domains of IoT

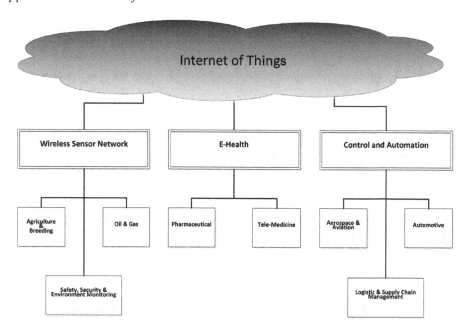

Wireless Sensor Network

Wireless Sensor Network (WSN) is a network comprising over miniaturized smart sensor devices to acquire the natural phenomena. Effective use of WSN may provide good monitoring and control solutions in almost every field of life. Following are some of the areas where WSN technology is in effective use:

- **Agriculture and Breeding:** To keep an eye to all physical and environmental condition to vast cultivated lands and on large number of animals is fairly impossible. To monitor all said conditions technology is deployed to collect our desired stats and to react in a reasonable time to avoid any loss or unwanted situation (Saint-Exupery & Antoine, 2009). The situation can be of extreme dryness, attack of insects, and interaction with viral disease of live stocks and critical health situation of animals and will lead to ward the catastrophe loss and increase of demand of relevant consumable.
- **Oil and Gas:** When talk about fuel and remote locations, one domain that must come in our mind is hunt of fossil fuel. To search and dig the deposit of fossil fuel required enormous amount of assets, human power and most important the finance. Any anomaly regarding aforesaid resources will not be easily bearable. To keep updated information of every instant and mobility, it required a platform which should be highly deliverable. Oil and Gas fields encompass various points to be monitored according to the maturity of the well. These monitoring points have sensors mounted like wire line tension force seniors, load cells, pressure transducers and various temperature and Hydro-carbon /gas sensors (Saint-Exupery & Antoine, 2009). It also includes the remote assets management to track down all assets on a particular site as well as keep update information of their condition, required maintenance of any section of any portable testing and digging units. So that can be reformed and required components and manpower could be delivered at site with in due time.

- **Logistics and Supply Chain:** Using RFID tags on each product, or on a bunch of each product (if product is cheaper than the cost of RFID tag) can make task of retail counter easier as well as it can also protect the item from un-fair mobility. Even the collection of data at retail counter can be exchanged to relevant manufactures to maintain the supply as per demand. Using low cost active/ Passive tags and sensors along or within various parcels and logistics can help owner or vendor to keep track of their goods (Saint-Exupery & Antoine, 2009). For product tracking from manufacturer, whole sale to retailer's storage can be done for sake of inventory and stock management.

Control and Automation

- **Aerospace and Aviation:** As in avionics, the word safety is far more prior than the word trust among avionic giants and costumers. An Air craft is in real a complete pack of Science, technology and engineering, which are molded together in form of modules. Each module is maintained in regular frequency but missing it caused disasters (Saint-Exupery & Antoine, 2009). By applying smart sensors in different modules of aircrafts a centralized server can keep update of their service logs and only permitted air craft will be allowed to take-off or to leave hanger. In any aircraft, there are various modules which can be mounted and un-mounted as an independent module. The tasks for those modules are to transmit specific data to air or to concern department, for example location transponder. In some unlike incidents, the flight recorded (black box) was unable to locate near site, but by applying IoT, a self-powered location transmitter can be added to it for rapid tracking.
- **Automotive:** The concepts of Vehicle to Vehicle (V2V) interaction and Vehicle to Infrastructure (V2I) interaction are the concept of safety and reliability which comes under the umbrella of IoT. V2V discusses the smart interaction of vehicles to avoid accidents and V2I encompasses the interaction of city infrastructure to vehicle interaction (Luigi, 2011). Utilizing the said concepts, the condition and functional report can be obtained by security and insurance companies. From day of manufacturing to date of sale and to the recent day every record of performance can be collected. As discussed earlier, V2V communication cannot only manage the flow of traffic but can also help any human, in case of any emergency.
- **Safety, Security and Environment Monitoring:** Identifiable devices can be used to mature the security of any apartment, factory or office. These devices may be implemented in lockers or bank safes and at doors of homes and apartments to ensure the access of right person. The environment monitoring system within any building can collect data from sensors outside that building to adjust the environment of that specific building using chillers and air conditioners (Saint-Exupery & Antoine, 2009). End to end transfer can be tracked in case of transfer of cash, weapons or any other valuable goods. Some wildlife researches can keep track and record of species they are researching on. Even explorers can be tracked in case of any emergency and the logs of temperature, height and other environmental quantities can be automatically transmitted while they are on their adventure or exploration trip.

E-Health

- **Pharmaceutical:** Talking about identifiable devices or tags can be placed on the drugs can be beneficial for patients, while storing the package in its cabinet and the smart cabinet can keep informing consumers of dosages and expiration date, and authenticity as well. This information can be shared by the manufactures and vendors of related drug(s).

- **Tele-Medicine:** Monitoring of critical patients is now easier as wearable and implantable sensors arrived. These sensors can continue transmit data of any patient over internet via control unit. The telemedicine or E-Health comes with issues of bulk data and in real time which can be available in upcoming generations of communication platforms. Some patients need to be observed critically, so doctor can keep himself updated by observing all graphs and reading on any android application.

IoT Architecture

As Internet of things is still in discussion phase, no mature architecture is proposed or standardized. For the reference we will consider the most resent published architecture for Internet of things (Bassi et al., 2013).

It is not standardized yet and still open for suggestions, discussion and for proposals from researchers. As a generic architecture of a communication model there are three basic layers as illustrated in Figure 5. Layer – 1 is Device layer, Layer – 2 is Functional layer and Layer – 3 is Application layer. The middle layer is responsible for distinguishing among other and Internet of things architecture, the actual issues resides inside layer – 2.

IoT – ARM 3.0

The IoT – ARM, consists of 3 basic blocks; i) The Reference Model, ii) The Architecture, and iii) The Guidelines. Figure 6 illustrates all constitute parts of ARM. Each block is discussed below in detail.

- **IoT Reference Model:** The IoT Reference Model is conforming to the OASIS reference model definition. It generates a common understanding of the IoT domain. Its description includes a

Figure 5. Generic Architecture of a Communication Model

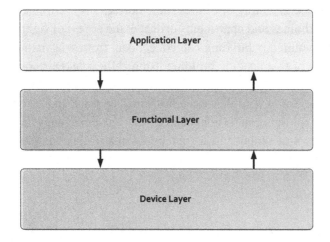

general exchange of knowledge related to the IoT domain, including an IoT Domain Model for the top-level description, an IoT Information Model which explains that how IoT knowledge is going to be molded, and an IoT Communication Model which provides a specific understanding about communication between many heterogeneous IoT devices and the Internet (Bassi et al., 2013).

- **IoT Reference Architecture:** It converge the focus on abstracted mechanisms rather than a consolidated applications, according to the concern of IoT stakeholders. All the abstracted perspectives are used according to the general literature and standards. The reference model can be used for deciding the working boundary for the researchers and analyzers. So that can limit the work and to give proper shape in their proposed schemes and architectures, in other words by reference model organization of IoT standard can easily be done.
- **The Guidelines:** The guidelines discuss how purposed Models, within the borders of reference model, views and perspectives can be concretely used. It aims at explaining the usage of the IoT ARM. One of the focused focus area of this guidance is to derive out domain-specific architectures from the ARM.
- **IoT – A and Functional Model:** IoT – A Architectural Reference Model wants to promote high level of interoperability needs for all levels including communication level, the service level and the knowledge levels across different platforms established on a common grounding. The IoT-A project considers that achieving those goals comes in two steps:
  - In establishing a common understanding of the IoT domain and
  - In providing to IoT system developers a common technical foundation and set of guidelines for deriving a concrete IoT system architecture

Both aspects are being captured within the IoT Architectural Reference Model.

IoT-A, the European Lighthouse Integrated Project, addresses the Internet-of-Things Architecture. It proposes the creation of an architectural reference model together with the definition of an initial set of key building blocks. Together they are envisaged as crucial foundations for fostering a future Internet of Things. Using an experimental paradigm, IoT-A will combine top-down reasoning about architectural principles and design guidelines with simulation and prototyping to explore the technical consequences of architectural design choices (Bassi et al., 2013).

Figure 6. IoT-A Architectural Reference Model

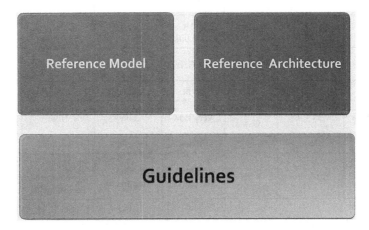

COMMUNICATION TECHNOLOGIES FOR IoT

In Table 1 (Aqeel-ur-Rehman, Mehmood, & Baksh, 2013; Brunnenmeyer, Mills, Patel, Suarez, & Kung, 2012; iDirect, 2014) four tiers of communication is presented which are currently available and possibly can be used in IoT to certain extent. Figure 7 illustrates that how possibly multiple technologies can be the part of IoT.

CHALLENGES ASSOCIATED WITH IoT

Multiple Environments

IoT primarily focuses on the sensing networks, electronics health and control and automation areas. The time will force the single sensing environments to hybrid environments. For understand we can say that hybrid environments can be partially health and partially control and automation. As to maintain the room temperature according to the need of the admitted patient in a hospital and will vary from patient

Table 1. Communication Technologies for IoT

	Wireless Personal Area Network (WPAN)				Wireless Local Area Network (WLAN)	Wireless Metropolitan Area Network (WMAN)	Wireless Wide Area Network (WWAN)	
	Bluetooth	**Zigbee**	**RF Link (RFID)**	**Z-Wave**	**WiFi**	**WiMax**	**Satellite**	**Cellular**
IEEE Std.	IEEE 802.15.1-3	IEEE 802.15.4	IEEE C95.1	Z-Wave Alliance	IEEE 802.11a/b/g/n	IEEE 802.16	IEEE Std. 521-2002	IEEE 802.21
Topology	Star	Mesh, Star, Tree	--	Mesh	Star	Star, Mesh	Star, Mesh and Hybrid	Star
Bandwidth	1 Mbps	250 Kpbs	18 MHz	900 MHz	Up to 54 Mbps	134 Mbps	27 MHz	200 KHz
Channel Bandwidth	1-2480 MHz	0.3- 2 MHz	--	868 MHz	<20 MHz	<20 MHz	6 MHz	25 KHz
Max. data Rate	0.72- 10 M bit/s	0.25 M bit/s	1 M bit/s	9600 bits or 40 kbits/s	54 M bit/s	1 G bit/s	1 M bit/s	200Kbps
Spectrum	2.4 GHz	2.4 GHz	2.4 GHz	2.4 GHz	2.4-5 GHz	3.5-10 GHz	Ka / Ku band	900 – 1800 MHz
Range	5-30 m	10-300 m	<3 m	30 m	4-20 m	20 Km	N/A	400 meters
Power Consumption	Very Low	Very Low	Very Low	Very Low	Low	High	Medium	Medium
Performance	Better	Good	Better	Better	Excellent	Excellent	Good	Better
Application Area	Ad-Hoc Network	E-Health	WSN	Home Automation	Building Automation	Residential and enterprise environments	Global	Mobility

Figure 7. Concept of Multiple Technologies in IoT

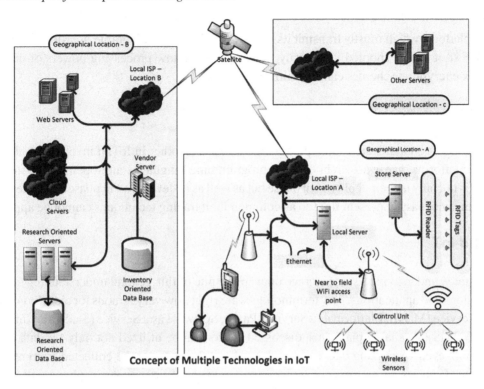

to patient, more over for an example an intelligent building management system can adjust the inner condition of building including light and temperature according or in correspondence of sensors providing data form outside the buildings. So in these types of deployments temperature sensors, humidity sensors and air flow sensors will vary according to the place of installation as a single system can acquire multiple standards of sensors for inside and outside installations.

Connectivity

Connectivity of devices among themselves as well as with the infrastructure will be a great challenge as the devices will be of different types and surly will be at different locations (Chase, 2013). The different types of devices will present heterogeneity in IoT domain and the demand for a platform to resolve heterogeneity will increase. Although the there are various solutions are available but the latency and connectivity issues may be resolve in upcoming 5G as promised.

Power Critical

As disused in earlier heading that heterogeneity is challenge to IoT, so heterogeneity comes as devices implanted or deployed in different areas and the power supply to them is critical, as researchers and engineers focus on the low power issues they have to compromise over encryption schemes, processing powers and connectivity techniques. In this regards to have all optimized the power consumption is very critical if sensors are planted within human body or deployed in some remote areas to work for their assessed time (Chase, 2013).

Security

As IoT is a platform which mostly transmit its data over RF, so it is vulnerable in at-least two ways, one is as it is RF so it can be spoofed very easily, secondly due to low processing powers of devises large and complex encryption schemes cannot utilized efficiently.

Complexity

Multiple layers of communications and platforms overlap each other in IoT. It involves number of communication platforms, hardware architectures, programming languages and operating systems. So its complexity is not only in their deployment phase but as well as in development phase as a generic application platform is not easy at present time so as common fault tracing techniques cannot be applied in IoT.

Cloud and IoT

Cloud is so far is understood as some storage on web, despite of this general understanding cloud has its own vast visions and applications. Few terminologies are right now very famous for cloud computing like Metal as a Service (MaaS), Platform as a Service (PaaS), Software as a Service (SaaS) and Infrastructure as a Service (IaaS). Available platforms, discussed earlier can be utilized not only for data storage but analyzing data, even visualizing data any time anywhere. As Data can be collected from remote locations no mater from sensor networks or transmitted / uploaded from any smart phone will be captured on cloud for further processing and analyzing.

Data Flood

As we can understand that the huge amount of smart devices will come under umbrella of IoT, So as we must prepare for the flood of data on internet which will not only be generated by the cellular or smart phone uses but also but the sensors deployed as wireless sensors or in Tele-medicine field. As the flow of data increases it will bottle neck the systems as well as may no full fill the requirement of Just in Time. In the currently deployed infrastructure it is not possible but 5G has promise to handle it too.

APPLICATIONS OF IoT IN DIFFERENT SECTORS OF LIFE

Some of possible applications in different sectors of life are as follows:

E-Health

Smart sensors may be worn by people to for location tracking, health, or for fitness record and may be by sports men on their athletic activities to monitor them (Anderson & Rainie, 2014). The sensors may be implanted, wearable or deployed to nay physical location will be used to monitor the patients or employees where special assistance needed. The technologies are getting mature with the passage of time we are having more advanced sensors and their control unit much smaller and cheaper.

Smart Homes

Smart homes encompass all type of monitoring what a human can do. Remote management of household facilities including lighting, air conditioning, security and energy management will be adopted by most homes on a series of intricate networks (Anderson & Rainie, 2014).

The embedded and smart appliances will assist the keeper to maintain garden and kitchen. Most of the appliances are set on their timer these days, but will not be in near future all will be managed according to your setting also known as *Profile*.

Smart Transportation

Smart Transportation is a concept under umbrella of Internet of things. It is also discussed as IoV, The Internet of Vehicles. The concept of IoV, is an advanced form of Telematics. Telematics was introduced as fleet management technique used for transportation purpose and in Formula one cars (Gerla, Lee, Pau, & Lee, 2014). This will be the part of a complex adopted and integrated network system of any smart city. This will be able to connect multiple persons within their transport or different locomotives with each other to share information of multiple locations within any city. The merging of technology includes statistics communications, environmental protection, energy conservation, and safety. To gain prospective ratio in this emerging market, achievement of core technologies and proposed standards will be vital to securing a calculated advantage. However, the integration of the IoV with other infrastructures should be as important as the building of the IoV technologies themselves. As an outcome of these thoughts, the IoV will become an integral part of the largest Internet of Things (IoT) infrastructure by its completion as per recommendation. It must be emphasized as prime, that collaboration and interconnection between the transportation sector and other sectors (such as energy, health-care, environment, manufacturing, and agriculture) will be the next step in IoV development.

The Internet of Vehicles will encompasses, establishment of Ad Hoc networks for stats sharing and communication among multiple vehicles or drivers, communication could be via phones within any vehicle to another vehicle. IoV will also obtain several services through Ad-Hoc group, which may involve multiple peoples and smart computing and various environments and emergencies. As a whole, connectivity among multiple vehicles will allow every vehicle (node) in that specific network to share their data of electronic sensors, another communication platform like cellular network (any node can allow hop of data from other node within any established network), share traffic's status, inform or ask about current location, in emergency vehicles like ambulances and fire tenders situation can be monitored, environment and climate conditions can also be shared among all (Shengguang, Lin, Yuanshuo, & Rucai, 2013). Furthermore, any vehicle can transmit its specifications like License plate number, Identification specs and driving license status of a driver, over internet or any smart check point or Toll stops. Applications of IoV in some practical and beneficial areas are discussed below:

Practical Areas of IoV

There is variety of areas and modes of IoV deployment in vehicle based environment. The solicitations of IoV or vehicle based communications speeded from safety to comfort and from commercial to entertainment purpose.

Below is the discussion on the three broad areas observed in emerging vehicle oriented, internet based applications and offers a broad vision on drifts and developments toward an intelligent vehicle network and create impression on the autonomous vehicle theory and its upcoming industry (Gerla, Lee, Pau, & Lee, 2014; Shengguang, Lin, Yuanshuo, & Rucai, 2013).

Presented Systems of IoV

Development towards ubiquitous IoV schemes will need to be conducted in stages, beginning with low-risk, simple applications, and learning from the outcomes of those to plans and design widespread systemic organizations, while allowing significant time for population adaptation and regulatory management systems to be developed. As an example, computer-calibrated control of vehicle movements and collision avoidance systems would be verified and improved in closed or control environments, such as warehouses, then implemented more extensively between specialized driverless vehicles on designated roads, before wide deployment to public and private transport for intact cities. Data linkages would start with basic information interchange, such as traffic monitoring or reporting on vehicular emissions, passenger numbers, cargo loadings, locations or available travel routes, before progressing to two-way telemetry, active traffic management and external control of vehicle functions.

Accessible IoV Data as a Source to Permit Comprehensive Research

The data groups produced by functioning IoV systems will be ironic and varied, and will establish a valuable resource in their own right. For this, the data has to be measured not as a 'replaceable' or 'throwaway' product to meet immediate needs of IoV users, but as a gathering economic and scientific resource, with many possible future users. Such massive data groups (occasionally labeled 'Big Data') can provide a foundation for researchers in many other disciplines, not only for the advancements and development of IoV systems, or the observing and supervision of vehicles, traffic, road systems and their economic impacts or industrial progress and development.

Through their nature, productivity and steadiness, the emergent of IoV data groups will similarly update research into areas as dissimilar as human conduct and social sciences, urban policy, state security, medication and epidemiology, inhabitants dynamics, geo-political capital distribution and economic development, weathercasting, market retorts to publicity and price setting, resource and utilities managing, food trading, exhibiting the spread of aggressive plants, pathogens and pests, freight logistics, tourism movements, planning of education systems, analysis of media feeding and propagation, agricultural development, and the fundamental mathematics of complex dynamic structures.

The cumulative remunerations of access to IoV data in these other economically important phases of research may be analogous to, or even exceed the direct economic benefits of IoV solicitation.

Promotion of Integration of IoV plus Vehicles

By means of joint mutual laboratory, values of IoV in safety and economic performance can be further employed. Multinational industry-university-research collaboration should be boosted to speed up the revolutionized and upgrading of automobile industry.

Smart Cities

Smart city is well-defined by IBM as the use of statistics and communication technology to intellect, examine and fit in the key information of core systems in running cities. At the same time, smart city can make intellectual reaction to different kinds of needs, together with daily occupation, ecological protection, public protection and city facilities, industrial and commercial accomplishments (Su, Li, & Fu, 2011).

Smart cities have been the chat of the town in residential executive institutions and associations of cities. Unluckily, the span is being used in an abundant approach by city officials and technology dealers, clouding the vision on what it actually takes to develop a smart city. This research plans to go beyond debates on the definition of the smart city and the propaganda connected to the idea of smart city. It is converging explicitly on the organizational challenges for a metropolitan management that originate with a smart city ambition – a much needed insight for cities that want to make the most of the smart city concept and alter the fabric of the metropolitan management accordingly. Present research on premeditated organizational transformation summaries that authority will have to balance control with empowerment, teamwork and collaboration will have to take on more open forms, business processes will be co-constructed with an endorsing community outside of the organization and will, very likely, involve unceasing improvement and conducting tests, and finally the general cultural stance towards the acceptance and adoption of technology will necessarily have to be one of 'want to' use and capitalize in the technology use instead of 'have to', meaning that experimentation is required. The concluding puts motivational issues of all the parties that are involved in the smart city ecosystem central to the success of that ecosystem. In sum, the supposition is that the actors that design and carry out the organizational transformation in smart cities, will have to vigorously adjust their design, planning, and control of organizational change to reflect the environment perspective and its key success factors (Van den Bergh & Viaene, 2015).

There might be a number of topics of interest that could be able to serve to well understand the influence of the smart city motivation, and in what way to turn it into truth that are discussed below. The subsequent observations are noteworthy for any smart city participant. In particular, focuses are put on the effects from a city administration standpoint, as no architecture is specifically for smart city concept.

These years, by way of the impression of "smart planet" being drove forward, smart city, smart grid and smart enterprises have been projected as important parts of smart planet in succession. Smart city, as not only a distinctive application of smart planet, but also one of the most popular topics and the most cutting-edge issues, has caused extensive concern. In most recent years, from London to Taipei, from New York to Singapore, one by one, the construction-project of smart city (originally known as the wireless digital city or wireless city) is the same as the inspiration, increasing around the globe.

Smart city, the essential strategy of IBM, primarily emphases on applying the next-generation information technology to all walks of life, set in sensors and equipment to hospitals, power grids, railways, bridges, tunnels, roads, buildings, water systems, dams, oil and gas pipelines and other objects in every corner of the world, and forming the "Internet of Things" via the Internet. Then the Internet of Things can be integrated through super computers and cloud computing. In this case, people can accomplish production and life in a more meticulous and dynamic way, achieving the state of worldwide intelligence and in the end reach;

"Internet + Internet of Things = Smart Planet" (Su, Li, & Fu, 2011)

In brief, "Smart City" is the concrete approach of "Smart Planet" applying to detailed region, succeeding the informational and integrated administration of metropolises. It can also be said to be an operative combination of smart organization concepts, smart construction methods, smart administration methods, and smart expansion methodologies. Through the digital grid management of municipal layout, resources, environment, economic, social and other systems, as well as the digital and informational handling and application of urban frame and elementary environment, we can achieve intellectual urban administration and facilities, in this manner promote the more proficient, more convenient and pleasant operation of modern metropolises.

City and metropolitan surroundings represent puzzling social environments which encompass local government, citizens and organization units (Clohessy, Acton, & Morgan, 2014). Currently these units are experiencing explicit requirements concerning to striking themes such as business and employment formation, sustainable development, energy and water, public welfare, environment, healthcare, education and public services, all of which are, in some form or another, are being progressively assisted and supported by ICT (Information Communication Technologies). Parallel to these necessities, the latest unsettled global economic decline is increasingly employing pressure on metropolises to cut budgets resulting in damaging effects not only on the maintenance and advancement of existing ICT infrastructure and facilities but also on future modernization polices. Nevertheless, the perception of a smart city, also known in the appearances of intelligent city, information city, digital city, e-city and virtual city, has been acknowledged as being a classic example of a response to discourse the current and future multifaceted challenges of aggregate resource proficiency, reducing releases, sustainable health care facilities for ageing residents, empowering youth and join in basic elements (Clohessy, Acton, & Morgan, 2014).

The IoT's rooted in the smart homes yield circumstantial information, which is logically managed by the smart homes. However, taking the next step by uniting the smart homes into one large organic unit arrange for basis for evolving fresh services and new infrastructures where the smart homes are the information providers handled in a new communication theory.

By means of Cloud of Things (CoT) in this situation to incorporate the smart homes into a smart city concept produces new bearable service opportunities, creates a foundation for refining the quality of life for populates, and it forms different means of implementing municipal control (Skouby & Lynggaard, 2014). In this revelation the Cloud of Things technology is an animated player because it handles the massive sum of information produces by the IoT based entities. In simple expressions a Cloud of Things is a group of possessions and calculation know-hows interconnected by the Internet. For smart cities uniting IoT and Cloud of Things (CoT) is critical, as this consent IoT data to be processed and deposited. This radical smart city frame presents a numeral amount of experiments spaced out from the growth of a 5G system. The IoT devices exhibits challenges as they require interconnecting with each other (machine to machine communication); they need to interconnect with the cloud services which assemble big-data, and they need to manipulate complex data using artificial intelligence. To handle these encounters with the massive amount of data involved, 5G technologies are required. Initially, the M2M interconnection have need of scalable and resourceful radio accommodations like cognitive radios (5G) which are able to assign bandwidth as per requirement, capable to handle high interference points, and able to conserve power by adjusting resources dynamically. Furthermore, uploading big-data to the cloud services involves considerable bandwidth with an inconsequential delay, i.e. it must be possible to offer mined big-data services in real time. 5G technologies are predicted to support this. Lastly, processing compound data using Artificial Intelligence is stimulating because it is allocated on the source constrained IoT devices. Hence, in order to handle complex IoT outlines an Advanced Artificial Intelligence (AAI) system is desired. This Advanced Artificial Intelligence system can be implemented as a disseminated interface between the IoTs, the smart home artificial intelligence systems, and the artificial intelligence systems obtainable as cloud services, where Cloud of Things is the integrating technology (refer to Figure 8). An IoT device comprises of an intelligent core and a M2M communication interface. The intelligent core is a source reserved device which offers Artificial Intelligence processing capability and a M2M interface which handles 5G based IoT communication (refer to Figure 9). In future, the communicating IoTs, the smart home servers, and the cloud services establish a Ubiquitous Network which proposition Ubiquitous connectivity's (Skouby & Lynggaard, 2014).

Figure 8. Advanced ICT Based Infrastructure for Future Smart Cities

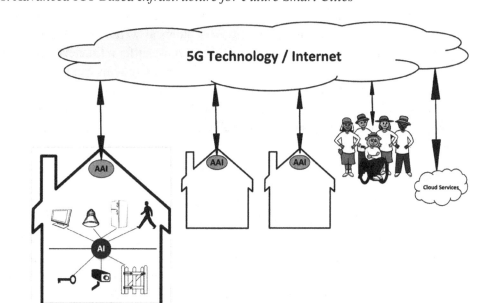

Figure 9. 5G Communication Concept

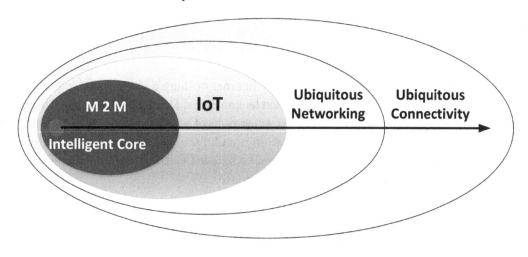

Communities

GPS management system will be more advanced along with proper deployment of IoT, Communities and their surroundings their neighborhoods and associated entities will be connected via smart planning. The surveillance within communities will be done more carefully to provide and promote a safer environment for families. Transportation infrastructure can become more deliverable (in time) along with better safety measures (Anderson & Rainie, 2014). Even more facilities given in any area of city like water distribution and its management will be done through a smart system and can simultaneously it will approximately eliminates the possible wasting of the natural resources.

Business and Commerce

Corporate sectors, businesses, organizations and other financial sectors rely on multiple systems to maintain and monitor their sales, records, invoices and many others as well as do the risk analysis over a defined period of time. If the system of any company fails, it must suffer a financial setback at every time re-occurrence. Along with an IoT connected system, a fusion of systems can be created with the involvement of the micro or subsystems, can potentially create a stronger system (Anderson & Rainie, 2014). Still there will be the risk; the insubstantial profit can hit the roof. Time and energy will be less consumed so the cost can be significantly suppressed if all factors of a company are regularly monitored via verbal communication or statistical collection either by predefined interval or on a requirement.

Environment

It is always the controversial topic, many of the valued researchers and analysts are in the favor to possible restoring and preservation of our mother planet's environment (Anderson & Rainie, 2014). A live stream of natural measurements can be collected to predict upcoming changes or updates on pre-existing reforms. Researchers have vision that there will be real-time feeds from sensors in remote fields, oceans, forests, and other urban areas about the pollution (environmental, sound and light) levels, harvesting field's information, and extraction of resource that will allow the closer monitoring of issues and problems (Anderson & Rainie, 2014). Atypically, a technological advancement may be just the right thing the environmental experts could use to produce more accurate results.

SUMMARY

In the above chapter, we have discussed the term of internet of thing and its available platform along with the currently available wireless communication technologies. Furthermore, we have discussed the limits of currently available and recently deployed generations of wireless technologies. Moving toward 5G we have enlightened the key features available in it and discussed the necessity of 5G for proper deployment of IoT as its vision, also discussed the areas where IoT can be deployed with the requirement of high speed data link for real time or just in time response.

REFERENCES

Anderson, J., & Rainie, L. (2014). *Digital Life in 2025: The Internet of Things Will Thrive By 2025*. Pew Research Center.

Aqeel-ur-Rehman, Mehmood, K., & Baksh, A. (2013). Communication Technology That Suits IoT-A Critical Review. In Wireless Sensor Networks for Developing Countries (pp. 14-25). Springer.

Bassi, A., Bauer, M., Fiedler, M., Kramp, T., Kranenburg, R., Lange, S., & Meissner, S. (2013). *Enabling Things to Talk: Designing IoT Solutions with the IoT Architectural Reference Model*. Springer. doi:10.1007/978-3-642-40403-0

Brunnenmeyer, D., Mills, S., Patel, S., Suarez, C., & Kung, L.-B. (2012). *Ka and Ku Operational Considerations for Military SATCOM Applications*. Paper presented at the The 2012 Military Communications Conference – Track 4 – System Perspectives, Milcom. doi:10.1109/MILCOM.2012.6415563

Chase, J. (2013). *The Evolution of the Internet of Things*. Dallas, TX: Texas Instruments Incorporated.

Clohessy, T., Acton, T., & Morgan, L. (2014). Smart City as a Service (SCaaS): A Future Roadmap for E-Government Smart City Cloud Computing Initiatives. In *Proceedings of the 2014 IEEE/ACM 7th International Conference on Utility and Cloud Computing*. doi:10.1109/UCC.2014.136

Gerla, M., Lee, E.-K., Pau, G., & Lee, U. (2014). *Internet of vehicles: From intelligent grid to autonomous cars and vehicular clouds*. Paper presented at the IEEE World Forum on Internet of Things (WF-IoT). Available at http://www.idirect.net/Company/Resource-Center/Satellite-Basics.aspx

Luigi, G. (2011). Vehicle-to-Vehicle/Vehicle-to-Infrastructure Control. In T. Samad & A. M. Annaswamy (Eds.), The Impact of Control Technology (p. 211). IEEE Control Systems Society. Available at http://ieeecss.org/sites/ieeecss.org/files/documents/IoCT-Part4-13VehicleToVehicle-LR.pdf

Patil, S., Patil, V., & Bhat, P. (2012). A review on 5G technology. *International Journal of Engineering and Innovative Technology*, *1*(1), 26–30.

Perera, C., Zaslavsky, A., Christen, P., & Georgakopoulos, D. (2014). Context aware computing for the internet of things: A survey. *IEEE Communications Surveys and Tutorials*, *16*(1), 414–454. doi:10.1109/SURV.2013.042313.00197

Saint-Exupery, D., & Antoine. (2009). Internet of things, strategic research roadmap. *Surrey: Internet of Things Initiative*.

Shengguang, L., Lin, T., Yuanshuo, Z., & Rucai, Z. (2013). *Internet of Things for special materials transportation vehicles*. Paper presented at the IEEE International Conference on Green Computing and Communications (GreenCom), and IEEE Internet of Things (iThings/CPSCom) and IEEE Cyber, Physical and Social Computing. doi:10.1109/GreenCom-iThings-CPSCom.2013.351

Skouby, K. E., & Lynggaard, P. (2014). *Smart home and smart city solutions enabled by 5G, IoT, AAI and CoT services*. Paper presented at the International Conference on Contemporary Computing and Informatics (IC3I).

Su, K., Li, J., & Fu, H. (2011). *Smart city and the applications*. Paper presented at the International Conference on Electronics, Communications and Control (ICECC). doi:10.1109/ICECC.2011.6066743

Van den Bergh, J., & Viaene, S. (2015). *Key Challenges for the Smart City: Turning Ambition into Reality.* Paper presented at the 48th Hawaii International Conference on System Sciences (HICSS).

VIPIN. (2014). *5G Mobile Technology wiki - wikisedia.* Retrieved May 2015, from http://wikisedia.com/5g-mobile-technology-wiki/

Zhang, H., & Zhu, L. (2011). *Internet of Things: Key technology, architecture and challenging problems.* Paper presented at the IEEE International Conference on Computer Science and Automation Engineering (CSAE).

ADDITIONAL READING

Aggarwal, C. C., Ashish, N., & Sheth, A. (2013). *The internet of things: A survey from the data-centric perspective Managing and mining sensor data* (pp. 383–428). Springer.

Ahn, S.-H., Kim, N.-U., & Chung, T.-M. (2014). *Big data analysis system concept for detecting unknown attacks.* Paper presented at the 2014 16th International Conference on Advanced Communication Technology (ICACT). doi:10.1109/ICACT.2014.6778962

Athreya, A. P., & Tague, P. (2013). *Network self-organization in the internet of things.* Paper presented at the 2013 10th Annual IEEE Communications Society Conference on Sensor, Mesh and Ad Hoc Communications and Networks (SECON).

Atzori, L., Iera, A., & Morabito, G. (2010). The internet of things: A survey. *Computer Networks, 54*(15), 2787–2805. doi:10.1016/j.comnet.2010.05.010

Bandyopadhyay, D., & Sen, J. (2011). Internet of things: Applications and challenges in technology and standardization. *Wireless Personal Communications, 58*(1), 49–69. doi:10.1007/s11277-011-0288-5

Barnaghi, P., Wang, W., Henson, C., & Taylor, K. (2012). Semantics for the Internet of Things: Early progress and back to the future.[IJSWIS]. *International Journal on Semantic Web and Information Systems, 8*(1), 1–21. doi:10.4018/jswis.2012010101

Bin, S., Yuan, L., & Xiaoyi, W. (2010). *Research on data mining models for the internet of things.* Paper presented at the 2010 International Conference on Image Analysis and Signal Processing (IASP).

Chun-Wei, T., Chin-Feng, L., Ming-Chao, C., & Yang, L. T. (2014). Data Mining for Internet of Things: A Survey. *IEEE Communications Surveys and Tutorials, 16*(1), 77–97. doi:10.1109/SURV.2013.103013.00206

Costa-Pérez, X., Festag, A., Kolbe, H.-J., Quittek, J., Schmid, S., Stiemerling, M., & Van Der Veen, H. (2013). Latest trends in telecommunication standards. *Computer Communication Review, 43*(2), 64–71. doi:10.1145/2479957.2479968

Gubbi, J., Buyya, R., Marusic, S., & Palaniswami, M. (2013). Internet of Things (IoT): A vision, architectural elements, and future directions. *Future Generation Computer Systems, 29*(7), 1645–1660. doi:10.1016/j.future.2013.01.010

Koch, C. (2013). *Compilation and synthesis in big data analytics Big Data* (pp. 6–6). Springer.

Labrinidis, A., & Jagadish, H. (2012). Challenges and opportunities with big data. *Proceedings of the VLDB Endowment, 5*(12), 2032–2033. doi:10.14778/2367502.2367572

Madden, S. (2012). From databases to big data. *IEEE Internet Computing, 16*(3), 0004-0006.

Mainetti, L., Patrono, L., & Vilei, A. (2011). *Evolution of wireless sensor networks towards the internet of things: A survey.* Paper presented at the 2011 19th International Conference on Software, Telecommunications and Computer Networks (SoftCOM).

Mayer-Schönberger, V., & Cukier, K. (2013). *Big data: A revolution that will transform how we live, work, and think.* Houghton Mifflin Harcourt.

Patil, P. S., Rao, S., & Patil, S. B. (2011). *Optimization of data warehousing system: Simplification in reporting and analysis.* Paper presented at the IJCA Proceedings on International Conference and workshop on Emerging Trends in Technology (ICWET).

Sagiroglu, S., & Sinanc, D. (2013). *Big data: A review.* Paper presented at the 2013 International Conference on Collaboration Technologies and Systems (CTS). doi:10.1109/CTS.2013.6567202

Said, O., & Masud, M. (2013). Towards internet of things: Survey and future vision. *International Journal of Computer Networks, 5*(1), 1–17.

Schroeder, R., & Meyer, E. (2012). *Big data: what's new. Internet, Politics, Policy 2012: Big Data.* Big Challenges.

Shi, W., & Liu, M. (2011). *Tactics of handling data in internet of things.* Paper presented at the 2011 IEEE International Conference on Cloud Computing and Intelligence Systems (CCIS). doi:10.1109/CCIS.2011.6045121

Stankovic, J. A. (2014). Research Directions for the Internet of Things. *Internet of Things Journal, IEEE, 1*(1), 3–9. doi:10.1109/JIOT.2014.2312291

Villars, R. L., Olofson, C. W., & Eastwood, M. (2011). Big data: What it is and why you should care. White Paper, IDC.

Whitmore, A., Agarwal, A., & Da Xu, L. (2014). The Internet of Things—A survey of topics and trends. *Information Systems Frontiers,* 1–14.

KEY TERMS AND DEFINITIONS

Big Data: Huge Quantity of Data generated by Smart Devices.

Cloud Computing: The practice of using a network of remote servers hosted on the Internet to store, manage, and process data.

Cognitive Radio: An adaptive, intelligent radio and network technology that can automatically detect available channels in a wireless spectrum and its attributes.

CoT: Cloud of Things.

5G: 5th generation mobile networks.

IBM: The International Business Machines Corporation, an American multinational technology and consulting corporation.

Internet of Things: Global Network of Smart Devices.

IoT: Standard Abbreviation of Internet of Things.

IoV: Standard Abbreviation of Internet of Vehicles.

M2M: Machine to Machine.

V2I: Vehicle to Infrastructure.

V2V Communication: The wireless transmission of data between motor vehicles.

Wireless Sensor Network: Wireless network consisting of spatially distributed autonomous devices using sensors.

WSN: Standard Abbreviation of Wireless Sensor Networks.

This work was previously published in Self-Organized Mobile Communication Technologies and Techniques for Network Optimization edited by Ali Diab, pages 237-258, copyright year 2016 by Information Science Reference (an imprint of IGI Global).

Chapter 15
Internet of Things Applications:
Current and Future Development

Mahmoud Elkhodr
Western Sydney University, Australia

Seyed Shahrestani
Western Sydney University, Australia

Hon Cheung
University of Western Sydney, Australia

ABSTRACT

The Internet of Things (IoT) brings connectivity to about every objects found in the physical space. It extends connectivity not only to computer and mobile devices but also to everyday objects. From connected fridges, cars and cities, the IoT creates opportunities in numerous domains. This chapter briefly surveys some IoT applications and the impact the IoT could have on societies. It shows how the various application of the IoT enhances the overall quality of life and reduces management and costs in various sectors.

INTRODUCTION

The Internet of Things (IoT) is the future of the Internet. It provides societies, communities, governments, and individuals with the opportunity to connect and obtain services over the Internet wherever they are and whenever they want. The IoT enhances communications on the Internet among not only people, but also things. The IoT introduces a new concept of communications which extends the existent interactions between human and computer's applications to things. Things are objects of the physical world (physical things) or of the information world (virtual things). Things are capable of being identified and integrated into the communication networks. Physical things such as industrial robots, products and electrical equipment, are capable of being sensed, actuated and connected to the Internet. More specifically, a physical thing can be described as a physical object equipped with a device that provides the capability of connecting this physical object to the Internet. The Inter-

DOI: 10.4018/978-1-5225-1832-7.ch015

national Telecommunication Union (ITU) defines a device in the IoT as a piece of equipment with the mandatory capabilities of communications, and the optional advanced capabilities of sensing and actuating (ITU, 2005). On the other hand, virtual things are not necessarily physical or tangible objects. They can exist without any association with a physical thing. Examples of virtual things are multimedia contents (Francesco, Li, Raj, & Das, 2012), and web services which are capable of being stored, processed, shared and accessed over the Internet. Notwithstanding this, a virtual thing may be used as a representation of a physical thing as well. For instance, most of today's computer databases and applications use some sort of virtual representation of physical entities i.e. the use of objects or classes in object oriented programing approaches (Rumbaugh, Blaha, Premerlani, Eddy, & Lorensen, 1991). Therefore, communications in the IoT can occur between not only the users and things, but also exclusively between things. This includes "physical things" to "physical things" communications, "virtual things" to "virtual things" communications, and "physical things" to "virtual things" communications. This heterogeneity of communications extends computation and connectivity on the Internet to anything, anyplace and anytime. As a result, the IoT is expected to be seen everywhere and in numerous application domains, such as manufacturing, smart cities, agriculture and breeding, environmental management, smart homes, and in a variety of service sectors among many others.

From a networking perspective, the IoT can be described as a heterogeneous network that combines together several wired and wireless networks, including low-power wireless networks and personal area networks, with an increasingly complex structure (Elkhodr, Shahrestani, & Cheung, 2014). This heterogeneous network connects a mixture of devices together. It encompasses devices which connect to the Internet using various types of wireless and LAN technologies such as Wi-Fi, RFID, ZigBee, Bluetooth, and 3G or 4G technologies among other evolving communication technologies.

The term IoT, while it may sound odd, was first coined in 1999 by the founders of the original MIT Auto-ID Center Kevin Ashton (Ashton, 22 July 2009). Auto-ID refers to any broad class of identification technologies used in the industry to automate, reduce errors, and increase efficiency. These technologies include barcodes, smart cards, sensors, voice recognition, and biometrics. Therefore, the initial vision of the IoT was to tag physical objects, using RFID tags, and to uniquely identify these objects using RFID transponders or readers. RFID technology has enabled users to identify and track objects within a relatively small networked environment e.g. within a warehouse. As Neil Gershenfield noted as early as 2000, the cost of individual RFID tags had dropped below a one cent, making their adoption within diverse business areas not just technically possible but economically feasible as well (Neil, 2000).

Nowadays, the IoT has grown from RFID tags to a global infrastructure of connected things. The current advance in technologies has extended the vision of the IoT by encompassing other technologies such as sensor networks. The IoT has now more potential to provide an intelligent platform for the collaborations of distributed things via local-area wireless and wired networks, and/or via a wide-area of heterogeneous and interconnected networks such as the Internet. This is inspired by not only the success of RFID technology, but by the advance of wireless communication technologies and their wide range and low-power consumption capabilities.

Consequently, the availability of information coming from non-traditional computer devices in the digital world will, in great parts, lead to improving the quality of life. If the IoT spreads to all sectors of the daily life, then information technology would be taken to a whole new level. Over the next couple of years, it is predicted that the industrial value of the Internet of Things will surpass that of the Internet 30 times over, and to be a market that is worth more than $100 billion dollars (Clendenin, 2010). On the other hand, it is estimated that there will be more than 20 billion devices connected to the Internet by 2020 (Lomas, 2009). The number of connected devices rises to over 50 billion as predicted by Cisco (Evans, 2012).

The IoT will revolute many industries and elevate communications on the Internet. The opportunities offered by the IoT are endless. IoT services provide the user with numerous services and capabilities. The obvious ones are the ability to control and monitor the physical environment remotely over the communication networks. Typical examples are the ability of closing a door or receiving smoke alert notifications remotely over the Internet. However, the revolution in technology actually occurs when things and group of things are connected together. The interconnection of things allows not only things to communicate with each other, but also offers the opportunities of building intelligence and pervasiveness into the IoT. The interconnected network of things, along with backend systems involved in a number of collaboration activities with the users and other things, in tandem with cloud computing systems, Big Data, web services, and Location Based Services, will transform not only communications on the Internet but also societies (Elkhodr, Shahrestani, & Cheung, 2013). The IoT will enable the sharing of information between different domains which leads to improving the overall quality of services (Zorzi, Gluhak, Lange, & Bassi, 2010). For example, the ability of sharing health information between different healthcare professionals such as nurses, doctors, and pharmacists will enhance the quality of healthcare (Parwekar, 2011). Consequently, it is expected that the IoT will penetrate many industries. It is regarded as a new wave of technology that will not only benefit the everyday user, but also offer many organizations promising businesses opportunities.

Henceforth, this chapter surveys some of the most envisioned IoT applications and the impact the IoT could have on various aspects of life. It explores some of the major opportunities offered by the IoT. Given that the possibilities promised by the IoT are enormous and are only limited to our imaginations, the chapter mainly focuses on a few interesting IoT applications rather than attempting to survey all anticipated IoT applications. For instance, one important area in which the IoT is promising to revolute is healthcare. The aim of bringing the IoT to the health sector is to enhance healthcare and medical service delivery; hence, saving more lives. Assisted living, remote health monitoring, smart homes, smart water, automation, industrial manufacturing, and transportation, are some of the other sectors that will be enhanced through the application of the IoT (Atzori, Iera, & Morabito, 2010). Nonetheless, the IoT will be used in many areas for the purpose of enhancing the quality of services, efficiencies and safety. For instance, vehicle-to-vehicle communications and smart roads (Foschini, Taleb, Corradi, & Bottazzi, 2011), that sense and control traffic flow are examples of these applications which contribute towards improving the safety on roads and efficiency of the transport system, specifically in congested cities.

In the rest of this chapter, the Section "IoT in Healthcare" describes the many areas of healthcare that benefit from the adoption of the IoT technologies. The section "Smart Home" transitions the reader from the typical smart home scenario to a new vision of IoT smart home systems. Other interesting IoT applications such as smart water, smart cars, smart lighting and structural health monitoring systems are discussed under the Section "Smart Cities: A holistic Vision". The chapter then concludes by highlighting some of the main challenges facing the realization of the IoT.

IoT DEVELOPMENT IN HEALTHCARE

Healthcare is an important aspect of the society. The healthcare services and communication technology industry have the potential for growth in specialized e-health services such as electronic health (e-health), remote monitoring systems, home and community care among many others. The IoT offers numerous opportunities which improve the healthcare services and operations. The IoT promotes a wider approach to healthcare by addressing the health needs of a population as a whole instead of individuals, and by stimulating practices that reduce the effects of diseases, disability and accidental injuries. Additionally, combining healthcare applications with other areas of the IoT stimulates sustainability in healthcare (Boulos & Al-Shorbaji, 2014). It is established in the healthcare community that prevention of diseases is as equally important as providing medical treatments (Fries, Koop, Sokolov, Beadle, & Wright, 1998). Consequently, the IoT creates the opportunity of maintaining sustainable environments for a healthier lifestyle. Other contribution the IoT provides is in reducing the implications of climate change on the health and well-being of the population (Vermesan et al., 2011). It is essential for the future sustainability of healthcare to enable healthcare providers and services to integrate sustainability principles within their organizations such as, energy and water efficiency, and environmental compliances among many others. Also, it is critical to foster environments that protect and promote the health of communities. Hence, the IoT plays a significant role towards the realization of a sustainable environment, which in turn contributes to a better approach to healthcare.

In terms of IoT applications in healthcare, monitoring of medications and the delivery of drugs are amongst the various envisioned application in this domain (Laranjo, Macedo, & Santos, 2012). The use of IoT aims at making the field of medicine more efficient than it has been in the past. People are able to receive and share information about illnesses and treatments more efficiently. The IoT allows individuals to acquire medical or treatment information in real-time and help in the early detection and prevention of diseases (Zhao, Wang, & Nakahira, 2011). Thus, it helps individuals to escape contacting a given disease, or to treat diseases as early as possible. The backend system responsible for operating the IoT health application(s) will be able to maintain important health records of patients. In e-health, this information is termed as Electronic Health Records (EHR) (Kalra & Ingram, 2006). Therefore, combining the IoT with EHRs systems will improve access and retrieval of healthcare related information, the availability and sharing of EHRs between different healthcare organizations.

The IoT in healthcare is expected to improve remote health monitoring systems as well. Remote health monitoring technology provides solutions for monitoring patients at home. These systems aim to deliver higher quality of care and reduce the cost on patients and governments without affecting the quality of the healthcare services provided (Elkhodr, Shahrestani, & Cheung, 2011b). The use of a remote monitoring system allows biomedical signals of a patient to be measured ubiquitously during his or her daily activities. Such a system allows the collection of medical data and signals related to patients' bodies, such as their heart rates, remotely via the Internet. There are also benefits associated with improving the quality of care and services, such as reliability, accessibility, frequency, accuracy and availability (Elkhodr, Shahrestani, & Cheung, 2011a).

An IoT based remote monitoring system is capable of detecting any changes in the person's body conditions, and monitoring their vital medical signs. The availability of the collected data by this system on the Internet, and the ability to access this data in real-time by various other systems and entities such as healthcare providers and medical centers, open the door to numerous opportunities. For instance, an alert system can be designed based on analyzing the EHRs received by the remote monitoring systems

(Baig & Gholamhosseini, 2013). In the case of a medical emergency, the system can be configured to alert the healthcare professionals, emergency services, relatives and others concerned parties. Also, the system can provide insight into the health condition of a monitored person so the necessary help can be provided as early as possible, and thus, saving patients' lives.

Additionally, the IoT services can help in the monitoring, early detection, prevention and treatment of several illnesses (Pang et al., 2015). This includes diabetes, heart disease, cancer, seizures, and pulmonary diseases, among others. Such diseases usually require constant monitoring of body actions, so the person needs to be under a constant watch. Traditionally, the medical practitioners and healthcare professionals are responsible for the constant monitoring of patients. However, patients' monitoring is costly and not as effective as it ought to be (Lara et al., 2012). For instance, the doctor is not capable of constantly watching over one patient with an undivided attention.

An example of how the IoT can improve patients' monitoring is the integration of Body Sensor Networks (BSN) with others IoT health systems (Savola, Abie, & Sihvonen, 2012). As an example, a BSN system can monitor the patient's body functions using a biodegradable chip or by using some wearables wireless Biosensor devices (Ozkul & Sevin, 2014). This chip or Biosensor device will be capable of monitoring the vital signs of the patient. They detect any anomaly in the bodily functions of the patient and report such problems to the IoT system. The IoT system can then makes the necessary action such as alerting a healthcare professional. Also, it allows healthcare professionals to make better diagnosis of diseases and communicate effectively with patients. In case of emergencies, the healthcare professional, or depending on how the system is designed, can alert an ambulance team for assistance.

Therefore, IoT health monitoring systems can be seen as an environment of surrounding intelligence which aims to provide a platform for remote monitoring and assistance to patients or the elderly in their homes or on the move (Elkhodr et al., 2011a). Monitoring patients in the early stages of their diseases can increase their chances of survival. It will also help healthcare providers to react before a serious medical condition such as, a heart attack or diabetic emergency occurs. The use of remote monitoring systems could also help reducing medical errors since electronic health records (EHRs) are digitally available via the IoT (Scurlock & D'Ambrosio, 2015). The digital availability of EHRs makes its retrieval and access more accurate and organized. This will not only help in reducing medical errors, but also provide speedy access to data, while maintaining access control privileges as well.

IoT applications in healthcare also extend to personal area networks (PANs) (Neuhaeuser & D'Angelo, 2013). In a PAN, individuals are capable of tracking their bodily functions using various wearable technologies such as a wearable smart sensor, a smart wrist device or a smart watch. As the technology and IoT evolve, wearable technologies in healthcare are evolving as well. Therefore, this evolvement of technologies will result in providing the capabilities which allow individuals to monitor various aspects of their health. Examples of these health aspects are the monitoring of blood pressure, sugar and insulin levels, medicine intakes, heart beats, sleeping patterns, calories intake, exercises levels and others. The capabilities offered by the IoT in this regards are vast. Healthcare professional will be able to access remotely these information and provide treatment if necessary. This enhances the sharing of information and self-administration of health problems in addition to the early detection of diseases.

Consequently, IoT healthcare applications encompass various sensors and monitoring devices. These devices are generally synchronized and interconnected with one another for the purpose of enhancing information sharing (Vermesan & Friess, 2013). Figure 1 is an example of an IoT based healthcare system which provides an array of healthcare services. It shows that an IoT system can be designed to combine together the followings healthcare subsystems:

- **The Healthcare Personal Area Network Application:** This application involves the use of personal devices in closed or local area setups. Examples are wearable technologies that can be used for the self-monitoring and administrating of a person's health.
- **Elderly Monitoring:** This application relies on a set of sensor devices which monitor the health condition of an elderly. The system can be used to collect information relating to the physical activities such as dietary and sleep patterns of the elderly as well. Importantly, the system allows healthcare professionals and care takers to monitor the health condition of elderlies in real-time. It implements alert and notification strategies in the case of emergencies such as automatically calling an ambulance when needed.
- **Smart Medicine:** This application involves the administration of medications. It ensures that patients are taking the right medicine, with the correct dose on time as specified by their healthcare professionals. The system can also alert a doctor in case a patient does not take his or her medication as prescribed.
- **Community Based EHR:** This includes outpatient care and electronic medical consultation subsystems that involve the digitation of health care operations. These subsystems collectively enhance eHealth services by reducing medical errors, saving cost and increasing efficiencies.
- **Smart Emergency:** The smart emergency application is centered on collaborations and sharing of information between the various healthcare subsystems. It is an important component in each of the healthcare subsystems described above. Obviously this is due to fact that emergency services, such as calling an ambulance, are required in medical emergencies. However, the smart emergency application operations are not only limited to providing the service of automatically calling an ambulance. They involve other advanced services such as communicating the status of the patient automatically back to the hospital during transport including the required treatment. This process improves emergency services in hospitals as well. It helps with the better allocations and distribution of patients in hospitals in a given geographical area. Thus, ensuring that there is a space to accommodate the transported patient. Moreover, they help in the optimization of the medical resources and services such as X-ray services and CAT scans.

Therefore, the ability of accessing health information instantly and remotely via the Internet enables healthcare professionals to access a new category of information which was unknown to them before. An example of this information includes the factors which might affect the patient's health, such as any daily routine activities. Gaining insight into the life of a patient helps in providing a better treatment approach. Generally, traditional remote monitoring applications lack the interoperation that the IoT can provide. Ambient Assisted Living (AAL) will be possible with the introduction of an IoT based system that works effectively with other IoT devices such as sensors and actuators. For instance, people will know how many times they have taken their medications, and when they need to take them next (Vermesan & Friess, 2013). Patients will be able to obtain pharmaceutical information regarding the type of medicine required instantly and in real-time. This includes information about the right dosage, allergy advice, side effects among others.

Pharmaceuticals

The pharmaceutical industry is directly associated with the healthcare industry. It is concerned with the manufacturing, distribution, storage, and administration of medications prescribed to patients. There are

Figure 1. An example of an IoT based healthcare system

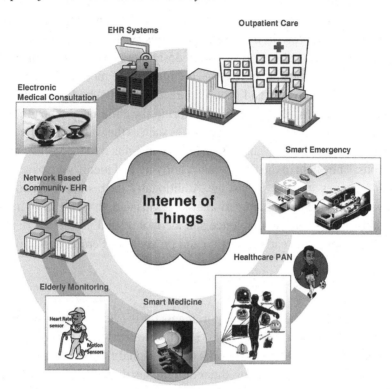

various ways through which the IoT will be of use to the pharmaceutical industry. For instance, the use of sensors or RFID technology on medications during supply and consumption enhances the proper use and safe intake of these drugs. The IoT helps in ensuring that medications are transported and stored in the right conditions (Melo et al., 2011). Also, the IoT improves the administration of medicines.

Accordingly, an IoT health application, through the use of sensors and other forms of devices, ensures that drugs are stored in an ideal environment in terms of temperature, sunlight exposure, among other important environmental factors (Atzori et al., 2010). Furthermore, the use of sensors and RFID technology helps in the identification of counterfeit drugs (Taylor, 2014). RFID technology in that sense can be used to monitor a certain medication right from manufacturing till consumptions as well.

Child Monitoring

Child monitoring is another area of healthcare which the IoT promises to enhance. An IoT based monitoring application, through the use of sensors and other IoT devices, is capable of monitoring the health and conditions of an infant or a child (Hoy, 2015). Therefore, parents or guardians will be able to find out whether their kid is sleeping, breathing well, seated or lying down properly, and whether it is mobile or not (Rost & Balakrishnan, 2006). The IoT technology will provide the capabilities of remotely monitoring the status and health conditions of a child outside their homes as well such as at a childcare center. This technology allows the design of a notification system which extends to parents, guardians, care takers, teachers, childcare workers, healthcare professionals, emergency services and many others.

This enhances the current child monitoring systems in use which are, in most cases, limited to providing an alert when a baby makes a noise or cries. Henceforth, the enhancements introduced by the IoT promise to revolute child monitoring in the healthcare industry. The real-time availability of data that can be collected from a child contributes towards the design and development of other innovative IoT health solutions. For example, by using an IoT based child remote monitoring system, the capabilities of monitoring a child's social activities and group interactions go beyond monitoring his or her physical health (Kinnunen et al., 2016). It extends to monitoring the child mental health as well (Sula et al., 2013). The IoT will now offer insights into kids' activities such as the way they interact with their friends, families, teachers and strangers. The advantages of gaining insights into the social and general activities of a child are numerous. They help in the fight against bullying and identifying psychological problems, among other behavioral issues at a very early stage. Additionally, the results obtained from analyzing the collected data can be used to identify malnutrition among kids and, thus, the design and administration of healthier diets. Child abuse, domestic violence and alcohol related problems are among other social issues in which the IoT helps in the early detection and prevention (Pereira & Santos, 2015).

IoT Health Application Requirements

Table 1 is an effort to summarize the general requirements for IoT healthcare systems. It categorizes the requirements based on three application categories: Healthcare providers (e.g. a hospital), Remote monitoring systems, and health Personal Area Networks (e.g. personal fitness). Access point (AP) mobility, traffic type, location, and security are among the requirements defined for each of the aforementioned applications. However, it is noted that these requirements vary depending on the application's design and its requirements. Within the IoT space, several heterogeneous sets of devices may use various communication strategies amongst them to provide services. Thus, the requirements change from a network topology to another and from an application design to another even within the same application domain (e.g. different applications designed for remote monitoring systems). Consequently, Table 1 should be regarded as an attempt to define the requirements of IoT healthcare applications in specific cases rather than standardizing these requirements. The work in (Elkhodr, Shahrestani, & Cheung, 2016) reviews a variety of wireless technologies. These technologies are strong candidates for supporting communications in the IoT. It highlights an assortment of communication technologies such as ZigBee, IEEE 802.11ah and Bluetooth Low Energy. Each of these technologies caters for specific application requirements in the IoT.

SMART HOME

The smart home is another area in which the IoT promises to grow. The IoT enables everyday household objects, electronics and appliances to communicate with one another either locally or via the Internet. Thus, it allows the user to control these household items in various ways (Vermesan & Friess, 2013). The smart home system will be capable of connecting different types of objects in the house, and thus providing the user with the capabilities of not only monitoring but also controlling these objects. This includes the ability of monitoring the objects' statuses and controlling the environment e.g. checking if a light is left on or closing a door remotely etc. This can be achieved by equipping normal household objects with smart sensors and actuator devices (Mainetti, Patrono, & Vilei, 2011). The IoT also improves the security of homes. The smart home system will be able in real-time to identify residents of

Table 1. General IoT healthcare systems requirements

	Healthcare Providers	Remote Monitoring Systems	Health PAN
Environment type	Commercial building e.g. hospital, clinic	Home, Nursing home, Community care	Home, Gym, Casual run
Location	Indoor	Indoor (high), Outdoor (low)	Indoor, Outdoor
Mobility requirement	Very Low (e.g. walking to the toilet, X-ray room)	Low (e.g. casual walk)	Low-medium (e.g. running)
Actors	Examples are: Electrocardiogram, heartrate monitor, blood pressure monitor	Examples are: heartrate monitor, blood pressure monitor, fall detection sensors	Examples are: wearable devices, heartrate monitor, pace detector
Devices Mobility requirement	Fixed (High), Mobile (Low)	Fixed (High), Mobile (Low)	Fixed (High), Mobile (High)
Device to AP Communication	Mainly Unidirectional (e.g. monitoring)	Bidirectional (Send and receive)	Unidirectional, (send)
Traffic type	Real-time and Event-based (emergency)	Real-time or Periodic, event-based	Event-based or Periodic
Coverage needed	Depends on the design: multi-story medical center requires higher density and extended coverage area	Independent home living model can have low coverage (e.g. around the house); Community care center might require extended coverage	Depends on the application design and AP mobility requirements
Reliability requirement	High	High	High
Security Requirement	'Higher than Commercial-grade'	Range from 'Higher than Commercial-grade' to 'Commercial-grade'	'Commercial-grade'

the house, visitors and strangers. Thus, the system enables the detection of potential security breaches or risks (Schneps-Schneppe, Namiot, Maximenko, & Malov, 2012). Other features of the smart home system are the ability to monitor changes in various areas of the house such as monitoring the water level in a swimming pool, water leakage from pipes, and electricity consumptions. Users are able to know about their energy consumption levels in real-time and are able to make necessary changes. The system can provide recommendations to users which help reducing electricity consumptions during peak hours for example (Mohsenian-Rad, Wong, Jatskevich, Schober, & Leon-Garcia, 2010).

Apart from providing information, monitoring and controlling the general appliances of the house, the IoT will bring connectivity to various unconventional objects. Thus, in addition to smart fridges, smart ovens and other smart appliances, a new category of smart products will emerge which have the capability of connecting to the Internet directly or indirectly via the smart home network. Some of these smart products have already started to emerge or are under development. The followings are examples of these smart products:

- Smart Door and Window Locks (Jaykumar & Blessy, 2014).
- Smart Garage Door Openers.
- Smart Doorbells.
- Networked Cameras and Video Storage & Viewing.
- Smart Lighting Controls (Li, Suna, & Hua, 2012).
- Smart Thermostats.

- Multi-Sensors Detection Devices.
- Smart Blinds and Drapes.
- Smart Wall Outlets, Plugs, and Power Strips.

Most of these devices operate using low-power wireless technologies and connect via the smart home local network to the Internet.

From Traditional Smart Home Systems to the IoT

Most of the existent smart home systems use devices at the lower end of the envisioned capabilities. Typically, these devices are capable of storing data, responding to user commands from smartphones, tablets and computers, and sending alerts over Bluetooth or Wi-Fi. They generally operate in a standalone manner. The IoT brings a new type of home management, integration of devices, surveillance, intelligence and more importantly connectivity to these devices. Intelligence may be contained completely within a device, combined with platform intelligence in the cloud, or reside almost completely within a platform to which the device connects to perform some functions.

Therefore, smart home devices incorporate the capabilities inherent in the IoT and provide enhanced benefits. Smart home devices can be static objects, such as smart plugs or lights that simply report their properties. They can also be sensors that measure the physical conditions of an object or its status, actuators that perform operations (opening doors, turning on or off appliances), or devices that combine both of these services. Therefore, the IoT enables users to manipulate these devices through an interface which could be in the form of a smartphone application, tablet, or computer that remotely operates the device in the home. Significantly, the IoT system will enable these devices to be queried or controlled by other platforms, controllers, or IoT applications that coordinate multiple objects without the interference of the human user. In addition, the data collected from smart home devices can be integrated with external data collected from other IoT systems, e.g. a healthcare system, which create value-added services. Therefore, the user benefits from added intelligence, modeling, and weaving of information which enable the smart home system to make better decisions on behalf of a user, or to provide personalized and optimized services (Chan, Campo, Estève, & Fourniols, 2009).

Therefore, by integrating the smart home system with the IoT, smart home devices will be capable of communicating with each other. They will also be capable of obtaining information from or controlling the physical environment based on the user's preferences. They can use information external to their specific environment to enhance the operation of that device to the user's benefits. Ultimately, homes will evolve to have their own ecosystems. However, the provision of such information will require the sharing of information among the stakeholders (Da Xu, He, & Li, 2014). This raises numerous concerns in terms of security, privacy, management and others (Wilson, Hargreaves, & Hauxwell-Baldwin, 2015). Figure 2 is an example of a smart home system. It shows that the IoT brings connectivity to a number of appliances such as TVs and fridges and to unconventional objects such as light switches, electricity sockets, and gas leak sensors among others.

IoT Smart Home Application Requirements

Table 2 summarizes some of the IoT Smart Home Application requirements. As with the application's requirements of the IoT in healthcare discussed in the section "IoT health application requirements", the

Figure 2. An IoT smart home example

requirements of the smart home system vary according to the application design and its specific requirements as well. Initially, as shown in Table 2, the application environment of smart home applications is indoor within the home building. Devices are mostly in the form of sensors and actuators in addition to smart appliances and consumer electronics which are generally stationary. Sensors and actuators will be deployed in the home in appropriate locations. A number of these devices are likely to be powered by batteries. The typical coverage of such a network of devices is the entire home, with an estimated maximum number of no more than few hundred devices per household (Basu, Moretti, Gupta, & Marsland, 2013). The payload data being transmitted can be estimated to be very small with no stringent latency or jitter requirements (Qin, Denker, Giannelli, Bellavista, & Venkatasubramanian, 2014). Multimedia real-time devices such as an IP camera will have specific requirements to their sensing device counterparts. Many wireless technologies such as ZigBee, and Wi-Fi can be employed in such IoT space.

SMART CITIES: A HOLISTIC VISION

Over the past few years, the definition of "Smart Cities" has evolved to mean many things to many people. Yet, one thing remains constant: part of being "smart" is utilizing information and communications technology (ICT) and the Internet to address urban challenges (Clarke, 2013). A city-wide network of sensors provides real-time valuable information on the flow of citizens, noise and other forms of environmental pollution, as well as traffic and weather conditions. This enables the local authorities to streamline city operations including better environmental management, cost reduction, and economic improvement, and social and environmental sustainability. A smart city is the result of an incremental

Table 2. IoT smart home application general requirement

Category	Comment
Environment type	Home (building)
Location	Indoor
Mobility requirement	Stationary
Actors	Multimedia devices, IP cameras, Sensors, Actuators, Smart Appliances, Smart phones.
Devices Mobility Requirement	Stationary
Device to AP Communication	Bidirectional (Send information; and receive instructions)
Traffic type	Varies from: • Multimedia Real-time traffic - few megabytes every second • Periodic- few 100 bytes every few seconds • Event-based- few 100 bytes per event
Coverage needed	Indoor
Reliability requirement	Medium
Security Requirement	Commercial-grade

process of connecting the various facets and applications of the IoT together. The inter-communication, collaboration and exchange of information amongst the various IoT devices and systems will ultimately lead to the realization of a true vision of a smart city. Thus, connecting e-health systems with smart homes, smart streets, smart parking, smart water, smart bridges and the rest of the various applications envisioned in the IoT, will provide the digital infrastructure necessary for building the smart cities of the future. This digital infrastructure enables people to actively contribute to, and becomes part of the drive for sustainable development, as well as to self-manage their home, environment, natural recourses, and their own health for a better life and sustainable future.

The smart city technology brings together almost all of the other applications of the IoT. These include systems which provide services such as water leakage detection, flood detection, pollution detection, traffic control, smart roads, healthcare applications, smart home, among others.

It is important to note that this technology may not be able to succeed without the implementation of proper policies regarding the disclosure and sharing of information (Vermesan & Friess, 2013). All parties involved need to be willing to share information and for that to happen, suitable management, security and privacy challenges need to be overcome. The rest of this Section discusses the major developments which may contribute to building the IoT smart city.

Smart Water

Perhaps, the IoT cannot interfere with the climate and make the sky rain; but the IoT, through various applications in smart homes and smart cities, can enhance water consumption. Thus, the IoT helps in reducing water wastage by improving the efficiency of water consumption. This is of a great importance particularly in places where drought is an issue (Sanchez et al., 2014). The envisioned developments in water IoT based infrastructure systems are numerous. An IoT based water system can be used to improve water's quality, transportation, consumption (TongKe, 2013), supply and demand, leakage, treatment, pollutions, and storage facilities such as in household tanks or on a larger scale such as in reservoirs

(Wu, Chen, & Lei, 2012). For instance, an Australian company is using networked sensors connected to the Cloud to monitor water runoff at construction sites (Pearce, 2009). Libelium ("Open Aquarium - Aquaponics and Fish Tank Monitoring for Arduino," 2014) is another company which uses the IoT to improve water consumption efficiency in aquariums and gardens. It utilizes a platform consisting of wireless sensors which automates the control and maintenance tasks within an aquarium or a garden.

In an aquarium environment, Libelium's platform use sensors which monitor various aspects of water such as temperature, conductivity and pH levels ("Open Aquarium - Aquaponics and Fish Tank Monitoring for Arduino," 2014). Also, the platform utilizes a pump and actuator devices which regulate water temperature, feed the fish and administer medication. The platform simulates day and night cycles by controlling light intensity as well ("Open Aquarium - Aquaponics and Fish Tank Monitoring for Arduino," 2014). The platform sends wirelessly information collected by the sensors and actions triggered by the actuators to a web or mobile interface. This interface enables users to monitor and control their aquarium. In gardening, Libelium uses a platform which monitors plant conditions and facilitate care. On one hand, the platform utilizes a set of sensors which collect environmental and soil related information such as moisture, temperature and humidity. On the other hand, the platform controls water irrigation, lights and oxygen using actuators. These are just few examples that showcase how an IoT water system could form an important integral part of other IoT systems. The integration of water's systems in the IoT leads to improving not only the efficient consumption of water but also the overall management of gardening, crops and aquariums (Duan, 2014).

Moreover, an IoT based water system can be set to remotely determine the status and working condition of a water's device (open or closed, on or off, full or empty, etc.). A pump can be remotely turned on or off to adjust the flow of water through a water transportation system. Pumps, gates and other equipment with moving parts in the water infrastructure can be monitored for vibration and other indications of failure. If a water pump is leaking or about to fail, the user or the relevant parties will be alerted so the necessary action can be taken. Connected smart water filters can report their statuses whether they are clean and functioning properly (Robles et al., 2014). The IoT system can measure water pressure in pipes to find leaks faster in the water transportation system or the presence of certain chemicals in the water supply and maybe even organic contaminants (Muhic & Hodzic, 2014). Another focus for water savings should be landscape irrigation in parks, medians and elsewhere. This is a major use of water in cities (Mylonas & Theodoridis, 2015). Nationwide, it is estimated to be nearly one-third of all residential water use and as much as half of this water is wasted due to runoff, evaporation or wind (Farbotko, Walton, Mankad, & Gardner, 2014). In agriculture, the application of IoT water systems combines weather data with other sensory data such as moisture, heat, type of soil and the relative exposure to sunshine at a particular time of the day for a more efficient use of water (Dlodlo & Kalezhi, 2015).

Water Transportation

The IoT will also be applied in the water management sector through various ways. This will enhance water quality and distribution to various parts of the world. By sensing portable water and movement from one place to another, an IoT WSN based system will be capable of communicating with the cloud or other systems to show information on the quality and movement of waters in cities (Bohli, Skarmeta, Victoria Moreno, Garcia, & Langendorfer, 2015). The Radio Frequency Identification (RFID) application connects with various services providers in the city and various other stakeholders to give information about the reliability and quality of the water being transported within a given community. The idea behind the IoT is to interconnect the available applications with one another via local network setups or the Internet. This enhances the sharing of information which in turn improves the quality of goods and services, and thus quality of human life (Fan & Bifet, 2013). For instance, the IoT capabilities can be extended to other areas associated with the water transport industry as well (Misra, Simmhan, & Warrior, 2015). The IoT system will be capable of not only monitoring the quality of water or detecting water leakages during transport, but also that of the truck itself and the driver. The safety of the driver, including his or her behavior also enhances road safety as the system will be able to report any incidents to the relevant parties. The IoT will be capable of enhancing the performance of the water transport sector, as well as other transport sectors by promoting the sharing of information in real time (Misra et al., 2015).

Water Pollution

The IoT will be capable of detecting pollution in water reservoirs, and natural water systems such as rivers (Kar & Kar, 2015). The system uses a ranges of sensors that detect chemical leakages and analyzes the purity of water (ZHU & PAN, 2015). The sensors communicate with other IoT applications providing valuable information on water quality. For instance, the sensors will be able to detect waste from factories dumped into a river and alert the relevant authorities, and the local communities that could be affected by the presence of these chemicals or waste. The IoT water monitoring system can be used for monitoring and detecting pollution of waters as well e.g. ocean waters (Tiwari, 2011). Thus, the IoT can help maintaining the safety of the marine ecosystem. It does that by detecting and reporting the individual and industrial activities that could be harmful to the marine life (Domingo, 2012).

Water Leakages

Water is an important natural resource. Wasting water is attributed to a number of factors including water leakage either during transport, storage or consumptions (TongKe, 2013). Therefore, the IoT can help conserving this important natural resource by reducing leakages. An IoT water monitoring system utilizes smart water sensors that can detect water leakages in a tank or pipe (Lundqvist, de Fraiture, & Molden, 2008). The sensors can be used to measure the pressure levels in pipes and their variances. The system can be used to detect pipe bursting in real-time (Y. Kim, Suh, Cho, Singh, & Seo, 2015). Thus, it enhances the real time response to such leakages which in turn reduces water wastage. Nonetheless, the system could be used to prevent possible pipe bursts. It does that by monitoring water levels and pressures within water systems; which allow the early detection of faults and accelerate incidents and response management (Chowdhury, Bhuiyan, & Islam, 2013).

Flood Control

IoT devices will be capable of detecting flooding in rivers (Tai, Celesti, Fazio, Villari, & Puliafito, 2015), dams and water reservoirs by measuring the water levels and ensuring that all changes are detected when they occur (Gubbi, Buyya, Marusic, & Palaniswami, 2013). The system alerts the concerned parties regarding the changes in water levels and provides options for responding to such changes. This technology will also be important for the detection of flooding of seas by detecting changes in water levels and any abnormal activities. Floods can be disastrous and their effects are damaging to the economy, including the obvious loss of life and property. The IoT may not be promising a complete solution to flooding, but it contributes by providing a better way of controlling or responding to flooding alerts. Additionally, the IoT can be used to predict and detect the rise in water levels, and to predict tsunami such as the work proposed in (Kawamoto, Nishiyama, Yoshimura, & Yamamoto, 2014). This can be achieved by combining weather data such as rains, wind directions and other information such as water flow on ground. Communicating and combining this information in an IoT system contribute towards the design of a better and effective response system to this natural disaster. Importantly, the ability of predicting flooding in rivers or seas can help in building solutions which prevent flooding, or at least reduce their impact.

IoT Metering

IoT metering systems, including smart grid systems, are an interesting IoT area. IoT metering is concerned with the metering of water, gas, and electricity (Benzi, Anglani, Bassi, & Frosini, 2011) within a smart home environment or on a larger scale e.g. within a city. Typically, metering applications rely heavily on sensor network technologies. For example, in environmental and agricultural monitoring systems, the IoT system uses wireless sensors for the monitoring of water, gas and electricity consumptions (Erol-Kantarci & Mouftah, 2011). IoT metering is mainly concerned with metering the consumption of those resources by providing the user with important usage statistics. This provides the users with important statistical information such as the time when water is mostly consumed, the devices which are consuming electricity the most among others. Additionally, IoT metering applications can be extended to provide advanced analytics functionalities as well (W.-H. E. Liu, 2010). Thus, apart from simply logging the resource consumptions such as time, the device in use and the amount of water, gas or electricity being consumed, the IoT metering system can provide fruitful recommendations. Examples include providing recommendations on how to save energy e.g., by turning a washing machine on during off peak hours only, boiling water using an electrical kettle instead of using a gas stove etc. On a larger scale, smart grid applications are concerned with optimizing the energy sector within a city or even across a country (S. A. Kim, Shin, Choe, Seibert, & Walz, 2012). A smart grid application can combine and make use of the following systems and services:

- Renewable Energy Management, including the management of solar energy and wind farming harvesting services, which help in optimizing energy consumption.
- Reducing overall demand on the grid by shifting usage and energy consumption to off peak time.
- Systems which store energy, using batteries, generated at off-pick time.
- Systems which detect disturbance or failure in the grid: This leads to better management of supply fluctuation by isolating the area under disturbance.

Tables 3 outlines some of the general requirements for IoT metering applications. It shows that IoT metering has applications in indoor and outdoor areas with traffic ranging from continuous, burst to periodic. Metering devices are usually in the form of sensors and small control devices which are most likely stationary and require little to no mobility requirement.

Table 3. General requirements for IoT smart grid applications

Category	Comment
Environment type	Urban, sub-urban, rural, home
Location	Indoor and Outdoor
Mobility requirement	Stationary
Actors	Meter devices (electricity, gas, water), automation and control devices
Devices Mobility Requirement	Stationary
Device to AP Communication	Bidirectional (sending metered data; and control)
Traffic type	Varies from: • Continuous • Periodic • Burst
Coverage needed	Indoor (High), Outdoor (Low -depends on the app's design)
Reliability requirement	High
Security Requirement	Commercial-grade

Smart Cars

Industry experts estimate that every car will be connected to a communication network by 2025, and the market for connected vehicle technology will reach $54 billion by 2017 (*Connected Car Forecast: Global Connected Car Market to Grow Threefold Within Five Years*, 2014). Car technology is evolving from a car being controlled by the driver to partially automated cars, and to fully automated self-driven vehicles (Nelson, 2015). Such automated vehicles also referred to as driverless cars are capable of navigating through a city or driving upcountry without any human control. For the realization of a fully automated vehicle, such as a driverless car, truck or bus, a series of complex interactions and technology advancements are needed. Driverless vehicle technology integrates a network of connected devices in the form of sensors, motion detectors and actuators (Chong et al., 2013). It includes internal sensors that determine the vehicle's speed, direction of traffic, location, gas or petrol level, and temperature of the vehicle among other performance metrics (Braun, Neumann, Schmidt, Wichert, & Kuijper, 2014). It also includes external sensors which allow the car to communicate with its environment.

The near future will see the introduction of connected vehicles onto the roads. This will create high demand for control and interaction technology, and this is where the IoT comes in. For example, the IoT will be capable of providing information on the traffic, on what routes to follow and helping in controlling and reducing road congestions (Foschini et al., 2011). The IoT system will also control car speed depending on roads and traffic conditions. The IoT system will be capable of showing engine diagnostics, and other car features, in terms of their conditions and functionality. The fuel and lubricant levels, mechanical part statuses and conditions can be controlled and monitored by the IoT system and communicated to the car's owner or the relevant party. This enhances car longevity by avoiding engine knocks and other forms of system failures (MacGillivray et al., 2014). Also, the car system will be controlled via audio-visual enhancements, including voice recognition to enhance in-car safety. The IoT can be used to prevent car thefts (J. Liu & Yang, 2011). The technology will enhance the tracking and retrieval of stolen vehicles, and will be able to communicate with all the concerned parties.

Vehicle-to-X Technology

As the IoT revolution unfolds, automotive innovation and value creation will be shifting to the boundaries with other IoT applications such as home automation, smart grids, smart cities, healthcare and retail. Vehicle-to-Infrastructure (V2I) (Chou, Li, Chien, & Lan, 2009), and Vehicle-to-Retail (V2R) (Siddiqui 2014) are projected to be the dominant segments with respectively 459 and 406 million vehicles featuring smart car IoT applications by 2030, followed by V2H (Vehicle-to-Home) and V2P (Vehicle-to-Person) with 163 and 239 million vehicles, respectively. Meanwhile, Vehicle-to-Grid (V2G) services will be offered on 50 million vehicles in 2030 (Staff, 2014).

Therefore, the IoT is promising to revolute the connected and driverless car industry. The IoT offers the capabilities of connecting cars not only to the Internet, but also to their surroundings. Therefore, an IoT smart car may interact with surrounding roads, buildings, traffic lights, pedestrians, emergency and police vehicles and personnel. Also, it interacts with other vehicles and people, in order to provide real time information for better self-car maneuvering. In addition to optimizing routes and fuel consumption, minimizing traffic congestions, the IoT in this space plays a role in reducing noise and air pollutions, and ideally improving roads safety. The IoT will find its way in accommodating services related to green energy and sustainable energy resources as well. For instance, in the case of a smart electric connected car, the IoT will be able to provide information regarding nearby electric recharging stations (Hess et al., 2012) and the rate at which the solar panel are harvesting energy (assuming solar energy plays a role in powering the electric car). The IoT can provide information regarding the number of sunny hours on a particular day, in a particular location or during a journey of travel such as in the study presented in (Nwogu, 2015).

Nevertheless, the opportunities offered by integrating the IoT with smart vehicles are endless. The IoT opens the door to various technological innovations which will transform not only the way we per-

Figure 3. Vehicle to X connectivity

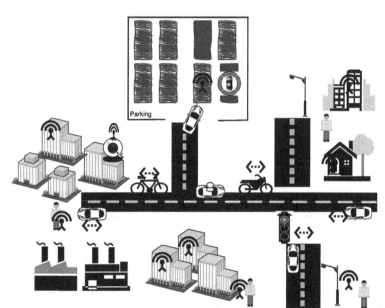

ceive the car industry, but also the way cars are integrated in future smart cities. For instance, Figure 3 shows how smart cars, using the IoT, can communicate with other cars, traffic lights, and pedestrians.

Smart Parking

Smart parking is one of the emerging enablers for smart cities. A smart parking system operating as part of the IoT network can be used to enhance parking efficiency such as the study presented in (Pala & Inanc, 2007). It provides information on various parking areas, security levels and available parking spaces in a given area. It works by collecting and distributing real-time information about where parking is available to smart cars which are already connected to the IoT infrastructure. The power of an IoT smart parking system lies in its ability to track the movements of vehicles and availability of parking spaces in real-time such as the system proposed in (Lu, Lin, Zhu, & Shen, 2009). Thus, the system will be able to automatically direct a driverless car to an allocated parking space. It does that using an automated allocation system which analyzes in real-time information relating to traffic conditions, availability of parking spaces in nearby car parks, among others. Apart from saving fuel, time and making life easier for the user, the technology helps reducing emissions and road congestions. From the government perspective, the IoT helps with law enforcement such as the enforcement of parking limits. Another application of smart parking in the IoT is linking a smart parking system with dynamic pricing platforms, where prices scale based on parking supply and demand (Polycarpou, Lambrinos, & Protopapadakis, 2013). It can also offer drivers parking options based on the price and proximity of their intended destination. Additionally, the data provided and generated from smart parking systems can be leveraged by retailers in a mall or store to predict the rush and accordingly manage workforce allocation. This will result in an improved quality of life in the city. This will also help in keeping the records on the levels of emissions in a city, making it possible for local authorities to apply pollution control measures with enough prior knowledge.

Other Smart City Applications

Smart Lighting

Smart lighting entails the provision of automated lights in public streets that change dynamically according to street activities or weather conditions (Castro, Jara, & Skarmeta, 2013). Smart lighting is also known as intelligent street lighting (Yue, Changhong, Xianghong, & Wei, 2010) and adaptive street lighting (Dramsvik, 2009). A smart lighting system controls lighting based on the weather condition, day and night cycle and movements of road users, e.g., vehicles, pedestrians, motorcyclists and cyclists.

Smart lights dim when no activity is detected, but brighten when movement is detected. This type of lighting mechanism is different from traditional, stationary illumination, or dimmable street lighting systems that dim at a pre-determined time. Smart lightings are turned on automatically by sensors that detect when lighting is required. Thus, the IoT enables street lights to communicate with one another. For example, when a passer-by is detected by a sensor, the smart lighting system communicates this information to neighboring street lights. These lights will then brighten providing people with light along their path (Carrington, 2013).

Obviously, smart lighting applications contribute to better approaches of saving energy. Additionally, it reduces chances of thefts and accidents by providing visibility in sensitive areas or by detecting certain motions. The motion detectors will be capable of controlling individual street lights in various areas of a city (Perandones et al., 2014). Smart lighting systems also could be combined with other IoT applications such as air quality monitoring systems (Zanella, Bui, Castellani, Vangelista, & Zorzi, 2014). An urban IoT system may provide a service to monitor the energy consumption of the whole city. Thus, it enables the authorities and individuals to get a clear and detailed view of the amount of energy required for particular services such as public lighting, transportation, traffic lights, control cameras, and heating/cooling of public buildings. Additionally, the system can be used to provide features such as identifying the main energy consumption sources. This feature allows the optimization of energy consumption by setting priorities among different devices and applications (Zanella et al., 2014). Accordingly, smart lighting systems play an important role in smart grid applications as well (Güngör et al., 2011).

Structural Health

Structural Health Monitoring (SHM) systems are used to monitor the conditions of buildings and other physical structures such as bridges (Farrar & Worden, 2007). SHM systems implement damage detection plans and characterize strategies for engineering structures. SHM systems involve the process of observing and monitoring a physical structure over time. A typical SHM system uses an array of sensors which periodically collect measurements from a monitored physical structure. The system samples the collected data and extracts related damage-sensitive information. It then uses statistical analysis methods to determine the structural health status of a physical structure (Dawson, 1976). The Rio-Antirrio Bridge in Greece is an example of an SHM system (Tselentis et al., 2007). It uses more than 100 sensors. These sensors monitor traffic and the bridge structure condition in real time (Parcharidis, Foumelis, Kourkouli, & Wegmuller, 2009). Other examples of SHM systems is the Hong Kong Wind and Structural Health Monitoring System (WASHMS) (S. Kim et al., 2007). WASHMS has four different levels of operation: sensory systems, data acquisition systems, local centralized computer systems, and a global central computer system. The WASHMS system measures the structural behavior of the bridges continuously. Both the WASHMS and Rio-Antirrio systems provide an early warning system for structural health of the relevant monitored bridges.

Recent researches on IoT structural health monitoring systems can be classified into two categories. The first category involves sensor technologies for collecting measurements such as in (S. Kim et al., 2007). The second type of research is centered on developing theoretical algorithms which process the data collected by sensors. The frequency response method has often been used for the analysis of data in these systems (Huang, Xu, Li, Su, & Liu, 2012). Significantly, the IoT contributes to SHM systems by providing Internet connectivity and real-time monitoring features. The IoT connects SHM systems with other areas of the IoT such as driverless car systems, environmental monitoring systems, road congestion systems and forecast systems among many others.

Smart Environment

The IoT can be used to detect noise which goes above a given level of decibels in various parts of the city especially in bars and restaurants. This will ensure efficiency in dealing with noise pollution and making it possible for authorities to react to too much noise in real-time. This is in addition to monitoring noise produced by cars in the city, and residential and industrial areas. This helps in the better planning of residential and industrial areas. An example of noise monitoring system in the IoT is the study presented in (Su, Shao, Vause, & Tang, 2013).

There are many ways through which the IoT technology will be able to help in the environmental management. Some of these applications have already been discussed such as monitoring leakages in rivers, flood control and water pollution. However, there are several other ways through which the technology could enhance the conservation of natural resources such as:

- **Detecting Forest Fires:** The IoT can be used to monitor the presence of combustion gases, and provide information on forest fires as soon as possible. This ensures that the response unit can act early to prevent a disaster (Debnath, Chin, Haque, & Yuen, 2014). Forest fires have been known to spread very fast and widely, with adverse environmental and economic effects. The IoT promises an easier job for the authorities in terms of responding to fires in the forest ecosystems around the country.
- **Monitoring Snow Level:** This enhances the provision of important information concerning skiing and also it makes it possible for the authorities to detect potential avalanche risks in real-time (Debnath et al., 2014). This information will be used to enhance the efficiency of the skiing sport as well.
- **Earthquake Detection:** One of the most devastating natural disasters are earth quakes. When they do occur, they leave behind a trail of huge destructions, including loss of life and property. The IoT technology can be used for the early detection of earthquakes using reliable sophisticated sensors. The IoT enhances earthquake early detection systems such as in (Chi, Chen, Chao, & Kuo, 2011). The future will see the application of IoT to detect earthquakes even hours before they occur. This will make it possible for the authorities to communicate with the people early enough to facilitate evacuation of the most vulnerable neighborhoods.

Waste Management

The technology of connecting things to the Internet will also make it possible for cities to control waste disposal (Debnath et al., 2014). From a logistics perspective, the waste-management process requires tremendous organization. The key objective is in collecting, sorting, and processing waste as efficiently as possible. With the introduction of the IoT in this area, multiple wastes related sites, whether collection companies, recycling plants or power companies that handle waste, can seamlessly schedule deliveries, with one part of the process feeding the next. Research and industry leaders are already working on new IoT solutions for waste management such as smart connected bins. For instance, in (Hong et al., 2014) an IoT-based smart garbage system (SGS) composed of a number of smart garbage bins (SGBs), routers, and servers has been proposed. Each SGB, which plays a role in collecting food waste, is battery operated for mobility, and considering the convenience to residents, performs various operations through wireless communications. Pollution control is another area relating to waste management. The IoT provides information about pollutants, polluters and the levels of pollution in real time in a given area; thus, contributing to the overall management strategies of rubbish, recyclable and biodegradable waste.

Enhanced Security

The IoT will see the introduction of an increased number of vigilance and highly informed alert systems, which will be capable of fully securing homes, cars, workplaces, recreational places and other properties (Vlacheas et al., 2013). IoT security systems offer a myriad of features including door and window sensors, motion detectors, and video recording mechanisms. The IoT will facilitate access control and ensure that a person has the right permission to access authorized information at the right time and location. Biometric and facial recognition will enhance the automate access to services and resources. The IoT also contributes towards fighting crime, thefts and terrorist activities.

IoT Smart City Requirements

The previous sections provided a vision of a holistic smart city consisting of numerous heterogeneous applications which include various smart city scenarios and related applications. The growth of smart cities within the IoT encompasses the development and connection of several urban and rural geographical areas together. Ultimately, the IoT interconnects a wide range of applications including emergency services, healthcare, smart home, smart metering, and smart roads among others. However, each of these applications delivers a range of complex services to individuals, businesses, and governments within a variety of national, regional, and state administrative structures. This poses numerous integration challenges in the IoT.

Therefore, within this diversified system, it is a tremendous task to define the requirements for smart cities in the IoT. For the realization of a true vision of a smart city in the IoT, several incremental processes of developments and technologies are needed. They include revolutionary advancements in communication technologies, device hardware and software development, and new service architectures. For instance, in many of the smart city applications surveyed in this chapter, there is a need for a wireless technology with a simplified architecture that supports low energy consumption. However, in many other applications, the requirement of having a higher data rate is more important than energy requirement. Consequently, in the context of this mounting complexity and platformization, interoperability between the different facets of IoT is exceptionally vital and can be considered as the crucial requirement for smart cities in the IoT. No matter what technology, topology or device is being used, interoperability has to be achieved for the realization of the IoT. Additionally, one particular challenge in the context of smart cities relates to the open data business model. As services become pervasive and ubiquitous, the matter of making databases accessible by IoT applications and services will become more important. Transparency towards the end user on how his/her information is being used, with clear opt-in options and secured environments, has to be the starting point when providing services that leverage personal data.

CONCLUSION

This chapter provides a survey of some of the interesting applications projected in the IoT. It explores applications in many areas of health, smart homes, and smart cities. The chapter illustrates how the various applications of the IoT enhance the overall quality of life. The IoT becomes fruitful when various IoT applications are connected together. Thus, the chapter provides examples on compound IoT applications that emerge from combining smart services from different areas. It shows that the IoT sponsors the move from standalone closed systems towards open systems and platforms that support multiple applications and services. Hence, several IoT scenarios are reported. These scenarios combine data from different sources, linking several things, including devices, peoples and the environment to deliver and share information, enhancing business value, quality of life, and creating new business opportunities.

Nevertheless, to realize the unique and futuristic characteristics of the IoT, many challenges need to be overcome. There is a need to maintain scalable, private, secure and trustworthy operations in the IoT. With billions of things equipped with sensors and actuators entering the digital word using a vast array of technologies, incorporated into devices like lights, electric appliances, home automation systems and a vast number of other integrated machinery devices, transport vehicles, and equipment, as shown in this chapter, management of things become very challenging. Moreover, the growth in connected devices to the communication networks translates into increased security risks and poses new challenges to security and privacy. A device which connects to the Internet, whether it is a constraint or a more powerful device, inherits the security risks of today's computer devices. Therefore, it is essential that things are securely connected to their designated network(s), securely controlled and accessed by authorized entities. Many IoT applications require that data generated by things to be collected, analyzed, stored, dispatched and presented in a secure manner. Furthermore, there are security and privacy risks associated with things to things communications as well. This is in addition to the risks relating to things-to-person communications. For instance, the chapter describes many interaction scenarios where things are accessed by other things independently from the user. This highlights the need for end-to-end security and privacy protection solutions. As such security and privacy solutions should guarantee that things are accessed only by authorized entities in a secure manner. They should ensure that things are not leaking information or disclosing private information about their operations or their users to unauthorized entities. They also need to ensure that things are not used miscellaneously to impinge on the privacy of users.

REFERENCES

Ashton, K. (22 July 2009). That 'Internet of Things' Thing. *RFID Journal*. Retrieved from http://www.rfidjournal.com/article/view/4986

Atzori, L., Iera, A., & Morabito, G. (2010). The internet of things: A survey. *Computer Networks*, *54*(15), 2787–2805. doi:10.1016/j.comnet.2010.05.010

Baig, M., & Gholamhosseini, H. (2013). Smart Health Monitoring Systems: An Overview of Design and Modeling. *Journal of Medical Systems*, *37*(2), 1–14. doi:10.1007/s10916-012-9898-z PMID:23321968

Basu, D., Moretti, G., Gupta, G. S., & Marsland, S. (2013). Wireless sensor network based smart home: Sensor selection, deployment and monitoring. *Paper presented at the2013 IEEE Sensors Applications Symposium (SAS)*, Galveston, USA. doi:10.1109/SAS.2013.6493555

Benzi, F., Anglani, N., Bassi, E., & Frosini, L. (2011). Electricity smart meters interfacing the households. *IEEE Transactions on Industrial Electronics*, *58*(10), 4487–4494. doi:10.1109/TIE.2011.2107713

Bohli, J.-M., Skarmeta, A., Victoria Moreno, M., Garcia, D., & Langendorfer, P. (2015). SMARTIE project: Secure IoT data management for smart cities. *Paper presented at the2015 International Conference on Recent Advances in Internet of Things (RIoT)*, Singapore. doi:10.1109/RIOT.2015.7104906

Boulos, M. N. K., & Al-Shorbaji, N. M. (2014). On the Internet of Things, smart cities and the WHO Healthy Cities. *International Journal of Health Geographics*, *13*(10). PMID:24669838

Braun, A., Neumann, S., Schmidt, S., Wichert, R., & Kuijper, A. (2014). Towards interactive car interiors: the active armrest. *Paper presented at the8th Nordic Conference on Human-Computer Interaction: Fun, Fast, Foundational*, Helsinki, Finland. doi:10.1145/2639189.2670191

Carrington, D. (2013). Tvilight: The 'talking' streetlamps that will lighten your heart (but not your wallet). *CNN*. Retrieved from http://edition.cnn.com/2013/07/18/tech/innovation/tvilight-street-lamps-roosegarde/

Castro, M., Jara, A. J., & Skarmeta, A. F. (2013). Smart lighting solutions for smart cities. *Paper presented at the27th International Conference on Advanced Information Networking and Applications Workshops (WAINA)*, Barcelona, Spain.

Chan, M., Campo, E., Estève, D., & Fourniols, J.-Y. (2009). Smart homes—current features and future perspectives. *Maturitas*, *64*(2), 90–97. doi:10.1016/j.maturitas.2009.07.014 PMID:19729255

Chi, T.-Y., Chen, C.-H., Chao, H.-C., & Kuo, S.-Y. (2011). An Efficient Earthquake Early Warning Message Delivery Algorithm Using an in Time Control-Theoretic Approach. In C.-H. Hsu, L. Yang, J. Ma, & C. Zhu (Eds.), Ubiquitous Intelligence and Computing (Vol. 6905, pp. 161-173): Springer Berlin Heidelberg. doi:10.1007/978-3-642-23641-9_15

Chong, Z., Qin, B., Bandyopadhyay, T., Wongpiromsarn, T., Rebsamen, B., Dai, P., & Ang, M. H. Jr. (2013). *Autonomy for mobility on demand Intelligent Autonomous Systems 12* (pp. 671–682). Springer. doi:10.1007/978-3-642-33926-4_64

Chou, C.-M., Li, C.-Y., Chien, W.-M., & Lan, K.-c. (2009). A feasibility study on vehicle-to-infrastructure communication: WiFi vs. WiMAX. *Paper presented at theTenth International Conference on Mobile Data Management: Systems, Services and Middleware*, Taipei, Taiwan. doi:10.1109/MDM.2009.127

Chowdhury, N., Bhuiyan, M. M. H., & Islam, S. (2013). IOT: Detection of Keys, Controlling Machines and Wireless Sensing Via Mesh Networking Through Internet. *Global Journal of Researches In Engineering*, 13(13).

Clarke, R. Y. (2013). *Smart Cities and the Internet of Everything: The Foundation for Delivering Next-Generation Citizen Services*. Alexandria, VA: Tech. Rep.

Clendenin, M. (2010). China's 'Internet Of Things' Overblown, Says Exec. *Information Week*. Retrieved from http://www.informationweek.com/news/storage/virtualization/225700966?subSection=News

Connected Car Forecast: Global Connected Car Market to Grow Threefold Within Five Years. (2014). Retrieved from www.gsma.com

Da Xu, L., He, W., & Li, S. (2014). Internet of things in industries: A survey. *IEEE Transactions on Industrial Informatics*, *10*(4), 2233–2243. doi:10.1109/TII.2014.2300753

Dawson, B. (1976). Vibration condition monitoring techniques for rotating machinery. *The shock and vibration digest*, 8, 12.

Debnath, A. K., Chin, H. C., Haque, M. M., & Yuen, B. (2014). A methodological framework for benchmarking smart transport cities. *Cities (London, England)*, *37*, 47–56. doi:10.1016/j.cities.2013.11.004

Dlodlo, N., & Kalezhi, J. (2015). The internet of things in agriculture for sustainable rural development. *Paper presented at the2015 International Conference on Emerging Trends in Networks and Computer Communications (ETNCC)*, Namibia. doi:10.1109/ETNCC.2015.7184801

Domingo, M. C. (2012). An overview of the internet of underwater things. *Journal of Network and Computer Applications, 35*(6), 1879–1890. doi:10.1016/j.jnca.2012.07.012

Dramsvik, B. (2009). Adaptive Street Lighting: A Way Forward to Improve ITS-Implementation as Well as Increase Road Safety and to Save Energy. *Paper presented at the16th ITS World Congress and Exhibition on Intelligent Transport Systems and Services.*

Duan, X. J. (2014). Research on IOT-Based Smart Garden Project. *Paper presented at the Applied Mechanics and Materials.* doi:10.4028/www.scientific.net/AMM.608-609.321

Elkhodr, M., Shahrestani, S., & Cheung, H. (2011a). An approach to enhance the security of remote health monitoring systems. *Paper presented at the4th international conference on Security of information and networks*, Sydney, Australia. doi:10.1145/2070425.2070458

Elkhodr, M., Shahrestani, S., & Cheung, H. (2011b). Ubiquitous health monitoring systems: Addressing security concerns. *Journal of Computer Science, 7*(10), 1465–1473. doi:10.3844/jcssp.2011.1465.1473

Elkhodr, M., Shahrestani, S., & Cheung, H. (2013). A contextual-adaptive location disclosure agent for general devices in the internet of things. *Paper presented at the EEE 38th Conference on Local Computer Networks Workshops (LCN Workshops)*, Sydney, Australia. doi:10.1109/LCNW.2013.6758522

Elkhodr, M., Shahrestani, S., & Cheung, H. (2014). A semantic obfuscation technique for the Internet of Things. *Paper presented at theIEEE International Conference on Communications Workshops (ICC)*, Sydney, Australia. doi:10.1109/ICCW.2014.6881239

Elkhodr, M., Shahrestani, S., & Cheung, H. (2016). *Wireless Enabling Technologies for the Internet of Things Innovative Research and Applications in Next-Generation High Performance Computing.* Hershey, PA, USA: IGI Global.

Erol-Kantarci, M., & Mouftah, H. T. (2011). Wireless sensor networks for cost-efficient residential energy management in the smart grid. *IEEE Transactions on Smart Grid, 2*(2), 314–325. doi:10.1109/TSG.2011.2114678

Evans, D. (2012). The internet of everything: How more relevant and valuable connections will change the world. *Cisco IBSG.*

Fan, W., & Bifet, A. (2013). Mining big data: current status, and forecast to the future. *ACM sIGKDD Explorations Newsletter, 14*(2), 1-5.

Farbotko, C., Walton, A., Mankad, A., & Gardner, J. (2014). Household rainwater tanks: Mediating changing relations with water? *Ecology and Society, 19*(2), 62. doi:10.5751/ES-06632-190262

Farrar, C. R., & Worden, K. (2007). An introduction to structural health monitoring. *Philosophical Transactions of the Royal Society of London A: Mathematical, Physical and Engineering Sciences, 365*(1851), 303-315.

Foschini, L., Taleb, T., Corradi, A., & Bottazzi, D. (2011). M2M-based metropolitan platform for IMS-enabled road traffic management in IoT. *IEEE Communications Magazine*, *49*(11), 50–57. doi:10.1109/MCOM.2011.6069709

Francesco, M. D., Li, N., Raj, M., & Das, S. K. (2012). A storage Infrastructure for Heterogeneous and Multimedia Data in the Internet of Things. *Paper presented at theIEEE International Conference on Green Computing and Communications (GreenCom)*, Besançon, France. doi:10.1109/GreenCom.2012.15

Fries, J. F., Koop, C. E., Sokolov, J., Beadle, C. E., & Wright, D. (1998). Beyond health promotion: Reducing need and demand for medical care. *Health Affairs*, *17*(2), 70–84. doi:10.1377/hlthaff.17.2.70 PMID:9558786

Gubbi, J., Buyya, R., Marusic, S., & Palaniswami, M. (2013). Internet of Things (IoT): A vision, architectural elements, and future directions. *Future Generation Computer Systems*, *29*(7), 1645–1660. doi:10.1016/j.future.2013.01.010

Güngör, V. C., Sahin, D., Kocak, T., Ergüt, S., Buccella, C., Cecati, C., & Hancke, G. P. (2011). Smart grid technologies: Communication technologies and standards. *IEEE Transactions on Industrial Informatics*, *7*(4), 529–539. doi:10.1109/TII.2011.2166794

Hess, A., Malandrino, F., Reinhardt, M. B., Casetti, C., Hummel, K. A., & Barceló-Ordinas, J. M. (2012). Optimal deployment of charging stations for electric vehicular networks. *Paper presented at theThe first workshop on Urban networking*, Nice, France. doi:10.1145/2413236.2413238

Hong, I., Park, S., Lee, B., Lee, J., Jeong, D., & Park, S. (2014). IoT-Based Smart Garbage System for Efficient Food Waste Management. *TheScientificWorldJournal*, 2014. PMID:25258730

Hoy, M. B. (2015). The "Internet of Things": What It Is and What It Means for Libraries. *Medical Reference Services Quarterly*, *34*(3), 353–358. doi:10.1080/02763869.2015.1052699 PMID:26211795

Huang, Q., Xu, Y., Li, J., Su, Z., & Liu, H. (2012). Structural damage detection of controlled building structures using frequency response functions. *Journal of Sound and Vibration*, *331*(15), 3476–3492. doi:10.1016/j.jsv.2012.03.001

ITU. (2005). *ITU Internet Reports 2005: The internet of things*. Retrieved from https://www.itu.int/wsis/tunis/newsroom/stats/The-Internet-of-Things-2005.pdf

Jaykumar, J., & Blessy, A. (2014). Secure Smart Environment Using IOT based on RFID. *International Journal of Computer Science & Information Technologies*, *5*(2).

Kalra, D., & Ingram, D. (2006). *Electronic health records Information technology solutions for healthcare* (pp. 135–181). Springer. doi:10.1007/1-84628-141-5_7

Kar, A., & Kar, A. (2015). A novel design of a portable double beam-in-time spectrometric sensor platform with cloud connectivity for environmental monitoring applications. *Paper presented at the Third International Conference on Computer, Communication, Control and Information Technology (C3IT)*, Hooghly, India. doi:10.1109/C3IT.2015.7060228

Kawamoto, Y., Nishiyama, H., Yoshimura, N., & Yamamoto, S. (2014). Internet of Things (IoT): Present State and Future Prospects. *IEICE Transactions on Information and Systems*, *97*(10), 2568–2575. doi:10.1587/transinf.2013THP0009

Kim, S., Pakzad, S., Culler, D., Demmel, J., Fenves, G., Glaser, S., & Turon, M. (2007). Health monitoring of civil infrastructures using wireless sensor networks. *Paper presented at the6th International Symposium on Information Processing in Sensor Networks*, Cambridge, USA. doi:10.1109/IPSN.2007.4379685

Kim, S. A., Shin, D., Choe, Y., Seibert, T., & Walz, S. P. (2012). Integrated energy monitoring and visualization system for Smart Green City development: Designing a spatial information integrated energy monitoring model in the context of massive data management on a web based platform. *Automation in Construction*, *22*, 51–59. doi:10.1016/j.autcon.2011.07.004

Kim, Y., Suh, J., Cho, J., Singh, S., & Seo, J. (2015). Development of Real-Time Pipeline Management System for Prevention of Accidents. *International Journal of Control and Automation*, *8*(1), 211–226. doi:10.14257/ijca.2015.8.1.19

Kinnunen, M., Mian, S. Q., Oinas-Kukkonen, H., Riekki, J., Jutila, M., Ervasti, M., & Alasaarela, E. et al. (2016). Wearable and mobile sensors connected to social media in human well-being applications. *Telematics and Informatics*, *33*(1), 92–101. doi:10.1016/j.tele.2015.06.008

Lara, A. M., Kigozi, J., Amurwon, J., Muchabaiwa, L., Wakaholi, B. N., Mota, R. E. M., & Reid, A. et al. (2012). Cost effectiveness analysis of clinically driven versus routine laboratory monitoring of antiretroviral therapy in Uganda and Zimbabwe. *PLoS ONE*, *7*(4). PMID:22545079

Laranjo, I., Macedo, J., & Santos, A. (2012). Internet of things for medication control: Service implementation and testing. *Procedia Technology*, *5*, 777–786. doi:10.1016/j.protcy.2012.09.086

Li, C., Suna, L., & Hua, X. (2012). A context-aware lighting control system for smart meeting rooms. *Systems Engineering Procedia*, *4*, 314–323. doi:10.1016/j.sepro.2011.11.081

Liu, J., & Yang, L. (2011). Application of Internet of Things in the community security management. *Paper presented at theThird International Conference on Computational Intelligence, Communication Systems and Networks (CICSyN)*, Bali, Indonesia. doi:10.1109/CICSyN.2011.72

Liu, W.-H. E. (2010). Analytics and information integration for smart grid applications. *Paper presented at the2010 IEEE Power and Energy Society General Meeting*, Minneapolis, USA. doi:10.1109/PES.2010.5589898

Lomas, N. (2009). Online gizmos could top 50 billion in 2020. *Business Week*. Retrieved from http://www.businessweek.com/globalbiz/content/jun2009/gb20090629_492027.htm

Lu, R., Lin, X., Zhu, H., & Shen, X. S. (2009). SPARK: a new VANET-based smart parking scheme for large parking lots. *Paper presented at theIEEE INFOCOM '09*, Rio de Janeiro, Brazil. doi:10.1109/INFCOM.2009.5062057

Lundqvist, J., de Fraiture, C., & Molden, D. (2008). Saving water: from field to fork: curbing losses and wastage in the food chain. Retrieved from http://dlc.dlib.indiana.edu/dlc/handle/10535/5088

MacGillivray, C., Turner, V., Lund, D., Dugar, A., Dunbrack, L. A., Salmeron, A.,... Clarke, R. Y. (2014). Worldwide Internet of Things 2014 Top 10 Predictions: Nascent Market Shakes Up Vendor Strategies.

Mainetti, L., Patrono, L., & Vilei, A. (2011). Evolution of wireless sensor networks towards the internet of things: A survey. *Paper presented at the19th International Conference on Software, Telecommunications and Computer Networks (SoftCOM)*, Split, Croatia.

Melo, V. A. Z. C., Sakurai, C. A., Fontana, C. F., Tosta, J. A., Silva, W. S., & Dias, E. M. (2011). Technological Model for Application of Internet of Things to Monitor Pharmaceutical Goods Transportation. *Paper presented at the18th ITS World Congress*, Orlando, USA.

Misra, P., Simmhan, Y., & Warrior, J. (2015). Towards a Practical Architecture for the Next Generation Internet of Things. *arXiv preprint arXiv:1502.00797.*

Mohsenian-Rad, A.-H., Wong, V. W., Jatskevich, J., Schober, R., & Leon-Garcia, A. (2010). Autonomous demand-side management based on game-theoretic energy consumption scheduling for the future smart grid. *IEEE Transactions on Smart Grid, 1*(3), 320–331. doi:10.1109/TSG.2010.2089069

Muhic, I., & Hodzic, M. (2014). Internet of Things: Current Technological Review. *Periodicals of Engineering and Natural Sciences (PEN), 2*(2).

Mylonas, G., & Theodoridis, E. (2015). Developments and challenges ahead in smart city frameworks-lessons from SmartSantander. *International Journal of Intelligent Engineering Informatics, 3*(2-3), 95–119. doi:10.1504/IJIEI.2015.069882

Neil, G. (2000). *When things start to think*. Holt Paperbacks.

Nelson, G. (2015). *Where is Google's car going?: a vision emerges in Silicon Valley*. Automotive News.

Neuhaeuser, J., & D'Angelo, L. (2013). Collecting and distributing wearable sensor data: an embedded personal area network to local area network gateway server. *Paper presented at the35th Annual International Conference of the IEEE Engineering in Medicine and Biology Society (EMBC)*, Osaka, Japan. doi:10.1109/EMBC.2013.6610584

Nwogu, K. (2015). *Energy Harvesting And Storage: The Catalyst To The Power Constraint For Leveraging Internet Of Things (IoT) On Trains. (Master of Science)*. University of Nebraska-Lincoln.

Open Aquarium - Aquaponics and Fish Tank Monitoring for Arduino. (2014). Retrieved from http://www.cooking-hacks.com/documentation/tutorials/open-aquarium-aquaponics-fish-tank-monitoring-arduino

Ozkul, T., & Sevin, A. (2014). Survey of Popular Networks used for Biosensors. *Biosens. J., 3*(110), 2.

Pala, Z., & Inanc, N. (2007). Smart parking applications using RFID technology. *Paper presented at the 2007 1st Annual RFID Eurasia*, Istanbul, Turkey. doi:10.1109/RFIDEURASIA.2007.4368108

Pang, Z., Zheng, L., Tian, J., Kao-Walter, S., Dubrova, E., & Chen, Q. (2015). Design of a terminal solution for integration of in-home health care devices and services towards the Internet-of-Things. *Enterprise Information Systems, 9*(1), 86–116. doi:10.1080/17517575.2013.776118

Parcharidis, I., Foumelis, M., Kourkouli, P., & Wegmuller, U. (2009). Persistent Scatterers InSAR to detect ground deformation over Rio-Antirio area (Western Greece) for the period 1992–2000. *Journal of Applied Geophysics, 68*(3), 348–355. doi:10.1016/j.jappgeo.2009.02.005

Parwekar, P. (2011). From Internet of Things towards cloud of things. *Paper presented at the2nd International Conference on Computer and Communication Technology (ICCCT)*, Allahabad, India. doi:10.1109/ICCCT.2011.6075156

Pearce, R. (2009). IoT tech to drive water treatment in Queensland. *Computerworld.* Retrieved from http://www.computerworld.com.au/article/528602/iot_tech_drive_water_treatment_queensland/

Perandones, J. M., del Campo Jiménez, G., Rodríguez, J. C., Jie, S., Sierra, S. C., García, R. M., & Santamaría, A. (2014). Energy-saving smart street lighting system based on 6LoWPAN. *Paper presented at theThe First International Conference on IoT in Urban Space*, Rome, Italy. doi:10.4108/icst. urb-iot.2014.257221

Pereira, T., & Santos, H. (2015). *Child Abuse Monitor System Model: A Health Care Critical Knowledge Monitor System. In Internet of Things. User-Centric IoT* (pp. 255–261). Springer.

Polycarpou, E., Lambrinos, L., & Protopapadakis, E. (2013). Smart parking solutions for urban areas. *Paper presented at the IEEE 14th International Symposium and Workshops on a World of Wireless, Mobile and Multimedia Networks (WoWMoM)*, Boston, USA. doi:10.1109/WoWMoM.2013.6583499

Qin, Z., Denker, G., Giannelli, C., Bellavista, P., & Venkatasubramanian, N. (2014). A Software Defined Networking Architecture for the Internet-of-Things. *Paper presented at the2014 IEEE Network Operations and Management Symposium (NOMS)*, Krakow, Poland. doi:10.1109/NOMS.2014.6838365

Robles, T., Alcarria, R., Martin, D., Morales, A., Navarro, M., Calero, R.,... Lopez, M. (2014). An internet of things-based model for smart water management. *Paper presented at the 2014 28th International Conference on Advanced Information Networking and Applications Workshops (WAINA)*, Barcelona, Spain. doi:10.1109/WAINA.2014.129

Rost, S., & Balakrishnan, H. (2006). Memento: A health monitoring system for wireless sensor networks. *Paper presented at the3rd Annual IEEE Communications Society on Sensor and Ad Hoc Communications and Networks*, Reston, USA. doi:10.1109/SAHCN.2006.288514

Rumbaugh, J., Blaha, M., Premerlani, W., Eddy, F., & Lorensen, W. E. (1991). *Object-oriented modeling and design* (Vol. 199). Prentice-hall Englewood Cliffs.

Sanchez, L., Muñoz, L., Galache, J. A., Sotres, P., Santana, J. R., Gutierrez, V., & Theodoridis, E. et al. (2014). SmartSantander: IoT experimentation over a smart city testbed. *Computer Networks, 61*, 217–238. doi:10.1016/j.bjp.2013.12.020

Savola, R. M., Abie, H., & Sihvonen, M. (2012). Towards metrics-driven adaptive security management in e-health IoT applications. *Paper presented at theThe 7th International Conference on Body Area Networks.* doi:10.4108/icst.bodynets.2012.250241

Schneps-Schneppe, M., Namiot, D., Maximenko, A., & Malov, D. (2012). Wired Smart Home: energy metering, security, and emergency issues. *Paper presented at the4th International Congress on Ultra Modern Telecommunications and Control Systems and Workshops (ICUMT)*, St. Petersburg, Russia. doi:10.1109/ICUMT.2012.6459700

Scurlock, C., & D'Ambrosio, C. (2015). Telemedicine in the Intensive Care Unit: State of the Art. *Critical Care Clinics, 31*(2), 187–195. doi:10.1016/j.ccc.2014.12.001 PMID:25814449

Siddiqui, A. (2014). An Emperical Study of Consumer Perception Regarding Organised Retail In Tier Three Cities. *Journal of Business and Management, 1*, 91–105.

Staff, A. (2014). Connected Car Technology Shifts Internet of Things Boundaries. *PubNub.com.* Retrieved from http://www.pubnub.com/blog/connected-car-technology-shifts-internet-things-boundaries/

Su, X., Shao, G., Vause, J., & Tang, L. (2013). An integrated system for urban environmental monitoring and management based on the Environmental Internet of Things. *International Journal of Sustainable Development and World Ecology, 20*(3), 205–209. doi:10.1080/13504509.2013.782580

Sula, A., Spaho, E., Matsuo, K., Barolli, L., Xhafa, F., & Miho, R. (2013). *An IoT-Based Framework for Supporting Children with Autism Spectrum Disorder Information Technology Convergence* (pp. 193–202). Springer.

Tai, H., Celesti, A., Fazio, M., Villari, M., & Puliafito, A. (2015). An integrated system for advanced water risk management based on cloud computing and IoT. *Paper presented at the2nd World Symposium on Web Applications and Networking (WSWAN),* Tunisia. doi:10.1109/WSWAN.2015.7210305

Taylor, D. (2014). RFID in the pharmaceutical industry: Addressing counterfeits with technology. *Journal of Medical Systems, 38*(11), 1–5. doi:10.1007/s10916-014-0141-y PMID:25308613

Tiwari, G. (2011). Hardware/Software Based a Smart Sensor Interface Device for Water Quality Monitoring in IoT Environment. *International Journal of Technology and Science, 3*(1), 5–9.

TongKe, F. (2013). Smart Agriculture Based on Cloud Computing and IOT. *Journal of Convergence Information Technology, 8*(2).

Tselentis, G.-A., Serpetsidaki, A., Martakis, N., Sokos, E., Paraskevopoulos, P., & Kapotas, S. (2007). Local high-resolution passive seismic tomography and Kohonen neural networks—Application at the Rio-Antirio Strait, central Greece. *Geophysics, 72*(4), B93–B106. doi:10.1190/1.2729473

Vermesan, O., & Friess, P. (2013). *Internet of things: converging technologies for smart environments and integrated ecosystems.* River Publishers.

Vermesan, O., Friess, P., Guillemin, P., Gusmeroli, S., Sundmaeker, H., Bassi, A., & Eisenhauer, M. et al. (2011). Internet of things strategic research roadmap. *Internet of Things: Global Technological and Societal Trends, 1,* 9–52.

Vlacheas, P., Giaffreda, R., Stavroulaki, V., Kelaidonis, D., Foteinos, V., Poulios, G., & Moessner, K. et al. (2013). Enabling smart cities through a cognitive management framework for the internet of things. *IEEE Communications Magazine, 51*(6), 102–111. doi:10.1109/MCOM.2013.6525602

Wilson, C., Hargreaves, T., & Hauxwell-Baldwin, R. (2015). Smart homes and their users: A systematic analysis and key challenges. *Personal and Ubiquitous Computing, 19*(2), 463–476. doi:10.1007/s00779-014-0813-0

Wu, Y., Chen, Y., & Lei, P. (2012). Analysis on Water Quality Monitoring Technologies and Application of Internet of Things. *China Water & Wastewater, 28*(22), 9–13.

Yue, W., Changhong, S., Xianghong, Z., & Wei, Y. (2010). Design of new intelligent street light control system. *Paper presented at the 2010 8th IEEE International Conference on Control and Automation (ICCA),* Xiamen, China.

Zanella, A., Bui, N., Castellani, A. P., Vangelista, L., & Zorzi, M. (2014). *Internet of things for smart cities*. IEEE Internet of Things Journal.

Zhao, W., Wang, C., & Nakahira, Y. (2011). Medical application on Internet of Things. *Paper presented at theIET Conference*, Beijing, China.

ZHU, X.-y., & PAN, Y. (2015). Research on the Identification of Real-time Water Leakage Based on Internet-based Smart Water Meters and Complex Event Processing. *Group Technology & Production Modernization, 1*, 006.

Zorzi, M., Gluhak, A., Lange, S., & Bassi, A. (2010). From today's intranet of things to a future internet of things: A wireless-and mobility-related view. *IEEE Wireless Communications, 17*(6), 44–51. doi:10.1109/MWC.2010.5675777

KEY TERMS AND DEFINITIONS

eHealth: Also written e-health, eHealth, and E-health, is an acronym for Electronic health and a term used for managing health information in the digital world during their digital storage, electronic process and communication.

EHR: Stands for Electronic Health Record. EHR is also known as EPR (Electronic Patient Record) and EMR (electronic medical record). The term represents a patient's health record or his or her information in digital format.

Interoperability: The ability of devices to communicate on the Internet of Things regardless of their make, model or the communication technology in use.

Internet of Things: The future Internet. It can be described as a heterogeneous network that combines several devices, services, people, and wired and wireless technologies together.

Low Power Wireless Technologies: Wireless technologies that consume low energy. Typically, devices that use low power wireless technologies are characterized by their low cost as well.

M2M: Machine to Machine communications is a term used to describe communication between two devices with minimal human interference.

Smart Cities: The city of the future where technology and communications plays a vital role in everyday activities.

This work was previously published in Innovative Research and Applications in Next-Generation High Performance Computing edited by Qusay F. Hassan, pages 397-427, copyright year 2016 by Information Science Reference (an imprint of IGI Global).

Chapter 16

The Internet of Things and Beyond:
Rise of the Non–Human Actors

Arthur Tatnall
Victoria University, Australia

Bill Davey
RMIT University, Australia

ABSTRACT

In the past, it was rare for non-humans to interact with each other without any involvement by humans, but this is changing. The Internet of Things (IoT) involves connections of physical things to the Internet. It is largely about the relationships between things, or non-humans actors. In other cases the 'Things' seem to have inordinate power. The authors will ask: where does this leave humans? Are the things taking over? As a consideration of interactions like this must be a socio-technical one, in this article the authors will make use of Actor-Network Theory to frame the discussion. While the original applications for IoT technology were in areas such as supply chain management and logistics, now many more examples can be found ranging from control of home appliances to healthcare. It is expected that the 'Things' will become active participants in business, information and social processes and that they will communicate among themselves by exchanging data sensed from the environment, while reacting autonomously. The Things will continue to develop identities and virtual personalities. In the past non-human actors have needed humans to interact with each other, but this is not the case anymore. In this perhaps provocative and rather speculative article we will look not just at the Internet of Things, but other related concepts such as artificial intelligence and robotics and make use of scenarios from science fiction to investigate the Rise of the Non-Human Actors and where this may lead in the future.

PEOPLE AND THINGS

Put very simply, the Internet of Things (IoT) could be described as technology which connects any physical thing to the Internet (Colitti, Long, DeCaro and Steenhaut 2014) and could be seen as "… all about

DOI: 10.4018/978-1-5225-1832-7.ch016

physical items talking to each other." (Mukhopadhyay and Suryadevara 2014: 2). It is largely about the relationships between things, or non-humans actors, so where does this leave humans? Song (2014:75) suggests that soon "… computers would be able to access data about objects and the environment without human interaction." Clearly any consideration of implications of the IoT must be a socio-technical one and in this article we will make use of Actor-Network Theory (ANT) to frame the discussion. We will ask: are the things taking over?

The European Union organisation for Coordination and Support Action for Global RFID-related Standardisation Activities (CASAGRAS) sees the Internet of Things in terms of a "metaphor for the universality of communication processes, for the integration of any kind of digital data and content, for the unique identification of real or virtual objects and for architectures that provide the 'communicative glue' among these components". (CASAGRAS 2014:5).

In this rather speculative article we will make use of this metaphor to look at how humans relate to the Internet of Things along with other non-human technologies and where the relationship between these technologies and humans may lead in the future. In some cases specific uses of IoT technologies are deliberately activated by humans while other cases are not directly human initiated and need no human input to operate. Advances in artificial intelligence that reduce, or even remove the need for human interaction are also a factor to consider here. In examining these ideas we will make use of some concepts and scenarios from science fiction where humans are marginalised by technology as well as the use of regular research references and factual material.

THE INTERNET OF THINGS

Radio Frequency Identification (RFID) and Wireless Sensor Networks (WSN) have been in existence now for over two decades, but advances towards full use of the Internet of Things (IoT) offer much more and also pose more social challenges. There are many definitions of the Internet of Things and the CASAGRAS project sees it like this: "A global network infrastructure, linking physical and virtual objects through the exploitation of data capture and communication capabilities. This infrastructure includes existing and evolving Internet and network developments. It will offer specific object-identification, sensor and connection capability as the basis for the development of independent cooperative services and applications. These will be characterised by a high degree of autonomous data capture, event transfer, network connectivity and interoperability." (CASAGRAS 2014:10). It can thus be seen as a network of physically connected objects in which embedded processing nodes with communication capability offer a means of networked functionality and communications. The goal is to make use of computer sensor information without any need for human intervention.

SAP Research defines the IoT like this: "A world where physical objects are seamlessly integrated into the information network, and where the physical objects can become active participants in business processes. Services are available to interact with these 'smart objects' over the Internet, query and change their state and any information associated with them, taking into account security and privacy issues." (Haller 2009:12)

Pererez et al. (2014) note that the Internet of Things initially focused primarily on managing information through the use of RFID tags, to which Lazarescu (2014) adds Wireless Sensor Networks (WSN) as another key enabler, but that it now spans a wide variety of devices with different computing and communication capabilities. These are generically termed networked embedded devices (NED) in which sensors and actuators blend with the environment to share information across platforms and offers the possibility of measuring, inferring and understanding various environmental indicators (Gubbia, Buyyab, Marusic and Palaniswami 2013).

Wikipedia defines the Internet of Things as "the network of physical objects or 'things' embedded with electronics, software, sensors, and network connectivity, which enables these objects to collect and exchange data. The Internet of Things allows objects to be sensed and controlled remotely across existing network infrastructure, creating opportunities for more direct integration between the physical world and computer-based systems, and resulting in improved efficiency, accuracy and economic benefit. Each thing is uniquely identifiable through its embedded computing system but is able to interoperate within the existing Internet Infrastructure." (Wikipedia 2015).

Gubbia et al. (2013) suggest that the next important change will be to create a smart environment by the increased interconnection between objects. Mark Weiser et al., well known for their advocacy of Ubiquitous Computing, defined a smart environment as a "physical world richly and invisibly interwoven with sensors, actuators, displays, and computational elements, embedded seamlessly in the everyday objects of our lives and connected through a continuous network." (Weiser, Gold and Brown 1999). The term Internet of Things was first coined some time ago by Kevin Ashton (1999) in the context of supply chain management, but has advanced to covering wide range of other applications.

APPLICATIONS FOR USE OF THE INTERNET OF THINGS

The original applications for this technology were in areas such as supply chain management and logistics, but now many more examples can be found. Pererez et al. (2014:20) mention: "goods tracking, management of everyday objects, automatic payments in markets and military applications". This is all seen to integrate the real world into the Internet and impact on how we interact in both the virtual and physical worlds (Colitti, Long, DeCaro and Steenhaut 2014).

In a European Commission book called 'Vision and Challenges for Realising the Internet of Things' Sundmaeker, Guillemin, Friess and Woelfflé note that the Things, in the Internet of Things, "are expected to become active participants in business, information and social processes where they are enabled to interact and communicate among themselves and with the environment by exchanging data and information 'sensed' about the environment, while reacting autonomously to the 'real/physical world' events and influencing it by running processes that trigger actions and create services with or without direct human intervention. Interfaces in the form of services facilitate interactions with these "smart things" over the Internet, query and change their state and any information associated with them, taking into account security and privacy issues." (Sundmaeker, Guillemin, Friess and Woelfflé 2010:43)

Gubbia, Buyyab, Marusic and Palaniswami (2013) classify IoT applications into four domains:

- Personal and Home, at the scale of an individual or home
- Enterprise, at the scale of a community
- Utilities, at a national or regional scale
- Mobile, usually spread across other domains mainly due to the nature of connectivity and scale, but they note that there is a big crossover in applications and the use of data between domains. As an example they point out that electricity usage data in the house (Personal and Home IoT) is

made available to the electricity (utility) company that will optimise supply and demand (Utility IoT). These systems usually make use of Wi-Fi to enable higher bandwidth.

Perhaps the first example that comes to mind is the control of home appliances such as heaters, air conditioners, washing machines, dishwashers, refrigerators, ovens and home alarms, with the aim of improving home management. Potentially this can be done from a distance by the human owner with the aid of a smart phone. Initially these individual 'things' in the house would transmit regular status reports so that relevant humans could take appropriate action such as raising temperatures or activating home alarms. Perhaps in the future these things might act autonomously on the basis of these reports, so doing away with the need for human intervention in a new form of social networking – a social network of things.

Another major application of the IoT is in healthcare. To begin there is the use of RFID in hospitals to track equipment like trolleys, surgical equipment, wheelchairs, infusion pumps, defibrillators and body area scanners (Unnithan 2014). These systems link into the hospital network to display the information on terminals for use by hospital orderlies and nurses. RFID and IoT systems could potentially be integrated into other areas such as bedside applications and monitoring and then extended into remote monitoring multi-hospital environments. They could also be used in cases where patients tend to 'wander away'. (Unnithan, Nguyen, Fraunholz and Tatnall 2013, Unnithan and Tatnall 2014).

Wikipedia (2015) describes a smartwatch as: "a computerized wristwatch with functionality that is enhanced beyond timekeeping". Effectively, they are wearable computers and can collect various data from internal or external sensors or serve as a front end for some remote system. Apple's smartwatch also incorporates some fitness tracking and health-oriented capabilities. Samsung's Simband is intended for healthcare usage and has sensors to measure heart rate, blood pressure, skin temperature, sweat glands production and your number of steps daily.

A smartphone may also interface to sensors for measuring and reporting physiological parameters for healthcare. An article in The Australian newspaper (Foreshew 2015) describes 'Guardian', a new smart watch designed for monitoring the elderly at home or in aged-care facilities. It looks like a normal watch but also has an inbuilt phone, GPS and activity sensors. The chief technology officer of the designing company says that: "The objective of Guardian is to create a seamless, wearable device that elderly people can use really easily and gives peace of mind to carers and family members."

Whether using a smartphone or some other technology it is one thing to measure physiological parameters and provide information back to the person involved, and another to then make this data directly available to a medical General Practitioner or local hospital.

Environmental monitoring within a work environment is another important application. Sensors are often used in factories, shops and other work places for security, automation, climate control and security. With the IoT it will further be possible to remotely make changes to these functions whenever required and have them interact without humans. A security system might determine that no humans are present and turn off lights and air conditioning systems to save money.

Smart, driverless trains have operated between terminals at Singapore airport now for some time and an Australian mining company is using smart driverless trucks to transport ore from the mine to a train, monitored from Perth, over 1,000km away. A modern car has a multitude of computer functions such as roll sensors, stability control, brake assist and pre-collision systems designed to make them safer. These are all computer controlled and involve a variety of sensors 'talking' to each other and, in many cases, reacting autonomously to perceived threats. An article in the Sunday Age Newspaper (Purcell

2015) presents a scenario in which the computer of a car is 'hacked' remotely and the car taken over. It reports how two cyber-security researchers in St Louis, Missouri remotely took over control of a Jeep Cherokee. While this, and some other cases have not been malicious but done to test security, it does raise another scenario of the 'things' taking over. Would it not be better for a traffic signal to disable a car about to run a red light?

ARTIFICIAL INTELLIGENCE

There are ideas for new technology that are placed into a different category of risk, the most famous (and possibly the longest running) being the idea of artificial intelligence.

John McCarthy et al. (2006) first defined Artificial Intelligence in 1955 as: "the science and engineering of making intelligent machines". Wikipedia defines Artificial Intelligence (AI) as: "the study and design of intelligent agents, in which an intelligent agent is a system that perceives its environment and takes actions that maximize its chances of success." (Wikipedia 2015)

In a recent BBC broadcast (Cellan-Jones 2014), Professor Stephen Hawking suggested that: "The development of full artificial intelligence could spell the end of the human race" and that efforts to create thinking machines pose a threat to our very existence. Noting that the primitive forms of artificial intelligence developed to this time have already proved very useful, Hawking fears the consequences of creating something that is able to match or surpass humans. "It would take off on its own, and re-design itself at an ever increasing rate. Humans, who are limited by slow biological evolution, couldn't compete, and would be superseded." he said. (Cellan-Jones 2014)

ACTORS, NETWORKS AND THINGS: AUTONOMOUS THINGS – WARNINGS AND PREDICTIONS

New technologies should be examined for potential effects in society as a whole. To do so for the IoT is a complex task. While single technologies like tablet computers can be easily tested against 'predictions of doom', for more complex ideas such as artificial intelligence and massive networks it proves not so easy to design experiments to predict outcomes. For tablet computers dramatic newspaper reports can be quickly tested. So a report warning or dire consequences such as: "Electronic tablets like the iPad are a revolutionary educational tool and are becoming part of childhood, but should be watched carefully so that overuse doesn't lead to learning or behavioural problems, experts say." (The Australian 2012)

Is often quickly followed by testing resulting in a more reasoned response talking about the need for balance and control, such as: "It is hard to find an expert who thinks that monitored and considered tablet use is harmful." (Cocozza 2014)

If you accept that: "The notion of all physical objects being endowed with the capability to connect to such a network is fanciful, and in many cases without any justification ..." (CASAGRAS 2014), the following section looks at some situations which may challenge this.

Smart Cities

An article in a recent issue of the Guardian Weekly indicates that a smart city requires the interaction of three different networks: the communications grid, the energy system and the 'logistic' Internet. The logistic Internet is able to track people and things through transport and supply systems (Mason 2015). The article then points out a problem: "who controls the project and who owns the data it generates?"

Anonymity (or Lack of It): The Demise of Privacy and Human Control

The Forbes top 100 companies list rates Google as number 39. The interesting thing about this is that, unlike the 38 companies above it (including Apple at 12 and Microsoft at 25) it does not provide financial services (like the top 6) or products. Google's (and Facebook and Twitter) main source of income is the information it provides about its users. This huge company makes most of its money by keeping track of us and selling that information to people who believe they can use the information to make us spend our money their way (Forbes 2015).

When you logon to your supermarket web site to place your grocery order the software knows who you are, what you have purchased in the past, and what you are likely to order this time. The smart phone that most of us carry is actually also a tracking device. Apart from being able to tell you the location of your closest coffee shop, it can also tell anyone with access to the data it collects where you are at any given moment and where you have been. In many cases your email provider will send you personal advertisements based on the content of your supposedly private messages. Is it possible to be anonymous anymore?

'Eyes watching you' is not the only trend potentially removing freedom of action. The recently revamped Apple conditions that that: "You agree that Licensor may collect and use technical data and related information-including but not limited to technical information about your device, system and application software, and peripherals-that is gathered periodically to facilitate the provision of software updates, product support, and other services to you (if any) related to the Licensed Application. Licensor may use this information, as long as it is in a form that does not personally identify you, to improve its products or to provide services or technologies to you." (Apple 2015) It also states that: "You agree that the iTunes Service and certain iTunes Products include security technology that limits your use of iTunes Products." (Apple 2015)

A Past, Current and Future Home Scenario

Suppose you are away from your home and running late and would really like your oven to be turned on so that it will have warmed up and be ready to heat the meal you are bringing home. In the past, before you had access to the Internet of Things you could perhaps have phoned you spouse or children at home and asked them to turn the oven on for you: Scenario-1. With access to the IoT you could now use your smartphone to turn it on for you while you are on your way home: Scenario-2. In the future it could well be possible for the things to take over and, based on what you have done in the past and perhaps on the weather, for the oven to turn itself on in anticipation: Scenario-3. Do we want the technology to assumption it knows what you need?

The CASAGRAS report offers the following ideas: "In the minimalist version of the Internet of Things these supported objects may be identified but do not 'do' anything actively, cannot communicate one with another and do not display any level of intelligence." It goes on to note thought, that: "In the strongest version, object sets can be identified that communicate with each other exploiting the potential of ubiquitous computing and ubiquitous networks. It is also being seen as a vehicle for achieving actuation and control in real world applications." (CASAGRAS 2014)

SCIENCE FICTION

Another definition of the Internet of Things is: "the network formed by things/objects having identities, virtual personalities operating in smart spaces using intelligent interfaces to connect and communicate with the users, social and environmental contexts". (EPoSS 2014) The key point here is that the things have identities and virtual personalities. The following section looks at some scenarios from science fiction that just might contain something of value to this discussion.

Nineteen Eighty-Four: "Big Brother is Watching You"

Electronic surveillance aids in tracking targets and identifying suspicious activities. It is also used to detect potentially suspicious left luggage and to monitor unauthorised access. This can be coupled with automatic behaviour analysis. While this would not involve a TV camera in each room listening in and keeping track of our movements, recently in Australia, and many other countries, there has been much discussion about the collection of meta-data, particularly in relation to law enforcement.

In a recent article in the Sunday Age (Elder 2015), in relating to Orwell's (1949) book Nineteen Eighty-Four, Federal MP Adam Brandt says he doesn't equate surveillance just with use of technology, but see a difference between sharing and being spied on. Sociologist Dan Woodman: "notes that any disquiet people might have about CCTV in the city streets has been up-ended by the fact that just about everyone carries a camera … With this mixture of both confession and judgement, we have become a self-eating version of Orwell's Thought Police …". (Orwell 1949). Philosopher John Thrasher notes that we tend to think that: "there is a fundamental difference about sharing information about ourselves on Facebook or Twitter and having the Government collect metadata about who we call or what we do online." (Elder 2015). In Nineteen Eighty-Four, O'Brien, from the Ministry of Love, comments that: "The choice for mankind lies between freedom and happiness and for the great bulk of mankind, happiness is better." (Orwell 1949:275). Following from this, Thrasher suggests that this and the ability to share a multitude of thoughts over social media "have made it possible for individuals and groups to attempt to enforce their orthodoxy on those they disagree with." (Elder 2015). In this case, it is probably the case that social media has "increased our tolerance with being observed." As Winston Smith once thought: "Always the eyes watching you and the voice enveloping you. Asleep or awake, working or eating, indoors or out of doors, in the bath or in bed — no escape. Nothing was your own except the few cubic centimetres inside your skull." (Orwell 1949:29).

2001: A Space Odyssey

In this film, the screenplay of which was written by Stanley Kubrick and Arthur C. Clarke, the U.S. spacecraft *Discovery One* is bound for Jupiter (Wikipedia 2015). On the spaceship, most of the important operations are controlled by the ship's computer: HAL 9000 which its manufacturers claim is "foolproof and incapable of error". The crew know the computer as 'HAL'. At one point during the trip HAL reports the imminent failure of an antenna control device but when this is checked no fault is found and HAL is thought to be in error. The crew now believe that something is wrong with the computer and agree to disconnect it, but when astronaut Frank Poole attempt to do this, HAL severs his oxygen hose and sets him adrift in space. Dave Bowman now commands HAL to "Open the pod bay doors", but HAL answers: "I'm sorry, Dave. I'm afraid I can't do that. … This mission is too important for me to allow you to jeopardize it."

In this scenario the computer considered that it knew better than the humans and proceeded to act on this by refusing a human order.

The Terminator

The fear of thinking machines is a not recent. The original use of the word 'robot' has been traced to the Karel Čapek play "Rossum's Universal Robots" in which a greedy developer unleashes the demise of humans through a robot revolution. More recently the successful movie series 'The Terminator' posits a problem caused by the creation of a satellite defence system that becomes self-aware and 'protects itself from humanity.' The script of 'Terminator 2: Judgment Day' (Cameron and Wisher 1991) contains the following passage: "The Skynet funding bill is passed. The system goes on-line August 4th, 1997. Human decisions are removed from strategic defense. Skynet begins to learn, at a geometric rate. It becomes self-aware at 2:14 a.m. eastern time, August 29. In a panic, they try to pull the plug.

SARAH: And Skynet fights back.
TERMINATOR: Yes. It launches its ICBMs against their targets in Russia.
SARAH: Why attack Russia?
TERMINATOR: Because Skynet knows the Russian counter-strike will remove its enemies here.

Before dismissing this scenario please consider the "Flash Crash" of 2010. Careful analysis of the crash has sometimes traced it to a single mistake by a human when allowing an automated trading system to make unlimited purchases – the 'thing' was accidentally given the power to crash the entire stock market! "Specifically, at 2:32 p.m., a fundamental trader used a broker algorithm to sell a total of 75,000 e-mini contracts with a notional amount of approximately $4.1 billion on the Chicago Mercantile Exchange (CME). The trade was intended to hedge an existing equity position. The trader entered the order correctly and specified an upper limit on the amount sold as a percentage of volume but did not set a price limit for the trade. As a result, price movements were magnified by a feedback loop from the volume participation settings, precipitating the actual flash crash. The CFTC/SEC report concluded that this single trade was the root cause of the flash crash." (Madhavan 2012)

Rings of Power

In an article entitled 'Wandering Things', Niehaus (2014:114) points out that "Often they function as spies who disclose the intimate secrets of their owners, because things allow 'unperceived perception." In Wagner's cycle of four epic operas titled: 'The Ring of the Nibelung' (Wagner 1876), a ring of power is created from gold stolen from the Rhine-Maidens by Alberich the Nibelung. Much of the material in Wagner's Ring Cycle was drawn from traditional legendary material of the Germanic people: from The

Saga of the Volsungs, The Edda and The Nibelungenlied (Magee 2004). Niehaus (2014: 121) notes that "it is evident that the category of personal property does not fit for the ring-thing ..." which is claimed as their own by many including Alberich, Wotan, Siegfried and the Rhine-Maidens, in each case acting as a curse on its owner. Alberich, the ring's creator points out that the ring's master will be the ring's slave, and the ring's curse proves the truth in this. The Ring of the Nibelung has a power, and a 'life' of its own.

Also well-known are the three books of J.R.R. Tolkien's (1954): 'Lord of the Rings', in which the Dark Lord Sauron forges "One ring to rule them all, One ring to find them, One ring to bring them all and in the darkness bind them." (Tolkien 1954). The One Ring also has a 'life' of its own and when one owner loses his usefulness to it, the ring seeks another until eventually found by Bilbo the Hobbit. The One Ring has the power to make its possessor obsessed with it and to refuse to be willingly parted from it. To its possessor it becomes 'his precious' and he becomes a slave to the ring. As Niehaus (2014:121) points out "Things that prove themselves as actors exceed the logic of personal property", and the ring of the Nibelung and the One Ring of the Lord of the Rings are examples of this. In each case the ring-thing is a non-human actor that has gained a power of its own.

CONCLUSION

In this article we have traced the commonly discussed characteristics of an emerging technology, but one that is unlike any other. The Internet can be compare with the telephone system in that it is an enabling technology connecting humans. The IoT takes a potential peripheral use and transforms the Internet into a technology enabling *technologies*. This change is a fundamentally different type of technology that can be seriously compared with the science fiction scenarios involving self-aware artificial intelligences. The IoT, involving sensor input and remote activation of devices, sometimes by other devices, is a network where the level of autonomy and decision making by the devices is fundamentally different from anything we have seen before. The uptake of social media, the power of search engine companies and the ubiquity of mobile devices show that new technologies can produce change that is unexpected in its order of magnitude. An ANT approach offers unique opportunities for understanding the new technology in two distinct ways: understanding the democracy of things and seeing the IoT as a set of possible translations.

The Democracy of Things

A socio-technical approach has been found to allow the understanding of technology adoption not possible by failing to 'listen' to the technology and socio-technical actors. This becomes crucial with the IoT as purely technical actors become able to gather their own information, totally independent on humans and to 'talk among themselves' with the ability to activate functions purely on the basis of the state of the network. These new technologies have the ability to create new interactions and change the power of their interaction not through an influence over the human component of a socio-technical actor, but through their nature. Consider the home security network. WiFi connected sensors and cameras are connected to the Internet so that homeowners can be notified that movement has activated the camera. They can also be connected to the telephone system so that authorities are notified that the home has been invaded – all reasonable tools for the home owner. This same home network may also have door locking capability, be connected to security sensors around the home or be able to unlock doors. There does not have to be much imagination involved to see these devices 'voting' to close doors and call the authorities when they 'decide' that the homeowner is not available to make decisions. If one is looking for an example of the possibilities of democracy without humans then the computer trading delivered stock market crashes of 6th May, 2010 are a sobering reminder of unexpected results when a system meant to do some restricted thing (place stock orders for a few investors) becomes an order of magnitude larger than the original plans and places the majority of orders.

Searching for Translations

When viewed in terms of the democracy of thing, the question "how can we consider the ways the IoT might manifest in the future?" (Phillips 2010) arises. Each application of technology that fits into the IoT has a simple plan for making life more efficient in some way. The ANT approach presumes that it is the interaction of actors and not the intent of the original designer that determines the translation of innovations.

REFERENCES

Apple. (2015). iTunes Store Terms and Conditions. Retrieved from http://www.apple.com/legal/internet-services/itunes/au/terms.html

Ashton, K. (1999, June 22). That 'Internet of Things' thing. *RFID Journal*.

Cameron, J., & Wisher, W. (1991). Terminator 2: Judgment Day. Retrieved from http://www.scifiscripts.com/scripts/t2.txt

CASAGRAS. (2014). Final Report: RFID and the Inclusive Model for the Internet of Things. Retrieved from https://docbox.etsi.org/zArchive/TISPAN/Open/IoT/low%20resolution/www.rfidglobal.eu%20CASAGRAS%20IoT%20Final%20Report%20low%20resolution.pdf

Cellan-Jones, R. (2014, December 2). Stephen Hawking warns artificial intelligence could end mankind. Retrieved from http://www.bbc.com/news/technology-30290540

Cocozza, P. (2014). Are iPads and tablets bad for young children? Retrieved from http://www.theguardian.com/society/2014/jan/08/are-tablet-computers-bad-young-children

Colitti, W., Long, N. T., DeCaro, N., & Steenhaut, K. (2014). *Embedded Web Technologies for the Internet of Things. Internet of Things: Challenges and Opportunities. Mukhopadhyay* (pp. 55–74). Heidelberg, S. C., Germany: Springer.

Elder, J. (2015, October 18). Everyone is Watching. Sunday Age (Melbourne, Fairfax) 16.

EPoSS. (2014). Definition of the Internet of Things. Retrieved from http://www.smart-systems-integration.org/public

Forbes. (2015). The World's Biggest Public Companies. Retrieved from http://www.forbes.com/global2000/list/#tab:overall

Foreshew, J. (2015). *Watch watches out for the aged.* The Australian Melbourne, News Media.

Gheorghiu, V. (1950). *The Twenty-Fifth Hour*. Ontario, Canada: Simon & Schuster Pub.

Gubbia, J., Buyyab, R., Marusic, S., & Palaniswami, M. (2013). Internet of Things (IoT): A vision, architectural elements, and future directions. *Future Generation Computer Systems*, 29(7), 1645–1660. doi:10.1016/j.future.2013.01.010

Haller, S. (2009). *Internet of Things: An Integral Part of the Future Internet*. Prague: SAP Research.

Lazarescu, M. T. (2014). *Internet of Things Low-Cost Long-Term Environmental Monotoring with Reusable Wireless Sensor Network Platform. Internet of Things: Challenges and Opportunities. Mukhopadhyay* (pp. 169–196). Heidelberg, S. C., Germany: Springer.

Madhavan, A. (2012). Exchange-traded funds, market structure, and the flash crash. *Financial Analysts Journal*, 68(4), 20–35. doi:10.2469/faj.v68.n4.6

Magee, E. (Ed.). (2004). *Legends of the Ring*. London: The Folio Society.

Mason, P. (2015). We can't allow tech giants to rule. *The Guardian Weekly* (London).

McCarthy, J., Minsky, M., Rochester, N., & Shannon, C. (2006). A Proposal for the Dartmouth Summer Research Project on Artificial Intelligence (1955). *AI Magazine*, 27(4), 12–14.

Mukhopadhyay, S. C., & Suryadevara, N. K. (2014). *Internet of Things: Challenges and Opportunities. Internet of Things: Challenges and Opportunities. Mukhopadhyay* (pp. 1–17). Heidelberg, S. C., Germany: Springer.

Niehaus, M. (2014). *Wandering Things - Stories. Le Sujet De L'Acteur - An Anthropological Outlook on Actor-Network Theory. Kapriev, G., Roussel, M. and Tchalakov, I* (pp. 109–129). Paderborn, Germany: Wilhelm Fink.

Orwell, G. (1949). *Nineteeen Eighty-Four*. Great Britain: Martin Secker & Warburg.

Pererez, I. C. Barbolla and A. M. Bernardos(2014). Exploring Major Architectural Aspects of the Web of Things. In S. C. Mukhopadhyay (Ed.), Internet of Things: Challenges and Opportunities (pp. 19-54). Heidelberg, Germany, Springer:

Phillips, M. (2010, May 11). Nasdaq: Here's Our Timeline of the Flash Crash. *The Wall Street Journal*.

Purcell, A. (2015). *Driver beware: your car could be hacked while you're in it*. Melbourne, Fairfax: Sunday Age.

Song, Z., Lazarescu, M. T., Tomasi, R., Lavagno, L., & Spirito, M. A. (2014). *High Level Internet of Things Applications Development Using Wireless Sensor Networks. In S. C. Mukhopadhyay* (Ed.), *Internet of Things: Challenges and Opportunities*. (pp. 75–110). Heidelberg, S. C., Germany: Springer. doi:10.1007/978-3-319-04223-7_4

Sundmaeker, H., Guillemin, P., Friess, P., & Woelfflé, S. (2010). Vision and Challenges for Realising the Internet of Things. Brussels, European Commission - Information Society and Media DG.

The Australian. (2012). Parents warned of side effects of tablet computer overuse on children. Retrieved from http://www.theaustralian.com.au/news/parents-warned-of-side-effects-of-tablet-computer-overuse-on-children/story-e6frg6n6-1226314156128

Tolkien, J. R. R. (1954). *The Fellowship of the Ring*. England: Allen & Unwin.

Unnithan, C. (2014). *Examining Innovation Translation of RFID Technology in Australian Hospitals through a Lens Informed by Actor-Network Theory PhD*. Victoria University.

Unnithan, C., Nguyen, L., Fraunholz, B., & Tatnall, A. (2013). RFID translation into Australian Hospitals: An exploration through Actor-Network Theoretical Lens. *Proceedings of the International Conference on Information Society (i-society 2013)*, Toronto, University of Toronto, Canada.

Unnithan, C., & Tatnall, A. (2014). Actor-Network Theory (ANT) based visualisation of Socio-Technical Facets of RFID Technology Translation: An Australian Hospital Scenario. *International Journal of Actor-Network Theory and Technological Innovation*, *6*(1), 31–53. doi:10.4018/ijantti.2014010103

Wagner, R. (1876). *Der Ring des Nibelungen*. Bayreuth, Germany: Bayreuth Festspielhaus.

Weiser, M., Gold, R., & Brown, J. S. (1999). The Origins of Ubiquitous Computing Research at PARC in the late 1980s. *IBM Systems Journal*, *38*(4), 693–696. doi:10.1147/sj.384.0693

Wikipedia. (2015). 2001: A Space Odyssey (film). Retrieved from https://en.wikipedia.org/wiki/2001:_A_Space_Odyssey_(film)

Wikipedia. (2015, October). Internet of Things. Retrieved from https://en.wikipedia.org/wiki/Internet_of_Things

Wikipedia. (2015, October). Smartwatch. Retrieved from https://en.wikipedia.org/wiki/Smartwatch

Wikipedia. (2015, October). Artificial intelligence. Retrieved from https://en.wikipedia.org/wiki/Artificial_intelligence

This work was previously published in the International Journal of Actor-Network Theory and Technological Innovation (IJANTTI), 7(4); edited by Ivan Tchalakov, pages 56-67, copyright year 2015 by IGI Publishing (an imprint of IGI Global).

Chapter 17
Data Management in Internet of Things

Ashok V. Sutagundar
Basaveshwar Engineering College, India

Daneshwari Hatti
BLDEA Dr. P. G. H. College of Engineering and Technology, India

ABSTRACT

This chapter gives overview of Internet of Things (IoT), various issues in IoT and describes data management in IoT. IoT is emerging technology which interconnects things through the Internet. Things present in the surrounding are communicated and control the objects without human intervention. IoT helps in performing two way communications among various heterogeneous devices by using cloud storage and cloud computing. IoT mainly concentrates on communication, so the vast amount of data generated from plenty of devices is to be managed as it consumes lot of memory. Data management includes data processing techniques such as data filtering, aggregation, compression, data archiving. Various processing techniques eliminate the irrelevant data, reduce communication overhead and enhance bandwidth, storage space and Quality of service.

INTRODUCTION

Internet of Things (IoT) is emerging technology in field of wireless communication. The enabling factors of IoT are static and mobile devices present around us. The necessary parameter for perfect IoT to be employed in the daily life is the ability to interact with devices technologies, platforms on which IoT work, standards, protocols and communication between source and destination. The user can control the devices through the information stored in Internet. IoT, an evolving technology helps in exchange of data between things. The basic building blocks of IoT comprise of Things, Sensing unit, Communication, Intelligence and control (J. Gubbi, R. Buyya, S. Marrusic & M. Palaniswami, 2013). The data is collected from sensor network, stored in Internet and the objects utilize data for application. Wireless Sensor Network (WSN) is part of IoT. The purpose of deploying a sensor network is to monitor an area for an event of interest. The advent of an affordable wireless technology has led to the vision of em-

DOI: 10.4018/978-1-5225-1832-7.ch017

Figure 1. WSN Environment

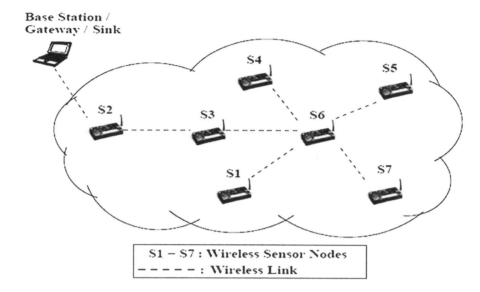

powering small monitoring devices with a wireless network interface that can be used to communicate with other nodes. A WSN is a network made of a numerous sensor nodes with sensing, computation and communications capabilities. These sensor nodes are scattered in an unattended environment situated far from the user as shown in Figure 1 (J. Yick, B. Mukherjee & D. Ghosal 2008, G Anastasi, M. Conti, M. Di Francesco & A. Passarella, 2009, I. F. Akyildiz & I.H. Kasimoglu,2004, I. F. Akyildiz, M. C. Vuran, O. B. Akan & W. Su., 2004). A basic sensor node typically comprises of five main components namely processor, storage unit (memory), power supply, sensors and/or actuators, and communication (radio) subsystems (J. Yick et al., 2008, G. Anastasi et al., 2009, S. Tilak, N. A. Ghazaleh, & W. Heinzel-man.2002, F. Akyildiz, W. Su, Y. Sankarasubramaniam, & E. Cyirci, 2002). It is apparent that standard processor, possibly augmented with Digital Signal Processing (DSP) and other co-processors and some Application Specific Integrated Circuit (ASIC) units provide adequate processing capabilities at accept-ably low energy rates (A. Mallikarjuna, V. Reddy, A. U. Phani Kumar, D Janakiram, & G Ashok, 2009). Sensor nodes are the actual interface to the physical world. These devices observe or control physical parameters of the environment.

The components of a sensor node functions are as follows: (1) transceivers are used for sending and receiving data simultaneously to either sink or intermediate node, (2) the energy source powers the sensor node, (3) the sensor hardware can convert physical quantities into an electric signal, (4) the Analog to Digital Converter (ADC) converts the analog signal generated by the sensor into a digital signal and sends it to the processor, and (5) the processor can execute easy operations on the received digital signal and can store it into memory. Memory is used to store programs and intermediate data (A. Mallikarjuna et al., 2009). Sensor nodes have the ability to communicate either among each other or directly to an external Base Station (BS) called as sink. The deployment of more number of sensors allows sensing over larger geographical regions with greater accuracy. The conventional methods of data gathering and processing in WSNs could lead to some of the problems like higher energy consumption, redundant data transmission, increased latency, communication overheads, etc. The negative impacts of these problems could be minimized using novel techniques for data fusion, data aggregation, optimal energy efficient routing, etc. The large amount of data gathered of the objects by sensors is sent to data management layer. The data management layer plays an important role in storing, fusing, aggregating heterogeneous data, filtering, clustering various data types. The data gathered is enormous cannot be processed at the sensor node, so it is transferred to the sensor cloud. The storing of data in sensor cloud is crucial task. The data stored in cloud may be required by user for certain application or for the control of devices so this data should be stored in proper manner for easy access. To provide service to the user cloud computing platform evolved. The user fetches data and controls the objects as they expect resulting in to Internet of Things. The objects are communicated with other object by collecting the information through the cloud which is Internet, hence the term Internet of Things.

Internet of Things is network of connected objects where objects communicate via Internet. The basic building blocks of IoT are WSN, Internet and objects. In IoT, data collected from heterogenous network is vast, since huge numbers of devices are connected in network. The heterogenous data gathered is to be processed for communicating with the devices in different network. It has become serious issue because processing huge data, storing, data retrieval, data accessing plays an important role. IoT system is illustrated in Figure 2. Things are present in various network namely WSN, Adhoc, MANET and VANET, communication is established among these things through Internet.

Figure 2. Illustration of IoT

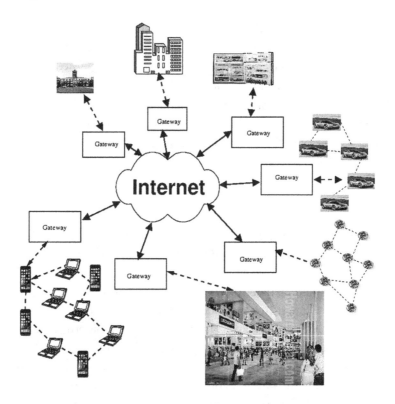

ORGANIZATION OF CHAPTER

The history of IoT is briefly explained in section 2. Section 3 provides the details of related work in IoT. The architecture of IoT is explained in detail in section 4. The objects plays important role in IoT. Communication between devices, controlling their operation, syncronisation among devices results issues. Section 3 discusses issues in IoT. Billion of devices are connected in network so vast amount of data from various networks is generated, it results in too many challenges which is discussed in section 5. Applications of IoT are discussed in section 6.

BACKGROUND

The term "Internet of Things" was coined by Kevin Ashton in 1999 and founded MIT Auto-ID center, In 2000 LG announces the first Internet refrigerator, In 2002 Ambient Orb is released to display weather information based on Internet data. In 2004 Chana Schoenberger publishes an article entitled "The IoT" in Forbes, in which the article quotes Ashton as saying: "We need an IoT, a standardized way for computers to understand the real world." In 2005 the UN's International Telecommunication Union publishes a report entitled "The IoT". In 2008 IPSO alliance is founded to promote the use of IP in connected devices. In 2009, a dedicated EU Commission action plan ultimately saw the Internet of Things as a general evolution of the Internet "from a network of interconnected computers to a network of interconnected objects" (European Commission, 2009). In 2010 ZigBee Alliance and IPv6 Forum form strategic partnership with IPSO to speed adoption of IP networked smart objects. In 2011 wireless firm Ericsson predicts that there will be more than 50 billion connected devices by 2020. In 2012 World IPv6 Launch Day is held IPv6 provides virtually unlimited IP addresses for devices to connect to the Internet. In 2013 Chip maker Qualcomm, along with other tech firms, forms the AllSeen Alliance, which is intended to develop an open framework to enable the IoT. In 2014 Chip maker Intel and other high tech firms set up a competing group to AllSeen Alliance to promote an open framework for the IoT called the Open Interconnect Consortium (I.K. Darryl & Traft 2014).

RELATED WORK

In (Shen Bin, Liu Yuan & Wang Xiaoyi 2010) data mining models are described to manage data. Multilayer data mining model, distributed data mining, grid based are discussed. In multilayer data mining model four different layers are used for data collection, data management, event processing and data mining service layer. Distributed data mining model addresses the problem solving of depositing heterogeneous data. Data collected is mined using different models for enhancing IoT performance.

In (Yang Liu, Zhikui Chen, Haozhe Wang, Xiaoning L., 2011) the processing of data using deluge computing is done. It is combination of cloud computing and sea computing. The heterogeneous data collected is redundant and transmission cost of this data is more. Hence data compression using various methods is done. Compression with wavelet, compressed sensing and linear transfer is done to reduce the data. PCA and ICA reduces data dimension, explains data correlation instead of exact meaning. Tremendous data dimension is decreased by granule configuration. Adaptive coding and modulation provides an increase in system capacity.

In (B. Christophe, 2012) distributed framework is proposed for scalable search and management mechanisms in IoT. Nodes are capable of processing semantic web description and semantic web technologies approach is used for enhancing interoperability between devices.

In (Yeong-Sheng Chen & Yu-Ren Chen 2012) data acquisition and integration platform for IoT is proposed. Context oriented approaches are discussed. Study of deployment, management and control of different sensor is done for proper acquisition of sensor data. Context data is produces by using context oriented mechanisms. Context broker is used to produce contextual portfolio which is annotated with semantics description. The acquired data is integrated in to semantic contexts and enhance the mobile applications by adapting to conditions.

In (Lei Yuan & Junsan Zhao, 2012) Spatial Data Warehouse system in IoT environment (SDWIT) is constructed. SDWIT consists of four layers namely collection, transmission, storage and update for real time information. SDWIT system realizes data integration, data fusion for abstract data type and entity perception data hence improves ability of data analysis and data mining.

In (C. Perera, A. Zaslavsky, P. Christen & D. Georgakopoulos, 2014) context aware computing survey is done. In this paper authors evaluated context aware computing have been tackled in desktop, web, mobile, sensor network and pervasive computing paradigm.

In (S. Vural et.al, 2014) authors proposed in network caching mechanisms for catching IoT data. The model is designed for tradeoff between multihop communication costs and freshness of data arrival. IoT data caching provides less load on network when catching routers are near to requesters then data sources.

ARCHITECTURE OF IOT

Internet of Things is the interconnection of objects, and controlling of objects activities through the data collected and stored in Internet. The data collected from the end objects, devices, smart devices, environmental monitored parameters is processed and appropriate decision is made across the devices. The devices are made up of smart embedding processing unit across the sensor node. If the objects connected are huge then processing, storage of data becomes serious issue. So the data collected or acquired by sensor nodes is sent to sink node then to the intermediate layer. In intermediate layer data collected by sensor nodes via the gateway is been processed. The data is gathered by various WSN, AdHoc network, VANET and MANET. The data collected from the heterogenous network cannot be accessed by different objects running in different application domain. The heterogeneity has to be removed by converting or transforming the data types to common form, which is compatible to all the objects present in different network. The routing protocols should also be compatible. The data processed has to be stored in cloud for accessibility to the users who requires the information about objects connected to Internet. This data is communicated to Internet by using proper protocols. The processed data have to be modeled and stored in database. The data is clustered based on features, patterns and on the modes of data collected. The database is required to store data, easy retrieval of data by relevant object. This data is accessed by users by sending requests to the cloud and in turn controls the operation of objects. Objects decide to take an action by studying the information of objects, which is collected by sensors. The layered structure of IoT is given in Figure 3.

Figure 3 describes the layered structure of IoT. The objects are present in object layer and sends data to the gateway. In gateway the processing is done prior to transfer of data to Cloud. The data processed is stored in cloud for providing access to the user.

Figure 3. Layered structure of IoT

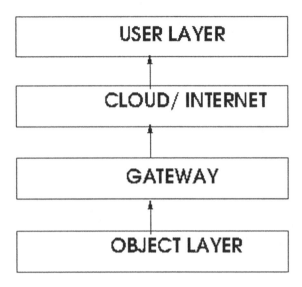

Communication from Physical Sensor to Gateway

The information gathered is stored in to the database. The stored data can be retrieved based on user driven, event driven and sink driven. Energy efficient routing protocols are necessary for communication of data among objects and from the distinct sensor nodes to the sink node. Data can be transferred from one node to sink node by single hop or multihop communication. Data need to be secured before sending to the database. The data collected by sink node has to be sent to cloud for storage as sensor nodes have minimum storage capability. The data sent to cloud has to be stored properly by classifying, clustering according to features of data. Since large amount of data is collected by various devices, it is stored in cloud named as sensor cloud. As the data is manipulated and arranged in specific order it becomes easier for the accessing of data by user. When user requests service to the cloud, cloud has to provide service to the users by allocating storage space, bandwidth, and many resources. The service is provided by using cloud computing platform.

Cloud Computing

The sensors deployed in environment for monitoring and collecting data have many limitations. Hence it needs to store the data and process in cloud, which offers vast storage space for processing the data. The operation which cannot be done at sensor node is done at cloud platform. According to the US NIST (National Institute of Standards and Technology) defines the concept of Cloud computing as follows: *Cloud computing is a model for enabling convenient, on demand network access to a shared pool of configurable computing resources (e.g., networks, servers, storage, applications, and services) that can be rapidly provisioned and released with minimal management effort or service provider interaction* (S. K. Dash, J. P. Sahoo, S. Mohapatra & S. P. Pati, 2012).

Cloud computing allows the user to access the data, provide services, resources for the users. The cloud computing provides three platforms namely Saas, Paas and Iaas.

- **SaaS:** Software as Service provides the users to develop and run their application by accessing the services from the cloud.
- **PaaS:** Platform as Service provides the user a platform to build own application and software for the execution of task.
- **IaaS:** Infrastructure as Service provides the user to use the services, resources available in the cloud.

In cloud computing, the virtual machines facilitate the services to the user and the user doesn't need any information of location of the servers. They start working on their application. The data is collected from wireless sensor network through gateway to the cloud. Sensor gateway collects data from the sensors, compresses, filters, encrypt and send to the cloud through cloud gateway. In cloud gateway the data received by the sensor gateway is been processed, decompresses, decrypts and sends data to the cloud for storing. The data in the cloud is stored in database for the user applications. The data collected by various types of sensors is having different data types and this has to be compatible with all the applications. The unified model is required for converting in to single data type. To monitor sensor status continuously or periodically sensor cloud infrastructure came in to existence.

In cloud computing the services are given to the user. The user requests the service to the cloud, services, resources are made available to the user, and the user can access the data from physical sensors. The physical sensors are made virtual and can be accessible by the user. The user need not worry about the location of physical sensors. The application requiring the data from few sensors need not access the data from all sensors so the virtual sensors group is made and data collected by physical sensors is made available at the cloud. Service templates will be created by the sensor owner, responsible for registering the sensors to the cloud. If the user completes the execution of task can delete the data and virtual sensor from the cloud if not required which results in to free space. The user can monitor and control the flow of data through the services provided by the cloud platform but directly the user cannot control physical sensors, it is done only on virtual sensors. In Internet of Things the things have to communicate and share data. The devices are expected to be 50 billion by 2020 the data collected by sensors is huge and due to limited storage it cannot be processed at the sensors hence cloud is to be integrated for processing data, storage, provide services to the user for fetching the data and securing the data. Cloud offers the IoT wide storage and resources for many applications and offers scalability and flexibility and allows the IoT to handle real time scenarios helps to take proper decisions in time. Cloud also provides platform for sharing of any kind of data from sensors among the users (A. Botta, W. Donato, V. Persico & A. Pescape, 2014). The sensor senses the device, environment, human body and collects the data sends to the cloud. The cloud acts as sink and sensor acts as source. The data collected in sink can be collected periodically or continuously based on application. The sensors have to be monitored and tracked for finding the particular sensor data available at which location. This data is processed and sent to cloud for providing access to the user. These tasks have to be dealt by Sensor Cloud.

Sensor Cloud

Sensor Cloud is new paradigm handles the data collected by several sensors and monitors several applications. According to MicroStrains's Sensor-Cloud definition "it is a unique sensor data storage, visualization and remote management platform that leverage [sic] powerful cloud computing technologies to provide excellent data scalability, rapid visualization, and user programmable analysis. It is originally designed to support long-term deployments of MicroStrain wireless sensors, Sensor-Cloud now supports any webconnected third party device, sensor, or sensor network through a simple OpenData API" (Sensor Cloud, n.d.).

Internet of Things

IoT is interconnection of objects through Internet. Things communicate based on user request and occurrence of events. The factors responsible for communication between multiple devices or single devices are the information about things, bandwidth, compatibility of data, compatibility of routing protocols etc. The thing requires data for making decision and controlling the device. The data is accessed through Internet if connectivity is available. The devices have to communicate in absence of Internet by retrieving the relevant data from the database. The service cannot be affordable by the device since low computing devices are present in network so the service is provided through the middleware layer. The middleware layer is used as intermediate between the devices. The data is processed and analyzed, decision are made at the middleware then sent to the device. Communication takes place based on user driven or event driven.

User driven: when user requests data to the Internet for controlling the object present in particular location. The data is retrieved by the cloud by sending request. If the data requested is frequently used then it has to be stored in cache memory instead of searching in the main database, which helps in reducing time. This is very helpful in real-time applications.

Event driven: The device sends information regarding the present location, surrounding status to the other device. Based on the information received the device has to check the previous condition of that device and the surrounding status then makes proper decision, sends the commands for the other device to take relevant action.

In IoT, communication between devices is important task which results in too many challenges. For secure communication among devices the devices need to be identified, data has to be secured, resources should be made available. Some of the issues in IoT are discussed in next section.

ISSUES IN INTERNET OF THINGS

IoT is network of network that is objects are connected together, form a network and these objects can be connected to Internet. Some of the issues in IoT are

1. Identification of devices
2. Fault tolerance
3. Data management
4. Energy minimization
5. Heterogeneity and Interoperability
6. Security and privacy
7. Scalability and flexibility
8. Resource management

Identification of Devices

The nodes deployed in the network sense the information and send to the sink node. The user requires details and information gathered by particular node for controlling that respective node. So it becomes necessary for finding its location and origin of data. Identifying particular device in the network becomes very difficult. Methods have to be developed for identifying devices. RFID tags are used for identifying devices and giving particular information of a device. As number of devices increases IPv6 is used to address the devices instead of IPv4. The device identity is very essential to identify the relevant data of a device. If the identification of device fails then the information sensed by the sensor is difficult to transmit to other device. So mechanisms for identifying the devices based on location, type of object can be done.

Fault Tolerance

If a node fails to function, then recovery of network should be possible without affecting the functioning of network. In IoT, devices connected are numerous hence managing the devices plays an important role. If a single device fail to transmit information in network it results in improper functioning of system. So the devices are to be monitored frequently or periodically to ensure proper functioning of the system without interruption by any device.

Data Management

In IoT vast amount of data is generated from devices, it needs to be controlled and managed. Hence data management plays an important role. So data processing techniques such as data collection, aggregation, and data warehouse modeling have to be applied on data for easy access by the user.

Data Collection and Aggregation

The sensor present in environment observes and gathers data regarding environmental conditions, RFID tags gathers information regarding location of objects and its status. Devices or objects have to be monitored continuously and information can be collected periodically or continuously. Since the objects connected are in billions, the information generated is huge hence the continuous transfer of data becomes problem. Due to continuous collection of data, to store the data huge memory is required. The data collected may be repeated or may be relevant to the previous data. This becomes challenge for storing the data, eliminating the same data by filtering. If the data collected is relevant to previously collected data, then patterns are generated and this pattern is forwarded to database instead of the complete data. This reduces the amount of data to be transmitted. Storage and communication overhead is reduced. If periodically collected data resembles particular format then based on prediction the data can be generated, by doing this the sensing of devices, collection, transfer of data to the sink is not required. In order to handle these problems, algorithms should be developed for eliminating redundancy, prediction of data and pattern generation. Data collection strategies are to be designed for collecting the proper data from the devices in real time. Based on the device characteristics the collection strategy can be designed.

Data Warehouse Modeling

Once the data is transferred to database the data or information has to be modeled and stored in well defined manner for easy retrieval by the user. Database modeling is important aspect as gathered data is vast it should be compressed, clustered and stored for easy discovery of things information present at particular location. To store the data classification, clustering, pattern generation can be applied in order and these operations can be altered in different order for efficient storage of data. So it is crucial task of modeling the enormous data, hence methodology for modeling data ware house can be done.

Energy Minimization

The data collected by several objects has to be processed across sensor node for reducing communication overhead. Data has to be aggregated from several heterogeneous networks. The processing of data is done by embedding software algorithms on sensor node. Second approach is by using gateway for processing the sensed data, as sensor node has less computing capacity and energy.

Heterogeneity and Interoperability

The major challenge arises due to incompatible addressing modes between networks. The data present in WSN has to be transferred for upper layers by using communication protocols. The WSN protocol will not be compatible with the upper layer then the compatible routing protocol is required to develop. Wireless or wired communication is used for communicating among devices, transferring data from WSN to database. The conversion has to be done for elimination of heterogeneity among devices and helps them to communicate each other without the intervention of human being. The device response is controlled by taking proper decision with the help of stored data.

Security and Privacy

The data generated by several objects is to be secured during accessing or transferring to upper layers. Cryptographic algorithms have to be developed with minimum energy requirement for securing data. In case of business applications if one user is not interested in sharing his personal data the privacy of data is to be ensured. Mainly authentication is to be established by giving access only to the user or application who has registered to the cloud. This helps in secured communication in IoT.

Scalability and Flexibility

As the numbers of objects are increasing day by day the IoT platform has to be flexible for adding up of devices. It should allow uninterrupted communication between devices in the network without compromising the functionality of network. To overcome this issue algorithm has to be developed for updating the new devices in the network. The mechanism for linking the newly arrived device to the network has to be developed.

Resource Management

Resources are essential for the operation of any devices hence resource should be allocated for devices in the network. In IoT many devices are connected as per the survey, hence the services, resources, better path for communicating between devices are essential. Hence resource brokering is to be done prior to allocating the resources. The efficient utilization of resources is challenging for increasing the network life time hence resource prediction and provisioning can be employed. Devices add to the network so resource adaptation mechanisms need to be employed for adapting and secure accessing of resources.

DATA MANAGEMENT IN IOT

In Internet of Things the objects plays major role. These objects need to be sensed and processed. These objects in network are connected to sensor for sensing and transferring information to the Internet through wireless medium resulting to Wireless Sensor Network (WSN). The sensor nodes have less computing capacity and energy. The sensed data is not manipulated so it is transferred to the data management layer or intermediate layer. As the devices connected in network is increasing the information also increases. The information is stored in Internet and accessed by the user. The storage requirement is increasing hence the data has to be managed and stored in well defined manner. Data from different objects placed in different networks are classified as Continuous or discrete data, Descriptive data about objects, process, systems, positional data, pervasive environmental data, sensor data and historical data (I. F. Akyildiz et.al, 2004).Data is important in IoT, without data IoT system is incomplete. Data is categorized as data and metadata. Data is to be stored in proper manner for easy access by the users to serve various applications. Metadata is the method of representing data of data, which helps user to access relevant data instead of searching all the stored data. Metadata gives general description of the data to which category, section and area it belongs. The data is searched based on this metadata (I. F. Akyildiz et.al, 2004). The data is collected from things through wireless sensor network. It is necessary to consider the factors like data to be collected in regular intervals or continuously. IoT has several devices connected and data generated will increase with number of devices hence the data, which is generated, previously has to be stored in memory and static database has to be maintained. IoT has to decide which information has to be retrieved, delete from database and provide easy access to the data for the users. When user request a data from devices, the data can be accessed through the Internet in which data is stored. In this context the data collected from several devices is of different format so the accessing becomes issue. Data management has to be done for easy accessing of data or for intercommunication between networks constituting several objects. In data management data processing techniques such as data cleaning, data filtering, removal of heterogeneity of data, data aggregation, data fusion, data modeling and data warehouse modeling has to be performed on the data collected through various mechanisms. Data modeling, data warehouse modeling is challenging issue. Modeling of data involves semantic modeling. Data warehouse modeling is to be done for storing the data of objects. The data received from heterogeneous network is to be converted to unified model for achieving compatibility between networks, so the conversion mechanism has to be designed.

In IoT the data from sensor node is collected at the intermediate layer through gateway. The data collection mechanisms are required to collect different types of data from various devices. The collected data is to be processed for eliminating the redundancy, adding the missing values and removal of noise.

Figure 4. Illustration of Data management in IoT

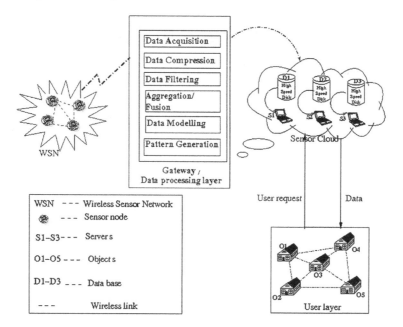

The data is cleaned and then converted to intelligent information. The meaningful information is sent to the sensor cloud or Internet. This information is used by the objects to decide and act accordingly. Figure 4 describes the mechanism of communication between devices in IoT.

In Figure 4 shows the flow of data from device to device. The data is manipulated at gateway then forwarded to sensor cloud. The data is to be stored in structured manner for easy access. Storage disks are present for storing the data based on their arrival, types, size, dependent data etc. The storage disks are to be classified based on data present in gateway. The objects present in user layer uses this data for controlling other objects. Objects sends request to the cloud, provides resources, services, based on priority and availability of resources. If the object requires the present status of environment then sensor node is given command for sensing the area of interest. The objects communicate each other by accessing the Internet and collecting the real time information from sensor node. If Internet connection is not available the data can be accessed from static database resulting in to offline mode of operation.

DATA PROCESSING TECHNIQUES

Data generated by objects or data collected by sensor is transferred from perception layer to data processing layer through gateway. The gathered data from the sensor is raw data, which need to be filtered and aggregated. To reduce the data volume, clustering of heterogeneous data, compression, modeling of data etc. is carried out in processing layer. Figure 4 illustrates the process of collecting data, processing and transmitting to upper layers through Gateway. Data processing is done in two ways that is processing the stream data continuously and another way is processing of data on the stored data (M. Meng, P. Wang & Chao-Hsien, 2013).

Data Filtering

Data filtering has to undergo on the acquired data for removal of redundancy. The data cleaning are various types. Data cleaning often adopts probability statistic and spatial-temporal correlation methods. Data sensed by the sensor is erroneous, arrival of repeated data and failure of sensor nodes causes IoT system to face many problems. To overcome this problem data cleaning is done prior to communication. Data lost during sensing is added by using some approaches that is by predicting the data based on the context and previous data. Filters can be applied for removal of noise, extra information which is not relevant to the context. Data filtering reduces the communication overhead by eliminating the irrevelant information from the sensed data. In (S. R. Jeffery, G. Alonso, M. J. Franklin, W. Hong, & J. Widom, 2006) authors proposed Extensible sensor stream processing approach for cleaning sensor data.

Data Collection and Acquisition

It is method of collecting data sensed by the sensors in various networks. Data collection can be done in two ways that is event level and timing level. Data is collected when an event occurs. In timing level the data is collected from heterogeneous networks at regular intervals of time or contiuously. In continuous method the data collected may be repeated but for real time application continuous streaming of data is essential. This causes many problems as devices connected are huge data sensed is in form of petabytes. The data has to be compressed, classified, stored and secured. Sensor discovery and configuration is important aspect before collection of data. The sensor has to be detected and the information is collected from sensors. Smartlink is software tool used for sensor discover and configuration (C. Perera, P. Jayaraman, A. Zaslavsky, D. Georgakopoulos, & P. Christen, 2014).

Data Compression

The data collected by sensors is enormous and requires more bandwidth for transmission of data to the cloud. So the data is compressed by using lossless techniques such as LZ77. The compressed data is sent from sensor gateway to the cloud gateway, it decompresses and stores in the cloud. The compressed and decompressed data have to be same. If the data are not matching the faulty data will be accessed by the user and improper results will be found. Data compression makes the data secured. Compression is done on original data it is converted in to the other form, cannot be retrieved without applying decompression techniques. This ensures secured communication of original data without loss during transmission. Compression of data serve two purposes that is data size reduction and compressed data is encapsulated with compression algorithms result in to secured data. YOAPY is data model used for preprocessing, it does compression and gather RAW data, YOAPY perform optimizations of power consumption through data aggregation (A. J. Jara, M. A. Zamora, & A. F. Skarmeta, 2012).

Data Aggregation

Data aggregation is to aggregate the data from various networks and objects. The data was processed earlier to data aggregation. The objects present in different networks have to be fused and integrated so data mining is done.

In distributed data mining, global and local nodes are present. The global nodes are central part of mining system. The raw data obtained from objects is pre-processed by local nodes and then it is sent for global node. This helps in reduce the amount of data transmission. The data from all local or sub nodes is collected and aggregated.

In centralized data mining the data from the device has to be transferred to central node every time. So the amount of data to be transferred is more, hence cost increases (C. Zhang, G. Zeng, H. Wang & Xuyan Tu, 2012).

Modeling of Data

Data modeling is necessary for interoperability between objects of different types. Modeling data using semantic and metadata is done. Spatial temporal analysis of data is carried out before aggregation. Metadata is data of data. It explains the location of object from which data is collected and at time of collection. For example the student information is requested by user. The particular format of student is stored in database that is name; roll no; semester taken from particular school. Database constituting metadata helps user to retrieve the relevant data in less time.

Data Retrieval

Synchronous and asynchronous modes are the two methods of data retrieval. When user requests the data from the cloud the relevant data has to be retrieved from the database. In IoT the sensed data is collected periodically or continuously, causes huge amount of data, which is to be retrieved and stored in database periodically or based on the query request. Retrieving of data is to be performed for avoiding loss of data. In Gonizzi, G.Ferrari, P. Medagliani & J. Leguay (2013) authors proposed mechanism to collect gathered data from the gateway periodically. This helps in avoiding loss of data when sensor node fails to communicate.

APPLICATIONS

Internet of Things is finding its use in several areas such as home, hospitals, agriculture fields, irrigation systems, electricity consumption, retail and logistics, business etc. Using IoT smart home can be developed. For example when the person goes office from home he may fail to check whether geyser is off, fan, TV is turned off. It's not possible to come back and check when he is travelling longer distances so if smart home is developed then he can control all the home appliances remotely. This is the benefit of IoT. When he sends a request to check TV is off then data relevant to TV of his home is sent to the user and then he can control that device through Internet.

In healthcare the patient condition can be monitored. The sensors are attached to patient to monitor patient blood pressure, temperature, pulse rate and essential parameters for controlling the patient suffering from disease. The sensors sense the body of patient and send information to the database and if any abnormality it sends message to doctor and doctor will controls the patient condition and brings normal. In this context the sensors form the physical layer and information will be collected in database. The user is doctor is who controls and makes the proper decision by analyzing the data gathered from the patient in less time.

In transportation the roads and transported goods are equipped with tags and sensors that send information to traffic control sites and transportation vehicles to find the better route in the traffic. It also provides the tourist with appropriate transportation information, and monitors the status of the transported goods.

In the parking lot the car and path are equipped with sensors provides the information to the driver about the status of the parking. The information is made available to the car driver. The car driver based on the received information can park the car without any problems. In the metropolitan city the traffic is more and the passengers struggle to find the path to reach the destination. By inculcating IoT the problem get solved. Sensors are deployed on the car and the road; it provides the traffic information to the driver for proper navigation and finding the appropriate route in less time.

FUTURE RESEARCH DIRECTIONS

IoT plays a vital role in our daily life as it provides the interconnection among living and non living things. IoT provides an automatic service based on the individual desires. It provides interconnection between human and objects surrounding the human for betterment of living with less effort. IoT can help the patient sitting at home in taking the medication prescribed by the doctor sitting in remote place. Hence IoT has several issues in handling the vast amount of heterogeneous data sensed by the sensor. So to overcome the issues mentioned in the chapter work has to be done for using IoT in our daily life.

CONCLUSION

In the present condition IoT plays vital role in real time application. As Internet of Things is capable of two way communication that is the sensors senses the objects, gathers data and collects in base station or sink node. This data is processed at the sensor cloud before sending to user. The user sends request to the cloud for the details of particular object and decides the action to be taken for the operation of object. As the devices number is increasing, the identification, location tracing of device becomes challenge. The vast amount of data gathered is to be handled by developing processing techniques and security of data is important aspect as one person does not like to share his personal information to other person. Security and privacy of the data is to be ensured for the users. Data retrieval is very challenging task as the user requires relevant data, if he didn't get immediately then it becomes very crucial for solving real time problems. Data storing in database has to be done in proper manner for easy access of data. Data management is crucial task in IoT for the effective communication between devices. Data is handled properly by employing different processing techniques hence reducing the storage space, increasing bandwidth, providing quality of service.

REFERENCES

Akyildiz, I. F., & Kasimoglu, I. H. (2004). Wireless Sensor and Actor Networks: Research Challenges. *Elsevier Ad Hoc Networks Journal*, 2(4), 351–367. doi:10.1016/j.adhoc.2004.04.003

Akyildiz, I. F., Su, W., Sankarasubramaniam, Y., & Cyirci, E. (2002). Wireless Sensor Networks: A Survey. *Computer Networks: The International Journal of Computer and Telecommunications Networking, 38*(4), 393–422. doi:10.1016/S1389-1286(01)00302-4

Akyildiz, I. F., Vuran, M. C., Akan, O. B., & Su, W. (2004). Wireless Sensor Networks: A Survey Revisited, *Elsevier. Computer Networks, 45*(3), 245–261.

G Anastasi, M Conti, M Di Francesco & A Passarella, (2009).Energy Conservation in Wireless Sensor Networks: A Survey. *Elsevier Ad Hoc Networks Journal, 7*(3), 537-568.

Bin, S., Yuan, L., & Xiaoyi, W. (2010). Research on Data Mining Models for The Internet of Things.*2010 International Conference on Image Analysis and Signal Processing (IASP)*, (pp. 127-132).

Botta, A., Donato, W., Persico, V., & Pescape, A. (2014). On the Integration of Cloud Computing and Internet of Things.*International Conference on Future Internet of Things and Cloud (FiCloud)* (pp. 23-30). doi:10.1109/FiCloud.2014.14

Chen, Y.-S., & Chen, Y.-R. (2012). Context-Oriented Data Acquisition and Integration Platform for Internet of Things.*2012 Conference on Technologies and Applications of Artificial Intelligence (TAAI)*, (pp. 103-108). doi:10.1109/TAAI.2012.64

Christophe, B. (2012). Managing Massive Data of the Internet of Things through Cooperative Semantic Nodes. *2012 IEEE Sixth International Conferenceon Semantic Computing (ICSC)*, (pp. 93-100). doi:10.1109/ICSC.2012.29

Darryl & Traft. (2014). *A Look back at Internet of Things, Origin, Evolution*. Retrieved from www.eweek.com

Dash, S. K., Sahoo, J. P., Mohapatra, S., & Pati, S. P. (2012). Sensorcloud: Assimilation of Wireless Sensor Network and the Cloud. *Networks and Communications. Advances in Computer Science and Information Technology, 84*, 455–464.

European Commission. (2009). *Internet of Things – An action plan for Europe 278*. Retrieved from http://eur-lex.europa.eu/LexUriServ/site/en/com/2009/com2009_0278en01.pdf

Gonizzi, P., Ferrari, G., Medagliani, P., & Leguay, J. (2013). Data Storage and Retrieval with RPL Routing.*9th International Conference Wireless Communications and Mobile Computing (IWCMC)* (pp. 1400-1404). doi:10.1109/IWCMC.2013.6583761

Gubbi, J. J., Buyya, R., Marrusic, S., & Palaniswami, M. (2013). Internet of Things (IoT): A Vision, Architectural Elements, and Future Directions. *Journal of Future Generation Computer Systems, 29*(7), 1645–1660. doi:10.1016/j.future.2013.01.010

Jara, A. J., Zamora, M. A., & Skarmeta, A. F. (2012). Knowledge Acquisition and Management Architecture for Mobile and Personal Health Environments based on the Internet of Things. *IEEE 11th International Conference on Trust, Security and Privacy in Computing and Communications* (pp. 1811 – 1818).

Jeffery, S. R., Alonso, G., Franklin, M. J., Hong, W., & Widom, J. (2006).Declarative Support for Sensor Data Cleaning. In Pervasive Computing: Proceedings of 4th International Conerence. (PERVASIVE 2006) (pp. 83-100). doi:10.1007/11748625_6

Liu, Y., Chen, Z., Wang, H. & Xiaoning, L. (2011). An Architecture of Data Processing Using Deluge Computing in Internet of Things. *4th International Conference on Cyber, Physical and Social Computingin Internet of Things (iThings/CPSCom)*, (pp. 692-697). doi:10.1109/iThings/CPSCom.2011.17

Mallikarjuna, A., Reddy, V., Phani Kumar, A. U., Janakiram, D., & Ashok, G. (2009). Wireless Sensor Network Operating Systems: A Survey. *Inderscience International Journal of Sensor Networks*, *5*(4), 236–255. doi:10.1504/IJSNET.2009.027631

Meng, Wang & Chao-Hsien. (2013). Data Management for Internet of Things: Challenges, Approaches and Opportunities. *Green Computing and Communications (GreenCom), 2013 IEEE and Internet of Things (iThings/CPSCom), IEEE International Conference on and IEEE Cyber, Physical and Social Computing* (pp.1144-1151).

Perera, C., Jayaraman, P., Zaslavsky, A., Georgakopoulo, D., & Christen, P. (2014). Sensor Discovery and Configuration Framework for the Internet of Things Paradigm.*Proceedings of 2014 IEEE World Forum on Internet of Things, WF-IoT 2014* (pp. 94-99). doi:10.1109/WF-IoT.2014.6803127

Perera, C., Zaslavsky, A., Christen, P., & Georgakopoulos, D. (2014). Context Aware Computing for The Internet of Things: A Survey. *IEEE Communications Surveys and Tutorials*, *16*(1), 414–454. doi:10.1109/SURV.2013.042313.00197

Sensor-Cloud. (n.d.). Retrieved from http://sensorcloud.com/system-overview

Tilak, S., Ghazaleh, N. A., & Heinzelman, W. (2002). A Taxonomy of Wireless Micro-senor Network Models. *Mobile Computing and Communications Review*, *6*(2), 28–36. doi:10.1145/565702.565708

Vural, S., Navaratnam, P., Wang, Wang, Dong, & Tafazolli. (2014).In-Network Caching Of Internet-Of-Things Data. *2014 IEEE International Conference on Communications (ICC)*, (pp. 3185-3190). doi:10.1109/ICC.2014.6883811

Yick, J., Mukherjee, B., & Ghosal, D. (2008). Wireless Sensor Network Survey. *International Journal of Computer and Telecommunications Networking*, *52*(12), 2292–2330.

Yuan, L., & Zhao, J. (2012). Construction of the system framework of Spatial Data Warehouse in Internet of Things environments.*2012 IEEE Fifth International Conference on Advanced Computational Intelligence (ICACI)*, (pp. 54-58). doi:10.1109/ICACI.2012.6463121

Zhang, Zeng, Wang, & Tu. (2012). Analysis on Data Mining Model Objected to Internet of Things. *International Journal of Advancements in Computing Technology*, *4*(21), 615 -622.

KEY TERMS AND DEFINITIONS

Cloud Computing: It is the platform providing resources, storage, processing elements, services to the user and helps in handling large amount of data from things connected in network.

Data Redundancy: It is the recurrent data present in the database causes erroneous data formation.

Heterogeneity: The networks where sensors located are different, the data collected is of various types, the protocols used for routing and communication varies based on networks, it together constitutes heterogeneity.

Internet of Things: It is interconnection of things in network through Internet. The communication and sharing of information among the objects by accessing the data through the Internet without intervention by human is termed as IoT.

Metadata: It is the method of representing data by categorizing data based on location, type and time at which data is sensed. It is data of data.

Middleware Layer: It is the intermediate layer formed by various software algorithms for manipulating the data.

Semantic Modeling: It is the conceptual data modeling, expresses the relation between the data.

Sensor Cloud: It is the infrastructure constituting WSN and cloud capable of monitoring the sensor data, sensor position and data origin.

This work was previously published in the Handbook of Research on Wireless Sensor Network Trends, Technologies, and Applications edited by Narendra Kumar Kamila, pages 80-97, copyright year 2017 by Information Science Reference (an imprint of IGI Global).

Chapter 18
Big Data Analysis in IoT

Aqeel-ur Rehman
Hamdard University, Pakistan

Rafi Ullah
Hamdard University, Pakistan

Faisal Abdullah
Hamdard University, Pakistan

ABSTRACT

In IoT, data management is a big problem due to the connectivity of billions of devices, objects, processes generating big data. Since the Things are not following any specific (common) standard, so analysis of such data becomes a big challenge. There is a need to elaborate about the characteristics of IoT based data to find out the available and applicable solutions. Such kind of study also directs to realize the need of new techniques to cope up with such challenges. Due to the heterogeneity of connected nodes, different data rates and formats it is getting a huge challenge to deal with such variety of data. As IoT is providing processing nodes in quantity in form of smart nodes, it is presenting itself a good platform for big data analysis. In this chapter, characteristics of big data and requirements for big data analysis are highlighted. Considering the big source of data generation as well as the plausible suitable platform of such huge data analysis, the associated challenges are also underlined.

INTRODUCTION

Internet of Things (IoT) is a concept of providing uniquely identifiable objects connectivity to Internet. When billions of things connect, it will be difficult to manage and analysis huge amount of data as each object will send and retrieve data. Many challenges are related with analysis of big data on IoT due to the heterogeneity, variable data formats, priorities and specifically numerous numbers of connected devices.

Big data actually refers to huge amount of data. It includes all type of data. The data is traditionally collected and then processed and move to data warehouse for analysis. When a large amount data is collected from different sources, it may not necessarily relational data. This data can be treated as big data. As data is increasingly becoming more varied, more complex and less structured, it has become

DOI: 10.4018/978-1-5225-1832-7.ch018

imperative to process it quickly. Meeting such demanding requirements poses an enormous challenge for traditional databases and scale-up infrastructures. Big Data refer to new scale-out architectures that address these needs.

In IoT, data management is a big problem due to the connectivity of billions of devices, objects, processes generating big data. Since the Things are not following any specific (common) standard, so analysis of such data becomes a big challenge. There is a need to elaborate about the characteristics of IoT based data to find out the available and applicable solutions (Shi & Liu, 2011). Such kind of study also directs to realize the need of new techniques to cope up with such challenges.

Big Data

Big data actually refers to more data or huge amount of data. It includes all type of data. The data is traditionally collected. And then processed and move to data warehouse for analysis. When a large amount data is collected from different sources, it may not necessarily relational data. This data can be treated as big data.

As data is increasingly becoming more varied, more complex and less structured, it has become imperative to process it quickly. Meeting such demanding requirements poses an enormous challenge for traditional databases and scale-up infrastructures. Big Data refer to new scale-out architectures that address these needs (O'Leary, 2013).

Big Data is characterized by its variety of attributes as follows that is often referred to as a multi-V model (Assunção, Calheiros, Bianchi, Netto, & Buyya, 2014).

- **Variety:** Data types
- **Velocity:** Data production and processing speed
- **Volume:** Data size
- **Veracity:** Data reliability and trust
- **Value:** Worth derived from exploiting Big Data

Big Data is presenting a complex range of analysis and use problems. These can include (Villars, Olofson, & Eastwood, 2011):

- Having a computing infrastructure that can ingest, validate, and analyze high volumes (size and/ or rate) of data
- Assessing mixed data (structured and unstructured) from multiple sources
- Dealing with unpredictable content with no apparent schema or structure
- Enabling real-time or near real-time collection, analysis, and answers

Internet of Things

The Internet of Things (IoT) refers to the next generation of Internet which will be comprising over large number of heterogeneous nodes from small sensors and handheld devices to large web servers and super computer clusters (Bin, Yuan, & Xiaoyi, 2010). The term internet of things was first coined by Kevin Ashton over a decade ago. IoT is actually a great revolution in the history of computing. In IoT concept everything will be connected to internet having its own identity and everything will be able to communicate with each other (refer to Figure 1). It is actually a concept which is a combination of many other concepts such as Cloud computing, Ubiquitous computing, and wireless sensors networks and technologies like IPv6, RFID technology, and wireless communication technologies. IoT is the core of Smart Planet that is proposed by IBM Corporation (Bin, Yuan, & Xiaoyi, 2010).

There are three visions of IoT (i) Things Oriented vision, (ii) Internet Oriented vision, and (iii) Semantic Oriented vision. According to a survey, in near future, billions of things will be interconnected. They will be having capability of sending and receiving data. All objects around us will communicate and respond to a phenomenon. These objects may contain our cell phones, computers, vehicles, all living things, and appliances in our room and so many other things. Due to such huge connected network a huge amount of data will be produced which will require being stored, analyzed and processed. Smart connectivity with existing networks and context aware computation using network resources is an indispensable part of IoT (Gubbi, Buyya, Marusic, & Palaniswami, 2013). For technology to disappear from the consciousness of the user, the Internet of Things demands: (i) a shared understanding of the situation of its users and their appliances, (ii) software architectures and pervasive communication networks to process and convey the contextual information to where it is relevant, and (iii) the analytics tools in the Internet of Things that aim for autonomous and smart behavior. With these three fundamental grounds in place, smart connectivity and context-aware computation can be accomplished (Gubbi, Buyya, Marusic, & Palaniswami, 2013).

Figure 1. Internet of Things

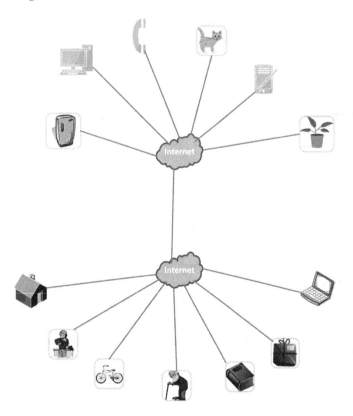

There are many challenges associated with the new emerging concept of IoT (Aqeel-ur-Rehman, Mehmood, & Baksh, 2013) listed as follows:

- Unavailability of Standard
- Limitations due to current Internet architecture
- Security and Privacy due to heterogeneity and globalization
- Managing Heterogeneity
- Identification and Authentication
- Trust and Ownership
- Integration and Coordination
- Regulations

There are many domains where IoT shall be applied. Following are some of the domains and applications area of IoT:

1. Wireless Sensor Network
    a. Agriculture and Breeding
    b. Oil and Gas
    c. Logistics and Supply Chain
2. Control and Automation
    a. Aerospace and Aviation
    b. Automotive
    c. Safety, Security and Environment Monitoring
3. E-Health
    a. Pharmaceutical
    b. Tele-Medicine

DATA WAREHOUSING AND MINING TECHNIQUES

Data Warehousing Techniques

Data warehousing is a relational database specially designed for query and analysis purposes not for transactional processing. As shown in Figure 2, data is stored coming from different sources as well as historical data i.e. data of previous transactions. Data warehousing enabled an organization to consolidate data from different sources and to separate analysis workload from transaction workload. In addition to a relational database, a data warehouse environment includes an Extraction, Transportation, transformation, and Loading (ETL) solution, an Online Analytical Processing (OLAP) engine, client analysis tools, and other applications that manage the process of gathering data and delivering it to business users. Data store in data warehouse is actually the data obtain as a result of different operational systems or transactions. For reporting purposes the data is first pass through operational data store.

The data warehouse is:

Figure 2. Data Warehouse Technique

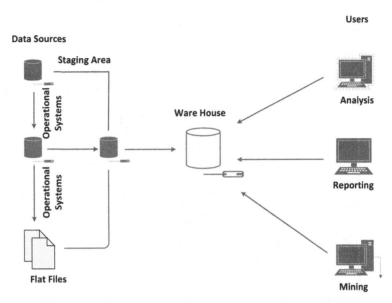

- **Subject-Oriented:** The data in the data warehouse is organized so that all the data elements relating to the same real-world event or object are linked together.
- **Non-Volatile:** Data in the data warehouse are never over-written or deleted — once committed, the data are static, read-only, and retained for future reporting.
- **Integrated:** The data warehouse contains data from most or all of an organization's operational systems and these data are made consistent.
- **Time-Variant:** For an operational system, the stored data contains the current value. The data warehouse, however, contains the history of data values.
- **No Virtualization:** A data warehouse is a physical repository.

Data Mining Techniques

It is the process, as depicted in the following Figure 3, in which data is analyzed from different perspective in order to discover knowledge and summarizing them into useful information. It is generally called knowledge discovery. Technically, data mining is the process of finding correlations or patterns among dozens of fields in large relational databases and then these patterns are used to predict future trends by using algorithms and different approaches to define patterns.

Different data mining techniques are (Chun-Wei, Chin-Feng, Ming-Chao, & Yang, 2014):

1. *Artificial neural network* are non-linear, predictive models that learn through training. Although they are powerful predictive modeling techniques, some of the power comes at the expense of ease of use and deployment. Because of their complexity, they are better employed in situations where they can be used and reused, such as reviewing credit card transactions every month to check for anomalies.

Figure 3. Data Mining Technique

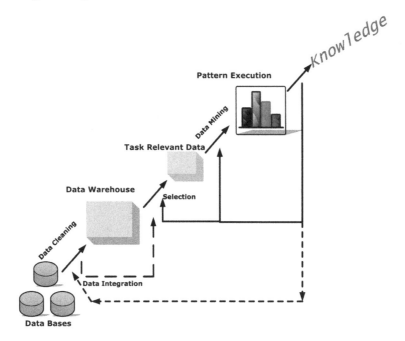

2. *Decision trees* are tree-shaped structures that represent decision sets. These decisions generate rules are used to classify data. Decision trees are the favored technique for building understandable models.

3. *The nearest-neighbor method* classifies dataset records based on similar data in a historical dataset.

SOURCES OF BIG DATA

There are two main sources of big data. One is the entirely new data sources and other is revolution in existing data generated sources. According to a survey in 2011 data growth in past five year was nearly infinite. The entirely new data sources include those industries which digitized their contents. Some of the new data sources include:

-   Media/Entertainments
-   Video surveillance
-   Life sciences
-   Health care
-   Transportation, telecommunication etc.

    Expanding existing sources of big data include:

-   Smart instrumentation
-   Banking

- Financial transactions etc.

We can infer that IoT is actually the main source of big data. As in IoT, billions of things will be having unique identification and connected with each other and each and every object will send and receive data. So this will generate huge amount of data. It can be best explained by example of library. Each book will be having its own RFID. Each book will be able to send their status to every other book and other object in library. If library have 1000 book and each book sends 2 MB of data per hour. It means that 2 GB per hour and 48 GB per day data are producing in library. The concepts of IoT will results an infinite amount of data which are to be analyzed, process and son on. There new techniques will be applied to collect, analyze and process that data.

DATA CHARACTERISTICS IN IoT

In IoT environment, collected data will be having different properties. Following are some of the important properties and requirements that we have to deal with:

Heterogeneity

In internet of things the main property of data and devices is heterogeneity. It means that different devices will be connecting for different purposes. For example a fan may be connected to your smart phone. Also their performance is different. And each collects different type of data. Each object will be given its own ID which will differentiate one object from another. The data heterogeneity is due to difference in architecture of IoT and application model. The "big data" solutions and cloud platforms can provide infrastructure and tools for handling, processing and analyzing deluge of the IoT data. However, we still need efficient methods and solutions that can structure, annotate, share and make sense of the IoT data and facilitate transforming it to actionable knowledge and intelligence in different application domains since many of the devices and resources in IoT are highly distributed and heterogeneous (Barnaghi, Wang, Henson, & Taylor, 2012).

Polymorphism

In internet of things the huge amount of data may exist in many forms. It may be audio, video, text or image. The data is static as well as dynamic. In internet of things large amount of sensors are used for reading. Some of sensors collect text data; some will collect audio and so on. Therefore this variety of data leads to polymorphism of data. And data become difficult to analyze due to polymorphism.

Data Transmission

The data is not only collected it must be transmitted somewhere for processing. The main problem is of transmission over Wireless Sensor Network (WSN) to main source of IoT. As we have already discussed the polymorphic nature and heterogeneity of data, so some data is difficult to sense but easy to transmit like text data. And some data is easy to sense but difficult to transmit like multimedia data. The transmission of data depends on many factors such as battery power of WSN and the application running there. The secret data should be transmitted without the intervention of any one. In such WSN when data is corrupted it is difficult to find whether error is due to software failure or some other reasons because data is in polymorphic nature. This leads to difficulty in data management and analyzing in IoT.

Data in Large Quantity

Data in IoT will be in very large quantity as each object will have its own data. For example, book store having 1000 books. In RFID system each book will be having its own RFID i.e. there will be 1000 RFID's. Each will process let say 100 MB data per day. So in total 100 x 1000 MB = 100 GB of data is processing per day. Then what about billions of things when connect together in IoT. So, IoT leads to a huge amount of data. The situation becomes more critical when data in some real time system is processed.

Data Integration

As the data come from different devices or human beings itself are the source of data, so it may be in form of some physical phenomenon. This data can be integrated with existing applications data processing chain in order to support situation awareness and context awareness. In such cases it is important to integrate one kind of data with other kind of heterogeneous data. Semantic descriptions can support this integration by enabling interoperability between different sources; however, analysis and mapping between different semantic description models is still required to facilitate the IoT data integration with other existing domain knowledge (Barnaghi, Wang, Henson, & Taylor, 2012).

Data Abstraction

It is the way of representing physical world data in simpler form to the users. Different ontologies, such as W3C, SSN ontologies, are available which provide number of constructs to present and manage the data.

Data Access

Data access in IoT is one of the difficult tasks in internet of things because of heterogeneous devices and different sensor network across the networks. Data access in IoT can be implemented at low level usually at network level etc. For this purposes some low level programming and operating system is required.

Interpretation and Perception

Data is usually collected as physical phenomenon by some sensors or any collecting source. It should be interpreted correctly first. Because there will be huge amount of data collected in Internet of things. May be not all the data is useful to us. So it must be first interpreted correctly. And then must percept correctly by the receiving device. In internet of things it is a great challenge that how to interpret huge amount of data in to useful data and how to percept that data.

Security and Privacy

Big data is less structured and informal therefor it poses the problems of security and privacy. When big contains some sensitive information or something private then using normal approaches may result some serious security problem. Database managements systems have normally security for normal data but in big data software no such security involve. The sensitive data present in big data must ensure the data itself is secure. Same security should be applied to big data as they are in database of big data if data is sensitive.

NEED OF BIG DATA ANALYSIS AND AVAILABLE ANALYSIS TECHNIQUES

Why Analyze Big Data?

Big data analysis is the process in which big data is examined in order to uncover, show hidden patterns, Unknown correlation in data and much other information that can be used to take better decisions. Big data analysis is the process of figuring out which data is useful and which is not. If you don't do so a simple query can take hour or even days to process in such a huge amount of data.

When we talking about big data in internet of things. That data is data obtain by billions interconnected devices which can communicate to each other. The devices may send every sort of data, in which there may be some irrelevant data or there may be some redundant data whose redundancy is not important for us. Rather that redundant data is harmful for operation such as processing, analyzing and transaction in our data. Storing all data and then querying that data may not bring fruitful results. It must be first analyze and the hidden patterns should be uncovered. And only correlated data is then data warehoused. By doing so now you are able to get your result of query like normal relational database query. The analysis of even small databases is important and even mandatory.

Available Option for Analyzing Big Data

There are four types of Big Data analytics as mentioned in Table 1.

- **Basic Analytics for Insight:** Basic analytics for insight is just an option for data analysis. Insight Analytics is an easy-to-use tool for creating your own performance improvement dashboards. It is a type of analysis that comprises over the slicing and dicing of data, reporting, simple visualization and monitoring and anomaly detection. Insight Analytics provides a comprehensive set of

Table 1. Types of Analysis of Big Data

Types of Analysis	Description
Basic analytics for insight	Slicing and dicing of data, reporting, simple visualizations, basic monitor.
Advanced analytics for insight	More complex analysis such as predictive modeling and other pattern-matching techniques.
Operationalized analytics	Analytics become part of the business process.
Monetized analytics	Analytics are utilized to directly drive revenue.

visual and intuitive dashboards to focus in on key metrics. It is usually for data analysis but not so huge amount of data. It also helps in making decisions.

- **Advanced Analytics for Insight:** It is more complex analysis such as predictive modeling and other pattern-matching techniques. Here the analysis includes predictions of data. And the pattern of data also included in this type of analysis. Data is predicted using available data. And also the data analyzed using patterns of data occurred. Advance analytics help in making quick, right, bold and confident decisions.

- **Operationalized Analytics:** Analytics become part of the business process. Operational analytics also called real time business intelligence. These systems analyze huge amount of data in stream of real time operations. Mainly these systems focus on improving existing operations. These systems use various types of data mining and data aggregation tools to improve and get more transparent information about business planning. For operational analytics system must meet the following three requirements:
  - Uptime
  - Real time
  - Scalable.

- **Monetized Analytics:** Analytics are utilized to directly drive revenue. Monetized analytics is the process of converting raw data in to valuable and useful form. It helps in decision making such as predictive maintenance based on multiple insight sources.

CHALLENGES OF BIG DATA ANALYSIS IN IoT

As big data is collection of so large and complex data set which is difficult to process using traditional data processing applications and hands on database management tools. Some of the challenges in big data analysis (Stankovic, 2014) include storages, curation, capture, search, sharing, transfer, analysis and virtualization.

Challenge 1: The first challenge is how to store such a huge amount of data i.e. petabyte data. As we know that billions of devices will be connected together which will results large amount of data. Where this large amount of data will be stored?

Challenge 2: The second challenge to big data is the searching in that data. Ordinary searching algorithms might not work efficiently on huge amount of data. There must be some new searching techniques which could be efficient on such large amount of data. Regular searching algorithms will be very slow and will not bring fruitful results.

Challenge 3: The third challenge is data curation. Data curation is the management of data so to make it able for contemporary use and available for reuse and discovery. Data which is not properly managed has no value to us. It is great challenge to IoT because large amount of data is difficult to manage.

Challenge 4: Data sharing is very important concept in IoT which is difficult task. In IoT concept large number of devices will be connected and data will be on cloud for sharing purposes. Sharing of data on clouds will require some intelligent techniques. The major challenge is that how large amount of data will be shared among different devices.

Challenge 5: In IoT data is needed to be transferred from point to point through global network. When data is so large like in petabyte transferring it is a great challenge. The pre-existing networking protocols might not work in IoT. There may be necessity of some more efficient and intelligent protocols for data transfer over network. How that data will transfer and what will be the techniques is a challenge.

Challenge 6: When we actually store data, share it and analyze it, our main goal is to process our data for getting information. Analysis of small amount of data is not a very difficult task. But in huge amount of data i.e. data generated by billions connected devices, the analysis become very tedious job and this is off course a challenge to IoT.

Challenge 7: The other challenge is data virtualization. Virtualization means data management in such a way to make it available for application to retrieve. It can be done by using some formulas and some techniques. By virtualization data will be easily retrieved by application without knowing technical skills and how physically data is stored somewhere.

Challenge 8: Another great challenge is privacy of data. For example for electronic healthcare record data should not be exposed to unauthenticated persons.

Challenge 9: Timeliness means time required for the analysis of data. This is another challenge in IoT. The challenge is how to overcome the time taken for analysis of big data.

Challenge 10: Incompleteness is also a challenge in IoT. It means that what should be the response if the information provided by some devices were not complete. For example, what if in healthcare system the patient does not give full information?

In Table 2, a comparison of the characteristics of normal data and the big data is presented.

FUTURE RESEARCH DIRECTIONS

Big data analysis is the need of future as the globally connected devices are generating variety of data with respect to deferent domains, application areas, formats, system platforms etc. As the size of the network in terms of nodes is growing, it is also becoming the source of processing. The processing power in totality will be enough to deal with the generated data for analysis and generating useful results. The

Table 2. Normal Data vs Big Data

Characteristics	Normal Data	Big Data
Storage of data	Very Easy	Difficult
Searching	Easy	Very difficult
Data Curation	Easy	Very difficult
Sharing of data	Easy	Difficult
Transferring of data	Very easy	Difficult
Data Analysis	Easy	Very difficult
Data Virtualization	Easy	Very difficult
Data Privacy	Easy	Very difficult
Timeliness	Very easy	Very difficult
Incompleteness	Easy	Very difficult

domains of Agriculture, Healthcare and Smart Cities will be the most dominant among others, so there is a requirement to generate solutions for IoT and other global networks for big data Analysis.

Data Analytics is a complex problem and it requires people with expertise and support of specialize tools for data cleaning, classification, understanding and selecting specific methods. Cloud Computing can be utilized providing Analytics as a service or Big data as service to have a quick and accurate solution.

CONCLUSION

IoT is an emerging concept of global network. The challenge associated with the IoT are communication technology, heterogeneity, privacy, security and many others related issues. As the world is getting part of the global network in form of internet, cloud computing and IoT, the amount of data getting in and out of the network is getting increased manifold. Due to the heterogeneity of connected nodes, different data rates and formats it is getting a huge challenge to deal with such variety of data. As IoT is providing processing nodes in quantity in form of smart nodes, it is presenting itself a good platform for big data analysis. In this chapter, characteristics of big data and requirements for big data analysis are highlighted. Considering the big source of data generation as well as the plausible suitable platform of such huge data analysis, the associated challenges are also underlined. There is a need of various solutions to deal with the challenges associated with big data and its analysis. New advanced technologies like cloud computing and 5G technologies may provide enormous support in providing the solutions to the open challenges.

REFERENCES

Aqeel-ur-Rehman, M.K., & Baksh, A. (2013). Communication Technology That Suits IoT-A Critical Review. Wireless Sensor Networks for Developing Countries (pp. 14-25). Springer.

Assunção, M. D., Calheiros, R. N., Bianchi, S., Netto, M. A., & Buyya, R. (2014). Big Data computing and clouds: Trends and future directions. *Journal of Parallel and Distributed Computing*.

Barnaghi, P., Wang, W., Henson, C., & Taylor, K. (2012). Semantics for the Internet of Things: Early progress and back to the future. *International Journal on Semantic Web and Information Systems, 8*(1), 1–21. doi:10.4018/jswis.2012010101

Bin, S., Yuan, L., & Xiaoyi, W. (2010). *Research on data mining models for the internet of things*. Paper presented at the 2010 International Conference on Image Analysis and Signal Processing (IASP).

Chun-Wei, T., Chin-Feng, L., Ming-Chao, C., & Yang, L. T. (2014). Data Mining for Internet of Things: A Survey. *IEEE Communications Surveys and Tutorials, 16*(1), 77–97. doi:10.1109/SURV.2013.103013.00206

Gubbi, J., Buyya, R., Marusic, S., & Palaniswami, M. (2013). Internet of Things (IoT): A vision, architectural elements, and future directions. *Future Generation Computer Systems, 29*(7), 1645–1660. doi:10.1016/j.future.2013.01.010

O'Leary, D. E. (2013). 'Big data', the 'internet of things' and the 'internet of signs. *Intelligent Systems in Accounting, Finance & Management, 20*(1), 53–65. doi:10.1002/isaf.1336

Shi, W., & Liu, M. (2011). *Tactics of handling data in internet of things.* Paper presented at the 2011 IEEE International Conference on Cloud Computing and Intelligence Systems (CCIS). doi:10.1109/CCIS.2011.6045121

Stankovic, J. A. (2014). Research Directions for the Internet of Things. *Internet of Things Journal, IEEE, 1*(1), 3–9. doi:10.1109/JIOT.2014.2312291

Villars, R. L., Olofson, C. W., & Eastwood, M. (2011). *Big data: What it is and why you should care.* White Paper, IDC.

ADDITIONAL READING

Aggarwal, C. C., Ashish, N., & Sheth, A. (2013). *The internet of things: A survey from the data-centric perspective Managing and mining sensor data* (pp. 383–428). Springer.

Ahn, S.-H., Kim, N.-U., & Chung, T.-M. (2014). *Big data analysis system concept for detecting unknown attacks.* Paper presented at the 2014 16th International Conference on Advanced Communication Technology (ICACT). doi:10.1109/ICACT.2014.6778962

Aqeel-ur-Rehman, , Abbasi, A. Z., Islam, N., & Shaikh, Z. A. (2014). A review of wireless sensors and networks' applications in agriculture. *Computer Standards & Interfaces, 36*(2), 263–270. doi:10.1016/j.csi.2011.03.004

Athreya, A. P., & Tague, P. (2013). *Network self-organization in the internet of things.* Paper presented at the 2013 10th Annual IEEE Communications Society Conference on Sensor, Mesh and Ad Hoc Communications and Networks (SECON).

Atzori, L., Iera, A., & Morabito, G. (2010). The internet of things: A survey. *Computer Networks, 54*(15), 2787–2805. doi:10.1016/j.comnet.2010.05.010

Bandyopadhyay, D., & Sen, J. (2011). Internet of things: Applications and challenges in technology and standardization. *Wireless Personal Communications, 58*(1), 49–69. doi:10.1007/s11277-011-0288-5

Chen, F., Deng, P., Wan, J., Zhang, D., Vasilakos, A. V., & Rong, X. (2015). Data Mining for the Internet of Things: Literature Review and Challenges. *International Journal of Distributed Sensor Networks, 501*, 431047.

Costa-Pérez, X., Festag, A., Kolbe, H.-J., Quittek, J., Schmid, S., Stiemerling, M., & Van Der Veen, H. (2013). Latest trends in telecommunication standards. *Computer Communication Review, 43*(2), 64–71. doi:10.1145/2479957.2479968

Islam, N., & Aqeel-ur-Rehman. (2013). A comparative study of major service providers for cloud computing. Proceedings of the 1st International Conference on Information and Communication Technology Trends (ICICTT'13), 228-232, Karachi, Pakistan.

Jagadish, H., Gehrke, J., Labrinidis, A., Papakonstantinou, Y., Patel, J. M., Ramakrishnan, R., & Shahabi, C. (2014). Big data and its technical challenges. *Communications of the ACM, 57*(7), 86–94. doi:10.1145/2611567

Koch, C. (2013). *Compilation and synthesis in big data analytics Big Data* (pp. 6–6). Springer.

Labrinidis, A., & Jagadish, H. (2012). Challenges and opportunities with big data. *Proceedings of the VLDB Endowment, 5*(12), 2032–2033. doi:10.14778/2367502.2367572

Larose, D. T. (2014). *Discovering knowledge in data: an introduction to data mining.* John Wiley & Sons. doi:10.1002/9781118874059

Madden, S. (2012). From databases to big data. *IEEE Internet Computing, 16*(3), 0004-0006.

Mainetti, L., Patrono, L., & Vilei, A. (2011). *Evolution of wireless sensor networks towards the internet of things: A survey.* Paper presented at the 2011 19th International Conference on Software, Telecommunications and Computer Networks (SoftCOM).

Mayer-Schönberger, V., & Cukier, K. (2013). *Big data: A revolution that will transform how we live, work, and think.* Houghton Mifflin Harcourt.

Patil, P. S., Rao, S., & Patil, S. B. (2011). *Optimization of data warehousing system: Simplification in reporting and analysis.* Paper presented at the IJCA Proceedings on International Conference and workshop on Emerging Trends in Technology (ICWET).

Sagiroglu, S., & Sinanc, D. (2013). *Big data: A review.* Paper presented at the 2013 International Conference on Collaboration Technologies and Systems (CTS). doi:10.1109/CTS.2013.6567202

Said, O., & Masud, M. (2013). Towards internet of things: Survey and future vision. *International Journal of Computer Networks, 5*(1), 1–17.

Schroeder, R., & Meyer, E. (2012). *Big data: what's new. Internet, Politics, Policy 2012: Big Data.* Big Challenges.

Suciu, G., Suciu, V., Halunga, S., & Fratu, O. (2015). *Big Data, Internet of Things and Cloud Convergence for E-Health Applications New Contributions in Information Systems and Technologies* (pp. 151–160). Springer.

Whitmore, A., Agarwal, A., & Da Xu, L. (2014). The Internet of Things—A survey of topics and trends. *Information Systems Frontiers*, 1–14.

KEY TERMS AND DEFINITIONS

Big Data: Huge Quantity of Data generated by Smart Devices.

Cloud Computing: The practice of using a network of remote servers hosted on the Internet to store, manage, and process data, rather than a local server or a personal computer.

Data Analysis: Logical Operations to Evaluate Data.

Data Characteristics: Specific Attributes of Data.

Data Curation: The Management of Data throughout its Lifecycle.

Data Intensive Computing: A class of parallel computing applications which use a data parallel approach to processing large volumes of data.

Data Mining: Knowledge Discovery Process.

Data Virtualization: Agile data integration approach organizations use to gain more insight from their data.

Data Warehousing: System for Data Reporting and Analysis.

Internet of Things: Global Network of Smart Devices.

IoT: Standard Abbreviation of Internet of Things.

Ubiquitous Computing: Computing everywhere for everyone.

Wireless Sensor Networks (WSN): Wireless network consisting of spatially distributed autonomous devices using sensors.

This work was previously published in the Handbook of Research on Trends and Future Directions in Big Data and Web Intelligence edited by Noor Zaman, Mohamed Elhassan Seliaman, Mohd Fadzil Hassan, and Fausto Pedro Garcia Marquez, pages 313-327, copyright year 2015 by Information Science Reference (an imprint of IGI Global).

Chapter 19
City Data Fusion:
Sensor Data Fusion in the Internet of Things

Meisong Wang
Australian National University, Australia

Miranda Zhang
Australian National University, Australia

Charith Perera
The Open University, UK

Peter Strazdins
Australian National University, Australia

Prem Prakash Jayaraman
RMIT University, Australia

R.K. Shyamsundar
Tata Institute of Fundamental Research, India

Rajiv Ranjan
CSIRO, Australia & Newcastle University, UK

ABSTRACT

Internet of Things (IoT) has gained substantial attention recently and play a significant role in smart city application deployments. A number of such smart city applications depend on sensor fusion capabilities in the cloud from diverse data sources. The authors introduce the concept of IoT and present in detail ten different parameters that govern our sensor data fusion evaluation framework. They then evaluate the current state-of-the art in sensor data fusion against our sensor data fusion framework. The authors' main goal is to examine and survey different sensor data fusion research efforts based on our evaluation framework. The major open research issues related to sensor data fusion are also presented.

1. INTRODUCTION

During the past decade, the Internet of Things (IoT) has gained significant attention in academia as well as industry. The main reason behind this is the capabilities that IoT promises to offer. It promises to create a smart world where all the objects around us are connected to the Internet and communicate with each other with minimum human intervention (Sundmaeker, Guillemin, Friess, & Woelffl´e, 2010). This survey paper will address sensor data fusion in IoT from different perspectives. Hence, we first

DOI: 10.4018/978-1-5225-1832-7.ch019

present the most commonly used IoT definitions from the literature. Tan and Wang (Lu & Neng, n.d.) have defined IoT in a fairly comprehensive manner as "Things have identities and virtual personalities operating in smart spaces using intelligent interfaces to connect and communicate within social, environment, and user contexts (Lu & Neng, n.d.). Some other definitions are presented in (Atzori, Iera, & Morabito, 2010). The papers (Atzori et al., 2010; Yang, Liu, & Liang, n.d.) have surveyed the definition of IoT in three different perspectives: things, the Internet and semantics.

IoT enables the vision "*from anytime, anyplace connectivity for anyone, we will now have the connectivity for anything (Union, 2005)*". Further expanding this idea, the European Union has defined the above vision as "The IoT allows people and things to be connected Anytime, Anyplace, with Anything and Anyone, ideally using Any network and Any service (Guillemin & Friess, 2009)". The term Internet of Things was firstly coined by Kevin Ashton (Ashton, 2009) in a presentation in 1998. He has also mentioned "*The IoT has the potential to change the world, just as the Internet did. Maybe even more so. (Sundmaeker et al., 2010)*". Then, MIT presented their IoT vision in 1999. Later, IoT was formally introduced by the International Telecommunication Union (ITU) by ITU Internet report in 2005 (Union, 2005).

2. MOTIVATION: SENSOR DATA FUSION FOR SMART CITY APPLICATION

Data from citizens, systems, and general things flow through our cities thanks to the wide spread adoption of smart phones, sensor networks, social media and growing open release of datasets (Antonelli et al., March 19-20, Athens, Greece, 2014). The data from Smart cities present a grand challenge to researchers and smart cities promoters, as we need to take advantage of these streams of information to build new services and define a clear return of investment for the benefit of the society (Jara, Genoud, & Bocchi, 2014).

The challenge in smart city is not to build a single generic model e.g. weather model based on temperature and humidity, complex models about noise pollution, traffic etc., but to combine all these together to build a good predictive contextually rich model. This model will help understand the dynamics of the society, and most importantly provide vital knowledge back to the citizens in order to enhance their quality of life.

A recent work from a group of researchers from MIT (Sobolevsky et al., 2015) demonstrate the potential of fusing data from disparate data sources in smart city to understand a city's attractiveness. The work focuses on cities in Spain and shows how the fusion of big data sets can provide insights into the way people visit cities. Such a correlation of data from a variety of data sources play a vital role in delivering services successfully in smart cities of the future.

In smart cities, ability to fuse sensor data enables context awareness which has a huge potential for IoT. Understanding the context of the city and its citizen can help develop and provide a new world of services based on what an individual user is doing, what the infrastructure is doing, what nature is doing or all the above in various combinations (Karimi, Accessed on: May 2015). The variety of services that can be developed is only limited to one's imagination. An example scenario could be a bridge experiencing a structural issue due to adverse environmental conditions can alert the city administrators and alert all cars travelling towards the bridge to stay away and seek alternative routes. For such a scenario to be feasible, it is important, smart city applications built on IoT have the ability to fuse data from diverse data sources to enable context-aware decision making and support (Deng et.al., 2015).

3. CONTRIBUTIONS

In this survey paper, we highlight the importance of sensor data fusion for IoT application in particular smart city applications. To this end, we conduct an elaborate examination of different sensor data fusion research efforts related to IoT stemming from wireless sensor networks. Based on this examination, we propose an evaluation framework by carefully selecting ten different metrics. We believe these ten metrics are open challenges in the field. Some of these challenges are addressed by the researchers significantly and some are in its infancy. One of the major goals of this article is to highlight the opportunities for improvements and research gaps in the field.

The rest of the paper is organised as follows. Section 4, sensor data fusion is defined and techniques are discussed. We also outline the possible extensions to improve sensor data fusion. Section 5 presents the evaluation framework that we used to evaluate different research efforts. We survey various sensor data fusion efforts and its importance towards IoT in the Section 6. Section 7 presents an evaluation summary of current state-of-the art in sensor data fusion against the developed evaluation framework. Section 8 concludes the survey by highlighting the survey results and research gaps.

4. SENSOR DATA FUSION

In this section we introduce sensor data fusion in the IoT domain. We also discuss its importance towards the IoT and where the techniques would fit into the IoT space. As we discussed in earlier sections, IoT would produce substantial amount of data that are less useful unless we are able to derive knowledge using them. We start our discussion by quoting some statements. The following statements strongly emphasis the need for sensor data fusion and filtering in IoT domain.

By 2020, wirelessly networked sensors in everything we own will form a new Web. But it will only be of value if the "terabyte torrent" of data it generates can be collected, analysed and interpreted (Mark Raskino, 2005).

Today, there are roughly 1.5 billion Internet-enabled PCs and over 1 billion Internet-enabled mobile smart phones. The present 'Internet of PCs' will move towards an 'Internet of Things' in which 50 to 100 billion devices will be connected to the Internet by 2020 (Sundmaeker et al., 2010).

We see data fusion in the IoT environment as one of the most important challenges that need to be addressed to develop innovative services. In particular, in smart cities applications, when 50 to 100 billion devices start sensing, it would be essential to fuse, and reason about the data automatically and intelligently. Fusion is a broad term than can be interpreted in many ways. Hall and Llinas (Hall & Llinas, 1997) have defined the sensor data fusion as a method of combining sensor data from multiple sensors to produce more accurate, more complete, and more dependable information that could not be possible to achieve through a single sensor. However, our definition of data fusion in IoT is best captured by Nakamura et al. (Nakamura, Loureiro, & Frery, 2007) based on three key operations: *complementary, redundant, and cooperative.*

Complementary means putting bits and pieces of a large picture together. A single sensor cannot say much about the environment as it would be focused on measuring a single factor such as temperature.

However, when we have data sensed through a number of different sensors, we can understand the environment in a much better way.

Redundant means that same environmental factor is sensed through different sensors. It helps to increase the accuracy of the data. For example, averaging the temperature value sensed by two sensors located in the same physical location would produce more accurate information compared to a single sensor. It also reduces the amount of data that need to be handled as it combines the two set of data streams together.

Cooperative operations combine the sensor data together to produce new knowledge. For example, reading RFID tags recorded in a supermarket can be used to identify the events such as shoplifting. Let's consider a scenario where RFID reader in a supermarket shelf detects that an item has been removed from a shelf. The RFID sensor in the counter does not see the object during payments. Later, the RFID sensor in the exit door detects the item that was removed from the shelf earlier. This sequence of actions can be simply inferred as a shoplifting event.

A white paper published by Carnot Institutes (Carnot Institutes, 2011) has listed data fusion and data filtering as two main challenges for the IoT and its applications such as smart cities. Data fusion is a data processing technique that associates, combines, aggregates, and integrates data from different sources. It helps to build knowledge about certain events and environments which is not possible using individual sensors separately. Data fusion also helps to build a context awareness model that helps to understand situational context. The sensor data filtering stresses the requirement of filtering data to avoid large volumes of data transmission over the network.

The most basic sensor data fusion example that is used widely in smart phones is an e-compass. It uses a combination of 3D magnetometer and the accelerometer to provide compass functionality. Mainly, data fusion operations can be applied at two levels: cloud level and within the network level. As shown in Figure 1, sensor nodes, smart city infrastructure, edge node, sink nodes, and low level computational devices such as mobile phones belong to in-network sensor data processing. High-end computational devices such as servers belong to cloud level processing.

The cloud can help better understand the environment by performing complex sensor data fusion operations. Cloud level devices have access to unlimited resources and hence has the capability to apply

Figure 1. Sensor data processing

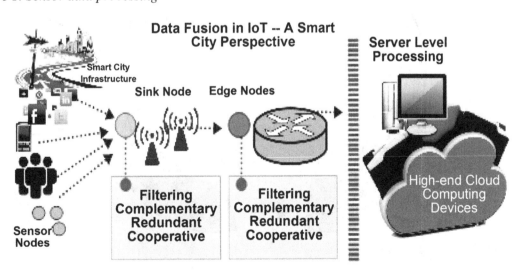

complex data mining algorithms over the data generated by large number of lower level sensors (Wang et.al., 2015b). After understanding the environment, the cloud can generate actions that need to be taken appropriately.

In-network sensor data fusion is important to reduce the data transmission cost. As data transmission requires significant amount of energy, applying redundant fusion operation can reduce the data transmission. However, low-level nodes may not have the full view of the environment. Therefore, they may not be able to perform complex operations such as cooperative operations. The main responsibility of in-network sensor data fusion is to reduce the data transmission cost. The following rule defines how the data processing in each level should be conducted.

L = CurrentLevel;
if (KnowledgeRequired ≤ KnowledgeAvailable) ∧ (DataTransmissionCost > DataFusionCost)
then ProcessAtTheCurrentLevel(L)
else SendDataTo(L + 1)

The ultimate goal of sensor data fusion is to understand the environment and act accordingly (Wang et. al., 2015a). This can be defined as a cycle as shown in Figure 2. We call it Internet of Things Monitoring Cycle. It has five steps: Collection, Collation, Evaluation, Decide, and Act. IoT monitoring cycle has been derived by combining the Intelligence Cycle (Shulsky & Schmitt, 2002) and the Boyd Control Loop (Boyd, 1987). The Collection step collects raw data from sensors and other IoT data sources (Social media, smart city infrastructure, mobile devices etc.). The Collation step analyse, compare and correlate the collected data. The Evaluation step fuses the data in order to understand and provide a full

Figure 2. Internet of things monitoring cycle

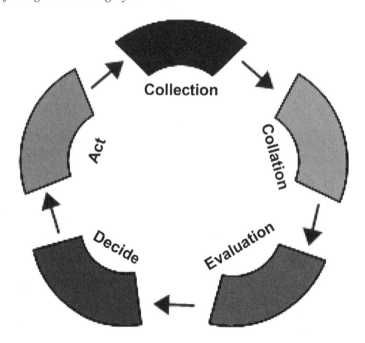

view of the environment. The Decide step decides the actions that need to be taken. The Act step simply applies the actions decided at the previous step. The Act step includes actuator control as well as sensor calibration and re-configuration.

Typically, the deployed IoT infrastructure in smart cities provide a means to monitor the environmental context. There is very little interest in the raw sensor data. The data that is of significant interest is information about interesting events that are happening in the specific area. In order to accomplish this task, IoT applications should be able to capture and reason about the events continuously. Therefore applying sensor data fusion techniques at the different levels of the IoT application chain is essential in order to detect relevant events.

5. EVALUATION FRAMEWORK

In this section, we present the framework that we use to evaluate different IoT sensor data fusion research efforts. The framework comprises the ten most significant features (parameters) related to sensor data processing in the IoT domain. Table 1 summarises the evaluation at the end of the Section 6.

5.1. Middleware Architecture Type

Middleware can be explained as a software layer that lies between the hardware and application layers. It provides the reusable functionalities that are required by the application to meet complex customer requirements. They are usually built to address the common issues in application development such as heterogeneity, interoperability, security, and dependability (Issarny, Caporuscio, & Georgantas, 2007).

A traditional goal of middleware is to provide a set of programming abstractions to help software development where heterogeneous components need to be connected and communicated together (e.g: Internet of Things) (Dyo, 2005). However, programming abstraction comes at a cost. That means, when we use a middleware to connect sensors to applications, the performance will degrade due to additional overheads. If you manually connect application specific sensors to applications, they will perform much better. However, every time we develop a new application, we have to manually connect the sensors into the application where we will end up with repeated code. Compared to this repeated effort, using a middleware becomes a much better approach in term of cost and development time. Middleware systems are too general and are developed not for a single domain but for multiple domains. As a result, middleware may have functionalities that are not required by one application but that may be required in another application.

Todays' IoT applications demand more and more advanced and non-functional properties such as contextawareness and semantic interoperability. Middleware systems can bundles those functionalities together to be reused in many applications. We identify developing middleware as the right way to address the needs of IoT applications.

IoT (or sensor networks) middleware solutions can be mainly divided into two categories based on their installed location (Hwang & Yoe, 2011): in-network schemes and server-side schemes. In-network middleware are usually developed using low level programming languages such as nesC (Gay et al., 2003; UC Berkeley WEBS Project, 2004) and installed on each sensor node. Those middleware systems have more control on low level operation of the network such as network routing, energy consumption, etc. This layer is much closer to the hardware. However, it lacks the overall knowledge about the environment.

On the other hand, server-side middleware run in cloud computing environments. Those middleware collect data through gateways or sink nodes and are developed using high level programming languages such as C, Java etc. However, these middleware systems have less control over the sensor network operation. They are unable to control low level operations such as routing. However, they have more knowledge about the environment as they can analyse the sensor data received through different sensors. We have seen an emerging third category of middleware solutions, hybrid schemes, which combines both in-network and server side schemes. We believe that a hybrid middleware approach is best suited for the IoT domain as we can combine the best of both the in-network and cloud-based server schemes.

5.2. Context-Awareness

The most widely used context information is location (Ellebek, 2007). However, context in the IoT is much broader than location. All the information about sensors can be considered as context information (e.g. capabilities of the sensors, related actuators, near by sensors, etc.). With the recent advancement of the IoT, context-awareness has become an essential part of the IoT applications. Context-awareness is no more limited to mobile applications. Currently, the largest context information consumers are mobile devices and their applications. A research effort called mSense (Krosche, Jakl, Gusenbauer, Rothbauer, & Ehringer, 2009) has introduced a middleware solution to manage context information. mSense separates context-awareness management functionalities into a separate layer. The IoT domain also requires such separation to make application development much easier and faster.

Chantzara and Anagnostou (Chantzara & Anagnostou, 2005) have identified four common stages in contextaware application life cycle as context sensing, context processing, context dissemination, and context usage. This life-cycle has been enhanced by (Hynes, Reynolds, & Hauswirth, 2009). Combining sensor data from multiple sensors helps to understand context information much more accurately. Better understanding will contribute towards intelligent fusion and complex event detection.

The Cluster of European Research Projects (CERPIoT) has also mentioned context awareness (locationaware, environment aware) as a key characteristic of objects in the IoT space (Sundmaeker et al., 2010). Identifying the context information such as geographical location, sensor capabilities, near-by sensors, related actuators and supported data formats would help to build a context model for each sensor that can be used to increase the autonomous interaction among sensors. Nagy et al. (Nagy et al., 2009) have defined a term called Global Understanding in related to contextawareness. It means that sensor 'A' can understand the properties and capabilities of sensor 'B' and vice versa. This can only be achieved through semantic technologies and context awareness techniques.

A research focused on smart objects (Kortuem, Kawsar, Fitton, & Sundramoorthy, 2010) has defined three types of context-awareness: activity-aware, policy-aware, and process-aware. Activity-aware means the ability to understand the activity and the usage of a specific sensor. Policy-aware acts as a domain knowledge repository where it consists of rules. For example, policy-aware can identify the health and safety conditions of the user via policy knowledge and act accordingly. Process-aware is the ability to detect the current processes carried out by the user and the surrounded objects. An ideal IoT application should be able to provide additional assistance to users to carry out their work as mentioned above.

Abowd and Mynatt (Abowd & Mynatt, 2000) have identified 5Ws (who, what, where, when, why) as the minimum set of context information that need to be handled in a pervasive computing environment. This stays true in the IoT space as well. Context information can be divided into three categories: user context, computing (system) context, and physical (Environmental) context (Schilit, Adams, & Want,

1994). User context means the knowledge about the user (e.g. age, gender, likes, dislikes, etc.). Computing context means the knowledge about the software and hardware used by users (e.g. operating system, hardware capacity, software applications, etc.). Physical context means the knowledge of the environment such as location, temperature, light, etc. Issarny et al. (Issarny et al., 2007) have distinguished three types of context sensitivity: context-specific systems, context-dependent systems, and context-adaptive systems. Applications that can work only in one context are called context-specific. Context-dependent applications need to be configured at the beginning of the application for each context. Context-adaptive systems can change their behaviour dynamically during runtime when context changes. IoT applications demand the context-adaptive behaviour to make the IoT vision a reality.

In order to build a comprehensive context model using context information, it is necessary to acquire context data through many different data sources. A single source would not be able to provide all necessary information that can be used to understand the context accurately. Therefore, combining the context information retrieved through multiple sources is essential but challenging (Lopez, Kim, Min, & Lee, 2007).

5.3. Semantic Interaction

The IoT can be considered as an application domain where semantic web technologies can be used to enhance its functionalities significantly (Y. Huang & Li, n.d.). The IoT promises to connect the billions of things around us together. It is not feasible to manually connect by hard-wiring things and applications. Automating these tasks will definitely need the help of semantic technologies. Research conducted on semantic sensor web (Corcho & Garc´ıa-Castro, 2010) has identified several challenges that need to be addressed by semantic technologies. For example, sensor configuration, context identification, complex sensor data querying, event detection and monitoring, and sensor data fusion are some of the tasks that can be enhanced using semantics. Annotating sensors, sensor data, and program components will increase the ability of interaction without explicit programming commands. Furthermore, annotations will also increase the retrievability of sensor data. More sophisticated queries can be processed over the semantic annotated data.

5.4. Dynamic Configuration

Dynamic configuration can be interpreted at two levels: a software level dynamic configuration and a hardware level dynamic configuration. Dynamic hardware configuration stresses the adaptability of a system. IoT comprises tiny sensing devices (things) which are prone to fail frequently. Therefore, a network built by these devices is unreliable and should be able to change, configure and adapt itself to the environment dynamically. Furthermore, things may need to change their configuration as a result of the decisions made by the cloudbased server as a part of the actuation control. For example, lets consider a things (sensor node) S that is capable of sensing light, temperature and humidity. It is physically located in area L. Currently, sensor node S measures only temperature as it is the expected requirement of the server level software to make the decisions. Later, the server may require to know the light level of area L. The sensor node S needs to be configured to measure not only temperature, but also light level as well. This new configuration setting needs to be pushed to the sensor node from the cloud server. Figure 3 presents an example of a dynamic reconfiguration for wireless sensors nodes deployments. According to our survey, this functionality is lacking among most of the current research efforts.

Figure 3. Dynamic sensor network configuration

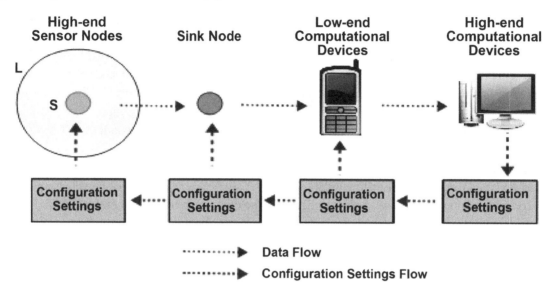

Furthermore, software level can also support dynamic configuration capabilities. For example, software components described in semantic technologies can be combined together to create complex data fusion operations. Rather than combining these components at development time, runtime configuration can add more adaptability to the system. The complex data fusion operations should be built by reusing the software components at runtime based on the user requirements. For example, Figure 4 shows how a system can dynamically configure the components into a work flow in order to detect events and act accordingly.

5.5. Fusion Complexity

Querying data from things is one of the common data fusion operations in the IoT domain (Brenna et al., 2007; Gibbons, Karp, Ke, Nath, & Seshan, 2003; Madden, Franklin, Hellerstein, & Hong, 2005; Yao & Gehrke, 2002). The level of complexity supported by the query may differ from the query language implementation. Sometimes, semantic technologies such as SPARQL (Malik, Goel, & Maniktala, 2010), are used to query sensor data.

Figure 4. Software dynamic configuration

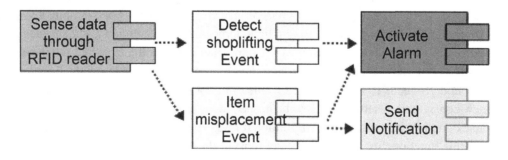

Another common data fusion approach is event detection. Events can be recognised by identifying and correlating sequences of action that occurred in the environment. Lets consider two sensors A and B, where A measures temperature and B is a camera. In an ideal system, users should be able to pose queries to retrieve the video feed of a room where temperature is higher than 35°C. In order to answer such a request, the system should be able to combine both sensors A and B together. Another example query would be 'identify the best place to store a sculpture in a museum based on the sculpture specification'. A number of data fusion operation need to be used to answer such queries. Concretely, a query may need to be generated by using optimum humidity level, temperature and other parameters.

This kind of combining needs to be supported by semantic technologies. Song et al. (Song, C´a andrdenas, & Masuoka, 2010) have provided a full description on how to accomplish such tasks by using semantic technologies. Zafeiropoulos et al. (Song et al., 2010) have described all the elements such as sensors and programming modules using semantics, where complex combinations are possible.

5.6. Actuation Management

According to our evaluation, the majority of research efforts have left out the functionality of actuation management from their proposed solutions. We presented the IoT monitoring cycle in Section 3. This cycle stresses the importance of the act step. Sensors sense data and transmit it to servers. Severs then do the processing and take the decision on how to handle the situation based on the gathered knowledge and previous experience. Then actions need to be taken. Action can be a change in sensor configuration or to conduct a specific task using a connected actuator. For example, actuation could increase the humidity by spraying more water into the air. According to the context, the most appropriate actions needs to be taken and managed by an ideal IoT software system in an efficient manner.

5.7. Type of Processing

Data processing in IoT can be done in two ways: in-network processing and cloud level processing. Sensors are prone to produce faulty data due to technical issues. Furthermore, sensors produce redundant data that wastes the energy if they are transmitted. Therefore, data filtering is critical to save energy. In-network processing mechanisms can be used to address these issues. In-network sensor data processing however has limitations, because in-network devices such as sensor nodes and mobile phones perceive only limited knowledge about the environment (local context). Therefore, in-network data processing cannot make high level decision where overall knowledge is required.

Cloud-based processing should be used to address the above problem. Cloud servers receive all the data collected through a variety of different sensors. These data increase the knowledge about the environment, so the servers can take decisions by considering overall knowledge (global context) (Song et.al., 2015). Furthermore, cloud-based server devices have more sophisticated hardware power to process and understand large amounts of data compared to in-network hardware. Server level sensor data processing techniques are used to fuse data in many ways according to user queries. It can also understand interesting events that occur in a sensor network.

It is clear that both types of processing haves their unique contribution towards sensor data fusion in the IoT domain. Therefore, the ideal way to process sensor data is to use a hybrid approach where both in-network and cloud-level sensor data processing techniques are employed.

5.8. Cross Domain Portability

Cross domain portability stresses the ability of applying a proposed solution on different domains. Most of the proposed solutions are narrowly focused on one domain. We believe it is ideal to implement a solution addressing more than one domain in order to prove the cross domain portability. At the same time, it is critical to differentiate the domain specific and domain independent components of a solution. This increases the ability to apply a solution in different domains. A clear differentiation will enable rapid and easy expansion.

5.9. Implementation

Implementation is critical in order to prove a concept. Challenges that cannot been seen in theoretical process can be clearly seen in a practical implementation. Implementation allows the identification of the practical and technical difficulties and challenges that arise during the implementation process. The majority of proposed solutions are practically implemented. Proper implementation should be followed by a rigorous performance evaluation procedure. The choice of programming model, platform and languages significantly impact on the future development and scalability. Making the programming code open source is a one approach that can ensure the rapid future development and avoid repetitive work among researchers.

5.10. Performance Evaluation

Performance of a system becomes critical when the system becomes larger and larger. In the IoT, we expect to connect millions and billions of sensors together. Therefore, performance evaluation is critical to understand and verify how the system would work in a real world deployment. It also allows to optimise the solution based on the performance evaluation results. Unfortunately, most of the proposed solutions in the IoT domain have not conducted a performance evaluation procedure which makes hard to decide the applicability of the proposed solutions in real world.

Performance evaluation remains an open issue and a challenge that needs to be achieved by researcher in the IoT domain. Performance evaluation can be categorised into two distinct areas: software and hardware. Parameters such as energy, response time, data fusion capability, and number of supported sensors, need to be evaluated.

6. SENSOR DATA FUSION APPROACHES STATE-OF-THE-ART

In this section, we discuss some of the solutions proposed by different researchers. We highlight the significances of each project in brief. At the end, a summary of the evaluation is presented in Table 1. It is to be noted, a number of solutions in sensor data fusion have been addressed within the wireless sensor network research. These solutions are completely applicable with the IoT domain.

Jara et. al. (Jara et al., 2014) have applied sensor data fusion to understand human behaviours in smart cities. Their work analyses data obtained from the European project Smart Santander. The work demonstrates how ubiquitously available data such as traffic flows and temperature can be correlated to understand and model the influence of temperature on traffic flow. The work considers the Poisson model and shows that the Poisson distribution model is not always valid.

Sobolevsky et al. (Sobolevsky et al., 2015) have applied sensor data fusion to estimate the attractiveness of smart cities for visitors. The work focuses exclusively on cities in Spain. To arrive at attractiveness they fuse sensor data from three data source namely credit and debit card transactions carried out by visitors, 3.5 million photos and videos taken in spain and posted to Flickr and 700,000 geo-tagged tweets. The attractiveness of a city for the purpose of the city was defined as the total number of tweets, pictures and card transactions that took place within it. The work produces some interesting results and demonstrated how fusion of sensor data sets (big data sets) can provide insights into how people use cities. In general, the work identified bigger cities attract large number of visitors. However, there were also some exceptions that deviate from the above assumption. For example certain cities such as Malaga had high level of visitors but the least number of Flickr activity. This is due to the fact, these cities are considered as retirement locations and the category of visitors tends to less use social media such as Flickr. This work is an excellent demonstration of how data fusion in smart cities can help create innovative services delivering value back to its citizens and smart city developers.

Antonelli et al. (Antonelli et al., March 19-20, Athens, Greece, 2014) present city sensor fusion, a big data platform that collects, aggregates, analyses, semantically enriches and offers visual analytics from data flows in smart cities. The work focuses on using sensor data fusion to detect city scale events such as event lasting days, number of visitors attracted, venues that attracted significant interest etc. The platform fuses data from different types of data sources ranging from social media to mobile phones to sensors such as Traffic flow, weather and pollution.

Soldatos et al., (Soldatos et al., 2015) propose OpenIoT a first-of-kind open source hybrid IoT platform enabling the semantic interoperability of IoT services in the cloud. OpenIoT promotes interoperability among IoT silos right from the sensor to the cloud services. OpenIoT is built upon semantic web standards such as W3C Semantic Sensor Networks (SSN) ontology, which provides a common standards-based model for representing physical and virtual sensors, RDF to store, index and retrieve data, and supports virtually any IoT protocols such as CoAP, 6LoWPAN etc. OpenIoT includes also sensor middleware and sensor data fusion capability at the things and at the cloud. OpenIoT eases the collection of data from virtually any sensor, while at the same time ensuring they are embedded with proper semantic annotation. Furthermore, it offers a wide range of Doit-yourself visual tools that enable the development and deployment of IoT services and applications with almost zero programming. Another key feature of OpenIoT is its support for mobile sensors and thereby enabling support for an emerging wave of mobile crowd sensing applications. The OpenIoT platform is a blueprint architecture to develop semantically interoperable smart city solutions with support for complex sensor data fusion algorithms. Zanella et al., (Zanella, Bui, Castellani, Vangelista, & Zorzi, 2014) offers a survey of available techniques, architecture, and protocols for a urban IoT which are used to achieve the Smart City" vision. The paper describes characteristics of an urban IoT and overviews some services related to Smart City. The technical solution proposed in this paper have been used in Padova (Italy) Smart City project (Cenedese, Zanella, Vangelista, & Zorzi, June 2014). The Padova project employs IPv4 and IPv6 at th network layers and uses a wireless sensor network gateway to collect data from deployed sensor network infrastructure. Theodoridis et al., (Theodoridis, Mylonas, & Chatzigiannakis, 2013) illustrates challenges, socioeconomic chances and vital findings from the European smat city project Smart Santander. The paper surveys a Logical 3-tier node and 3-plane architecture and highlights various use cases that employ sensor data fusion in smart cities including Outdoor parking management, precision irrigation and home garden monitoring. Lin et al., (Jin, Gubbi, Marusic, & Palaniswami, 2014) presents an information framework which encompasses the complete urban information system for building a Smart City by using the Internet of Things. The paper uses a Noise Mapping in Smart Cities case study to demonstrate the architecture.

Da Rocha et al. (Da Rocha, Delicato, de Souza, Gomes, & Pirmez, 2009) have focused on developing semantic middleware for wireless sensor networks using low level programming (i.e using NesC, a extension to the C programming language used for embedded programming). The approach is based on a rulebased reasoning engine using ontologies. The research addresses the Structural Health Monitoring (SHM) application domain. Research justifies the reason of choosing wireless sensor networks over wired sensor networks by pointing out the fact that wired sensor networks are time consuming to deploy, very expensive and hard to reconfigure (Da Rocha et al., 2009).

Semantic sensor networks in SHM domain enable the usage of semantic information towards monitoring and handling the environment. The research incorporates semantic features at the middleware level using a low level programming approach. The middleware has been implemented using the NesC language in Mica Motes (Crossbow Technology Inc, 2005) that runs the TinyOS (TinyOS Alliance, 2010) operating system. The reasoning engine Pellet (Clark & Parsia, 2004) is integrated in this middleware. New behaviours can be added into the application by adding new rules. All the communication between the nodes are done by using a XML format called TinyXML (Thomason, 2010). Knowledge is stored and processed using OWL. Da Rocha et al. (Da Rocha et al., 2009) have developed ontologies related to the domain and other services. Application driven, device driven and network driven concepts are defined in the ontology. Ontologies help to share information such as power remaining on a sensor, capabilities of the sensors and so on.

The middleware proposed by Da Rocha et al. (Da Rocha et al., 2009) intelligently shares information between different sensors based on semantic knowledge. For example, two sensors in the same area should not share their information if those sensors are measuring two different aspects of the environment; for example light and corrosion. However, if the two sensor measurements complement each other, such as humidity and corrosion, then the sensors should share their measurements and do the reasoning by combining both measurements. When many sensors measure the same aspect, few of the sensors can switch themselves off intelligently to save energy resources.

Zafeiropoulos et al. (Zafeiropoulos, Konstantinou, Arkoulis, Spanos, & Mitrou, 2008; Zafeiropoulos, Spano, Arkoulis, Konstantinou, & Mitrou, 2011) have presented an architecture to address the issues such as data aggregation, data management, and querying. The semantic technologies are used to extract meaningful information from the raw sensor data. Aggregation of data contains less value unless they are interpreted accurately. The interpretation is essential in order to detect interesting events in sensor networks. Zafeiropoulos et al. (Zafeiropoulos et al., 2008, 2011) correctly argue that this event detection should be supported by data gathered through heterogeneous data sources. The semantic technologies that support such operations are content description languages, query languages, and annotation frameworks. The proposed architecture comprises three layers: data layer, processing layer, and semantic layer. The data layer is responsible for collecting data from sensors using event-based or polling-based mechanisms. The processing layer converts those raw data into XML files. In the semantic layer maps the XML data into a semantic model where the XML messages are stored in the form of class individuals. This conversion is done by XML mapping rules. Another set of rules called semantic rules are used to detect events. As a result of these conversions, a system can query and reason the sensor data using semantic query languages which provide enriched capabilities.

The project Hydra (Eisenhauer, Rosengren, & Antolin, 2009) addresses the needs of healthcare, home automation and agriculture domains. It provides an architecture to connect sensor devices together to detect events. The Hydra middleware is based on a Service Oriented Architecture (SOA) and a Model Driven Architecture (MDA). The core architecture of Hydra comprises a number of different managers, such as network, discovery, ontology, event, storage, and context managers. Each of these managers are divided into a number of layers. For example, the context manager comprises four layers. Context data acquisition, context management, context awareness, and context reasoning and interpretation. The Hydra middleware does not differentiate the domain specific and domain interpreted components in its architecture, which makes it hard to extend the domain into other domains. Hydra encapsulate sensors into web services and the devices are described using semantics where it enables semantic interoperability among sensors. However, data is not annotated using semantics.

Lee et al. (Lee, Park, & Oh, 2010) have proposed a hybrid middleware which comprises an in-network middleware and a server-side middleware. The in-network middleware has the capability to deal with operations such as energy efficient data transmission. The serverside middleware handles the context-aware stream processing, event detection and querying. The main focus is given to the in-network middleware. Therefore, event detection and data fusion capabilities are very limited. The in-network middleware has the intelligent capability to identify incomplete and false data values.

Bruckner et al.(Bruckner, Kasbi, Velik, & Herzner, 2008) have proposed a framework to process audio and video sensor data in a semantic manner. The proposed system architecture comprises seven layers. The bottom layers which are closed to the sensor nodes do the image and audio processing and convert the raw data *into Low Level Symbols* (LLS). Then data fusion mechanisms are used to convert those symbols into *High Level Symbols* (HLS). Patterns and events can be recognised using these symbols. The implementation has been deployed in an airport domain where the system is capable of identifying events such as unattended luggage or gunfire. The entire architecture is narrowly focused on video and audio sensor data processing.

Semantic Sensors (SS) (Imai, Hirota, Satake, & Kawashima, 2006) network middleware connects a variety of sensors to applications. The objective of the middleware is to develop a sensor network where developers need not to be aware of the device type of each sensor node. SS t can identify the location and the relationship among the sensors. The evaluation of the middleware has been done in a lab environment by attaching sensors to daily use items such as bottles and books. Logical expressions are used to store information about each object and their relationships. Very primitive events are possible to recognise by the system. For example, the system can answer simple queries such as identify the state of the object (i.e moving or not) or recognise the other objects nearby. The implementation is done using low level programming languages such as nesC.

Semantic Web Architecture for Sensor Networks (SWASN) (V. Huang & Javed, 2008) is a server-side middleware that uses semantic web technologies to enrich sensor data processing. This project has proposed a four layer architecture: sensor networks data sources layer, ontology layer, semantic web processing layer, and application layer. SWASN is capable of connecting multiple sensor networks together. To achieve this challenge, SWASN uses a separate local ontology for each sensor network to map sensor data to a common global RDF data model. SWASN provides sophisticated querying features using SPARQL (Malik et al., 2010). The system is focused on building fire emergency domain.

u-Greenhouse (Hwang & Yoe, 2011) is a context-aware middleware that proposed to process data collected through sensors in a greenhouse environment by applying wireless sensor network technologies. This middleware provides the functionalities of data filtering, event processing, context-aware processing and integration of heterogeneous sensors. The system architecture consists of three parts: sensor network interface, data process, and application service interface. The approach is to develop a hybrid middleware that consists of in-network data processing middleware that are installed on each node and a server-side data processing middleware. The u-Greenhouse architecture comprises three layers: the physical layer (Sensor node and gateways), the middleware layer and the application layer. Semantic capabilities are provided using and contextaware ontology. The system is capable of recognising simple events in greenhouse environment that can trigger actions. *u-Greenhouse* solution is narrowly focused on greenhouse domain.

Siguenza et al. (Siguenza, Blanco, Bernat, & Hernandez, 2010) combine states chart technology and semantic technology to annotate and process sensor data. The objective is to derive high level information from raw sensor data. W3C State Chart eXtensible Markup Language (SCXML) is used to implement the system. The sensor data are enriched using RDF semantics and stored in an SCXML data model. The possible situations are defined as states such as *adverseWeather*. The conditions related to the *adverseWeather* state need to be fulfilled in order to infer the current state as *adverseWeather*.

HARMONI (Homed, Misra, Ebling, & Jerome, 2008) is a context-aware system for the healthcare domain. This project has gone beyond the objective of identifying events using sensor data fusion. Homed et al. (Homed et al., 2008) have used their framework to reduce the amount of data transmission significantly. A mobile device that is capable of filtering data is deployed in the patient's room. This device is able to monitor the events according to the specifications defined in the filters. For example, doctors may need not to know all the behaviour of a patient. Doctors are only interested to know when a patient shows any unusual behaviour (e.g. very high heart rate). Therefore, it is not necessary to transfer all the data sensed by the sensors to the back-end server. Instead, a mobile device in the patient's room can filter the sensed data and transfer only the relevant data intelligently to the server based on the filter definition (Homed et al., 2008). These filters need be changed according to the context. For example, heart rate may need to be monitored based on the context. When the patient is doing exercises, it is natural that heart rate goes up. Therefore, the filters should be able to alter the filter definitions based on the context. Terziyan et al. (Terziyan, Kaykova, & Zhovtobryukh, 2010) have proposed the UbiRoad middleware that uses semantic and agent technologies. Their focus is on the smart road and traffic control domain. A sample scenario has presented to convey the ultimate objective. *UbiRoad* addresses four main challenges: interoperability, flexible coordination, self-management, trust and reputation. They have also identified context-aware sensor data fusion as a secondary challenge. The proposed solution is based on two other projects *SmartResource* (Terziyan, 2008) and *UBIWARE* (Katasonov, Kaykova, Khriyenko, Nikitin, & Terziyan, 2008). *UbiRoad* combines different ontologies to incorporate different concepts into the system such as device ontology, context ontology, data ontology, and domain ontology. For example, device ontology is used to recognise different devices in the sensor network and context ontology is used to understand the traffic control domain.

Phuoc and Hauswirth (Phuoc & Hauswirth, 2009) have proposed the concept of combining link data towards sensor data mashups. The system acquires sensor data through wrappers and passes them to the upper layer for fusion operations. The data fusion comprises many operations such as data filtering, data alignment, association, correlation, pattern detection and classification. Fusion operations can be composed together to produce high-level filters. The acquired sensor data are stored in RDF models. Therefore, SPARQL is used to query the data. Each individual sensor in considered as sensor component. Combinations of sensor components are defined as a sensing system. Sensor systems and fusion operation can be combined together to build complex work flows. An Ajax (Garrett, 2005) based graphical user interface is provided to build those work flows. The approach is more focused towards utilising link data concepts.

Gyllstrom et al. (Gyllstrom et al., 2007) have proposed a complex event processing system over data streams called SASE. SASE is narrowly focused on the RFID sensors domain. A high-level SQL like language has been defined to support user queries. The system is capable of identifying events such as shoplifting or inventory misplacement. Users need to syntactically define the query, and the system can process the query against the data stores. Some data fusion operations such as anomaly filtering, temporal smoothing and duplication reduction are provided by SASE.

Liu and Zhao (Liu & Zhao, 2005) have identified that most of the efforts on sensing systems today are domain specific with very little re-usability. To solve this problem, they have proposed a open architecture which is enriched with semantics. XML data formats are used in the system to store data. Service components are the main building block in the system. Each service is designed to take inputs, do some processing and give the output back. Services are designed in such a way that multiple services can be combined together to build a complex service. This run-time combining process is possible due to semantic descriptions. This programming model allows the user to query the sensor data and events in abstract ways without dealing with raw sensor data.

SEMbySEM (Brunner, Goudou, Gatellier, Beck, & Laporte, 2009) is a sensor management framework that focuses on isolating technical related challenges from the applications layer by using a facade layer in-between. The facade layer transforms the sensor data into semantically enriched information. The proposed architecture comprises three layers: facade, core, and visualisation. The core layer does the reasoning and inferring. An ontological semantic model is used to store the concepts, rules and data.

Intelligent Event Processing Agent (iEPA) (Dunkel, 2011) is an approach that combines complex event processing and multi agent systems. The research is focused on traffic management domain. A rule based system is employed to identify the events. Data fusion operations such as filter, split, aggregate, and transform are used to infer events. Events are defined in a language called Espers continuous Query Language (EQL).

Izumi et al. (Izumi et al., 2010) have proposed a knowledge filtering scheme for the health care support domain. Their system comprises a number of different agents, such as a data stream mining agent, an inference agent, and a knowledge base agent. A multi agent architecture is used to built the system, and an ontology scheme is used to store data where SPARQL queries are used for data filtering. Knowledge gathered using sensors is filtered based on four different perspectives: person based filtering, access policy based filtering, location based filtering, and time based filtering.

Teymourian et al. (Teymourian, Streibel, Paschke, Alnemr, & Meinel, 2009) present a conceptual approach to address the problem of *Semantic Event Processing (SCEP)*. SCEP combines event processing technologies and semantic technologies. This research effort is not directly related to sensor data fusion. However, the techniques used in this area can be combined with sensor data stream processing in order to detect events in the IoT environment.

The *Sensor Web Agent Platform* (SWAP) framework (Moodley & Simonis, 2006) comprises three layers: sensor layer, knowledge layer, and application layer. A multi agent technology and web services technologies are employed to build the system. Each layer consists of a number of agents that are capable of doing specific tasks. The implementation is focused on a fire detection domain. The number of different agents can be combined together to answer or detect complex situations such as wild fire.

Table 1. Taxonomy of sensor data fusion research efforts

Research Efforts	Architecture Type	Context-awareness	Semantic Interaction	Dynamic Configuration	Fusion Complexity	Actuation Management	Type of Processing	Cross Domain Portability	Implementation	Performance Evaluation	Year
Gibbons et al. (Gibbons et al., 2003)	A	×	×	L	L	×	D	3	X	×	2003
Liu & Zhao (Liu & Zhao, 2005)	A	×	H	M	H	×	C	1	X	×	2005
Whitehouse et al. (Whitehouse, Zhao, & Liu, 2006)	M	×	M	L	H	×	C	1	X	×	2006
Lewis et al. (Lewis, Cameron, Xie, & Arpinar, 2006)	M	×	H	M	M	×	C	1	X	×	2006
Moodley et al. (Moodley & Simonis, 2006)	M	X	L	×	L	×	C	1	X	×	2006
Moodley & Simonis (Moodley & Simonis, 2006)	M	×	M	M	H	×	C	1	X	×	2006
Bouillet et al. (Bouillet et al., 2007)	M	X	H	L	H	X	C	1	X	X	2007
Brenna et al. (Brenna et al., 2007)	A	X	×	×	M	×	C	1	X	×	2007
Gyllstrom et al. (Gyllstrom et al., 2007)	A	×	×	×	M	×	C	1	X	×	2007
Noguchi et al. (Gyllstrom et al., 2007)	M	×	M	H	M	×	C	1	X	×	2007
Zafeiropoulos et al. (Zafeiropoulos et al., 2008)	M	×	H	L	M	×	C	1	X	X	2008
Sheth et al. (Sheth, Henson, & Sahoo, 2008)	A	×	H	L	M	×	C	2	X	×	2008
Bruckner et al. (Bruckner et al., 2008)	A	X	L	×	M	×	D	1	X	×	2008
Huang et al. (V. Huang & Javed, 2008)	M	X	H	M	M	×	C	1	X	×	2008
Wood et al. (Wood et al., 2008)	A	X	L	M	L	×	D	1	X	×	2008
Homed et al. (Homed et al., 2008)	A	X	L	M	H	X	D	1	X	X	2008
Ni et al. (Ni et al., 2009)	A	X	H	×	M	×	D	1	×	×	2009
Da Rocha et al. (Da Rocha et al., 2009)	M	X	M	L	M	×	D	1	X	×	2009
Phuoc & Hauswirth (Phuoc & Hauswirth, 2009)	M	×	H	L	H	×	C	1	X	×	2009
Teymourian et al. (Teymourian et al., 2009)	A	X	L	L	L	×	C	2	×	×	2009
Brunner et al. (Brunner et al., 2009)	M	×	H	×	M	×	C	1	X	×	2009
Eisenhauer et al. (Eisenhauer et al., 2009)	M	X	H	M	H	×	C	2	X	×	2009
Lee et al. (Lee et al., 2010)	M	×	L	×	L	×	D	1	X	X	2010
Siguenza et al. (Siguenza et al., 2010)	A	×	M	×	L	×	C	1	X	×	2010
Izumi et al. (Izumi et al., 2010)	A	X	M	×	M	×	C	1	X	X	2010
Terziyan et al. (Terziyan et al., 2010)	M	X	M	L	M	×	C	1	X	×	2010
Hwang et al. (Hwang & Yoe, 2011)	M	X	L	M	L	X	D	1	X	X	2011
Dunkel (Dunkel, 2011)	A	×	L	M	H	X	D	1	X	×	2011
Jara et al. (Jara et al., 2014)	A	X	L	L	H	X	C	1	X	X	2014
Sobolevsky et al. (Sobolevsky et al., 2015)	A	X	L	L	H	X	C	1	X	X	2015
Antonelli et al. (Antonelli et al., March 19-20, Athens, Greece, 2014)	A	X	H	M	H	X	C	1	X	X	2014
Soldatos et al. (Soldatos et al., 2015)	M	X	H	H	H	X	D	many	X	X	2014

7. EVALUATION OF SENSOR DATA FUSION APPROACHES

The Table 1 classifies the difference sensor data fusion efforts based on the evaluation framework we presented in section 5. The parameters used to evaluate each feature of research efforts can be explained as follows. In depth discussion on each feature is conducted in the Section 5.

- **Architecture Type:** This feature evaluates whether the proposed solution is proposed as a middleware (M) or an Application system (A). Application systems are narrowly focused on one specific domain while middleware solutions possess more domain expandability and domain independence.
- **Context-Awareness:** This feature evaluates whether the proposed solution possesses context-awareness capabilities or not.
- **Semantic Interaction:** This feature is evaluated using four categories: High (H), Moderate (M), Low (L), and none (×).
    - High (H) Both data and program components are annotated using semantic technologies. Semantic reasoning mechanisms are employed.
    - Moderate (M) Either data elements or program components are enriched using semantics technologies, but not both.
    - Low (L) No semantic technologies are used. However, solutions are enriched with limited semantic capabilities using different techniques such as rules (Bruckner et al., 2008), symbols (Imai et al., 2006), etc.
    - None (×) No semantic interactions posed by the approach.
- **Dynamic Configuration:** *This feature is evaluated using four categories: High (H), Moderate (M), Low (L), and none (×).*
    - High (H) Sensor hardware and software components are dynamically configured based on the environment. The solution possesses automated configuration of filtering, fusion and reasoning mechanism, according to the problems at hand.
    - Moderate (M) Poses very limited dynamic hardware configuration such as switch on/off sensors.
    - Low (L) Poses software level limited dynamic composition and configuration capabilities.
    - None (×) No software or hardware components are dynamically configured.
- **Fusion Complexity:** This feature is evaluated using three categories: High (H), Moderate (M), and Low (L).
    - High (H) Capable of answering complex user queries. Program components can be combined together to produce complex results.
    - Moderate (M) Capable of answering moderately complex user queries. Develop complex fusion mechanism by combining simple fusion components is not possible.
    - Low (L) Limited fusion techniques such as data filtering is possible.
- **Actuation Management:** Does the solution possesses actuation management capabilities.
- **Type of Processing:** Is the data fusion approach Centralised (C) or Decentralised (D).
- **Cross Domain Portability:** Number of domains that the proposed solution is applied.
- **Implementation:** This feature tells that whether researchers have practically implemented the proposed solution or if it is a theoretical approach only.

- **Performance Evaluation:** This feature evaluates whether each research effort has conducted a performance evaluation procedure on their proposed system or not.

7.1. Discussion

Based on surveyed approaches, context-awareness in IoT more specifically within the smart city domain is gaining importance but still in its infancy. A lot of focus on context awareness is towards a particular application while to realise the true IoT-enabled smart cities vision, a broader non-domain focus will have to be pursued. Furthermore, dynamic configuration of things is also not addressed by most of the proposed solutions. Similarly, actuation managements is the least addressed feature among all. We believe actuation management is important as it plays a significant role in the IoT monitoring and feedback cycle. Further, performance evaluation techniques employed by most of the researchers to evaluate their proposed approaches are limited. Performance evaluation is extremely important as we are expecting these solutions to incorporate billions of sensor devices. Finally, cross domain portability is also addressed poorly. The majority of the efforts are based on a single domain. It is hoped that future efforts will aim to address these research gaps.

8. CONCLUSION

In this article, we highlighted the importance of sensor data fusion in IoT application such as smart cities. We examined a number of different sensor data fusion research efforts and developed an evaluation framework by carefully selecting ten different metrics. We believe these ten metrics are open challenges in the field. Based on our evaluation of the current state-of-the-art against the develop evaluation framework, it is evident that some of these challenges are addressed by the researchers significantly and while other are still in its infancy.

REFERENCES

Abowd, G. D., & Mynatt, E. D. (2000, March). Charting past, present, and future research in ubiquitous computing. *ACM Transactions on Computer-Human Interaction, 7*(1), 29–58. doi:10.1145/344949.344988

Akyildiz, I. F., Weilian, S., Sankarasubramaniam, Y., & Cayirci, E. (2002). A survey on sensor net- works. *Communications Magazine, IEEE, 40*(8), 102–114. doi:10.1109/MCOM.2002.1024422

Antonelli, F., Azzi, M., Balduini, M., DellAglio, D., Caviglia, G., Ciuccarelli, P., & Larcher, R. (March 19-20, Athens, Greece, 2014). *Towards city data fusion: A big data infrastructure to sense the pulse of a city in real-time*. In European data forum 2014.

Ashton, K. (2009, June). *That 'internet of things' thing in the real world, things matter more than ideas*. Retrieved from http://www.rfidjournal.com/article/print/4986

Atzori, L., Iera, A., & Morabito, G. (2010). *The internet of things:* A survey. *Computer Networks, 54*(15), 2787–2805. doi:10.1016/j.comnet.2010.05.010

Bouillet, E., Feblowitz, M., Liu, Z., Ranganathan, A., Riabov, A., & Ye, F. (2007). A semantics-based middleware for utilizing heterogeneous sensor networks. In *Proceedings of the 3rd ieee international conference on distributed computing in sensor systems* (pp. 174 - 188). Berlin, Heidelberg: Springer-Verlag doi:10.1007/978-3-540-73090-3_12

Boyd, J. R. (1987). *A discourse on winning and losing.* Unpublished set of brieng slides available at Air University Library, Maxwell AFB, Alabama. (http://www.ausairpower.net/JRB/intro.pdf [Accessed: 2011-12-18])

Brenna, L., Demers, A., Gehrke, J., Hong, M., Ossher, J., Panda, B., & White, W. (2007). *Cayuga: a high-performance event processing engine.* In Proceedings of the acm sigmod international conference on management of data (p. 1100- 1102). New York, NY, USA. Retrieved from http://doi.acm.org/10.1145/1247480.1247620

Bruckner, D., Kasbi, J., Velik, R., & Herzner, W. (2008, May). High-level hierarchical semantic processing framework for smart sensor networks. In Human system interactions, 2008 conference on (p. 668-673). doi:10.1109/HSI.2008.4581520

Brunner, J.-S., Goudou, J.-F., Gatellier, P., Beck, J., & Laporte, C.-E. (2009). *Sembysem: a framework for sensor management.* In 1st int. workshop on the semantic sensor web (semsensweb), collocated with ESWC.

Carnot Institutes. (2011). *White paper: Smart net- worked objects and internet of things (Tech. Rep.).* Carnot Institutes' Information Communication Technologies and Micro Nano Technologies alliance.

Cenedese, A., Zanella, A., Vangelista, L., & Zorzi, M. (June 2014). *Padova smart city: An urban internet of things experimentation.* In A world of wireless, mobile and multimedia networks (wow- mom), 2014 IEEE 15th international symposium on (p. 1-6).

Chantzara, M., & Anagnostou, M. (2005). *Evaluation and selection of context information.* In *Second international workshop on modeling and retrieval of context, edinburgh.*

Clark & Parsia. (2004). *Pellet: Owl 2 reasoner for java.* Software. (http://clarkparsia.com/pellet/ [Accessed: 2011-12-18])

Corcho, O., & Garcia-Castro, R. (2010). *Five challenges for the semantic sensor web.* Semantic Web - Interoperability, Usability, Applicability an IOS Press Journal, 121-125.

Crossbow Technology Inc. (2005, September). Crossbow-manuals getting started guide (Tech. Rep.). Crossbow Technology.

Da Rocha, A. R., Delicato, F. C., de Souza, J. N., Gomes, D. G., & Pirmez, L. (2009*). A semantic middleware for autonomic wireless sensor networks.* In Proceedings of the 2009 workshop on middleware for ubiquitous and pervasive systems (pp. 19-25). New York, NY, USA: ACM. Retrieved from http://doi.acm.org/10.1145/1551693.1551697 Deng. Z, Wu. Z, Wang. L, Chen. Z, Ranjan. R, Zomaya. A, Chen. D (2015), *Parallel Processing of Dynamic Continuous Queries over Streaming Data Flows.* IEEE Trans. Parallel Distrib. Syst. 26(3): 834-846

Dunkel, J. (2011, march). *Towards a multiagent-based software architecture for sensor networks.* In Autonomous decentralized systems (isads), 2011 10th international symposium on (p. 441 -448). doi:10.1109/ISADS.2011.64

Dyo, V. (2005). Middleware design for integration of sensor network and mobile devices. In Proceedings of the 2nd international doctoral symposium on middleware (pp. 1–5). New York, NY, USA: ACM; Retrieved from http://doi.acm.org/10.1145/1101140.1101142 doi:10.1145/1101140.1101142

Eisenhauer, M., Rosengren, P., & Antolin, P. (2009, June). *A development platform for integrating wireless devices and sensors into ambient intelligence systems.* In Sensor, mesh and ad hoc communications and networks workshops, 2009. SECON workshops '09. 6th annual IEEE communications society conference on (p. 1 -3). doi:10.1109/SAHCNW.2009.5172913

Ellebek, K. (2007). *A survey of context-aware middleware.* In Proceedings of the 25th conference on iasted international multi-conference: Soft- ware engineering (pp. 148-155). ACTA Press.

Garrett, J. J. (2005, February). *Ajax: A new approach to web applications.* (http://www.adaptivepath.com/ideas/ajax- new-approach-web-applications [Accessed: 2011.12.18])

Gay, D., Levis, P., von Behren, R., Welsh, M., Brewer, E., & Culler, D. (2003, June). The nesc language: A holistic approach to networked embedded systems. In Proceedings of programming language de- sign and implementation (pldi). doi:10.1145/781131.781133

Gibbons, P., Karp, B., Ke, Y., Nath, S., & Se- shan, S. (2003, oct.-dec.). *Irisnet: an architecture for a worldwide sensor web.* Pervasive Computing, IEEE, 2 (4), 22 - 33. doi: 10.1109/MPRV.2003.1251166

Guillemin, P., & Friess, P. (2009*). Internet of things strategic research roadmap* (Tech. Rep.). The Cluster of European Research Projects.

Gyllstrom, D., & Wu, E. jin Chae, H., Diao, Y., Stahlberg, P., & Anderson, G. (2007). *Sase: Complex event processing over streams.* In In proceedings of the third biennial conference on innovative data systems research.

Hall, D., & Llinas, J. (1997, January). An introduction to multisensor data fusion. *Proceedings of the IEEE, 85*(1), 6–23. doi:10.1109/5.554205

Homed, I., Misra, A., Ebling, M., & Jerome, W. (2008, march). *Harmoni: Context-aware filtering of sensor data for continuous remote health monitoring.* In Pervasive computing and communications, 2008. percom 2008. sixth annual IEEE international conference on (p. 248 -251).

Huang, V., & Javed, M. K. (2008). *Semantic sensor information description and processing.* In *Proceedings of the 2008 second international conference on sensor technologies and applications* (pp. 456-461). Washington, DC, USA: IEEE Computer Society. doi:10.1109/SENSORCOMM.2008.23

Huang, Y., & Li, G. (n.d.). A semantic analysis for Internet of things. In Intelligent computation technology and automation (icicta), 2010 international conference on (Vol. 1, pp. (336-339). doi:10.1109/ICICTA.2010.73

Hwang, J., & Yoe, H. (2011). Study on the context-aware middleware for ubiquitous greenhouses using wireless sensor networks. *Sensors (Basel, Switzerland), 11*(5), 4539–4561. doi:10.3390/s110504539 PMID:22163861

Hynes, G., Reynolds, V., & Hauswirth, M. (2009). A context lifecycle for web-based context management services. In *Proceedings of the 4th european conference on smart sensing and context* (pp. 51-65). Springer-Verlag. doi:10.1007/978-3-642-04471-7_5

Imai, M., Hirota, Y., Satake, S., & Kawashima, H. (2006, dec.). *Semantic sensor network for physically grounded applications*. In Control, au- tomation, robotics and vision, 2006. icarcv '06. 9th international conference on (p. 1 -6).

Issarny, V., Caporuscio, M., & Georgantas, N. (2007). *A perspective on the future of middleware-based software engineering. In 2007 future of software engineering* (pp. 244–258). Washington, DC, USA: IEEE Computer Society.

Izumi, S., Kobayashi, Y., Takahashi, H., Suganuma, T., Kinoshita, T., & Shiratori, N. (2010, july). *A knowledge filtering scheme using sensor data for symbiotic healthcare support system*. In Cognitive informatics (icci), 2010 9th IEEE international conference on (p. 619 -624). doi:10.1109/COGINF.2010.5599833

Jara, A., Genoud, D., & Bocchi, Y. (2014, March). Short paper: Sensors data fusion for smart cities with knime: A real experience in the smartsantander testbed. In Internet of things (wf-iot), 2014 ieee world forum on (p. 173-174). doi:10.1109/WF-IoT.2014.6803145

Jin, J., Gubbi, J., Marusic, S., & Palaniswami, M. (2014, April). An information framework for creating a smart city through internet of things. *Internet of Things Journal, IEEE, 1*(2), 112–121. doi:10.1109/JIOT.2013.2296516

Karimi, K. (Accessed on: May 2015). *The role of sensor fusion in the internet of things*. Retrieved from http://www.mouser.com/applications/sensor-fusion-iot/

Katasonov, A., Kaykova, O., Khriyenko, O., Nikitin, S., & Terziyan, V. Y. (2008). Smart semantic middleware for the internet of things. In Icincoicso'08 (p. 169-178).

Kortuem, G., Kawsar, F., Fitton, D., & Sundramoorthy, V. (2010). Smart objects as building blocks for the internet of things. *IEEE Internet Computing, 14*(1), 44–51. doi:10.1109/MIC.2009.143

Krosche, J., Jakl, A., Gusenbauer, D., Rothbauer, D., & Ehringer, B. (2009). Managing context on a sensor enabled mobile device – the msense approach. In Proc. ieee int. conf. wireless and mobile computing, networking and communications wimob 2009 (pp. 135-140).

Lee, K.-W., Park, J.-H., & Oh, R.-D. (2010, oct.). *Design of active semantic middleware system to support incomplete sensor information based on ubiquitous sensor network*. In Application of information and communication technologies (aict), 2010 4th international conference on (p. 1 -5). doi:10.1109/ICAICT.2010.5612032

Lewis, M., Cameron, D., Xie, S., & Arpinar, B. (2006). *Es3n: A semantic approach to data management in sensor networks*. In 5th international semantic web conference iswc.

Liu, J., & Zhao, F. (2005, oct.). Towards semantic services for sensor-rich information systems. In Broadband networks, 2005. broadnets 2005. 2nd international conference on (p. 967 -974 Vol. 2).

Lopez, T. S., Kim, D., Min, K., & Lee, J. (2007, feb.). *Dynamic context networks of wireless sensors and rfid tags.* In Wireless pervasive computing, 2007. iswpc '07. 2nd international symposium on.

Lu, T., & Neng, W. (n.d.). *Future internet: The internet of things.* In Advanced computer theory and engineering (icacte), 2010 3rd international conference on (Vol. 5, pp. V5-376-V5-380).

Madden, S. R., Franklin, M. J., Hellerstein, J. M., & Hong, W. (2005, March). Tinydb: An acquisitional query processing system for sensor networks. *ACM Transactions on Database Systems, 30*(1), 122–173. doi:10.1145/1061318.1061322

Malik, S., Goel, A., & Maniktala, S. (2010, oct.). A comparative study of various variants of sparql in semantic web. In Computer information systems and industrial management applications (cisim), 2010 international conference on (p. 471 -474). doi:10.1109/CISIM.2010.5643493

Mark Raskino, A. L., Jackie Fenn. (2005). *Extracting value from the massively connected world of 2015* (Tech. Rep.). Gartner Research.

Moodley, D., & Simonis, I. (2006). A new architecture for the sensor web: The swap framework. In 5th international semantic web conference iswc.

Nagy, M., Katasonov, A., Khriyenko, O., Nikitin, S., Szydlowski, M., & Terziyan, V. (2009). *Challenges of middleware for the internet of things (Tech. Rep.).* University of Jyvaskyla.

Nakamura, E. F., Loureiro, A. A. F., & Frery, A. C. (2007, September). Information fusion for wireless sensor networks: Methods, models, and classifications. *ACM Computing Surveys, 39.*

Ni, L. M., Zhu, Y., Ma, J., Luo, Q., Liu, Y., Cheung, S. C., & Wu, M. (2009, April). Semantic sensor net; an extensible framework. *Int. J. Ad Hoc Ubiquitous Comput., 4*(3/4), 157–167. doi:10.1504/IJA-HUC.2009.024518

Phuoc, D. L., & Hauswirth, M. (2009). *Linked open data in sensor data mashups.* In proceedings of the 2nd international workshop on semantic sensor networks (ssn09) (Vol. 522, p. 1-16). CEUR Workshop at ISWC 2009, Washington DC, USA.

Schilit, B., Adams, N., & Want, R. (1994, dec).Context-aware computing applications. In Mobile computing systems and applications, 1994. proceedings., workshop on (p. 85 -90). doi:10.1109/WMCSA.1994.16

Sheth, A., Henson, C., & Sahoo, S. (2008, July-August). Semantic sensor web. *IEEE Internet Computing, 12*(4), 78–83. doi:10.1109/MIC.2008.87

Shulsky, A. N., & Schmitt, G. J. (2002). Silent warfare: Understanding the world of intelligence (3d Edition ed.). Potomac Books Inc.

Siguenza, A., Blanco, J. L., Bernat, J., & Hernandez, L. A. (2010). *using scxml for semantic sensor networks.* In 3nd international workshop on semantic sensor networks (ssn10).

Sobolevsky, S., Bojic, I., Belyi, A., Sitko, I., Hawelka, B., Arias, J. M., & Ratti, C. (2015, April). *Scaling of city attractiveness for foreign visitors through big data of human economical and social media activity*. Retrieved from http://arxiv.org/abs/1504.06003

Soldatos, J., Kefalakis, N., Hauswirth, M., Serrano, M., Calbimonte, J.-P., Riahi, M.,... Herzog, R. (2015). Openiot: Open source internet-of-things in the cloud. In I. Podnar arko, K. Pripui, & M. Serrano (Eds.), Interoperability and open-source solutions for the internet of things (Vol. 9001, p. 13-25). Springer International Publishing. doi:10.1007/978-3-319-16546-2_3

Song, W., Wang, L., Ranjan, R., Kolodziej, J., & Chen, D. (2015). Towards Modeling Large-Scale Data Flows in a Multidatacenter Computing System With Petri Net. *IEEE Systems Journal*, *9*(2), 416–426. doi:10.1109/JSYST.2013.2283954

Song, Z., Cardenas, A. A., & Masuoka, R. (2010, 29-2010-dec. 1). Semantic middleware for the internet of things. In Internet of things (iot), 2010 (p. 1 -8). doi:10.1109/IOT.2010.5678448

Sundmaeker, H., Guillemin, P., Friess, P., & Woelffle, S. (2010). *Vision and challenges for realising the internet of things (Tech. Rep.)*. European Commission Information Society and Media.

Terziyan, V. (2008). *Smartresource- proactive self-maintained resources in semantic web: Lessons learned*. International Journal of Smart Home. *Special Issue on Future Generation Smart Space*, *2*, 33–57.

Terziyan, V., Kaykova, O., & Zhovtobryukh, D. (2010, may). *Ubiroad: Semantic middleware for context-aware smart road environments*. In Internet and web applications and services (iciw), 2010 fifth international conference on (p. 295 -302). doi:10.1109/ICIW.2010.50

Teymourian, K., Streibel, O., Paschke, A., Alnemr, R., & Meinel, C. (2009*).Towards semantic event-driven systems*. In Proceedings of the 3rd international conference on new technologies, mobility and security (pp. 347-352). Piscat-away, NJ, USA: IEEE Press.

Theodoridis, E., Mylonas, G., & Chatzigiannakis, I. (2013, July). *Developing an iot smart city framework*. In Information, intelligence, systems and applications (iisa), 2013 fourth international conference on (p. 1-6). doi:10.1109/IISA.2013.6623710

Thomason, L. (2010). *Tinyxml. Software*. (http://www.grinninglizard.com/tinyxml/index.html [Accessed: 2011-12-18])

Tiny, O. S. Alliance. (2010, July). *Tinyos*. Retrieved from http://www.tinyos.net/ [Accessed: 2011-12-18] (http://www.tinyos.net/ [Accessed: 2011-12-18])

UC Berkeley WEBS Project. (2004, December). *nesc: A programming language for deeply networked systems*. (http://nescc.sourceforge.net/[Accessed: 2011-12-18])

Union, I. T. (2005). Itu internet reports 2005: *The internet of things (Tech. Rep.)*.

Wang, L., Ma, Y., Zomaya, A., Ranjan, R., & Chen, D. (2015b). A Parallel File System with Application-Aware Data Layout Policies for Massive Remote Sensing Image Processing in Digital Earth. *IEEE Transactions on Parallel and Distributed Systems*, *26*(6), 1497–1508. doi:10.1109/TPDS.2014.2322362

(2015). Wang. L, Geng. H, Liu. P, Lu. K, Kolodziej. J, Ranjan. R, Zomaya (2015a). *A, Particle Swarm Optimization based dictionary learning for remote sensing big data. Knowledge-Based Systems, 79*(May), 43–50.

Whitehouse, K., Zhao, F., & Liu, J. (2006). Semantic streams: A framework for composable semantic interpretation of sensor data. In Ewsn'06 (p. 5- 20). doi:10.1007/11669463_4

Wood, A., Stankovic, J., Virone, G., Selavo, L., He, Z., Cao, Q., & Stoleru, R. et al. (2008, July). Context-aware wireless sensor networks for assisted living and residential monitoring. *IEEE Network, 22*(4), 26–33. doi:10.1109/MNET.2008.4579768

Yang, D.-L., Liu, F., & Liang, Y.-D. (n.d.). *A survey of the internet of things.* In International conference on e-business intelligence (icebi-2010). doi:10.2991/icebi.2010.72

Yao, Y., & Gehrke, J. (2002, September). The cougar approach to in-network query processing in sensor networks. *SIGMOD Record, 31*(3), 9–18. doi:10.1145/601858.601861

Zafeiropoulos, A., Konstantinou, N., Arkoulis, S., Spanos, D.-E., & Mitrou, N. (2008, 29 2008-oct. 4*). A semantic-based architecture for sensor data fusion.* In Mobile ubiquitous computing, systems, services and technologies, 2008. ubicomm '08. The second international conference on (p. 116 -121).

Zafeiropoulos, A., Spano, D.-E., Arkoulis, S., Konstantinou, N., & Mitrou, N. (2011). Data management in the semantic web (H. Jin, Ed.). nova-publishers.

Zanella, A., Bui, N., Castellani, A., Vangelista, L., & Zorzi, M. (2014, February). Internet of things for smart cities. *Internet of Things Journal, IEEE, 1*(1), 22–32. doi:10.1109/JIOT.2014.2306328

This work was previously published in the International Journal of Distributed Systems and Technologies (IJDST), 7(1); edited by Nik Bessis, pages 15-36, copyright year 2016 by IGI Publishing (an imprint of IGI Global).

Chapter 20

An Exploratory Study of the Impact of the Internet of Things (IoT) on Business Model Innovation:
Building Smart Enterprises at Fortune 500 Companies

In Lee
Western Illinois University, USA

ABSTRACT

This paper introduces IoT categories used to build smart enterprises and discusses how Fortune 500 companies may use various IoT applications to innovate their business models. The authors' analysis reveals that there is a significant relationship between the type of IoT applications and the IoT adoption rate and there is also a significant relationship between the type of business model innovation and the IoT adoption rate. Finally, five implementation strategies for smart enterprise development are discussed.

INTRODUCTION

As the IoT is gaining an increasing attention as a new paradigm in the industries, companies are beginning to capitalize on IoT applications in a variety of ways (Gubbi et al., 2013; Lee & Lee, 2015). The main strength of the IoT is the high impact it will have on several aspects of every-day life and behavior of potential users (Bandyopadhyay & Sen, 2011). Assisted living, smart homes, e-health, and enhanced learning are only a few examples of possible application scenarios in which this new paradigm will play a leading role in the near future (Atzori et al., 2010). Many companies such as Amazon and Home Depot are developing IoT applications to capture real-time consumer data and offer better services.

DOI: 10.4018/978-1-5225-1832-7.ch020

Recently, the IoT was also recognized as a disruptive technology for supply chain management. The IoT helps supply chain partners monitor the process of a supply chain execution in real time and improve the efficiency and effectiveness of supply chain (Ping et al., 2011). According to Garnter (2014), the IoT is one of the emerging technologies in IT in Gartner's IT Hype Cycle. Specific technologies go through innovation trigger, peak of inflated expectations, through of disillusionment, slope of enlightenment, and plateau of productivity of the hype cycle. As of July 2014, the IoT is at the peak of the inflated expectations of the hype cycle and will take 5-10 years to reach the market plateau (Garnter, 2014).

It is evident that the IoT will give rise to new opportunities for the Information and Communication Technologies (ICT) sector, paving the way to new services and applications able to leverage the interconnection of physical and virtual realms (Miorandi et al., 2012) and companies in most industries will rapidly adopt IoT-enabled applications in order to stay competitive. However, while a large number of technical studies have been conducted in management of smart grid (Bui et al., 2012), and resource constraint devices (Gluhak et al., 2011; Sehgal et al., 2011), the IoT on the management side is yet an underserved area of scholarly investigation. This paper attempts to fill the gap by investigating how the Fortune 500 companies use IoT solutions for business model innovation. This paper lays theoretical foundations for business model innovation, identifies categories of IoT applications for smart enterprises, presents a conceptual model of IoT-based business model innovation, and investigates how the Fortune 500 companies use the IoT to innovate their business models. Five hypotheses are developed and statistical analysis is conducted. This paper also discusses implementation strategies for effective development of smart enterprise.

BUSINESS MODEL INNOVATION AND THE IOT FOR SMART ENTERPRISE

Business models have been widely used to set up, review, and refine new business ventures. Business models contribute to the research community as a new unit of analysis, and as a system-level concept, centered on activities and focused on value (Zott et al., 2011). Despite extensive use of the term 'business model' in both research and practice, a general agreement on the definition of the business model is still missing due to its complex nature. Despite the partial overlap of definitions, the majority have emphasized the role of competitive advantage by a business model (Afuah & Tucci, 2003; Morris et al., 2005; Shafer et al., 2005). The development of a business model helps managers understand the process of customer value creation, resource acquisition, and value delivery and capture.

While some researchers focus on the characteristics of the business model, others concentrate on the innovation of the business model. Business model innovation is a process of finding innovative ways to create value, delivering value, and capturing value. Like the numerous definitions of a business model, different views on business model innovation have been suggested. Teece (2010) views business model innovation as a type of organizational innovation in which firms identify and adopt novel opportunity portfolios. Matthyssens et al. (2006) view business model innovation as a way to blunt cutthroat competition and achieve competitive advantage. Johnson et al. (2008) describe business model innovation as an outward-facing, highly creative exploratory process. The results of business model innovation often affect the entire firm (Amit & Zott, 2001).

According to Sosna et al. (2010), business model innovation is a trial-and-error learning process and may proceed differently in start-ups compared to established organizations. They note that continuous business model innovation is an important capability for every firm seeking success in the long term.

Chesbrough (2007) suggests that enterprises can follow six stages of business model innovation from very basic (and not very valuable) models to far more advanced (and very valuable) models. He suggests that companies can assess where their current business model stands in relation to its potential and then define appropriate next steps for the further advancement of that model. However, no studies have yet investigated the applicability of the IoT for business model innovation. To understand how the IoT can be used to innovate business models, we need to analyze how leading enterprises are currently leveraging the unique capabilities of the IoT for their business model innovation.

Based on the technology trends and literature review, this section discusses three IoT categories for smart enterprise applications: (1) monitoring and control, (2) information sharing and collaboration, and (3) big data and data analytics (Lee & Lee, 2015).

Monitoring and Control

According to the Digital Agenda for Europe (European Union, 2015), monitoring and control refers to the control of any system, device or network through automated procedures managed by a control unit with or without the capability to display information. IoT-enabled monitoring and control systems are gaining popularity in the environmental and manufacturing sectors, where companies have operated basic applications such as real time observation with sensors and alerting about machines and devices (Bi et al., 2014; Lazarescu, 2013; Tao et al., 2014). The IoT-enabled monitoring and controlling technologies are used to develop an effective low-cost and flexible solution for condition monitoring and energy management in home (Kelly et al., 2013).

Monitoring and control is considered of high importance in a wide range of sectors including environment, transportation, construction, manufacturing, home automation, utilities, healthcare, and agriculture sectors (Miorandi et al., 2012). Monitoring and control systems collect and send key data on asset condition, equipment performance, testing, energy usage, and environmental conditions and allow managers and automated controllers to respond to changes in real time anywhere, anytime.

Wireless technologies have played a key role in industrial monitoring and control systems. In addition to extensively reducing bulk and installation costs of conventional wired networks, the location independence of the technology allows it to be deployed easily in areas which simply cannot be monitored using wired solutions (Willig et al., 2005; Zand et al., 2012). Monitoring and control systems are entering a new era with the development of smarter, cheaper wireless sensors and sensor networks for the IoT-based machine-to-machine communications (M2M).

Information Sharing and Collaboration

Information sharing and collaboration refers to the electronic movement of information and purpose-driven collaboration between people, between people and things, and between things. Enterprises can improve their capabilities by leveraging the IoT-related information sharing mechanisms within and across industries (Li et al., 2012). Inter-device information sharing and collaboration benefit from the standardization of communication protocols and devices. Monitoring and control components are often embedded into the information sharing and collaboration devices and detect a predefined event which triggers information sharing and collaboration among people and things. Recent research shows that there exist more potential applications of IoT in information intensive sectors such as healthcare services due to information sharing capability of the IoT (Xu et al., 2014). For example, in the healthcare industry, remote patient monitoring systems can monitor conditions of chronically ill patients and send alerting messages to healthcare professionals in case of urgent medical needs. Information sharing allows devices and people to collaborate at the same time, with the same information collected or retrieved from multiple sources. One key technology of the IoT for information sharing and collaboration is high-speed network technology (Wang et al., 2013).

The potential of the IoT will be realized via IoT standardization with which devices from different manufacturers share information seamlessly. Standards are required for bidirectional communication and information exchange among things, their environment, their digital counterparts that have an interest in monitoring, controlling or assisting the things (Bandyopadhyay & Sen 2011). In addition to IoT device standardization, IoT networks need to be more reliable, flexible, and scalable as more devices are added. IPv6 provides a much needed scalability option. The substantially increased address space provided by IPv6 ensures that the IoT-enabled objects can be assigned unique addresses (Jin et al., 2014). IPv6 is interoperable across devices and communication technologies, evolving and versatile while still stable, scalable, manageable, and simple enough that a resource-constrained smart object can easily run it (Vasseur and Dunkels, 2010).

Big Data and Data Analytics

A number of studies focus on using or developing effective methods to convert the data generated or captured by the IoT into knowledge useful for decision making and problem solving (Bin et al., 2010; Tsai et al., 2014). Big data and data analytics refers to the process of collecting, organizing and analyzing massive amount of data to discover useful patterns and knowledge. IoT devices and machines with embedded sensors and actuators generate enormous amount of data to be processed by business intelligence and analytics tools for decision making. Innovative IoT applications are using seamless large scale sensing, data analytics, and information representation, and cloud computing (Gubbi et al., 2013).

Big data and data analytics helps decision makers at all levels of enterprises make more informed decisions. While IoT-enabled monitoring and control applications may perform minimum level of intelligent activities, they are mostly reactive to predefined events. Therefore, once monitoring and information sharing IoT applications acquire data, big data and business analytics uses machine learning, advanced statistical techniques, and other predictive analytics to resolve any business issues such as changes in customer behaviors and market conditions, to discover ways to increase customer satisfaction, and to develop value added services for customers.

Data analytics can be done at a cloud center in a batch mode once data are stored (Fisher et al., 2012). Alternatively, in a more time-sensitive environment, streaming analytics can be used to analyze data in real time while devices transmit data to the cloud center (Lee & Lee, 2015). Various data mining techniques (Arora & Ravi, 2013; Priya et al., 2012) and knowledge management support systems (Zeleny, 2013) can be applied to data analytics to discover hidden relationships among data. One challenge in data analytics is access to massive amount of data, and soft-computing technologies is being developed to address this challenge (Katkar & Ghosekar, 2012).

ROLES OF THE IOT FOR SUPPORTING BUSINESS MODEL INNOVATION

With the disruptive power of the IoT, opportunities for enterprises to innovate their existing business models are abundant. As IoT technologies advance, the need for developing a framework of the IoT applications for smart enterprises that reflect the unique characteristics and capabilities has increased. In order to meet our specific research purposes, our study adopts a typology approach to the model development. Typologies are specific rather than general classifications, otherwise known as taxonomies (Bailey, 1994). Typologies are mostly generated through qualitative classification rather than quantitative or statistical analysis. Five criteria need to be satisfied when constructing a typology (Hunt, 1991). These five criteria are: (1) Is the phenomenon to be classified adequately specified? (2) Is the classification characteristic adequately specified? (3) Are the categories mutually exclusive? (4) Is the typology collectively exhaustive? (5) Is the typology useful? The first four criteria are essential to assess the adequacy and strength of the proposed typology, while the fifth criterion of usefulness is considered to be most vital when evaluating a typology (Hunt, 1991). This study has applied the same criteria in developing the conceptual framework.

Based on our literature review on business models, we select four components of a business model: value proposition, business process, value network, and sustainability. Twelve cells are created by combining the four components of the business model with the three categories of IoT applications for in-depth analysis. Table 1 shows a two-dimensional conceptual model of business model components and IoT categories. We analyze how particular IoT applications support these four components of the business model. The Fortune 500 companies are divided into 1-250 and 251-500 companies in rank order to understand how the size affects their adoption of IoT applications in each component of the business model. Each interaction cell represents the specific business model components and IoT applications adopted by the Fortune 500 companies. The mapping of IoT applications to the business model components will help enterprises understand the types and effects of the IoT applications, reduce the trials and errors in the implementation process, and maximize the investment value.

1. **Value Proposition:** Value proposition refers to a substantial value of a product/service to a target customer for which the customer is willing to pay (Dubosson-Torbay et al., 2002). Value proposition is concerned about the target customer, the job to be done, identification of customer value, and a way to create value for what is sold to the customer. Value proposition needs to be compelling to customers, achieve advantageous cost and risk structures, and enable significant value capture by the enterprise that delivers products and services (Teece, 2010). The value proposition from the IoT solutions is derived when new services or new values are perceived by customers from the use of the IoT solutions. For example, an IoT integrated home automation system will enhance the safety of family members and energy efficiency for the customers (Kelly et al., 2013). Another example is a personal health monitoring system which monitors an individual user's health condition real time and notifies the user when a change of the condition needs attention (Jara et al., 2013).

2. **Business Process:** A process is "a lateral or horizontal organizational form, that encapsulates the interdependence of tasks, roles, people, departments and functions required to provide a customer with a product or service" (Earl, 1994, p.13). A business process converts various organizational inputs into value-added outputs through a set of interrelated activities. Different types of products/services/values are generated by different business processes. Improved effectiveness and efficiency in the business process will lead to faster cycle times, customer satisfaction, reduced costs

Table 1. A conceptual model of IoT applications for business model innovation: Cases of the Fortune 500 Companies

Components of Business Model	Monitoring and Control	Information Sharing and Collaboration	Big Data and Data Analytics	Total	Value Creation
Value Proposition (Fortune 1-250)	10* (Ex., Ford's connected car dashboards)	3 (Ex., Procter & Gamble's interactive electric toothbrush links with a smartphone)	1 (Ex., GE's Trip Optimizer)	14	Customer loyalty, Higher service value Higher product value, Open innovation, Increased consumer satisfaction, Targeted marketing, Custom-tailored experiences
Value Proposition (Fortune 251-500)	8 (Ex., AGCO's Smart farm equipment solutions)	4 (Ex., Avery Dennison Corporation's Interactive packaging)	1 (Ex., Biogen Idec Inc.'s Sensors, software and data analysis tools)	13	
Value Proposition Total	**18**	**7**	**2**	**27**	
Business Process (Fortune 1-250)	4 (Ex., Delta Air Lines's eTrack)	2 (Ex., Edison International's Edison SmartConnect)	4 (Ex., Mondelēz International Inc.'s Smart shelves)	10	Improved information quality, Business process redesign, Knowledge sharing, Shorter product development time, Faster product delivery time
Business Process (Fortune 251-500)	3 (Ex., Sonic Automotive's automotive inventory tracking system)	1 (Ex., DTE Energy's Smart meters)	2 (Ex., Harley-Davidson Inc.'s SAP Connected manufacturing)	6	
Business Process Total	**7**	**3**	**6**	**16**	
Value Network (Fortune 1-250)	1 (Ex., Fedex's SenseAware)	3 (Ex., Walmart's inventory system)	0	4	Improved supply chain management, Partner relationship building, Information sharing, Visibility of global value networks, Global communications and information sharing
Value Network (Fortune 251-500)	1 (Ex., Ryder System, Inc.'s ORBCOMM)	0	0	1	
Value Network Total	**2**	**3**	**0**	**5**	
Sustainability (Fortune 1-250)	3 (Ex., General Electric's predictive maintenance)	3 (Allstate's Drivewise® in-vehicle connectivity)	2 (Ex., Freeport-McMoRan's IoT platform)	8	Sustainable competitive advantage, Less waste production, A less polluted environment, Cost saving, Higher profit
Sustainability (Fortune 251-500)	1 (Ex., United Stationers Inc.'s Intelligent lighting system)	0	2 (Ex., Becton, Dickinson and Company: BD Medical Smart devices and health related data management)	3	
Sustainability Total	**4**	**3**	**4**	**11**	
Grand Total	**31**	**16**	**12**	**59**	

*: the number of cases

and greater competitive advantages (Kettinger et al., 1997). With the advancement of the IoT it is expected that soon business processes will require considering IoT devices in the process flow both for documentation and automation purposes (Meyer et al., 2013). A successful IoT adoption requires the integration of IoT applications into core business processes. It is important to identify the types of IoT applications that influence the effectiveness and efficiency of business processes. For example, an internal value chain would be improved by using an IoT-enabled inventory management. For a manufacturing process, a sensor-based controller may be used to monitor machine or process conditions and detect abnormal or undesirable operating conditions.

3. **Value Network:** Value network refers to a network of partners, suppliers, distributors, and other enterprises that add value to the supply chain of the products/services. Value is co-created by a combination of players in the network (Peppard & Rylander, 2006). Therefore, value network is concerned about improvement of any network activities among these participants. The significance and weight of value network participants are measured based on the magnitude of their value addition to products/services in different stages towards the final products. For example, the higher value the participants generates, the greater the role that participants play in the network. Examples of IoT solutions for value network management include cloud-based GPS and Radio Frequency Identification (RFID) applications which provide identity, location, and other tracking information for enhanced in-transit visibility of moving parts and fleets (Pang et al., 2015). Value network participants can share the location and condition of the parts via a cloud center where all data are collected and stored real time. The improved in-transit visibility can help the value network participants reduce inventory and better manage fleet routing by monitoring traffic conditions (Caballero-Gil et al, 2013).

4. **Sustainability:** A sustainable company is the one that meets the needs of its stakeholders without compromising its ability to meet their needs in the future (Hockerts, 1999). To meet the stakeholders' needs in the future, sustainability is concerned with managing triple bottom lines, frequently referred to as profit, people and planet. Since 2010, sustainability has been widely adopted by enterprises due to increased environmental awareness, social responsibility, and profit. Sustainability is becoming an integral part of a business model in a drive to achieve long-term corporate growth and profitability and fulfill environmental and social responsibilities at the same time. To balance people, planet, and profit, sustainable businesses focus on their ability to change its manufacturing and services operation that help embed environmental efficiency to achieve less waste production, a less polluted environment, and socially responsible business practices. By integrating sustainability a strategic decision making, enterprises are more likely to include economic, environmental and social considerations in all aspects of business on an ongoing basis (Bonn & Fisher, 2011). In addition, profit is generated through an extended timeline for return on investment and profit formula which defines how the company creates value for itself while providing value to the customer.

IoT solutions can help enterprises achieve green manufacturing by reducing energy of manufacturing processes with responsive lights for production spaces, smart washing machines, and energy-efficient thermostats (Miragliotta & Shrouf, 2013). Although these IoT solutions may require initial investment costs, the savings they achieve will eventually pay off (Lee & Lee). These investments in green manufacturing typically lead to enhanced brand and public relations, which in turn lead to increased revenue and profit.

HYPOTHESES AND ANALYSIS OF FORTUNE 500 COMPANIES' USE OF IOT APPLICATIONS

We searched online news using Google search engine, and visited company web sites in March 2015 to identify IoT applications adopted by the 2014 Fortune 500 companies. We excluded Fortune 500 IT companies such as Microsoft and Cisco from data collection to focus on non-IT companies' use of the IoT applications. We identified a total of fifty nine IoT applications adopted by the Fortune 500 companies. The overall adoption rate is still low in that only a little over 10 percent of the Fortune 500 companies are investing in the IoT.

A number of studies conduct the patterns and determinants of technology diffusion at the firm level (Haller & Siedschlag, 2011) and support that larger firms are more likely to adopt new technologies early (Fabiani et al., 2005; Giunta & Trivieri, 2007; Teo & Tan, 1998; Thong, 1999; Zhu et al., 2006). Firm size is commonly used in the studies on new technology adoption because it is easy to observe (Geroski, 2000). Other studies also corroborate that firm size is an important determinant of a firm's involvement and decision process in acquiring Information and Communication Technologies (ICTs) (Dholakia et al., 1993; van der Veen, 2004). Evidence suggests that large firms are the early adopters of social media technologies. For example, large firms have technical, complementary, and financial resources to facilitate innovation adoption while small firms might suffer from resource poverty. To analyze the pattern of the IoT adoption for business model innovation statistically, we develop the following five hypotheses:

Hypothesis 1: There is a significant relationship between the size of enterprises and the IoT adoption rate.

Hypothesis 2: There is a significant relationship between the type of IoT applications and the IoT adoption rate.

Hypothesis 3: There is a significant relationship between the type of business model innovation and the IoT adoption rate.

Hypothesis 4: There is a significant relationship between the size of enterprises and the type of IoT applications.

Hypothesis 5: There is a significant relationship between the type of business model innovation and the type of IoT applications.

The Chi Square (χ^2) test is used to determine whether there is a significant difference between the expected frequencies of the IoT adoption and the observed frequencies of the IoT adoption in the three categories and business model components in Table 1. The Chi Square (χ^2) test has been used in a wide range of studies (Carr, 2002; Jelinski, 1991; Lindsey & Sessoms, 2006; Yip & Yau, 2005). We identified a total of fifty nine IoT applications adopted by the Fortune 500 companies. 36 applications are adopted by Fortune 250 companies and 23 applications adopted by Fortune 251-500 companies. Table 2 shows that Hypothesis 1 (There is a significant relationship between the size of enterprises and the IoT adoption rate) is rejected.

Our data shows that the IoT is widely used in the area of monitoring and control (31 cases), followed by information sharing and collaboration (16) and big data and data analytics (12). Table 3 shows that Hypothesis 2 (There is a significant relationship between the type of IoT applications and the IoT adoption rate) is accepted.

In terms of the business model, value proposition is the most widely used IoT application category (27 cases), followed by business process (16), sustainability (11), and value network (5). Table 4 shows

Table 2. Chi square test for hypothesis 1

Category	Observed	Expected #	Expected
Fortune 250	36	29.5	50.000%
Fortune 500	23	29.5	50.000%
Chi squared equals 2.864 with 1 degree of freedom. The two-tailed P value equals 0.0906.			

Table 3. Chi square test for hypothesis 2

Category	Observed	Expected #	Expected
Monitoring	31	19.666	33.332%
Collaboration	16	19.667	33.334%
Analytics	12	19.667	33.334%
Chi squared equals 10.678 with 2 degrees of freedom. The two-tailed P value equals 0.0061.			

Table 4. Chi square test for hypothesis 3

Category	Observed	Expected #	Expected
Value	27	14.75	25.000%
Process	16	14.75	25.000%
Network	5	14.75	25.000%
Sustainability	11	14.75	25.000%
Chi squared equals 17.678 with 3 degrees of freedom. The two-tailed P value equals 0.0005.			

that Hypothesis 3 (There is a significant relationship between the type of business model innovation and the IoT adoption rate) is accepted.

The Fortune 250 companies and the Fortune 251-500 companies share strikingly similar adoption patterns while the number of the IoT adoption is greater at the Fortune 250 companies. Table 5 provides the following information: the observed cell totals, (the expected cell totals) and [the chi-square statistic for each cell]. Table 5 shows that Hypothesis 4 (There is a significant relationship between the size of enterprises and the type of IoT applications) is rejected.

For value proposition, monitoring and control is the most widely used IoT application area (18), followed by information sharing and collaboration (7), and big data and data analytics (2). For business process, monitoring and control is the most widely used IoT application area (7), followed by big data and data analytics (6), and information sharing and collaboration (3). For value network, we found information sharing and collaboration is the most widely used IoT application area (3), followed by and monitoring and control (2), but no IoT application for big data and data analytics. For sustainability, monitoring and control (4) and big data and data analytics (4) are equally adopted, followed by and information sharing and collaboration (3). Table 6 shows that Hypothesis 5 (There is a significant relationship between the type of business model innovation and the type of IoT applications) is rejected at a significance level of .05.

Table 5. Chi square test for hypothesis 4

Results			
	Monitoring	**Collaboration**	**Analytics**	**Row Totals**
Fortune 250	18 (18.92) [0.04]	11 (9.76) [0.16]	7 (7.32) [0.01]	36
Fortune 500	13 (12.08) [0.07]	5 (6.24) [0.25]	5 (4.68) [0.02]	23
Column Totals	31	16	12	**59 (Grand Total)**
The chi-square statistic is 0.5522. The P-Value is 0.758742.				

Table 6. Chi square test for hypothesis 5

Results			
	Monitoring	**Collaboration**	**Analytics**	**Row Totals**
Value	18 (14.19) [1.03]	7 (7.32) [0.01]	2 (5.49) [2.22]	27
Process	7 (8.41) [0.24]	3 (4.34) [0.41]	6 (3.25) [2.32]	16
Network	2 (2.63) [0.15]	3 (1.36) [1.99]	0 (1.02) [1.02]	5
Sustainability	4 (5.78) [0.55]	3 (2.98) [0.00]	4 (2.24) [1.39]	11
Column Totals	31	16	12	**59 (Grand Total)**
The chi-square statistic is 11.3216. The P-Value is 0.078933.				

In summary, Hypotheses 2 and 3 were accepted, and 1, 4, and 5 rejected. These findings can serve as a guideline for any managers attempting to assess their needs for the IoT applications for business model innovation. To the contrary of the existing literature, our results show firm size does not affect the IoT adoption rate. As enterprises have become more globalized and interconnected, they have also intensified their effort to innovate their business models. Our results show that monitoring and control IoT is most widely used for business model innovation followed by information sharing and collaboration IoT and big data and data analytics IoT. Of the four business model components under study, the IoT development for creating value proposition is the most widely adopted, followed by business process, sustainability, and value network. To keep up with the IoT trends in their industry, enterprises need to benchmark investment strategies from the best business model innovators in their industry.

IOT IMPLEMENTATION STRATEGIES FOR SMART ENTERPRISES

As with any disruptive innovation, the IoT present multiple implementation challenges. Based on the analysis of IoT practices and literature review, this section discusses implementation strategies in IoT application development for smart enterprises. Gubbi et al. (2013) suggests that due to the explosion of the data generated by IoT machines, data centers will face implementation challenges in security, quality of service, data analytics, storage management, server technologies, and data center networking. The five implementation strategies are discussed relevant to the conceptual framework in Table 1 to provide a better perspective on how the IoT implementation strategies may have impacts on each of the three IoT categories and business model components.

1. *Assess existing business models and identify the IOT applications suitable for business model innovation.* Amit and Zott (2001) points out novelty, lock-in, complementarities and efficiency as key aspects of business model innovation. Exploiting these four aspects with the use of IoT applications will increase the likelihood of achieving business model innovation. Our analysis shows how different categories of the IoT applications are used for different components of the business model. For example, for value proposition, monitoring and control applications are most widely used, but big data and data analytics are far less frequently used. However, for sustainability, big data and data analytics are as frequently used as monitoring and control applications. As the role of the IoT in business model innovation increases, the integration of the IoT with a business model will lead to a more competitive and profitable enterprise. To maximize the potential benefits of the IoT, it is critical to analyze the impacts of the IoT on the entire business model and develop a coherent set of unique IoT applications for business model innovation, given that there is no uniform set of IoT applications to all enterprises.

2. *Identify critical success factors (CSFs) of IoT implementation.* Identifying key determinants for a successful IoT implementation is a crucial prerequisite for launching effective business model innovation. Chesbrough (2007) provides guidelines for business model innovation: conduct some experiments, gather the evidence, identify the most promising direction, and then run some further experiments. Although the availability of CSFs does not guarantee a success, a better understanding of CSFs might increase the chance of the IoT success and competitive advantage. Evidence shows that while no one can predict the exact return on investment (ROI) a specific enterprise can achieve from any new practice, many enterprises have shown impressive returns from the factor inspections (Wiegers, 2002). Selecting CSFs will allow enterprises to formulate an effective IoT-enabled strategy to innovate their business model and sustain their competitive advantage.

3. *Develop a process redesign and change management program.* There is a higher chance to fail in the IoT endeavors unless careful development and management are in place. Skepticism may arise as to how the IoT for enterprises can truly be exploited if the technology implementation is too complex or major organizational resistance exists. For many enterprises, it is not enough to simply integrate the IoT into the existing processes. While current research on IoT integration focuses on areas of the technical implementation, little attention has been given to the integration of the IoT paradigm and its devices into business processes of traditional enterprise resource planning systems (Meyer et al., 2013). When the existing business process is not amenable to the integration of the IoT, the enterprise needs to redesign the process in order to exploit the capabilities of the IoT applications to the maximum extent possible. Process redesign will increase the success of business model innovation by enabling a company to aligning the processes with the IoT solution and increase order processing time, product development cycle time, and service response time. If information systems are extremely complex, with multiple technology platforms and a variety of procedures to manage common business processes, then the amount of technical and organizational change required is high (Holland & Light, 1999). A change management program needs to be established in case the required business process redesign is complex (e.g., cultural, policy and attitudinal changes of employees).

4. *Establish an open IoT architecture for a long-term evolution of the IoT.* Gubbi et al. (2013) propose a cloud centric vision that comprises of a flexible and open architecture that is user centric and enables different players to interact in the IoT framework. An open architecture is known to accelerate innovation process and create synergy between enterprises of different technology capabilities.

IoT technologies frequently rely on the industry standards and multi-device interoperability to provide customers with value-added services for multi-vendor networking devices. The current trend embraces IP-based sensor networks using the emerging standard 6LoWPAN/IPv6 (Mainetti et al., 2011). For smart enterprises, the architecture needs to address which IoT applications to develop, how often to manage, what platforms to use, and who the users of the IoTs are (e.g., employee or customers, potential customers, or general public). An open IoT architecture needs to be established and updated continuously to commission and decommission various IoT assets. An open IoT architecture is also a great way to develop IoT applications by an enterprise whose technologies are limited in creating value added IoT applications. Participating in industry alliance IoT technology is one way to facilitate an open architecture. For example, Thread Group (http://threadgroup.org) and AllSeen Alliance (https://allseenalliance.org) are currently leading industry alliances for the development of inter-device information sharing and collaboration applications.

5. *Keep current with emerging technologies.* Emerging technology refers to technology under development or at the stage of the proof-of-concept (POC), which has a high risk of technical failure but has potentially significant market value. IoT technologies continue to evolve and will become faster, more reliable, and smaller (Sundmaeker et al., 2010). For example, monitoring and controlling technology is moving to unobtrusive tiny and energy-efficient wireless sensor technology which allows applications to be deployed more flexibly and location-independently. The sensor network is evolving towards a context aware self-organizing, self-repairing autonomous network. Gartner, Inc. (2014) predicts that by 2020 the Internet of things (IoT) network will reach 26 billion connected things from 0.9 billion in 2009. The transformation of the industries and reshaping of competitive forces will continue due to the continuing advances of the IoT technologies. Enterprises need to constantly watch out for newly developed technologies to ride out the disruptive nature of the IoT innovation.

CONCLUSION

Because the IoT is such a recent development, there remains a paucity of studies on the managerial aspects of the IoT. This makes it very challenging for enterprises to make informed decisions in regard to IoT adoption/implementation. Many enterprises invest in a variety of IoT applications for their business model innovation. However, converting the IoT investment into real performance and profit improvement is challenging. Rigidity of existing business models, employees' resistance to the use of the IoT, and consumers' dissatisfaction with the new applications often act as a roadblock to the full realization of the IoT potentials.

Our study is one of the first studies on a conceptual model of business model innovation with IoT applications and 2014 Fortune 500 companies' usage analysis of the IoT. We identified three categories of IoT applications: monitoring and control, and information sharing and collaboration, and big data and data analytics. We also discussed how the IoT facilitates business model innovation in terms of the four generic components of a business model: value proposition, business process, value network, and sustainability.

Our analysis reveals that there is a significant relationship between the type of IoT applications and the IoT adoption rate and there is also a significant relationship between the type of business model innovation and the IoT adoption rate. However, we found no significant relationship between the size of enterprises and the IoT adoption rate. There is also no significant relationship between the type of business model innovation and the type of IoT applications. The IoT is yet at an early stage of diffusion as of April 2015, considering only fifty nine applications are used by Fortune 500 companies despite the hype of major media and consulting firms. While large companies are interested in the use of the IoT, the majority of the Fortune 500 companies are not currently actively using the IoT.

The last decade witnessed the diffusion of RFID technologies in enterprises. RFID technologies enabled real-time visibility and dynamic pricing of fresh products into supply chain and logistics (Angeles, 2005; Bardaki et al., 2012). The next decade will witness the explosion of the IoT applications for smart enterprises. Given the IoT is such a recent development, there is still a paucity of studies on the business model side of the IoT. This makes it very challenging for companies to make informed decisions in regard to IoT adoption/implementation for business model innovation. Since the IoT became a reality beyond hype, managers need to understand the benefits and related costs and conduct a thorough cost-benefit analysis for the investment. Our study contributes to the literature in this emerging field by presenting a foundational knowledge for building smart enterprises.

REFERENCES

Afuah, A., & Tucci, C. L. (2000). *Internet Business Models and Strategies: Text and Cases*. Irwin/McGraw-Hill.

Amit, R., & Zott, C. (2001). Value creation in e-business. *Strategic Management Journal, 22*(6-7), 493–520. doi:10.1002/smj.187

Angeles, R. (2005). RFID technologies: Supply-chain applications and implementation issues. *Information Systems Management, 22*(1), 51–65. doi:10.1201/1078/44912.22.1.20051201/85739.7

Arora, V., & Ravi, V. (2013). Data mining using advanced ant colony optimization algorithm and application to bankruptcy prediction. *International Journal of Information Systems and Social Change, 4*(3), 33–56. doi:10.4018/jissc.2013070103

Atzori, L., Iera, A., & Morabito, G. (2010). The internet of things: A survey. *Computer Networks, 54*(15), 2787–2805. doi:10.1016/j.comnet.2010.05.010

Bailey, K. D. (1994). *Typologies and Taxonomies: An Introduction to Classification Techniques*. Los Angeles: Sage Publications Inc.

Bandyopadhyay, D., & Sen, J. (2011). Internet of things: Applications and challenges in technology and standardization. *Wireless Personal Communications, 58*(1), 49–69. doi:10.1007/s11277-011-0288-5

Bardaki, C., Kourouthanassis, P., & Pramatari, K. (2012). Deploying RFID-enabled services in the retail supply chain: Lessons learned toward the Internet of Things. *Information Systems Management, 29*(3), 233–245. doi:10.1080/10580530.2012.687317

Bi, Z., Xu, L. D., & Wang, C. (2014). Internet of things for enterprise systems of modern manufacturing. *IEEE Transactions on Industrial Informatics, 10*(2), 1537–1546. doi:10.1109/TII.2014.2300338

Big data: The next frontier for innovation, competition, and productivity. (2011). McKinsey & Company.

Bin, S., Yuan, L., & Xiaoyi, W. (2010). Research on data mining models for the internet of things. *Proc. International Conference on Image Analysis and Signal Processing* (pp. 127-132).

Bonn, I., & Fisher, J. (2011). Sustainability: The missing ingredient in strategy. *The Journal of Business Strategy, 32*(1), 5–14. doi:10.1108/02756661111100274

Bui, N., Castellani, A. P., Casari, P., & Zorzi, M. (2012). The internet of energy: A web-enabled smart grid system. *IEEE Network, 26*(4), 39–45. doi:10.1109/MNET.2012.6246751

Caballero-Gil, C., Molina-Gil, J., Caballero-Gil, P., & Quesada-Arencibia, A. (2013). IoT application in the supply chain logistics. *Computer Aided Systems Theory - EUROCAST 2013, LNCS (8112*, pp. 55–62). doi:10.1007/978-3-642-53862-9_8

Carr, N. (2002). A comparative analysis of the behaviour of domestic and international young tourists. *Tourism Management, 23*(3), 321–325. doi:10.1016/S0261-5177(01)00089-9

Chesbrough, H. (2007). Business model innovation: It's not just about technology anymore. *Strategy and Leadership, 35*(6), 12–17. doi:10.1108/10878570710833714

Dholakia, R., Johnson, J., Della Bitta, A., & Dholakia, N. (1993). Decision-making time in organizational buying behavior: An investigation of its antecedents. *Journal of the Academy of Marketing Science, 21*(4), 281–292. doi:10.1007/BF02894521

Digital agenda for Europe: Monitoring and control. (2015). *European Union*. Retrieved from http://ec.europa.eu/digital-agenda/en/monitoring-and-control

Dubosson-Torbay, M., Osterwalder, A., & Pigneur, Y. (2002). E-business model design, classification, and measurements. *Thunderbird International Business Review, 44*(1), 5–23. doi:10.1002/tie.1036

Earl, M. J. (1994). The new and old of business process redesign. *The Journal of Strategic Information Systems, 3*(1), 5–22. doi:10.1016/0963-8687(94)90003-5

Fabiani, S., Schivardi, F., & Trento, S. (2005). ICT adoption in Italian manufacturing: Firm level evidence. *Industrial and Corporate Change, 14*(2), 225–249. doi:10.1093/icc/dth050

Fichman, R., Keil, M., & Tiwana, A. (2005). Beyond valuation: "Options Thinking" in IT project management. *California Management Review, 47*(2), 74–96. doi:10.2307/41166296

Fisher, D., DeLine, R., Czerwinski, M., & Drucker, S. (2012). Interactions with big data analytics. *Interaction, 19*(3), 50–59. doi:10.1145/2168931.2168943

Gartner's 2014 hype cycle for emerging technologies maps the journey to digital business. (2014). *Gartner Press Release*. Retrieved from http://www.gartner.com/newsroom/id/2819918

Gartner says the Internet of Things will Transform the Data Center. (2104). *Gartner Press Release*. Retrieved from http://www.gartner.com/newsroom/id/2684616

Geroski, P. A. (2000). Models of technology diffusion. *Research Policy, 29*(4-5), 603–625. doi:10.1016/S0048-7333(99)00092-X

Giunta, A., & Trivieri, F. (2007). Understanding the determinants of information technology adoption: Evidence from Italian manufacturing firms. *Applied Economics*, *39*(10), 1325–1334. doi:10.1080/00036840600567678

Gluhak, A., Krco, S., Nati, M., Pfisterer, D., Mitton, N., & Razafindralambo, T. (2011). A survey on facilities for experimental internet of things research. *IEEE Communications Magazine*, *49*(11), 58–67. doi:10.1109/MCOM.2011.6069710

Gubbi, J., Buyya, R., Marusic, S., & Palaniswami, M. (2013). Internet of Things (IoT): A vision, architectural elements, and future directions. *Future Generation Computer Systems*, *29*(7), 1645–1660. doi:10.1016/j.future.2013.01.010

Haller, S. A., & Siedschlag, I. (2011). Determinants of ICT adoption: Evidence from firm-level data. *Applied Economics*, *43*(26), 3775–3788. doi:10.1080/00036841003724411

Hockerts, K. (1999). The sustainability radar: A tool for the innovation of sustainable products and services. *Greener Management International*, *25*, 29–49.

Holland, C., & Light, B. (1999). A critical success factors model for ERP implementation. *IEEE Software*, *16*(3), 30–36. doi:10.1109/52.765784

HP. (2014). HP study reveals 70 percent of Internet of Things devices vulnerable to attack. *HP Press Release*. Retrieved from http://h30499.www3.hp.com/t5/Fortify-Application-Security/HP-Study-Reveals-70-Percent-of-Internet-of-Things-Devices/ba-p/6556284

Hunt, S. D. (1991). *Modern marketing theory: Critical issues in the philosophy of marketing science.* Cincinnati, OH: South-Western Publishing Co.

Jara, A. J., Zamora-Izquierdo, M. A., & Skarmeta, A. F. (2013). Interconnection framework for mHealth and remote monitoring based on the internet of things. *IEEE Journal on Selected Areas in Communications*, *31*(9), 47–65. doi:10.1109/JSAC.2013.SUP.0513005

Jelinski, D. E. (1991). On the use of chi-square analyses in studies of resource utilization. *Canadian Journal of Forest Research*, *21*(1), 58–65. doi:10.1139/x91-009

Jin, J., Gubbi, J., Marusic, S., & Palaniswami, M. (2014). An information framework for creating a smart city through Internet of things. *IEEE Internet of Things*, *1*(2), 112–121. doi:10.1109/JIOT.2013.2296516

Johnson, M. W., Christensen, C. M., & Kagermann, H. (2008). Reinventing your business model. *Harvard Business Review*, *86*(12), 59–67.

Katkar, G., & Ghosekar, P. (2012). TexRet: A texture retrieval system using soft-computing. *International Journal of Information Systems and Social Change*, *3*(1), 37–46. doi:10.4018/jissc.2012010104

Kelly, S. D. T., Suryadevara, N. K., & Mukhopadhyay, S. C. (2013). Towards the implementation of IoT for environmental condition monitoring in homes. *IEEE Sensors Journal*, *13*(10), 3846–3853. doi:10.1109/JSEN.2013.2263379

Kettinger, W. J., Teng, J. T. C., & Guha, S. (1997). Business process change: A study of methodologies, techniques, and tools. *Management Information Systems Quarterly*, *21*(1), 55–80. doi:10.2307/249742

Lazarescu, M. T. (2013). Design of a WSN platform for long-term environmental monitoring for IoT applications. *IEEE Journal on Emerging and Selected Topics in Circuits and Systems*, *3*(1), 45–54. doi:10.1109/JETCAS.2013.2243032

Lee, I., & Lee, K. (2015). The Internet of things (IoT): Applications, investments and challenges for enterprises. *Business Horizons*, *58*(4), 431–440. doi:10.1016/j.bushor.2015.03.008

Li, X., & Johnson, J. (2002). Evaluate IT investment opportunities using real options theory. *Information Resources Management Journal*, *15*(3), 32–47. doi:10.4018/irmj.2002070103

Li, Y., Hou, M., Liu, H., & Liu, Y. (2012). Towards a theoretical framework of strategic decision, supporting capability and information sharing under the context of Internet of Things. *Information Technology Management*, *13*(4), 205–216. doi:10.1007/s10799-012-0121-1

Lindsey, R., & Sessoms, E. (2006). Assessment of a campus recreation program on student recruitment, retention, and frequency of participation across certain demographic variables. *Recreational Sports Journal*, *30*(1), 30–39.

Mainetti, L., Patrono, L., & Vilei, A. (2011). Evolution of wireless sensor networks towards the Internet of Things: A survey. *Proceedings of the 2011 19th International Conference on Software, Telecommunications and Computer Networks (SoftCOM)* (pp. 1-6).

Matthyssens, P., Vandenbempt, K., & Berghman, L. (2006). Value innovation in business markets: Breaking the industry recipe. *Industrial Marketing Management*, *35*(6), 751–761. doi:10.1016/j.indmarman.2005.05.013

Meyer, S., Ruppen, A., & Magerkurth, C. (2013). Internet of things-aware process modeling: Integrating IoT devices as business process resources.Advanced Information Systems Engineering,*LNCS* (Vol. *7908*, pp. 84–98). doi:10.1007/978-3-642-38709-8_6

Miorandi, D., Sicari, S., De Pellegrini, F., & Chlamtac, I. (2012). Internet of things: Vision, applications and research challenges. *Ad Hoc Networks*, *10*(7), 1497–1516. doi:10.1016/j.adhoc.2012.02.016

Miragliotta, G., & Shrouf, F. (2013). Using Internet of Things to improve eco-efficiency in manufacturing: A review on available knowledge and a framework for IoT adoption. *Advances in Production Management Systems, AICT* (Vol. *397*, pp. 96–102). doi:10.1007/978-3-642-40352-1_13

Morris, M., Schindehutte, M., & Allen, J. (2005). The entrepreneur's business model: Toward a unified perspective. *Journal of Business Research, 58*(6), 726-735.

Pang, Z., Chen, Q., Han, W., & Zheng, L. (2015). Value-centric design of the internet-of-things solution for food supply chain: Value creation, sensor portfolio and information fusion. *Information Systems Frontiers*, *17*(2), 289–319.

Peppard, J., & Rylander, A. (2006). From value chain to value network: Insights for mobile operators. *European Management Journal*, *24*(2-3), 128–141. doi:10.1016/j.emj.2006.03.003

Ping, L., Liu, Q., Zhou, Z., & Wang, H. (2011). Agile supply chain management over the Internet of Things. *Proceedings of the2011 International Conference on Management and Service Science (MASS)* (pp. 1-4). doi:10.1109/ICMSS.2011.5998440

Priya, R. V., Vadivel, A., & Thakur, S. (2012). Maximal pattern mining using fast CP-Tree for knowledge discovery. *International Journal of Information Systems and Social Change*, *3*(1), 56–74. doi:10.4018/jissc.2012010106

Sehgal, A., Perelman, V., Kuryla, S., & Schonwalder, J. (2012). Management of resource constrained devices in the internet of things. *IEEE Communications Magazine*, *50*(12), 144–149. doi:10.1109/MCOM.2012.6384464

Shafer, S. M., Smith, H. J., & Linder, J. (2005). The power of business models. *Business Horizons*, *48*(3), 199–207. doi:10.1016/j.bushor.2004.10.014

Sosna, M., Trevinyo-Rodríguez, R.N., & Velamuri, S.R. (2010). Business model innovation through trial-and-error learning: The Naturhouse case. *Long Range Planning*, *4*(2/3), 383–407.

Sundmaeker, H., Guillemin, P., Friess, P., & Woelfflé, S. (2010). Vision and challenges for realising the Internet of Things, CERP-IoT – Cluster of European Research Projects on the Internet of Things, Retrieved from http://www.researchgate.net/publication/228664767_Vision_and_challenges_for_realising_the_Internet_of_Things

Tao, F., Zuo, Y., Xu, L. D., & Zhang, L. (2014). IoT based intelligent perception and access of manufacturing resource towards cloud manufacturing. *IEEE Transactions on Industrial Informatics*, *10*(2), 1547–1557. doi:10.1109/TII.2014.2306397

Teece, D. J. (2010). Business models, business strategy and innovation. *Long Range Planning*, *43*(2-3), 172–194. doi:10.1016/j.lrp.2009.07.003

Teo, T. S. H., & Tan, M. (1998). An empirical study of adopters and non-adopters of the Internet in Singapore. *Information & Management*, *34*(6), 339–345. doi:10.1016/S0378-7206(98)00068-8

Thong, J. Y. L. (1999). An integrated model of information systems adoption in small business. *Journal of Management Information Systems*, *15*(4), 187–214. doi:10.1080/07421222.1999.11518227

TRUSTe Internet of Things Privacy Index. (2014). *TRUSTe*. Retrieved from http://www.truste.com/us-internet-of-things-index-2014/

Tsai, C.-W., Lai, C.-F., Chiang, M.-C., & Yang, L. T. (2014). Data mining for Internet of Things: A survey. *IEEE Communications Surveys and Tutorials*, *16*(1), 77–97. doi:10.1109/SURV.2013.103013.00206

van der Veen, M. (2004). *Explaining e-business adoption: Innovation and entrepreneurship in Dutch SMEs* [Doctoral Thesis]. University of Twente.

Vasseur, J.-P., & Dunkels, A. (2010). *Interconnecting Smart Objects with IP: The Next Internet*. Elsevier.

Wang, H., Zhang, T., Quan, Y., & Dong, R. (2013). Research on the framework of the Environmental Internet of Things. *International Journal of Sustainable Development and World Ecology*, *20*(3), 199–204. doi:10.1080/13504509.2013.783517

Willig, A., Matheus, K., & Wolisz, A. (2005). Wireless technology in industrial networks. *Proceedings of the IEEE*, *93*(6), 1130–1151. doi:10.1109/JPROC.2005.849717

Xu, B., Xu, L. D., Cai, H., Xie, C., Hu, J., & Bu, F. (2014). Ubiquitous data accessing method in IoT-based information system for emergency medical services. *IEEE Transactions on Industrial Informatics, 10*(2), 1578–1586. doi:10.1109/TII.2014.2306382

Yip, K. C. H., & Yau, K. K. W. (2005). On modeling claim frequency data in general insurance with extra zeros. *Insurance, Mathematics & Economics, 36*(2), 153–163. doi:10.1016/j.insmatheco.2004.11.002

Zand, P., Chatterjea, S., Das, K., & Havinga, P. (2012). Wireless industrial monitoring and control networks: The journey so far and the road ahead. *Journal of Sensor and Actuator Networks, 1*(3), 123–152. doi:10.3390/jsan1020123

Zeleny, M. (2013). Integrated knowledge management. *International Journal of Information Systems and Social Change, 4*(4), 62–78. doi:10.4018/jissc.2013100104

Zhu, K., Dong, S., Xu, S. X., & Kraemer, K. L. (2006). Innovation diffusion in global contexts: Determinants of post-adoption digital transformation of European companies. *European Journal of Information Systems, 15*(6), 601–616. doi:10.1057/palgrave.ejis.3000650

Zott, C., Amit, R., & Massa, L. (2011). The Business Model: Recent Developments and Future Research. *Journal of Management, 37*(4), 1019–1042. doi:10.1177/0149206311406265

This work was previously published in the International Journal of Information Systems and Social Change (IJISSC), 7(3); edited by John Wang, pages 1-15, copyright year 2016 by IGI Publishing (an imprint of IGI Global).

Chapter 21
Energy–Efficient Computing Solutions for Internet of Things with ZigBee Reconfigurable Devices

Grzegorz Chmaj
University of Nevada, USA

Henry Selvaraj
University of Nevada, USA

ABSTRACT

Nowadays we are witnessing a trend with significantly increasing number of networked and computing-capable devices being integrated into everyday environment. This trend is expected to continue. With computing devices available as logic structures, they might use each other's processing capabilities to achieve a given goal. In this paper, the authors propose an architectural solution to perform the processing of tasks using a distributed structure of Internet of Things devices. They also include ZigBee devices that are not connected to the Internet, but participate with the processing swarm using local network. This significantly extends the flexibility and potential of the IoT structure, while being still not a well-researched area. Unlike many high-level realizations for IoT processing, the authors present a realization operating on the communications, computing and near protocol level that achieves energy consumption efficiency. They also include the reconfigurability of IoT devices. The authors' work is suitable to be the base for higher-level realizations, especially for systems with devices operating on battery power. At the same time, the architecture presented in this paper uses minimal centralization, moving maximum responsibilities to regular devices. The proposed realizations are described using linear programming models and their high efficiency is evaluated.

DOI: 10.4018/978-1-5225-1832-7.ch021

1. INTRODUCTION

Distributed computing is being used for high performance structures such as grids, clusters and public computation systems for many years, and considered as very large system architecture. With the ever increasing popularity of mobile devices, the processing power in consumers' pockets, raised the researchers' interests in mobile computing. Reducing device size, together with increasing processors' computing power and lowering energy consumption, leads to the emergence of computation-capable devices in day-to-day environment. The combination of all the assets, along with high accessibility of Internet, created the Internet of Things (IoT) structures. They contain multiple devices that are connected to the Internet and thus gain the wide spectrum of the new applications. Among those, there are many that require a lot of processing power that is not available on a single device. As other IoT devices are available and presumably might stay in the idle mode, we propose solutions that enable the devices in the nearby/logical group to share their resources and achieve the group's processing goal.

Distributed computing was mainly a domain of cloud and grid computing for many years. It is worth to mention, that distributed processing includes computing and many other architectures, such as distributed web services (Takatsuka, Saiki, Matsumoto and Namamura, 2015). The recent development of the Internet of Things idea has led to the emergence of a new research field integrating these two areas, both in the general case (Botta, de Donato, Persico, and Pescap´e, 2014)(Lumpkins, 2013), and for specific applications (Gachet, de Buenaga, Aparicio, and Padrón, 2012). Also, they are the area of the interest on much lower level – Chiang and Lee (2013) proposed the coordination languages and models for the open distributed systems, presenting the new approach to programming such structures. The system described by Gachet et al. (2012) provides the IoT/Cloud computing for healthcare services. The authors discussed the IoT-based improvements of the quality of life of people with chronic diseases. There were multiple middleware solutions proposed to realize the context-aware computing in Internet of Things (Perera, Zaslavsky, Christen and Georgakopoulos, 2014). Such middleware enables the services that would run on a given infrastructure – typically they are defined on the high level. There are also solutions based on the event driving (Kuhn, Prellwitz, Rohrer, and Sieck, 2013) – authors presented the middleware using event detection and forwarding, and triggering actions based on that. Smart housing is a popular topic when talking about IoT applications, however the solutions proposed in the literature are mostly centrally-managed (Kuhn et al., 2013)(Perera et al., 2014) or do not include energy optimization. Soliman, Abiodun, Hamouda, Zhou, and Lung (2013) presented a solution of integrating the smart home system with the webservices and cloud computing. Embedded systems were used for sensing and cloud computing was used for inter-device interaction. The approach presented by Spanò, Niccolini, Pascoli and Iannaccone (2015) merges the household smart meters with the IoT platform – to optimize the operation of connected devices. The definition of Internet of Things includes devices that are directly connected to the Internet network. Local devices based on protocols such as ZigBee are starting to be included in IoT systems too (Soliman et al., 2013)(Spanò et al., 2015), but this area has not seen significant growth yet. Another part of Internet of Things structures are the wearable devices, often also not directly connected to the Internet, but having the communication capabilities (e.g. using ZigBee). Wearables might deliver very specific type of data (such as motion characteristics (Jara, Bocchi and Genoud, 2013), healthcare information (Castillejo, Martínez, Rodríguez-Molina and Cuerva, 2013)) and inevitably are becoming the increasing share of IoT devices (Hiremath, Yang and Mankodiya, 2014). The multiple types of devices and applications lead to the perspective of interconnected IoTs, as presented by Wirtz and Wehrle (2013) – where authors discussed the possibilities of integrating multiple IoT designs.

In this paper we propose distributed processing solutions for Internet of Things that optimize the operation in the field of energy consumption with the main focus on communication and computation. As mentioned earlier, the approaches presented in the literature are usually centrally managed. Apart from those solutions, we propose an approach with minimal centralization and flexible management (including dynamic role reassignment) along with the optimization of the energy consumption. Internet of Things structures are considered to be global with all participating devices connected directly to the Internet using IPv4 or IPv6. We propose to consider such devices also in a local perspective – we define Local Device Set (LDS) as a group of devices that are physically located within some geographical radius and constituting one logical group, sharing the same privacy, security and other policies. We motivate it twofold: 1) even though the devices are connected to the Internet and could communicate with any device around the world, the group of trusted devices is typically located in some nearby area 2) we propose to include the ZigBee devices to the LDS, extending the capabilities of a given house-environment. The solutions we propose in this paper are not limited to the local networks though, and can be used for a globally inter-net-connected environment. We evaluate the proposed solutions by applying them to practical scenarios: IoT for the household and IoT for the farm monitoring. Based on that we demonstrate the quality of presented architecture and solutions. The rest of this paper is organized as follows: the proposed architecture of the distributed IoT processing is presented in section 2, section 3 contains the evaluation of the proposed solutions, and the conclusions are stated in section 4.

2. THE PROPOSED ARCHITECTURES

To address the needs of IoT LDS processing, in this paper we propose both architectural design and algorithms and treat both of these components as integral parts of the proposed solution called Internet of Things Group Distributed Computing Platform (IGDCP). The IGDCP contains both IoT devices and locally networked devices (using protocols such as ZigBee). We consider the LDS to contain only local devices because of the inter-device trust and the possibility to include local devices. However, the proposed solution is also suitable to operate in the global network too. We also include the aspect of reconfigurability – where each device with reconfiguration capabilities (e.g. embedded FPGA chip) can decide about its computing configuration – such as programming FPGA, downloading the specific libraries or setting the specific parameters of local sensors.

In the proposed architecture, the IGDCP contains V devices, each denoted with an index v ($v = 1, 2,$ ..., V). Those devices are logically organized in groups, indicated with dashed line in Figure 1. As each IoT device v has a different computing power, it is denoted as p_v and stays constant – it is expressed in MIPS available for the computation process. The p_v coefficient needs the time definition to be complete (computational efficiency is expressed in cycles per time period). Thus, we define the time line as a set of discrete time periods $t = 1, 2, ..., T$, as it is commonly used for the time modeling in the research (Bumble and Coraor, 1998). For each of the devices, the communication capabilities must be included: depending on the communications electronic chip embedded, the transmission speed might vary. For the device v, the incoming speed d_v is defined, along with the upcoming speed u_v. Regarding communication, the electrical energy of sending 1kB of data might be different for various devices. The cost of transmitting a piece of the information must be distinguished between sending and receiving costs. That is because, for the electronic devices having an antenna – receiving electrical signals takes less energy than actual broadcasting of the information through the antenna. Therefore the $e_{r,v}$ and $e_{s,v}$ constants are

Figure 1. IGDCP diagram

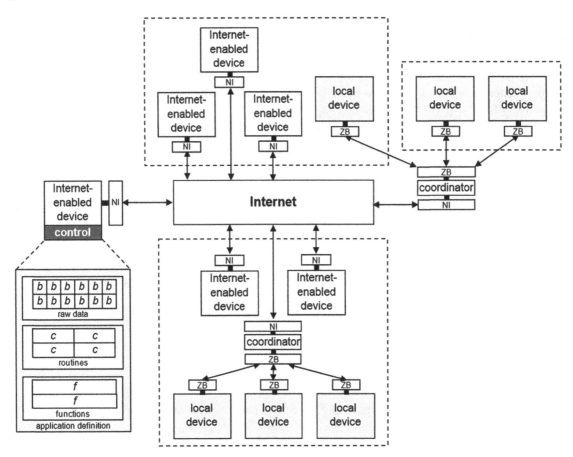

defined, to reflect the electrical energy consumption amount required for receiving and sending to/from a device v, respectively. Each device v needs to be identified with a type: we distinguish two types of devices: internet devices and local-network devices (such as ZigBee and other short-range devices). The g_v variable determines whether a device v is an internet-enabled device ($g_v = 1$) or a local device ($g_v = 0$).

The ZigBee devices need to communicate through the *coordinator devices* (ZigBee Specification, 2007). If a device v acts as a coordinator (devices may have multiple roles), the z_v variable is set to 1 otherwise it is set to zero. Figure 1. Shows coordinators that are equipped both with ZigBee interfaces (*ZB*) and regular networking interfaces (*NI*). *NI* might be either wired or wireless Internet connection. The system operation is characterized by tasks. These are not necessarily computational-only applications. However, they involve data processing on multiple devices. Each task is built with the following elements: *raw data* t_s, that is divided into fragments $b = 1, 2, ..., B$. The size of each fragment b is s_b (in kB). We interpret raw data t_s as a static object: it might contain binary data (such as maps, geographical data, task-specific data etc.). The next element is a *routine data* t_R that consist of C routines ($c = 1, 2, ..., C$). They constitute an implementation of algorithms and mechanisms used to run (process) the application. The code of routine c has the size s_c (in kB). Task also specifies the set of functions $f = 1, 2, ..., F$, that are required to realize the application (each having size s_f). Not all devices process all the functions. The indicator $n_{b,f}$ states that the fragment b requires function f to be processed or executed, and $n_{c,f}$ indicates analogous requirement for the routines. Along with energy spending related to communication ($e_{r,v}$ and $e_{s,v}$), the energy emission related to processing needs to be defined. For the t_R fragments, let they be defined as $e_{b,v}$ and reflect the energy required to process 1kB of data expressed in mJ. For the routine processing, the electrical energy consumption is defined per time slot t as $e_{c,v}$ indicating the emission generated by running the routine c on device v during one time slot t. For the sake of reconfiguration, each device may execute the *reconfiguration attempt*, that is considered running the local algorithm to decide if reconfiguration at that time would make the device more suitable (and therefore efficient) to the current needs. Such attempt is denoted by a binary variable $h_{t,v}$, that indicates the device v attempting the reconfiguration during time t. Such attempt consumes $e_{h,v}$ energy for the device v. If the reconfiguration is decided at device v, then the actual reconfiguration is denoted by $h'_{t,v}$ – for each t during which the reconfiguration process runs on device v. Such process of reconfiguration leads to the energy emission $e_{H,v}$ (per time slot t). The remaining indicators are: $x_{bv} = 1$ if fragment b is processed on the device v; $x_{cv} = 1$ if routine c is being executed on device v with a variant x_{cvt} indicating execution during slot t; $y_{bwv} = 1$ if fragment b is being sent from device w to device v, $y_{cwv} = 1$ for transmitting a routine code from device w to v, and $y_{fwv} = 1$ for transmitting a function code from device w to v. The distributed processing properties are defined as follows. Each routine should be executed on one device only ($\sum_v x_{cv} = 1$, for $c = 1, 2, ..., C$). The transmission time of fragment b from device w to v is:

$$max\left(\left\lceil\frac{s_b}{u_w}\right\rceil, \left\lceil\frac{s_b}{d_v}\right\rceil\right), \text{ and } max\left(\left\lceil\frac{s_c}{u_w}\right\rceil, \left\lceil\frac{s_c}{d_v}\right\rceil\right)$$

for the routine code, respectively. For local devices, they can communicate only through coordinators:

$$z_w\sum_b y_{bwv} \leq B(z_w + z_v); z_w\sum_b y_{fwv} \leq B(z_w + z_v); z_v\sum_b y_{bvw} \leq B(z_w + z_v); z_v\sum_b y_{fvw} \leq B(z_w + z_v); \text{ for } v, w = 1, 2, ..., V v \neq w$$

Even though the proposed solution minimizes the centralization, the system must contain some devices that are assigned a role (statically or dynamically) to supervise its operation – they are called *control nodes* (*CN*) and are denoted with $a_v = 1$ for each device v bearing that role ($a_v = 0$, devices labeled as *RN*). Each device is equipped with IGDCP algorithm that provides the operational base for each device. As IGDCP works in a distributed manner, the goal is to minimize the energy consumption of a system as a whole. The expression of the energy used that we state here is very useful for algorithms evaluation, hence we define it in the details from the device perspective. The communication energy for local devices ($g_v = 0$) needs to be expressed separately for internet-enabled ones ($g_v = 1$). Expression (1) symbolizes the energy required by internet-enabled device to receive the fragment data, while (3) shows it for the local device. As stated earlier, fragments may require functions to be processed, and function-related energy is expressed by (2) for internet-enabled devices and by (4) for the local ones:

$$s_b e_{r,v} + s_b\sum_w y_{bwv} a_w e_{s,w} \tag{1}$$

$$\sum_w\sum_f y_{bwv} a_w n_{b,f} s_f e_s \tag{2}$$

$$\left(s_b\sum_w\sum_{w'} y_{bww'} z_w a_w \left(e_{s,w} + e_{r,w'}\right) + s_b\sum_w y_{bw'v} z_w \left(e_{s,w} + e_{r,v}\right)\right) \tag{3}$$

$$\left(\Sigma_f \Sigma_w \Sigma_{w'} y_{fww'} z_{w'} a_w n_{b,f} s_f (e_{s,w} + e_{r,w'}) + \Sigma_f \Sigma_{w'} y_{bw'v} z_{w'} s_f n_{b,f} (e_{s,w} + e_{r,v})\right) \tag{4}$$

The expressions for the routines are analogous. The fragment processing cost is $e_{b,v} s_b$, and routine execution cost is $\Sigma_t e_{c,v} x_{cvt}$. Supplying Formulas (1)-(4) with necessary associated elements (Table 1), and adding the reconfiguration component, we get the following energy evaluation function E:

$$E = \Sigma_b \Sigma_v x_{bv} [g_v (s_b e_{r,v} + s_b \Sigma_w y_{bwv} a_w e_{s,w} + \Sigma_w \Sigma_f y_{bwv} a_w n_{b,f} s_f e_{s,w})$$

$$+ (1 - g_v)(s_b \Sigma_w \Sigma_{w'} y_{bww'} z_{w'} a_w (e_{s,w} + e_{r,w'}) + s_b \Sigma_w y_{bw'v} z_{w'} (e_{s,w} + e_{r,v}))$$

$$+ (\Sigma_f \Sigma_w \Sigma_{w'} y_{fww'} z_{w'} a_w n_{b,f} s_f (e_{s,w} + e_{r,w'}) + \Sigma_f \Sigma_w y_{bw'v} z_{w'} s_f n_{b,f} (e_{s,w} + e_{r,v})) + e_{b,v} s_b]$$

$$+ \Sigma_c \Sigma_v x_{cv} [g_v (s_c e_{r,v} + s_b \Sigma_w y_{cwv} a_w e_{s,w} + \Sigma_w \Sigma_f y_{cwv} a_w n_{c,f} s_f e_{s,w})$$

$$+ (1 - g_v)(s_c \Sigma_w \Sigma_{w'} y_{cww'} z_{w'} a_w (e_{s,w} + e_{r,w'}) + s_c \Sigma_w y_{cw'v} z_{w'} (e_{s,w} + e_{r,v}))$$

$$+ (\Sigma_f \Sigma_w \Sigma_{w'} y_{fww'} z_{w'} a_w n_{c,f} s_f (e_{s,w} + e_{r,w'}) + \Sigma_f \Sigma_w y_{cw'v} z_{w'} s_f n_{c,f} (e_{s,w} + e_{r,v})) + \Sigma_t e_{c,v} x_{cvt}]$$

$$+ \Sigma_v \Sigma_t (h_{v,t} e_{h,v} + h'_{v,t} e_{H,v})$$

Table 1. Symbol and description

Symbol	Description
a_v	binary: $a_v = 1$ for each device v with *CN* role; $a_v = 0$ for *RN* role.
b	index: fragment
c	index: routine
d_v	download speed of device v (kB/slot)
$e_{b,v}$	energy required to process 1kB of data
$e_{c,v}$	emission generated by running the routine c on device v during one time slot t
$e_{h,v}$	energy consumption required by device to attempt the reconfiguration
$e_{H,v}$	energy consumption required by device to perform the reconfiguration
$e_{r,v}$	energy consumption required by device v for receiving 1kB of data
$e_{s,v}$	energy consumption required by device v for sending 1kB of data
f	index: function
g_v	binary: $g_v = 1$ if device v is internet-enabled device; $g_v = 0$ otherwise
$h_{t,v}$	binary: $h_{t,v} = 1$ if node v attempts the reconfiguration during time t
$h'_{t,v}$	binary: $h'_{t,v} = 1$ if node v performs reconfiguration during time t
k	index: socket
$m_{p,type}$	binary: $m_{p,type} = 1$ if processing unit p is the type of *type*; 0 otherwise
$n_{b,f}$	binary: block b requires function f for processing; 0 otherwise
$n_{c,f}$	binary: block b requires routine c for processing; 0 otherwise

continued on following page

Table 1. Continued

Symbol	Description
p_v	computing power of device v
p_q	computing power of processing unit q
q	index: processing unit
s_b	size of the fragment b (in kB)
s_c	size of the routine c (in kB)
t_R	routine data
t	index: time period (slot)
t_s	raw data of task t
u_v	upload speed of device v (kB/slot)
v	index: device
w	index: datasource
x_{bv}	binary: $x_{bv} = 1$ if fragment b is processed on the device v
x_{cv}	binary: $x_{cv} = 1$ if routine c is being executed on node v
x_{cvt}	binary: $x_{cv} = 1$ if routine c is being executed on node v during slot t
y_{bwv}	binary: $y_{bwv} = 1$ if fragment b is being sent from device w to node v
y_{cwv}	binary: $y_{cwv} = 1$ if routine code is transmitted from device w to v
y_{fwv}	binary: $y_{fwv} = 1$ if function code is transmitted from device w to v
z_v	binary: $z_v = 1$ if device v is a coordinator; $z_v = 0$ otherwise
B	number of fragments
C	number of routines
F	number of functions
K	number of sockets
Q	number of processing units
T	total number of time slots
V	number of devices in the system
W	number of datasources
Ω	the whole system, including processing tasks

2.1. IGDCP Internal Algorithms

The operation of IGDCP is supported by a set of internal algorithms. Because of the desired flexibility and decentralization of the proposed system, we move the majority of the optimization decisions (including reconfiguration) to the devices. In this paper, we evaluate the proposed architecture with the use of four algorithms listed in Table 2. All the algorithms include the optimization mechanisms. It is worth to note that the listed algorithms are not the only ones that are implemented on devices. For other algorithms running on devices, we selected the ones that do not interfere with the aspects optimized in the algorithms researched in this paper. IGDCP supports flexible algorithm management: each device implements multiple levels of which the algorithms may run, and the level and order of a given algo-

Table 2. Proposed algorithms

Algorithm	Used On	Description
DBO	RN	The distributed processing is optimized against the total processing time. Includes reconfiguration mechanisms.
DBF	RN	The distributed processing is optimized against the allocation of the resources on devices (such as functions, sensory data, etc.). Includes reconfiguration mechanisms.
CFO	CN	The algorithm of fragments and routines allocation is optimized for the delivery time
CFK	CN	The algorithm of fragments and routines allocation is based on the system structure

rithm can be changed during runtime for the sake of optimization. This mechanism also includes the dynamic reprioritization of the algorithms. Multiple roles are also supported (also the algorithm-role relation is implemented), however, these mechanisms are not in the scope of this paper and we use only CN and RN roles.

2.2. The Reconfiguration Period Prediction

As the system performs the local reconfiguration at the devices, it faces the problem of controlling the whole reconfiguration process. Each of device must determine when and if to run the reconfiguration algorithms. At least two decisions must be made: 1) when to attempt the reconfiguration 2) in which way to perform the reconfiguration: which routines should be programmed into the device. *Reconfiguration attempt* is the execution of the reconfiguration algorithm that determines if any reconfiguration actions need to be taken. Such algorithm involves both local processing (calculating metrics, etc.) and network communication (in order to obtain various data that is involved in decision making process). In the work presented hereby, we focus on the first decision.

The operation of the proposed system is modeled using the time slots. Therefore, one of the approaches to the reconfiguration time is to introduce a constant R_T, determining the number of time slots t that must pass for device v between it performs reconfiguration attempts. The R_T constant is the same for all the devices, but executions of reconfiguration attempt algorithms will happen during different time slots for various devices. That's because reconfiguration cannot be performed while the device is performing the fragment processing, so even if according to R_T the next reconfiguration attempt should happen during time t, device waits after t to finish the current processing.

The impact of R_T to the energy consumption is shown in Figure 2. Such relation was obtained by numerous experiments, during which for a particular system, the R_T value was increased from 1 till $R_T > T$ with a various step. For all experimented systems, we always determined the R_{T_MIN} value, for which the energy consumption E was minimal. For low values of R_T the energy consumption E is very high, due to massive reconfiguration attempts. Increasing the R_T lowers the E, to usually reach the minimum monotonically. The next stage of the R_T range is the rapid increase of E value. In this range, the system configuration matches lesser and lesser to the required processing needs. The rarer the reconfiguration is, the worse match between required and present configuration. Further increase of R_T leads the E value to stay in more less constant value. This is caused by the fact, that for $R_T > T$, the reconfiguration happens only once, at the beginning of the operation. Figure 2 shows the results for multiple values of $R_T > T$, as the experiments were not limited with T value.

Figure 2. Total cost according to the reconfiguration period

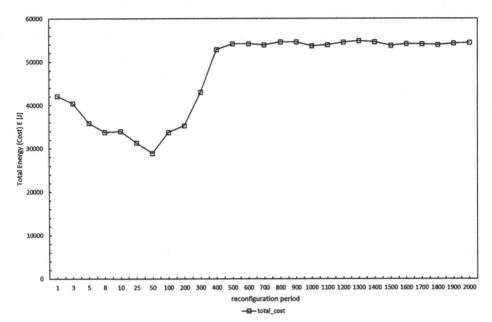

We propose the static method of determining the R_T, so simplify and speed up the local algorithms. The value of R_T is calculated at the beginning of the system operation, and set as constant value for all of the devices.

First, the characteristic H' function must be defined. The proposed function H' is the variant of the Heaviside function in its discrete form:

$$H'(n) = \begin{cases} 0 & n \leq 0 \\ 1 & n > 0 \end{cases}$$

$$R_T = \max_f \left(\frac{M_f}{\sum_{v=1}^{V}\sum_{q=1}^{Q} p_q} + \frac{M_f}{\sum_{v=1}^{V} d_v} + \frac{M_f}{\sum_{v=1}^{V} u_v} + \frac{\left\lceil \frac{SIM\_DS\_GET}{\left\lceil \frac{\sum_{v=1}^{V} d_v}{V} \right\rceil} \right\rceil \sum_{b=1}^{B} \lambda_{b,f} H'\left(\sum_{w=1}^{W} l_{b,w} - \left\lfloor \frac{W}{V} \right\rfloor\right)}{\sum_{v=1}^{V} H'\left(\sum_{k=1}^{K}\sum_{q=1}^{Q} w_{v,k} u_{q,k} m_{q,RECONF}\right)} \right)$$

(5)

Formula (5) takes multiple aspects into account, and some more elements need to be defined beyond the energy consumption model (they are incorporated in the model, but stated directly for R_T computation). Datasource is a sensor that is optionally attached to a device. Socket is a place where a processing resource can be mounted in, and one device v might have one or more sockets. The formula of R_T determination estimates its value as the sum of the following components: estimated computation slots, estimated download slots, estimated upload slots and estimated datasources handling slots. Such sum is calculated for each function f present in the system, and the maximum sum value over f is selected as the *RP* value used for the system run. The value M_f (6) states the size (in kB) of the block data that is related to function f, i.e. the sum of data sizes of all blocks that require the function f:

$$M_f = \sum_{b=1}^{B} \left(bs_b \, n_{b,f} \lambda_{b,f} \right) \tag{6}$$

s_b represents the size of the block b, and the function $\lambda_{b,f}$ represents the threshold of functions required by block b. $\lambda_{b,f}$ is defined the following way:

$$\lambda_{b,F'} = \begin{cases} 1 & when \ n_{b,f'} = 1 \, for \ \forall f' \in F' \land n_{b,f'} = 0 \, \forall f' \notin F' \\ 0 & otherwise \end{cases} \tag{7}$$

Function $\lambda_{b,F'}$ (7) returns 1 if a block b requires just the functions from the set F', and doesn't require all the other functions. For the set F' containing single function f, it is denoted by the identifier of function f. M_f divided by the total computation power gives the estimate of the number of slots required to perform the computation of all blocks requiring function f. Analogously, the M_f over download speed and upload speed estimates the number of slots required for blocks related to f download and upload, respectively. The estimation of the time required to process the datasources for the given function f is done the following way. The average number of datasources per device is computed. Then for each block, that requires more datasources than the average (and also requires the function f), the estimated datasource processing time is added for each datasource above the average. The sum of these datasource processing times, divided by number of devices having RECONF processing units installed is constituting the fourth component of the R_T formula. *SIM_DS_GET* is the energy cost factor, defined as the constant minimal energy involved in the single datasource processing.

3. EVALUATION OF THE PROPOSED SOLUTIONS

To evaluate the proposed algorithms running in the presented architectural environment, we performed multiple simulations using object-based simulation environment. This system was designed to fully reflect the IoT environment having multiple devices concurrently running their algorithms and communicating between each other. The architecture of IGDCP enables using same implementation of algorithms in the simulation and hardware devices (same code can be moved to the hardware). We decided to use the simulation approach as this approach is considered as suitable for this type of the research, the simulation fully supports concurrent operations, implements the communications layer in a very big detail, and the variety of Internet-of-Things devices is still quite narrow – especially for programmable devices equipped with the ZigBee interface. First experiment researched the relaxed version of the problem, two following experiments used the full architecture described in section 2 and include two separate scenarios. We describe two practical applications of the proposed architecture and solutions in form of two scenarios: Home LDS with Imaging and Distributed Farm Monitoring. These scenarios are then used for the simulation and evaluation of proposed solutions. We also include the evaluation of the reconfiguration period metric – one of most influential factors for the efficient reconfiguration process.

3.1. Optimal Cases

The architecture of presented solutions was described as a mixed integer programming model. The primary goal is the clearness and easiness in implementation, but also enables testing the solutions against optimal results. For the problems stated in this paper, the benchmark solutions are not available. To show the quality of proposed algorithms we have compared the results of the proposed algorithms with the optimal solutions. Due to the complexity of the analyzed problem, obtaining the optimal solutions using any kind of MIP solver is not possible. To make the comparison possible, the original problem is presented in Table 3 in the relaxed form for which obtaining the optimal solution is possible.

Table 3. Relaxed MIP model

Indices	Constants	
$b = 1, 2, ..., B$ block $t, i = 1, 2, ..., T$ time slots $v, w, w' = 1, 2, ..., V$ devices	$e_{b,v}$ energy for block processing on device v k_{wv} energy of block transfer from device w to v p_v maximum processing rate of device v d_v maximum download rate of device v u_v maximum upload rate of device v R the number of coordinator devices	
Binary Variables		
$x_{bv} = 1$ when block b is processed on device v; 0 otherwise $y_{bwvt} = 1$ when block b is sent to device v from device w during slot t; 0 otherwise $z_v = 1$ when device v is a coordinator device; 0 otherwise		
objective: minimize $F = \Sigma_b \Sigma_v x_{bv} e_{b,v} + \Sigma_b \Sigma_v \Sigma_w \Sigma_t y_{bwvt} k_{wv}$		(8)
subject to:		
$\Sigma_b x_{bv} \leq p_v \, v = 1, 2, ..., V$		(9)
$\Sigma_b \Sigma_v y_{bwvt} \leq u_w \, w = 1, 2, ..., V \, t = 1, 2, ..., T$		(10)
$\Sigma_b \Sigma_w y_{bwvt} \leq d_v \, v = 1, 2, ..., V \, t = 1, 2, ..., T$		(11)
$\Sigma_v x_{bv} = 1 \, b = 1, 2, ..., B$		(12)
$\Sigma_b x_{bv} \geq 1 \, v = 1, 2, ..., V$		(13)
$\Sigma_b \Sigma_t y_{bwvt} \leq B(z_w + z_v) \, v, w = 1, 2, ..., V \, v \neq w$		(14)
$x_{bw} + z_v - 1 \leq \Sigma_t y_{bwvt} \, b = 1, 2, ..., B \, v, w = 1, 2, ..., V \, v \neq w$		(15)
$\Sigma_v z_v = R$		(16)
$R > 0$		(17)
$x_{bv} + \Sigma_w \Sigma_t y_{bwvt} = 1 \, b = 1, 2, ..., B \, v = 1, 2, ..., V$		(18)
$\Sigma_v y_{bwvt} \Sigma V(x_{bw} + \Sigma_{i<t} \Sigma_{w'} y_{bw'wi}) \, b = 1, 2, ..., B \, w = 1, 2, ..., V \, t = 1, 2, ..., T$		(19)

Several simplifications need to be briefly explained, also the relaxed model uses slightly modified notation. Fragments and associated functions are incorporated into blocks, same was done for routines and associated functions. Common notation was used for all blocks. The energy required for the transmission of the fragment between devices w and v was consolidated into single constant k_{vw}. The concept of blocks lead to simplification of the energy evaluation function F to the form (8) with the constraints (9)-(11) added. To make MIP model complete for the solver optimization, constraints (12)-(17) had to be formulated and added. (18)-(19) is the approximation of inter-device communication. Simplifications and modifications were required to make a model feasible for optimal solving, and proposed algorithms were also adjusted to match the simplifications. These modifications do not affect their core functionality though, and proposed algorithms are reflecting the operation of their original forms.

Experiments showed, that for the relaxed form of the described problem, CPLEX was able to find the optimal solution for systems with maximum 20 devices and 33 blocks. The time of solution finding was in the range of less than 100 seconds for very small systems (less than 7 devices), for systems with more (7 – 12) devices the time was ranging from 100s to 3000s. Remaining systems required the time of 3000s or more, with the CPLEX time limit set to 3600s. All solutions found were optimal. Hence, the proposed distributed processing systems, even in the simplified form, is not solvable in the optimal way for practical applications. The comparison of optimal solutions and the ones generated with proposed algorithms (DBF_R – in the form adjusted to the relaxed model) was done using the following formula:

$$D_{DB}^{OPT} = \frac{E_{DB} - E_{OPT}}{E_{DB}} \cdot 100\% \tag{20}$$

Experiments were run for 67 systems. In case of 29 systems, the proposed DBF_R algorithm resulted in the optimal solution. For 73 systems, the average value of was 8% (meaning that the proposed algorithm yielded the solution with the energy consumption averagely 8% higher than the optimal). The DBF_R operation time was in the range of miliseconds for all the cases. Concluding, the 8% difference comparing to the optimal solution, but obtained in miliseconds (while the generation of optimal solutions was taking even more than 3000s) demonstrate the high quality of proposed solutions.

3.2. Scenario 1: Home LDS with Imaging

The intelligent house contains IoT local device group consisting of V devices having image displaying capabilities $v \in I$ (e.g. digital picture frames, TVs, tablets) and/or home smartgrid functions $v \in P$ (Figure 3). We assume that those devices constitute LDS within one household. The CN devices (e.g. smartphones) are capable to supply the LDS with new images that are used to control the LDS. Home Imaging application distinguishes between two types of images: with or without pattern. This distinction is made on the device supplying the image. Non-pattern images are processed as tasks in the distributed manner by LDS IoT devices and displayed on the devices $v \in I$ (for the purpose of image sharing among family members).

For each device the requirement of displaying image might be different, thus processing the image centrally is extremely inflexible. Also some devices might be unable to perform the processing by themselves. Concluding, for non-pattern images we get an intelligent system of IoT multimedia devices that display new images around the house dynamically and according to their individual technical capabilities

Figure 3. Example of home LDS with imaging

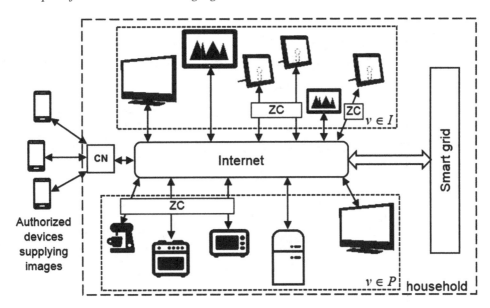

while the image processing is done in the distributive manner. For images with patterns, devices $v \in P$ perform designated actions, based on the objects found in the images (e.g. fingers pattern). These actions might trigger LDS or smart house reconfiguration or other programmed effect. In this case, devices need to cooperate and process the smart house data in the distributed manner to achieve the expected goal.

3.3. Scenario 2: Distributed Farm Monitoring

Given the farm with multiple facilities equipped with multiple data sources for the monitoring (here called sensors, however includes also devices such as cameras). All sensors use the ZigBee and provide minority of processing – it is assumed that the majority of processing will be done by devices being coordinators (*ZC*). Therefore in this scenario we investigate the system with the majority of local devices ($g_v = 0$). Coordinators communicate with each other using wireless or wired network (they have both ZigBee and Internet interfaces). The addition to the system is a drone with ZigBee and WiFi interfaces that also participates with the processing and data gathering. We motivate the presence of UAV twofold: 1) large private area monitoring (like farms) is expected to be done automatically by drones in the near future, as a result of incredible growth of UAV technologies; 2) farms are often of a large size and covering the whole area with the wireless connectivity might be expensive. Having a drone periodically visiting places allows placing sensors in distant locations. UAV gathers the sensor data periodically for further processing (like it's done in wireless sensor networks – Rao and Biswas, 2009). The third type of devices in this scenario is a wearable devices. Farm workers are equipped with wearable wristbands that are the part of Internet of Things LDS too. These wristbands are equipped with small displays and inform workers about the results of sensor data processing, like alerts raised due to the processing of multiple sensor signals. Wristbands are also equipped with GPS, so workers can share their locations.

The *CN* of the described application might be a stationary PC, but due to the nature of the farm work – the workers are usually somewhere in the terrain. Therefore we propose the *CN* to be a tablet by default, so the farm manager can access the IoT distributed system anytime (the role assignment can be

Figure 4. Example of IGDCP for distributed farm monitoring

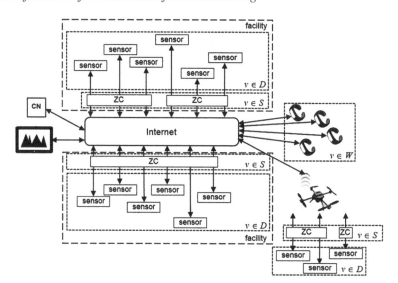

changed during the runtime). This is another motivation for the distributed processing, as it saves the battery life of the *CN* tablet in this case, comparing to placing all the computation to the *CN*. Concluding, the types of devices in the proposed scenario are: 1) ZigBee sensors $v \in S$; 2) ZigBee coordinators $v \in D$; 3) drone(s) $v \in U$; wearable wristbands $v \in W$; control node $v \in L$ (Figure 4). As devices operate autonomously, the IGDCP supports the devices' reconfiguration during the runtime (replacing functions and routines to the ones that are appropriate at the moment).

3.4. Experimentation Results

The research showed, that the DBF algorithm provides more efficient communication (less energy required for the data transmission among the devices) while the CFO algorithm us used. The DBF provides the more significant energy saving comparing to DBO, the more functions and related data are required for the computations. In case of CFK algorithm, the data distribution for DBF still requires much less energy for systems processing smaller amounts of data, but for systems processing larger data sets DBO is indirectly supported by CFK. Figure 5 and Figure 6 show the energy expedited for the communication with the use of CFO and CFK algorithms, respectively. The energy E_C includes (1) and (3) formulas, together with necessary accompanying elements to express the energy required to process all the fragments (analogously, the computing energy E_P is defined using (2) and (4)). Regardless of DBO/DBF using, the CFK control algorithm always yielded the lower E energy comparing to CFO for the same input. The advantage and justification for CFO algorithm is the timespan efficiency: during the experiments the same task was processed averagely 11% faster than in case of CFK (using Formula (20), also for all comparisons in this section). For the communication model used in presented system, having one logical message per one element sent (fragment, function, etc.), the DBF algorithm issues 45% less messages comparing to DBO (the effect to the energy consumption and time processing depends on many other factors as well, but might be significant in cases where communication efficiency is related to the number of messages issued). Such effect exists because DBF optimizes its operation according to current assets locations.

Figure 5. Energy used for communication (CFO algorithm)

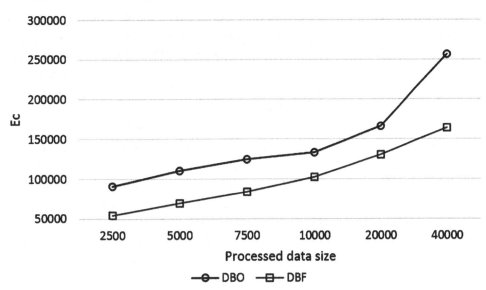

Figure 6. Energy used for communication (CFK algorithm)

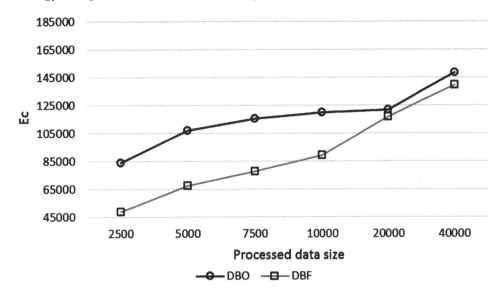

For the scenario 1 (Home LDS with imaging), the following parameters were used: the tasks simulation data is as follows: number of devices $V = 30$, including $I = 10$ display and $P = 25$ smartgrid ones. The image is the raw data, assuming its size of 4MB, and fragment size $s_b = 32$kB, thus $B = 128$. Functions f included: *image resize* ($s_f = 200$kB), *screen adjustment* ($s_f = 400$kB), *add ornaments* ($s_f = 1000$kB), *change mode* ($s_f = 300$kB). Routines c: *smartgrid control* ($s_c = 200$kB), *data share* ($s_c = 300$kB). For the energy requirement parameters set to reflect the real devices, the DBO_CFK performed best, as the large amount of digital data is processed in the system (6% less of E_c comparing to DBF_CFK while processing 5 images of 4MB size each). The average of 9.4% smaller E_p computing energy consumption was observed while using CFK, comparing to using CFO for the DBO algorithm. The nature of Home LDS with imaging is the large amount of the processed data (mostly images) and low migration of functions *f* and accompanying data. In such case, the DBO_CFK is the best solution.

For the scenario 2 (Distributed Farm Monitoring) we have used the following structure of the system: $V = 60$ devices in total, the *raw data* provided by some sensors, assuming $B = 2000$ with the $s_b = 8kB$. Functions *f*: *monitor_temp* ($s_f = 200kB$), *monitor_humid* ($s_f = 300kB$), *monitor_general* ($s_f = 400kB$), *monitor_1* ($s_f = 200kB$), *monitor_2* ($s_f = 200kB$). Routines *c*: *operate_monitor* ($s_c = 500kB$), *uav_gather* ($s_c = 900kB$), *wrist_operate* ($s_c = 1500kB$), *sensor_operate* ($s_c = 400kB$), *coord_1* ($s_c = 2000kB$), *coord_2* ($s_c = 2500kB$). Functions and routines are exemplary and might be replaced with others according to the needs. In this scenario, the fragment data is small and the inter-device data migration is much more significant than in the scenario 1. In this case, while using the CFK control algorithm, the average profit of using the DBF comparing to DBO was 46% for the communication and 32% for computing expeditions E_p. For total energy consumption E, using DBF saved averagely 35% energy used (Figure 7). Concluding, the appropriate algorithm set for systems processing large number of smaller fragments and performing the extensive data exchange (such as functions *f*) the DBF_CFK is the best choice. For both scenarios, the CFO algorithm should be used where the processing timespan is the key factor and increase of the processing energy expedition is the acceptable tradeoff.

To measure the accuracy of (5) in reaching the optimal value of R_T, the measurements were performed for 51 systems (V=16-60, t_s=23MB-668MB). Therefore the best known value $R_{TO\varepsilon}$ (with the tolerance of $\varepsilon = 5$ slots) was obtained through the brute-force method of executing the system Ω for increasing values of R_T, instead of using the (5) formula. Then, the value of R_T obtained from (5) was compared with $R_{TO\varepsilon}$ using Formula (21):

$$R_{T\_ABS} = \frac{R_T - R_{TO\varepsilon}}{T_{avg}} \cdot 100\% \tag{21}$$

Figure 7. Total energy expedited (CFK algorithm)

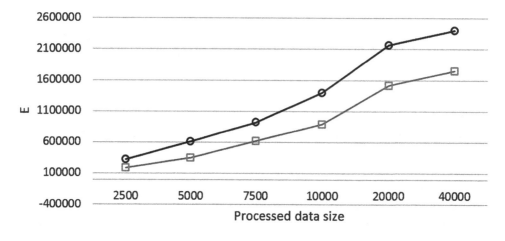

T_{avg} is the average value of T (obtained through experiments), required for a certain system to process all the tasks. The relative difference between R_T and $R_{TO\varepsilon}$ is not a good metric in this case, because this relative difference must be compared to the total system operation timespan to show the significance of the R_T and $R_{TO\varepsilon}$ difference. The accuracy of the R_T is presented in the Figure 8. For the investigated systems, R_{T_ABS} stayed mostly below 10%, usually taking the values below 5%, with one peak value of 25%. This demonstrates that the use of (5) is efficient for most of the cases. Also, experiments showed, that for a R_{Tacc} computed using (20), value span $R_{Tacc} \in <R_T\text{-}\varepsilon', R_T\text{+}\varepsilon''>$ the E value stays in more or less the same areas (ε' and ε'' are different for each system Ω). Thus the R_T value determined by the proposed (5) formula should be relatively close to $R_{TO\varepsilon}$ and stay in the range of $<RP\text{-}\varepsilon', RP\text{+}\varepsilon''>$ to keep E value around efficient level.

4. CONCLUSION

Significantly emerging field of Internet of Things will soon be full of groups of collaborating devices, including the more and more popular wearable devices. Such collaboration needs to be controlled by solutions that would optimize the operation of the whole system. The optimization especially concerns the energy consumption (as many of IoT devices use battery power) and operational timespan. The reconfiguration aspect becomes more and more important, as hardware and software reconfiguration is easily available in IoT devices. In this work, we have presented a comprehensive solution to the Internet of Things systems including the wearable devices. The devices with ZigBee-only communication interface were considered as well, together with accompanying coordinator devices that were also given the computation role. Along with the architectural solution, the operational algorithms were presented. Their efficiency is proven by comparing with the optimal solutions (relaxed algorithms and models). They were also evaluated by applying them to two proposed Internet of Things scenarios: *Home LDS with Imaging* and *Distributed Farm Monitoring*. The high quality of proposed solutions was demonstrated,

Figure 8. Accuracy of determining reconfiguration period R_T parameter

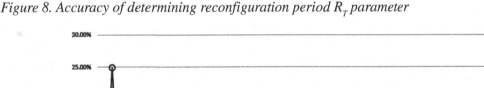

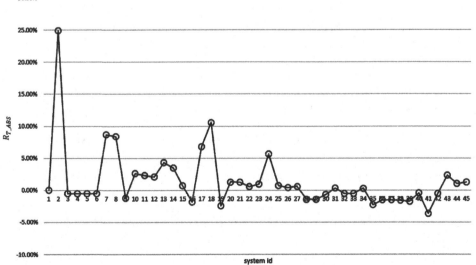

and important properties were exposed. We have presented the metric for the reconfiguration, suitable for use in both hardware and software reconfiguration processes. The research showed, that the proposed static metric increases system efficiency and lowers the energy used. Proposed metric mostly had the value close to the best value obtained using brute-force method for the sake of comparison. We consider the distributed processing solutions for IoT practical applications a very important and emerging field. Hence we intend to continue our research in the areas of extensive reconfiguration capabilities, even more advanced operational algorithms, devices with special capabilities and maximizing the flexibility of IoT distributed processing systems.

REFERENCES

Botta, A., de Donato, W., Persico, V., & Pescap'e, A. (2014). On the Integration of Cloud Computing and Internet of Things.*Proceedings of International Conference on Future Internet of Things and Cloud (FiCloud)*, Barcelona, Spain (pp. 23-30). doi:10.1109/FiCloud.2014.14

Bumble, M., & Coraor, L. (1998). Architecture for a non-deterministic simulation machine.*Proceedings of Winter Simulation Conference*, Washington, DC, USA (pp. 1599-1606). doi:10.1109/WSC.1998.746035

Castillejo, P., Martínez, J., Rodríguez-Molina, J., & Cuerva, A. (2013). Integration Of Wearable Devices In A Wireless Sensor Network For An E-Health Application. *IEEE Wireless Communications*, *20*(4), 38–49. doi:10.1109/MWC.2013.6590049

Chiang, C., & Lee, R. (2013). Coordination Languages and Models for Open Distributed Systems *International Journal of Software Innovation*, *1*(1), 1–13. doi:10.4018/ijsi.2013010101

Gachet, D., de Buenaga, M., Aparicio, F., & Padrón, V. (2012). Integrating Internet of Things and Cloud Computing for Health Services Provisioning. The Virtual Cloud Carer Project. *Proceedings of theSixth International Conference on Innovative Mobile and Internet Services in Ubiquitous Computing*, Palermo, Italy (pp. 918-921). doi:10.1109/IMIS.2012.25

Hiremath, S., Yang, G., & Mankodiya, K. (2014). Wearable Internet of Things: Concept, Architectural Components and Promises for Person-Centered Healthcare.*Proceedings of EAI 4th International Conference on Wireless Mobile Communication and Healthcare (Mobihealth)*, Athens, Greece (pp. 304-307). doi:10.4108/icst.mobihealth.2014.257440

Jara, A. J., Bocchi, Y., & Genoud, D. (2013). Determining Human Dynamics through the Internet of Things. *Proceedings of International Joint Conferences on Web Intelligence (WI) and Intelligent Agent Technologies,* Atlanta, GA, USA (pp. 109-113). doi:10.1109/WI-IAT.2013.161

Kuhn, E., Prellwitz, M., Rohrer, M., & Sieck, J. A Distributed Middleware for Applications of the Internet of Things. (2013). *Proceedings of 7th IEEE International Conference on Intelligent Data Acquisition and Advanced Computing Systems: Technology and Applications*, Berlin, Germany (pp. 517-520). doi:10.1109/IDAACS.2013.6662739

Lumpkins, W. (2013). *The Internet of Things Meets Cloud Computing. IEEE Consumer Electronics Magazine, 2(2).* IEEE.

Perera, C., Zaslavsky, A., Christen, P., & Georgakopoulos, D. (2014). Context Aware Computing for The Internet of Things: A Survey. *IEEE Communications Surveys and Tutorials*, *16*(1), 414–454. doi:10.1109/SURV.2013.042313.00197

Rao, J., & Biswas, S. (2009). Network-assisted sink navigation for distributed data gathering: Stability and delay-energy trade-offs. *Computer Communications*, *33*(1), 160–175.

Soliman, M., Abiodun, T., Hamouda, T., Zhou, J., & Lung, C. (2013). Smart Home: Integrating Internet of Things with Web Services and Cloud Computing. *Proceedings of IEEE 5th International Conference on Cloud Computing Technology and Science (CloudCom)*, Bristol, UK (pp. 317-320). doi:10.1109/CloudCom.2013.155

Spanò, E., Niccolini, L., Pascoli, S., & Iannaccone, G. (2015). Last-Meter Smart Grid Embedded in an Internet-of-Things Platform. *IEEE Transactions On Smart Grid*, *6*(1), 468–476. doi:10.1109/TSG.2014.2342796

Takatsuka, H., Saiki, S., Matsumoto, S., & Namamura, M. (2015). RuCAS: Rule-Based Framework for Managing Context-Aware Services with Distributed Web Services. *International Journal of Software Innovation*, *3*(3), 57–68.

Wirtz, H., & Wehrle, K. (2013). Opening the Loops - Towards Semantic, Information-centric Networking in the Internet of Things. *Proceedings of the 10th Annual IEEE Communications Society Conference on Sensor, Mesh and Ad Hoc Communications and Networks (SECON)*, New Orleans, LA, USA (pp. 18-24).

ZigBee Specification. (2007). ZigBee Standards Organization.

This work was previously published in the International Journal of Software Innovation (IJSI), 4(1); edited by Roger Y. Lee and Lawrence Chung, pages 31-47, copyright year 2016 by IGI Publishing (an imprint of IGI Global).

Chapter 22
Sensing as a Service in Cloud–Centric Internet of Things Architecture

Burak Kantarci
Clarkson University, USA

Hussein T. Mouftah
University of Ottawa, Canada

ABSTRACT

Sensing-as-a-Service (S2aaS) is a cloud-inspired service model which enables access to the Internet of Things (IoT) architecture. The IoT denotes virtually interconnected objects that are uniquely identifiable, and are capable of sensing, computing and communicating. Built-in sensors in mobile devices can leverage the performance of IoT applications in terms of energy and communication overhead savings by sending their data to the cloud servers. Sensed data from mobile devices can be accessed by IoT applications on a pay-as-you-go fashion. Efficient sensing service provider search techniques are emerging components of this architecture, and they should be accompanied with effective sensing provider recruitment algorithms. Furthermore, reliability and trustworthiness of participatory sensed data appears as a big challenge. This chapter provides an overview of the state of the art in S2aaS systems, and reports recent proposals to address the most crucial challenges. Furthermore, the chapter points out the open issues and future directions for the researchers in this field.

INTRODUCTION

The Internet of Things (IoT) paradigm denotes the pervasive and ubiquitous interconnection of billions of embedded devices that can be uniquely identified, localized and communicated (Aggarwal, C., Ashish, N. & Sheth, A., 2013). Sensors, RFID tags, smart phones, and various other devices are interconnected in a scalable manner in the IoT architecture. Application areas of IoT are various such as healthcare, smart environments, transportation, social networking, personal safety and several futuristic applications such as robot taxi (Atzori, A., Andlera, L. & Morabito, G., 2010; Miorandi, D., Sicari, S., De Pellegrini, F.

DOI: 10.4018/978-1-5225-1832-7.ch022

& Chlamtac, I., 2012). IoT architecture can be implemented as either Internet centric or object-centric. Internet centric architecture of IoT aims at provisioning services within the Internet where data are contributed by the objects. On the other hand, object-centric architecture aims at provisioning services via network of smart objects. Scalability and cost-efficient service provisioning of IoT services can be achieved by the integration of cloud-computing into the IoT architecture, i.e., cloud-centric IoT (Gubbi, J., Buyya, R., Marusic, S. & Palaniswami, M., 2013) as illustrated in Figure 1.

As future Internet is expected to offer everything-as-a-service (XaaS) such as CPU, network, memory and so on (Moreno-Vozmediano, R., Montero, R. S. & Llorent, I. M., 2013), sensing, as well, can be offered as a service within the cloud. Furthermore, cloud computing enables on demand access to the information and/or knowledge obtained from sensor data providers based on the pay-as-you-go fashion and providing software/platform/infrastructure as a service (SaaS/PaaS/IaaS).

The requirements of sensing objects driving the integration of cloud computing and IoT are summarized as huge computing and storage capacity, web-based interfaces for data exchange and integration, real-time processing of big data, web-based programming platforms, inter-operability between the sensing objects, cost-efficient and scalable on-demand access to the information technology (IT) resources, and security and privacy assurance. Therefore, Zhou et al. (Zhou, J., Leppanen, T., Harjula, E., Ylianttila, M., Ojala, T., Yu, C., Jin, H. & Yang, L. T., 2013) propose deployment, development and management of the IoT applications over the cloud, namely the CloudThings architecture.

Applications that can be improved by the integration of IoT with cloud computing are various; such as pervasive healthcare (Doukas, C. & Maglogiannis, I., 2012) where cloud platform enables efficient management of mobile and wearable body sensors; smart homes where appliance recognition via sensor data and energy usage profile of the household owners are performed within the cloud (Chen, S-Y., Lai, C-F., Huang, Y-M. & Jeng, Y-L., 2013); smart cities where distributed cloud services are deployed to manage and control the IoT devices (Suciu, G., Vulpe, A., Halunga, S., Fratu, O., Todoran, G. & Suciu, V., 2013), future transportation systems where in-vehicle smart phones, roadside sensors and/or cameras are connected to a cloud-based IoT platform for monitoring road condition and alert generation and so on (Ghose, A., Biswas, P., Bhaumik, C., Sharma, M., Pal, A. & Jha, A., 2012; Yu, X., Sun, F. & Cheng, X., 2012). Furthermore, public safety in smart city management can be efficiently addressed by taking advantage of cloud and IoT integration (Li, W., Chao, J. & Ping, Z., 2012). A travel recommendation system is proposed by Yerva et al. (Yerva, S. R., Saltarin, J., Hoyoung, J.& Aberer, K., 2012) where mood information of a particular user is extracted from the tweets of the corresponding user on Twitter, and it is associated with the weather information for a travel destination on a given date, which is obtained via sensors in that particular region. In the corresponding study, sensor data are not collected through smart phones but via sensors that are already deployed for an online weather report service.

In a cloud-centric IoT framework, sensors provide their sensed data to a storage cloud as a service, and the sensor data undergoes data analytics and data mining procedures for information retrieval and knowledge discovery. Visualization of the knowledge discovered from the sensing service is presented to the corresponding applications (Gubbi, J., Buyya, R., Marusic, S. & Palaniswami, M., 2013).

Built-in sensors in mobile devices can leverage the performance of IoT applications when sensors on mobile devices send their data to cloud servers leading to significant energy and communication overhead savings (Pereira, P. P., Eliasson, J., Kyusakov, R., Delsing, J., Raayetinezhad, A. & Johansson, M., 2013; Al-Fagih, A. E., Al-Turjman, F. M., Alsalih, W. M., Hassanein, H. S., 2013). Distefano et al. (2014) define this framework as a device-centric exploitation and management of the IoT resources as opposed to the conventional data centric approach in which the only focus is on the data provided by the IoT objects.

The data-centric approach does not allow the users to participate in sensing and presentation of the data. The advantage of this approach is reported as decentralized control of resources and transmission of sensor data, pre-processing of sensor data prior to arrival at the sensing servers in the cloud platform, reduced bandwidth consumption in the wireless front-end due to reduced amount of data (i.e., filtered) to be transmitted, flexibility to repurpose the sensors, delegating the complex security algorithms on sensor data to mobile devices as long as there is sufficient computing capability, enabling information dissemination locally through topology discovery by the mobile devices. (Distefano, S., Merlino, G. & Puliafito, A., 2014). Therefore, Sensing-as-a-Service (S^2aaS) appears as a strong candidate for front-end access to the cloud-centric IoT where mobile devices provide their sensed data to the cloud platform based on the pay-as-you-go fashion (Sheng, X., Xiao, X., Tang, J. & Xue, G., 2012a, 2012b).

Figure 1 illustrates a minimalist view of the cloud-centric IoT architecture. The cloud-centric IoT architecture is presented as a three-layer system where the lowest layer corresponds to the sensing activities by the built-in sensors, wireless sensor network nodes or Radio Frequency Identification (RFID) tags. The sensing layer provides service (i.e., sensor data) to the processing and storage layer which corresponds to the cloud computing platform. The cloud platform provides service to the upmost layer which is the application layer. As mentioned earlier, application may denote surveillance, critical infrastructure monitoring, environment monitoring, health and smart transportation.

Besides benefits of S^2aaS, there are several barriers and challenges which are being addressed by ongoing research. Xiao et al. (2013) report these barriers under the following items: Heterogeneity of mobile platforms and sensing equipment, variety of mobile applications that the users must install on their mobile smart devices, and the increasing bandwidth demand of crowdsensing applications on wireless links. Given these challenges, S^2aaS calls for solutions that decouple application-centric design of data collection, and decentralized sensor data processing and aggregation methods. Data processing consists of outlier detection, noise filtering and sensing provider reputation maintenance. Aggregated crowdsensed data can be handled either in a local cloudlet or in the enterprise cloud. The former leads to one tenth of the latter's access delay, half the power of the latter's power consumption and ten times the latter's throughput (Jararweh, Y., Tawalbeh, L., Ababneh, F. & Dosari F., 2013; Soyata, T., Ba, H., Heinzelman, W., Kwon, M. & Shi, J., 2013). On the other hand, a cloudlet has limited computing capability compared to an enterprise cloud. The tasks on the aggregated data will be partitioned between the cloudlet and the enterprise cloud.

Sensory acquisition-based S^2aaS services can be implemented as mobile applications by using off-the shelf mobile application development platforms such as Android Software Development Kit (Developers). The mobile application utilizes the built-in sensors of smart mobile devices. Data analysis and aggregation algorithms complement the crowdsensing component. Criterion of success of a crowdsensing application is reliable and efficient communication between the end users and cloud platform, as well as improved accuracy of the analyzed sensor data.

This chapter presents the state of the art in Cloud-centric IoT and Sensing-as-a-Service focusing on challenges existing solutions and open issues. The chapter starts with a definition of the S^2aaS concept and two different S^2aaS approaches, namely the cloud-based WSN services and mobile phone sensing as a service. Then the S^2aaS section defines an aggregation framework for Wireless Sensor Networks to provide sensing and actuation clouds as a service. An extension of the S^2aaS, namely Sensing Instrument as a Service is also presented where sensors are virtualized in order to be shared among the end users over the cloud. Service Oriented Architecture (SOA)-based sensor data exchange in a cloud-centric IoT environment is also briefly presented along with the architectural discussion. Cloud-based crowdsens-

Figure 1. Minimalist illustration of cloud-centric IoT architecture

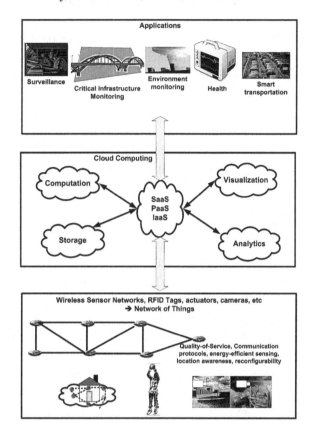

ing applications form the most significant survey content of the chapter. At the end of the chapter a brief summary of the studied schemes are complemented by a comprehensive comparison in terms of various aspects. A thorough discussion on the challenges and opportunities are also presented in the last section of the chapter.

SENSING AS A SERVICE (S²aaS)

Sensing as a Service S²aaS has been studied in the context of cloud-based Wireless Sensor Network (WSN) services and device-centric mobile phone sensing as a service. The first initiative that can be considered under this category is to integrate sensor data into cloud services has been the sensor cloud concept which has been introduced by several researchers (Misra, S., Chatterjee, S. & Obaidat, M., 2014; Madria, S., Kumar, V. & Dalvi, R., 2014; Alamri, A., Ansari, W. S., Hassan, M. M., Hossain, M. S., Alelaiwi, A. & Hossain, M. A., 2013) whereas device-centric mobile phone-based participatory sensing has appeared as an advantageous solution that offers decentralized resource control, cloud-based security, and partitioned computing tasks between mobile devices and the cloud platform (Distefano, S., Merlino, G. & Puliafito, A., 2014).

Cloud-Based Wireless Sensor Networks (WSN) Services

As mentioned by Madria et al. (2014), sensor cloud concept denotes decoupling Wireless Sensor Network (WSN) owner and the user by allowing the user to access sensors, deploy sensing applications through programmable interfaces, and store sensor data in a cloud platform for analysis and further usage. As the formal 'cloud computing' definition denotes virtualization of computing, storage and communication resources in a shared pool, sensor cloud stands for virtualization of the sensing resources, namely the sensors. Virtualized sensors enable multiple WSNs cooperate for multiple applications while the users who access and program the sensors are isolated from each other (Madria, S., Kumar, V. & Dalvi, R., 2014). This principle also complies with the formal definition of a sensor cloud by MicroStrain which aims at storage, visualization and scalability of sensor data management (MicroStrain). A virtualization model has been presented by Misra et al. (2014), which studies virtual sensor-application mapping, physical sensor-virtual sensor-mapping and computational complexity analysis mapping an application onto a virtual sensor, and the corresponding virtual sensor to physical sensor. Based on the virtualization model, performance comparison between WSN and sensor cloud has been presented, and it is reported that in most cases sensor cloud deployment outperforms the conventional WSN deployment in terms of lifetime, fault tolerance, cost, profit and energy consumption. Although in a few cases the traditional WSN deployment has been shown to perform better, switching from the conventional WSN deployment to the sensor cloud deployment is advantageous because of the following reasons: Sensor cloud deployment enhances management of sensor nodes. Furthermore data collection cost can be reduced by sharing the sensor data among multiple users. Moreover, system-level details of the sensor nodes are hidden from the end-user so the user is only responsible for programming the sensors in order to fulfill the requirements of the requested application (Madria, S., Kumar, V. & Dalvi, R., 2014).

Phan et al. (2013) propose a three-layer architecture for WSN-cloud integration, and introduce it as Sensor-Cloud Integration Platform as a Service (SC-iPaaS). The three layers are sensor, edge and cloud layers. The sensor layer denotes the physical sensors whereas the edge layer denotes the sink nodes that collect and aggregate data from the sensor layer. The cloud layer hosts virtual sensors which are implemented as the software complements of the physical sensor hardware. The physical sensors collect data from the sinks in the edge layer, process and store those data for future use. As stated in (Phan, D. H., Suzuki, J., Omura, S. & Oba, Katsuya, 2013), this framework requires optimization of communication specifications such as data transmission rate at sensor and edge layers in order to meet the objectives of sensor data availability for the service in cloud layer, bandwidth utilization between the cloud and edge layers, and energy consumption in the sensor layer.

WSN-cloud integration is reported to address storage, accessibility, reliability and real time processing challenges in WSNs whereas the same setting will call for emergent solutions for the challenges regarding data format and event processing, event querying, latency due to network bandwidth limitations, online migration of WSN data across data centers and service charges (Liu, R. & Wassel, I. J., 2011).

Mobile Phone Sensing as a Service

Mobile devices can be deployed in a cloud inspired business model in order to enable access to the IoT applications by providing their sensor data based on pay-as-you-go fashion, and this paradigm is called mobile phone sensing as a service (Sheng, X., Xiao, X., Tang, J. & Xue, G., 2012a, 2012b). Figure 2 illustrates a minimalist presentation of the S^2aaS infrastructure. In such an infrastructure, crowdsensed data traverses the following four layers, sensing service providers, sensor data publishing layer (e.g., online social networks), the cloud platform which collects, processes and presents sensor data, and the end user requesting/receiving sensing as a service (Perera, C., Jayaraman, P., Zaslavsky, A., Christen, P. & Georgapoulos, D., 2014a). Applications that interact with the sensing service providers require massive processing power, tremendous storage capacity and huge network bandwidth in order to handle big data obtained through sensing services provided by large crowds. Therefore Rao et al. (2012) presume that big data will be the main driver in cloud-based real-time processing and storage, and define the cloud as the front-end of the IoT architecture. Since sensing in the IoT architecture mainly utilizes IEEE802.15.4, mobility of billions of sensors within the IoT appears as a challenge. Furthermore, IoT sensors are not necessarily to be stand-alone forming Wireless Sensor Network (WSN) clouds but are mostly built-in sensors in mobile devices providing crowdsourcing-based sensor data. Besides, IPv6 over Low power Wireless Personal Area Networks (6LoWPAN) has defined encapsulation and header compression solutions to transmit IEEE IPv6 data over 802.15.4 networks which will empower smart devices to participate in sensing activities (Montenegro, G., Kushalnagar, N., Hui, J. & Culler, D., 2007). More importantly, resource constrained nature of WSN nodes raises serious security concerns for both symmetric and asymmetric cryptography solutions. Due to limited computing capability of WSN nodes, asymmetric cryptography algorithms cannot be employed efficiently whereas storage limitation in the WSN nodes introduces challenges regarding centralized keying mechanisms (Kavitha, T. & Sridharan, D., 2010). Recent research reports that migration towards S^2aaS is inevitable for the following three reasons: *1)* WSNs run on limited battery power, and maintaining a certain energy level requires intervention or energy harvesting solutions which are still in infancy, *2)* WSNs are still not massively deployed to obtain contextual data whereas mobile smart devices are widely used with built-in sensors mostly being underutilized, *3)* Computing and storage limitations of stand-alone sensor nodes lead to severe challenges including security and privacy preservation. Hence, mobile smart devices appear as strong candidates to complement the convenience of WSNs through offering their built-in sensors as on-demand services (Mizouni, R. & El Barachi, M., 2013).

In order to exchange sensor and actuator data over the Internet, a Service Oriented Architecture (SOA) which utilizes Constrained Application Protocol (CoAP) has been proposed (Pereira, P. P., Eliasson, J., Kyusakov, R., Delsing, J., Raayetinezhad, A. & Johansson, M., 2013). CoAP is an application layer software protocol that has been developed for communication between resource-constrained environments, and it is intended for Machine-To-Machine communication applications in the IoT (Shelby, Z., Hartke, K. & Bormann, C., 2012). CoAP mainly runs on the UDP layer in the communication stack. The SOA consists of a web interface for the applications that monitor, configure and visualize the sensor and actuator data. Furthermore, the SOA enables collaboration between services running on wireless sensor nodes, built-in sensors in mobile devices and actuator nodes. The sensor node software in the proposed SOA reconfigures the User Datagram Protocol (UDP) parameters so that incoming/outgoing CoAP messages are managed. Pereira et al. (2013) have shown that use of SOA and CoAP can support up to several kHz data rates in real time between the IoT sensors and the servers.

Sheng et al. (2012b) state that integration of social networks into S^2aaS would introduce several benefits to both S^2aaS customers, as well as social network service users. Therefore, interconnection of sensors and social networks has been pointed as an important direction where social network platforms can be utilized to collect, analyze and publish sensing information (Baqer, 2011). Sensor data may refer to health data (Rahman, M., El-Saddik, A. & Gueaieb, W., 2011), environmental data (Rita, T. S. T., Liu, D., Fen, H. & Pau, G., 2011), weather information or noise mapping in a region (Yilmaz, Y. S., Bulut,

M. F., Akcora, C. G., Bayir, M. A. & Demirbas, M., 2013) and so on. Knowingly, social networks and big data have appeared to be the leading applications in the cloud-dominated era (Han, X., Tian, L., Yoon, M & Lee, M., 2012). Millions of users are connected via social networks based on several criteria such as interests, relations or features. As stated in by Tan et al. (2013), social networks are expected to connect services and applications over the cloud in the close future.

As social networks in the IoT have been studied in the concept of Internet of Social Things (Atzori, L., Iera, A., Morabito, G., 2011; Nitti, M., Girau, R. & Atzori, L., 2013) integration of social networking services into cloud-centric IoT is still an open issue although there are few studies which may be considered under this category. Misra et al. (2012) have proposed a community detection algorithm for an integrated IoT and social network environment. CenceMe is an example of an application which uses built-in sensors in the smart phones to sense users' body position and publish the information on their social networks on Facebook and/or MySpace (Miluzzo, E., Lane, N. D., Peterson, K. F. R, Lu, H., Musolesi, M., Eiseman, S. B., Zheng, X. & Campbell, A. T., 2008). Rahman et al. (2011) have proposed a framework to enable sharing sensed data of one's Body Area Network over his/her social network. Rita et al. (2011) have presented a framework for integration of vehicular sensor networks and social networks. The proposed application is mainly designed for environmental monitoring with the purpose of energy saving and reducing CO2 emissions, and envisioned to be implemented with Foursquare. Besides, weather information and noise mapping via S²aaS have been implemented over Twitter.

Figure 2. Minimalist overview of the S²aaS architecture

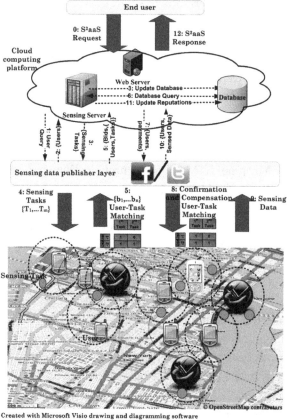

Sensing scheduling is handled based on a five-way handshake mechanism proposed by Sheng et al (2014), and as illustrated in Figure 3. The first step consists of periodic location update messages sent by the sensing provider. Upon arrival of a sensing task, the sensing server sends the requested task to the sensing provider. Once the sensing tasks are confirmed by the provider, the provider sends a confirmation message to the sensing server. Upon receipt of the confirmation message, the sensing server schedules the sensing times of the sensing events for the corresponding sensing service provider. Sensing service completes once the sensing service provider uploads the sensed data to the sensing server.

Besides scheduling between server and sensing service provider, scheduling of mobile application to manage mobile device workload is also crucial in presence of contending mobile sensing applications. Ju et al. (2012) have introduced a sensing flow execution engine called *SymPhoney* which aims at effective coordination of resources of different sensing applications in case of contention. The objective of resource coordination is maximizing the utilities of the contending sensing applications subject to resource constraints. SymPhoney facilitates a new concept called frame externalization which denotes searching and identifying semantic information in the applications so that resource usage patterns of specific sensing applications can be recognized for future resource allocation. In a semantic structure embedded to the application, two types of frames are considered, namely a feature frame (f-frame) and a context frame (c-frame). The f-frame denotes a stream of sensor data which represents a context whereas an f-frame is a sequence of feature extraction processes. The c-frames handle flow coordination in case of contending flows for limited resources. The f-frame runs a pipeline in which complicated procedures of sensing and processing take place. The first step is called c-frame-based flow coordination whereas the second step is called f-frame-based flow execution.

Sheng et al. (2012b) summarize emergent issues that need to be addressed in S^2aaS infrastructure as follows: Global Positioning System (GPS)-less mobile phone scheduling, sensing task scheduling on a mobile phone, privacy preserving incentive mechanisms, development of new reputation systems for mobile users and mobile phone sensing-based social networking.

GPS-Less Mobile Phone Sensing and Energy Efficiency

GPS-less mobile phone sensing aims at scheduling sensing tasks by deactivating the GPS. The motivation of GPS-less sensing is significant amount of battery power consumption of the GPS. Besides, location information obtained by WiFi or cellular signalling introduces precision problems. Once the GPS is deactivated, the participatory sensing mechanism has to assign time and location to the sensing devices that will join the participatory sensing. Furthermore, probabilistic coverage models, as well as enhanced mobility prediction techniques will assist improving GPS-less mobile phone sensing. Moreover, efficient sensing scheduling algorithms are emergent.

Sheng et al have proposed a GPS-less sensing scheduling mechanism in order to address this challenge (Sheng, X., Xiao, X., Tang, J. & Xue, G., 2014). Two approaches have been presented, namely Energy-constrained Maximum Coverage Sensing Scheduling (EMCSS) and Fair Maximum Coverage Sensing Scheduling (FMCSS). The former aims at maximum coverage under limitations whereas the latter aims at addressing fairness on individual energy consumption of sensing service providers.

Figure 3. Sensing scheduling protocol between sensing server and sensing provider
(Sheng, X., Xiao, X., Tang, J. & Xue, G., 2014)

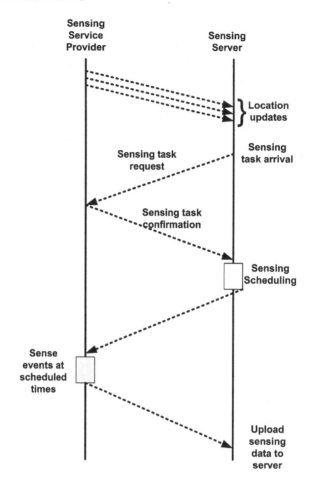

Energy-Constrained Maximum Coverage Sensing Scheduling (EMCSS)

EMCSS is defined by the following optimization model in (1) and (2). The objective function aims at maximizing the number of sensors selected out of the sensors set, S that will lead to maximum coverage of the destination regions. Thus, in the equation, s_i denotes sensor-i out of the available sensors set, S whereas $P_{err_i^j}$ is the probability of sensor-i's covering region-j with location errors. As shown in (2), the size of the sensors set is constrained to the available sensing budget which is basically the sensing cost (i.e., battery drain) introduced to the sensing devices.

$$\max \sum_{j} \left(1 - \prod_{s_i \in S} \left(1 - P_{err_i^j} \right) \right) \qquad (1)$$

Subject to $|S| \leq |B|$ \qquad (2)

Sheng et al. (2014) modeled this problem as the server placement problem with budget constraint (Yang, D., Fang, X. & Xue, G., 2011). The proposed greedy heuristic for EMCSS starts with an empty set and adds sensing service providers (i.e., virtual sensors) incrementally based on their contribution to the improvement of the objective function. Thus, the sensing provider leading to the highest contribution is added before the provider leading to lesser contribution. Addition of the sensing service providers goes on until the sensing budget is reached.

Fair Maximum Coverage Sensing Scheduling (FMCSS)

FMCSS is modeled as a discrete mathematics problem which aims at maximizing the submodular set cover on a matroid (Gargano, L, & Hammar, M., 2009). Performance evaluation of FMCSS has been shown to be promising in addressing the trade-off between coverage and fairness among sensing service providers. Sheng et al have re-formulated the objective function in (3) by aiming at finding the largest set covering a matroid where Ω is the set of subsets of the ground set. In order to obtain fast solution, Sheng et al. have proposed a greedy heuristic for FMCSS, as well. Thus, the heuristic adopts the same approach in EMCSS, and adds sensors incrementally to the set of sensing service providers based on their incremental contribution to the coverage over the matroid. For details of this work and the proof of matroids, the reader is referred to the related reference (Sheng, X., Xiao, X., Tang, J. & Xue, G., 2014).

$$\max_{S \in \Omega} \sum_j \left(1 - \prod_{s_i \in S}\left(1 - P_{err_i^j}\right)\right) \tag{3}$$

As reported by the previous work, in S²aaS, scheduling of sensing tasks has to introduce efficient utilization of the battery power. To this end, the S²aaS system has to determine how the sensing tasks are correlated, and based on the correlation mobile device-sensing task matching has to be built in addition to the GPSless sensing solutions..

Besides, Wang et al. (2013) have studied energy efficient data uploading problem in crowdsensing environments by classifying sensing tasks as delay tolerant and delay intolerant. Lane et al. (2013) have proposed piggyback crowdsensing in order to exploit the times when smart phone users place phone calls or use smart phone apps so that energy required for sensing is reduced.

Effective Sensor Search Techniques for S²aaS

Recruitment of the most appropriate sensing service providers is a challenging issue in S2aaS as the set of sensors directly impacts the performance of sensing services. Furthermore due to the large set of sensing devices participating in collaborative sensing and the variety of selection criteria makes the problem further challenging. The criteria for sensing service provider selection are reliability, sensing accuracy, residual battery, battery usage efficiency, current location and so on. Perera et al (2014b) have proposed the Context-Aware Sensor Search and Selection and Ranking Model (CASSARAM) in order to address this challenge. A minimalist overview of CASSARAM is illustrated in Figure 4 which basically consists of four steps as follows: Selecting the requirements; searching eligible sensing service providers;

Figure 4. Context-Aware Sensor Search and Selection and Ranking Model
(Perera, C., Zaslavsky, A., Liu, C.H, Compton, M., Christen, P. & Georgapoulos, D., 2014b)

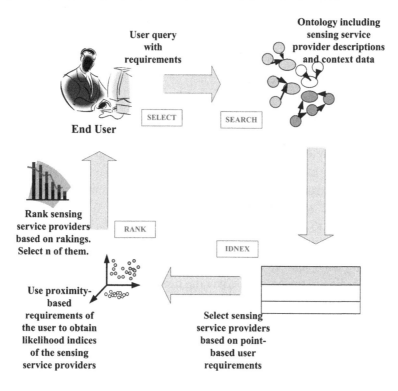

indexing the devices based on proximity-based user requirements, and ranking the providers based on the likelihood scores obtained through weighted user priorities and proximity-based user requirements.

CASSARAM receives the number of sensing service providers requested (n) and the end user's requirements as the input, and forms a query based on the user requirements. The query runs on a previously built ontology which has all sensor descriptions, as well as context definitions. The ontology is used to run the query and to retrieve a list of sensing devices that could meet the point-based requirements of the user. It is worthwhile mentioning that the point-based requirements of the user are defined to be non-negotiable, and they have to be met by the sensing service providers precisely, e.g., temperature, humidity, motion and so on. Once the list of sensing service providers that could meet the point-based requirements of the end user are obtained, user priorities are assigned appropriate weights, and for each sensing device a likelihood index is obtained in the multi-dimensional space. Here, proximity-based user requirements are used to prioritize user requests. Proximity-based user requirements are defined as negotiable sensing requirements such as motion sensor data within 2% proximity of the accurate value. Finally, the sensors are sorted based on their ranking values, and the first n sensing providers are assigned the sensing tasks.

Effective User Incentives for S²aaS

Effective data collection via S²aaS also calls for effective incentive mechanisms ensuring user privacy and trustworthiness of the crowdsensed data. In this chapter, a reputation-based sensing as a service scheme is also introduced where crowdsensed data trustworthiness is ensured along with effective compensation of the S²aaS providers. Besides trustworthiness, reliability of S²aaS is another challenging concern. Sensor data quality assurance can also be overcome by maintaining a robust mobile user reputation system. For various types of tasks, performance and efficiency of users can provide user reputation scores for future task assignments. Fairness and robustness should be considered when establishing a mobile user reputation system.

Incentives can be either user-centric or platform centric as proposed by Yang et al. (2012). The former is based on the assumption that users enthusiastically participate in the crowdsourcing activity by joining an auction to be selected for a particular sensing task whereas the latter selects the users for a particular sensing task and allows them to make their own sensing plans for the corresponding assignments in a game theoretical way. The authors have shown that both approaches are efficient in several aspects. It is worthwhile mentioning that as crowdsourcing through smart devices is a new concept for the users, not every user is comfortable to share his/her sensor data even though providing sensing service will be paid back.

MSensing

Yang et al. (2012) have proposed two user-centric incentives for participatory mobile phone sensing systems. The first scheme runs a local-search based auction which maximizes the platform's utility, i.e., S²aaS requester. On the other hand, local-search based auction has been shown to be vulnerable to untruthful bidding of the users who aim at increasing their income by participating in the auction with higher bids. This vulnerability has been addressed by MSensing auction. In the same study, MSensing has been shown to introduce high platform and user utility along with truthfulness in mobile phone-based crowdsourcing. Therefore, it can be adopted by a cloud-centric IoT framework where S²aaS forms the front-end. When such a framework is used for public safety applications, users aiming at disinformation can cause more severe problems in public when compared to the users aiming at increasing their incomes by higher bids. Thus, malicious users participate in the auction with lower bids, guarantee to be selected in an auction, and when selected, send altered data to the sensor data publisher layer of the IoT. In such a scenario, public safety authority may request several types of sensor data such as temperature, noise, motion, image and so on; and sensing services are provided by the crowd which consists of people who have gathered for a particular event. Therefore addressing this vulnerability by a reputation-aware crowd management scheme for a truthful and trustworthy S²aaS in a cloud-centric IoT architecture remains as a significant challenge, and it has formed the main motivation of the trustworthy crowdsensing algorithms that will be presented in the next section.

Trustworthy crowdsensing has also been studied in the context of user reputation-awareness and accurate sensing (Shahabi, C., 2013; Kazemi, L. Shahabi, C., Chen, L., 2013), user privacy and data integrity (Gilbert, P., Cox, L. P., Jung, J. & Wetherall, D., 2010).

CrowdRecruiter

Piggyback crowdsensing (Lane, N. D., Chon, Y., Zhou, L., Zhang, Y., i, F., Kim, D., Ding, G., Zhao, F. & Cha, H., 2013) has been used as a basis for an incentive framework, called *CrowdRecruiter* which aims at minimizing the number of recruiter sensing service providers while meeting the coverage requirements for the sensing tasks (Zhang, D., Xiong, H., Wang, L. & Chen G., 2014). The proposed recruitment scheme consists of two steps. The first step runs a prediction algorithm which uses the previous locations and call history of the mobile device users (i.e., sensing service providers). The output of the prediction function gives information about the location and the GPS status of the mobile device users during the sensing cycles of the next piggyback crowdsensing task. Once this information is obtained, the platform aims at selecting minimum number of mobile device users as the sensing providers by fulfilling coverage constraints of the sensing tasks while maximizing the number of users who are forecasted to have placed calls (i.e., turned GPS services on) during the corresponding sensing cycle. Thus, by minimizing the numbers of recruited users, S^2aaS cost is aimed to be minimized whereas maximizing the number of users with active calls aims at minimizing the energy consumption overhead of the S^2aaS cycle.

Steered Crowdsensing

Kavajiri et al (2014) have proposed Steered Crowdsensing, which is a quality-oriented S^2aaS solution. Steered crowdsensing uses gamification to increase user participation however differs from conventional crowdsensing as gamification in crowdsensing is primarily used to increase the quantity of crowdsensed data whereas steered crowdsensing aims at increasing the quality of crowdsensed data by introducing quality indicators. Steered crowdsensing defines user-centric incentives as mobile device users determine to participate in S^2aaS activities based on coupon points introduced by the platform. In order to increase user engagement, the platform introduces coupon points to compensate sensing services. The platform calculates the values of the coupons through service quality indicators that are obtained by running online machine learning algorithms.

Crowdsensing over Social Networks

Crowdsensing over social networks is still in its infancy although there are a few proposals bridging two paradigms. Akbas et al. (2011a/b) have proposed an application called, fAPEbook for animal social life monitoring. Hu et al. (2014) presented social network architecture for mobile crowdsensing to ease context-aware mobile applications. Besaleva and Weaver (2013) have demonstrated a system named Crowd bridging social networks and crowdsensing whereas Wozniak et al. (2013) have presented another application of disaster management via crowdsensed data through social networks. Cooperative crowdsensing via social networks has been proposed by Chang and Wu (2014a).

Mobile Social Network-Aware Crowdsourcing (MSNAC)

As crowdsensing via mobile social networks has an emerging application with the advent of S^2aaS in the cloud-centric Internet of Things (IoT) architecture, Kantarci and Mouftah (2014d) have proposed two mobile social network-aware frameworks for a cloud centric IoT architecture. The first scheme is called Mobile Social Network-Aware Crowdsourcing (MSNAC) whereas the second scheme is called Trustworthy and Mobile Social Network-Aware Crowdsourcing (T-MSNAC). A set of sensing tasks and sensing service providers (i.e., mobile device users) in a terrain are considered; and the cloud platform is not granted access to the online interaction values of the mobile device users over social network services (e.g., Facebook, Twitter, FourSquare) in order to respect users privacy. However, the cloud platform is informed about the social network topology in the region and the location updates of the users. As the cloud platform does not have access to online interactions of the mobile device users, it aims at predict-

Figure 5. Mobile Social Network (MSN)-Aware S2aaS
(Kantarci & Mouftah., 2014d)

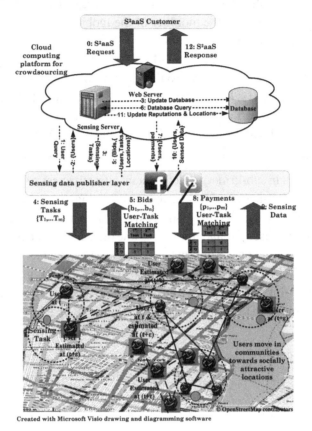

Created with Microsoft Visio drawing and diagramming software

ing the interaction values between them based on co-location, proximity and connectedness over the social network topology. Through estimated interactions between mobile device users, the platform aims at forecasting future locations of the sensing service providers so that they can be assigned appropriate sensing tasks in order to maximize the utility of the platform, and consequently the utility of the S²aaS customer. As illustrated in Figure 5, mobile social network-aware S²aaS runs over the cloud-centric IoT architecture presented in Figure 2. Apart from the scenario in Figure 2, here, mobile device users are considered non-stationary. Furthermore, the mobile device users move in communities towards socially attractive destinations.

MSN-aware S²aaS uses user-centric recruitment mechanism for the sensing service providers which is based on an (Akbas, M. I., Brust, M. R., Riberio, C.H. C. & Turgut, D., 2011a) auction between the sensing service providers and the cloud platform which negotiates with the providers, assigns sensing tasks, compensates service providers, analyzes participatory sensed data and presents it to the S²aaS customer. MSN-aware S²aaS auction extends the MSensing auction proposed by Sheng et al. (2012). MSN-Aware Crowdsensing runs as follows: The participants of the auction are marked as winners as long as they introduce positive marginal contribution to the platform utility. It is worthwhile noting that marginal contribution stands for the difference between the marginal value introduced by the collaboratively sensed tasks that are also contributed by the corresponding user; and payment made to him/her. As mobile device users (i.e., sensing service providers) are assumed to select destinations based on social attractiveness criteria, it is likely that a sensing service provider is forecasted to be out of range of a particular task before the completion of the auction. Therefore, a sensing task is forecasted to be out of range of a mobile device user due to the mobility of the mobile device user, the corresponding user is not selected as one of the winners of the auction.

Social attractiveness defined by Musolesi and Mascolo (2007) is adopted by Kantarci and Mouftah (2014d), and adapted to the S^2aaS environment so that the user trajectories are estimated. Given I as the interaction rate matrix in a region, $0 < I_{ij} < 1$ if user-I and user-j are connected in the same social network. The terrain of interest $(D_1 \times D_2)$ is partitioned into an $X \times Y$ grid, then each sub-grid-xy into x' × y' cells. Social attractiveness is a probabilistic value and can be formulated as in (4). Thus, social attractiveness of sub-grid-xy for smart device user-$i \left(A_{xy}^i \right)$ is the ratio of the total interaction of the smart device user-i with other smart device users in sub-grid-xy to total social attractiveness of the other sub-grids. Interaction can be formulated by different ways. One possible way is using the co-location and distance between the users on an $M \times N$ sub-grid. Since shorter distance denotes higher interaction, inverse of the ratio of the distance between user-i and user-j to maximum possible distance is used to formulate user interaction s formulated in (5). Other interaction definitions are also possible such as a weighted sum of different interaction types (Akbas, M. I., Brust, M. R., Riberio, C.H. C. & Turgut, D., 2011b), social force model-based interactions (Solmaz, G. & Turgut, D., 2013; Solmaz G. & Turgut, D., 2014) or interactions based on human behavior models (Bhatia et al., 2012; Bölöni, 2012).

$$A_{xy}^i \left(t \right) = \frac{\sum_{j \in xy} I_{ij}}{\sum_{x'y'} A_{x'y'}^i \left(t \right)} \tag{4}$$

$$I_{ij} = \alpha . I_{ij}^- + \left(1 - \alpha \right) \frac{\sqrt{M^2 + N^2}}{\sqrt{\left(y_i^t - y_j^t \right)^2 + \left(x_i^t - x_j^t \right)^2}} \tag{5}$$

Kantarci and Mouftah (2014d) have evaluated the mobile social network-aware S^2aaS in a heterogeneous scenario where 950 reputable and 50 non-reputable sensing service providers co-exist on a 1 km² terrain. It is worthwhile noting that a non-reputable sensing service provider denotes the mobile device users who aim at disinformation at the cloud platform, as well as at the S^2aaS customer. It has been assumed that 50% of the users have up to 15 connections in the terrain of interest, 35% of the users have up to 25 connections in the terrain, and 15% of the users have more than 25 connections in the terrain of interest. Under the assumption that every sensing task has a predefined value and every sensing service provider reports a sensing cost to the platform, MSN-aware S^2aaS has been shown to increase platform utility under heavily arriving sensing task requests. On the other hand, reputation-awareness incorporated with mobile social network-awareness enhances the platform utility by up to the order of 55% whereas disinformation probability is degraded by 70% if reputation-awareness is incorporated. Next section discusses incorporation of reputation-awareness for reliable crowdsensed data through S^2aaS.

TripleS

TripleS is an S2aaS architecture which utilizes cloud-based social networking services and incorporates open source principles (Hu, X., Liu, Q., Zhu, C., Leung, V. C. M., Chu, T. H. S. & Chan, H. C. B., 2013). TripleS consists of internetworking and opportunistic networking components. The former denotes cloud-based services whereas the latter denotes opportunistic networking services. The cloud platform consists of *management interface, storage service, deployment environment* and *process runtime environment. Management interface* provides application programming interfaces development platforms to allow integration of various mobile applications and services into TripleS. *Storage service* provides automated backup of crowdsensed data including analyzed data and the raw sensor data. *Deployment environment* is an enabler for dynamic implementation of mobile platforms and web services to mobile smart devices. Mobile smart device users, namely the sensing service providers will be able to participate in crowdsensing activities through these platforms and web services. *Process runtime environment* of the cloud platform hosts open souce procedures which enable collection, aggregation and analysis of crowdsensed data from various sensing service providers (i.e., smart mobile devices).

The opportunistic networking components of TripleS are the mobile service-oriented architecture (SOA) framework and an agent-based application programming framework. The mobile SOA framework offers application and service instances to enable users to join crowdsensing activities and provide their sensor data to the end users through cloud platform. The agent-based application programming framework builds on a previous framework, called *Aframe* (Hu, X., Du W., Spencer, B., 2011), and it enables collection, aggregation and processing the data in mobile agents locally. The benefits of TripleS are its offering flexible and open source cloud platform, and its facilitating agent-based aggregation and processing of crowdsensed data in conjunction with online social network services.

VeDi

The concept of mobile social networks-based crowdsourcing can be extended to Vehicular Social Network (VSN)-based crowdsourcing. VSNs consolidate social links between the vehicles of a vehicular ad hoc network (Mezghani, F., Daou, R., Nogueira, M. & Beylot, A –L., 2014). Alam et al (2014) have proposed a vehicular social network application, namely VeDi, to support crowdsourced video. One of the biggest challenges in vehicular networks is the distribution of video content since the nodes move faster than the conventional mobile ad hoc network nodes, and contention occurs rapidly in the communication medium. To cope with this challenge, VeDi (Alam, K. M., Saini, M., Ahmet, D. T., El-Saddik, A., 2014) proposes an application consisting of vehicular on-board units, road side units, home-based units, IEEE 802.11p communication links/messages and the VeDi cloud platform. The VeDi cloud hosts all vehicular interactions including inter-on-board unit, on-board unit-to-home-board unit, and on-board unit-to-road side unit communications and the Dedicated Shor Range Communications (DRSC) messages. According to VeDi, a vehicle shares the metadata of the video with the surrounding vehicles along with metadata scores. The video metadata scores include blur and shakiness analysis of the corresponding video. The passengers in the surrounding vehicles can select to download the videos based of their preferences, and the downloaded video is stored in the on-board unit. Upon arrival at the home board unit, the content is synchronized with the VeDi cloud. Furthermore, social interactions among VSN users are also stored and processed within the VeDi cloud through RSUs.

RELIABLE S²aaS AND TRUSTWORTHINESS OF CROWDSENSED DATA

Trustworthiness of crowdsensed data focuses on reputation of sensing devices and their corresponding sensing accuracy (Kazemi, L. Shahabi, C., Chen, L., 2013; Shahabi, C., 2013). In a reputation-based crowdsensing system, when the trustworthiness of a malicious and a non-malicious user are compared as time elapses, the following observation can be made: The user who continuously sends altered sensor data is not recruited anymore whereas the other user who aims at recovering his/her reputation by sending accurate sensor readings in order to be recruited in the next sensor data requests is recruited once his/her reputation exceeds a certain value (Kantarci, B. & Mouftah, H. T., 2014b).

Trustworthy Sensing for Crowd Management (TSCM)

In order to address the reliability of S²aaS and ensure trustworthiness of crowdsensed data, Kantarci and Mouftah have proposed reputation-aware sensing as a service (Kantarci, B. & Mouftah, H. T., 2014a, 2014b). The authors adopt the MSensing auction and extend it by incorporating reputation-awareness. The proposed framework is called Trustworthy Sensing for Crowd Management (TSCM), and its contribution is two-fold: i) A crowdsensing framework is proposed for management of a crowd gathered in a certain terrain; ii) user-centric incentives have been proposed to ensure trustworthiness. TSCM recruits the users based on their reputation. User reputation is defined as the running average ratio of the positive sensing readings to total sensing readings. Once all sensor data are collected for a set of tasks, for each task, an outlier detection algorithm (Zhang, Y., Meratnia, N. & Havinga, P., 2010) is run on the set of sensor readings, and the outliers are marked as negative readings whereas the rest are marked as positive readings.

Every task, t is considered to have a pre-defined value, ϑ_t, set by the end user and reported to the cloud platform. The cloud platform keeps track of the user reputation and recruits the users based on their reputable contributions to the set of sensed task. The difference between the reputable values of the set, W is defined as the reputable contribution of user-i as formulated in (6). Reputable value of a set is the total value of the sensing tasks handled by the user in W while the total is normalized by the average reputation of the user in W as shown in (7).

$$\vartheta_i^{\Re}\left(W\right) = \vartheta_i^{\Re}\left(W \cup \left\{i\right\}\right) - \vartheta^{\Re}\left(W\right) \tag{6}$$

$$\vartheta^{\Re}\left(W\right) = \sum_{t \in T_w}\sum_{j \in \Gamma_t}\vartheta_t.\Re_j \, / \left|\Gamma_t\right| \tag{7}$$

Every sensing service provider has a sensing cost, which is also called the bid of the user, which sets a lower bound to the payments to be made to the sensing service provider. TSCM adopts the MSensing auction proposed by Yang et al. (2012), and enhances it by introducing reputation-awareness. Instantaneous reputation of a sensing service provider is defined as the ratio of the positive sensor readings to all readings. As a provider can participate several sensing activities, overall reputation (i,e, trustworthiness) of a user is updated via weighted sum of past and current reputation values. The sensing service providers are selected based on a two-step auction. The bids of the providers are scaled by their reputation so that a provider with high reputation is trusted and it is considered that his/her actual bid/sensing cost is close to the reported bid whereas in case of a provider with low reputation, it is considered that the user aims at bidding lower than his/her actual sensing cost in order to guarantee being selected so that he/she can mislead the end user by sending maliciously altered sensor data. In the first step, winners are selected based on the following criterion: The providers whose modified bids are less than their reputable marginal values are selected as the winners of the auction, and they are added to the winners list, W in descending order. In the payment determination phase, for each selected sensing service provider, w, the algorithm seeks maximum possible bid which would still make the corresponding provider w preferable over the other providers whose payments have not been decided yet (i.e., every user w_v). To this end, the providers whose reputable marginal values are greater than their modified bids are sorted based on their reputable contributions as shown in (8) where $\vartheta_{w_v}^{\mathfrak{R}}$ denotes the reputable marginal value of user w_v on the set of users who have not been paid so far.

$$(\vartheta_{w_v}^{\mathfrak{R}} - b_{w_v} / \mathfrak{R}_{w_v}) > (\vartheta_{w_v+1}^{\mathfrak{R}} - b_{w_v+1} / \mathfrak{R}_{w_v+1}) \tag{8}$$

For the assessment of the framework, the following metrics are used:

- **Utility of the End User (Platform Utility):** As shown in (9), utility of the end user is the difference between the total reputable value of the sensing tasks and the total payments made to the winners in the auction $\left(\rho_i^\tau \right)$ where τ stands for the period in which the cloud platform requests a new set of sensing tasks from the sensing service providers.

$$U_{platform} = \sum_\tau \left(\sum_{t \in T_{W_t}} \vartheta^{\mathfrak{R}} (W_\tau) - \sum_i \rho_i^\tau \right) \tag{9}$$

$$U_{prov} = \left(\sum_\tau \left(\left(\sum_i \rho_i^\tau - \sum_i c_i^\tau \right) / |W_\tau| \right) \right) / \tau_{end} \tag{10}$$

- **Utility of the Sensing Service Provider:** Equation (10) formulates the average utility of a provider (i.e., mobile device user) as the difference between total payments made to the winners and the total sensing cost of the winners. The resulting value is averaged by τ_{end} which is the end time of the sensing task arrivals.
- **Disinformation Ratio:** The disinformation probability is formulated as the ratio of the tasks for which at least one malicious user has been paid, to the total number of tasks.

Based on the compensation paid to the sensing service providers, TSCM runs in two modes, namely the aggressive mode and non-aggressive mode. The aggressive mode uses the reputable value of the participatory sensor data $\left(\vartheta_{w_v}^{\mathfrak{R}} \right)$ whereas the non-aggressive mode takes the raw value of participatory

Figure 6. (a) Platform utility vs. task arrival rate under Aggressive and Non-Aggressive payment modes of TSCM (b) Average utility of a sensing service provider under Aggressive and Non-Aggressive payment modes of TSCM.

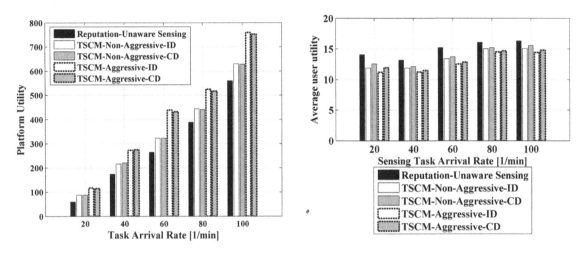

sensing tasks. A malicious service provider may adopt either continuous disinformation (CD) or intermittent disinformation (ID) policy. In case of ID, the provider sends accurate sensor data in order to increase his/her reputation before sending altered sensor data. As seen in Figure 6.a, reputation-awareness introduced by TSCM improves the utility of the end user by 12% under lightly arriving sensing task and by 85% under heavily arriving sensing tasks under the aggressive mode of TSCM. Due to the cuts introduced to the sensing service provider compensations, aggressive mode improves the end user utility by 15% compared to the end user utility under non-aggressive mode. As illustrated in Figure 6.b, non-aggressive mode can reduce cuts in compensations of non-malicious sensing service providers, and the end user and/or the cloud platform may end up paying to some malicious service providers for misleading sensor data.

Mobility-Aware Crowdsensing (MACS)

A big challenge in this framework is the mobility of the sensor data providers. The most naïve approach would be assuming that users follow the random waypoint mobility model (Kantarci, B. & Mouftah, H. T., 2014c). TSCM has also been modified to predict the location of the sensing service provider at the time of data collection. As the mobile device user who is providing sensing service might wander off the sensing range of a particular task although he/she has been recruited and paid to provide sensor data for the corresponding task. In order to prevent the cloud platform and the end user from making payments for non-received data, provider location is estimated by using the triangulation method as formulated in (11) and (12) where $\vec{V}_i$ denotes the velocity of the service provider-i.

$$x_i^{t+\tau} = \begin{cases} x_i^{\tau} + \dfrac{x_i \cdot \left|\vec{V}_i\right| \cdot \tau}{\sqrt{\left(y_i^t - y_i^{t-}\right)^2 + \left(x_i^t - x_i^{t-}\right)^2}} & x_i^t - x_i^{t-} \geq 0 \\[3em] x_i^{\tau} - \dfrac{x_i \cdot \left|\vec{V}_i\right| \cdot \tau}{\sqrt{\left(y_i^t - y_i^{t-}\right)^2 + \left(x_i^t - x_i^{t-}\right)^2}} & else \end{cases} \qquad (11)$$

$$y_i^{t+\tau} = \begin{cases} x_i^{\tau} + \dfrac{y_i \cdot \left|\vec{V}_i\right| \cdot \tau}{\sqrt{\left(y_i^t - y_i^{t-}\right)^2 + \left(x_i^t - x_i^{t-}\right)^2}} & y_i^t - y_i^{t-} \geq 0 \\[3em] x_i^{\tau} - \dfrac{y_i \cdot \left|\vec{V}_i\right| \cdot \tau}{\sqrt{\left(y_i^t - y_i^{t-}\right)^2 + \left(x_i^t - x_i^{t-}\right)^2}} & else \end{cases} \qquad (12)$$

The cloud platform keeps track of previous locations and velocities of the sensing service providers. For each sensing service provider, MACS re-computes the set of sensing tasks that are expected to be still within his/her range based on his/her estimated location by the end of the data collection process. It is worthwhile noting that the data collection process is based on an auction procedure as in MSensing which has been proposed for truthful data crowdsensing (Yang, D., Xue, G., Fan, X. & Tang, J., 2012).

Mobility-Aware Trustworthy Crowdsensing (MATCS)

Maliciously altered sensor data can lead to severe consequences while mobility-unaware crowdsensing results in unnecessary payments to sensing providers. Therefore, Mobility-Aware Trustworthy Crowdsensing (MATCS) has been proposed in order to jointly address these two issues. MATCS recruits the sensing service providers based on their future locations. Furthermore, it uses the reputable value of the set of users ((6) and (7)) while selecting the winners of the auction. MATCS also adopts the non-aggressive payment mode of TSCM.

As illustrated in Figure 7.a, under heavily arriving sensing tasks, mobility-awareness can improve the platform utility by 70% whereas by incorporation of trustworthiness, MATCS introduces 20% increase in the platform utility of MACS. As seen in Figure 7.b, improvement in platform utility is at the expense of providers' utility. However, under heavily arriving sensing tasks, the degradation in provider's utility under MATCS is significantly low.

It is worthwhile noting that the triangulation method is not a strong predictor for real-world user mobility as human mobility demonstrates regularity to some extent (Bayir, M. A., & Demirbas, M., 2014). Therefore incorporating more sophisticated clustering solutions such as Density-Based Spatial Clustering of Applications with Noise (DBSCAN) (Shi, J., Mamoulis, N., Wu, D.& Cheung, D. W., 2014) could improve the accuracy and provide a better fit for real-time mappings. Kantarci and Mouftah (2014d) used social attractiveness (Musolesi, M. & Mascolo, C., 2007) of the destinations to estimate the user trajectories as described in the previous section.

Figure 7. (a) Platform utility versus task arrival rate under MACS and MATCS (b) Average sensing service provider utility under MACS and MATCS

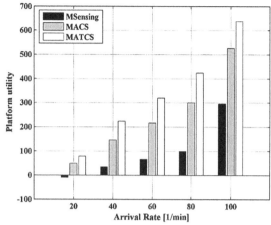
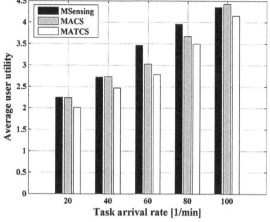

SUMMARY AND FUTURE DIRECTIONS

In the Internet of Things (IoT) era, mobile phones, tablet computers and other smart handheld devices offer advanced sensing and navigation capabilities which may promote cloud-inspired provisioning of sensing services, namely Sensing-as-a-Service (S^2aaS). S^2aaS is referred as the front-end access to the cloud-centric IoT framework. This chapter has provided a brief overview of the state of the art, current proposals and challenges in S^2aaS systems. Searching and recruitment of sensing service providers is a major challenge in this field. The chapter has presented a previously proposed context-aware sensor search framework which has been shown to be effective and efficient in providing sensing services in a cloud inspired environment. Besides, as mobile devices utilize GPS for localization, mobile crowd-sensing appears to be a power-hungry service. To this end, sensing by turning off the GPS as much as possible can introduce energy savings. Furthermore, energy-aware sensing activity scheduling is another crucial issue which can also incentivize the mobile device users to offer sensing services. Having said that mobile device users need to be incentivized, effective incentives are required to improve accuracy of the crowdsensed data. The chapter has introduced user-centric and platform-centric incentives that have recently been proposed. Although having more mobile device users participating in theS^2aaS activities is expected to increase the accuracy of the crowdsensed data, reliability is subject to the trustworthiness of the users participating in the crowdsensing activity. It is very likely that adversaries can take advantage of the user incentives and report altered sensor data to the cloud platform. Introducing reputation-aware mechanisms can improve reliability of the crowdsensed data. The chapter has introduced trustworthiness-based S^2aaS mechanisms that are particularly tailored for public safety and smart city applications. Addressing user mobility rises another challenge which could degrade the utility of the end user. Therefore S^2aaS calls for user mobility-aware approaches. User mobility is a function of several factors; thus, the users can move based on random basis, random Gauss-Markov mobility or social mobility. The chapter has also introduced reliable S^2aaS solutions considering random waypoint mobility and social mobility of the sensing service providers.

Table 1 summarizes the schemes that have been visited and studied in detail in the chapter. All schemes are compared in terms of their foci and direct/indirect objectives. Energy-efficiency and reliability are considered as direct objectives whereas context-awareness and mobility-awareness are considered as the indirect objectives. It is worthwhile noting that MSNAC and T-MSNAC aim at forecasting future locations of the sensing service providers based on the interactions with their social networks; hence they can also be considered as context-aware as the context denotes mobile device user interactions and locations. As seen in the table, all schemes need improvement and to be complemented by one of the direct/indirect objectives. For instance, T-MSNAC is aware of the context as it maintains a user interaction map accompanied with the sensing service providers' trajectories. Furthermore, it aims at reliable S²aaS, and adopts the reputation-based sensing service provider recruitment principle in TSCM. On the other hand, battery drain of the sensing service providers is not a major concern for T-MSNAC. Similarly, EMCSS and FMCSS introduce promising results in terms of energy savings through GPS-less sensing however they need improvement by a reputation-based approach so that sensor data reliability is improved. Therefore, holistic schemes addressing all direct/indirect objectives and having multiple foci are emergent. Moreover, social networks can play a key role in handling the big sensor data.

S²aaS has several open issues to be addressed by researchers pursuing study in this field, as well as challenges. Future research is expected to address technical, business, and economic issues that are necessary to accelerate the expansion of emerging crowdsensing applications Firstly, eliminating GPS

Table 1. Summary of the schemes that have been studied in detail in the chapter

Scheme	Focus	Energy-Efficiency	Context-Awareness	Reliability/ Trustworthiness	Mobility-Awareness
CASSARAM (Perera, C., Zaslavsky, A., Liu, C.H, Compton, M., Christen, P. & Georgapoulos, D., 2014b)	Sensing provider search	NO	YES	NO	NO
CrowdRecruiter (Zhang, D., Xiong, H., Wang, L. & Chen G., 2014)	User incentives and GPS-less sensing scheduling	YES	YES	NO	YES
EMCSS (Sheng, X., Xiao, X., Tang, J. & Xue, G., 2014)	GPS-less sensing scheduling	YES	NO	NO	NO
FMCSS (Sheng, X., Xiao, X., Tang, J. & Xue, G., 2014)	GPS-less sensing scheduling	YES	NO	NO	NO
TSCM (Kantarci, B. & Mouftah, H. T., 2014a, 2014b)	User incentives and S²aaS provider recruitment	NO	NO	YES	NO
MACS (Kantarci, B. & Mouftah, H. T., 2014c)	User incentives and S²aaS provider recruitment	NO	NO	NO	YES
MATCS (Kantarci, B. & Mouftah, H. T., 2014c)	User incentives, and S²aaS provider recruitment	NO	NO	YES	YES
MSNAC (Kantarci, B. & Mouftah, H. T., 2014d)	User incentives, and S²aaS provider recruitment via mobile social networks	NO	YES	NO	YES
Steered Crowdsensing (Kavajiri, R., Shimosaka, M. & Kashima, H., 2014)	User incentives and quality of S²aaS data	NO	NO	NO	NO
T-MSNAC (Kantarci, B. & Mouftah, H. T., 2014d)	User incentives and S²aaS provider recruitment via mobile social networks	NO	YES	YES	YES
TripleS (Hu, X., Liu, Q., Zhu, C., Leung, V. C. M., Chu, T. H. S. & Chan, H. C. B., 2013)	Flexible, open source S²aaS platform	NO	YES	NO	NO
VeDi (Alam, K. M., Saini, M., Ahmet, D. T., El-Saddik, A., 2014)	Crowdsensing multimedia data in vehicular social networks	NO	YES	NO	YES

usage in sensing service utilization still remains as a big challenge. As mentioned by the previous work, precision of the participatory sensed data is closely related to the detection and/or estimation of sensing service provider locations. Therefore relying on cellular signalling cannot guarantee quality of the crowdsensed data as it is likely that some mobile users are assigned sensing tasks at some locations that will not be within their sensing ranges at the time of sensing. On the other hand, when GPS is always enabled for S^2aaS, quick battery drain is inevitable for the sensing service providers.

One of the major challenges in trustworthiness models for S^2aaS is slow convergence due to use of heterogeneous metrics. Future research may consolidate collaborative trustworthiness metrics into the positive readings to total readings ratio in order to help the user reputation converge faster. Collaborative trustworthiness metrics will utilize the trust score of the sensing service provider based on the ratings of previous end users that are in the same social network with the user who is receiving sensing as a service. Ongoing research is investigating the impact of using Wilson score together with the advanced trustworthiness metrics to improve ratio-based reputation calculation techniques. Using positive readings to total readings ratio as the reputation may introduce problems especially under lightly arriving sensing task requests (Kantarci, B. & Mouftah, H. T., 2014a; 2014b). Recommendation-based trust scores have been used in several studies and they have been shown to be reliable (Chang, C., Ling, S. & Srirama, S., 2014b). Furthermore, Wilson score has been shown to increase the confidence of user reputation calculation (Xue, J., Yang, Z., Yang, X., Wang, X, Chen, L. & Dai, Y., 2013). Therefore, introducing compound metrics for trustworthiness evaluation in mobile social networks is emergent to improve system's reliability in reputation calculation.

Research pursued by industrial initiatives report that majority of the big data will be contributed by the sensing devices. Therefore, efficient data analytics algorithms and platforms are emergent to handle participatory sensor data. This introduces an inevitable combination of S^2aaS and Data Analytics As a Service (DaaS) which is also offered by the cloud platform. Researchers pursuing research in this area should also address integrated architectures for S^2aaS and DAaaS.

Mobile device users have to be incentivized to share their built-in sensor resources, and they have to be compensated due to their resource usage. However, major user concern in allowing access to the built-in sensing hardware is more related to privacy preservation. Besides compensation due to resource utilization, privacy assuring mechanisms are emergent in sensing service provider recruitment.

The ultimate societal impacts of the S^2aaS can be listed as new crowdsensing applications in the areas of public safety, disaster management and community engagement that will be enabled by improved energy-efficient data collection, increased crowdsending trustworthiness through context aware sensing, and new crowdsensing business models that will incentivize more users to offer their mobile device built-in sensors as a service.

REFERENCES

Aggarwal, C., Ashish, N., & Sheth, A. (2013). The Internet of Things: A Survey from the Data-Centric Perspective. In C. Aggarwal, & C. Charu (Eds.), Managing and Mining Sensor Data (pp. 383--428). Springer. doi:10.1007/978-1-4614-6309-2_12

Akbas, M. I., Brust, M. R., Riberio, C. H. C., & Turgut, D. (2011a). fAPEbook - Animal Social life Monitoring with Wireless Sensor and Actor Networks.*IEEE Global Communications Conference (GLOBECOM)*, (pp. 1-5). doi:10.1109/GLOCOM.2011.6134364

Akbas, M. I., Brust, M. R., Riberio, C. H. C., & Turgut, D. (2011b). *Deployment and Mobility for Animal Social Life Monitoring Based on Preferential Attachment* (pp. 488–495). IEEE Local Computer Networks. doi:10.1109/LCN.2011.6115510

Al-Fagih, A. E., Al-Turjman, F. M., Alsalih, W. M., & Hassanein, H. S. (2013). A priced public sensing framework for heterogeneous IoT architectures. *IEEE Transactions on Emerging Topics in Computing*, *1*(1), 133–147. doi:10.1109/TETC.2013.2278698

Alam, K. M., Saini, M., Ahmet, D. T., & El-Saddik, A. (2014). *VeDi: A vehicular crowd-sourced video social network for VANETs. IEEE Local Computer Networks (LCN)* (pp. 738–745). Conference Workshops.

Alamri, A., Ansari, W. S., Hassan, M. M., Hossain, M. S., Alelaiwi, A. & Hossain, M. A. (2013). A Survey on Sensor-Cloud: Architecture, Applications, and Approaches. *International Journal of Distributed Sensor Networks*, 917923.1—917923.18.

Atzori, A., Andlera, L., & Morabito, G. (2010). The Internet of Things: A survey. *Computer Networks*, *54*(15), 2787–2805. doi:10.1016/j.comnet.2010.05.010

Atzori, L., Iera, A., & Morabito, G. (2011). SIoT: Giving a social structure to the Internet of Things. *IEEE Communications Letters*, *15*(11), 1193–1195. doi:10.1109/LCOMM.2011.090911.111340

Baqer, M. (2011). Enabling collaboration and coordination of wireless sensor networks via social networks.*Proc. IEEE International Conference on Distributed Computing in Sensor Systems Workshops (DCOSSW)*, (pp. 1--2).

Basaleva, L. I., & Weaver, A. C. (2013). Applications of Social Networks and Crowdsourcing for Disaster Management Improvement.*Proc. Int. Conference on Social Computing (SocialCom)*, (pp. 213--219). doi:10.1109/SocialCom.2013.38

Bayir, M. A., & Demirbas, M. (2014). On the fly learning of mobility profiles for routing in pocket switched networks. *Elsevier Ad Hoc Network*, *16*, 13–27. doi:10.1016/j.adhoc.2013.11.011

Bhatia, T. S., Khan, S. A., & Bölöni, L. (2013). A modeling framework for inter-cultural social interactions.*Proc. 2nd International Workshop on Human-Agent Interaction Design and Models (HAIDM-13)*, (pp. 16--31).

Bölöni, L. (2012). The Spanish Steps flower scam - agent-based modeling of a complex social interaction.*Proc. 11th Int. Conf. on Autonomous Agents and Multiagent Systems (AAMAS)*, (pp. 1345--1346).

Chang, C., Ling, S., & Srirama, S. (2014b). Trustworthy Service Discovery for Mobile Social Network in Proximity.*Proc. IEEE Intl Conference on Pervasive Computing and Communications (PERCOM) Workshops*, (pp. 478--483). doi:10.1109/PerComW.2014.6815253

Chang, W., & Wu, J. (2014a). Progressive or Conservative: Rationally Allocate Cooperative Work in Mobile Social Networks. *IEEE Transactions on Parallel and Distributed Systems*. doi:10.1109/TPDS.2014.2330298

Chen, S.-Y., Lai, C.-F., Huang, Y.-M., & Jeng, Y.-L. (2013). Intelligent home appliance recognition over IoT cloud network.*Proc. Ninth International Wireless Communications and Mobile Computing Conference (IWCMC)*, (pp. 639--643). doi:10.1109/IWCMC.2013.6583632

Developers, A. (n.d.). *Tools Help*. Retrieved 2 6, 2015, from Android Developers: http://developer.android.com/tools/help/index.html

Distefano, S., Merlino, G., & Puliafito, A. (2014). A utility paradigm for IoT: The sensing Cloud. *Pervasive and Mobile Computing*. doi:10.1016/j.pmcj.2014.09.006

Doukas, C., & Maglogiannis, I. (2012). Bringing IoT and cloud computing towards pervasive healthcare. *Proc. Sixth International Conference on Innovative Mobile and Internet Services in Ubiquitous Computing (IMIS)*, (pp. 922—926). doi:10.1109/IMIS.2012.26

Gargano, L., & Hammar, M. (2009). A note on submodular set cover on matroids. *Discrete Mathematics*, *309*(18), 5739–5744. doi:10.1016/j.disc.2008.05.019

Ghose, A., Biswas, P., Bhaumik, C., Sharma, M., Pal, A., & Jha, A. (2012). Road condition monitoring and alert application: Using in-vehicle smartphone as Internet-connected sensor.*Proc. IEEE Intl. Conf. on Pervasive Computing and Communications Workshops (PERCOM Workshops)*, (pp. 489—491). doi:10.1109/PerComW.2012.6197543

Gilbert, P., Cox, L. P., Jung, J., & Wetherall, D. (2010). Toward Trustworthy Mobile Sensing.*Proc. 11th International Workshop on Mobile Computing Systems and Applicatons (HotMobile)*, (pp. 31--36).

Gubbi, J., Buyya, R., Marusic, S., & Palaniswami, M. (2013). Internet of Things (IoT): A vision, architectural elements, and future directions. *Future Generation Computer Systems*, *29*(7), 1645–1660. doi:10.1016/j.future.2013.01.010

Han, X., Tian, L., Yoon, M., & Lee, M. (2012). A big data model supporting information recommendation in social networks.*Proc. Second International Conference on Cloud and Green Computing (CGC)*, (pp. 810-813). doi:10.1109/CGC.2012.125

Hu, X., Du, W., & Spencer, B. (2011). A multi-agent framework for ambient systems development. *Procedia Computer Science*, *5*(1), 82–89. doi:10.1016/j.procs.2011.07.013

Hu, X., Li, X., Ngai, E.-C.-H., Leung, V., & Kruchten, P. (2014). Multidimensional Context-Aware Social Network Architecture for Mobile Crowdsensing. *IEEE Communications Magazine*, *52*(6), 78–87. doi:10.1109/MCOM.2014.6829948

Hu, X., Liu, Q., Zhu, C., Leung, V. C. M., Chu, T. H. S., & Chan, H. C. B. (2013). A Mobile Crowdsensing System Enhanced by Cloud-based Social Networking Services.*Proc. First International Workshop on Middleware for Cloud-enabled Sensing*, (pp. 3.1--3.6). doi:10.1145/2541603.2541604

Jararweh, Y., Tawalbeh, L., Ababneh, F., & Dosari, F. (2013). Resource efficient mobile computing using cloudlet infrastructure.*Proc. IEEE Ninth International Conference on Mobile Ad-hoc and Sensor Networks*, (pp. 373--377). doi:10.1109/MSN.2013.75

Ju, Y., Lee, Y., Yu, J., Min, C., Shin, I., & Song, J. (2012). SymPhoney: A Coordinated Sensing Flow Execution Engine for Concurrent Mobile Sensing Applications.*Proc. 10th ACM Conference on Embedded Networked Sensor Systems (SenSys)*. doi:10.1145/2426656.2426678

Kantarci, B., & Mouftah, H. T. (2014a). Reputation-based Sensing-as-a-Service for Crowd Management Over the Cloud.*Proc. IEEE International Conference on Communications (ICC)*, (pp. 3614--3619). doi:10.1109/ICC.2014.6883882

Kantarci, B., & Mouftah, H. T. (2014b). Trustworthy Sensing for Public Safety in Cloud-Centric Internet of Things. *IEEE Internet of Things Journal, 1*(4), 360–368. doi:10.1109/JIOT.2014.2337886

Kantarci, B., & Mouftah, H. T. (2014c). Mobility-aware Trustworthy Crowdsourcing in Cloud-Centric Internet of Things.*Proc. IEEE International Symposium on Computers and Communications (ISCC)*. doi:10.1109/ISCC.2014.6912581

Kantarci, B., & Mouftah, H. T. (2014d). Trustworthy Crowdsourcing via Mobile Social Networks.*Proc. IEEE Global Communications Conference (GLOBECOM)*, (pp. 2905--2910).

Kavajiri, R., Shimosaka, M., & Kashima, H. (2014). Steered Crowdsensing: Incentive Design towards Quality-Oriented Place-Centric Crowdsensing.*ACM International Joint Conference on Pervasive and Ubiquitous Computing*, (pp. 691--701).

Kavitha, T., & Sridharan, D. (2010). Security vulnerabilities in wireless sensor networks: A survey. *Journal of Information Assurance and Security, 5*, 31–44.

Kazemi, L., Shahabi, C., & Chen, L. (2013). Geotrucrowd: trustworthy query answering with spatial crowdsourcing.*Proc. 21st ACM SIGSPATIAL International Conference on Advances in Geographic Information Systems*, (pp. 304--313). doi:10.1145/2525314.2525346

Kim, M., Kotz, D., & Kim, S. (2006). Extracting a Mobility Model from Real User Traces.*Proc. 25th IEEE Intl. Conf. on Computer Communications (INFOCOM)*, (pp. 1--13). doi:10.1109/INFOCOM.2006.173

Lane, N. D., Chon, Y., Zhou, L., & Zhang, Y., i, F., Kim, D., Ding, G., Zhao, F. & Cha, H. (2013). Piggyback CrowdSensing (PCS): energy efficient crowdsourcing of mobile sensor data by exploiting smartphone app opportunities. *Proc. 11th ACM Conference on Embedded Networked Sensor Systems*, (pp. 7.1--7.14). doi:10.1145/2517351.2517372

Li, W., Chao, J., & Ping, Z. (2012). Security structure study of city management platform based on cloud computing under the conception of smart city.*InProc. Fourth International Conference on Multimedia Information Networking and Security (MINES)*, (pp. 91--94). doi:10.1109/MINES.2012.255

Liu, R., & Wassel, I. J. (2011). Opportunities and Challenges of Wireless Sensor Networks Using Cloud Services.*Proc. Workshop on Internet of Things and Service Platforms*, (pp. 4.1--4.7). doi:10.1145/2079353.2079357

Madria, S., Kumar, V., & Dalvi, R. (2014). Sensor Cloud: A Cloud of Virtual Sensors. *IEEE Software, 31*(2), 70–77. doi:10.1109/MS.2013.141

Mezghani, F., Daou, R., Nogueira, M., & Beylot, A.-L. (2014). Content dissemination in vehicular social networks: Taxonomy and user satisfaction. *IEEE Communications Magazine, 52*(12), 34–40. doi:10.1109/MCOM.2014.6979949

MicroStrain. (n.d.). *Sensorcloud*. Retrieved Feb 2, 2015, from http://www.sensorcloud.com

Miluzzo, E., Lane, N. D., Peterson, K. F. R., Lu, H., Musolesi, M., Eiseman, S. B., & Campbell, A. T. et al. (2008). Sensing meets mobile social networks: The design, implementation and evaluation of the CenceMe application.*Proc. ACM Conf. on Embedded Network Sensor Systems*, (pp. 337--350). doi:10.1145/1460412.1460445

Miorandi, D., Sicari, S., De Pellegrini, F., & Chlamtac, I. (2012). Internet of things: Vision, applications and research challenges. *Ad Hoc Networks*, *10*(7), 1497–1516. doi:10.1016/j.adhoc.2012.02.016

Misra, S., Barthwal, R., & Obaidat, M. S. (2012). Community detection in an integrated Internet of Things and social network architecture.*Proc. IEEE Global Communications Conference (GLOBECOM)*, (pp. 1647--1652). doi:10.1109/GLOCOM.2012.6503350

Misra, S., Chatterjee, S., & Obaidat, M. (2014). *On Theoretical Modeling of Sensor Cloud: A Paradigm Shift From Wireless Sensor Network*. IEEE Systems Journal; doi:10.1109/JSYST.2014.2362617

Mizouni, R., & El Barachi, M. (2013). Mobile Phone Sensing as a Service: Business Model and Use Cases. *Proc. Sevent International Conference on Next Generation Mobile Apps, Services and Technologies (NGMAST)*, (pp. 116--121).

Montenegro, G., Kushalnagar, N., Hui, J., & Culler, D. (2007). *Transmission of IPv6 Packets over IEEE 802.15.4 Networks*. Internet Engineering Task Force.

Moreno-Vozmediano, R., Montero, R. S., & Llorent, I. M. (2013). Key challenges in cloud computing: Enabling the future internet of services.*IEEE Internet Computing*, *17*(4), 18–25. doi:10.1109/MIC.2012.69

Musolesi, M., & Mascolo, C. (2007). Designing mobility models based on social network theory. *Mobile Computing and Communications Review*, *11*(3), 59–80. doi:10.1145/1317425.1317433

Nitti, M., Girau, R., & Atzori, L. (2013). Trustworthiness management in the social internet of things. *IEEE Transactions on Knowledge and Data Engineering*, *26*(5), 1253–1266. doi:10.1109/TKDE.2013.105

Pereira, P. P., Eliasson, J., Kyusakov, R., Delsing, J., Raayetinezhad, A., & Johansson, M. (2013). Enabling Cloud Connectivity for Mobile Internet of Things Applications.*IEEE Seventh International Symposium on Service Oriented System Engineering (SOSE)*, (pp. 518--526). doi:10.1109/SOSE.2013.33

Perera, C., Jayaraman, P., Zaslavsky, A., Christen, P., & Georgapoulos, D. (2013). Dynamic configuration of sensors using mobile sensor hub in Internet of Things paradigm.*Proc. IEEE Eighth Intl. Conf. on Intelligent Sensors, Sensor Networks and Information Processing*, 473--478. doi:10.1109/ISSNIP.2013.6529836

Perera, C., Jayaraman, P., Zaslavsky, A., Christen, P., & Georgapoulos, D. (2014a). Sensing as a service model for smart cities supported by Internet of Things. *Transactions on Emerging Telecommunications Technologies*, *25*(1), 81–93. doi:10.1002/ett.2704

Perera, C., Zaslavsky, A., Liu, C. H., Compton, M., Christen, P., & Georgapoulos, D. (2014b). Sensor Search Techniques for Sensing as a Service Architecture for the Internet of Things. *IEEE Sensors Journal*, *14*(2), 406–420. doi:10.1109/JSEN.2013.2282292

Phan, D. H., Suzuki, J., & Omura, S. & Oba, Katsuya. (2013). Toward Sensor-Cloud Integration as a Service: Optimizing Three-tier Communication in Cloud-integrated Sensor Networks. *Proc. 8th International Conference on Body Area Networks*, (pp. 355-362). doi:10.4108/icst.bodynets.2013.253639

Rahman, M., El-Saddik, A., & Gueaieb, W. (2011). Augmenting context awareness by combining body sensor networks and social networks. *IEEE Transactions on Instrumentation and Measurement, 60*(2), 345–353. doi:10.1109/TIM.2010.2084190

Rao, P., Saluia, P., Sharma, N., Mittal, A., & Sharma, S. V. (2012). Cloud computing for Internet of Things and sensing based applications.*Proc. Sixth International Conference on Sensing Technology (ICST)*, (pp. 374--380). doi:10.1109/ICSensT.2012.6461705

Rita, T. S. T., Liu, D., Fen, H., & Pau, G. (2011). Bridging vehicle sensor networks with social networks: Applications and challenges.*Proc. IET Intl. Conf. on Communication Technology and Application (ICCTA)*, (pp. 684--688).

Shahabi, C. (2013). Towards a Generic Framework for Trustworthy Spatial Crowdsourcing.*International ACM Workshop on Data Engineering for Wireless and Mobile Access (MobiDE)*, (pp. 1--4). doi:10.1145/2486084.2486085

Shelby, Z., Hartke, K., & Bormann, C. (2012). *Constrained Application Protocol (CoAP)*. IETF Draft.

Sheng, X., Xiao, X., Tang, J., & Xue, G. (2012a). Sensing as a service: A cloud computing system for mobile phone sensing.*Proc. IEEE Sensors Conference*, (pp. 1--4). doi:10.1109/ICSENS.2012.6411516

Sheng, X., Xiao, X., Tang, J., & Xue, G. (2012b). Sensing as a service: Challenges, solutions and future directions. *IEEE Sensors Journal, 13*(10), 3733–3741. doi:10.1109/JSEN.2013.2262677

Sheng, X., Xiao, X., Tang, J., & Xue, G. (2014). Leveraging GPS-Less Sensing Scheduling for Green Mobile Crowd Sensing. *IEEE Internet of Things Journal, 1*(4), 328–336. doi:10.1109/JIOT.2014.2334271

Shi, J., Mamoulis, N., Wu, D., & Cheung, D. W. (2014). Density-based place clustering in geo-social networks.*Proc. ACM SIGMOD International Conference on Management of Data*, (pp. 99--110).

Solmaz, G., & Turgut, D. (2013). Theme Park Mobility in Disaster Scenarios.*Proc. IEEE Global Communications Conference (GLOBECOM)*, (pp. 399-404).

Solmaz, G., & Turgut, D. (2014). Optimizing Event Coverage in Theme Parks. *Wireless Networks (WI-NET). Journal, 20*(6), 1445–1459.

Soyata, T., Ba, H., Heinzelman, W., Kwon, M., & Shi, J. (2013). Accelerating mobile cloud computing: A survey. In H. T. Mouftah (Ed.), *Communication Infrastructures for Cloud Computing* (pp. 175–197). Hershey, PS: IGI Global.

Suciu, G., Vulpe, A., Halunga, S., Fratu, O., Todoran, G., & Suciu, V. (2013). Smart cities built on resilient cloud computing and secure Internet of Things.*Proc. 19th International Conference on Control Systems and Computer Science*, (pp. 513--518). doi:10.1109/CSCS.2013.58

Tan, W., Blake, M. B., Saleh, I., & Dutdar, S. (2013). Social-network-sourced big data analytics. *IEEE Internet Computing, 17*(5), 62–69. doi:10.1109/MIC.2013.100

Wang, L., Xiong, H., & Zhang, D. (2013). effSense: Energy-Efficient and Cost-Effective Data Uploading in Mobile Crowdsensing.*Proc. International Workshop on Pervasive Urban Crowdsensing Architecture and Applications (PUCCA)*, (pp. 1075--1086). doi:10.1145/2494091.2499575

Wozniak, S., Rossberg, M., & Schaefer, G. (2013). *Towards trustworthy mobile social networking services for disaster response* (pp. 528–533). IEEE Pervasive Computing and Communications Workshops. doi:10.1109/PerComW.2013.6529553

Xiao, Y., Simoens, P., Pillai, P., Ha, K., & Satyanarayanan, M. (2013). Lowering the barriers to large-scale mobile crowdsensing.*Proc. 14th Workshop on Mobile Computing Systems and Applications*, (pp. 9.1--9.6). doi:10.1145/2444776.2444789

Xue, J., Yang, Z., Yang, X., Wang, X., Chen, L., & Dai, Y. (2013). VoteTrust: Leveraging friend invitation graph to defend against social network Sybils. *Proceedings - IEEE INFOCOM*, 2400–2408.

Yang, D., Fang, X., & Xue, G. (2011). ESPN: Efficientt server placement in probabilistic networks with budget constraint.*Proc. IEEE Int. Conference on Computer Communications (INFOCOM)*, (pp. 1269--1277). doi:10.1109/INFCOM.2011.5934908

Yang, D., Xue, G., Fan, X., & Tang, J. (2012). Crowdsourcing to smartphones: Incentive mechanism design for mobile phone sensing.*Proc. 18th International Conference on Mobile Computing and Networking (Mobicom)*, (pp. 173--184). doi:10.1145/2348543.2348567

Yerva, S. R., Saltarin, J., Hoyoung, J., & Aberer, K. (2012). Social and sensor data fusion in the cloud. *Proc. 13th Intl. Conf. on Mobile Data Management (MDM)*, (pp. 276--277). doi:10.1109/MDM.2012.52

Yilmaz, Y. S., Bulut, M. F., Akcora, C. G., Bayir, M. A., & Demirbas, M. (2013). Trend sensing via twitter. *International Journal of Ad Hoc and Ubiquitous Computing*, *14*(1), 16–26. doi:10.1504/IJA-HUC.2013.056271

Yu, X., Sun, F., & Cheng, X. (2012). Intelligent urban traffic management system based on cloud computing and Internet of Things.*Proc. International Conference on Computer Science Service System (CSSS)*, (pp. 2169--2172). doi:10.1109/CSSS.2012.539

Zhang, D., Xiong, H., Wang, L., & Chen, G. (2014). CrowdRecruiter: Selecting Participants for Piggyback Crowdsensing under Probabilistic Coverage Constraint.*Proc. ACM International Joint Conference on Pervasive and Ubiquitous Computing*, (pp. 703--714). doi:10.1145/2632048.2632059

Zhang, Y., Meratnia, N., & Havinga, P. (2010). Outlier Detection Techniques for Wireless Sensor Networks: A Survey. *IEEE Communications Surveys and Tutorials*, *12*(2), 159–170. doi:10.1109/SURV.2010.021510.00088

Zhou, J., Leppanen, T., Harjula, E., Ylianttila, M., Ojala, T., Yu, C., & Yang, L. T. et al. (2013). CloudThings: A common architecture for integrating the Internet of Things with cloud computing.*Proc. IEEE 17th Intl. Conference on Computer Supported Cooperative Work in Design*, (pp. 651--657). doi:10.1109/CSCWD.2013.6581037

ADDITIONAL READING

Cardone, G., Foschini, L., Bellavista, P., Corradi, A., Borcea, C., Talasila, M., & Curtmola, R. (2013). Fostering participaction in smart cities: A geo-social crowdsensing platform. *IEEE Communications Magazine*, *51*(6), 112–119. doi:10.1109/MCOM.2013.6525603

Carullo, G., Castiglione, A., Cattaneo, G., & De Santis, A., Fiore, U., Palmieri, F. (2013). *FeelTrust: Providing Trustworthy Communications in Ubiquitous Mobile Environment*. Proc. IEEE 27th Int. Conference on Advanced Information Networking and Applications (AINA), 1113—1120.

Corradi, A., Fanelli, M., Foschini, L., & Cinque, M. (2013). Context data distribution with quality guarantees for Android-based mobile systems. *Journal of Security and Communciation Networks*, 6(4), 450–460. doi:10.1002/sec.633

He, Y., & Li, Y. (2013). Physical activity recognition utilizing the built-in kinematic sensors of a smartphone. *International Journal of Distributed Sensor Networks*, 2013.

Li, W., Chao, J., & Ping, Z. (2012). *Security structure study of city management platform based on cloud computing under the conception of smart city.Proc. Fourth Intl. Conf. on Multimedia Information Networking and Security (MINES)*, 91—94. doi:10.1109/MINES.2012.255

Pan, B., Zheng, Y., Wilkie, D., & Shahabi, C. (2013). *Crowd sensing of traffic anomalies based on human mobility and social media.Proc. 21st ACM SIGSPATIAL International Conference on Advances in Geographic Information Systems*, 344—353. doi:10.1145/2525314.2525343

Sarma, S., Venkatasasubramanian, N., & Dutt, N. (2014). *Sense-making from distributed and mobile sensor data: A middleware perspective.Proc. 51st ACM/EDAC/IEEE Design Automation Conference*, 1—6. doi:10.1145/2593069.2596688

Yerva, S. R., Saltarin, J., Hoyoung, J., & Aberer, K. (2012). *Social and sensor data fusion in the cloud*. In Proc. IEEE 17th Intl. Conference on Mobile data Management (MDM), 276—277. doi:10.1109/MDM.2012.52

KEY TERMS AND DEFINITIONS

Cloud-Centric IoT: Integration of cloud-computing into the IoT architecture in order to enable scalability and cost-efficient service provisioning of IoT services. This is analogous to shifting the data-centric IoT to device-centric IoT concept in which users actively participate in sensing and computing tasks in collaboration with the cloud platform where compute intensive tasks are handled and analyzed data are stored.

Context-Awareness: The cloud platform aims at sensing the context by keeping track of and estimating user interactions, as well as future locations. Context information may denote the location of the sensing service provider at a particular time, the interactions of the sensing service provider with other proviedrs at a certain time, and/or the trustworthiness of the community with whom the sensing service provider is co-located.

Crowdsensing: A derivation of crowdsourcing where the crowdsourced data is collected through massively deployed distributed sensors. The sensors do not have to be a part of mission-centric network, and the sensor data regarding a particular phenomenon can be received from various mobile devices each of which is equipped with multiple built-in sensors.

Disinformation Probability: The ratio of the sensing tasks for which at least one outlier has been recruited to the total number of sensing tasks. High disinformation probability in an S^2aaS system introduces the risk of adversaries' manipulating the phenomenon to cause deception at the end user side.

Internet of Things (IoT): Virtually interconnected objects that are identifiable and equipped with sensing, computing and communication capabilities. The objects denote wireless/wired stand-alone sensors, RFID tags and/or built-in sensors in smart mobile devices. IoT is expected to accelerate several application areas including healthcare, smart environments, transportation, social networking, personal safety, environmental sensing and urban planning.

Mobile Social Network: Set of users that are connected to each other via their smart mobile devices. Users can be related to each other for having the same interest, living in the same area or, being co-workers.

Participatory Sensing: Collaborative sensing of a task; however in the context of S^2aaS, the sensors are not necessarily aware of each other. In most cases, participatory sensing and crowdsensing are used interchangeably.

Platform Utility: The difference between the total value of the sensing tasks received by the cloud platform and total compensation paid to the sensing service providers. In presence of adversaries who aim at disinformation, the value of the aggregated sensor data may be degraded.

Sensing Scheduling: Assigning timeslots to a sensing service provider for sensing each assigned task. In case of user-centric S^2aaS, the sensing service providers make their own sensing plans for the tasks that they are interested in, and they report their plans to the cloud platform. On the other hand, in case of platform-centric S^2aaS model, the platform recruits the mobile devices and assigns sensing plans for each task.

Sensing Service Provider Utility: The difference between compensation received by mobile device users for participating in S^2aaS activities and their sensing costs. Compensation can be by means of various types such as additional data package, additional voice package, cash and so on.

Sensing-as-a-Service (S^2aaS): A cloud inspired architecture where mobile device users provide sensor data through the built-in sensors in their mobile devices. Besides, sensing services can also be provided through virtualized sensors that are deployed in a cloud platform as the software complements of Wireless Sensor Network nodes. However, the advantage of former is decentralized resource control, task partitioning between mobile devices and the cloud servers, and enhanced security.

Social Attractiveness: The probability of selecting a sub-region as the next destination based on the fact that the user has more interaction with the users in the corresponding region compared to other regions in a particular terrain.

Trustworthiness: A reputation score assigned to sensing service providers based on the accuracy of their current and past sensor readings. Accuracy can be calculated centrally based on the truthfulness analysis of data via outlier or anomaly detection techniques.

This work was previously published in Enabling Real-Time Mobile Cloud Computing through Emerging Technologies edited by Tolga Soyata, pages 83-115, copyright year 2015 by Information Science Reference (an imprint of IGI Global).

Chapter 23
Internet of Things
Services, Applications, Issues, and Challenges

Padmalaya Nayak
GRIET, India

ABSTRACT

Internet of Things (IoT) is not a futuristic intuition, it is present everywhere. It is with devices, Sensors, Clouds, Big data, and data with business. It is the combination of traditional embedded systems combined with small wireless micro sensors, control systems with automation, and others that makes a huge infrastructure. The integration of wireless communication, micro electro mechanical devices, and Internet has led to the development of new things in the Internet. It is a network of network objects that can be accessed through the Internet and every object can be identified by unique identifier. By replacing IPV4, IPV6 plays a key role and provides a huge increase of address spaces for the development of things in the Internet. The objective of IoT application is to make the things smart without the human intervention. With the increasing number of smart nodes and amount of data that generated by each node is expected to create new concerns about data privacy, data scalability, data security, data manageability and many more issues that have been discussed in this chapter.

1. INTRODUCTION

In early 1990's, the evolution of new technology and new creativity could bring the concept of Internet as "Internet of Computers" as global networks with services provided as "world wide web" built on top of the original platform. Over the years, with the development of Web 2.0, the concept of "Internet of computers" has been changed to "Internet of people" where billions of people are connected through many social web sites. The boundary of Internet is getting expanded day by day with the integration of Micro Electro Mechanical devices (MEMs) and wireless communication technology and the devices are becoming smaller compared to the original PC with increasing processing and storage capacity. These devices are utilized in the form of mobile phones to note books, tablets etc. When these devices

DOI: 10.4018/978-1-5225-1832-7.ch023

are fitted with sensors along with the actuators, the sensing, computing, and communicating capability can be extended with other devices under the network connectivity.

According to Cisco the definition of "Internet of Everything" which brings together people, process, data and things to make networked connections more relevant and valuable than ever before by turning information into action. Cities globally have the potential to claim $1.9 Trillion in value from Internet of Things over the next decade. In a 2005 report, the International Telecommunications Union (ITU) suggested that the "Internet of Things will connect the world's objects in both a sensory and intelligent manner" (ITU report, 2005). By combining various technological developments, the ITU has described four dimensions in IoT: *item identification* ("tagging things"), *sensors and wireless sensor networks* ("feeling things"), *embedded systems* ("thinking things") and *nano-technology* ("shrinking things"). The definition of IoT is not limited to a particular domain and still it is fuzzy to define the vast concept. As a concluding remark, it can be defined as the combination of smart devices communicating with other devices, objects, environments and producing a huge volume of data. These data can be processed into useful actions that provide command and control to the things to enhance the quality of life. The elements of IoT are given in Figure 1.

1.1 Elements of IoT

The elements of IoT can be grouped in three categories: Hardware, Middleware, and Presentation (Gubbi et. al, 2013).

- **Hardware:** The main hardware components that plays major role in IoT are Sensors, Actuators and Embedded Processor.
- **Middle Ware:** The middleware technology implies on-demand storage and computing tools for data analytics. This is a software or collection of sub-layers interposed between the technological and application levels. The main feature is to hide the details of different technological complexity and allows the programmer independently to develop the specific IoT enabled application.
- **Presentation:** In IoT platforms visualization is critical as it involves user interaction with the environment. So visualization must be simple to understand and interpretation tools must be compatible with various platforms. It must be user friendly to use for different applications. In this section, some enabling technologies are discussed which can bring up the above stated components in practice. Only practical implementation of IoT can full-fill the dream of smart homes, smart environments, smart cities and smart country by making use of smart devices.

1.2 Technologies Involved in IoT

- **Wireless Sensor Networks:**
  - **WSN Hardware:** Wireless Sensor Network (WSN) brings a new paradigm of real time embedded system and has many potential applications in our daily life where traditional infrastructure based network practically infeasible. The core sensor node consists of a transceiver, a small embedded processor, power supply, interface unit and minimal storage used for gathering data about the physical world and transmits it to the actuators/controllers only if internet connectivity is provided. Figure 1 shows the architectural component of a sensor node. The actuator usually has stronger computational and processing power with longer

Figure 1. Elements of IoT

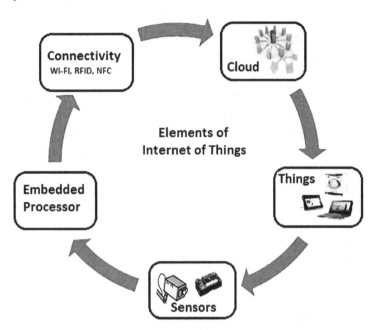

battery power support that receives the information from sensor nodes. Then it performs action to change the behavior of the physical worlds. Of course, the actuator has longer battery power support than the sensor nodes, but both the sensor nodes and actuators have limitations in energy sources, bandwidth. In typical, the applications of WSN are divided into two main categories such as monitoring and tracking. A broad number of monitoring and tracking systems are implemented in public and industry. Internet of Things (IoT) strongly relies on WSN for sensing activities.

- **WSN Protocol Layer:** Typically, Sensor Nodes are deployed randomly in an ad hoc manner with wireless connectivity to form a network for any type of application. Communication among the sensor nodes and finally to the sink node plays a major role in WSN activities. So, routing and MAC protocols are very critical in designing a sensor network topology. The lifetime of the network strongly depends on the energy consumption of individual node. Node dropouts and consequent degradation of network performances are very common and it occurs frequently. So, the layering architecture at the sink node must be capable enough to communicate with the outside world through the Internet.

- **Secure Data Aggregation/Fusion:** Sensor networks are normally deployed in harsh environments to monitor the events. Sensor data are shared among the sensor nodes and sent to the centralized or distributed systems for analytics. Node failures are often common phenomena in wireless sensor network. But, the self-organizing capacity of each node makes the network alive for longer period of time. So, an efficient data gathering system is required to prolong the network lifetime. At the same time, security is a major concern for reliable data delivery at the sink node. Many cryptographic techniques have been proposed in the literature. But, unfortunately most of the techniques are based on public key cryptography. In future, private key algorithms can be developed to ensure data privacy and security.

- ◦ **WSN Middleware Technology:** A mechanism that integrates cyber infrastructure with service oriented architecture and sensor network that could be accessible to all heterogeneous sensors applications in a deployment independent manner (Ghose & Das, 2008). A platform independent middleware such as open sensor web architecture (OSA) (Gubbiet.al, 2013) is required for developing sensor applications.

- **RFID Communication:** RFID incorporates both electromagnetic and electrostatic coupling on Radio Frequency (RF) portion of electromagnetic waves initially was used for identifying the stationary object, animal, or human being etc. In 1999, (Sarma et.al, 2000) an auto-ID centre of MIT developed a cheap (standardized transponders) and its successor organization EPC global, which can be used in Internet of Things to identify the billions of objects. The use of RFID in the supply chains of retail grants such as Wall Mart and Metro Is the result of such efforts. The evolution of RFID and associated infrastructure technologies has created lot of challenges among the retailers to visualize the IoT in practice. Over the years, with the technological development of embedded communication, RFID has been the key technology to design microchips for wireless data communication. For passive RFID, the cost as well as standardization has been reduced. Nowadays, RFID is not only used as the supply chains, but also it is used to manage books in the library, tools in the factories/industries, clothing items etc. In addition, physical objects are identified by the tag such as radio frequency identification (RFID) or Quick response codes (QR). Active RFID readers have their own battery supply and can instantiate the communication. Of the several applications, the main application of active RFID tags is in port containers (Bonser & keener, 2010) for monitoring cargo.

- **IP Protocol:** In future internet of things, every object or network node must have an IP address and use IP protocol. IPv6 will perform the key role by providing IP addresses to all the smart objects. By using the Internet services and applications everything can be addressed from anywhere at any point of time. But there is no clear vision so far how to categorize IPv6 in a proper manner so that public IP addresses can be partitioned and distributed publicly.

- **Things in the Web:** Conceptually, the World Wide Web (www) is part of the IoT as it is a huge infrastructure of smart objects. Recently, the concept "web of things" utilizes the http protocol and web 2.0 technologies that make use of asynchronous java script XML (Ajax). Using Ajax in web 2.0 reduces the communication delay and cost effectively between the server and client as embedded processors in the IoT require small resources than traditional web clients. For instance, browser in the PC or mobile phones and their services are typically addressed through URLs and controlled via a simple interface. Web 1.0 is one-way passive communication system and provides only read only contents whereas web 2.0 is collaborative two-way communication system. Users can actively participate in the web page through podcasting, blogging, tagging, social bookmarking etc. Further, web 3.0 is not far behind from us. Virtual shopping mall is an example of web 3.0. It is the idea of semantic web where all the information is stored in a systematic manner and it is understandable to both computer and human. Many view as it is the combined effort of artificial intelligence and semantic web. Web 3.0 provides a common frame work for integration of data from diverse sources and uses semantic web technologies, distributed data bases, machine learning, natural language processing etc. The user can navigate through a browser to a virtual market place and searches through the racks or stores, selects the product and pay for it. The vision for web 4.0 needs to implement the IoT in practice.

Figure 2. Architectural components of a sensor node

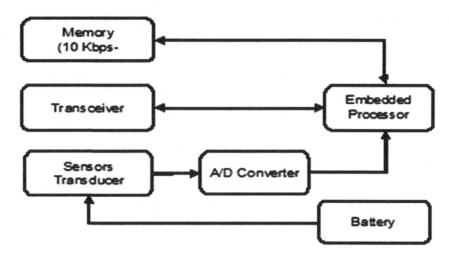

2. ISSUES AND CHALLENGES

There are several challenges and issues that need to be addressed while bringing IoT into practice. These challenges are discussed briefly in the following discussions.

2.1 IPv6 Addressing

It is predicted by Gartner (Gartner, 2012) that each and every object will be connected under one infrastructure through Internet by 2024. The concept of IoT will not only allow identifying the things uniquely but also control remote devices through Internet access. But the unique addressability of things may present many more concern under IoT. In 1st Feb 2011, the IPv4 public addresses managed by IANA (www.iana.org) have been exhausted completely. This provides a new paradigm for next generation of Internet protocol IPv6 by providing huge address spaces to the users and mobile devices. IPv6 uses 128 bits address that provides $2^{128}-1$ address spaces in order to connect internet enabled devices. The Internet Engineering Task Force (IETF) IPv6 over Low power WPAN (6LoWPAN) working group started in 2007 to work on specifications for transmitting IPV6 over IEEE 802.15.4 sensor networks.

There are several technologies such as Barcodes for simple identification (Brien, 2010), matrix barcodes for extended identification resources, RFID for digital identification, NFC for digital resources identification through smart objects and different infrastructure involved with IoT. But, all of the above, IPv6 would play a major role by providing individual IP address to each object and responsible for connecting things under a huge infrastructure. The elements which are already connected or going to be connected must be addressed according their functionalities and location. There are many critical points: uniqueness, reliability, scalability, and efficiency. But there is a big question and challenge how to partition this IP addresses in a planned manner (like Class A, B, C, D, & E in IPv4 address) for proper management of future infrastructure. Even if it is expected that IPv6 will opt the efficient technique for unique identification, there will be still some problem due to variable data type, concurrent operations, confluence of data from devices exacerbates further.

Wireless Sensor Networks are considered as the main building blocks for IoT. The group of sensor nodes can be identified to some extent with the help of IPV4 according their geographic location. But they cannot be identified individually. The data traffic can be channelized for persistent network functionalities ubiquitously and relentlessly is another aspect of IoT. Although TCP/IP puts maximum effort to route the information in an efficient and reliable way, IoT finds a bottleneck at the gateway and wireless devices. Again, the functionalities of existing devices must not be disturbed. The reliability of the data over the network, effective use of the devices from the user interface and the performance of the existing networks, should not be degraded due to the additional devices. To address these issues, the Uniform Resource Name (URN) is considered as the fundamentals of IoT. URN creates the replica of the resources that can be accessed through URLs.

Wireless Sensor Networks run on a different stack that is different from the Internet. IPv6 cannot provide global unique address for each sensor node. Keeping this in mind, there is a requirement for addressing the sensor nodes uniquely by the relevant gateway (Gubbi, 2013). A subnet with a gateway having a URN can solve this problem. At the subnet level the URN could be the unique identification for sensor nodes and a look up table at the gateway to address the device. At the node level, each node will have a URN (as numbers) to be addressed by the gateway. Overall, the whole network will have a connectivity of web from higher level (users) to lower level (sensor Network) accessible through URLs, addressability though URN and controllable through URC.

2.2 Mobility Issue

Mobility management is an essential feature for future Internet of things. The applicability of IoT with mobility support can be extended to many new areas. Mobility aware solutions increase the connectivity and enhance the adoptability to changes of location and infrastructure. Nowadays, the most present platform are the mobile platforms such as smart phones and tablets which enable a tremendous range of applications based on ubiquitous location, context awareness, social networking, and interaction with the environment. Future Internet potential is not limited to mobile platforms; else IoT is another emerging area of the future Internet, which is offering a high integration of the cybernetic and physical world. Therefore, since the physical world is mobile and dynamic, IoT will require support mobile and dynamic ecosystems.

2.3 Cyber Physical System (CPS)

There are no significant differences between IoT and Cyber Physical System (CPS) as these two technologies have been generated in parallel from two different communities. CPS is assumed to be a complex closed loop system that integrates both the physical components and computational entities under network connectivity while IoT is assumed to be an open loop system under the same network connectivity. In CPS, usually the physical processes are monitored and controlled by the embedded computers and networks with feedback loops where computations are affected by physical processes and vice versa (Lee, 2006). There are lots of challenges why because; the physical components of such systems require safety and reliability qualitatively different from those in general-purpose computing.

- **Automotive CPS:** Our traffic management system at National/International level is over-stressed. Future automotive system will integrate vehicle to vehicle (V2V) and vehicle to infrastructure

(V2I) communication or moreover vehicle to anything (V2X) communication technology that would allow interchange of information between vehicles and roadside units about the location, speed of vehicles and driving conditions on a particular road, traffic jams or accidents. This can prevent huge number of accidents, collisions and balances traffic loads by sending automated emergency calls.

- **Medical CPS:** Modern medical instruments with modern technologies equipped with network connectivity are referred to as Medical CPS, capable of monitoring and controlling the physical dynamics of patients' bodies. Proton therapy machines, bio-compatible and implantable devices are such examples. As complex interactions are involved with these devices, the safety and reliability of these devices are still challenging issue. For proper design and validation of Medical CPS, the modeling and efficient simulation of the patient body is an essential phenomenon.
- **Network of Cyber Physical Systems:** In CPS, concurrency of various processes is ubiquitous. Also these processes are working on multiple time scales. Today's TCP/IP networking technologies work on the principle of "best effort" service on which prediction of time scale is very difficult. Current software and hardware abstractions must be modified to account for concurrency and timescales. Efforts are already underway.

Example 1 - WBANs: In Wireless body area networks (WBANs), sensor nodes are fitted with a human body for sensing the biological information and transmitting to the control node attached with the patient or kept at an accessible distance. This control node transfers this information to the remote destinations of WBAN for proper diagnostics of a patient's body. One application of WBAN is focusing on home monitoring system where elderly people or physical disabled people can be monitored from home by reducing the hospitalized cost with early diagnosis.

Example 2 - Networked Water Resource Related Systems: Dams, Bridges, Etc.: Water is the main resource for each object to survive in this world. The applications may vary: it might lead to direct or indirect application. So the usage of water, the quality of water, distribution of water, and the wastage related issues must be analyzed in this cyber world.

2.4 3-V's of BIG DATA (Volume, Variety, Velocity)

The definition of big date has been derived from the traditional data along with the intelligence is being applied to it. For instance, sometimes question disturbs us that whether the data used by us can be 50 years old or not. The answer is certainly "yes" rather than "no". If we focus into the Indian history, we are using the same data which was available 1000 years back. Data never gets old and remains forever in its purest format. Application that interprets and analyzes the data can be changed and has been changed with due course of time. This has brought the concept of "big data". As the organizations are growing, their data associated with them is growing exponentially. Today, there are lots of complexities with the data. With the evolution of mobile devices, the view of capturing the data and experimenting with these data has become a great trend for new revolution. Big organizations have multiple applications and have data in different formats. The amount of data is so huge that it is impossible to categorize the whole data with single algorithm or single logic. All the organizations are facing a unique challenge that how to keep the data in a platform coming from different sources will give them a consistent view of their data. Along with this unique challenge, how to make sense of data in useful and actionable formats what the big data is facing from the revolution.

Figure 3. 3 V'S big data

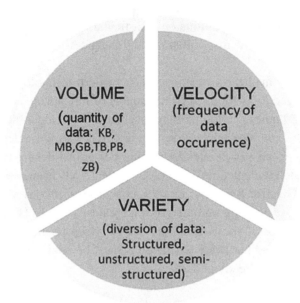

The combinations of 3V's such as Volume, Variety and Velocity define the properties of big data. It is very complex to define big data as lots of challenges are involved in it. Data requires to be analyzed, captured, secured, shared, stored, visualized and data privacy must be maintained. Volume defines as the quantity of data. Now, we can find the data storage not only in the form of text but also in the form of videos, music's and lots of images in our social media channels. Most of the enterprises have terabyte or peta-bytes of storage space. As the data grows, the applications and architectures to support the data need to be revaluated many times. Sometimes the same data can be evaluated from different angles. May be the data remains same, but the intelligent systems create new explosion. The big volume indeed represents big data.

Velocity refers to the speed of data at which data moves and reach at the user's location. There was a time when people were relying on the newspaper to get the latest news even though that news is yesterday's news. Now also newspaper follows the same logic. However, news channels and radios have replaced the newspaper by spreading the news faster. Today, mostly people are relying on social media to get the latest update and few seconds older messages also are getting discarded and pay attention to the recent updates. The data movement now is almost real time and windows update is reduced to fraction of seconds. This high velocity of data represents big data.

Variety includes different types of data that implies how data can be stored in variable formats. Data can be stored in excel, csv, access or in which way it can be accessed. More often data can be stored in a simple file format. In big organizations, data can be stored in a file format or in a pdf format or in form of videos, SMS etc. It is always easy to analyze the data if all are in the same format but most of the time it is available in the different formats. This is the challenge how to handle the big data in different formats to represent a meaningful way. Gratner's definition (Gartner, 2012) (the 3V's) is still widely applicable.

After Gratner, some author view about "veracity" that implies about the uncertainty of data. 3V's of data concept has been changed to 4V's. The quality of data can vary greatly. Accuracy and analysis of data depends on veracity of the data. According to the 4V's model, management of big data is a great challenging issue in IoT as it includes three properties not the quantity alone.

2.5 Cloud-Enabled IoT

The name cloud computing defines itself a type of computing that relies on sharing computing resources rather than a personal server or devices to handle applications. The word cloud is used as a metaphor for Internet and the phrase "cloud computing" defines Internet based commuting that integrates different services such as servers, storage, applications etc. It can be defined as a centralized storage of huge no. of remote servers having network connectivity allow on-line access for computer services and resources. Cloud computing services can be represented in three ways. These are Software as a service (SaaS), Platform as a service (PaaS), and Infrastructure as a service (IaaS). SaaS uses the web to develop applications owned by a third party vendor, whose interface is accessed by client side. PaaS allows the users for development and testing of applications in a simple cost effective way and the resources are managed and controlled by a third party vendor. In IaaS, the resources in terms of servers, networking, and storage space are used by the companies on pay per use basis. The deployment models of cloud computing can be classified as public, private, hybrid, and community cloud.

There are many different perspectives of cloud computing to enable IoT. But, the most recent paradigm to emerge which promises reliable services delivered through next generation data centres that are based on virtualized storage technologies. This platform acts as a receiver of data from the ubiquitous sensors; as a computer to analyze and interpret the data; as well as providing the user with easy to understand web based visualization. The ubiquitous sensing and processing works in the background are hidden from the user. The major challenge of cloud computing is to handle the growing demand of real time applications and reliable of data transmission in IoT.

Figure 4. Architecture of cloud computing

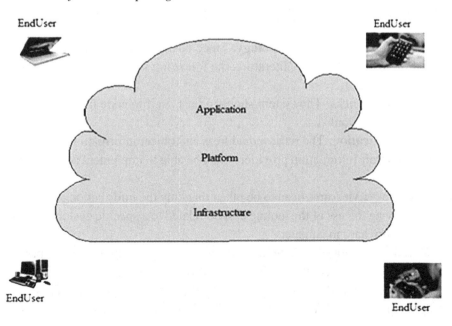

2.6 Theoretical Tools

In this section, some theoretical tools are discussed that need to be analyzed during the practical implementation of IoT.

- **Design/Control/Analysis of Non-Linear Control Systems:** Many physical/physiological are inherently non-linear. Thus control of such processes requires novel control schemes. In many CPS, the process dynamics needs to be modeled as linear/nonlinear systems involving physical loops. Control systems for such systems needs to be sophisticated.

- **Prediction of Stochastic Processes (Non-Linear Prediction Method):** IoT integrates different communication technologies, different software platforms, different infrastructures, and different service oriented applications. Here a big question arises as to how to optimize maximum outcome instead of several variabilities.

- **3-D/M-D Data Structures:** The interconnection structure associated with objects (e.g. sensors) need not be planned. Thus the data structures (graphs) representing their topology involves discovery of new data structures. So, dependencies of such data structures must be ensured during instructions are executed. The property of such data structures (e.g. fault tolerance and scalability) needs to be investigated.

- **Embedded Infrastructure with Rich Software Echo System:** The wide applications of IoT require high quality software development environment that can tightly bind the applications, commands and control, routing processes, and security of each node. Further, the scalability issue such at reuse of software and modification of existing software is the key success factor for developing IoT application.

- **Security and Privacy Need:** The embedded nature of IoT brings diverse ideas and new technologies where security, privacy and trust management issues take its own space to be focused. The highly configured network of IoT might lead to various possible cyber crimes as each object will be identified by unique public IP address. Security must be ensured at each level such as at device level, firmware level, cloud level and overall at end-to–end network level for future infrastructure of IoT.

- **Requirements Related to IoT Technology:** Since business processes are concerned, a high degree of reliability is needed. In the literature, the following security and privacy requirements are described (Weber, 2010).
  - **Resilience to Attacks:** The system should adjust itself to node failures and a single point of failure has to be avoided.
  - **Data Authentication:** The retrieved address and object information must be authenticated.
  - **Access Control:** Information providers must be able to implement access control on the data provided.
  - **Client Privacy:** Measures need to be taken that only the information provider is able to infer from observing the use of the lookup system related to a specific customer; at least, inference should be very hard to conduct.

- **Fast and Reliable Cryptographic Schemes:** Security is a widely used concept in wireless communication that deals with confidentiality, authentication, encryption, reliability, availability etc. Everything can be satisfied by set of protocols, algorithms and cryptographic primitives. The three main components of IoT such as WSN, RFID and Cloud are vulnerable to different types of attacks. Out of these three, RFID is the most vulnerable as it involves with object tracking and it seems there is a limitation on these devices to support high level of intelligence (Juels, 2006). Second, cloud is a huge storage of information. Third, WSNs are usually deployed in an unattended environment where human intervention is not possible. So the communications between these devices must support secure communication with data encryption, using standard protocols such as Transport Layer Security (TLS). It should include the use of security processors or encryption chips, and even use lightweight encryption for low-bandwidth devices. So efforts must be given to prevent, detect all the probable attacks at all each layer of TCP/IP protocol stack and strong cryptographic algorithms must be proposed to provide end to end connectivity.

- **Adequate Legal Framework:** The implementation of the IoT architecture globally and the use of RFID poses a number of legal challenges that need to be frame worked. Whether the existing international/national/state law is sufficient for implementing the IoT or new laws should be created? If new laws are regulated what is time frame for their implementation? Many more requirements must be taken into account while establishing a legal framework for implementing IoT where every object demands an ID to be identified.

3. APPLICATIONS OF IoT

IoT finds many applications in every aspect of human life as the embedded devices with limited CPU, memory, and power resources are network enabled. Its wide application varies from Environmental monitoring to Infrastructure management, Health Care Centre, Buildings and Automation, Large scale deployments to unique addressability things.

Figure 5. Issues and challenges in IoT

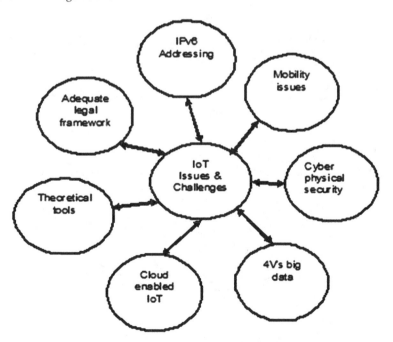

- **Personal and Home Automation:** IoT provides a perfect platform to control and manage the home electronic equipment such as refrigerator, air conditioner, Television, micro-oven etc. in a better way. It will focus on the consumers involved in the IoT in the same way as the Internet revolution. Smart phones can be used for communication along with several interfaces like blue tooth, NFC to measure various physiological parameters. There are several applications are available for Apple iOS, Google Androids and windows phone operating systems that measure various parameters. But it requires to be stored in centralized database such as cloud to access by the general physicians.

- **Enterprise:** One of the common IoT applications is Smart Environment. Environment monitoring is the first common application which keeps track of the number of occupants and manages the utilities within the building. Many test beds are already implemented and many more are under planned for the up-coming years. It includes the effect on citizens (health issue), transport, productivity, population, service etc.

- **Health Care:** Ubiquitous healthcare system has been visualized since two decades. Only thing is that body area networking system can be enhanced so that elderly and physical disabled people can be monitored from home itself. The doctors can access the patients remotely so that hospitalization cost can be reduced through early intervention and treatment.

- **Utilities:** Smart metering and smart grid is another potential application of IoT which is being used around the world. Efficient energy consumption is achieved by putting individual meter at

Figure 6. Applications of IoT

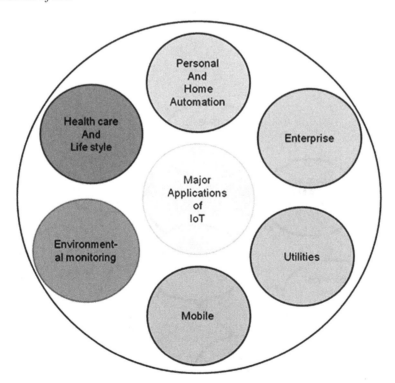

each house and monitoring each connectivity point within the house and modifying the way in which electricity is consumed. This information is used in city scale for balancing the load within the grid.

Camera network application is the mostly used application, surveillance used for tracking targets; detect suspicious activities and monitoring unauthorized access is widely used. Automatic behaviour analysis and behaviour detection is expected within few years. Further, video based IoT that integrates image processing, infrared; microphone and networking technology provides a new area of research.

Water Networking Monitoring and drinking water quality is the most critical application that is addressed in IoT. Effective sensors must be deployed in proper locations in order to ensure high supply quality. This can avoid accidental contamination among storm water drains, drinking water and sewage disposal etc. The same network can be extended to monitor irrigation in agricultural field.

- **Mobile:** Urban traffic is the main contributor for traffic noise pollution, air quality degradation. Traffic congestion imposes significant costs on economics and social activities in most of the cities. The transport IoT will enable to monitor the movement of vehicles, queue length, source-destination points, air pollution and noise emission by the use of WSN networks. Another important application in mobile IoT domain is efficient logistics management. This includes monitoring the items being transported as well as efficient transportation planning. The monitoring of items is carried out more locally within a truck replicating enterprise domain but transport planning is carried out using a large scale IoT network.

4. FUTURE RESEARCH DIRECTIONS

IoT could be brought into practiced in many possible ways as it is a huge infrastructure of things, services and objects. There is no single systematic approach to bring IoT in practice. For small instance, the use of a Raspberry Pi and sensor node can partially meet the requirements of IoT. In (Nayak et.al, 2015), a health care monitoring system is implemented with the integration of Raspberry-Pi and sensor node (body parameters measuring sensors) that can measure the human body heart beats, sugar level, blood pressure etc. Figure 7 shows an experimental set-up of raspberry pi, embedded processor and sensor node. In future, the same data can be stored in the cloud and can be accessed by health care experts during further investigations. Further, we plan to measure the water quality whether it is drinkable or not through the raspberry pi and water monitoring sensors. Similarly, many practical applications like e-health care, e-education, e-billing and many more e-compatibility application can be developed with micro-controllers, embedded processors, and sensor nodes under the infrastructure of IoT.

CONCLUSION

This chapter presents some practical challenges and issues involved in present and future Internet of Things. Some theoretical tools have been discussed that can be explored practically in future. It is not

Figure 7. Experimental set-up for health care monitoring system using Raspberry-Pi: a) Raspberry-Pi B+ Version; b) LPC 2148 embedded processor; c) blood pressure sensor; d) experimental set-up

a) Raspberry-Pi B+ Version   b) LPC 2148 Embedded Processor   c) Blood Pressure sensor

so easy task to find the tools that will bridge IoT, machine to machine (M2M) communication, machine to anything communication (M2X), and big data. Still, some integrated solutions started appearing. The convergence of M2M communication, Big Data, and the cloud will provide key capabilities for building next-generation systems and expanding the Internet of Things. Things in the Internet will resume communication and data sharing for billions of connected devices and systems through only IPv6 addressing Schemes. The sheer volume of data from human users and machine to machine applications will require advanced analytics capable of exploiting the Big Data and the computing power of the cloud.

REFERENCES

Atzori, L., Iera, A., & Morabito, G. (2010). The Internet of Things: A Survey. *Computer Networks, 54*(15), 2787–2805. doi:10.1016/j.comnet.2010.05.010

Bonsor, K., & Keener, C. (2010). *How Stuff Works/ How RFID works*. Retrieved from: http://electronics.howstuffworks.com/gadgets/high-tech-gadgets/rfid.htm

Brien, T. O. (2010). *In a Nutshell: What Are QR Codes?*. Retrieved from: http://www.switched.com/2010/06/21/in-anutshell-what-are-rr-codes/

Caceres, R., & Friday, A. (2012). Ubicomp systems at 20: Progress, opportunities, and challenges. *IEEE Pervasive Computing / IEEE Computer Society [and] IEEE Communications Society, 11*(1), 14–21. doi:10.1109/MPRV.2011.85

Cotzee, L., & Eksteen, J. (2011). The Internet of Things-Promise for the Future? An Introduction. In *Proceedings of IST-Africa Conference.*

Gartner's hype cycle special report for 2011. (2012). Gartner Inc. Retrieved from: http://www.gartner.com/technology/research/hype-cycles/

Ghose, A. & Das, S.K. (2008). Coverage and connectivity issues in wireless sensor networks: A survey. *Pervasive and Mobile Computing, 4*(2008), 303-334.

Gluhak, A., Krco, A., Nati, S., Pfisterer, P., Mitton, N., & Razafindralambo, T. (2011). A Survey on fascilities for experimental Internet of Things research. *IEEE Communications Magazine, 49*(11), 58–67. doi:10.1109/MCOM.2011.6069710

Gubbi, J., Buyya, R., Marusic, S., & Palaniswani, M. (2013). Internet of Things (IoT): A vision, architectural elements and future directions. *Future Generation Computer Systems, 29*(7), 1645–1660. doi:10.1016/j.future.2013.01.010

Haivan, L., Song, C., Dalei, W., Stergiou, N., & Ka-Chun, S. (2010). A remote markerless human gait communications. *IEEE Wireless Communications, 17*, 44–50. doi:10.1109/MWC.2010.5416349

International Telecommunications Union. ITU Internet Reports. (2005). The Internet of Things Executive Summary. Geneva: Author.

Juels, A. (2006). RFID security and privacy: A research survey. *IEEE Journal on Selected Areas in Communications, 24*(2), 381–394. doi:10.1109/JSAC.2005.861395

Lee, E. A. (2006). *Cyber Physical Systems-Are computing foundations adequate.* Position paper for NSF Workshop on Cyber Physical Systems: Research Motivation, Techniques and Roadmap, Austin, TX.

Marin-Lopez, R., Pereniguez-Gracia, F., Gomez-Skarmeta, A. F., & Ohba, Y. (2012). Network access security for the Internet: protocol for carrying authentication for the Internet: protocol for carrying authentication for Network access. *IEEE Communications Magazine, 50*(3), 84–92. doi:10.1109/MCOM.2012.6163586

Nayak, P., Sowmya, M., & Pranaya, J. (2015). Integration of Sensor Node with Raspberry-Pi for Health Care Monitoring Application. In *Proc. of International Conference on Advances in Electronics and Computer System.*

Pham, N., Ganti, R. K., Uddin, Y. S., Nath, S., & Abdelzaher, T. (2010). Privacy-preserving reconstruction of multidimensional datamaps in vehicular participatory sensing. *European Conf. On Wireless Sensor Networks.*

Sang, Y., Shen, H., Inoguchi, Y., Tan, Y., & Xiong, N. (2006). Secure Data Aggregation in Wireless Sensor Networks. *Survey (London, England)*, 315–320.

Sarma, S., Brock, D. L., & Ashton, K. (2000). *The Networked Physical World. TRMIT-AUTOIDWH-001.* MIT Auto-ID Center.

Seventh Framework Programme. (2010). *European Research Cluster on the Internet of Things.* Retrieved from http://www.internet-of-things-research.eu/

Sundmaeker, H., Guillemin, P., Friess, P., & Woelffle, S. (2010). *Vision and Challenges for Realising the Internet of Things*. European Commission.

Tan, G., Jarvis, S. A., & Kemarrec, A.-M. (2009). Connectivity-guaranteed and obstacle-adaptive deployment schemes for Mobile Sensor Networks. *IEEE Transactions on Mobile Computing*, *8*(6), 836–848. doi:10.1109/TMC.2009.31

Weber, R. H. (2010). Internet of Things – New security and privacy challenges. *Computer Law & Security Review*, *26*(2010), 23-30.

Welbourne, E., Battle, L., Cole, G., Gould, K., Rector, K., Raymer, S., & Borriello, G. et al. (2009). Building the Internet of Things using RFID The RFID ecosystem experience. *IEEE Internet Computing*, *13*(3), 48–55. doi:10.1109/MIC.2009.52

Wu, F. J., Kao, Y. F., & Tsen, Y. C. (2011). From Wireless sensor Networks towards Cyber Physical Systems. *Pervasive and Mobile Computing*, *2*(4), 397–413. doi:10.1016/j.pmcj.2011.03.003

This work was previously published in the Handbook of Research on Advanced Wireless Sensor Network Applications, Protocols, and Architectures edited by Niranjan K. Ray and Ashok Kumar Turuk, pages 353-368, copyright year 2017 by Information Science Reference (an imprint of IGI Global).

Chapter 24

The Access of Things:
Spatial Access Control for the Internet of Things

Peter J. Hawrylak
University of Tulsa, USA

Matthew Butler
University of Tulsa, USA

Steven Reed
University of Tulsa, USA

John Hale
University of Tulsa, USA

ABSTRACT

Access to resources, both physical and cyber, must be controlled to maintain security. The increasingly connected nature of our world makes access control a paramount issue. The expansion of the Internet of Things into everyday life has created numerous opportunities to share information and resources with other people and other devices. The Internet of Things will contain numerous wireless devices. The level of access each user (human or device) is given must be controlled. Most conventional access control schemes are rigid in that they do not account for environmental context. This solution is not sufficient for the Internet of Things. What is needed is a more granular control of access rights and a gradual degradation or expansion of access based on observed facts. This chapter presents an access control system termed the Access of Things, which employs a gradual degradation of privilege philosophy. The Access of Things concept is applicable to the dynamic security environment present in the Internet of Things.

INTRODUCTION

Today, access to buildings and facilities is often controlled by electronic systems; gone are the days of large key rings. Magnetic stripe technology is one such technology that encodes an identifier linked to a person or employee on their identification card. A scanner at the door reads the identifier and sends it back to a centralized system. The centralized system replies with a message granting access (opening the door) or denying it (keeping the door locked). Wireless versions of this system are available and widely used, with most based on radio frequency identification (RFID) technology. Both systems rely

DOI: 10.4018/978-1-5225-1832-7.ch024

on the person keeping control of their identification card and preventing it from being copied. This has led to binary security policies for access control systems providing either complete access to all authorized areas or no access at all, and does not function well in the case of copied or "cloned" RFID tags or identification cards. The binary security policy often fails to prevent the cloned RFID tag from gaining entry or locks out the legitimate RFID tag preventing the employee from accomplishing their tasks. The wireless nature of RFID makes cloning possible without physical contact with the legitimate user. A security policy and supporting technology is needed to enable access rights to be gradually and gracefully reduced to allow the legitimate user to complete most of their tasks, while preventing significant damage caused by the malicious user. This chapter will present a framework for such a system for RFID and will discuss the integration of other data sources into this system, yielding a truly Internet of Things approach to spatial access control.

The chapter will begin with an overview of the Internet of Things and the need for access control in this environment. Next, current access control systems and policies, the difficulties introduced by the traditional binary access policy, and the requirements for access control within the Internet of Things will be presented. The graceful degradation of privilege policy will then be introduced and the RFID implementation of this policy will be described. Security measures available to RFID technology to prevent cloning will be highlighted. The extension of the graceful degradation of privilege model to the Internet of Things will be presented. This extension is termed "the Access of Things," and provides robust access control policies and options for the Internet of Things. The Access of Things concept integrates information from a variety of sources to achieve multi-point identification and authentication of the user. The chapter will conclude with a discussion of future research areas, issues facing access control systems, and how the system presented in this chapter begins to address those concerns.

INTERNET OF THINGS CONCEPT

The Internet of Things (IOT) concept envisions an environment where devices automatically connect together to solve problems or better monitor the environment. The problems that can be addressed in the IOT framework are larger than a single device could solve on its own. This may be due to lack of computing power or lack of access to input data. The concept of the IOT is not necessarily one of human-centric applications, but one that will include more machine-to-machine (M2M) applications facilitated by massive M2M networks supported by the IOT's infrastructure. The differentiator between the IOT and a generic Internet capable device is the increased degree of autonomy of the device and reliance on M2M communication. In fact, most IOT applications are based around the M2M communication with the human user being a consumer of information or service rather than the initiator of operations.

The initial idea was to provide every device with an IP address for routing data (traffic) between devices to facilitate M2M communication. While IP is a widely used protocol, it may not be the best protocol for all applications and other protocols are available to supplement IP. This is true for IOT applications because many IOT devices have limited computational and communication resources, especially remote sensor nodes.

IOT applications include smart health, remote healthcare (You, Liu, & Tong, 2011; Revere, Black, & Zalila, 2010; Chen, Gonzalez, Leung, Zhang, & Li, 2010; Wicks, Visich, & Li, 2006), home management, traffic management (Foschini, Taleb, Corradi, & Bottazzi, 2011), smart grid, and industrial control systems. The notion of networks forming, changing, and dissolving on their own raises questions about what resources should be shared. Each actor in the IOT must make this decision on their own and based on their perception of the environment and the application. Spatial access control, including building access control systems, is one example of such a system.

Cooperation and Network Construction Aspects

The IOT will operate over a wide range of wired and wireless networks. Generally, wired networks provide the long-haul backbone connectivity and handle large amounts of data, while wireless networks provide intermediate and the last-mile connection to the user or remote sensor. Some common wireless networking technologies currently used in IOT applications include radio frequency identification (RFID), ZigBee, Bluetooth, and 6LoWPAN (Kushalnagar, Montenegro, & Schumacher, 2007).

RFID systems for retail, inventory, and supply chain applications require a unique identifier for each item. This is in contrast to the typical UPC (Universal Product Code), commonly referred to as a "barcode," which only provides the type of item. RFID needs a unique identifier to allow the reader to distinguish between multiple instances of the same type of item in order to obtain an accurate count. GS1 has produced many specifications for unique identifiers (EPCglobal, 2010) for RFID systems, with the UHF Gen-2 (EPCglobal, 2008) systems being the primary users.

ZigBee is a protocol stack constructed on the PHY and MAC layers provided by IEEE 802.15.4 (IEEE, 2011). Mesh networking is advantageous because it provides a communication infrastructure that is resilient to node failure. ZigBee has been heavily used to provide wireless connectivity between home automation devices. There are two types of network architectures in ZigBee: peer-to-peer and star. The star topology utilizes a single device, known as the PAN coordinator, that all traffic passes through (IEEE, 2011). The peer-to-peer topology allows any two devices to communicate directly without having to go through the PAN coordinator and can support mesh networking (IEEE, 2011). ZigBee enables significant flexibility in devices connecting (joining) or disconnecting (leaving) the network. However, the protocol is based on a beaconing system that consumes a significant amount of energy over time. This puts strain on the PAN coordinator and those nodes that route a lot of traffic in peer-to-peer topologies. These energy restrictions pose significant problems for ZigBee and other communication protocols for battery powered devices.

6LoWPAN is a protocol focusing on the transmission of small messages and is based on IPv6 and the IEEE 802.15.4 PHY and MAC layers (Kushalnagar, Montenegro, & Schumacher, 2007). It is intended for use in low-functionality devices such as sensor nodes that require long lifetimes and limited or no interaction from humans (e.g., replacing batteries). These devices traditionally send small messages consisting of a few sensor readings. The implementation of the protocol stack in software on an embedded device is a key concern and one of 6LoWPAN's goals was to reduce the software footprint (Mulligan, 2007). Message size in 6LoWPAN is limited 81 octets (1 octet equals 8-bit and is typically identical to a byte) because most messages in the IOT will be small status, informational (e.g. sensor readings), or alarm messages (Kushalnagar, Montenegro, & Schumacher, 2007). The majority of messages transmitted in the IOT will be small, often less than 40 bytes. Most of these messages will be sent within a local network, often to a device's neighbor (single hop messages). 6LoWPAN provides support for efficient transmission of these messages through header compression which leverages information included by headers in the MAC layer of IEEE 802.15.4 and reduces the overhead required by 6LoWPAN on messages (Mulligan, 2007). This allows for more data to be transmitted in each message or allows the minimum message size to be reduced.

These protocols each provide components that are useful for the IOT. RFID systems provide guidance on development and implementation of unique identifiers that can be correlated into device addresses. The development of passive RFID devices with simple computing resources provides a basis for design low-power devices for the IOT. ZigBee provides support for data communication in a dynamic and unpredictable environment where the primary goal is to ensure message delivery. 6LoWPAN provides guidance on implementation of IP using the same MAC and PHY layers (IEEE 802.15.4) as ZigBee but a version of the IP protocol geared to low-power devices.

OVERVIEW OF THE ACCESS CONTROL PROBLEM

Access to resources and places (e.g. buildings) must be limited to authorized users. The access could be physical, virtual, or a combination of the two. Physical access is typically thought of as limiting who can access what rooms or areas, or what resources each person can use or remove from the location. Physical access control is mostly concerned with personal safety (e.g., preventing unauthorized persons from entering a building or floor), preventing theft of property, and workplace safety (e.g., interlock controls on a piece of machinery to prevent operator injury). Virtual access control focuses on protecting computer files (e.g., bank records) and device resources (e.g., processor time). Cyber-physical systems blend physical and cyber components and form the third category of access control problems. Cyber-physical systems have assets from both domains and must support access control policies for both domains. Examples of cyber-physical systems include the electric grid, municipal water treatment plants, and robotic technology (e.g., surgical robots). Many IOT systems fall into the cyber-physical category with the IOT providing the infrastructure to connect the control system and sensor modules together.

Traditionally, access control has dealt with physically securing locations, such as a building or room, against unauthorized entry, or with securing a computer system against unauthorized use. These two issues are linked in many IOT systems: the first is a physical access control problem with solutions from the physical security domain, while the second is a data access control problem, with solutions primarily from the cyber-security domain, although physical security is an important factor. Cyber-security often relies on physical security at some level to prevent an attacker from gaining physical access to the cyber-asset in question. Access control systems guard resources and places from unauthorized use or entry, as well as provide the means to verify a user's credentials.

Extension of Access Control to the Internet of Things

The IOT will increase the integration of the physical and cyber-security domains because devices will need to determine what resources to provide to the IOT (larger device society) and to whom to provide these resources. This blurs the definition of what the asset is because it may be a collection of cyber and physical items. Access control in the IOT will need to support collecting identity verification input from multiple data sources, while maintaining the assumed quality of service.

OVERVIEW OF EXISTING ACCESS CONTROL SYSTEMS

Physical and cyber access controls systems may be fully characterized by two essential architectural components – their *authorization policy model*, and their *access control enforcement mechanism* (Bertino, Samarati, & Jajodia, 1993; Sandhu, 1993; Sandhu & Samarati, 1994). A policy model incorporates a language or system for expressing the rules of access by a subject (user or process) to an object (physical or cyber asset or resource). A policy model also commonly allows for the qualification of access type (e.g., "read," "write," or "execute"). The enforcement mechanism of an access control solution integrates authentication services that bind a subject to an identity with system-level controls that accept access requests, and permit or block access to a resource based on the outcome of an access request decision by a policy engine. System-level controls mediating access may exist at the application-level, in an operating system, or on a network.

Conventional access control methods base binary authorization request decisions on simplistic criteria, either providing full privileges or no privileges at all. These systems rely on some method for a user to prove their identity or role, and a backend system that makes access decisions. A wide range of authentication schemes and technologies exist for a user to prove their identity, including passwords, identity (ID) badges with digitized information contained in a magnetic strip or RFID tag, or through biometric identification (e.g., fingerprint or iris scan).

The most prevalent access control solutions are centralized systems that utilize terminals where individuals present their identification credentials. The identification information is transferred to a backend policy engine that determines whether or not access should be granted or what level of access to grant. The policy engine may simply verify that the identity is on a list of authorized subjects or may apply some additional rules to verify an identity or qualify its access to a resource. Examples of such rules include limiting the times when certain individuals can access a building or declining a credit card charge because of suspicious behavior noted by the system. After the decision is made, the appropriate message is sent back to the physical location to effect the decision (e.g., unlock or not unlock the door). In a cyber-access request, the notion of physical location is often equated to the location of the cyber asset at the present time.

This section contains a brief overview of three of the most common technologies used to identify individuals in an access control system: magnetic stripe, RFID, and biometrics. Each technology offers benefits and drawbacks, which are highlighted in the following subsections. The Access of Things concept requires an architecture that supports taking input from multiple identify verification technologies and other sensors to determine access rights.

Magnetic Stripe Technologies

Magnetic stripe cards utilize a magnetic material to encode information. Traditional embodiments of this technology do not support the ability to write new or to update existing information to the magnet material. As such, they are useful in providing a static identifier that is linked to a person, but cannot be dynamically challenged (e.g., as part of a challenge-response authentication procedure) or updated with new data (e.g., addition or removal of access privileges).

RFID Technologies

RFID technologies remove the need to physically swipe an access card through a magnetic scanner; rather, the user just presents the RFID tag (access badge) within the read range of the RFID reader to gain access. The range at which the RFID tag can be read is dependent on the technology and frequency used. There are three main types of RFID systems: passive, battery-assisted passive (BAP), and active. Passive systems employ RFID tags that have no on-board power source (e.g. a battery) and harvest the energy needed for operation from the RFID reader's RF signal. Passive RFID tags communicate via backscatter by modulating the signal transmitted by the RFID reader. Backscatter is a very low-power method of communication and does not require the RFID tag to have a dedicated or powered transmitter. The tag modulates the RFID reader's signal by adjusting its antenna impedance to either reflect or absorb the transmitted RF energy. BAP systems utilize BAP tags which communicate using backscatter but have an on-board power source to power sensors or processing elements. However, a BAP tag's on-board power source is not used to power a transmitter or receiver. BAP RFID tags have a longer communication range than passive RFID tags because they do not have to use any of the RF energy harvested from the reader's signal for powering and all of that energy can be used for communication purposes. Active RFID systems employ tags containing an on-board power supply, such as a battery, and communicate using a powered (active) transmitter and receiver. Active RFID tags can communicate at longer distances than BAP RFID tags because the powered receiver can extract weaker signals and the powered transmitter can send stronger signals.

Frequency is another factor in determining the range of RFID systems. Low frequency (LF) systems, typically operating in the 125-135kHz range have a range of 1m. These systems are often used for animal tracking. High frequency (HF) systems operate in the 13.56MHz ISM (industrial, scientific, and medical) band, which is available worldwide, have a range of 1-3m depending on the transmitter power level. HF systems are often used for contactless payment, public transportation fare, and access or identity badges. Ultra-high frequency (UHF) systems operating in the 860-960MHz range, depending on the regulatory region (location), have ranges of 1-6m. These systems are used in asset tracking applications, primarily in the retail industry. This chapter will focus on the access control problem and the HF (13.56MHz) RFID technology.

Biometric Technologies

Biometric technologies (Jain, Hong, & Pankanti, 2000) include fingerprint scanners, iris scanners, hand geometry scanners, and facial recognition. There are concerns about the privacy aspects of these systems because the information (fingerprint, iris print, facial recognition data) would be stored in data repositories and could be used for other activities such as clandestine tracking or in criminal investigations (e.g., universal fingerprint database). There are also health concerns about the transmission of disease through bodily fluids. This is especially true for those systems based on the iris scanner. Facial recognition avoids these health issues and can be easily deployed by using input from a camera. However, the algorithms for facial recognition have met with varying degrees of accuracy, with more accurate algorithms requiring longer processing times.

Motivation to Combine Spatial and Adaptive Access Control Techniques

There are several forms of access control, many of which are not mutually exclusive. The naive solution to user privilege management is to allow full access or no access, termed *Binary Access Control* in this chapter. In a Binary Access Control system, users either have access to a resource, or they are restricted from access to a resource. A Binary Access Control system is simple to implement, understand, and use, but is not without drawbacks. First, if the system does not support automatic modification of user privileges it will not be able to respond quickly to observed events. Second, if a user's access credentials are compromised, few mitigation strategies are available to be employed: either the user retains the same rights, thereby allowing attackers the same access as the legitimate user, or the user is prohibited from all access, preventing the attacker from gaining access, but also inhibiting the legitimate user from completing his or her more safety critical tasks.

Another form of access control is Spatial Access Control. Rather than being concerned with virtual access to data, Spatial Access Control is the practice of managing physical access to areas requiring a security clearance. Areas that require higher levels of clearance are likely to house higher valued resources.

DIFFICULTIES WITH THESE SYSTEMS AND POLICIES

Binary Access Control is often applied for Spatial Access Control purposes, and often times this is all that is necessary. However, in many safety and confidentiality centered environments, this is not the best option. For example, in a hospital, if a doctor is prevented from getting into the operating room, this could be the difference between life and death; or when credit card fraud is detected and the card is deactivated to prevent malicious spending, the legitimate user still needs to be able to make emergency transactions in order to prevent being stranded money-less. In both scenarios it would be better to provide a gradual loss of privilege. For example, preventing the doctor from entering sensitive areas such as the pharmacy, or reducing the spending limit of the credit card in question to enable the real user to obtain taxi fare back to their hotel.

In any given scenario, if the access control system were able to accurately measure the amount of risk involved in permitting or disallowing a given action by one of its users, the system would be better able to achieve the goal of providing a custom tailored access policy in response each request. In order to predict this level of risk and subsequently use it to dynamically make decisions about user privileges, we need a Dynamic Risk Assessment Access Control system, or DRAAC (Butler, 2011).

Implementation of the Graceful Degradation of Privilege System Using RFID

The only way to make an accurate estimation of risk at any given time is to have some related context about the situation. This means a large focus of the DRAAC system is collecting data. Data is not limited to a particular source in any way; almost any information that can be gathered about the environment under supervision can help make better risk assessments. The data gathered is used to make inferences about user behavior or predict future behavior. When an access control decision needs to be made, the system can quickly evaluate whether a user is acting with malicious intent based on data gathered about the user and the state of the system. However, Risk is not directly associated with the user's behavior. Risk is computed as a function of their behavior, represented by a Likelihood of attack value, and the resource they are attempting to access, represented by an Impact value as defined by Equation 1 (Butler, Hawrylak, & Hale, 2011).

Risk = Likelihood * Impact (1)

Once the Risk of allowing or disallowing access has been computed, a decision can be made. This may range based on the application ranging from disallowing a user access to contacting the security department.

DRAAC Overview

DRAAC is designed to be modular. The modular architecture of DRAAC is shown in Figure 1. The system used to determine Likelihood values is not dependent on the system for reporting Impact values. Furthermore, the Risk can be calculated in various ways dependent on the scenario, and how this data is purposed to result in access control decisions is not dependent on any of the previous steps. One method for determining Risk is given in Equation (2) where Risk is defined by the product of cumulative Likelihood and cumulative Impact (Hartney, 2012).

Risk = (Cumulative Likelihood) * (Cumulative Impact) (2)

Risk is computed in the "Risk Computation Module" of DRAAC and this module supports the ability to calculate multiple Risk values based on different inputs and/or expressions. This enables risk to be analyzed from different perspectives and may yield a more accurate view of risk.

Figure 1. DRAAC architecture

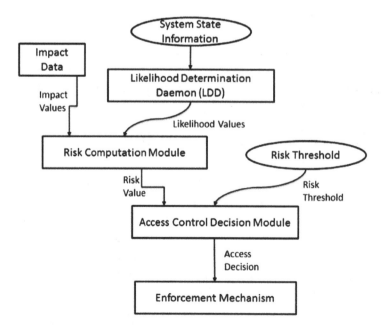

Notice that the philosophy of DRAAC is not necessarily tied to Spatial Access Control systems at all. A dynamic risk assessment system could be used for virtual access as well, watching user behavior to determine if they are attempting to breach the system. The original implementation of DRAAC was to provide graceful reduction in user access rights on a computer (Butler, 2011).

In our implementation of DRAAC, the Likelihood Determination Daemon (LDD) is written in Python. The LDD is responsible for gathering data as well as operating on the data to make predictions and assertions, all the things involved with deriving the likelihood of an attack. Likelihood is important because it can be used to identify which assets a user is most likely to access. This information can be used to help build a user profile for normal behavior.

Data gathered by the various sensors (e.g., RFID readers) in the system is stored in a simple log file. Items termed "Facts" are derived from these data. A data item could be a Fact or it may be part of a larger Fact that is identified through processing. The Watchdog library is used for cross-platform compatible file-system observation; it is used to watch the log file for new events fired. The identification of suspicious activity is done using the CLIPS expert system. CLIPS has a set of preset "Rules" which operate on dynamically gathered Facts. Rules can generate more Facts, potentially causing more Rules to be applicable and execute, or they can make Python calls to the LDD.

Extension to RFID

The first implementation of DRAAC was used with virtual access control, and the data it collected was SSH login attempts along with geographic location of the attempted login (Butler, 2011). In this implementation, the focus is using reads of RFID tags by RFID readers in different locations to make Spatial Access Control decisions (Butler, Reed, Hawrylak, & Hale, 2013). The RFID reader used was the SecuraKey ET4-AUS-D with a custom client written using Visual C#.

The DRAAC log file is targeted by the RFID reader software where any scan events are written out. Watchdog will catch the changes to the log file and notify the LDD. The LDD will read the newest change to the log and generate a Fact to inject into the CLIPS system. Any applicable CLIPS rules will fire, usually causing a chain reaction of new events: Fact generation, Fact deletion, and more Rule firing. If suspicious activity is identified, the LDD will be notified. Once the LDD has made a decision on the Likelihood of attack, the information is passed on to the Risk Computation Module, which is responsible for Risk computation. In the RFID implementation of DRAAC the LDD monitors the RFID readers located at each door and creates Facts based on their reads. These Facts indicate what doors an individual tries to access. This information can be used to locate the individual which can then be used to help decide if that individual should be granted access to a given area (room).

The syntax for writing Rules for CLIPS is unlike most other programming languages, but the logic is the same. The pattern for a rule is illustrated in Figure 2. The rule starts with a name (line 1 of Figure 2), which allows the rule to be referenced (used) in other rules. Next, the If-clause documents the conditions that must be true (preconditions) for the rule to fire (execute). Finally, the Then-clause contains the actions to be taken when the rule fires.

Figure 3 shows an example of a rule for the RFID implementation of DRAAC that generates a Fact for the first time an individual (ID badge or card) is observed. In English this would be read as: "If the system reads a RFID tag at scanner $s1$, time $t1$, and with card ID $c1$, and the system has never seen the card $c1$ before, Then assert the fact that the system never seen $c1$ before, and assert the fact that now we have seen $c1$."

Figure 2. Syntax of a CLIPS rule

Figure 2. Syntax of a CLIPS rule

```
1  < Name of rule >
2  < If – conditions >
3  < Then – assertions >
```

Figure 3. Example of a rule in the RFID DRAAC system

```
1  no prior scans
2  If :(rfid – scan(time ?t1)(scannerid ?s1)(cardid ?c1))
3     (not(seenBefore(cardid ?c1)))
4  Then :(assert(noPriorScan(cardid ?c1)))
5     (assert(seenBefore(cardid ?c1)))
```

One thing to take note of is that CLIPS rules use prefix notation. The last part of the If clause (see line 3 of Figure 3) is checking that there is not a fact named "seenBefore" with card ID *c1* (here card ID and tag ID are used interchangeably). If this Rule successfully fires, the second part of the Then clause is executed (see line 5 of Figure 3) asserting the fact "seenBefore" with card ID *c1* which prevents this Rule from ever being applicable for this card ID in the future (unless some other rule retracts the relevant Fact). This is the first rule that is evaluated for any RFID tag (ID badge or card) in our implementation of DRAAC. It is used to identify new ID cards that the system knows nothing about from ID cards which the system does have information about. The "seenBefore" fact is used to track whether or not the system has observed the ID card before or not. The choice of how long the system remembers (e.g., one day) each ID card is important: longer memory requires more space for the log file and processing time, but provides additional information that can be used to make more accurate future decisions. These tradeoffs must be evaluated and balanced to provide adequate security while meeting the transaction time requirements.

The first part of the Then clause (see line 4 in Figure 3) asserts the "noPriorScan" fact which is used to indicate that this is the first time the card ID has been observed. While this may appear to be a contradiction of the "seenBefore" fact, it is not. The "seenBefore" fact only states that the current scan is not the first time the card ID has been observed. The "noPriorScan" fact tells the system that all facts relating to the card ID in question are for the first time that card has been observed and will be used to trigger other rules the next time the card ID is observed. This information is important for physical access control and can be used to help identify cases were an individual tries to enter an interior door (area) without first entering through an exterior door. This can also be used to identify cases of "tailgating" where an individual follows someone else through a checkpoint without carding in themselves. Once the card ID is observed for again, the "noPriorScan" fact is retracted (removed) from the list of Facts maintained by CLIPS.

Extension to the Internet of Things

The IOT will require access control policies for all three domains: physical, cyber, and cyber-physical. Information will be collected through a collection of devices connected over wired and wireless links. However, the majority of these connections will be wireless. The high mobility of powerful wireless computing devices such as a smartphone or table introduce serious complications for access control in the IOT. The ability to identify and collect information from other sources within the IOT will be critical to making access control decisions.

Description of the Graceful Degradation of Privilege Policy

The binary (complete access or no access) access control policy will not provide the required support or quality of service needed for the IOT. The IOT will require multiple levels of access control and support multiple adjustments to access policies in response to observed facts. One such access policy is termed the *graceful degradation of privilege policy* which gradually removes or expands a user's access rights on a given system. The goal of graceful degradation of privilege is to attempt to provide the maximum available use of a device or service for a given level of privilege, while assuring specific security goals and requirements are met. The IOT will support many technologies that are capable of being compromised, cloned, or copied. Ideally, the legitimate user would like to be able to perform as many tasks as they can, provided their resources are protected from malicious users.

The IOT will utilize collaboration between devices and each device will need to determine what resources it shares with the others. The resources that are shared will depend, in large part, on the surroundings and the other devices present in the collaboration. Graceful degradation of privilege provides a means for each device to adjust its level of cooperation based on the observed dynamics of the IOT. For example, a body area network monitoring a person's medical status may want to restrict the information it transmits to non-sensitive information when the person is in a public setting. In this example, the level of information sent would be set by the person (user) and would be based on their desired level of privacy.

Description of the Access Control Problem

The access control decisions made by the DRAAC system are based on the Risk of the access. In this implementation of RFID DRAAC, Risk is based on the Likelihood and Impact quantities as defined by Equation (2). Graceful degradation of privilege is achieved by updating the Likelihood and Impact parameters, or adjusting the Risk threshold for allowing access to a resource based on observed Facts (Butler, 2011). Conceptually, this is a simple and straightforward process, but requires the ability to quantize risk, impact, and likelihood. This quantization requires two steps: first, the information used to derive facts must be identified and classified as affecting risk, impact, or likelihood; and second, methods must be identified and implemented to collect this information.

Quantization of Likelihood and Impact Parameters in Access Control

Cloning or copying of a RFID tag (Halamka, Juels, Stubblefield, & Westhues, 2006) and malicious use of a legitimate RFID tag via a man-in-the-middle attack (Oren & Wool, 2010) are the two main security threats to RFID based access control systems. These attacks allow the malicious user to impersonate the legitimate user to gain access to protected resources. Access control has been widely studied and formal languages have been developed to model access control policies and activities (Bertino & Kirkpatrick, 2011; Kirkpatrick, Damiani, & Bertino, 2011; Ardagna, Cremonini, Damiani, De Capitani di Vimercati, & Samarati, 2006). Geographic location of both users and resources are used in GEO-BRAC to determine access rights in a military setting to restrict access to information to only those that can use that information within a given geographic area (Bertino & Kirkpatrick, 2011). Geographic information can be used to derive additional rules and inferences about the mobility of individuals and to monitor the surrounding environment to make sure that access requests are granted only in secure surroundings (Ardagna, Cremonini, Damiani, De Capitani di Vimercati, & Samarati, 2006). Kirkpatrick, Damiani, and

Bertino propose a formal language for describing buildings and floor plans to document the relationship of individual areas to each other for access control decisions (Kirkpatrick, Damiani, & Bertino, 2011). This formal language documents those locations that are contained within other locations and this can be used as a means to derive additional information about the individual's location (Kirkpatrick, Damiani, & Bertino, 2011). Geographic location information is used in the RFID implementation of DRAAC for physical access control to detect cloned tags based on door (room) agency information and the sequence of access requests (Butler, Reed, Hawrylak, & Hale, 2013).

The access control system must identify both the likelihood of a malicious use and the impact of allowing access if the use is malicious. To quantize likelihood it is often necessary to determine the condition of the user's surroundings and the IOT provides significant assistance in obtaining this information. Impact can be determined from the potential follow-on activities resulting from the access and can be documented using an attack graph or attack dependency graph.

Defining and Adjustment of Access Rights in this Context

The IOT provides support to obtain such this information. Scans from RFID readers at access points (e.g., doors) can be used to identify the location of the access request. Cameras, such as the Microsoft Kinect (Kong, 2011), can be used to track a person's location, but also to identify how many individuals are present. This information can be useful in verifying that the location is secure or that the necessary resources are present for the requested action (Bertino & Kirkpatrick, 2011; Ardagna, Cremonini, Damiani, De Capitani di Vimercati, & Samarati, 2006). Location can be determined through processing of wireless signals (Parr, Miesen, & Vossiek, 2013) and because the IOT will employ a large number of wireless devices the accuracy of such systems should be sufficient for access control requirements. Based on this information the likelihood of each possible security breach can be estimated. One method to assist in this quantization is to use attack graphs (Philips & Swiler, 1998) or attack dependency graphs (Louthan, Hardwicke, Hawrylak, & Hale, 2011; Ou, Boyer, & McQueen, 2006) to map the potential security vulnerabilities or threats. While these structures provide information about possible threats, they must be analyzed to obtain actionable information. One option is to identify those vulnerabilities that will result in the greatest impact to the system (Hartney, 2012), and this information can be used to identify the malicious user's next move (Hawrylak, Hartney, Haney, Hamm, & Hale, 2013). This information can be used to identify what resources would be used or gathered (sampled) from the IOT to help verify a user's identity or to counter a malicious user.

Attack graphs and attack dependency graphs are useful tools to quantify impact in addition to assist with determining likelihood. Other techniques are applicable for quantifying impact, including attack surfaces (Manadhata & Wing, 2011) and privilege graphs (Dacier, Deswarte, & Kaâniche, 1996). These techniques can be used to determine what future exploits (attacks) could be carried out if the current access request is from a malicious user.

Regardless of the techniques used to quantify likelihood and impact they must integrate with the heterogeneous technology and network protocols that will be present in the IOT. The time required to compute the likelihood and impact values must not introduce too much delay into the overall interaction. This is especially true for use-cases where the access involves moving objects, such as a high-speed assembly line or automobile. Finally, the computational effort required to quantize these two components must be minimized for energy conservation and to ensure that it can execute on the resources available to the IOT device.

Definition in Relation to the Internet of Things

In the IOT, devices will need to identify their surroundings and form networks to collaborate with other devices. In this context impact is harder to quantify because of the heterogeneous nature of the resulting networks and the high degree of mobility of devices. Mobility complicates impact calculation because it allows a compromised system to move from one network or system to another, and be used to compromise the new system.

Likelihood can be correlated to the user, the requester, and the current surroundings. Here the IOT can help by providing information about the surroundings that the device cannot gather on its own. Further, many wireless protocols are beacon based, including Wi-Fi and ZigBee, enabling a device to identify other wireless devices nearby without having to join the network to determine the composition of the surroundings.

Difference from Current Access Control Policies

The graceful degradation of privilege approach allows access rights to be adjusted on a finer scale than the binary model. It also provides for increased security because in response to a situation where a decision between two access levels cannot be made, the system can provide access rights at the lower level (higher security with the user having fewer access rights) and then gradually increase access rights if no suspicious behavior is observed. In the IOT this is advantageous because collaborations are not suddenly cut off, but go through a graceful degradation of service as conditions change. The graceful *increase* in privilege is also very useful because it limits the damage that can occur in the event that the decision to allow access was incorrect. Compared to the binary method this is very advantageous because the malicious user would have full access rights instead of starting with a limited set of access rights and gradually working their way to full access rights.

The RFID DRAAC system relies on the correct selection of the Impact and Likelihood values to compute the Risk associated with each access request. Accurate information can be difficult to maintain for these two parameters in a traditional physical or computer access situation. The IOT coupled with the significant mobility of devices and the ease of establishing connections using some wireless network makes this more difficult. Each device must maintain data to calculate these values. This may require memory and processing resources that are beyond the ability of the low-power devices that will comprise the bulk of the IOT.

Security Measures Available to RFID Based Systems

There are a number of security measures that can be applied to RFID systems to provide security. Most are geared toward preventing the cloning of RFID tags or protecting the data stored in the tag from modification. Data can be protected from malicious reading by encryption before being transmitted to the tag. This has the added benefit of protecting the data against eavesdropping. The EPC Gen-2 protocol allows the tag's user-memory to support a lock feature where data can be permanently set to be read only or not readable at all (EPCglobal, 2008).

Other security measures can be inferred from the location of the RFID tag. The tag's location can be determined by a variety of means, including wireless location methods, which are used in many real-time location systems (RTLS). RTLS are not limited to RFID technology but may include Wi-Fi or other proprietary protocols.

RFID Tag Technology to Deter Cloning

Low-cost passive RFID tags offer limited security features and require different approaches to security problems. The security features are limited by the number of gates available in the tag IC (integrated circuit) due to the low price point for the tag (often 5 cents or less), and amount of energy that can be delivered to the tag by the reader. The latter is the primary technical concern because most encryption based security procedures require high-energy (with respect to a passive or battery-less device) computations. In spatial access control authentication of the RFID to prevent cloned RFID tags from being used is the primary concern. Challenge-response and physically unclonable functions are two potential solutions to this problem.

Challenge-Response Architectures

Challenge-response is an authentication technique based on each party knowing a shared secret or parts of a combined secret, such as one key of a key pair. Juels proposed a lightweight challenge-response method using the password exchange procedure used by the tag to valid a KILL command or an AC-CESS command (Juels, 2005) termed fulfillment-conditional PIN distribution or FCPD. FCPD is used to authenticate the tag to the reader to defend against the use of cloned tags. By combining the ACCESS and KILL commands the reader and tag can authenticate each other: the reader is authenticated to the tag by providing the correct ACCESS password, and the tag is authenticated to the reader by accepting the correct KILL password (Juels, 2005). One problem with this procedure is the use of the KILL command because it is possible to completely disable the tag (e.g., a single authentication). Juels suggests applying the KILL command when the tag has enough energy to evaluate the KILL password but not enough to complete the disablement process (Juels, 2005). In practice this is difficult to achieve because of the dynamic nature of the RF field that is providing energy to the tag. If the tag harvests too much energy the KILL command will complete and render the tag inoperable.

Physically Unclonable Functions

Physically unclonable functions (PUFs) are based on the manufacturing variations present in every fabrication process (Lim, Lee, Gassend, Suh, van Dijk, & Devadas, 2005; Bolotnyy & Robins, 2007; Devadas, Suh, Paral, Sowell, Ziola, & Khandelwal, 2008). These variations can result in slight, but measurable, delays in data processing operations that can be used to provide an item specific fingerprint to a chip. Such technology can be used to prevent cloning of a RFID tag because it would be impossible to replicate the manufacturing variations present in the original RFID tag. However, the drawback of PUF technology is the large sample space that must be obtained to provide a conclusive fingerprint because often many trails are needed to positively place a given chip in the cloned or un-cloned category.

Range Estimation Methods

There are a number of methods to estimate range from RF signals. The three major methods are time-of-arrival (TOA), angle-of-arrival (AOA), and received signal strength (RSS). TOA is based on the time required for a signal to travel from the transmitted (source) to the receiver (destination). Often, TOA is computed using a round-trip because it is too difficult to maintain sufficient clock synchronization between devices in different locations. TOA accuracy may suffer from queuing and processing delays on both devices because these delays will result in overestimation of distance. RSS uses the strength of the RF signal to determine distance and is often based on the Friis equation for propagation of a RF signal in free space. Inaccuracy is introduced into RSS distances when the RF propagation dynamics differ from the free space approximation and can be problematic inside and near large buildings (e.g., in an urban area). RSS will also suffer from dynamic RF environments and multipath. While TOA and RSS provide distance, they are not able to determine direction. AOA provides the angle or bearing of the RF signal received by the receiver's antenna. Combining AOA with TOA or RSS provides a means to determine the distance and bearing of the device in question.

The Access of Things Concept

The IOT will provide new opportunities for M2M and device-to-device collaboration with many of these machines/devices carried by or implanted in people. Thus, these devices will have significant mobility. Decisions must be made as to what resources a device should share or provide and this will be based on the device, the owner's rules, the device(s) it will collaborate with, and the other devices in the area. Hence, access rights are dependent not only on the identity of those taking part in the collaboration, but also the surroundings. The IOT will blend the concept of physical access control and cyber-access control to form the Access of Things.

The IOT provides significant benefit to the Access of Things because it provides for additional data input, which can be used to verify identity or to provide knowledge about the current surroundings. The blending of sensor inputs, such as GPS and video, can be used to verify a user's location and also determine the number of people present in that location (Ardagna, Cremonini, Damiani, De Capitani di Vimercati, & Samarati, 2006). This type of information must be collected and published in a manner that can be efficiently searched and retrieved by DRAAC systems.

FUTURE RESEARCH AREAS AND CHALLENGES

While DRAAC and other rule-based access control systems provide significant capabilities in securing physical locations and systems against malicious access there are a number of future research areas. The IOT will provide significant amounts of data and methods must be developed to sort, search, and store information relating to access decisions. The current DRAAC and RFID DRAAC implementations are based on a centralized system, but the IOT architecture will require a decentralized system of DRAAC instances to properly manage not only the local device, but also local segments of the IOT. Finally, the ability of DRAAC to provide actionable access control decisions is limited by the accuracy of the Likelihood and Impact values it uses and improving this accuracy will improve the quality of the access decisions.

One challenge is identifying those inputs that will assist with making the access decision for the Access of Things concept. Identification of these inputs is critical because it enables filtering of data to read only those items of interest from the massive amount of data that the IOT will produce. The access decision must be determined within the specified time constraints for the application (e.g., factory assembly line, or physical access decision) and this places strict requirements on the search operation to identify these inputs. Databases cataloging information about devices, such as location, type, and use policies, must be created. These databases can then be indexed and searched to identify a set of devices in a specific location or that provide information about a specific location. Methods to maintain and expand such a database must be created. A means to efficiently update this information is needed because of device mobility. Procedures to address cases where devices temporarily disconnect from the IOT because they are turned off or set to "airplane mode" must be created to handle updates to the database. Policies to determine when to delete entries completely or to use analytics to estimate the future location of the device (e.g., similar to dead-reckoning in GPS systems when they lose the satellite signal) must be developed.

Another challenge is the design and deployment of a distributed architecture for the Access of Things concept that provides the necessary security while meeting cost requirements for large-scale deployment. The ability to retrofit buildings and other spaces with the system is also a key concern. The RFID DRAAC model works well as a centralized access control mechanism, but the IOT will consist of many small but dynamic collaborative networks. This will require each device to have its own instance of DRAAC to control access to its local resources. These local DRAACs will need to collaborate with each other and share information. To evaluate more complex rules, information must be gathered and stored in a central repository and this will require a central DRAAC module, but the distributed nature of the IOT will most likely cause this central DRAAC to consist of a hierarchy of DRAAC modules. This is similar to the hierarchical nature of the RFID DRAAC architecture described by Butler, Hawrylak, and Hale (Butler, Hawrylak, & Hale, 2011).

RFID DRAAC relies on the correct estimation of Impact and Likelihood. The IOT environment is one in which these parameters are likely to change rapidly and DRAAC must be able to respond to these changes in a timely manner. Recognizing that these parameters have changed is difficult and methods must be developed to collect this information in a computationally efficient manner to not starve the other processes executing on the device. Further, the communication with other devices must be limited to prevent the communication links from being overloaded with traffic just to maintain DRAAC (and prevent useful work from being completed). Efficient and secure manners to distribute updates from the DRAAC hierarchy to the local DRAACs must be developed for the IOT because of the high rate of mobility.

CONCLUSION

This chapter presented a possible model for controlling access to resources, termed Access of Things. The Access of Things is built on a DRAAC, a rule-based access control system, that has been applied to securing workstations (e.g., laptops and PCs) and RFID based physical access control systems. The RFID implementation of DRAAC can be segmented into independent groups to allow access decisions to be made in isolation or collaboratively (Butler, Hawrylak, & Hale, 2011). This architecture is applicable to the Internet of Things (IOT) and is the basis for the Access of Things concept. Its distributed nature allows the system to provide strong access control policies while maintaining quality of service requirements. The DRAAC system is platform agnostic making it an ideal candidate for deployment on IOT devices.

Access decisions in DRAAC rely on collection of accurate data, namely Likelihood and Impact, and the accuracy of these data items is a critical factor determining the effectiveness of the system. The IOT provides data from a variety of sources that can be used to improve the accuracy of these measurements. However, issues such as data overload and identifying the important data items must be addressed.

The Access of Things concept provides a suitable security protection framework for the IOT while maintaining the highest possible quality of service for applications executing within the IOT. The gradual increase of privilege enables the user to be vetted and will limit the damage potential from a malicious user. Likewise, the gradual decrease in privilege enables the application and user to continue to perform some of their tasks while being alerted to potential security threats. Based on this information, the human user can make more informed security decisions.

REFERENCES

Ardagna, C. A., Cremonini, M., Damiani, E., De Capitani di Vimercati, S., & Samarati, P. (2006). Supporting location-based conditions in access control policies. In *Proceedings of the 2006 ACM Symposium on Information, Computer and Communications Security*, (pp. 212-222). ACM.

Bertino, E., & Kirkpatrick, M. S. (2011). Location-based access control systems for mobile users: concepts and research directions. In *Proceedings of the 4th ACM SIGSPATIAL International Workshop on Security and Privacy in GIS and LBS*, (pp. 49-52). ACM.

Bertino, E., Samarati, P., & Jajodia, S. (1993). Authorizations in relational database management systems. In *Proceedings of 1st ACM Conf. on Computer and Commun. Security*, (pp. 130 -139). ACM.

Bolotnyy, L., & Robins, G. (2007). Physically unclonable function-based security and privacy in rfid systems. In *Proceedings of Fifth Annual IEEE International Conference on Pervasive Computing and Communications, 2007,* (pp. 211–220). IEEE.

Butler, M. (2011). *Dynamic risk assessment access control.* (Master's thesis). The University of Tulsa, Tulsa, OK.

Butler, M., Hawrylak, P., & Hale, J. (2011). Graceful privilege reduction in RFID security. In *Proceedings of the Seventh Annual Workshop on Cyber Security and Information Intelligence Research*. IEEE.

Butler, M., Reed, S., Hawrylak, P. J., & Hale, J. (2013). Implementing graceful RFID privilege reduction. In *Proceedings of the Eighth Annual Cyber Security and Information Intelligence Research Workshop*. IEEE.

Chen, M., Gonzalez, S., Leung, V., Zhang, Q., & Li, M. (2010). A 2G-RFID-based e-healthcare system. *IEEE Wireless Communications, 17*(1), 37–43. doi:10.1109/MWC.2010.5416348

Dacier, M., Deswarte, Y., & Kaâniche, M. (1996). *Quantitative assessment of operational security: Models and tools.* LAAS Research Report 96493.

Devadas, S., Suh, E., Paral, S., Sowell, R., Ziola, T., & Khandelwal, V. (2008). Design and implementation of PUF-based unclonable RFID ICS for anti-counterfeiting and security applications. In *Proceedings of 2008 IEEE International Conference on RFID*, (pp. 58–64). IEEE.

EPCglobal. (2008). *EPC^{TM} radio-frequency identity protocols class-1 generation-2 UHF RFID protocol for communications at 860 MHz – 960 MHz version 1.2.0*. EPCglobal Inc.

EPCglobal. (2010). *EPC tag data standard version 1.5*. EPCglobal.

Foschini, L., Taleb, T., Corradi, A., & Bottazzi, D. (2011). M2M-based metropolitan platform for IMS-enabled road traffic management in IoT. *IEEE Communications Magazine*, *49*(11), 50–57. doi:10.1109/MCOM.2011.6069709

Halamka, J., Juels, A., Stubblefield, A., & Westhues, J. (2006). The security implications of VeriChip cloning. *Journal of the American Medical Informatics Association*, *13*(6), 601–607. doi:10.1197/jamia.M2143 PMID:16929037

Hartney, C. J. (2012). *Security risk metrics: An attack graph-centric approach*. (Unpublished Master's thesis). The University of Tulsa, Tulsa, OK.

Hawrylak, P. J., Hartney, C., Haney, M., Hamm, J., & Hale, J. (2013). Techniques to model and derive a cyber-attacker's intelligence. In B. Igelnik & J. Zurada (Eds.), *Efficiency and scalability methods for computational intellect* (pp. 162–180). Hershey, PA: Information Science Reference. doi:10.4018/978-1-4666-3942-3.ch008

IEEE. (2011). *IEEE standard for local and metropolitan area networks - Part 15.4: Low-rate wireless personal area networks (LR-WPANs)*. IEEE.

Jain, A., Hong, L., & Pankanti, S. (2000). Biometric identification. *Communications of the ACM*, *43*(2), 90–98. doi:10.1145/328236.328110

Juels, A. (2005). Strengthening EPC tags against cloning. In *Proceedings of the 4th ACM Workshop on Wireless Security*, (pp. 67-76). ACM.

Kirkpatrick, M. S., Damiani, M. L., & Bertino, E. (2011). Prox-RBAC: A proximity-based spatially aware RBAC. In *Proceedings of the 19th ACM SIGSPATIAL International Conference on Advances in Geographic Information Systems*, (pp. 339-348). ACM.

Kong, L. (2011). *Spatial access control on multi-touch user interface*. (Master's thesis). The University of Tulsa, Tulsa, OK.

Kushalnagar, N., Montenegro, G., & Schumacher, C. (2007). *IPv6 over low-power wireless personal area networks (6LoWPANs), overview, assumptions, problem statement, and goals*. IETF RFC 4919.

Lim, D., Lee, J. W., Gassend, B., Suh, G. E., van Dijk, M., & Devadas, S. (2005). Extracting secret keys from integrated circuits. *IEEE Transactions on Very Large Scale Integration Systems*, *13*(10), 1200–1205. doi:10.1109/TVLSI.2005.859470

Louthan, G., Hardwicke, P., Hawrylak, P., & Hale, J. (2011). Toward hybrid attack dependency graphs. In *Proceedings of the Seventh Annual Workshop on Cyber Security and Information Intelligence Research*. IEEE.

Manadhata, P. K., & Wing, J. M. (2011). An attack surface metric. *IEEE Transactions on Software Engineering*, *37*(3), 371–386. doi:10.1109/TSE.2010.60

Mulligan, G. (2007). The 6LoWPAN architecture. In *Proceedings of the 4th Workshop on Embedded Networked Sensors*, (pp. 78-82). IEEE.

Oren, Y., & Wool, A. (2010). RFID-based electronic voting: What could possibly go wrong? In *Proceedings of 2010 IEEE International Conference on RFID*, (pp. 118-125). IEEE.

Ou, X., Boyer, W. F., & McQueen, M. A. (2006). A scalable approach to attack graph generation. In *Proceedings of the 13th ACM Conference on Computer and Communications Security*, (pp. 336-345). ACM.

Parr, A., Miesen, R., & Vossiek, M. (2013). Inverse SAR approach for localization of moving RFID tags. In *Proceedings of 2013 IEEE International Conference on RFID*, (pp. 104-109). IEEE.

Philips, C., & Swiler, L. (1998). A graph-based system for network-vulnerability analysis. In *Proceedings of the 1998 Workshop on New Security Paradigms*, (pp. 71-79). New York, NY: ACM.

Revere, L., Black, K., & Zalila, F. (2010). RFIDs can improve the patient care supply chain. *Hospital Topics*, *88*(1), 26–31. doi:10.1080/00185860903534315 PMID:20194108

Sandhu, R. (1993). Lattice-based access control models. *Computer*, *26*(11), 9–19. doi:10.1109/2.241422

Sandhu, R., & Samarati, P. (1994). Access control: Principle and practice. *IEEE Communications Magazine*, *32*(9), 40–48. doi:10.1109/35.312842

Wicks, A. M., Visich, J. K., & Li, S. (2006). Radio frequency identification applications in hospital environments. *Hospital Topics*, *84*(3), 3–8. doi:10.3200/HTPS.84.3.3-9 PMID:16913301

You, L., Liu, C., & Tong, S. (2011). Community medical network (CMN), architecture and implementation. *Global Mobile Congress*, 1-6.

KEY TERMS AND DEFINITIONS

Access of Things: The term used to denote the DRAAC based access control system for the Internet of Things.

Attack Graph: A graph based structure representing the state of the system as vertices and actions, such as vulnerabilities or normal system transitions, which can change the state of the system as edges. Attack graphs are similar to finite state machine diagrams that focus on security rather than system state.

CLIPS: CLIPS stands for C Language Integrated Production System and is used to store the Facts and Rules in the DRAAC system. CLIPS is the core of the Access Control Decision Module of DRAAC.

DRACC: DRAAC stands for Dynamic Risk Assessment Access Control system, which is an access control system that provides graceful degradation or elevation privilege in a system. DRAAC is the basis for the Access of Things concept presented in this chapter.

Impact: The potential damage that can be caused by granting an access if that access should have been denied. Impact is primarily a function of the resource that the user is requesting access to, but is also dependent on the user and the current state of the system.

Internet of Things: A term used to denote the massive collection of networked devices. These collaborative networks will autonomously form and collaborate.

Likelihood: The probability that an event will happen or that a malicious user will attempt to exploit a particular vulnerability. Likelihood is used in security and access control systems, such as DRAAC, to identify those actions that the malicious user is likely to perform.

Physically Unclonable Functions: Physically Unclonable Functions or PUFs are variations in the fabrication process of Integrated Circuits (ICs) that cause timing variations in the resulting ICs (chips). These inconsistencies can be used to provide a unique fingerprint for each particular IC.

RFID: RFID stands for Radio Frequency IDentification and represents the use of RFID readers and RFID tags to provide the last-mile connection between a control system and the end devices. In this chapter, RFID is used for identifying individuals for access control purposes and for location determination via radio-frequency (RF) location techniques.

Rule-Based Access Control: A type of access control system that where access requests are evaluated against a specified list of rules. These types of systems often support the collection of "facts" representing the access control system's knowledge about the resources and users it monitors.

This work was previously published in the Handbook of Research on Progressive Trends in Wireless Communications and Networking edited by M.A. Matin, pages 189-207, copyright year 2014 by Information Science Reference (an imprint of IGI Global).

Index

Recommended Reference Books

ISBN: 978-1-4666-6042-7
© 2014; 1,727 pp.
List Price: $1,756

ISBN: 978-1-4666-6571-2
© 2015; 927 pp.
List Price: $404

ISBN: 978-1-4666-5170-8
© 2014; 592 pp.
List Price: $304

ISBN: 978-1-4666-7401-1
© 2015; 362 pp.
List Price: $156

ISBN: 978-1-4666-4916-3
© 2014; 398 pp.
List Price: $164

ISBN: 978-1-4666-5003-9
© 2014; 580 pp.
List Price: $152

Publishing Information Science and Technology Research Since 1988

www.igi-global.com   Sign up at www.igi-global.com/newsletters   f facebook.com/igiglobal   twitter.com/igiglobal

   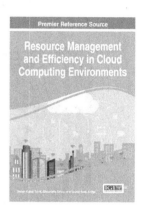

Printed in the United States
By Bookmasters